DARK WATERS, STARRY SKIES

OSPREY
PUBLISHING

JEFFREY R. COX

THE GUADALCANAL-SOLOMONS CAMPAIGN
MARCH–OCTOBER 1943

DARK WATERS, STARRY SKIES

OSPREY PUBLISHING
Bloomsbury Publishing Plc
Kemp House, Chawley Park, Cumnor Hill, Oxford, OX2 9PH, UK
29 Earlsfort Terrace, Dublin 2, Ireland
1385 Broadway, 5th Floor, New York, NY 10018, USA
E-mail: info@ospreypublishing.com
www.ospreypublishing.com

OSPREY is a trademark of Osprey Publishing Ltd

First published in Great Britain in 2023

A catalog record for this book is available from the British Library.

ISBN: HB 978 1 4728 4989 2; PB 978 1 4728 4987 8; eBook 978 1 4728 4988 5;
ePDF 978 1 4728 4985 4; XML 978 1 4728 4986 1

23 24 25 26 27 10 9 8 7 6 5 4 3 2 1

Maps by www.bounford.com
Index by Zoe Ross

AUTHOR'S NOTE:
The author would like to thank the Society of the Divine Word for their gracious assistance during the research process.

EDITOR'S NOTE:
The maps in the plate section were previously published in Campaign 326 *The Solomons 1943–44* by Mark Stille. Note that some of the times in the maps do not perfectly align with the times in the narrative. But there are few original reports where the times do agree.

Typeset by Deanta Global Publishing Services, Chennai, India
Printed and bound in Great Britain by CPI (Group) UK Ltd, Croydon CR0 4YY

CONTENTS

PROLOGUE:

VIA DOLOROSA[*]

He stood there quietly, waiting for the next question.

A servant of God, or, in his own words, "A servant of the servants of God," he had spent most of his life bringing the Word of God to some of the most remote, hostile, and dangerous places – and people – on Earth.[1] But he had been nowhere and met no one as remote, hostile, and dangerous as where he was and whom he was facing now: on a Japanese warship.

He along with 61 others were supposedly being transported to the Japanese base at Rabaul. Crammed into the forward crew quarters with little to do except wait. Wait and worry. Until their captors, who had called him and his people "spies," came to take each of them away for questioning.[2]

He was a man of God on a warship. An accused spy on a warship. But he was not known as "The Fighting Bishop" for nothing.[3] He was not one to be easily intimidated. He stood there quietly, waiting for the next question while his captors were writing down his answers on a notepad.[4]

He was 66-year-old Josef Lörks, Vicar Apostolic of the Roman Catholic Vicariate Apostolic of Central New Guinea.[5]

The presence of Bishop Lörks and the other missionaries was a legacy of one of the more curious experiments in European colonialism. In 1871, the Hall of Mirrors at Versailles had witnessed the unification of Germany under the leadership of the Prussian Hohenzollern dynasty. But having been unified only in 1871, Germany was late to the Great Power colonialism party and was left with just the unwanted scraps, like German Southwest Africa (now Namibia),[6] German East Africa (now Tanzania, Rwanda, Burundi, and part of Kenya and Mozambique), Kameruns (now Cameroon and part of Nigeria), Togoland (now Togo and Ghana) – and part of New Guinea.

---

[*] The *Via Dolorosa* is the processional route through Old Jerusalem that recreates the journey Jesus would have taken on his way to his crucifixion.

Europeans had descended on New Guinea and sliced it up like buzzards on a pizza. The Dutch, seeking an extension of their neighboring East Indies, took the western half of the island, with a border that was a virtual straight line, almost certainly drawn with a ruler, at 114 degrees East longitude. East of 114 degrees East was divided into northern and southern halves, albeit not with a ruler. The northern half became the domain of the Hohenzollerns, who called it "German New Guinea" (Deutsch-Neuguinea). To these holdings were added the appropriately named Bismarck Archipelago and the northern Solomon Islands.

It was 1875 when a German priest named Arnold Janssen formed a new missionary order of the Roman Catholic Church called the Society of the Divine Word (Societas Verbi Divini). Because of the persecution of Catholics in Germany as an outgrowth of *Kulturkampf,* the legal and philosophical battle taking place at that time between the Protestant Hohenzollerns and the Vatican, Father Janssen was compelled to set up his new order's headquarters in the small Dutch town of Steyl across the border. There he had a ready supply of exiled German Catholic clergy to be recruited as missionaries. In 1892, after the aforementioned *Kulturkampf* between Prussia and the Vatican had been resolved, many of those exiled German Catholic clergy were on the Society's first expedition to German New Guinea.

With the Kaiserreich's defeat in World War I, German New Guinea was legally turned over to Australia, who had taken it during the war. The Australians initially viewed these German nationals in their midst with suspicion. But the Society's mission continued to expand across the region. In 1932, a new ecclesiastical jurisdiction was set up, the "Vicariate Apostolic of Central New Guinea," covering Wewak on the coast of the Bismarck Sea and remote areas near the Sepik River. And a veteran priest who had initially come to New Guinea in 1900, Josef Lörks, was appointed as its Vicar Apostolic, or bishop.[7]

Being a bishop in this remote location, Lörks usually had to eschew most of the trappings and luxuries that most bishops usually enjoy. He was often seen sweating in his shirt sleeves and shorts doing as much manual labor as anyone to do what the mission needed to survive.[8] Lörks often had to juggle between the Melanesian locals who needed attention, care, and ministry; priests who wanted to immediately convert all Melanesians to Catholic Christianity without first winning their loyalty and trust; and Australian government officials who wanted to immediately bring the region under full government control, also without first winning loyalty and trust.[9]

After the war started in Europe in 1939, a fourth ball was added: convincing suspicious Australian officials that Lörks and the other missionaries who were citizens of Germany, with whom Australia was now at war – again – were not threats. Though the Australian authorities placed a few restrictions on the missionaries, including a 6pm-to-6am curfew, that Josef Lörks' name is usually anglicized as "Joseph Loerks" in most histories is suggestive of his success in this endeavor.[10]

Yet that success would be of no help once Japan entered the war. Though the Japanese moved into New Guinea in early 1942, they had mostly confined themselves to Papua and the Huon Peninsula in the eastern part of the island. But with the Japanese decision in late 1942 to withdraw from Guadalcanal, all that changed. Their defenses in New Guinea were to be reinforced. To that end, on the night of December 18, 1942, the armed merchant cruiser *Kiyosumi Maru*, escorted by the destroyers *Yugumo*, *Kazagumo*, and *Makigumo*, landed some 2,000 troops from a battalion of the 11th Infantry Regiment from the Imperial Japanese Army's 5th Division and the Imperial Japanese Navy's recently formed 2nd Special Base Force unopposed on a two-mile-long beach between Wewak and the Catholic mission at Wirui – the heart of Bishop Lörks' vicariate. Their objective was to complete the Japanese occupation of northern New Guinea and to begin turning Wewak into a major air base, supply depot, and staging area for Japanese forces.[11]

Now the Japanese were presented with the Gordian knot of the status of these missionaries. Almost all of them were citizens of Germany, an Axis ally of Imperial Japan. But though Adolf Hitler and Heinrich Himmler were ostensibly Catholic, their adherence to Catholic teachings left room for improvement, to put it mildly. Moreover, the Nazi regime was in general not a big fan of the Roman Catholic Church or its priests.[12] The Third Reich displayed little if any interest in the affairs of its Catholic missionary citizens on the other side of the world. The Society's missionaries were also subject to the jurisdiction of the Vatican, which was officially neutral. But the little papal city was completely surrounded by Fascist Italy, another Axis ally of Nazi Germany. The Society was on its own. With that, the Japanese simply cut its Gordian knot by declaring the missionaries "neutrals," often describing them as "neutral civilians" or "citizens of the third country."[13] They never used the expression "Allied civilians" or "hostile civilians," but they might as well have.[14] Because when the Japanese landed at and around Wewak, they immediately began interrogating the missionaries and lay staff including the St John's Catholic Mission at Bagaram on Kairiru Island northwest of Wewak, where Bishop Lörks was driven out at the point of a bayonet, and was injured when the bayonet slashed him.[15] The Catholic missionaries, the Japanese said, had "a pronounced uncooperative attitude."[16] The missionaries were mystified at the hostility shown by the Japanese, especially since most of the clergy were citizens of Germany. "You are Germans," the Japanese would explain. "Why did the Australians leave you here? Had you been loyal Germans, the Australians would have interned you. Since they have left you here, we must take it for granted that you are spies for the Australians and the Americans."[17]

It was around New Year's when Rear Admiral Kamata Michiaki, commander of the 2nd Special Base Force, ordered all the missionaries confined to Kairiru. The Japanese said the confinement would last only a few days, but the few days became a few weeks with no end in sight. Missionary work became impossible because almost all of the clergy were confined to Kairiru and, not knowing the true war situation, many of the local Melanesians had subscribed to what has become known as the "cargo cult," which at this point in time saw the Japanese as basically the strong horse and switched allegiance to them.[18] That impression was strengthened on January 20 when all of Wewak witnessed an American B-24 Liberator being shot down offshore near Wokeo Island.

That impression of being the strong horse came with some interruptions, however. Bishop Lörks had spent a decade as skipper of a schooner, a position he thoroughly enjoyed. The

Japanese ships around Wewak fascinated him. Too much, the Japanese decided. On one occasion, he was watching a large ship lazily maneuver in the harbor when it suddenly seemed to take evasive action, only to be stopped after a large plume of water erupted at its side. Lörks knew immediately what had happened. "Submarine, submarine!" he exclaimed, probably more as a reflex than anything else. But his exclamation got back to the Japanese, who blamed him for the ship's torpedoing and accused him of communicating with the enemy.[19] Mission property was torn apart as the Japanese looked for the alleged radio transmitter.[20] They accused one of the priests, Father Arthur Manion, Lörks' secretary and a US citizen, of using a coding machine. Exasperated missionaries replied that he was using a typewriter.

The best that could be said of the missionaries' life on Kairiru was that they were in one of their own missions in St John's, and they were free to move about the island. But it was impossible to continue their missionary work and there was not enough food on Kairiru to keep them fed.

The Japanese presence in the Wewak area continued to increase, and their losses from Allied submarines and air attacks continued to increase as well. The 2nd Special Base Force, responsible for security at Wewak, received reinforcements in mid-January and tightened the screws on the missionaries. They were convinced the mission was sending intelligence to the Allies, but despite their best efforts, they could not locate the means by which that intelligence was sent.

The situation for the Roman Catholic missionaries was rapidly becoming more and more precarious. Next door, in the Vicariate Apostolic of Eastern New Guinea, on or about February 19, Chicago-native Father Joseph Kotrba was interrogated by the Japanese and revealed he had at one time been an auxiliary chaplain for American troops – and was promptly beheaded.[21] The Japanese in the neighboring Vicariate Apostolic of Rabaul by this time had already killed three Marist brothers on Bougainville; one Sacred Heart priest from Ireland on New Ireland; and two more Sacred Heart priests, one from Ireland, the other from Australia, on New Britain.[22] A number of these murdered priests were, the Japanese claimed, guilty of "espionage" simply for giving Allied forces (usually downed aviators) not weapons, but just medicine, food or clothing.[23]

It is not clear if the Divine Word missionaries had heard about these events; given their isolation on Kairiru, more than likely they did not. But they certainly were aware of what happened on February 25, when two Divine Word priests from But Catholic Mission, west of Wewak, were taken out and shot for no apparent reason.[24]

The Divine Word feared it would be next, because it was about to have more contact with Allied airmen. Around the beginning of March, a letter was smuggled in for Father Manion. It was from US Army Air Force Lieutenant James A. McMurria of the 321st Bombardment Squadron of the 90th Bombardment Group. McMurria had been a pilot of the B-24 Liberator seen shot down at sea off Wewak on January 20. Two of his crew had been killed. The eight surviving crew members clung to a tiny rubber raft for two days out of sight of any land until they were washed up on Wokeo Island by a storm.[25] They spent almost two months on Wokeo as – mostly – friendly Melanesian locals nursed them back to health.

One still needed treatment for his injuries, particularly medicine. McMurria found out there was an American priest on Kairiru and was told there were no Japanese on the island as far as anyone on Wokeo knew. McMurria wrote a short message requesting medicine for that crew member, as well as "other supplies."[26] The note was hidden inside a bamboo capsule and surreptitiously delivered.[27]

This was the proverbial hot potato that the Catholic missionaries, given their increasingly perilous position, did not need, but Father Manion decided to help Lieutenant McMurria and his crew regardless. He asked Sister Adelaide Koetter, an American school teacher, and Sister Arildis Engelbrecht, a German who ran the Kairiru hospital, to put medicine, bandages, and other goods, along with razor blades and newspapers for trading with the islanders, into an empty copra sack for the airmen. Manion added a message for McMurria that reportedly advised him and his crew turn themselves in to the Japanese.[28] Friendly Melanesians smuggled it out the following night.[29] By now, Father Manion and the others should have known better than to suggest surrendering to the Japanese, and, after their own experiences with the Japanese, they probably did. In all likelihood, Manion did not intend for the note to be taken seriously by McMurria and did not expect it to be. The note was probably to give himself and the Divine Word some cover if they were found out or if the smuggled goods were seized by the Japanese.

It was probably March 14 when Lieutenant Commander Yagura Satoshi, the assistant chief of staff for the 2nd Special Base Force, arrived on Kairiru with Sublieutenant Kai Yajiro, who was attached to the staff of the 2nd.[30] Either that day or the morning of Monday, March 15, was when they informed Bishop Lörks that he and his missionaries were being moved from the Wewak area to the main Japanese base in the South Pacific at Rabaul.

On that March 15, at 1:30pm, an Imperial Japanese Navy destroyer, the *Akikaze*, dropped anchor off Bagaram. A barge sailed out from shore to the destroyer's starboard side near the stern carrying Lieutenant Commander Yagura, Sublieutenant Kai, and Bishop Lörks. They were introduced to the *Akikaze*'s skipper, Lieutenant Commander Sabe Tsurukichi, who met them on deck. All four proceeded to an area on the starboard side where a table had been set up underneath an awning that stretched from beneath the bridge. Here they met two other Japanese officers whose identities are not certain. One was probably Sabe's superior Captain Amaya Yoshishige, commander of Destroyer Division 34, to which the *Akikaze* was assigned. It has been reasonably speculated that the other officer was Sublieutenant Terada Takeo, the destroyer's executive or senior officer. All sat down for a conference. Sublieutenant Kai served as interpreter.[31]

It is not clear what was said at this conference, which lasted about an hour, but afterwards Sublieutenant Terada told Lieutenant Takahashi Manroku, the *Akikaze*'s "First Divisional" (gunnery) officer, "Since all of these passengers are being returned to their native country, we are returning to the base at Rabaul." Lieutenant Commander Yagura and Lieutenant Kai returned Bishop Lörks to shore, where he went to his room at St John's Mission to pack his things.

By around 3:30pm, six Divine Word priests, 14 Divine Word brothers, and eight sisters from the Servants of the Holy Spirit had congregated on the coast ready to leave. Among them were two Dutch and three American citizens: Father Manion, Sister Koetter, and Brother Victor Salois. The rest were Germans, though three were from Austria. Three lay people were with them. One was a native Melanesian woman, Magdalena Aiwaul, a candidate for sisterhood who refused to go home and insisted on staying with the missionaries. The remaining two were Chinese toddlers, believed to be children of Wewak storekeeper Ning Hee, in the care of the nuns. Lieutenant Commander Yagura and Sublieutenant Kai took roll call of the civilians. These 20 men, 19 women, and two children totaled 41.[32] There were supposed to be 42. Everyone noticed the one missing: Bishop Lörks.

Displaying what might be called a pronounced uncooperative attitude, Bishop Lörks did not want to leave St John's Mission – and made sure everyone knew it. He was, at least to observers, very sluggish in departing. Josef Lörks appeared wearing the most prominent symbols of his office: his mitre and the large pectoral cross; and carrying another prominent symbol of his office, the crozier, a shepherd's staff. An impatient Lieutenant Commander Yagura sent a burly naval guard to hurry the bishop along. After fixing his bayonet, the sailor charged at the bishop, tearing Lörks' clothing and breaking the chain to his pectoral cross, sending both clattering to the ground. A second charge by the sailor, this one from behind, was deftly avoided by the bishop, who nevertheless headed for the waiting barge.[33]

While Bishop Lörks was undoubtedly angry at being forced to leave what had become his home, much of what he did here was probably calculated. Instead of hiding them to be recovered later, as had been done in some of the missions in his vicariate, Lörks chose to display the symbols of his office. That visibility would have served two, maybe three purposes. First, it increased the probability that witnesses would remember what the Japanese had done to him and what they had forced him to do here, which would be needed for anyone to piece together these events after the fact. Moreover, Bishop Lörks was the head of the Roman Catholic Church in central New Guinea, the most prominent symbol of the Church in the Sepik River area. This was a statement that the Church was not abandoning its flock willingly, but was being physically forced out at the point of a bayonet, at the barrel of a gun. Finally, there is the implicit question to anyone watching or hearing the story of these events: "If the Japanese can do this to a bishop, what can they do to everyone else?"

The missionaries were herded onto the barge, where they were guarded by Lieutenant Commander Yagura, Sublieutenant Kai, and five naval infantrymen. The barge left the shore and went to the *Akikaze*. Bishop Lörks boarded the destroyer at the head of the procession of his priests, his religious, and the lay people.[34] The time was 3:35pm.[35] The civilians were housed in one compartment: the crew quarters in the after part of the ship. They were provided water, tea, milk, and bread. The *Akikaze's* medical officer, Dr. Sugiura Yoshio, treated those internees who had medical issues, including seasickness. The *Akikaze* headed for Manus, in the Admiralty Islands. She had another appointment to keep.[36]

For which she was apparently late. A little before 1:00pm on March 16, the *Akikaze* stopped at Manus in the Admiralty Islands and anchored maybe five miles west of Lorengau off a village called Lugos, where the headquarters of the Lutheran Liebenzell Mission was located.[37] She was there to pick up another group of "about 20 foreign nationals;" the exact number remains unclear.[38] This group included six Lutherans, of which five were missionaries from the aforementioned Liebenzell Mission: Reverend Friedrich Doepke, the head of the Liebenzell Mission, and his wife; Reverend Julius Gareis and his wife and infant child Leni, all Germans. Also taken from the Liebenzell Mission was Sister Maria Molnar, a Deaconess Nursing Sister from Hungary, another ally of Imperial Japan.[39]

At this time, missionaries from the Roman Catholic Sacred Heart Mission were also taken. They included three Sisters from the Dutch Province of the Daughters of Our Lady of the Sacred Heart; and three Missionaries of the Sacred Heart, of whom two were German and one was Dutch.[40] Joining this group of civilian internees was Carl Muenster, a native German and naturalized Australian who lived in Lorengau, near which he owned a plantation; and Peter Mathies, a plantation manager and yet another German.[41] After these 14, the number and identification of the civilians to be interned becomes less clear.[42] Two were Chinese, known only by their nicknames. Four others were called "Chamorra;" these are believed to have been Indian, Burmese, or Malayan.[43]

The situation with the missionaries on Manus had been a lot different than the situation at Wewak, with far fewer of the ominous rumblings. In fact, the Liebenzell Mission had enjoyed generally good relations with the small Japanese garrison of 20 naval infantry led by Chief Petty Officer Ichinose Harukichi. The food situation on Manus was a little different than on Kairiru, but Ichinose periodically provided the missionaries with food and even occasionally had them over for dinner.[44] And while there was most likely an unconscious element of coercion involved to some extent, there were no accusations of violence.

Ichinose himself, probably a few naval guards, and the missionaries went out in a boat to meet the destroyer. "Just three months and you will be back," the Japanese reassured them. Reverend Doepke was not buying it. "The Lord has made clear to me that we shall not return," he whispered to one of his Melanesian assistants. "The Japanese will kill us."[45] When they arrived at the *Akikaze*, Chief Petty Officer Ichinose handed a list of the civilians' names to Lieutenant Commander Sabe. Ichinose also informed Dr Sugiura that one of the Germans, the aforementioned Reverend Doepke, had a fever. This second batch of civilians was housed in the forward crew quarters. With his work done, Ichinose left the destroyer after a visit of some two hours and 40 minutes. As soon as he left, the *Akikaze* sailed from Lorengau. News that the missionaries were being taken away had spread through the Melanesian population, and as the destroyer pulled away, the ship was surrounded by Melanisians in canoes, who had followed the Catholic missionaries over.[46]

But the curious, worried canoeists dropped away as the *Akikaze* sailed off into the Bismarck Sea. The destroyer headed for the Japanese base at Kavieng on New Ireland. The civilians received bread, water, and tea. The chief medical officer treated Reverend Doepke for his fever and continued treating the other civilians for seasickness. That night, with their quarters turned over to the missionaries, most of the destroyer's crew slept on deck. There seem to have been few complaints about being forced out of their hot, stuffy cabins for one night. It was 8:30am when the *Akikaze* arrived at Kavieng. The destroyer stopped her engines just off the entrance to the port, but, curiously, did not drop her anchor. As far as the missionaries could tell, the destroyer had just stopped for a few hours. No cargo or supplies were taken on board, no one seemed to embark or disembark, though a boat came over to the destroyer and headed back after a few moments. It was very strange.[47] And it got stranger still, because after she left the harbor area at 10:13am, the *Akikaze*'s engines got very loud. Bishop Lörks knew what it meant: the destroyer was running at high speed.[48]

Shortly after leaving Kavieng, the Divine Word priests, religious, and lay people were moved from the crew quarters in the after part of the ship to the forward part of the ship where the civilians from Manus were staying. Sublieutenant Kai, still serving as interpreter, explained that the maid had to clean the after quarters, or something like that. The mood of the officers and crew on the *Akikaze* had taken a sudden turn for the worse, far more somber than the day before, or even earlier that morning.[49]

About an hour later, Sublieutenant Kai returned to the cabin with some guards, telling the civilians he had to gather personal information from each of them. So they would all be questioned.[50] One at a time. Bishop Lörks is believed to have been called first.[51]

Lörks was led from the crew compartment by Sublieutenant Kai and two naval guards. In somber, officious tones, Sublieutenant Kai asked the bishop his name, his age, his nationality, and other identifying details, writing this information on a note pad. When the questioning was complete, Kai turned him over to the pair of escorts.[52]

Those escorts took Bishop Lörks underneath the bridge on the starboard side on the main deck heading towards the after part of the *Akikaze* and the cabin from which they had just been ejected. He noticed that there was now a large canvas tarp hiding the after part of the ship . . .

The bishop suddenly felt the hands of his "escorts" physically seizing him. One grabbed one arm, the other grabbed the other. They crowned him with a cloth that served as a blindfold, tying it over his eyes. The bishop could feel being maneuvered towards the stern.[53]

The bishop was stopped. He felt hands tugging at his clothes, heard ripping sounds, and felt his skin exposed to the sun. Then he felt his wrists being tied in front of him.[54] He was maneuvered ahead again. Then he could feel himself being forced onto a platform that creaked, like it was made of wood. Like a gallows or Golgotha.

The bishop was pushed a little further, then turned around. His arms were lifted up so they were above his head. Then they were pulled upwards, lifting him off until he was hanging from some kind of cross. Josef Lörks was all alone. In a world – a mortal world, at least – by himself. He could see nothing. Because of the wind, the engines, and the churning of the water, he could hear nothing else. His feet pulled back by the speed of the ship, he felt nothing except the pain in his wrists and shoulders, the wind and the spray on his skin. No doubt the bishop would have focused on his prayers to the exclusion of all else.

But if Josef Lörks was listening very closely, over the sound of the wind, the engines, the churning waters, he might have heard muffled voices speaking a language he did not understand. And the faint clicks of a single bolt-action rifle chambering a round ...[55]

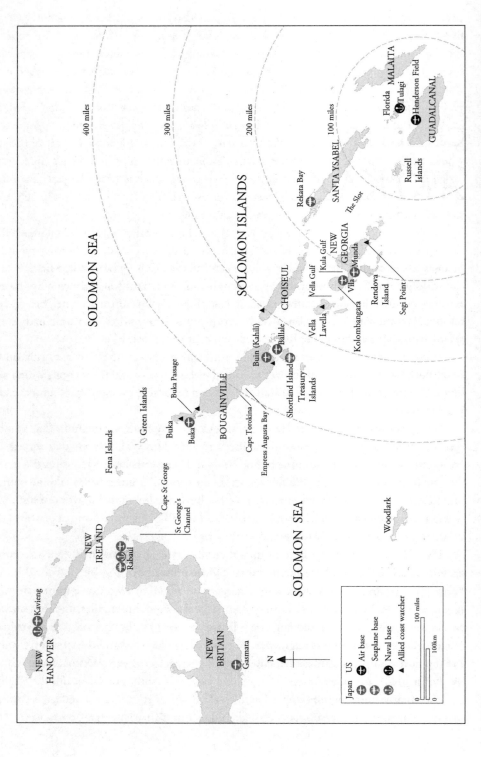

SOUTH PACIFIC 1943

SOLOMON SEA

SOLOMON SEA

SOLOMON ISLANDS

NEW
HANOVER

NEW
IRELAND

Kavieng

Rabaul

NEW
BRITAIN

Gasmata

St George's
Channel

Cape St George

Fena Islands

Green Islands

Buka Passage

Buka
Buka

BOUGAINVILLE

Cape Torokina

Empress Augusta Bay

Buin (Kahili)

Ballale

Shortland Island

Treasury
Islands

Woodlark

CHOISEUL

Vella Gulf

Kula Gulf

Vella
Lavella

Kolombangara

NEW
GEORGIA

Vila   Munda

Rendova
Island

Segi Point

Rekata Bay

SANTA YSABEL

The Slot

Russell
Islands

Florida   Tulagi

MALAITA

Henderson Field

GUADALCANAL

100 miles

200 miles

300 miles

400 miles

N

Japan   US

Air base

Seaplane base

Naval base

Allied coast watcher

0   100 miles

0   100km

CHAPTER 1

AKIKAZE

At about the same time Bishop Lörks was traveling his own personal *Via Dolorosa*, Lieutenant Commander Roy S. Benson of the US Navy was hunting a Japanese convoy as it traveled between the great Japanese fortress of Truk and Japanese bases in the Bismarck Sea such as Rabaul, Kavieng, and Wewak. But while Benson's mission was not as star-crossed as that of the civilians trapped aboard the *Akikaze* this day, it was star-crossed nonetheless.

When she left the US submarine base at, of all places, Midway on February 13, 1943, Lieutenant Commander Benson's submarine USS *Trigger* was assigned to patrol the Palau Islands on the route between Truk and the Japanese Home Islands. It was presumed that these would be good hunting waters.

Good hunting, but not necessarily good killing. She was on the surface in the early evening of February 20 when an unknown ship rapidly came into view dead ahead. The officer of the deck ordered submergence. They would track the ship with a periscope, but the ship was not seen again. "Undoubtedly," Lieutenant Commander Benson lamented, "the Officer of the Deck dived too soon," but it was a judgment call that had to be made quickly. "No fault can be found with that."[1]

The submarine's luck did not get much better. Three nights later she sighted a flare, but investigation found nothing. Benson decided to try his luck in a different patrol area: the route between Palau and Wewak. She arrived there on February 26.[2] Yet, if anything, the *Trigger*'s luck got worse. Just after submerging in the early morning hours of February 27, Lieutenant Commander Benson sighted an unescorted freighter off Palau. He quickly developed a firing solution and launched four torpedoes. The target turned away and all the torpedoes missed. About ten minutes later, the *Trigger* heard two "terrific" explosions. Benson guessed it was Japanese aircraft dropping bombs. He moved off, blaming himself for the "wasted" torpedoes.[3]

In the early morning hours of March 1, the *Trigger* sighted … something. Maybe a small destroyer, maybe a submarine chaser. Lieutenant Commander Benson started an approach on the surface, at which point the something opened fire. The submarine dove, but could not get into a position to fire her torpedoes. Later on, more enemy antisubmarine craft showed up, but no one attacked the *Trigger*.[4]

That was about the only good news. Two days later, the submarine sighted three freighters escorted by another small antisubmarine craft. Benson approached, but once again could not get into attack position, and the little convoy escaped.[5]

The next day, March 4, the *Trigger* sighted a freighter sailing alone. Lieutenant Commander Benson moved in to attack and then a squall intervened, making the target difficult to see. Benson managed to get the submarine into position to fire three torpedoes. The cargo ship apparently saw the torpedoes and took evasive action. All three torpedoes missed, but in one case that was a good thing. One of the torpedoes had made that special maneuver that seems unique to American torpedoes – the so-called Circular Torpedo Run, in which the torpedo is launched, and, instead of heading for the target on the assigned gyro angle, it circles around threatening to hit the submarine that launched it.[6] The *Trigger* was fortunate that the torpedo missed.

The fortnight of futility and frustration continued, as on March 5 the *Trigger* spotted a tanker. Again, she could not get into attack position. Then began a week of … nothing. No contacts, no attacks.[7] Near dusk on March 12, Lieutenant Commander Benson's boat sighted smoke on the horizon. He was able to get close enough to determine that it was coming from the funnel of a ship, but once again could not get into position to attack.[8]

But on March 15, when she was on the Equator about 190 miles northwest of Lorengau, where Liebenzell and the Sacred Heart missionaries were preparing for their removal as best they could, the *Trigger* caught a break. Finally. It was 10:35am when the submarine:

> Picked up smoke on the horizon bearing 103. Commenced approach. Turned out to be a convoy of two columns, 2 freighters in the right hand column and three in the left. There was an escort, small destroyer or other type, on each outboard bow. The convoy was zigzagging with escorts patrolling station. We worked into position ahead in order to get between the columns. Maneuvers were successful.[9]

Those maneuvers were complete at 12:15pm. Then the *Trigger*:

> Fired three stern tubes at the leading ship in the right hand column at 1600 yards 90 port track. Two hits.

But there was a catch.

> While these torpedoes were on the way got set up on the leading ship of the left hand column. The last zig had placed the columns in echelon so that the angle on the bow of our new target was 10 degrees starboard, relative bearing 300 and at a range of 2000 yards. The first firing, due to smooth sea, disclosed our position. Our new target headed for us. There was not time for us to turn.

So, two minutes later, at 12:17:

> Fired three bow tubes at zero angle on the bow range 700 yards, gyro angles about 45 degrees. Used normal dispersion as the spread. Two hits. Went deep on firing to avoid the target. The escorts were after us with depth charges instantly, alternating listening and dropping. The sea was smooth and sound conditions excellent so could not at the time come up to take a look. During the quiet periods the sounds associated with the breaking up and sinking of a ship were heard in the direction of our first target.[10]

The attacks kept the *Trigger* down for slightly more than two hours. Lieutenant Commander Benson raised the periscope at 2:20pm:

> Nothing in sound. Came to periscope depth. Nothing in sight.

Nothing he could see, but at 2:37 there was something he could hear.

> Depth charges at a distance. Nothing in sight. Assumed they were from planes. These distant explosions continued for the next hour.

A little more than a half hour later at 3:15, Benson:

> Sighted smoke on the horizon. Started approach. Its bearing remains constant.

Tracking down the target took almost two hours. At 5:05pm, he:

> Could now see a ship's masts. Continued the approach submerged. The new target was a ship which looked like our earlier second target, the one which we have fired and hit twice at 700 yards zero angle on the bow. Alongside of her on the far side and sticking out astern was the smaller ship resembling the freighter which had been third ship in the left hand column. This smaller ship was furnishing buoyancy and propulsion; speed about 2 knots, course 190. The pair was being protected by two small destroyers or corvettes. Continued the approach.

And a long approach it was – more than four hours. Finally, at 9:42pm:

> Fired three bow tubes at 700 yards 90 port track to run at 15 feet. Apparently the torpedoes did not get up to the targets' keels in time. Sound tracked them straight on the targets' bearing. Immediately escorts started running around but apparently did not know where to look. It was bright moonlight. We reversed course and took position for stern shots. Possibly we had been too close but we turned and reversed course at one-third speed without crossing the target's track so it is believed that the range at firing was sufficient. The torpedoes, in any event, did not get up to the target's keel depth.

The *Trigger*'s bad luck had returned, but Lieutenant Commander Benson persisted, and at 10:01pm:

Fired three stern shots at 1100 yards 100 port track to run at 15 feet.

But the *Trigger*'s bad luck had returned with a vengeance.

The only one sound heard ran circles; ran right over our engine room.

The Circular Torpedo Run. Again. Twice in the same patrol.

The commanding officer's confidence in himself and his weapons was so shaken that he considered further action by this vessel against these targets futile. After the escorts gave up, surfaced an [sic] sent contact report. We were not able to get any station to respond to our calls and therefore sent it blind on two frequencies.

March 17 was not quite 90 minutes old when the *Trigger* spotted a convoy. Six ships with one escort. This looked like a jackpot. Lieutenant Commander Benson spent the entire day tracking this convoy, finally maneuvering into attack position at 11:19pm. And then, after more than 22 hours of tracking this plethora of targets … a squall hit, obliterating the convoy from view. The *Trigger* was not able to find it again.[11]

With fuel getting critically low, Lieutenant Commander Benson had the *Trigger* start back toward Midway. En route, the submarine came across one last convoy. Four freighters. As she started tracking the convoy, another cargo ship, operating independently, came into view. Benson ignored this target to focus on the convoy. After slightly more than six hours of tracking, at 2:10pm, Benson fired three torpedoes from the submarine's bow tubes at the lead ship. One hit, or so he thought. The target, later determined to have been the auxiliary gunboat *Choan Maru No. 2 Go*, listed and slowed, but soon corrected her list and was back in formation with little reduction in speed. Benson concluded the hit had been "a detonation of low order." Without enough fuel to continue pursuing the convoy, with only two torpedoes left and those in his stern tubes, Benson disgustedly concluded the patrol and headed back to Midway, where she arrived on April 1.[12]

It had been a frustrating patrol. Few targets early on, then when targets appeared, the *Trigger* could not get into position to attack. Then when she did attack, her torpedoes malfunctioned, sometimes dangerously so. One ship sunk. Two ships potentially damaged.

What Lieutenant Commander Benson and the crew of the *Trigger* could not have known was the role they had unwittingly played in two tragedies then unfolding in the South Pacific.

While the *Trigger* was slowly crawling along on one engine in an effort to save fuel, the destroyer *Akikaze* was speeding along, much faster than was normally necessary. As if she was trying to escape the long line of human remains she was dumping over her stern at regular intervals.

Through the roughly 15 months of war, the Japanese had fielded destroyers that were revolutionary – sleek, fast, and deadly men-of-war who could expect to hold their own against any surface opponent. And they also fielded the *Akikaze*.

Completed in 1921, the *Akikaze* ("Autumn Wind") was like the "four-piper" destroyers that had formed the bulk of the US naval surface forces operating in Asiatic waters at the beginning of the Pacific War. She had been built too late to serve in World War I and too early to be considered a front-line unit in World War II.

The *Minekaze* class of destroyers, of which the *Akikaze* was a member, was actually built as a result of World War I. After the war, the Japanese had received as reparations five Imperial German destroyers. The Japanese examined the ships and incorporated several elements into the *Minekaze*s, which, for their time, were advanced. Once completed, their main gun battery consisted of four 4.7-inch guns in open single mounts – one forward, one aft, and two amidships – with gunshields. Their torpedo armament consisted of three twin mounts for 21-inch torpedoes – not the famous 24-inch Type 93 "Long Lance" that would become the crown jewel of the Imperial Japanese Navy surface fleet and the best torpedo in the world; that had not been invented yet, but the 21-inch was a decent torpedo nonetheless.

For more than a decade, the *Akikaze* and destroyers like her were the backbone of the Japanese destroyer contingent, as were the four-pipers for the US Navy's. Ultimately, however, the *Minekaze*s were but a transition class to the truly revolutionary *Fubuki*-class destroyers and their progeny.

By the time the Pacific War was on the not-too-distant horizon, it had become clear that the aging *Minekaze*s were no longer up to taking point in that war. As with their American four-piper analogues, they were now second-class units, at best. But unlike their American four-piper analogues, they would not be pressed into service on the front lines. Not quite, anyway. Two of the *Minekaze*s were converted into destroyer-transports, again, as were several of the four-piper US Navy destroyers. One *Minekaze* was stripped of its armament so she could be used as an aircraft rescue ship off Tateyama Air Station; how having weapons inhibited her ability to rescue downed pilots was never explained. The ten remaining *Minekaze*s, including the *Akikaze*, were to be used to protect convoys from air and submarine attack, and were modified in line with their new mission. The midships guns and the two aft twin torpedo mounts were removed, as was minesweeping equipment. Amidships was now home to 25mm antiaircraft guns, as many as ten. The fantail was now home to four depth charge launchers and 36 depth charges.[13]

That was the *Akikaze* when, in late 1941 and early 1942, the Japanese swept across southeast Asia and the Pacific with a speed and ferocity that rivaled anything the panzers and Stukas of the Wehrmacht had done. The brainchild of Admiral Yamamoto Isoroku, commander of the Combined Fleet, the oceangoing battle element of the Imperial

Japanese Navy – and, irony of ironies, an opponent of war with the United States. "The Centrifugal Offensive," some postwar historians would call Yamamoto's plan. "Spectacular," yet more historians would call it.

And spectacular it was. Reaching halfway across the Pacific to Pearl Harbor were the *Akagi, Kaga, Hiryu, Soryu, Shokaku,* and *Zuikaku,* the aircraft carriers of what was officially called the 1st Air Fleet and unofficially known as *Kido Butai* – the Japanese Carrier Striking Force. The carriers fielded the best aircrews in the world, dive bombing the enemy with Aichi D3A Type 99 carrier bombers, launching aerial torpedoes at the enemy with devastating Nakajima B5N Type 97 carrier attack planes, and shooting down the enemy with the shocking (to the Allies) Mitsubishi A6M Type 0 carrier fighter, popularly known to both Allies and Axis as the "Zero." Escorting the carriers were two old battlecruisers now converted into fast battleships, the *Hiei* and *Kirishima*; two weird-looking heavy cruiser-seaplane carrier hybrids *Tone* and *Chikuma*; and light cruiser *Abukuma,* leading the 1st Destroyer Flotilla with *Urakaze, Isokaze, Tanikaze, Hamakaze, Kagero, Shiranuhi, Arare, Kasumi, Sazanami,* and *Ushio.* They were led by a who's who of the Combined Fleet's (allegedly) best commanders; names that would appear again and again in the months ahead. The destroyer flotilla was led by Rear Admiral Omori Sentaro; the cruiser-seaplane carrier hybrids by Rear Admiral Abe Hiroaki; the battleships by Rear Admiral Mikawa Gunichi; and the carriers and the force overall by Vice Admiral Nagumo Chuichi. Admiral Yamamoto was certainly not happy about that last one. Yamamoto was a visionary, a gambler.[14] Nagumo was conservative and formulaic. That differential did not matter much at Pearl Harbor, however, or so it seemed. The "Sea Eagles" of the Japanese Naval Air Force operating from those carriers left all the battleships of the US Pacific Fleet immobilized, two permanently.

Several hours after Pearl Harbor came yet more spectacular success. More Sea Eagles, these of the 11th Air Fleet, the Combined Fleet's land-based air component, showed up uninvited over the American air base complex centered on Clark Field in the Philippines with the blazing-fast twin engine Mitsubishi G3M Type 96 and G4M Type 1 land attack planes and even more Zeros, destroying most of the US Army's Far East Air Force on the ground. It was the first domino in the Far East to fall that would eventually lead to the stunning conquest during the Java Sea Campaign of what Japan called the "Southern Resources Area" – Malaya (Malaysia), Singapore, and the Netherlands East Indies (Indonesia) – Japan's objective in starting the Pacific War.

To be effective, a spear needs not just a sharp tip but a strong shaft. The Sea Eagles of *Kido Butai* and Base Air Force got assigned the tip of the spear. For the spectacular destruction of Pearl Harbor, Clark Field, and, shortly thereafter, the Royal Navy's "Force Z" (battleship *Prince of Wales* and battlecruiser *Repulse*) and the US Navy's Cavite Navy Yard, the Sea Eagles got the glory. Other elements of the Imperial Japanese Navy, like the *Akikaze,* got the shaft.

In those first days of the Pacific War, the *Akikaze*'s entire unit, three modified *Minekaze*s of Destroyer Division 34, had been serving as air-sea rescue ships for the 11th Air Fleet.

The *Akikaze* and sister ship *Tachikaze* loitered in the waters between Formosa (now Taiwan) and Luzon, just in case any of the Japanese aircraft crashed or had to ditch during the Clark Field attacks.[15] The third member of the division, the *Hakaze*, was assigned a similar role off French Indochina in the South China Sea for the attacks on Force Z.[16] It was an important role, to be sure, but it was the closest the *Akikaze* and her division-mates had gotten to the tip of the spear.

Since those first days, however, the *Akikaze* had gotten nothing but the butt end of the shaft.[17] By the time the Japanese were landing on Malaya and the Philippines in December 1941, the *Akikaze* had been given her new mission – escorting convoys.[18]

While the Japanese were landing in the Netherlands East Indies in January 1942, the *Akikaze* was operating out of recently captured Davao on the southern Philippine island of Mindanao, escorting convoys. While the Japanese were completing their conquest of Malaya, Singapore, and the Netherlands East Indies in February 1942, the *Akikaze* was operating out of recently captured Ambon in the aforementioned Netherlands East Indies, escorting convoys. While the Japanese were trying to land at Port Moresby in Papua New Guinea and later at Midway in May and early June 1942, in the process losing four of the six carriers (*Akagi*, *Kaga*, *Hiryu*, and *Soryu*) that had attacked Pearl Harbor, the *Akikaze* was not escorting convoys. She was in drydock for maintenance, which was a better fate than that of her sister ship *Yakaze*, who was stripped of her weaponry and turned into a target ship.[19]

It was in late June and early July 1942 that the *Akikaze* had her second brush with the tip of the spear. Operating out of recently captured Rabaul, the *Akikaze* escorted aircraft transports *Mogamigawa* and *Kinryu Marus* to the lower end of the Solomon Islands. The *Mogamigawa Maru* brought reinforcements and supplies to the new seaplane base at Tulagi. The *Kinryu Maru* dropped off the 11th and 13th Construction Units and elements of the 3rd Kure Special Naval Landing Force to begin construction of an air base near Lunga Point on a little-known island called Guadalcanal.[20] At the time, neither the *Akikaze* nor the *Mogamigawa Maru* nor the *Kinryu Maru* could have known just how significant this convoy would become.

The *Akikaze* would escort convoys throughout the long Guadalcanal campaign from the American capture of the air base in August 1942 through to the evacuation of the remaining Japanese troops from the island in February 1943. Seemingly, no matter what the Imperial Japanese Navy did, the *Akikaze* would be escorting convoys. Mostly supply convoys but also individual ships: tankers, freighters, ammunition ships. Rather remarkable for a navy that did not yet have an organized convoy system, which was itself remarkable for a navy that had put so much effort before the war into building up its merchant marine.[21] Lest the assignment of the *Akikaze* to escorting convoys makes anyone believe the Japanese were taking the threat to merchant ships seriously, as American military analysts later explained:

The Japanese apparently went into the war without providing adequately for the vulnerability of their merchant marine to attack. In the early months of the war, merchant vessels were not armed, and no effective convoy system was in use. Until about March 1944 there were only about 25 vessels regularly assigned to convoy escort duty. An additional 40 subchasers too small for open-water sailing were distributed among the various naval bases for local defense. Convoying was not regularly begun until 1943 and then only on the Singapore run. But escort was provided to some degree, at least in the southern area, early in the war. What few convoying ships there were were stepchildren of the Navy, wornout vessels that were no longer of use to the fleet.[22]

"[W]ornout vessels that were no longer of use to the fleet" sounds a lot like the *Akikaze*. She and her division-mates were definitely stepchildren of the Combined Fleet inasmuch as they were not even in a surface fleet per se, but under the command of the 11th Air Fleet that had been given the rather unimaginative operational name "Base Air Force." The *Akikaze* in particular was also often lent out to the recently promoted Vice Admiral Mikawa's 8th Fleet (or "Outer South Seas Fleet"), based in Rabaul.[23]

The Imperial Navy's own disinterest in protecting its merchant marine was starting to take a serious toll as US Navy submarines became much more effective. Part of the reason for that disinterest was the Imperial Navy projecting its own doctrine onto the US Navy. Japanese submarines generally targeted warships, and so far had actually been fairly successful doing so, as the carriers *Yorktown*, *Wasp*, and *Saratoga* and the battleship *North Carolina* could attest. Japanese submariners did not like attacking the seemingly far less important (or exciting) targets such as tankers and freighters.[24] It just wasn't sporting. The US Navy followed a similar doctrine the Japanese believed.

Wrongly. While US Navy submarines would attack warships as targets of opportunity, they were generally used strategically. If, say, a carrier was nearby, they'd try to attack it, but otherwise they'd be on the prowl for tankers, freighters, ammunition ships, and the like. The way the US Navy saw it, every tanker or freighter sunk meant one less tanker load of oil or ship load of supplies, one less tanker or freighter for the Japanese merchant marine, and one more tanker or freighter the Japanese had to replace with their very limited supply of steel that had to be split between military and civilian uses. For the US Navy it was a war of attrition.

A war the Imperial Japanese Navy was not interested in fighting, in part because that was a war it could not win, which was why it was so obsessed with the idea of one large "decisive battle" deciding the Pacific War. Additionally, and perhaps more importantly, escorting convoys was boring, tedious duty. Spending long hours watching for an attack that, they believed, would probably not happen. They did not see how they could win glory for the emperor by guarding, say, a freighter full of rice.

They still didn't, but things were changing. The first sign was in August 1942, two months after the catastrophic defeat and loss of two thirds of *Kido Butai* at Midway. The Japanese construction of the airfield on Guadalcanal had been part of a strategic effort resumed after Midway to cut off Australia from the US with a network of bases at Lae, Salamaua, Buna, and Gona in Papua New Guinea; existing bases at Kavieng on New

Ireland, Rabaul on New Britain, and the Shortland Islands off Bougainville; and new bases running down through the Solomon Islands into the New Hebrides, New Caledonia, and even Fiji and Samoa.[25] The Imperial Army's efforts to complete the takeover of New Guinea by capturing Port Moresby continued to be stymied. Now the Combined Fleet's move down the Solomons was short-circuited by the Allies' surprise seizure in August of the Lunga airfield on Guadalcanal.

The Japanese had captured airfields before, especially in the Netherlands East Indies during the Java Sea Campaign. How hard could retaking this one be? The Japanese were encouraged when, the day after the enemy landing on Guadalcanal, Admiral Mikawa sailed down with a force of mostly cruisers to attack the invaders at night and managed to sink most of the warships protecting the invasion transports. But he left before going after the transports themselves because he feared US Navy air attacks after dawn and wanted to be as far away from the airfield and any lurking US Navy aircraft carriers as possible. Admiral Yamamoto was livid with Mikawa for this omission, but Mikawa had established a theme that would manifest itself throughout the upcoming Guadalcanal campaign.

The Combined Fleet turned to its designated "amphibious expert" Rear Admiral Tanaka Raizo, who had shepherded convoys landing troops in the Netherlands East Indies during the Centrifugal Offensive, and put him in charge of running troops to Guadalcanal to retake the airfield. It was not an assignment Tanaka wanted. The enormous convoys of troopships that landed on Java in March 1942 had done so with minimal interference from Allied aircraft. This time Tanaka was being ordered to land troops in the teeth of an occupied, equipped, and alerted enemy air base. And he was being ordered to do so with no fighter protection of his own. Tanaka tried to warn his superiors, but being the designated "amphibious expert" did not mean the higher brass would listen to his expertise. It only meant that when they wanted to do something amphibiously, they assigned it to Tanaka and then let him handle it. Which worked as long as the Japanese had aerial dominance as they had in the Netherlands East Indies.

This time, they didn't. Initially, the Japanese started by running troops to Guadalcanal on destroyers, who would land the troops at night then scurry to be out of range of Allied aircraft by daylight. The troops got through to Guadalcanal all right, but once landed, proved to be not nearly enough to retake the aforementioned airfield.

No matter. The Japanese tried to run two concurrent convoys full of troops – one with transports, one with destroyers – to Guadalcanal to retake the aforementioned airfield. Though these convoys were operating during daylight, Admiral Yamamoto refused to commit the two remaining members of *Kido Butai*, the *Shokaku* and *Zuikaku*, to actively provide air cover for it. Admiral Tanaka saw what was coming.

American aircraft, most of which were from that Guadalcanal air base from which the Americans had so rudely evicted the Japanese, sank one transport and one destroyer, and damaged one destroyer as well as Admiral Tanaka's beloved flagship, light cruiser *Jintsu*, in the process conking the admiral on his head. The separate convoy of four destroyers making a run to Guadalcanal was turned back after having one of their number sunk and a second disabled. Tanaka's and Mikawa's fears were realized.

But Tanaka Raizo was intelligent, cool under fire, and resourceful. He found an effective, if very inefficient, way of running troops to Guadalcanal. Those early convoys consisted of troops on destroyers who would run to Guadalcanal at night, drop the troops off, and leave, making sure to be out of the range of air attacks by daylight. And they had gotten through. Tanaka would continue using what worked. The Japanese would, rather derisively, call it "rat transportation." The Americans and their allies would call it something different: "The Tokyo Express."

This effort to retake the airfield settled into a pattern. During the day, Base Air Force would bomb the airfield, usually facing ferocious fighter opposition from US Marine and Army Air Force fighters, and, curiously, US Navy carrier planes based at the airfield. At night, Admiral Mikawa, now Admiral Tanaka's immediate superior, would send down the rat transports carrying Imperial Army troops with some escorts, who would often bombard the airfield from offshore. Then the whole bunch would skedaddle back toward Shortland to be out of range of Allied air attacks from Guadalcanal by dawn. Repeat *ad infinitum*.

Yet, because destroyers were notorious fuel hogs, rat transportation used a disproportionately large amount of fuel, the lack of which was Imperial Japan's reason for starting the Pacific War in the first place. Moreover, while rat transportation could get some troops to Guadalcanal, it could not get enough troops and supplies or any heavy weapons to Guadalcanal to form the critical mass of combat power needed to recapture the airfield. For that, they needed those slow, fat transports.

Which brought the Japanese back to their original problem of getting those slow, fat transports to Guadalcanal. The Japanese could not capture the airfield without the critical mass of troops; they could not get that critical mass of troops to Guadalcanal without capturing the airfield. And now the Japanese had to face this conundrum with an additional bigger, far more ominous complication: the aerial dominance *Kido Butai* and Base Air Force had provided to the Japanese surface fleet at the start of the Pacific War was long gone.

Worse, that particular balance was starting to tip in the other direction. By November 1942, of the original six carriers of *Kido Butai* that had attacked Pearl Harbor, only the *Shokaku* and *Zuikaku* were still afloat. And *Shokaku* was laid up in a shipyard. Worse still, of the 765 elite carrier aviators from *Kido Butai* who had attacked Pearl Harbor, 409 were now dead.[26] About 100 of that 409 were lost at the recent Japanese "victory" over the US Pacific Fleet off the Santa Cruz Islands in late October in which, Admiral Yamamoto believed, four US Navy carriers had been sunk, leaving none left in the South Pacific. Admiral Nagumo would later call Santa Cruz "a tactical win but a shattering strategic loss for Japan."[27]

By the second week of November, the *Shokaku* and the light carrier *Zuiho* (a recent addition to *Kido Butai* to try to make up for the four carriers lost at Midway) were laid up for repairs, and the *Zuikaku* was in the Home Islands training a new air group – again. The only Japanese aircraft carrier left on station in the South Pacific was the *Junyo*, that odd ship with the heart of a warship, the flight deck of a fleet carrier, and the engines of a cruise liner. And even after cannibalizing the pitiful remnants of the *Zuikaku*'s and the *Zuiho*'s old air groups, she could only field a partial complement of 27 Zeros, 12 Type 99 carrier bombers, and nine Type 97 carrier attack planes.[28]

When the *Zuikaku* would be back with her new air group was anybody's guess. At the beginning of the war, the Japanese Naval Air Force had 3,500 Sea Eagles. They had anticipated needing as many as 15,000 new pilots for the war, but they only trained "several hundred" per year.[29] Admiral Yamamoto and the Combined Fleet did not consider it a major issue for the time being. With, they believed, no US Navy carriers to oppose them, they could make do with Base Air Force and the *Junyo*'s aviators.

Except Base Air Force had not been able to suppress the Guadalcanal airfield in three months of attacks, first flying from bases around Rabaul and later from an advance base at Buin on southern Bougainville. The long distance the Japanese aviators had to fly between their bases and Guadalcanal greatly limited the times of day during which they could attack the Lunga airfield. And the enemy's possession of radar and seeding of spies throughout the Solomon Islands who reported Japanese ship and aircraft movements not only meant surprise was almost impossible to achieve, but that the Americans usually would be able to scramble fighters to meet the Japanese attackers. Additionally, that long distance made the return of aircraft damaged in combat problematic, recovery of downed aircrews even more so.

Finally, the Japanese were discovering a sad truth about war: it is extremely difficult to destroy or even seriously disrupt an airfield made out of dirt. Base Air Force would bomb the airfield; Combined Fleet would send ships, including at one point two battleships, to shell the airfield. They would put big holes in the dirt runways. The Americans would just take the dirt and fill the holes in again, often within an hour. It was Sisyphean. When the Americans added Marston matting (standardized perforated steel planking) to the runways to enable more efficient operations in the mud that comes with the frequent rainstorms in the Solomons, Japanese efforts at disruption had no more success because the Americans had plenty of extra matting on hand that they kept close to the runways to replace matting destroyed in the bombing raids.

Nevertheless, the Japanese thought they had "suppressed" the airfield in mid-October when, in an effort to cover the arrival of a convoy of those slow transports supplemented by faster convoys of seaplane carriers *Nisshin* and *Chitose* (who actually could carry some tanks and heavy artillery), and more rat transports, those two battleships, the *Kongo* and the *Haruna*, escorted by Admiral Tanaka, had blasted the airfield.[30] Using their 14-inch guns to lob mostly incendiary antiaircraft shells for some 90 minutes, the two battleships turned the airfield into a lake of fire worthy of Milton.

Even so, the next morning, the Americans sent up their scouts and fighter patrols as they usually did, to the shock and extreme consternation of the Japanese. Air attacks by the G4Ms of Base Air Force and the seaplanes of the cryptically named "R-Area Air Force," an organization Admiral Mikawa had created in August 1942 by pooling all the 8th Fleet's seaplanes and their parent tenders, continued to meet ferocious air opposition. Even after another night bombardment, this time by Admiral Mikawa's 8-inch-gun cruisers, the Americans continued to send up air attacks. Three of those precious slow, fat transports were so badly damaged they had to be beached on Guadalcanal to prevent their sinking, though they were able to land their Imperial Japanese Army troops.

Not that the Imperial Japanese Army had exactly been covering itself in glory during the Guadalcanal campaign. Three times they had tried to retake the airfield. The first time, in August, a light, badly outnumbered force of Japanese troops decided to attack by mounting what became known as a "banzai charge." That practice involved this relatively modern army complete with rifles, machine guns, and mortars, waiting until nightfall, fixing bayonets, then shouting "Banzai!" or "Totsugeki!" ("Charge!") as they charged en masse at US Marine positions. Like the Japanese, the Marines were armed with modern rifles, machine guns, and mortars. Unlike the Japanese, they were very happy to use them, along with antitank guns and heavy artillery, during these banzai charges. Seemingly every Imperial Japanese Army attack had to have at least one banzai charge. The August effort had three. Three times the Japanese banzai charged in droves and three times they were gunned down in droves, until some 90 percent of the 1,000-man force was dead.

No matter. Admiral Tanaka's failed transport effort in August and his subsequent development of rat transportation had been intended to land a much larger force on Guadalcanal. This one would burrow into the jungle and launch a banzai charge at the airfield from a completely different direction. The night of September 13–14, Imperial Army troops kept charging over a ridge that became known as Edson's Ridge in droves and kept getting gunned down in droves. But because they had almost fooled the US Marines, the Japanese had local numerical superiority over the defenders on the ridge (about 3.5 to 1) and almost reached the airfield.

Almost. Maybe they would have if one of the Japanese commanders had not gotten lost in the jungle, leaving his unit twiddling its thumbs while listening to their comrades being shot, bayonetted (sometimes by each other), and blown up. Or if starving Japanese troops had not been distracted by an American supply cache of food and stopped to gorge themselves. (Even at this early date in the Guadalcanal campaign, supplies were becoming an issue for the Japanese. Especially food, which eventually earned Guadalcanal the nickname "Starvation Island." It put into a new light the disgust members of the Imperial Navy felt at guarding, say, a freighter full of rice.) Nevertheless, the Japanese did not reach the airfield, let alone capture it. And, once again, their personnel losses from the repeated banzai charges had been devastating.

No matter. That bombardment by the *Kongo* and *Haruna* had covered, mostly, yet another series of convoys intended to culminate in a third major attack to recapture the Lunga airfield. Admiral Yamamoto sent the Combined Fleet, with *Kido Butai* under Admiral Nagumo and the battleship force under Admiral Kondo Nobutake, to sea in order to be ready to hunt for the remaining American carriers as soon as he got the word the airfield was in Japanese hands. Unfortunately for the Japanese, it took them almost two more weeks to have their troops burrow into the jungle again and position themselves for the attack, with the Combined Fleet at sea, every minute burning more of that precious fuel. The army's third major attack against the air base's perimeter had been from the same area in which the second attack was launched. The twist here was that the attack was two-pronged. Sure enough, on the morning of October 25, Admiral Yamamoto received word from the Imperial Army that the airfield had been captured. The long national nightmare was over.

There were some nagging uncertainties about the Japanese seizure of the airfield, however. Such as Japanese scout planes that were sent to check out the airfield being shot down by antiaircraft fire. Finally, the Imperial Army had to admit that it was mistaken: the airfield was not in Japanese hands. The left prong had, by now, the usual tactic of the Japanese troops banzai charging in droves and being gunned down in droves. The right prong, who had actually gotten lost and missed the Allied positions almost entirely, became convinced it had captured the airfield when, in fact, it had merely captured an open field.

Even with this new information, Admiral Yamamoto went ahead with sending *Kido Butai* and the battleship force forward. The result was the previously mentioned Battle of the Santa Cruz Islands. At least that's what the Americans called it. Yamamoto believed it cost the US Navy four aircraft carriers, kind of like a reverse Midway. But he did not treat it like much of a victory. Afterwards, Yamamoto took the opportunity to finally replace the cautious Nagumo, an officer who, he believed, should never have commanded *Kido Butai* in the first place. Nagumo was replaced with someone who he and many others believed should have had that command, Vice Admiral Ozawa Jisaburo.

By early November, after three months of air attacks, rat transportation, convoy runs, carrier battles, nighttime naval battles, and three major land attacks, the Japanese were no closer to recapturing the Lunga airfield. The Combined Fleet and the Imperial Army did what any self-respecting bureaucracy would do: more of the same and hope for a different result. In November 1942, Admiral Tanaka was ordered, despite his warnings, to bring a convoy of 11 "fast" transports carrying some 12,000 Japanese troops and some 10,000 tons of supplies to Guadalcanal. They were counting on suppressing the Lunga airfield with another night bombardment by battleships. This time, it would be the *Kongo*'s and *Haruna*'s sister ships, the *Hiei* and *Kirishima*, doing the shelling. The recently promoted Vice Admiral Abe, who normally commanded the *Hiei* and *Kirishima* as surface escorts for *Kido Butai*, was in charge of this operation.

After sailing through a storm, Admiral Abe's force arrived off Lunga and were shocked to find American warships waiting for them. As if that was not enough, maneuvering in the storm had left the Japanese formation in such disarray that the Imperial Navy ships found US Navy ships in their midst, "mingled like minnows in a bucket."[31]

The result was the "Friday the 13th Action," a frenzied ferocious fracas more reminiscent of Salamis than the South Pacific, "a no-holds-barred barroom brawl, in which someone turned out the lights and everyone started swinging in every direction."[32] The close quarters nature of the contest was such that Admiral Abe's flagship *Hiei* was besieged, facing a flock of American destroyers to her front and unable to shoot at them because her main and secondary batteries could not depress their guns low enough to hit them, while the destroyers were so close that they could not launch their torpedoes. One of the destroyers was almost run over by the *Hiei*, scooching clear of the flagship's bow by less than 10 meters.

But the destroyers punched well above their weight. With their guns unable to penetrate the *Hiei*'s hull armor, the tin cans instead aimed their 5-inch main batteries, their 20mm guns, and even their machine guns at the battleship's superstructure, especially her pagoda-like tower mast where her bridge was located. In so doing, they unintentionally targeted the weakest link in the Japanese chain. The maelstrom of white-hot steel smashed the battleship's bridge, killing or wounding almost everyone there, including Abe, who was hit in the face with shrapnel and likely suffered a concussion.

While the *Hiei* was tangling with the little destroyers in front of her, her 14-inch main battery was dealing with a cruiser off to starboard. A cruiser's 8-inch shells could not penetrate a battleship's armor, normally, but this time one such projectile got a lucky hit and started flooding in the battleship's steering compartment, shorting out the steering motor and forcing the men there to hold the rudder in place so the *Hiei* could be steered by engine. But for the close quarter nature of the combat, the injuries to the battleship's bridge and steering compartment would not have been realistically possible.

Barely conscious, Admiral Abe scrubbed the bombardment mission and had his force turn away, which was difficult for the *Hiei* with her rudder out of order. It apparently never occurred to anyone to try to stop the flooding in the steering compartment before the men holding the rudder in place had to abandon it, after which the rudder swung hard to starboard and jammed. Dawn found the *Hiei* only able to move in circles and unable to get away from the Lunga airfield that had gone from being the hunted to being the hunter. US Marine dive bombers, Army Air Force bombers, and, curiously, US Navy carrier planes, spent the daylight hours of November 13 trying to put the battleship under. Abe ordered the *Hiei* abandoned and left the battleship to sink sometime that night. A stunned Admiral Yamamoto was livid over Abe's actions and forced him into retirement.

As a result of the failed battleship bombardment, Admiral Tanaka was forced to delay his convoy by a day. Not that he minded. Indeed, he would have preferred to delay it indefinitely. Admiral Mikawa came down with his cruisers and, finding no naval opposition, proceeded to lob 8-inch shells at the airfield. But he sped back up toward Rabaul knowing his bombardment was ineffective.

That particular point was driven home the next morning, when Admiral Mikawa and his cruisers were not quite out of the range of the airfield. Repeated attacks by US Marine aviators and US Navy carrier planes sank one of his cruisers, fortunately an old one, not that the Imperial Navy could afford to be picky about surface ships. Heading in the other direction, Admiral Tanaka had watched the American aircraft hunting Mikawa's ships with a sense of dread, hoping against hope that they had not seen his group of transports.

It was a fool's hope, and Admiral Tanaka knew it. The Americans knew exactly where he was. He did have fighter protection, in the form of Zeros from Rabaul and Buin. But they did an inept job protecting his transports from the swarms of US Army Air Force B-17s, Marine dive bombers, and Navy carrier planes. For a navy that allegedly had no aircraft carriers left in the Pacific, the US Pacific Fleet was sending an awful lot of carrier planes against him. A bit of an explanation was provided when a Japanese scout plane reported sighting one enemy carrier that was not quite as sunk as Admiral Yamamoto had believed.

Not that it did Admiral Tanaka any good. He spent the day watching the Americans bomb, torpedo, and shoot up his transports, ultimately sinking six and forcing a seventh to retreat to Shortland, where she was sunk by air attack in short order. Almost all of the troops were rescued, but none of the supplies could be recovered.

Seemingly oblivious to the losses they were incurring, Admiral Yamamoto insisted on pressing ahead with the reinforcement convoy. This time Admiral Kondo, Yamamoto's second-in-command who commanded the Combined Fleet's 2nd Fleet, assembled an "Emergency Bombardment Unit" to, once again, blast the Lunga airfield with 14-inch incendiary shells. But while he had three 14-inch armed battleships, the *Kirishima*, *Kongo*, and *Haruna*, for reasons known only to Kondo, he took only the *Kirishima* with him to Guadalcanal.

When Admiral Kondo arrived off Guadalcanal, he proceeded to divide his 14-ship force four different ways.[33] Kondo held the part with the *Kirishima* back while the other three, consisting of two light cruisers and seven destroyers, dealt with a US Navy force that was rather inconsiderately blocking the way. It should not have been a problem, Kondo believed, because the American force consisted of only two cruisers and four destroyers. The enemy destroyers were neutralized, but the supporting Japanese divisions could not lay a glove on the two cruisers, which, they reported, were actually battleships. Nonsense, Kondo thought. Until his supporting divisions got tangled up with each other, leaving him face-to-face with one of them and, sure enough, it was a battleship. The *Kongo* and *Haruna* might have been useful right about now. Kondo's cruisers and the *Kirishima* got a few damaging licks in on it, but the second enemy battleship delivered an abject pummeling to the *Kirishima*, sending her to join her sister ship *Hiei* on the bottom. With no battleship to shell the airfield – the *Kongo* and *Haruna* might have been useful here, too – Kondo called off the bombardment.

Leaving Admiral Tanaka and his transports exposed to air attack once again. And he knew it. Desperate to get *something* to Guadalcanal, Tanaka, with the backing of his superiors, ordered his four remaining transports to run themselves aground on the island and unload their troops. Then he skedaddled out of there. The transports indeed ran themselves up on the beaches, from which they could never be recovered, and proceeded to unload their troops and supplies, or tried to, in the face of incessant US Marine, Army Air Force, and Navy air attacks, as well as shelling by US Marine artillery and at least one US Navy destroyer. Out of the 12,000 Japanese troops and some 10,000 tons of supplies the Japanese tried to send to Guadalcanal, only about 2,000 men landed and five tons of supplies reached the island. At a cost of two battleships, a heavy cruiser, three destroyers, and ten very valuable and very scarce transports. It was an abject catastrophe for Japan.

But old habits die hard. There were still thousands of Japanese troops on Guadalcanal to supply. That November convoy did not suggest so much as scream that supplying them was going to be a problem. The Japanese tried sending in supplies by submarine. "Mole transportation," they would call it. But the moles did not like this type of operation, and these particular moles were not designed for supplying, say, 10,000 troops. And on more than a few occasions when these moles would poke their heads out of the water, they would find an enemy naval unit waiting to whack them.

Then someone came up with the brilliant idea of taking some unused oil drums, scrubbing them clean (hopefully), and filling them with food so that destroyers could run to Guadalcanal at night and push the drums into the water, from where the Japanese troops ashore could recover them. Admiral Tanaka was among the first to try this ridiculous theory when he ran a force of destroyers to Guadalcanal intending to drop off these drums. Then a large force of enemy cruisers showed up. Tanaka stopped what he was doing, ordered his destroyers to "attack," which in the Japanese naval parlance meant "launch torpedoes," and scurry away.

One of his destroyers fired her guns and paid for it, attracting all the enemy gunfire and getting herself sunk. But the other Japanese destroyers held their gunfire, thus not revealing themselves in the dark, and just launched torpedoes and fled. They left one US Navy cruiser sunk and three others severely damaged. It was an incredible Japanese victory, one of the most spectacular of the war. But Tanaka could not get past the loss of one of his destroyers. And his superiors could not get past his failure to deliver the supply drums as he was ordered.

"Tenacious Tanaka," as he was nicknamed, would get another shot. He led another force of destroyers with drums. This time he flew his flag on the destroyer *Teruzuki*, the second commissioned member of what the Japanese called the "Type B" class of destroyers and Westerners called the *Akizuki* class designed primarily for air defense. They were "the finest class of destroyers Japan fielded during the war," according to respected Imperial Japanese Navy historian Jonathan Parshall.[34] They were also "the largest, most handsome, and, in the Japanese estimation, most successful destroyers in the Imperial fleet," according to respected Imperial Japanese Navy historian Allyn Nevitt.[35]

The only problem was that Tanaka's supply force found US Navy PT boats waiting for them. Having developed a well-earned reputation for shooting at anything that moved – friend or foe – but hitting nothing, the PTs managed to plunk an unusually damaging torpedo into the *Teruzuki*, giving Tanaka another conk on the head and knocking him out – again. When he came to, the *Teruzuki* was being abandoned, the torpedo having disabled the destroyer and started a nasty fire that ultimately detonated her depth charge stowage, eventually sending her to the bottom.

"The loss of my flagship, our newest and best destroyer, to such inferior enemy strength was a serious responsibility," Tanaka would later write. "I have often thought that it would have been easier for me to have been killed in that first explosion."[36] He was hospitalized in Rabaul. Deeply depressed about losing the *Teruzuki* and failing his mission, in pain from his injuries, and probably suffering from the effects of a concussion, Tanaka dictated a memorandum to his superiors recommending the evacuation of Guadalcanal.[37] His superiors had already decided to evacuate Guadalcanal, in effect, admitting defeat in the Guadalcanal Campaign, but, in their eyes, that was no excuse for Tanaka himself to admit defeat. Moreover, someone had to be blamed for the defeat, and it certainly would not be them. They reassigned Tanaka, their best destroyer admiral, to that hot-bed of naval activity: Burma (now Myanmar). Combined Fleet's message was all too clear: the defeat on Guadalcanal was all *his* fault. It was a sign of things to come.

Yet Tanaka Raizo's legacy would far outlive his now-ruined naval career. His system of running destroyers at night to convey troops and supplies to bases would continue. And be modified further. In late January and early February 1943, the Japanese used three nocturnal runs of destroyers to evacuate 10,652 of their troops from Guadalcanal – right under the noses of the Allies, and at the cost of just one destroyer sunk. They did not dare call it a "retreat," let alone a "defeat." Imperial General Headquarters, that weird Imperial Japanese institution in which the army and navy general staffs would negotiate what policies and strategies to follow, had coined the term *tenshin* – "turn around and advance."[38]

Having turned around and advanced from Guadalcanal back the way they had come, the strategic concept of isolating Australia was out the window. Still in the window was retrenchment. Holding what they already had, the Japanese military, now with a much needed dose of humility provided by the Guadalcanal Campaign, conceded, would be difficult enough. The Japanese would fortify their holdings in New Guinea at Wewak, Madang, the Lae-Salamaua area, and the Buna-Gona area, the defense of which was entrusted to the 18th Army under Lieutenant General Adachi Hatazo, though the Imperial Navy would have a presence as well. Wewak, in particular, was to be an army and navy base, airfield, supply depot, and staging area. Plans were hurriedly completed to rush the Imperial Army's 20th and 41st Divisions there.

In the interim, advance ground units were rushed to Wewak, Madang, and Hollandia (now Jayapura), the last of which was theoretically part of Netherlands New Guinea (now part of Indonesia). This Operation *Mu*, as it was designated, was a bit more exciting than the Japanese had intended. The reinforcements were given air cover by Vice Admiral Kakuta Kakuji's carrier *Junyo*, escorted by the new light cruiser *Agano* and destroyers *Isokaze* and *Hamakaze* operating in the Bismarck Sea. Shortly before midnight on December 18, they spotted a surfaced submarine. Gunfire from the destroyers convinced the boat, veteran Lieutenant Commander Lucius H. Chappell's USS *Sculpin*, to submerge and move along.[39]

The initial reinforcement to Wewak was successfully completed on December 18, as previously described, while the reinforcement of Madang had even more excitement than the *Junyo*'s experience. The armed merchant cruisers *Aikoku* and *Gokoku Maru*s had embarked passengers from multiple units of the 5th Division, including the 21st and

42nd Infantry Regiments, 58th Field Antiaircraft Artillery Battalion, 6th Airfield Construction Unit, road construction, and communications units. Escorting them were destroyers *Isonami*, *Inazuma*, *Suzukaze* and *Arashio* and the old light cruiser *Tenryu* led by Rear Admiral Matsuyama Mitsuharu. The convoy got to Madang in good order on December 18, but the *Gokoku Maru* took a bomb in the forecastle from American B-17s from the 43rd Bombardment Group of the 5th Air Force. The bomb started a small fire but otherwise did little serious damage. At 9:15pm, as they were starting to leave, three torpedoes intended for the *Gokoku Maru* bubbled past their target, only for two of those torpedoes to burrow their way into the stern of the *Tenryu*. The old cruiser's steering gear was wrecked, her engine rooms flooded, and she lost power. Matsuyama had to transfer his flag to the *Isonami*, who, with the *Suzukaze*, dropped four depth charges on the assailant, Lieutenant Richard C. Lake's USS *Albacore*, without apparent effect. The *Suzukaze* took off the cruiser's crew and the *Tenryu*, a pest with a history of punching well above her weight, sank at 11:20pm, with 23 killed and 21 injured.[40]

While the Imperial Navy was losing the *Tenryu* off New Guinea, in the Solomons it was adding what it should have added before building that airfield on Guadalcanal: several intermediate airfields. The most important of these new airfields was at Cape Munda, at the southwestern tip of New Georgia in the central Solomons. To support Munda, they built a second airfield at an old plantation at Vila on the neighboring island of Kolombangara; to support Vila and ultimately Munda, they constructed shipping facilities at the neighboring Stanmore plantation, earning the Kolombangara complex the rare hyphenated base name of "Vila-Stanmore." In addition, the Japanese had finished construction of still another airfield, this one running the length of a tiny island in the Shortlands off southern Bougainville named Ballale.[41]

These new and/or improved bases would mean more convoys in the region, which meant more work for the *Akikaze*. And more danger, because the Japanese had not been having good experiences with convoys or single supply ships as of late. But things seemed to get a little better with the coming of the new year 1943 and what was called Operation *18*. The operation was to get a convoy carrying elements of the Imperial Army's 51st Division from Rabaul to Lae. It consisted of the transports *Brazil*, *Nichiryu*, *Clyde*, *Chifuku*, and *Myoko Maru*s, escorted by destroyers *Urakaze*, *Tanikaze*, *Isokaze*, *Hamakaze*, and *Maikaze*. Despite fierce air attacks from General Douglas MacArthur's 5th Air Force, only two of the transports – *Nichiryu* and *Myoko Maru*s – were sunk, with most of the troops saved and most of the supplies salvaged.

Yet the relative success of Operation *18* was overshadowed by a disaster: the Japanese loss of Buna on the north coast of Papua on January 2, 1943. Buna had only fallen to the Japanese the previous July. The Imperial Army had hoped to use Buna as a jumping-off point for heading south to the Kokoda Trail that crosses the 14,000-foot Owen Stanley mountain range, and taking Port Moresby on Papua's southern coast.[42] Unfortunately for the Japanese, the Kokoda Trail was only the width of about one person and the Imperial Army could not break through to Port Moresby. Even more unfortunately, Douglas

MacArthur's army of American and Australian troops was later able to cross the Owen Stanleys and, after a brutal campaign, finally take Buna.

For the Imperial Japanese Navy, this was a problem. Vice Admiral Ugaki Matome, Admiral Yamamoto's chief of staff, had warned about what the loss of Buna would mean: the Allies could build airfields there that would move Allied bombers closer to Rabaul.

The Japanese had set up Rabaul, on the northeastern tip of New Britain, as a veritable fortress because it had the finest harbor in the South Pacific. Rabaul also had the finest set of volcanoes in the South Pacific, if not the world. Rabaul is set above a ring fracture in the Earth's crust with the highest concentration-per-square-inch of volcanoes, most of which ring the town to the east and on the appropriately named "Crater Peninsula," of which Vulcan and Tavurvur were (and are) particularly active. With a volcano of their own – Fujiyama – seen as something of a national symbol, the Japanese were hardly concerned about volcanoes and chose to make Rabaul their biggest base in the South Pacific. In so doing, they turned Simpson Harbor into a major anchorage for the Combined Fleet, operated two airfields built by the Australians before the war, and sited the headquarters of the Southeast Area Fleet, the 8th Area Army, Base Air Force, and 8th Fleet.

That anchorage in Simpson Harbor and those two airfields would be major factors in the war in the South Pacific. One air base, Vunakanau, 11 miles south-southwest of Rabaul near Keravia Bay, became the primary base for twin-engine bombers like the Mitsubishi G3M and G4M.[43] The other air base was located at Lakunai, 2 miles southeast of Rabaul between Simpson Harbor and Matupit Harbor, and became the primary base for fighters.[44] But while volcanoes can have a value all their own, their activities are not conducive to air operations. Vunakanau was close to Vulcan, while Lakunai was almost at the base of Tavurvur, and close to other volcanoes on the Crater Peninsula. The ash and noxious gases spewing from Vulcan and, especially, Tavurvur, created maintenance problems for aircraft and runways, and left Rabaul at constant risk for becoming a Pacific Pompeii.

The Japanese could deal with the earthquakes, the sulfuric fumes, and the volcanic ash that would periodically coat their aircraft.[45] But they could not deal with the loss of Buna. Not even the almost 400 antiaircraft guns they had positioned around Rabaul could handle the increased air attacks that would come from Buna. "[A]ir raids upon Rabaul," Admiral Ugaki said, "would be intensified, ultimately making it impossible for us to hold there."[46]

Sure enough, the Americans and the Australians built up a complex of air bases around Buna, especially around a village called Dobodura. But the Allies were hemmed in by the major Japanese bases in northern New Guinea: Lae and Salamaua, which would be the next objectives of the Allied advance. The Japanese had to fortify their hold on northern New Guinea in order to stop that advance and hopefully retake Buna.

Part of the fortification of the Lae-Salamaua area involved an attempt by those recently landed Japanese troops to seize the tiny and isolated yet strangely strategically important town of Wau. Capturing Wau, southeast of Salamaua at the southern end of a long valley, would give the Japanese another airfield, albeit a bizarre, barely usable one.[47] More importantly, securing Wau would secure the western flank of the Lae-Salamaua position.

Only a superhuman effort by the Allies to airlift troops into Wau using its bizarre, barely usable airfield – sometimes while being shot at by the Japanese – enabled the Allies to beat back this offensive. But the campaign was far from over.

The failure to capture Wau underscored the Japanese need to both reinforce the Lae-Salamaua sector and build up the sectors behind it at Madang, Wewak, and Hollandia. The Japanese were laboring, however, under two *katana*s of Damocles; enemy air power and enemy submarines. The US Army Air Force had developed a habit of bombing from high altitude, above the range of heavy antiaircraft guns. It thus kept the bombers and their crews safe, at least from antiaircraft fire, but at the expense of bombing accuracy. While high-altitude bombing could damage immovable land installations, against moving ships at sea it was almost completely ineffective. The bombers were so high up the targets could just look up, see the bombs falling down, and turn to be well away from the bombs when they splashed into the water. The Japanese had to hope the Army Air Force would not figure out that high-altitude bombing didn't work, because with the Allied capture of Buna and the construction of the Dobodura air base complex, as well as the expansion of the now-American-held Lunga airfield, the US Army Air Force would be getting more opportunities to bomb the Japanese, which meant more opportunities to get a lucky hit or, worse, to learn what they were doing wrong and correct it.

Complicating things further was that the Allies were advancing on two different vectors: Papua New Guinea and the Solomons. That meant Vice Admiral Kusaka Jinichi, who commanded the Southeast Area Fleet, the parent organization of both Admiral Mikawa's 8th Fleet and Base Air Force, but also commanded Base Air Force directly, had to juggle his Japanese Naval Air Force units between what – for now – were two widely separated axes.

For their part, enemy submarines were not on two separated axes so much as, it seemed, everywhere the Japanese did not want them to be. Nevertheless, up until the beginning of 1943 or so, US Navy submarines had been more entertaining than dangerous, what with their targets usually experiencing the thunk of dud American torpedoes against their hulls, if those torpedoes reached their hulls at all without exploding prematurely, running wild, or passing under them. However, as the sinking of the *Tenryu* helped emphasize, recently their entertainment value had been going down while their menace was increasing exponentially.

The result was that places that used to be safe for the Japanese, such as the waters around the bases in the Bismarcks and Shortlands, were no longer. They were not the front lines, at least not yet, but they were now simmering with submarine attacks and small air raids, picking off supply ships and occasionally warships the Japanese could ill afford to lose. And even when the Japanese were not losing ships to submarines, the mere presence of those submarines was unnerving enough, almost as though they had known the Japanese were coming and were waiting for them. In the wee hours of January 9, a small convoy of the general transport *Kisaragi Maru* and auxiliary transport *Yoshinogawa Maru*, escorted by a patrol boat reported to be the *PB-39* (the former destroyer *Tade*), was creeping along about 22 miles east of Bougainville in the Solomon Islands. At some point, the *Yoshinogawa Maru* apparently sighted a submarine and turned to engage with depth charges, but was unsuccessful. For her troubles, at about 3:30am, the *Yoshinogawa Maru* was hit by a torpedo, one of three launched by the USS *Nautilus* under the command of Lieutenant Commander William H. Brockman, Jr. Attempts to tow the disabled transport came to nothing and she sank with the loss of eight of her crew.[48]

The Japanese got some measure of revenge the next day, January 10. As the remaining transports from the Operation *18* convoy headed back to Rabaul empty, an aircraft attached to Base Air Force's 582 Air Group spotted a submerged submarine and dropped bombs to call the attention of the escorting destroyers to its position.[49] One of them, *Maikaze*, raced out to the spot and dropped several depth charges. Shortly thereafter, the submarine's large bow broke the surface at a steep angle. The *Maikaze* was joined by the *Isokaze* in circling the gravely injured boat, pumping the exposed bow full of 5-inch shells. The bow slid back into the sea, leaving some gruesome debris. According to the Japanese, the "destroyed top of the sub floated."[50] All of these activities were conducted under the watchful eyes of a US Army Air Force bomber who did nothing to interfere. Evidently it had emptied its bomb racks attacking the convoy.

At around midnight on January 12, it was the turn of one of the *Akikaze's* former sister ships. About 10 miles southwest of the Tingwon Islands, located just southwest of the northern tip of New Hanover in the Bismarcks, the old *Shimakaze*, now renamed the *PB-1*, was escorting the tanker *Akebono Maru*, whose claim to fame was taking a torpedo from a nocturnal attack by US Navy flying boats at Midway, when she fell foul of another submarine, the USS *Guardfish* under Lieutenant Commander Thomas Klakring. And the former destroyer's lengthy if not exactly glorious career came to an inglorious end in these waters west of Kavieng.[51]

Two days later it was the oiler *Toa Maru*, which was the target of a quintet of tin fish off Bougainville, again compliments of the *Nautilus*. One found its mark, leaving an unsightly dent but not exploding.[52] But this return to what had been the normal performance for US Navy submarines would be short lived. The morning of January 16, a convoy consisting of the *Brazil*, *India*, *Clyde*, *Delagoa*, *Uchide*, *Chifuku*, *Fukoku*, and *Fukuyo Marus*, escorted by the minesweepers *W-17* and *W-21*, left Rabaul bound for Palau. At 9:00am, only 90 minutes after leaving Simpson Harbor, the *Chifuku Maru* was torpedoed and sunk by Lieutenant Commander Howard W. Gilmore's USS *Growler*. The submarine evaded counterattacks by the escorting minesweepers, who rescued all but one of the ship's crew.[53]

At 6:00pm that same day, the auxiliary transport *Kimposan Maru*, en route to Rabaul from Yokosuka, was traveling alone west of Kavieng, about 8 miles northeast of Los Reyes Island in the Admiralties, when her engine room was the unhappy recipient of at least one torpedo. Without power, the ship sank very quickly. She evidently got off a distress call, for the subchaser *Ch-17* cut short her return to Rabaul from picket duty to drive the *Kimposan Maru's* undersea assailant, Lieutenant Commander Henry C. Bruton's

USS *Greenling*, deep. Then the subchaser proceeded to pick up survivors. The *Kimposan Maru* lost 31 killed.[54]

US Navy submarines seemed to be everywhere, as if they were waiting for the Japanese. In the early morning hours of January 18 that old entertainment factor reappeared for one rather weird ship. The *Soya*, designated an "auxiliary ammunition ship/survey vessel," was returning to Rabaul from a mission to Kieta. In Queen Carola Channel, off New Britain, she was reportedly the target of four torpedoes, all of which either exploded or hit but not both. Her crew hoisted a dud Mark 14 torpedo up to her deck as a war trophy. The attack has been attributed to the submarine *Greenling*.[55]

A lot of Japanese ships traveled alone. Though the Japanese would employ convoys for specific purposes, such as Admiral Tanaka's disastrous Guadalcanal reinforcement convoy the previous November or Operation *18* in early January, they still did not have much of a convoy system for run-of-the-mill supply ships. The auxiliary transport *Senzan Maru*, whose somewhat checkered past included a collision and a grounding, was traveling alone from the Home Islands to Rabaul with a cargo of gasoline. Around dawn on January 16, she picked up an escort in the form of subchaser *Ch-16*, who would accompany her the rest of the way to Rabaul. But a lone subchaser was a poor defense against air attack, even from high altitude. Off Kavieng, she was found by B-24 Liberators from the 90th Bombardment Group. They hit the *Senzan Maru*, igniting her cargo of gasoline and sending her to the bottom. *Ch-16* rescued survivors, but seven were killed.[56]

It was around this time that one of those instances of the Japanese employing convoys for specific purposes entered the South Pacific picture. This purpose was to get the Imperial Army's 20th and 41st Divisions from the Asian mainland to Wewak. The method chosen was a rather complicated set of convoys given the umbrella title of Operation "C" (*Hei-Go*). Wewak was at the edge of the range of Allied air power, accessible only by heavy bombers like the B-17 and B-24, at least until the Dobodura air complex was fully operational. But while the air threat was reduced, the increasing submarine threat remained.

That may have been the thinking behind the complicated operational plan which generally had the 20th Division moved first and the 41st Division moved second, often using the same ships, but which, instead of using one big convoy as Admiral Tanaka had tried at Guadalcanal the previous November, divided it into bite-sized pieces. One such savor-sized piece completed its part on January 19, when the old, weird light cruiser-fast transport hybrids *Oi* and *Kitakami* and the former seaplane tenders *Sanuki* and *Sagara Marus* reached Wewak with elements of the 20th Division.[57] To combat the still-present threat of air attack, the carrier *Junyo*, escorted by destroyers *Asagumo* and *Samidare*, provided their air cover by staging 21 Zeros and six attack planes, all under the command of air officer Lieutenant Commander Hashiguchi Takashi, into the Wirui airfield formerly used by the Divine Word mission.[58] Just a day after the convoy's arrival, a B-24 Liberator was sighted snooping over the base. While the *Junyo*'s Zeros at the airfield quickly scrambled and forced it down at sea, it was another unwanted reminder that the reach of enemy air power was getting longer and longer.[59] In another unwanted reminder, shortly thereafter, the *Junyo* got another submarine scare, so she and her escorts returned to Truk.[60]

Next came the *Gokoku Maru*, making her second appearance in the reinforcement of Wewak, with a host of passengers including reinforcements for the 2nd Special Base Force. Just short of her scheduled pit stop in Palau on January 17, she was the target of three submarine torpedoes from Lieutenant Commander Hiram Cassedy's USS *Searaven*. One torpedo hit, but failed to explode. Now with an entertaining story to tell, the *Gokoku Maru* continued on alone from Palau, arriving in Wewak late in the afternoon of January 21.[61]

Still another part of this very complicated reinforcement had the submarine tender *Yasukuni Maru*, the auxiliary transport *Hakozaki Maru*, and the ammunition ship *Aratama Maru* carrying more troops of the 20th Infantry Division, all escorted by the destroyer *Hatsuyuki*. It could not have been a fun trip for the 897 soldiers on the *Aratama Maru*, contemplating the results if a submarine torpedo hit their ammunition ship. As it was, at the convoy's scheduled pit stop in Palau, the *Aratama Maru* was held back, perhaps out of such concerns. The *Hatsuyuki*, *Yasukuni*, and *Hakozaki Maru*s took their leave on January 18, only for the *Yasukuni Maru* to run aground. The *Hatsuyuki* and *Hakozaki Maru* continued onward, arriving safely at Wewak the morning of January 21. They left that evening, but the *Hatsuyuki* split off when they came across the *Yasukuni Maru* the next day, having taken a day to work herself free. Then the destroyer escorted the *Yasukuni Maru* to Wewak. Both ships departed that afternoon.[62]

The *Aratama Maru* had been left behind in Palau, but only for about a day. She left the morning of January 19 with the next part of the reinforcement: transports *Shinkyo* and *Juzan Maru*s, all carrying more troops and equipment of the 20th Division, escorted by destroyer *Yugure*. They all arrived in Wewak in the wee hours of January 23, quickly offloaded their passengers and cargo, and left late that same morning.[63]

That completed the move of the bulk of the 20th Division. But while the transport ships of Operation "C" were heading back to the Asian mainland to pick up the 41st Division, back in Wewak the Imperial Army and Navy troops were getting a reminder of how dangerous US Navy submarines had become.

In the early afternoon of January 24, the destroyer *Harusame*, a veteran of the vicious November battles off Guadalcanal, was getting under way in the harbor when three torpedo wakes passed astern. When a fourth torpedo was spotted approaching, skipper Commander Kamiyama Masao had the destroyer turn away to starboard so that torpedo missed as well. Kamiyama had the destroyer continue its starboard turn 270 degrees until she was facing the direction from which the torpedoes had come. Then she charged, like a bull in the ring, intending to gore the submarine who had launched them.

Crewmen gathered on deck to watch the spectacle of the *Harusame* stampeding toward what they could see was a periscope sticking out of the water. On Kairiru, Bishop Lörks of the Divine Word mission was apparently watching the unfolding events as well.[64] This submarine had gotten deep into Wewak Harbor. Another torpedo came and passed them.

The periscope remained, like it was taunting them, less than 1,000 meters away. The snarling *Harusame* was almost there …

The charge was stopped abruptly by an explosion along the destroyer's hull below the waterline. The bullfighter had stuck one of his swords into the *Harusame* amidships. Her damage was severe; the torpedo had broken off most of her bow and buckled her keel. A keel is generally the bottom of a ship, but specifically, it is the bottom longitudinal girder on which the entire weight of the ship rests. A broken keel is often called a "broken back," as if it were like a human spine, but the analogy is imperfect. The keel helps keep the ship together; there is no redundant structural system to the keel. If the keel is broken, then the ship is held together only by its hull and its internal bulkheads, which are not designed to take all the weight or resist the stresses that would normally be handled with the keel.

The *Harusame* painfully crawled her way to shallow water, where she ran herself aground in sinking condition. She would sit half-sunk on that sandbar for the next month or so, serving as a very visible reminder of the submarine menace, until she was towed all the way to Truk, where she would get emergency repairs to enable her to return to Japan. The *Harusame* would be out of action for the rest of the year. It would have been of cold comfort for Commander Kamiyama and his crew that they had been hit by the soon-to-be-legendary US Navy Lieutenant Commander Dudley W. "Mush" Morton, chief of the *Wahoo*, who easily escaped Wewak Harbor despite air attacks and gunfire from shore batteries.[65]

The *Wahoo* would soon be leaving the South Pacific, creeping along the north coast of New Guinea into Netherlands New Guinea to cause even more mayhem. But even without the wild, wonderful *Wahoo*, the nicks and cuts in the Bismarck Sea would continue. While the convoys of Operation "C" had arrived safely at their destinations, the same could not be said of the "No. 6 Go Transportation Operation: Convoy No. 35," whose mission was to transport to the South Pacific the Imperial Japanese Army's 6th Kumamoto Division, a veteran unit of the war in China and notorious for its role in the Rape of Nanking. The convoy consisted of 11 transports divided into three elements traveling separately and counting among its escorts the *Akikaze*'s old sister ship *Hokaze*.[66]

It did not matter. When each element arrived in the South Pacific, it was almost like the submarines were waiting for them. In the early afternoon of January 19, 1943, the transport *Myoho Maru* was torpedoed and sunk northeast of Buin, courtesy of the US submarine *Swordfish* under Lieutenant Commander Jack H. Lewis. Having received the convoy's distress signal, Admiral Mikawa sent out the big, bad new destroyer *Akizuki* and the minelayer *Hatsutaka* to assist the convoy in reaching Shortland. At 9:30 that night, the *Akizuki* sighted a surfaced submarine. Guns blazing, the big antiaircraft destroyer turned toward the submarine and went to full speed to run it down. But it was not the usual submarine. It was the large and veteran USS *Nautilus*. The *Nautilus* had an experienced skipper in Lieutenant Commander Brockman. Together they had stared down *Kido Butai* at Midway, harassing the task force and indirectly helping to lead the pivotal US air strike to its doomed targets.[67] Brockman was not going to be intimidated by a destroyer coming right at him. And he wasn't, sending two torpedoes into the destroyer's starboard side. One hit under the Number 2 3.9-inch mount with a thunk, but any amusement the Japanese felt at yet another dud American torpedo was cut short by the second, which detonated under the bridge. It ripped a 26-foot gash in the starboard side, flooded a boiler room and the starboard engine room, and caused severe vibrations to the keel. The *Akizuki* suffered 14 killed and 63 injured. She staggered into the Shortlands anchorage two days later for emergency repairs to enable her to get back to a shipyard in Japan.[68]

There was plenty more where that came from. On January 20, en route from Truk to Shortland, the *Meiu* and *Surabaya Maru*s were recipients of American torpedoes with the compliments of Lieutenant Commander Creed C. Burlingame and his submarine *Silversides*. The *Meiu Maru* sank in about 80 minutes, taking with her about 400 of the nearly 3,000 troops she was carrying; the *Surabaya Maru* was evacuated, to be scuttled the next day, with 462 Imperial Army troops killed. Meanwhile, the transport *Kenkon Maru* was torpedoed by Lieutenant Commander Robert J. Foley's submarine USS *Gato*, causing a fire that detonated ammunition the transport was carrying, necessitating her scuttling.

On January 22, the veteran seaplane carrier *Akitsushima* started making the rounds between Kavieng, Möwe, Rabaul, Buka, and Shortland. Seaplanes were good at fishing out submerged submarines. Usually. At 4:45pm on January 23, when the *Akitsushima* was 15 miles southwest of Kavieng, her escort, the *Akikaze*'s division-mate *Hakaze*, detected a submarine and moved to attack. But the submarine, the busy USS *Guardfish*, beat her to the punch, torpedoing the old destroyer in the starboard side. The *Hakaze* quickly jackknifed and sank. The *Akitsushima* moved in to rescue survivors, of which there were 124, including skipper Lieutenant Commander Kashima Masanori, but 13 were killed.[69] It was more evidence that not even destroyers, traditionally the most dangerous enemy of submarines, were immune from these resurgent US submarines.

With their supplies of destroyers starting to run low, the Japanese resorted more and more to dedicated subchasers. Not that the subchasers were much more effective, but they were at least cheaper and easier to build. On January 29, the cargo ship *Nichiun Maru*, only requisitioned by the Imperial Japanese Army on January 1, was heading from Vila-Stanmore to Rabaul with the subchaser *Ch-22* as escort. She was hit by one torpedo forward and quickly sank by the bow. Her assailant, Lieutenant Commander Foley's *Gato*, managed to evade the *Ch-22* and escape.[70]

On the last day of January, it was the turn of the transport *Toa Maru No. 2* (not the tanker christened *Toa Maru* that took a dud torpedo from the *Nautilus* on January 14. The *Toa Maru No. 2* was making a run to Vila-Stanmore carrying Rear Admiral Ota Minoru, commander of the 8th Combined Special Naval Landing Force, his staff, 107 of his troops, two light tanks, a side-car motorcycle, ammunition, and cement. She was accompanied by the torpedo boat *Hiyodori* and the subchaser *Ch-23*. So she had decent protection against submarines, but what about air attacks? Aerial escort was provided by four Mitsubishi F1M Type 0 Reconnaissance Seaplanes from the R-Area Air Force's 958 Air Group as well as four to eight Nakajima Ki-43 Army Type 1 Fighters from the Imperial Army's 11th Air Regiment, operating from that new airfield at Munda.

The sun was going down when one of the 8th Combined Special Naval Landing Force's staff officers remarked, "[T]he sunset is coming soon, so we won't have to worry about an enemy attack." Naturally, right after he said this came an air attack from that cursed Lunga airfield. The *Toa Maru No. 2*'s purported air cover did nothing to stop or even mildly hinder the SBD Dauntless dive bombers and TBF Avenger torpedo bombers, but they did harass them after their bombing runs on their way back to base, which has to count for something. Not that it did the *Toa Maru No. 2* any good. At least one, probably two bomb hits and several near misses had caused fires on deck and flooding in the holds – which turned the bags of cement into concrete that weighed the ship down. The burning *Toa Maru No. 2* was abandoned that night. Almost all of her passengers and crew were rescued, with only one crewman and two soldiers killed, though perhaps as many as 40 were injured. The surviving naval infantry were all taken to Vila, and subsequently to Munda. None of their vehicles or supplies could be salvaged. The Japanese did not scuttle the *Toa Maru No. 2*, and the burning derelict drifted in the southern Vella Gulf for another three days or so before finally foundering in Kololuka Bay north of Gizo Island.

All through the waters of Papua New Guinea, the Bismarcks, and the Solomons, there was this constant pattern of nicks and cuts. None was strategically fatal or even particularly debilitating by itself, but a nick here and a cut there and soon you were talking about real blood loss. Consider the *Keiyo Maru*. In the middle of the afternoon of February 2, the *Keiyo Maru*, an "armed auxiliary aircraft transport," was caught by fighter and heavy bombers of the 13th Air Force during a raid on the Shortlands anchorage, something else that was happening much more often these days. She suffered bomb damage, but was able to continue operations.

The Americans were not through with the *Keiyo Maru*, however. On February 18 off New Britain, she was "lightly damage[d]" by a submarine torpedo, apparently a low order or premature detonation or a dud. The next day, she was attacked again by a submarine. This time the results were "unknown," but the *Keiyo Maru* remained afloat and ambulatory. Both attacks have been attributed to the submarine USS *Grampus* under Lieutenant Commander John R. Craig.[71]

That this "armed auxiliary aircraft transport" was still afloat after two submarine attacks in two days that left her "lightly damaged" did not speak well for US torpedoes. That the Japanese had not sunk or at least scared off the submarine after the first attack did not speak well for their antisubmarine competence, but they tried to change that. Later on February 19, the 958 Air Group sent out several seaplanes, probably Aichi E13A Type 0 reconnaissance seaplanes, to bother the bothersome boat.[72] They found a submarine southeast of New Britain, evidently at periscope depth, and proceeded to bomb it. They reported one direct hit on the conning tower and a large amount of oil on the surface after the attack.[73]

This was a busy period for Japanese antisubmarine activity. Three days earlier, on February 16, a convoy consisting of the busy torpedo boat *Hiyodori* and the submarine chaser *Ch-18* escorting the transport *Noshiro Maru* (with air cover provided by a seaplane, probably an Aichi E13A Type 0 reconnaissance seaplane, from the 958 Air Group) left Rabaul for Kolombangara. In midafternoon, they were off Cape St George when they spotted four torpedo tracks off the starboard beam. The torpedoes were successfully avoided.[74]

About six minutes later, the seaplane located the attacking submarine and dropped several depth charges. At 3:40, the *Hiyodori* arrived on site and dropped nine depth charges on the submarine's suspected location. Some five minutes later, the *Ch-18* got a fix on the boat and dropped six depth charges. This last attack brought oil welling to the surface. As the oil slick expanded, in the middle of it a conning tower appeared, its upper section bursting through the surface. That's generally a bad sign for the submarine. Before the Japanese could train their guns on it, however, the tower disappeared back into the oil slick.[75]

Smelling blood or at least oil in the water, *Ch-18* dropped three more depth charges, and would have dropped still more except "parts of the hull" floated to the surface. That was it for the combat. The Japanese milled around looking for more debris. At 4:42pm, the *Hiyodori* recovered several items, including a life raft printed with the words "Philadelphia Navy Yard." The Japanese recorded it as a sinking.[76]

These were only fingers in the proverbial dyke. On February 15, the auxiliary store ship *Suruga Maru* was torpedoed and sunk 35 miles northeast of Buin by Lieutenant Commander Foley's very busy USS *Gato*.[77] Four days later the *Gato* was at it again off eastern Bougainville, torpedoing the transport *Hibari Maru*, who was beached off Buin to prevent her sinking. It did no good. During another Allied air attack on the Shortlands anchorage, TBF Avenger torpedo bombers of Escort Scouting 111 finished off the wreck.[78]

On February 18, the destroyers *Arashio* and *Oshio* left Wewak in tandem with the minelayer *Shirataka* bound for Rabaul. Just before 6:00am on February 20, when the little flotilla was 70 miles northwest of Manus, the *Oshio* suffered an underwater explosion in the forward part of the starboard engine room, leaving a 35-foot gash in the hull. The Number 3 boiler room flooded and the *Oshio* went dead in the water. Ten minutes later, the *Arashio* dodged torpedoes. She vengefully dropped 21 depth charges on their assailant, the busy USS *Albacore*, to no apparent effect, then went to help her disabled sister ship. But the *Oshio*'s condition was grave. The *Arashio* tried to tow the *Oshio*, but the torpedo had buckled and probably snapped the destroyer's keel, making a tow extremely dangerous. Sure enough, after a half hour of flooding and increasing groaning and grinding sounds, at 6:30am the *Oshio* jackknifed at the Number 2 smokestack and quickly sank. The *Arashio* was able to rescue all but eight of her crew. It was the end of an Allied nemesis with a history of punching well above her weight, especially during the Java Sea Campaign.[79]

This dark period for the Japanese in the South Pacific did have a bright spot in the completion of Operation "C." On February 20, Wewak saw the return of the light-cruiser–fast-transport hybrids *Oi* and *Kitakami* and the former seaplane tenders *Sanuki* and *Sagara Maru*s, now fortified with the escorting destroyers *Yugumo* and *Kazagumo*, and bringing much of the 41st Division with them.[80] February 24 saw the return of the *Yasukuni Maru*, this time with the seaplane tender *Kiyokawa Maru* and the armed merchant cruiser *Ukishima Maru*. Their escort consisted of destroyers *Isonami*, *Akigumo*, and *Nagatsuki*.[81] Arriving on February 26 was the *Aratama Maru*, again with the *Shinkyo* and *Juzan Maru*s, all carrying more troops and equipment of the 41st Division, again escorted by destroyer *Yugure*, but also the *Satsuki* and *Fumizuki*.[82]

The final part of that reinforcement comprised a five-ship convoy carrying elements of the 239th Infantry Regiment from China to Wewak. The Headquarters and 1st Battalions were on board the *Aikoku Maru*, the 2nd Battalion (less 7th and 8th Companies) on the *Kiyosumi Maru*, and the 3rd Battalion on the *Gokoku Maru*. The *Gokoku Maru* was making her third appearance in this reinforcement, the other two ships their second. Escorting them were the destroyers *Asagumo* and *Samidare*. Just before 3:00pm on February 19, not even two hours after the convoy had left Palau, the wakes of four torpedoes harmlessly passed the *Samidare*. Three more torpedoes aimed at one of the transports missed as well. The convoy had run into the submarine *Runner* under Lieutenant Commander Frank W. Fenno, but the convoy had a guardian angel overhead, or at least a guardian aircraft, in the form of an Aichi E13A Navy Type 0 Reconnaissance Seaplane from the 902 Air Group out of Palau.[83] The biplane dropped a single 250kg depth charge that detonated close to the *Runner*, disabling both of her periscopes, her sound gear, and her magnetic and gyro compasses. The submarine had to terminate her war patrol and return to Pearl Harbor for repairs. The convoy arrived safely at Wewak on February 26, though not without another submarine scare as a Nakajima B5N carrier attack plane saw fit to drop a bomb on a shadow in the water.[84]

With that, the move of the bulk of the 41st Division was complete, and the Japanese would have defense in depth. But what they really needed to do was reinforce Lae and Salamaua, to which the front lines were moving closer and closer with the fall of the Buna sector. Lae was garrisoned by only 3,500 troops. While Operation "C" was entirely successful, Operation 6 had carried a high price when the submarine katana of Damocles came down. How could the Japanese get more troops to Lae?

While Imperial General Headquarters was wrestling with this question, February would end with a very curious incident in the Solomons. At 9:00am on February 27, the 3,829-ton cargo ship *Kirikawa Maru* left Buin, packed with elements of the 7th Yokosuka Special Naval Landing Force, two 140mm guns, four 80mm guns, and 600 tons of supplies. Escorted by the subchaser *Ch-26* and minesweeper *W-22*, the *Kirikawa Maru* started on a reinforcement run for Kolombangara.

She almost made it. Northeast of Vella Lavella, she was ambushed by US Navy and Marine aircraft and US Army Air Force fighter bombers operating from what was becoming a multi-runway complex at Lunga. The *Kirikawa Maru* was heavily damaged and her ammunition stores were set afire. The cargo ship was scuttled with three shots from one of the escorts, but the record is not clear as to whether it was the *Ch-26* or the

W-22.[85] Putting together the pieces of this incomplete puzzle, it would seem that after the air attack, the *Ch-26* headed back to Shortland while the larger *W-22* was left to rescue survivors of the *Kirikawa Maru* and probably to scuttle the ship as well.[86]

In any event, later that day the *W-22* found herself off Kolombangara, apparently alone. It was during this time that the minesweeper was the recipient of a submarine attack. Not a very good submarine attack, as the minesweeper was not sunk and is usually listed as "possibly" damaged.[87] Since she went back to Shortland and was immediately sent out again, whatever damage was inflicted seems to have been minor, though she was down for ten days at the end of March for repairs in Rabaul.[88] Maybe another low order or premature detonation, or dud.

As March 1943 began, the Japanese in the South Pacific were putting the finishing touches on a massive convoy they dubbed Operation *81*. The goal was to move 6,900 more troops from the 51st Division to Lae into the teeth, or at least the lips and gums, of Allied airpower at Port Moresby, especially, but also Milne Bay and Buna.

Lieutenant General Inamura Hitoshi, commander of the 8th Area Army (the Imperial Army's version of an army group, though its size was closer to that of a field army) and Admiral Mikawa devised a plan to move those troops directly to Lae. It would involve moving slow transports into the range of Allied air power at Buna, Port Moresby, and Milne Bay. The staff of the 18th Army, the Imperial Army's command authority in New Guinea, war-gamed the scenario, concluding the operation could lose 40 percent of the transports and between 30 and 40 aircraft. The alternative to a convoy of slow transports to Lae itself was to land the troops at Madang and march them some 140 miles to Lae through jungle, swamps, and even mountains. To be sure, Mikawa's staff favored this option, but it was felt, not unreasonably, that the march-through would take too long and be too hard on the troops, so it was rejected.[89]

To avoid a repeat of Admiral Tanaka's disastrous November convoy, Admiral Mikawa and General Inamura planned and plotted this reinforcement action to take advantage of advantageous storm fronts and minimize exposure to Allied air power. For actual fighter protection, Admiral Kusaka contributed Zeros from Base Air Force's 204, 252, and 253 air groups, plus some from the *Zuiho* operating from land bases for the time being.[90] These Zeros would operate from and stage between Rabaul, Gasmata, and Kavieng. The Japanese Army Air Force contributed its 1st and 11th Air Regiments and their Nakajima Ki-43 Type 1 fighters, operating from and staging between Rabaul and Lae itself.[91] In total, these units had maybe 100 fighters.

The Japanese would need them all. The normal difficulties of providing long-range fighter protection were compounded by several self-inflicted factors. One was that the Army's Nakajima Ki-43s did not have the endurance of the Navy's Zeros. Second and far worse was the recurring issue of communications. The Army fighters did not have radios compatible with those of the Navy air units or the ships, while the Navy's Zero fighters typically did not have radios at all. The Sea Eagle fighter jocks considered the radios unreliable and thus dead weight when they needed every knot of speed. How the Japanese planned to conduct this long-range fighter protection over these important ships without radios is unclear, but the Japanese air forces had always done it that way.[92]

The convoy set sail from Rabaul's Simpson Harbor a half hour before midnight on March 1 and turned northwest to follow the northern coast of New Britain. Eight transports and cargo ships carrying 6,004 troops and 750 drums of fuel, escorted by eight destroyers (who, just as they had on Admiral Tanaka's rat convoys, themselves carried troops, in this case a total of 958) of the 3rd Destroyer Flotilla under the command of recently promoted Rear Admiral Kimura Masatomi.[93]

It started off decently enough. The morning of March 2, Allied scouts found the convoy in the Bismarck Sea. B-17s plastered the *Kyokusei Maru*, a former POW "hell ship," with at least two and as many as five bomb hits. The destroyers *Yukikaze* and *Asagumo* picked up 819 men and salvaged 110 drums of oil and quickly ran them all to Lae.[94] If the Japanese could get this convoy to Lae with only one ship sunk, they would consider themselves quite lucky.

But maybe they had used up their stores of good luck getting those huge convoys to Java and those smaller convoys to Wewak. The next morning, March 3, in the Huon Gulf some 80 miles off Lae, only hours before they were to make port, the convoy ships found a massive aerial armada waiting for them, an aerial ambush the likes of which the Japanese had never seen before. While Base Air Force did have fighters overhead, they did the same inept job protecting this convoy that they had protecting Admiral Tanaka's Guadalcanal convoy. For once, Allied bombers attacked from low altitude – very low altitude. It was murderously effective. Admiral Kimura's flagship *Shirayuki* was an early victim. All seven remaining transports were sunk, as well as destroyers *Arashio*, *Asashio*, and *Tokitsukaze*. Only some 900 Imperial Army troops of the 51st Division got to Lae.

It was a sucker punch, far worse than Admiral Tanaka's convoy, far worse than all of their projections. Even more shocking to the Japanese was an unusual savagery shown by the US Army Air Force aircraft. Lifeboats, rafts, anything that floated or could be used as a flotation device were the targets of strafing runs. Large groups of survivors in the water were ruthlessly machine gunned, leaving swaths of the Huon Gulf colored a dark red. The Japanese were mystified as to what could have led to this ferocity. Kimura and his surviving destroyers were literally chased from the scene by American and Australian aircraft, only returning after dark to haul in the pitifully few survivors, who were being hunted by US Navy PT boats.

This air-sea engagement in which one ship was sunk in the Bismarck Sea and 11 sunk in the Huon Gulf is thus known as the Battle of the Bismarck Sea. It was an abject catastrophe for Japan, as if a meteor had crashed into the Huon Gulf and left a giant smoking crater where Japanese strategy had been. The shockwaves reached across the Pacific all the way to Tokyo, where an outraged Emperor Hirohito immediately asked the obvious question: Why had the Navy not immediately shifted gears and landed the troops elsewhere than Lae? He knew the answer: Imperial General Headquarters had failed to learn the lessons of the Guadalcanal convoy battles.[95] Admiral Yamamoto, who had been reluctant to commit eight destroyers to the convoy, "was greatly incensed."[96]

The war that the Japanese had started gave them no chance to compose themselves after the catastrophe in the Huon Gulf. While that convoy of slow, fat transports was meeting its fate, another convoy of slow, fat transports, this one designated Convoy "F2," had left Rabaul at 6:00pm on March 2 headed for Palau. The convoy consisted of the transports *Kiriha*, *Mito*, *Nagano*, and *Ryuzan Maru*s, escorted by the destroyer *Yuzuki*. At around noon on March 6, the convoy was some 150 miles west of the Manus when a torpedo burrowed its way into the stern of the *Kiriha Maru*. Another torpedo seems to have thunked off the bow of the *Mito Maru* without exploding but leaving an unsightly dent. The *Kiriha Maru* was not so lucky and sank with four of her crew lost. The *Yuzuki* rescued her survivors while keeping at bay her assailant, the submarine *Triton* under Lieutenant Commander George K. MacKenzie, Jr.[97]

To the Japanese in the Bismarck Sea area, it seemed that every time they moved a ship, enemy aircraft or submarines or even both were waiting for it. It sure seemed that Admiral Tanaka's rat transportation was much safer than sending those slow, fat transports. As if to emphasize the point, when the destroyers *Murasame* and *Minegumo* left the Shortlands on the evening of March 5 to make a supply run to Vila-Stanmore, they passed *Uranami* and *Hatsuyuki* coming in with survivors of the Bismarck Sea.[98] That evidence of an enemy ambush could not have been encouraging.

They steamed through the southern end of the Vella Gulf and went through the Blackett Strait to make their stop at Vila-Stanmore. After they had dropped off their supplies, Destroyer Division 2's commodore Captain Tachibana Masao decided not to go back the way he had come, but instead to go through the Kula Gulf around Kolombangara and back to the Shortlands. When March 6 was still very young, his *Murasame* led the *Minegumo* north deeper into the Kula Gulf.

And into the arms of the Americans. Not aircraft or submarines, but a surface force of US Navy cruisers and destroyers. The Japanese were so stunned that the *Murasame* could not get a shot off before she was hit by a torpedo that detonated both aft magazines in a cataclysmic explosion that mortally wounded the destroyer. The *Minegumo* got off only a few shots from her main battery before she was overwhelmed by gunfire. Both ships were permanently consigned to the depths of the Kula Gulf. Then the Americans gave a thorough shelling to the Vila airfield, though the Japanese described the bombardment's effects as "none in particular."[99]

As Japanese destroyer commander Hara Tameichi would later point out, "Admiral Tanaka carried out a series of brilliant transport operations to Guadalcanal in November and December 1942. When other destroyer groups, led by officers of lesser ability, tried the same kind of operation it frequently led to such debacles as the March 5 massacre in Kula Gulf."[100]

While describing the sinking of two destroyers as a "massacre" might be a bit of a stretch – especially considering what had just happened in the Huon Gulf – adding it to the ever-growing list of nicks and cuts was not. Another nick was from a convoy called "Hansa No. 1," with transports *No. 1 Shinsei*, *Momoyama*, *Yasushima*, *Oyo*, *Aso*, *Teiryu*, and *Sydney Maru*s, carrying even more elements of the 20th Division, this time to, oddly enough, Hansa Bay, about halfway between Wewak and Madang. It left Palau on March 6 with the escort of destroyers *Kazagumo*, carrying the commander of Destroyer Division 10, Captain Yoshimura Matake; *Yugumo*, *Satsuki*, *Akigumo*, and *Samidare*. On the first morning out, March 7, the *Samidare* depth charged a submarine and spent more than an hour staying over it to keep it too deep to make an attack while the convoy got clear. On March 11, the *Satsuki* dropped six depth charges on a suspected submarine, with "results unknown."[101]

The convoy arrived at Hansa Bay on March 12. Offloading was completed in a day. Captain Yoshimura was ordered to take the *Kazagumo*, *Yugumo*, and *Satsuki* to Rabaul, where they were to make supply runs in the Solomons, so they headed out together. The *Akigumo* and *Samidare* got the privilege of escorting the transports back to Palau. As the transports made their way out of Hansa Bay slowly, as slow, fat transports tend to be, at about 6:30pm on March 13, they were caught by five B-17s from the 5th Air Force's 63rd Bombardment Squadron, who managed to hit the *Momoyama Maru*, killing nine and leaving the transport disabled. The *Akigumo* took survivors on board and scuttled the hulk with one torpedo.[102]

A second convoy left Rabaul on March 12, 1943, also bound for Palau. It consisted of the *Tonei*, *Asaka*, *Nishiyama* (*Seizan*), *Momoha*, *Toho*, *Tasmania*, and *Florida Maru*s, with an escort of the old destroyer *Mochizuki* and the repair vessel *Nagaura*.[103] The use of a repair ship as escort was either an instance of Japanese prescience or an example of Japanese desperation to find escorts for its noncombatant ships; the destruction of the Lae convoy and two destroyers off Vila-Stanmore had left 8th Fleet short of destroyers.[104] Not part of the convoy were the subchasers *Ch-23* and *Ch-24*, but they left Rabaul the same day and apparently were serving as escorts until they had to leave to meet a second, incoming convoy for escort.[105]

The trip was uneventful until March 15, when at 12:15pm the *Momoha Maru* was hit by a torpedo in the engine room and lost power. She sank five minutes later, with no casualties.[106] The *Nagaura* was detailed to pick up survivors. She was transferring the survivors to the *Florida Maru* when, just before 3:00pm, the *Florida Maru* took a torpedo and was disabled.

Subchaser *Ch-23* was directed to pick up her survivors.[107] At about this time, the *Tonei Maru* moved to tow the *Florida Maru*. Evidently, that attempt failed or was abandoned for the time being. The *Florida Maru* was abandoned as well, and the convoy moved on, arriving in Palau on March 19.[108]

Meanwhile, the *Ch-22*, already heading for Palau, was in the area and seems to have been vectored in to assist in finding the undersea assailants.[109] The *Ch-24*, who had been with *Ch-23*, went out to help her sister *Ch-22* get a fix on the submarine. The subchasers conducted multiple depth charge attacks. Reportedly, after these attacks, the Japanese saw "a great quantity of oil, pieces of wood, cork and manufactured goods bearing the mark 'Made in U.S.A.'"[110]

This bizarre episode was not quite over. On March 18, the *Mochizuki* and the *Tonei Maru* returned to retrieve the abandoned *Florida Maru*, which was still afloat. With the *Mochizuki* as escort, the *Tonei Maru* towed the derelict to Möwe anchorage, New Hanover, where they arrived March 24.[111]

It seemed to be getting to the point that no matter where the Japanese went in the Bismarck Sea, the Huon Gulf, the Solomon Sea, or the Solomon Islands, an enemy submarine, air attack, or even surface force was waiting for them. The disastrous Operation *81* convoy, the "massacre" of the *Murasame* and *Minegumo*, the ugly half-sunk wreck of the *Harusame* that had sat for a month off Wewak until February 17, when the destroyers *Amatsukaze* and *Urakaze* and salvage tug *Ojima* managed to yank her off the reef and start to slowly tow her to Truk, dramatically drove that point home.

How was this possible? How was it possible that every time the Japanese moved in the Bismarck Sea there were enemy aircraft or submarines or both to meet it? Though it had been in the South Pacific for less than three months, the 2nd Special Base Force in Wewak believed it had found the cause:

Catholic missionaries.

Indeed, the 2nd Special Base Force remained convinced the Divine Word missionaries and lay people were sending intelligence to the Allies, despite their inability to locate the means by which that intelligence was sent. It got to the point where some even thought that a priest had the power to transmit messages while saying Mass.[112] Maybe using incense to send smoke signals. Passing on convoy information in Gregorian chants. Forwarding that information to their Allied handlers in Latin.

In fairness, during the Guadalcanal Campaign, the Japanese became aware that the Solomon Islands and New Guinea were seeded with what the Allies called "coastwatchers" who reported on Japanese ship, air, and troop movements. The early warning provided by these coastwatchers had crippled Japanese efforts to secure Guadalcanal. Admiral Mikawa later explained that:

> [W]henever our warships and air forces began operations, a wireless was dispatched, always from the jungles of the neighboring shore, as if to inform the enemy. We were frequently attacked by enemy aircraft, as if in reply to the wireless messages. So the Air Fleet and ship crews often earnestly requested my headquarters to eliminate those with enemy characteristics living on the shore. However, the naval landing forces under my command were lacking in strength and, even if I consulted the Army, it also lacked strength. So we were unable to execute any operations of this type. The Air Fleet and ship crews were considerably dissatisfied with my headquarters on this point. For the above-mentioned reason[,] Air Fleet personnel and ship crews seemed to be extremely cautious of persons with enemy characteristics living on the shore.[113]

In other words, they were racists. Someone's nationality did not matter nearly as much as the color of their skin.

But the Bismarck Sea was not the Solomon Islands. For starters, it had far fewer islands, which placed a much lower limit on how often the coastwatchers could see anything to report. It was also ringed with Japanese bases, so while someone watching a base could see the comings and goings, they could not necessarily see from and in what directions were the comings and goings. It was more difficult to tell where, say, a convoy of ships was heading. Plus, the alleged spies in this case were Catholic missionaries. While there were clergy who were spies serving the Allied cause – including one who was a coastwatcher in the Solomon Islands – they were very few and very far between. Finally, coastwatchers were generally well armed and usually traveled with a squad of armed Melanesian locals who served as bodyguards, porters, messengers, spies, and support personnel. Divine Word missionaries were unarmed and gave no indication they had any such support.

All the same, the 2nd Special Base Force had wasted little time after its arrival in complaining to Rabaul about the Divine Word missionaries. Just after the 2nd's December 1942 arrival, Admiral Kamata had reported to 8th Fleet headquarters in Rabaul "that on Kairiru Island there was an influential Catholic church, and that in this area there were two or three chapters of the church with 20 or more missionaries."[114] Rabaul ordered the missionaries gathered on Kairiru and kept there, with freedom to move about the island, but prohibited from leaving. Kamata had a list of their names forwarded to 8th Fleet.[115]

It seems to have had the desired effect. The means of the missionaries' transportation had returned to Rabaul. On February 27 the *Akikaze* had left Jaluit in the Marshall Islands. She arrived at Simpson Harbor at 5:28am on March 3. There was no rest for the wicked, however, and that night the destroyer had to escort the heavy cruiser *Aoba* to Kavieng. The *Aoba* had just returned from four months at the Kure Navy Yard, repairing the severe battle damage she had suffered off Guadalcanal at the hands of a US Navy force of cruisers and destroyers the previous October. Well, "repairing" might be a strong word. Her aft 8-inch turret had been wrecked and rendered inoperable; at Kure it was replaced by a Type 96 triple-mount 25mm antiaircraft gun. Even though the *Aoba* was old and not the ship she had been, the *Akikaze* rarely got chances to escort major warships.[116]

The *Akikaze* was back in Rabaul at 4:28pm on March 4 – just in time to see the survivors of the massacre of the Lae convoy crawl in to Simpson Harbor. Men were fished out of a Huon Gulf covered in oil, themselves badly wounded, bleeding, the results of devastating new tactics used by the US Army Air Force and the Royal Australian Air Force. Watching the wretched survivors being brought in caused a sense of abject humiliation among the Japanese in Rabaul. One author called it "the greatest humiliation and the greatest defeat that the Japanese Army, Navy, and Air Fleet in the Southwest Pacific had ever suffered," an opinion that seems to have been common among the Japanese, whether army or navy.[117]

The consequences of the catastrophe were still revealing themselves, and would be for months to come. But for now, according to Admiral Mikawa, "operations in the Rabaul area ... were in a state of great confusion and the psychological state of mind of the men had changed somewhat from the usual." Mikawa admitted this confusion permeated the chain of command, including flag levels. Unusually sensitive to the age of the ships under his command, Mikawa later suggested that watching the survivors of Operation *81* come in was especially humiliating for the crew of the *Akikaze* because there was no prospect of their striking back at the enemy since their ship was "an extremely old-type destroyer and could not be used in ordinary operations because of its poor fighting capacity."[118]

But the *Akikaze* would get her chance to respond, albeit not in the way her crew preferred. At 7:20pm on March 8, the *Akikaze* left Rabaul bound for Kairiru on "transport duty" for the 8th Fleet, who had specifically requested her because of the shortage of destroyers.[119] She was carrying materials for construction of a seaplane base for use by the "R-Area Air Force."[120] The *Akikaze* arrived the morning of March 10, and began unloading the supplies.[121] As she did so, Commander Miyazawa Kanshin, who had been dispatched from Rabaul aboard the *Akikaze* along with members of the 8th Fleet staff, headed to Wewak in a small boat. Miyazawa would apparently be overseeing construction of the new seaplane base, but for now he was just a messenger. He had orders for Admiral Kamata; curiously, they were only verbal orders. The admiral told his senior staff officer those orders were that "the missionaries on Kairiru Island were to be sent to Rabaul on board the *Akikaze* on orders of the 8th Fleet."[122]

It was a misleading description. The 8th Fleet was ordering the removal of the missionaries from Kairiru because Admiral Kamata had requested it, even had his assistant chief of staff, Lieutenant Commander Yagura, draft the request. As Yagura later explained it, Kamata wanted the missionaries removed "because, if Kairiru Island were made a naval base and people of neutral countries were present, it would be difficult to maintain secrecy. Furthermore, it was in order to conceal the various installations at the base, disposition of forces, and the like, from the enemy."[123]

In the meantime, the *Akikaze* had finished dropping off the construction materials at Kairiru and left at 2:45pm, heading for Kavieng, where she arrived on March 11 at about 9:30pm. The plan that was developed called for the *Akikaze* to load up on fuel and ammunition from the mostly heavy cruiser *Aoba*, return to Kairiru to drop these supplies off on March 15, then embark the missionaries and take them to Rabaul.[124]

To that end, the *Akikaze* left Kavieng in the pre-dawn hours of March 14.[125] The old destroyer got a rare bit of excitement as well as her first brush with the increasing submarine danger when, still north of Manus, she dropped depth charges on a suspected submarine with "results unknown."[126] For the first time in the Pacific War, the *Akikaze* had fired shots at the enemy. Or a suspected enemy, anyway.

Less exciting but more intriguing was the amount of effort and attention that was being given to the Christian missionaries. Admiral Kamata sent two officers to Kairiru to deal with the matter. One was Lieutenant Commander Yagura. Kamata had said to him, "Since the *Akikaze* will arrive in order to intern the missionaries, go to Kairiru and make preparations for their embarkation." Yagura was to officially transfer them from the charge of the 2nd Special Base Force to the charge of the captain of the *Akikaze*.

The second officer was Sublieutenant Kai. Kai was supposed to go to Rabaul on official business anyway, so Admiral Kamata piggybacked another rather ambiguously worded mission "to take care of the citizens of neutral countries who were to be transported to Rabaul from Kairiru on board the *Akikaze*." Kai was also "to act as an interpreter between the foreigners and the ship's crew and officers" because he could speak "a little English."[127]

With all those bases covered and with the submarine scare literally behind them for the moment, the *Akikaze* arrived at Kairiru on schedule and took in the Divine Word missionaries and lay people. Lieutenant Commander Yagura formally delivered them to Lieutenant Commander Sabe, then left. As planned, Sublieutenant Kai remained aboard the destroyer as she left Kairiru.[128]

Also as planned, after the civilians were taken from Kairiru, truckloads of Japanese troops were sent to the mission plantations to burn down the churches, clinics, and houses. Converts were bayonetted. The five decades of works performed by the Society of the Divine Word in the Wewak area would be swept away. There were undoubtedly some practical considerations involved; the Japanese were turning Wewak into a major military base, airfield complex, and staging area, and it is difficult to build military facilities on ground where, say, a church was already standing. But the bayonetting of converts demonstrates a definite ideological element to these activities. To the Japanese, the work of the Divine Word was just more European imperialism. There was no place for Europeans or their philosophy in the Greater East Asia Co-prosperity Sphere, although Wewak was neither in Asia nor prosperous. The Imperial Japanese firmly believed that Asia should be ruled by Asians. So long as those Asians are Japanese.

Also neither in Asia nor prosperous was the *Akikaze*'s next stop, Manus, where a more intriguing situation awaited than on Kairiru. Although the move of the Divine Word missionaries from Kairiru had been motivated by complaints from Admiral Kamata and the missionaries' geographic position on Kairiru that both overlooked a major base and was located on the site of another base under construction, somehow the Liebenzell Mission and the Sacred Heart missionaries on Manus were roped into this move as well. This despite the fact that none of these missionaries was connected to the Divine Word, and the Liebenzell missionaries were Lutherans. They were evidently close enough for the Japanese.[129] Moreover, Manus was not under the authority of the 2nd Special Base Force at Wewak, but the 8th Base Force under the command of Rear Admiral Tokunaga Sakae in Rabaul. As best as can be determined, no one had complained about their presence on Manus, even though the Japanese had an air base there.

All the same, Senior Staff Officer Matsumoto Hideshi at the 8th Base Force headquarters later testified, "I received orders from the 8th Fleet Headquarters to assemble the missionaries and nationals of neutral countries residing in Lorengau and to make shipping preparations for their transportation to Rabaul." Admiral Tokunaga signed them and forwarded them to the 81st Guard Unit.[130]

It was in early March 1943 when Chief Petty Officer Ichinose received a joint order from "the chief of staff of the 8th Fleet and the headquarters of the 81st Naval Garrison

(Guard) Unit" to prepare for the civilians to be taken to Rabaul.[131] Ichinose was surprised by the orders and did not take them seriously at first. He did not even give the missionaries a heads-up:

> Then, about two or three days later (I don't remember the exact date), I received another telegram. It stated that the destroyer *Akikaze* would go to Lorengau with the foreigners from Kairiru Island aboard, and advised me to make preparations. The telegram arrived about two days before the set date. I hurriedly took steps, had natives in their canoes go after the people, and barely got ready by the time mentioned in the telegram.[132]

Fortunately for Ichinose if not the missionaries, the destroyer arrived five or six hours late. And when she did arrive, she went to the wrong place. Ichinose had the internees board a landing barge, which he took with them out to the *Akikaze*. There, according to Ichinose, he "met the captain and reported to him that there were about twenty foreigners and also handed him the roster and the shipping manifest. At this point the captain said for me to go to the enlisted men's quarters, so I immediately went there."[133]

At which point the following rather extraordinary exchange took place:

> When I got there, I saw that it was filled with foreigners who had been put aboard at Kairiru Island and that they were suffering considerably from the heat. I felt that it would not do to crowd them any more, so I spoke to the captain and told him that I would like to have some other enlisted men's quarters assigned for just the foreigners from Lorengau. The captain agreed and said that he would assign them enlisted men's quarters forward. I took the people forward and made certain that they all got into the room. Furthermore, I mentioned to the medical officer of the *Akikaze* that there was a fever patient [Doepke, the Protestant missionary] and asked him to take care of him. I asked the captain to look after everything and disembarked.[134]

Lieutenant Commander Sabe wasted no time in starting the *Akikaze*'s engines and leaving Manus. It was 3:30pm.[135]

Throughout the night, the *Akikaze* headed for Kavieng. Despite the night air, the atmosphere remained extremely hot and humid. "Because of the severe heat," Sublieutenant Kai later said, "I had a movable cot set up outside on the deck, where I slept for the most part." Many of the enlisted men kicked out of their compartments for the night were quartered on the boat deck. There appear to have been few if any complaints from the sailors at being kicked out of their hot, stuffy quarters for the night.

The first thing the next morning, roll call was taken among the civilian internees because, obviously, of the danger they could escape and swim a hundred miles to the nearest land. The *Akikaze* arrived at Kavieng at about 8:30am and stopped her engines just outside the port entrance. According to Sublieutenant Kai, "a liaison boat came out from the shore and immediately returned. No one came aboard at Kavieng."[136]

But something had changed aboard the *Akikaze*. When she left at 10:13am, she passed through a channel and set a course for Rabaul. Not at the relatively relaxed speed of around 15 knots at which she had been traveling, but much faster. Lieutenant Takahashi, the gunnery officer, noticed the change immediately. "I remember that the speed was increased from high speed to first battle speed," Takahashi would later explain, "and it appeared that the urgent mission was to deliver the internees to the headquarters at the base at Rabaul, if possible, by today at the latest." Running at this high speed, maybe 28 knots, was not easy for the old engines on the old destroyer.[137]

Meanwhile, Sublieutenant Kai was standing on the main deck when Lieutenant Commander Sabe leaned over the bridge railing above and told him "that an order came from the 8th Fleet to execute the missionary passengers, the Third Party Nationals."[138]

Captain Amaya, the commander of the Destroyer Division 34, was with Sabe. Amaya's presence on the destroyer was largely superfluous. Of the three ships of Destroyer Division 34, the *Hakaze* had been sunk by a submarine in late January, while the *Tachikaze* was still returning from the Home Islands, leaving the *Akikaze* as the only ship in the division for the time being. And commanding the *Akikaze* was Sabe's job, while commanding the entire destroyer division was Amaya's job. Nevertheless, Amaya was "a very close friend" of Sabe's. They appear to have discussed the new orders – termed "confidential orders" – which had been delivered in a sealed and secured envelope for the skipper's eyes only by the liaison on that boat in Kavieng.[139]

"The Commander and the Captain were pale and appeared worried," Kai would later say. "They both said that they were opposed to the idea but that, since it was an order, there was no help for it."[140]

Indeed, more than even the Wehrmacht and the Red Army, in the military of Imperial Japan, orders were sacrosanct. Orders were explicitly given "in the name of the emperor," and everyone in the exceptionally brutal Imperial Japanese military – army or navy, officer or enlisted – was conditioned "to obey orders as if they came from the Emperor himself."[141] This order was no different. On the *Akikaze*, no thought was given to disobeying them by anyone in attendance, including Lieutenant Commander Sabe and Captain Amaya. For that matter, given the unusually secretive means by which these orders had been issued, Sabe could not even question his superiors about them.

Subsequently, according to Lieutenant Takahashi, "All Division Officers and above were ordered by the Captain to report to the bridge." When Takahashi got there:

> The Captain's face was pale, and he disclosed substantially the following information which still rings in my ears. He stated: "This order has just arrived and compels us to dispose of all internees on board. Have all men other than those on duty make preparations. The Executive Officer will have the responsibility of its supervision. Commence preparations immediately." We were all taken aback by the enormity of the order, but since it was a military order, we had no alternative but to commence preparations.[142]

The order seems to have cast a pall over the crew, or so they later said. The officers had lunch early and finished before noon. Those in the wardroom included Dr. Sugiura and Lieutenant Commander Sabe. "I seem to recall that the ship captain said after dinner that he had received a very difficult order," Sugiura later explained. "The captain had spoken in the manner of complaint ... to myself and two or three others who were there."[143]

The skipper had put his executive officer, Sublieutenant Terada, in charge of the executions. Terada, in turn, put the Master-at-Arms, Petty Officer Inoue Yokichi, in charge of setting up the executions. To conceal the preparations, which Inoue decided would be at the stern, Sublieutenant Kai was ordered to move all Catholics housed in the quarters near the stern to the forward quarters, using the excuse that the aft cabin was to be cleaned. Inoue had a wooden platform built almost right at the stern railing. He had the platform covered with straw mats to absorb the blood. A 10-foot-tall gallows was built above the platform, with a pulley in the middle of the crossbeam. A hoisting rope with a large hook at one end was run through the pulley. A 7.7mm Lewis machine gun was positioned in front of the structure. Two sailors with rifles were positioned on each side of the machine gun. Behind these five sailors was Sublieutenant Terada.[144]

While the execution area was under construction, the Japanese set up screens to hide what was going on in the stern area. Two canvas tarps were strung up on the main deck at the bridge in parallel rows that ran the width of the ship, like a corridor, with an entry way screened by curtains.[145]

"At a little past midday when we had reached a point approximately sixty nautical miles on the sea south of Kavieng," Sublieutenant Kai later said, "all the arrangements were completed." An all-hands-at-their-stations order was issued just before the executions began.[146]

The internees had been told that they would be called up one at a time for "questioning." Sublieutenant Kai indicated it was more for identification purposes than anything else. He now returned to the forward crew quarters and began calling names off the list. According to Lieutenant Takahashi, who had been assigned bridge duty and was able to see most of the ship from his position, the first person called was "a missionary," a term Takahashi had used to refer to Bishop Lörks.[147]

Sublieutenant Kai led the bishop out of the crew compartment and to the main deck for a "brief interrogation." It's not clear exactly where the questioning took place, but it seems to have been in the area of the bridge, though not on the bridge itself. Nor is it clear why the Japanese questioned the civilians at all, but many historians who have studied this massacre believe it was merely to give the impression of a routine survey. The answers were written down on a note pad. Once Kai finished his "brief interrogation," he turned Bishop Lörks over to two sailors and returned to the forward crew quarters to summon the next individual for questioning.[148]

Bishop Lörks was escorted by the two sailors, one on each side, under the bridge and through the entrance of the canvas corridor. At that point, the Japanese crew members seized the bishop's arms. A tight blindfold was tied over Lörks' eyes. The sailors maneuvered the bishop toward the stern.

When Bishop Lörks and his captors had reached – of all places – the after latrine, for reasons known only to the Japanese, Lörks' clothing was removed and thrown overboard, leaving the bishop in his underwear. The sailors resumed manhandling Lörks toward the stern and the platform where his mortal life would end.

According to Lieutenant Takahashi, watching from the bridge, after Bishop Lörks and other internees who followed him reached the platform, they "were faced toward the bow [and] suspended by their hands by means of a hook attached to a pulley[.]" Reportedly, by this time a crowd had gathered to watch the proceedings, "includ[ing] the Captain, the gunnery officer, the supply officer, the medical officer, two or three other officers, and over sixty petty officers and men."[149]

While Sublieutenant Terada had the firing squad and the machine gun on hand, the executive officer chose to handle this first victim himself with a Model 38 rifle.[150] It was a curious decision, suggesting the discomfort with this action reported by the officers, at least after the fact, might have been shared by the enlisted personnel. Terada may have shot Bishop Lörks himself to try to mitigate that discomfort.

In any event, Sublieutenant Terada shot and killed Josef Lörks himself. Lieutenant Takahashi "saw someone cut the rope by which the victim had been hanging and watched the body fall into the sea."[151]

An identical procedure was followed for the other internees, except that Sublieutenant Terada did not shoot any of them himself. Rather:

[A]t the order of the commander (Terada), [they] were executed by machine gun and rifle fire. After the completion of the execution the suspension rope was slackened, and it had been so planned that when the rope binding the hands was cut, the body would fall backwards off the stern due to the speed of the ship ... Thus, in this way, first the men and then the women were executed.[152]

Throughout the executions, Sublieutenant Kai continued to act as summoner and questioner. The civilians in the forward enlisted men's compartments apparently got anxious at how their people were called out for questioning and then never returned, so he went down several times "to reassure them."[153]

But Kai was in front of the bridge; he could not see the stern area because of the tarps. Nor could he hear the executions. "Because of the sound of the wind and the engines running at top speed, I could not hear the firing of the machine gun," he said later.[154]

Lieutenant Takahashi, the gunnery officer who was given duty on the bridge, from where he was watching the executions, also could not hear it. Though each victim was the victim of four riflemen and a 4- or 5-shot burst from the machine gun, "[w]ith the wind and the high speed of the ship, I could barely hear the shots from where I stood. I knew from the slight movement of the bodies and the sagging of the heads that they had been shot and were dead." That was by design of Lieutenant Commander Sabe. The tarps kept the civilians from seeing the executions, and the noise generated by the high speed of the ship kept them from hearing it.[155]

Lieutenant Takahashi later said it was too much for him. "I recall seeing 12 to 14 foreigners being executed in the above-described manner," he later explained. "I could not bear to watch the scene any more so I refrained from watching."[156]

All of the adults were handled in this way, at a rate of one execution every three minutes. Interestingly enough, there were no reports that the victims struggled or screamed. There was likely at least one exception to the lack of struggling or screaming, and that is when it came to the three children. "The woman missionary took the Chinese children […]," Sublieutenant Kai later reported. After the nuns passed through the curtain, the children were reportedly taken out of the Sisters' arms by a noncommissioned officer. While the Imperial Japanese Army would not only shoot infants, but toss them in the air and catch them on their bayonets, shooting or stabbing an infant was just too barbaric for the Imperial Navy. Instead, the children were each given a banana, then thrown overboard. So much more civilized.[157]

After two hours and 50 minutes, the executions were complete. Sublieutenant Terada went up to the bridge and reported it to Lieutenant Commander Sabe. Upon his orders, the gallows was dismantled and the blood- and gore-saturated matting was dumped over the stern. The deck was hosed down and then thoroughly scrubbed to remove any trace of the blood. The *Akikaze*'s speed was reduced.[158] The notes of the internees' answers to Sublieutenant Kai's questions were carefully collected, reviewed, and thrown out.[159]

At 7:06 that evening – after sunset – the *Akikaze* arrived in Simpson Harbor. Before the crew was allowed to disembark and experience the bright lights and glitz that is Rabaul, Lieutenant Commander Sabe assembled all officers and enlisted men. According to Machinist Petty Officer Ishigami Shinichi:

> The captain stood in front of us and said that the killing of these foreigners was done in accordance with orders received from higher up, that it was a very regrettable incident, and that we should not discuss this matter with our friends or comrades or with anyone after reaching port.[160]

The area of the stern where the executions had been conducted was then purified, offerings were made, and services for the dead were held in the presence of Lieutenant Commander Sabe and the entire crew. Three members of the crew who had been Buddhist priests before entering the navy chanted Buddhist scriptures "for the solace of the spirits of the departed." After that, Lieutenant Takahashi recalled, "it somehow seemed as if the spirits of all were restored." Ishigami opined that the fact that the victims murdered by the Japanese "were accorded due ceremony, shows the true Japanese character."[161]

The *Akikaze* completed docking. Waiting at the dock was Lieutenant Commander Yamamoto Kotohiko, the engineering staff officer of the 8th Base Force. Yamamoto, who was in charge of barracks for internees, had brought a truck to transport the civilians to their internment camp. He was puzzled when no civilians disembarked from the *Akikaze*. His repeated inquiries as to their status were met with silence, until it was explained to him "that the foreign nationals had fallen overboard due to a storm." A storm that swept overboard only foreign nationals? Yamamoto knew what that excuse meant.[162]

As that was going on, Lieutenant Commander Sabe, Captain Amaya, and Sublieutenant Kai picked their way through the darkened streets of Rabaul to 8th Fleet headquarters. They arrived at about 10:00pm, and found the lights still on in the ground floor offices and Lieutenant Kami Shigenori, Senior Staff Officer, on duty. While under normal circumstances, the senior officer, in this case Amaya, would have made the report, it appears that in accordance with his "confidential orders," it was Sabe who was to report to 8th Fleet headquarters concerning the completion of these orders.[163]

There is the hint that Lieutenant Commander Sabe was angry and sullen and, initially, ambiguous. Sabe appears to have started off by telling Lieutenant Kami that if he ever received orders like these again, he would not comply. He went on to say he "was greatly astonished at this act since Germany was a wartime ally of Japan, and there were Germans among those killed." Kami blurted out, "What! Were they killed?"[164]

"We were warned by Staff Officer Kami never to reveal this incident," Sublieutenant Kai recalled. "The captain was talking of taking ashore the baggage of the citizens of neutral countries the next day. I stayed for about five minutes but did not converse with Staff Officer Kami other than to report my arrival." Kai left alone and went to the headquarters of the 8th Base Force, which was close by, where he spent the night.[165]

Some time later, Lieutenant Commander Sabe followed Kai to 8th Base Force headquarters, but on a very different mission. Sabe was looking for Lieutenant Commander Kuroki Ikichiro, gunnery officer of the 8th Base Force and a close friend from their days at the naval academy.

Lieutenant Commander Kuroki found Sabe looking "shocked and dejected," so much so that he feared Sabe "did not have long to live."

"I have just returned from Kairiru Island and reported to the 8th Fleet Headquarters," Sabe said. "This last voyage was very unpleasant."

"What happened?" Kuroki asked.

"On orders from the 8th Fleet Headquarters we stopped over at Lorengau Island and took several missionaries aboard my ship, the *Akikaze*. On the return trip to Rabaul, an order for the disposal (*Shobun*) of the missionaries was received from 8th Fleet Headquarters, and although I felt that the order was mysterious, we had to dispose of the missionaries before reaching port in accordance with this order."

Lieutenant Commander Sabe went on to describe the exchange he had at 8th Fleet headquarters with Lieutenant Kami, that if he ever got an order like that again, he would not comply. Sabe was dumbfounded that he had been ordered to kill Germans, when Germany was an ally of Japan.

Gingerly, given the skipper's mood, Lieutenant Commander Kuroki probed Sabe for details of the order. It was clear to both that something did not add up about the order.

Sabe called the order "mysterious"; he did not know if 8th Fleet had the authority to issue such an order. Kuroki wondered if 8th Fleet had actually issued such an order at all. Kuroki knew Admiral Mikawa and his chief of staff Rear Admiral Onishi Shinzo personally and could not believe either of them would issue such an order. He wondered if it was sent out without their authorization. And both wondered about a particular member of Admiral Mikawa's staff ...

But there it had to wait. Lieutenant Commander Sabe went back to the *Akikaze* to try to sleep, if he could. The next morning, March 18, he sent ashore the victims' luggage. That night his ship left Simpson Harbor to begin escorting convoys from Rabaul to Kusai and Saipan, eventually ending in the Home Islands. The *Akikaze* and the central figure in the massacre now permanently attached to her name were shipped far away from the scene of the crime – and people who might want to look into that crime. The destroyer and her skipper would not return until early June, about two-and-a-half months. A lot can change in two-and-a-half months.

For that matter, a lot had changed in the past two-and-a-half months. A lot had changed in the past two-and-a-half weeks. The aerial massacre of the Lae convoy. The ambush of the *Murasame* and *Minegumo* off Vila-Stanmore. The constant grip of enemy submarines on the Japanese throat in the South Pacific now increasing.

For the Japanese, it was shocking, frustrating, and humiliating.

For someone, it was apparently so infuriating that he decided to take it out on 62 innocent civilians who had done him no wrong whatsoever. It was the worst kind of decision made in war: a decision based not on strategy or logic, but emotion. In this case, emotion alone. Military decisions based on emotion rarely work out well. In this case, the only ones paying the price had been 62 innocent civilians. But the Japanese would soon make other military decisions based on emotion.

The catastrophe of the Battle of the Bismarck Sea was but one domino. The toppling of this one domino started others toppling. One of those dominoes was the massacre aboard the *Akikaze*. But that was just one branch. There remained other branches in which the dominoes were starting to fall that would lead to an even worse catastrophe in the days ahead.

CHAPTER 2

PUTTING THE CARTWHEEL BEFORE THE HORSE

The American public had little love for Adolf Hitler or National Socialism, but it remained, at best, ambivalent about entering yet another war in Europe. After the Japanese bombed Pearl Harbor, in the words of John Kenneth Galbraith, "The mood of the American people was obvious – they were determined that the Japanese had to be punished. We could have been forced to concentrate all our efforts on the Pacific, unable from then on to give more than purely peripheral help to Britain."[1] But Hitler's declaration of war against the United States changed that equation.

It was in late December 1941 and early January 1942, as the Japanese sweep across Southeast Asia and the Pacific gained momentum, that US President Franklin Roosevelt and British Prime Minister Winston Churchill were having their first secret conference, codenamed "Arcadia." It was at Arcadia that the "Europe First" policy – in other words, "Germany First" – was firmly established by the US and Britain. It required a bit of a sales job to the American people. The Japanese – not the Germans – had bombed Pearl Harbor. The Japanese – not the Germans – had bombed Clark Field, Cavite Navy Yard, Guam, Wake. The Germans had only declared war against the US; it must be noted that this was before substantial evidence of the horrific Nazi crimes against the Jews, Poles, Roma, Ukrainians, and other ethnic groups the Nazis deemed "subhuman" was public knowledge. The emotional preferences of the American people can be illustrated by a common question among the American public at the time: "Where were you when you first heard about the Japanese attack on Pearl Harbor?" Few, if any, asked, "Where were you when you first heard about Germany declaring war against us?"

Nevertheless, Germany First was the policy. It was explained to the American people that the Japanese were just doing the bidding of the Germans, which was true – from a certain point of view. Japanese actions in the Pacific would have served to distract the US from taking action against Germany, the argument went. The leadership of the US Army, in the form of General George C. Marshall and Army Air Force General Henry H. "Hap" Arnold, was committed to the Germany First policy. Taking much of their cue from General Dwight Eisenhower, soon to become the Supreme Commander of the Allied Expeditionary Forces in the European Theatre, Marshall and Arnold were determined to quash any offensive actions in the Pacific and not send any reinforcements there.

The third piece of the Joint Chiefs, Admiral Ernest J. King, Commander in Chief of the US Fleet and, after March 1942, Chief of Naval Operations, disagreed, to put it mildly. King wanted to press the Pacific War against the Japanese, not drain it to support the fight against Germany. And because of that disagreement, King was hated by such a distinguished cast of characters who supported Germany First as Secretary of War Henry Stimson; Prime Minister Churchill; Chief of the Imperial General Staff Field Marshal Sir Alan Brooke; and Royal Navy Admiral Sir Andrew Cunningham.[2] None came close to the opinion of General Dwight Eisenhower. The man who could make friends with pretty much everyone once said, "One thing that might help win this war is to get someone to shoot King. He's the antithesis of cooperation, a deliberately rude person, which means he's a mental bully."[3]

Of course, cooperation is a two-way street, and the determination of both the British and Generals Marshall and Arnold to enforce the "Germany First" policy to the point of starving the Pacific of resources suggested their version of "cooperation" was that King would get nothing and like it.

Admiral King would countenance neither. Even though the agreement out of Arcadia was very clearly "Germany First" for resources and efforts, King managed to slip in a few lines about the war against Japan. The carefully worded and intentionally vague declaration said efforts in the Pacific would involve "Maintaining only such positions in the [Pacific] theatre as will safeguard vital interests and deny to Japan access to raw materials vital to her continuous war effort while we are concentrating on the defeat of Germany."[4] "Vital interests" was conspicuously left undefined, though the term was used a second time, as a title for a tiny section:

The Safeguarding of Vital Interests in the Eastern Theatre
    18. The security of Australia, New Zealand, and India must be maintained and Chinese resistance supported. Secondly, points of vantage from which an offensive against Japan can eventually be developed must be secured.[5]

It was from Arcadia that, on December 31, 1941, Admiral King issued his first substantive orders to Admiral Chester Nimitz, the new Commander in Chief of the Pacific Fleet, the battleships of which were sitting in the mud at Pearl Harbor. The Pacific Fleet was, first, to hold the line at Hawaii-Midway and protect the lines of communication with the West Coast. Second, and "only in small degree less important," the fleet was to protect the lines of communication with Australia.[6] But Admiral King was aware of the US Army's lack of interest in fighting Japan. Despite his dark and humorless personality, King had a can-do philosophy. He approached the war against Japan with the idea of "Make the best of what you have:"

> There must be no tendency to excuse incomplete readiness for war on the premise of future acquisition of trained personnel or modernized material ... personnel shall be trained and rendered competent ... existing material shall be maintained and utilized at its maximum effectiveness at all times.[7]

With the thin reed of resources available in the Pacific at this time and the determination of the US Army leadership to prevent additional resources from being sent its way, it was an essential philosophy. General Arnold later said, "it was impossible not to get the impression that the Navy was determined to carry on the campaign in that theater, and determined to do it with as little help from the Army as possible."[8]

At a March 2 meeting of the newly formed Joint Chiefs of Staff, Admiral King handed Generals Marshall and Arnold a memorandum detailing his proposal, summarized in nine words: "Hold Hawaii; Support Australasia; Drive northwestward from New Hebrides."[9] "The general scheme or concept of operations is not only to protect the lines of communication with Australia," he wrote, "but in so doing to set up 'strong points' from which a step-by-step general advance can be made through the New Hebrides, Solomons, and Bismarck Archipelago."[10] For this proposal, King said he needed two, maybe three Army divisions and maybe eight groups of aircraft.

Despite the Arcadia declaration, however, the leadership of the US Army was not sold on the necessity of keeping the lines of communication open to Australia. On February 28, 1942, General Eisenhower had told General Marshall:

> The United States' interest in maintaining contact with Australia and in preventing further Japanese expansion to the Southeastward is apparent ... but ... they are not immediately vital to the successful outcome of the war. The problem is one of determining what we can spare for the effort in that region, without seriously impairing performance of our mandatory tasks.[11]

While sacrificing Australia to Japan to free up more resources for the war against Germany – minus, of course, the Australians who were already fighting Germany under the Union Jack – may sound like an extreme position today, this was far from an extreme position within the US Army leadership. General Arnold, in particular, appeared willing to sacrifice not just Australia, but everything up to and including the western continental US as far east as the Rocky Mountains in order to squeeze more resources for the war against Germany.

The Army's refusal to provide additional units to the Pacific or to agree to offensive action there softened, curiously enough, when General Douglas MacArthur was rescued from the fall of the Philippines in March 1942. When the Japanese first attacked the Philippines on December 8, 1941, MacArthur "demonstrated his unique leadership style: when he was good, he was very, very good[;] when he was bad, he was horrid."[12] And, in those critical hours immediately after the Pearl Harbor attack, MacArthur was horrid – at best.

After long predicting the Japanese could not attack until spring of 1942, General MacArthur had refused to consider evidence that a Japanese attack was, in fact, imminent. Then, after being informed of the Pearl Harbor attack, MacArthur disappeared for the next several hours, the first hours of the war, apparently shell-shocked that his predictions were actually wrong. Most of his aircraft were destroyed on the ground at the Clark Field base complex by a Japanese air attack, due largely to MacArthur's willful violation of orders from Washington to attack Japanese air bases on Formosa and make sure his aircraft were not destroyed on the ground. The result was an inability to even contest Japanese control of the air over the Philippines and, later, the Netherlands East Indies.

His blunders did not stop there. While the long-held war plans contemplated US troops holding the Bataan Peninsula to deny the Japanese the use of Manila Bay, General MacArthur refused to position supplies on the Bataan Peninsula for a protracted campaign because the idea of withdrawing there was "defeatist," so that when MacArthur ultimately did withdraw there, his troops had neither the ammunition nor the food for prolonged resistance. With the defense of the Philippines coming to a conclusion, though not nearly as rapid a conclusion as the Japanese had hoped, Roosevelt ordered MacArthur to go to Australia, leaving the troops he had so poorly served behind.

But Douglas MacArthur was still a national hero, with a formidable public relations machine that covered up much of his horrid performance – and made him a domestic political threat to Roosevelt. Keeping him on the sidelines was out of the question. Now, all of a sudden, the Army was interested in reinforcing the Pacific – but only for the purpose of turning it into *The Douglas MacArthur Show*.

The Army's about-face brought up the question of whether the Pacific needed to be like Europe and have one theater commander. Generals Marshall and Arnold thought there should be a unified Pacific command – under Douglas MacArthur. "[General Marshall's] basic trouble," Admiral King later said, "was that like all Army officers he knew nothing about sea power and very little about air power."[13] So, the admiral had "to 'educate' the Army people."[14] King told Marshall that he had agreed to have an Army general in command of the European theater – "unity of command" – because it would be fought primarily by the Army. The Pacific was being fought primarily by the Navy and Marine Corps, hence it made more sense to have a Navy admiral in charge. The offensive "must be conducted under the direction of [the Commander in Chief of the Pacific Fleet] and cannot be conducted in any other way."[15] Europe was a land war, so put the Army in charge. The Pacific was a sea war, so put the Navy in charge. This wasn't rocket surgery. But in the face of this undeniable logic the Army still believed that Douglas MacArthur should be in charge of the Pacific. His record spoke for itself.

On that, the Navy agreed: his record did speak for itself. To the Navy leadership, MacArthur was the one who had constantly berated the Asiatic Fleet and its commander Admiral Hart as not being worthy of the name; allowed the Japanese to completely destroy their main Far East base at Cavite; then, to top it off, blamed the fleet for the collapsing situation in the Philippines. Finding MacArthur's performance in the Philippines horrid and believing MacArthur knew nothing about sea power – he didn't – Admiral King, with the full backing of the Navy leadership, vowed that MacArthur would never have operational command of the Pacific Fleet.[16] The Army believed MacArthur bore no responsibility for the disaster in the Philippines – that public relations machine at work – and would not agree to command by a Navy admiral.

Moreover, it was that same institutional arrogance and myopia that was behind the relentless drive to put Douglas MacArthur in that role of Pacific supreme commander. MacArthur's performance in the 1941–42 Philippines Campaign was so wracked with ineptitude, arrogance, and willful violation of orders that investigation and possible court martial were warranted. That such steps were impossible due to MacArthur's reputation is perhaps understandable, but that does not excuse the refusal by Generals Marshall and Arnold to acknowledge even privately that MacArthur's performance in the Philippines was perhaps below his usual standards, or to understand why the US Navy, slandered, abused, and blamed by MacArthur for the loss of the Philippines, did not want to serve under him or cater to his inability to accept being under anyone else's command. The possibility that Generals Marshall and Arnold would be able to ram a unified Pacific command under MacArthur down the Navy's throat hung over everything Admiral Nimitz and the Pacific Fleet did.

To break the impasse, on March 9, the Joint Chiefs created two command areas of the Pacific theater. One, a "Southwest Pacific Command" comprising the Philippines, the Netherlands East Indies, Australia, the Solomon Islands, and adjoining ocean areas. Most of these were not currently under Allied control. It would be up to its commander, General MacArthur, to retake them. These areas would require the bulk of the land combat in the Pacific. As part of the command, MacArthur even got his own little navy to abuse just as he had Admiral Hart and the Asiatic Fleet. At his new headquarters in Melbourne, MacArthur told a reporter, "[T]he best navy in the world is the Japanese navy. A first-class navy. Then comes the British navy. The US Navy is a fourth-class navy, not even as good as the Italian navy."[17]

Admiral Nimitz got the rest as part of a "Pacific Ocean Area," with him, as with General MacArthur, reporting to their respective service chiefs on the Joint Chiefs of Staff, who would be conducting this Pacific War by committee. Nimitz's Pacific Ocean Area was further divided into three regions, North, Central, and South, with boundaries at 40 degrees north latitude and the equator. Admiral Nimitz could directly command the first two, but the new South Pacific Command for the area south of the equator would have to be handed off to a subordinate; Vice Admiral Robert L. Ghormley, who had just finished his term as Special Naval Observer in London, was eventually selected.[18]

With that can kicked down the road, on April 16, Admiral King's assistant chief of staff for planning Rear Admiral Richmond Kelly Turner presented a four-phase "Pacific Ocean Campaign Plan" that was based on King's concept of "Driv[ing] northwestward from New Hebrides." Phase One of Turner's plan was the buildup of forces and bases in the South Pacific to secure the area and position for an offensive against the Japanese. Phase Two was an offensive from the New Hebrides Islands northwestward through the Solomons and New Guinea to seize the Bismarck and Admiralty Islands. Phase Three would extend that offensive to the Central Pacific, such as the Marshall and especially the Caroline Islands. Phase Four would involve a drive into the Philippines or the Netherlands East Indies, "whichever offers the more promising and enduring results." This document would become the basic plan for the US Navy in the Pacific.[19] Naturally, because fighting a war is not complicated enough, the planned strategy, at least initially, would center on that controversial command boundary between MacArthur's Southwest Pacific Command and Ghormley's South Pacific Command.

To make this plan work, Admiral Turner, who went by his middle name "Kelly," earlier had also recommended the establishment of an amphibious assault force in the South Pacific. King agreed and ordered Admiral Nimitz to create it. When Nimitz arrived back in Hawaii after his April 23–24 conference with Admiral King in San Francisco, he was carrying the specific directive to Admiral Ghormley to "prepare to launch a major amphibious offensive against positions held by the Japanese." The Pacific Fleet staff conducted studies that examined the Santa Cruz and lower Solomon Islands. King made Turner commander of this new amphibious force. Turner, very uncharacteristically, admitted that he knew little of the subject. King responded, "Kelly, you will learn."[20] It was a new war, with new weapons, new tactics, and new ways of thinking. How this all interacted, no one knew. They would have to learn on the fly, something that American officers would later call "makee learnee."[21]

And there things sat while carrier battles took place in the Coral Sea, in which the Japanese invasion force directed at Port Moresby on the southern coast of Papua was turned back; and near Midway, in which four Japanese carriers were sunk. Despite the losses of the carriers *Lexington* and *Yorktown*, destroyers *Sims* and *Hammann*, and oiler *Neosho*, the positive effects of both actions, especially Midway, on sagging American morale cannot be overstated. But the American victory at Midway would not have been possible without *Magic*.

Magic was a subset of what is more commonly and famously known as *Ultra*, the term adopted by the Allies to reference signals intelligence (in military acronym SIGINT) obtained by breaking encrypted enemy radio and wireless telegraph communications. While *Ultra* covered all such intelligence, the US adopted the term *Magic* for its decrypts specifically from Japanese sources. In the case of Coral Sea and Midway, a breakthrough had come in the Japanese naval high-level command and control communications code the Allies called "JN-25."[22] The Allied breakthrough had been the result of painstaking intelligence work. With the Japanese unaware of the breach, *Magic* and signals intelligence would be the gift that kept on giving.

For now, however, the victory at Midway was giving some headaches. General MacArthur took the opportunity to propose his own offensive in the South Pacific and demanded resources from the Pacific Fleet to carry out that offensive. Admiral King would have none of it, and instead proposed his own offensive based on Admiral Turner's proposal to drive northwestward from the New Hebrides.

To break this second impasse, during the last two days of June, Marshall and Admiral King hammered out the "Joint Directive for Offensive Operations in the Southwest Pacific Area Agreed on by the United States Chiefs of Staff" that consisted of three phases. Phase One, already given its own code name of *Watchtower*, would involve the seizure of Tulagi and the Santa Cruz Islands. This task would be completed by the Pacific Fleet. MacArthur's Southwest Pacific Command boundary would be moved up to the Solomons so this phase would lie entirely within the South Pacific Command. MacArthur himself would interdict "enemy air and naval activities westward of operating area," meaning Rabaul and New Guinea.[23] Phase Two would be the capture of Lae, Salamaua, and the rest of the northeast coast of New Guinea; and the central Solomons. Phase Three would involve the reduction and capture of Rabaul. Phases Two and Three would be under the command of General MacArthur. This three-part plan was given the cheerful name of *Pestilence*.

Admiral King and General Marshall – curiously not General Arnold – formally adopted *Pestilence* on July 2.[24] Phase One – *Watchtower*, involving the capture of the Santa Cruz Islands, Tulagi, and "adjacent positions" – was scheduled to begin August 1. Admiral Nimitz had been working on *Watchtower* and expanded the planned attack on Tulagi to include the capture of an unspecified airfield site, if not a finished airfield.[25]

This was about the time when things started getting complicated. Well, more complicated. Those coastwatchers of whom the Japanese thought the Divine Word, Sacred Heart, and Liebenzell missionaries were members – these particular clergy were not – were a uniquely useful form of Allied intelligence gathering in the South Pacific: an organization christened *Ferdinand*. Named after the children's story *Ferdinand the Bull*, whose title character preferred smelling flowers to fighting, *Ferdinand* was the brainchild of Australian naval reservist Lieutenant Commander Eric A. Feldt, a veteran of the British Grand Fleet in World War I. Feldt had been local affairs administrator on New Guinea, where he became familiar with the talented, temperamental, and fiercely independent Melanesian natives. When Feldt was recalled to service, he came up with the idea of enrolling plantation managers, government administrators, missionaries, and anyone who wanted to serve, but not to fight, not to be noticed, not to cause any trouble for the Japanese, except to watch and warn of Japanese movements, actions, and other developments. By December 1939, *Ferdinand* had 800 members, located everywhere in New Guinea, the Bismarcks, and the Solomons, including chief observers trained to communicate by radio.[26] These were the "coastwatchers."

Upon the arrival of the Japanese, the coastwatchers became dependent on the goodwill of the local Melanesians. Whether due to the respect and humanity with which the Australian local colonial officials had treated them, the general brutality with which the Japanese treated everybody including them, or both, the vast majority of Melanesians remained loyal to the Allied cause. They became essential to the Allies by gathering information, carrying equipment and supplies, providing cover, and infiltrating Japanese construction details.

As the Japanese advanced and began consolidating their hold on the Solomons, the coastwatchers, directed from Townsville, Australia, became eyes and ears – but not hands – for the Allies. (Though a few of the coastwatchers did try to be the hands.)

Be that as it may, in early July, a pair of those eyes that belonged to one Martin Clemens reported that the Japanese were building an airfield at Lunga Point on Guadalcanal, across from Tulagi. The work on the airfield was soon corroborated by *Magic* and air reconnaissance.

As a result, *Watchtower* was modified to encompass the capture of Tulagi and this new Guadalcanal airfield; the capture of the Santa Cruz Islands was delayed and eventually scrapped due in large part to the islands' unique, virulent form of cerebral malaria – to which the natives were immune – that did not make the travel brochures. And *Watchtower* was put on a clock: it had to take place before the Japanese completed that airfield. Because once the airfield was completed, the New Hebrides, from where Admirals King and Turner wanted to launch the counteroffensive up the Solomon Islands and where the construction of bases was proceeding in a rushed, lurching fashion for that purpose, would be dangerously exposed to attack, especially by air. In that case, more than likely, the Allies would not be able to use the New Hebrides as that staging area for the counteroffensive. They would have to use someplace much further away, such as New Caledonia, which would complicate things immensely and probably lengthen the war substantially.

Of course, having to launch this offensive in the tight, uncertain timeframe presented by the airfield complicated things on its own. Admiral Turner had been assigned the job of assembling an amphibious force for the South Pacific. For *Watchtower*, that force would transport the 1st Marine Division, which Marine General Alexander Vandegrift was still in the process of training. Intelligence estimated that the Japanese would complete the airfield in the first week of August. Admiral King had set August 1 as the date for the *Watchtower* offensive. It was pushed back a week, but they did not dare push it back further. Admiral Ghormley thought there was no way they could launch the offensive. Vice Admiral Frank "Jack" Fletcher, who had commanded the carriers during the Coral Sea and Midway battles, thought the operation would fail. There simply was not enough time. They would not be ready; yet that did not matter. They had to be ready.

Then the Japanese changed the equation somewhat. Having failed to take Port Moresby amphibiously in what became the Battle of the Coral Sea, the Japanese tried another tack and prepared to move by land on Port Moresby, the only major position in Papua New Guinea held by the Allies. Port Moresby was near the southern end of the Kokoda Trail, which ran north over the Owen Stanley Mountains to end near Buna on the north coast of Papua. While the Japanese held Lae and Salamaua on New Guinea's north coast, they did not hold Buna. That was about to change.

Allied intelligence had long believed the Japanese were interested in Buna, but General MacArthur made no effort to get there first. When intelligence revealed a Japanese invasion convoy leaving Rabaul on July 13, Colonel Kenneth Wills, senior intelligence staff officer for the Australian 1st Army, determined it was headed for Buna.[27] However, MacArthur's chief of staff, the "highly irritable" Major General Richard K. Sutherland, refused to believe it, saying he had no hard evidence that Buna was their destination.[28] The convoy was spotted on July 19 heading for Buna by a B-17 from the 19th Heavy Bombardment Group.[29] Sure enough, that night, the Japanese landed at Buna. Multiple heavy air attacks the next day by the 5th Air Force against the Japanese transports off Buna were too little, too late, and futile.[30] The Japanese were at Buna in force. At least Sutherland now had his hard evidence.

Having given Buna away, General MacArthur would have to pay dearly to get it back. Or, more precisely, make others pay dearly to get it back. Worse than having given away a major strategic position, as it had been with the disasters at Clark Field and Bataan, MacArthur had made a costly and very public mistake. That was not just intolerable; that was impossible. It just didn't happen. Someone else must be at fault, because Douglas MacArthur obviously was not, because he was Douglas MacArthur. The general and his senior staff would become utterly ruthless and unreasonable, looking for scapegoats, whipping everyone to correct his mistake or at least cover it up. He had done it after Clark Field. He would do it again with Buna.

Now there was the prospect of two major campaigns going on in the South Pacific at the same time. One was in Papua, where the Imperial Japanese Army would move south from Buna down the Kokoda Trail to try and capture Port Moresby and thus remove the great northern shield of Australia. Meanwhile, all the way across the Coral Sea, an Allied armada of 82 ships and 19,000 Marines sailed toward Guadalcanal. It was the largest armada yet assembled by the US Navy in the Pacific. It included three aircraft carriers, one brand-new battleship, and two brand-new light cruisers that would ultimately be used for antiaircraft work. The impressive picture was misleading as to just how desperate the circumstances in the Pacific were for the Allies, inasmuch as this was almost all of the operational ships of the Pacific Fleet.

But the landings came off successfully. On land, the only opposition came from some Special Naval Landing Force troops at Tulagi and its outlying islands, who fought tenaciously; and some wild pigs on Guadalcanal, who fought in a style all their own. The airfield was quickly captured. The Japanese attacked the invasion force by air, but aside from fatally damaging one destroyer and one transport and damaging a second destroyer, they accomplished little while incurring catastrophic losses among their aircrews.

Which brought to the forefront two significant problems. One was unloading the transports and cargo ships. This was still "makee learnee" and no one had yet come up with the idea of "combat loading" – that is, loading transports and cargo ships so the most essential items, such as ammunition and perishable food, were at the edge of the cargo bays and thus first to be unloaded. Moreover, there were not enough stevedores to unload the supplies. The result was a logjam of ships trying to unload on the beach and a logjam of supplies on the beach, so much so that the offloading of supplies had to be halted for a time so part of the beach could be cleared by moving some of the supplies inland. The jam would prove critical.

But it was the second issue that was much more of a problem with the potential to derail the entire *Watchtower* offensive. It had proven to be a problem throughout history: a military operation that is led by a commander who does not support it. It can be a recipe for disaster, as the ancient Athenians found out with Nicias and their ill-fated invasion of Sicily.

Admiral Fletcher, in command of the entire armada, had made it painfully clear that he was not a supporter of *Watchtower* and did not believe it would succeed. Although he had led US Navy carriers to victories at Coral Sea (which was a strategic victory if not a tactical one) and Midway, he had lost the carrier *Lexington* at Coral Sea and *Yorktown* at Midway. While both losses were arguably cases of bad luck – the *Lexington* had survived her battle damage, only to be destroyed by fuel air explosions; while the damaged *Yorktown*, disabled but under tow, had fallen victim to a Japanese submarine – it was still two carriers lost on his watch. Fletcher did not want to lose a third, so he decided to pull the carriers out after the second day of *Watchtower* operations. Without air cover, the rest of the armada, including Admiral Turner's transports, which were struggling to unload their supplies, would lose their fighter protection and have to pull out as well.

It was a fateful decision. While some have defended Admiral Fletcher's decision to pull the three aircraft carriers out – and there is a legitimate defense to be made – that decision set off a chain of events that resulted in what the US Navy calls The Battle of Savo Island and what the Marines on Guadalcanal disgustedly called "The Battle of the Four (or Five) Sitting Ducks," in which Admiral Mikawa showed up off Guadalcanal with his cruisers and sank three American heavy cruisers and fatally damaged an Australian cruiser in what remains the worst defeat in the history of the US Navy. It was only dumb luck for the Americans that the largely defenseless transports and cargo ships were not themselves attacked and sunk. As it was, the four sunken cruisers earned the waters off Savo Island and Guadalcanal the nickname "Ironbottom Sound." Late the next day, after continuing to discharge supplies despite the lack of air cover, Admiral Turner pulled the remaining ships out from off Guadalcanal. The 1st Marine Division was left behind – one member of General Vandegrift's staff cheekily renamed it "The 1st Maroon Division" – with nowhere near the amount of supplies they would need to finish and defend the airfield.[31] Admiral Fletcher's decision to withdraw the aircraft carriers is bitterly remembered by the US Marine Corps to this day.

After a surprisingly successful landing, the Savo Island debacle had sent *Watchtower* off to a rumbling, bumbling, stumbling start. But General Vandegrift and the 1st Maroon Division made the best of it. Living off supplies the Japanese had left behind at the airfield, the Marines established a defensive perimeter, dug themselves in, and got used to their new and very alien jungle surroundings. And, as one Marine said, "what a putrefying shithole it really was."[32]

It might be hard to imagine Guadalcanal. The island that, as many a writer has opined, looks like paradise but is more like Paradise Lost. The Solomon Islands have more than a few other Guadalcanals such as, say, New Georgia and Vella Lavella. But all share the same basic elements. The heat. And it's not a dry heat; the air is completely saturated. The public affairs officer Major Frank O. Hough described it, saying, "No air stirs here and the hot humidity is beyond the imagination of anyone who has not lived in it."[33] With the humidity comes the rain. Technically, the Solomons have two seasons, "dry" and "wet," though to the Marines the seasons were more like "wet" and "really wet." In the *New York Times*, F. Tillman Durdin wrote, "It rains almost every night – weepy tropical rain that soaks into the bed rolls and seeps through the tarpaulin. The nights are passed in wet chill and discomfort and the days in mud and filth."[34] It rained so much that standing water and drainage issues were common. And with standing water came Guadalcanal's most numerous resident: the mosquito. Not just any mosquitoes, either. These seemed larger than normal. It also was apparently a requirement for every mosquito on Guadalcanal to carry malaria.

The mosquito was hardly the animal kingdom's only bugbear to the jugheads. The aforementioned coastwatcher Martin Clemens described some of the others:

> On the inside she was a poisonous morass. Crocodiles hid in her creeks or patrolled her turgid backwaters. Her jungles were alive with slithering, crawling, scuttling things; with giant lizards that barked like dogs, with huge red furry spiders, with centipedes and leeches and scorpions, with rats and bats and fiddler crabs and one big species of landcrab which moved through the bush with all the stealth of a steamroller.[35]

But at least one could physically see the animals. One could not see the microbes that bred in the dark, damp places in the jungle so deep that light rarely reached the ground so it never truly dried. Not just malaria, but yellow fever, typhus, dengue fever, dysentery, and so many different fungal infections (especially the infamous "jungle rot") that literally every wound, every scratch, became infected.

Even the plants were hostile. Towering palm trees bombed the unwary with coconuts. Bamboo grew faster than it could be cut. Hidden roots tripped and vines with thorns and hooks cut and slashed clothing and flesh. Lean against a tree and it just might fall over because it is dead, rotted, hollowed out inside, and full of bugs. And there was the infamous crown jewel of the arboretum of assault: kunai grass, which could grow to ten feet tall, was stiff, serrated, and sharp. Kunai, too, cut and slashed clothing and flesh. Like walking through a field of swords.

It all added up to an atmosphere to which few who had visited wanted to return. The travel writer Jack London rather famously once wrote, "If I were king, the worst punishment I could inflict on my enemies would be to banish them to the Solomons." But he quickly added, "On second thought, king or no king, I don't think I'd have the heart to do it."[36]

Yet, here they were, the men of the 1st Maroon Division, making the best of what they had. First, the Marines had – using captured Japanese equipment and supplies, which sustained them during this early period – completed the airfield. Inspired by Major Lofton Henderson, who led 16 green Marine dive bomber pilots in a futile, fatal attack on the Japanese carrier *Hiryu* at Midway, the airstrip was named "Henderson Field." It was not until the afternoon of August 20, almost two weeks after the capture of the airfield, almost one week after the airfield was declared operational, that it finally got some actual aircraft: 19 Marine F4F Wildcat fighters from Marine Fighter Squadron 223 and 12 Douglas SBD Dauntless dive bombers of Marine Scout Bombing Squadron 232 from Marine Air Group 23, 1st Marine Air Wing. With their arrival on Guadalcanal, whose Allies code name was "Cactus," the "Cactus Air Force" was born.

That birth helped end that feeling of being the 1st Maroon Division. That same night, the Imperial Japanese Army made its first attack to recapture the base. Some 800 Japanese troops who had been transported by destroyers marched straight down the beach, fixed their bayonets, and, just after midnight on August 21, yelled "Banzai!" and charged en masse into the Marine perimeter across the sandbar that spanned Alligator Creek. Three times these 800 Japanese charged – a "banzai charge" was what the Allies called it – into the teeth of 15,000 US Marines with machine guns and artillery, and three times they were driven back with horrific losses. About 770 of the roughly 800 Japanese who attacked were killed.

This American victory in what is variously known as "The Battle of the Tenaru River" (though the Tenaru River was further east), "The Battle of Alligator Creek" (though it had no alligators and was not a creek), or "The Battle of the Ilu River" (though the Ilu was not a river but a tidal lagoon) was a major boost in the confidence and morale of the formerly green Marines.

Just in time for the Japanese to make another push to send reinforcements to the island with support from their aircraft carriers *Shokaku* and *Zuikaku*, after Midway the only two carriers remaining out of the original six carriers of *Kido Butai*. Admiral Fletcher chose to show up with his aircraft carriers *Saratoga*, *Enterprise*, and *Wasp* to give the Americans an overwhelming advantage. Then he proceeded to throw that advantage away by sending the *Wasp* off to refuel in what Admiral King would call another one of Fletcher's "inopportune refuelings." Even so, the Americans managed to sink the light carrier *Ryujo* while Marine and *Enterprise* dive bombers drove back the Japanese reinforcement convoy, sinking one transport, and B-17s from the 11th Heavy Bombardment Group out of Espiritu Santo sank a rescue destroyer that was strangely stationary. All at the cost of damage to the *Enterprise* that necessitated her return to Pearl Harbor. Fletcher never did find the *Shokaku* or the *Zuikaku*, but *Kido Butai* lost a good number of its aircrews this day. It was called, in US Navy circles, the Battle of the Eastern Solomons. And, in a rare bit of honesty in the Guadalcanal Campaign, it actually took place around the Eastern Solomons.

From there the Guadalcanal Campaign settled down into a campaign and a routine that was monotonous albeit not boring. A routine that involved a very curious and unique changing of the control of the seas around Guadalcanal every time the sun crossed the horizon. Every morning, when the sun rose, the aircraft of the Cactus Air Force would control the skies. The Japanese would send down raids comprising Mitsubishi G4M bombers – the Allies gave this aircraft the reporting name "Betty" – and Zero fighters – the Allies gave this aircraft the reporting name "Zeke," but it never really caught on and everyone kept calling this fighter the Zero. The problem for the Japanese was that their bases at Rabaul were so far away that their Zeros and Bettys, even when they had numerical superiority, were very limited in when they could appear and for how long they could stay over Guadalcanal. Moreover, the Americans would usually get warning from coastwatchers and radar, allowing them to scramble fighters. The bombers would be driven to high altitude by the Marines' heavy antiaircraft guns. The Japanese bombing would cause some damage but would be largely ineffective. Wildcats would tangle with Zeros and Bettys, the Japanese and Marines would each suffer losses, and the Japanese would make the return trip to Rabaul, the length of that trip making the recovery of downed pilots and the return of aircraft damaged in combat extremely difficult.

Conversely, the Cactus Air Force had the home field advantage, so to speak. Operating close to their Henderson Field base, the Cactus Air Force could operate around Guadalcanal throughout daylight, and any Japanese ship it caught in its range was vulnerable. Pilots who were shot down had a good chance of making it back to Henderson Field and returning to duty. During the day, Allied ships would discharge supplies, move between Guadalcanal and Tulagi, and generally run errands. Every morning, the Stars and Stripes controlled the seas around Guadalcanal.

But when the sun went below the horizon, the situation reversed. Allied ships left Ironbottom Sound, and in the midnight air the Rising Sun assumed control. Having learned their lesson about trying to send transports or even destroyers full of troops to Guadalcanal during the day, the Japanese took to running in destroyers full of troops by night. Typically, a convoy of Japanese destroyers would sail from their anchorage off Shortland, the name of the island off Bougainville, and also, confusingly, its accompanying island group. The destroyers would sail down the New Georgia Sound – the area between the double line of the Solomons that looked like a slot and was thus nicknamed, "The Slot." But they would not enter the range of Henderson Field until after dark. Then they would dash in and land their troops and supplies. They would often be accompanied by a cruiser floatplane, operating from a seaplane base the Japanese established in Rekata Bay, Santa Ysabel, that made an annoyance of itself.[37] The floatplane would drop flares to light the landing areas and to illuminate the airfield so the destroyers could bombard it for a bit. The floatplane would also drop a few bombs, just to keep the Marines awake. It was nicknamed "Louie the Louse." Another nocturnal visitor to Henderson Field was a twin-engine Betty – badly tuned, to make the engines loud and annoying, it would seem – that also dropped bombs and flares, just to keep the Marines awake. How thoughtful. The Betty was nicknamed "Washing Machine Charlie."

In any event, the Japanese destroyers, sometimes accompanied by a light cruiser, would go into Ironbottom Sound where any Allied ship they caught was vulnerable. Consequently,

Allied ships and boats generally stayed out of Ironbottom Sound while the sun was down. Once the Japanese destroyers had landed their troops and supplies, perhaps lobbed a few shells into Henderson Field, and maybe even sunk an Allied ship, they would scooch back up The Slot to be out of range of the Cactus Air Force by daylight. The frustrated Marines could not respond at all. Not until September 1, when 5-inch coastal defense guns – the same guns that were on US destroyers and the same guns left on the cargo ships on August 9 – of the 3rd Defense Battalion arrived. Even then, it was difficult to pick out their targets in the darkness of Ironbottom Sound. The Marines had a nickname – war typically involves a lot of nicknames – for these convoys: "The Cactus Express." But "Cactus" was a code name, so a different nickname got past the censors to the news media and the public, with whom it would become famous: "The Tokyo Express," an epithet that eventually came to mean any Japanese convoy of troops or supplies.

Every day involved a combination of some or all of these elements. Warning from coastwatchers or radar of approaching Japanese aircraft. Scrambling fighters. Air attack by Base Air Force between 11:00am and 3:00pm. Air battle over Henderson Field and Ironbottom Sound. Tokyo Express. Louie the Louse. Washing Machine Charlie. Every day. Repeat *ad infinitum*.

But the monotony of the Guadalcanal Campaign could not mask its deceptive and increasingly desperate character. What seemed like victories could actually be defeats and vice versa. Just when one side had the upper hand and thought it had turned the corner, 24 hours later the situation would be reversed. It was a veritable tug of war between the Japanese, with their main South Pacific fortress at Rabaul, the excellent harbor just northwest of the Solomons on New Britain, and their forward base in the Shortlands off Bougainville, and the Allies, with their main base at Nouméa, French New Caledonia, and their forward base at Espiritu Santo in the New Hebrides. One side would pull the rope toward them but could not get the traction to hold it or pull it further, and so the other side would pull it back, not get the traction to hold it or pull it further, and so the first side would take it again. Repeat *ad infinitum*.

It was a frustrating position for the Marines on Guadalcanal. They were more than holding their own, and they knew it. A mid-September Japanese attack did come close to reaching Henderson Field, due in part to a rare misjudgment by General Vandegrift that left a ridge in a critical part of the perimeter too thin. But the Japanese had not reached Henderson Field, thanks in large part to an incredible performance by Colonel Merritt Edson and his 1st Marine Raider Battalion, but also due to another inept performance by the Imperial Japanese Army, whose repeated banzai charges continued to lead to only more Japanese casualties. It was another morale booster for the Marines. They were confident they could continue to hold Henderson Field, but that was subject to change if the Navy could not stop the Tokyo Express runs.

This was where that old problem of a military operation that is led by a commander who does not support it manifested itself again and again. Admiral Fletcher's conservatism with the Pacific Fleet's carriers off Guadalcanal hampered the Marines' efforts to hold Henderson

Field and gained nothing: barely a month into the campaign, all three of Fletcher's carriers were out of action, the *Enterprise* damaged at Eastern Solomons, Fletcher's own flagship *Saratoga* torpedoed and damaged, and the *Wasp* torpedoed and sunk while escorting Admiral Turner's convoy of Marine reinforcements to Guadalcanal. Fletcher was removed.

But if Admiral Fletcher played not to lose, Admiral Ghormley played as if he had already lost. One war correspondent told Admiral Nimitz the poor results of the South Pacific campaign so far had come from "overcaution and the defensive complex," an outgrowth of defeatism.[38] A second one opined, "It seemed to me some officers thought only of NOT losing more ships, and it was in that mood that we undertook our early operations in the Solomons."[39] Ghormley had never visited Guadalcanal, had never even left his flagship *Argonne* in Nouméa.[40]

One major example was the deployment of the carrier *Hornet*. The *Hornet* was moved up to hold the line while the *Enterprise* and *Saratoga* were under repair at Pearl Harbor, but Ghormley insisted she be kept so far away from Guadalcanal that she was unable to support Henderson Field, much to the disgust of the carrier's task force commander, Rear Admiral George Murray. With a few notable exceptions, Ghormley also kept supplies, ships, and aircraft, all of which were needed at Guadalcanal, at rear area bases so that when *Watchtower* failed, as Ghormley knew it would, those bases would be defended. As a result, the Marines were starved of supplies and reinforcements, and naval efforts to stop the Tokyo Express were few and far between. One sortie in mid-October by US Navy cruisers and destroyers under Rear Admiral Norman Scott stopped a force of Japanese cruisers from bombarding Henderson Field, resulting in the first US Navy victory in a surface action since January 1942 during the Java Sea Campaign, but managed to miss the reinforcement force that accompanied those cruisers.

Two nights later, October 13–14, the dark turned into "All Hell's Eve" when Henderson Field was the unhappy recipient of "The Bombardment," in which the Japanese battleships *Kongo* and *Haruna* lazily cruised offshore and lobbed 14-inch shells, many of which were incendiaries with the vaguely menacing name of *sanshikidan* ("Type 3 shell") initially intended for antiaircraft work. To be sure, the Type 3s were used as antiaircraft shells here, destroying many of the Cactus Air Force's aircraft, albeit on the ground, but not enough to force a suspension of air operations. Perhaps counterintuitively, the runways were operational by dawn. Aside from the 41 deaths caused by "The Bombardment," the worst damage it had done was to the Cactus Air Force's supply of aviation fuel, which was almost all destroyed. The only opposition the battleships had was a flock of newly arrived PT boats, whose energy was not matched by effectiveness and were consequently brushed aside.

The Bombardment was followed by harassing fire from Japanese 150mm guns that were dubbed "Millimeter Mike," or, more popularly for those averse to the metric system, "Pistol Pete."[41] The next night saw another bombardment, this by 8-inch-armed cruisers, followed by the Japanese brazenly landing troops on Guadalcanal in full view of Henderson Field. The Marines and newly arrived US Army troops were left grumbling that the US did not have a navy.

Vice Admiral Aubrey Fitch, the commander of land-based air forces in the South Pacific, rushed toward Guadalcanal whatever aircraft, supplies, and, especially, fuel he could scrounge up from his rear area bases. In contrast, "The Night of the Battleships" left Admiral Ghormley in a state of panic, repeatedly signaling to anyone who would listen that his forces were "inadequate" to meet the Japanese offensive. It was the last straw for Admiral Nimitz, who, with Admiral King's full backing, sacked Ghormley and replaced him with Vice Admiral William F. Halsey.

"Bill" Halsey, as he was called by his contemporaries – "Bull" Halsey, as he is called by many historians – was considered the Pacific Fleet's top carrier commander. He had arrived in Nouméa to take command of a carrier task force centered on the freshly repaired *Enterprise* when he received his new orders to take over Allied forces in the South Pacific. "Jesus Christ and General Jackson! This is the hottest potato they ever handed me!"[42]

The news of Admiral Halsey's appointment spread like the proverbial wildfire across the South Pacific. The effect was electric. Cheers and celebration among the officers and sailors of the fleet. "We were absolutely elated when we heard the news," said Assistant Gunnery Officer Ed Hooper of the battleship *Washington*. "It was a shot of adrenalin for the whole command; things had been getting pretty wishy-washy down there."[43] The light antiaircraft cruiser *Atlanta's* Robert Graff took a slightly different angle:

> During wartime it's important how the leadership, starting with the Chief of Naval Operations, gets a message across to everybody in every ship, submarine, airplane, and shore station. You need to hear it said that that this is an extraordinary moment in your life and in the life of the country, and that you're not going to let it down. Until that day, we had received no such message.[44]

If the effect on the fleet was electric, the effect on Guadalcanal was nuclear. Lieutenant Commander Roger Kent, an air information officer there, described the atmosphere upon hearing the news: "One minute we were too limp with malaria to crawl out of our foxholes; the next we were running around whooping like kids."[45]

Admiral Halsey went straight to work. By word-of-mouth and even by posted signs he made everyone aware of his wartime credo: "Kill Japs! Kill Japs! Kill more Japs!" He told Pearl Harbor he would need his best staffers sent down to serve at his headquarters; Admiral Ghormley's old staffers had absorbed his defeatism, which Halsey did not want on his staff. The new South Pacific commander worked hard to eliminate distinctions, and thus rivalries, between the services. People would not be of the navy or the army any more, just warriors of the South Pacific Fighting Forces. He would pull in Army technicians to service the fleet and bases, and he wanted their cooperation publicized. "I would like to see it widely advertised that the army is helping us here. I have never seen anything like the spirit here in this neck of woods. It is a real United States service."[46]

Since the centerpiece of the South Pacific campaign was Guadalcanal, Admiral Halsey wanted to know everything about the island and its environs. On the night of October 20,

Admiral Halsey met with General Vandegrift; Major General Alexander M. Patch, commander of the US Army's American Division that was arriving on Guadalcanal to eventually take over from the Marines; Major General Millard Harmon, the senior Army officer in the South Pacific; Lieutenant General Thomas Holcomb, the Commandant of the Marine Corps, who was in Nouméa on an inspection tour; Major General C. Barney Vogel, who had just arrived as commander of the I Marine Amphibious Corps; Admiral Turner and Ghormley's other subordinate commanders; and Halsey's staff.

Generals Vandegrift and Harmon told their stories to Admiral Halsey. Vandegrift said his troops were "practically worn out," with not nearly enough sleep or food but more than enough combat for the past two months.[47] He said his troops needed material support and eventual relief, emphasizing that General Patch's American Division be sent in as well as the remainder of the 2nd Marine Division.[48] It was necessarily a very, very long briefing. When they finished, Halsey cut to the chase. "Are we going to evacuate or hold?" Vandegrift replied, "I can hold, but I've got to get more active support than I've been getting." Halsey was decisive. He nodded. "All right. Go on back. I'll promise you everything I've got."[49]

And Halsey made good on that promise, but at this time everything he had did not amount to much. He would be on his own for responding to the Japanese combined arms offensive that Pacific Fleet intelligence knew was coming. The Japanese now had some 20,000 troops on Guadalcanal, enough for an attack on the Marine perimeter. An attack that came the evening of October 24.

This time, however, the Marines were very much ready. The Japanese attacked with half their intended force, as the right prong of the two-pronged attack got lost in the jungle and ended up moving tangentially to the Marine line, with very few of the Japanese troops seeing any action. The left prong drove straight into the fortified Marine positions. Once again, the Japanese made their banzai charges with bayonets into machine guns, mortars, and heavy artillery fire. They managed to carve a salient in the middle of the Marine line at a cost, once again, of horrendous casualties. The Marines eliminated the salient the next day.

The Combined Fleet was positioning itself in support of the Imperial Army's attack on the Henderson Field perimeter. Yet this was a "combined arms" offensive, and that meant *Kido Butai*, with the carriers *Shokaku* and *Zuikaku* and the light carrier *Zuiho* in its current iteration. But Admiral Halsey was ready for them. Or at least he thought he was ready. Because on October 24, mere hours before the Japanese were to attack Henderson Field, the *Enterprise* and her escort group met the *Hornet* group northeast of the New Hebrides. In Admiral Halsey's words, "Until the *Enterprise* arrived, our plight had been almost hopeless. Now we had a fighting chance."[50] As he told Admiral Nimitz a few weeks later, Admiral Halsey knew "I had to begin throwing punches almost immediately. As a consequence quick decisions had to be made."[51]

And Admiral Halsey made them, sending out orders to Rear Admiral Thomas C. Kinkaid, who commanded the combined *Enterprise* and *Hornet* task forces: "[M]ake a sweep around north Santa Cruz Islands thence southwesterly east of San Cristobal to area in Coral Sea in position to intercept enemy forces approaching [Guadalcanal-Tulagi.]"[52] It was a bold, aggressive move, unlike anything seen out of Admiral Ghormley, going outside the air cover, such as it was, of Espiritu Santo, into waters visited by no American carrier in two months. The idea was to place the *Enterprise* and *Hornet* outside the range of Japanese air power on Rabaul, but able to strike from the east at the flank of, and hopefully ambush, the Japanese carriers.[53] In short, it was to be another Midway. These were the same maneuvers that enabled the badly outnumbered US Navy to win at Midway. But past performance is no guarantee of future results.

And this Midway II was already not going nearly as smoothly as Midway I, due to Admiral Halsey himself. Halsey's plan for another Midway by having the carriers "[M]ake a sweep around north Santa Cruz Islands" had, as he explained to Admiral Nimitz about a week later, one caveat: the carriers were to sweep past Santa Cruz only "if no enemy comes down." In other words, if no large enemy force appeared north of the Solomons. Somehow, that particular aspect of the plan did not make it into Halsey's orders to Admiral Kinkaid.[54] It would not be the last misunderstanding of Halsey's orders or intentions.

As Admiral Kinkaid sped northward – too far – they received a report of Japanese carriers launching within striking distance of Henderson Field.[55] Monitoring all the sighting reports from Nouméa, Admiral Halsey dispatched an order to Admiral Kinkaid and Rear Admiral Willis Augustus Lee, who commanded the escorting battleships, that would encapsulate the new attitude emanating out of Nouméa and electrify the men fighting in the South Pacific. The order read simply, "Strike, Repeat, Strike."[56]

They would, but so would the Japanese. October 26 started out with a pair of scouts putting two bombs into the aft flight deck of the Japanese carrier *Zuiho*, wrecking her arrester gear and rendering her useless for the remainder of the battle. Then it turned into an exchange of airstrikes between the *Enterprise* and *Hornet* on one side and *Kido Butai* on the other.

But the *Enterprise* and *Hornet* struggled in their air operations. The American airstrikes were sent up in driblets, stayed aloft in driblets, and broke up into even smaller driblets. Only one driblet actually reached *Kido Butai*. Defending Zeros hacked mercilessly at them, but the "hell divers," as the Japanese called the SBD Dauntlesses, made their attack all the same. In a very impressive performance, they got anywhere from four to six or more hits by 1,000lb bombs on the *Shokaku*. The *Shokaku*'s flight deck amidships was pummeled, so shattered it "looked like an earthquake fault zone."[57] While her damage was heavy, her watertight integrity was not impacted and her engines remained functional. She would make it back home for repairs.

No, this was not Midway. Sixteen Val dive bombers and 20 Nakajima B5N Type 97 Carrier Attack Planes – "Kate," the Allies would call this aircraft – attacked the *Hornet* in the face of extremely heavy antiaircraft fire, especially from the escorting light antiaircraft cruisers *San Diego* and *Juneau*. The *Hornet* was left dead in the water and burning. Admiral Kinkaid radioed Admiral Halsey with two words: "*Hornet* hurt."[58]

The Japanese soon found the *Enterprise* and launched repeated air strikes to put her under. "The Big E" now had to mix metaphors and juggle a lot of chickens in the air, both her own aircraft and those from the *Hornet*, while dancing like a ballerina, too, to avoid incoming torpedoes. The carrier struggled trying to recover her aircraft, put up a strike, and put up and keep up air cover. A traffic jam was built both on and over the flight deck. She tried to keep the air cover by landing a few Wildcats, refueling and reloading them right on the flight deck, then spotting and launching them immediately, like a pit stop in auto racing.

Nevertheless, the *Enterprise* ended up relying on antiaircraft fire, especially the light antiaircraft cruiser *San Juan* and the battleship *South Dakota* with her very large antiaircraft battery. And while under repair at Pearl Harbor, the *Enterprise* had 16 of the powerful 40mm Bofors antiaircraft gun in four quadruple mounts. On top of that, the *Enterprise* had received fire direction radar for her eight 5-inch guns and an increase in the number of 20mm Oerlikons, which were also effective antiaircraft guns.

The result was a typhoon of white-hot steel directed at the incoming Japanese. In the face of this typhoon, the Japanese still managed two bomb hits and two very damaging near misses on the *Enterprise*. Her forward elevator was jammed, her hull plating was ripped open near both the bow and the stern, and three oil tanks were ruptured, causing the carrier to trail a large oil slick. Nevertheless, the *Enterprise* was not crippled and was still operational, though her ability to juggle her chickens in the air was hampered by the jammed Number 1 elevator. The Japanese also managed one bomb hit each on the *South Dakota* and *San Juan*, causing moderate damage to both ships. One Kate crashed into the destroyer *Smith*, causing a large fire but leaving behind a copy of the current Japanese aircraft code. It was a present for *Magic*.

At one point a little before noon, in the air were no fewer than 73 *Enterprise* and *Hornet* aircraft, all critically low on fuel. The *Enterprise* had to recover as many planes as possible, managing to recover 47 planes – 23 Wildcats and 24 Dauntlesses – in 43 minutes without an accident. In so doing, the carrier saved American naval air power in the South Pacific.

Admiral Kinkaid knew they were lucky. The *Enterprise* was still – barely – operational. Kinkaid had to make a very difficult and painful decision to get the *Enterprise* out of danger, which meant he could provide no air cover for the disabled *Hornet*.

It was a veritable death sentence for the *Hornet*. Efforts to tow the carrier or to restore power were permanently thwarted by a small Japanese air strike that got a torpedo hit in the only remaining undamaged engine room. Efforts to scuttle the carrier were also thwarted by the ineffectiveness of the US Navy's Mark 15 torpedo. Japanese surface forces were so close that they chased away the destroyers tasked with putting the *Hornet* under and ended up scuttling the now-burning carrier themselves.

So ended the carrier engagement the US Navy would call the Battle of the Santa Cruz Islands, another bit of rare honesty in the Guadalcanal Campaign inasmuch as it took place near the aforementioned Santa Cruz Islands and their rare, deadly strain of cerebral malaria. The Japanese had literally chased the Americans from the area. In so doing, the Japanese had sunk one aircraft carrier. The Americans had sunk one destroyer. That's an uneven exchange even before considering that the destroyer the Americans had sunk was one of their own, the *Porter*, through a mishap with one of those quality US Navy torpedoes. It was thus a Japanese tactical victory. Strategically, though the Japanese did have two operational aircraft carriers after Santa Cruz and the Americans had maybe half of an operational carrier, the result was less clear due to the severe losses among Japanese aviators.

Since the start of the Guadalcanal Campaign the Americans had been aware of the declining skill level of Japanese aviators. Those skills had eroded to the point where the old rule learned early in the Pacific War of "Never, ever dogfight a Zero" was tossed aside. It was not just Zeros. While both the *Enterprise* and *Hornet* had been heavily damaged at Santa Cruz, the latter fatally so, the later Japanese efforts to torpedo and bomb the *Hornet* while the disabled carrier was almost stationary were underwhelming. The *Enterprise*'s recovery of aviators from both the *Enterprise* and the *Hornet* at the end of Santa Cruz had given her the best carrier air group in the Pacific. And they had an unsinkable airfield on Guadalcanal that had resisted all Japanese attempts to capture or reduce it.

Admiral Halsey called the senior officers of all branches in Nouméa and told them to pool their mechanics for the repairs to the *Enterprise* and other ships and aircraft.[59] He went so far as to ask Admiral Nimitz to get one or more British aircraft carriers sent to the South Pacific. Nimitz forwarded the request to King. In turn, Nimitz ordered Halsey to prepare a coordinated defense plan for the rear bases. They were bracing for the worst.[60]

And the worst looked more and more likely. The *Enterprise* limped into Nouméa where she got a prognosis from the repair ship *Vulcan* – three weeks to repair the carrier.[61] That wasn't good. But unlike his predecessor, Admiral Halsey was defiant in the face of adversity. In an October 31 letter to Admiral Nimitz, Halsey vowed to "patch up what we have and go with them." He went on to say, "I will not send any ship back to Pearl Harbor unless it is absolutely necessary. This may mean operating the *Enterprise* with a slightly reduced complement of planes and under difficulties, but under the present circumstances, a half a loaf is better than none."[62]

The Americans would need that half a loaf because the Japanese were coming. On November 6, the fleet intelligence summary commented, "All indications … point to continued preparations for offensive action." On November 11 intelligence predicted that the attack would begin the next day or the day after.[63] Thanks to *Magic*, Admiral Yamamoto's operations order for the new offensive ended up at Pearl Harbor.[64] When Admiral Halsey returned to Nouméa on November 9 from a visit to Henderson Field, "[Chief of Staff] Miles Browning was waiting for me, with news that another enemy offensive was brewing, one that would employ a vast number of ships and planes."[65] Intelligence estimated the Japanese would launch heavy aircraft attacks on November 11, a naval bombardment the night of November 12, and carrier air raids on November 13, to be followed by the landing of troops.

To meet this new threat, Admiral Halsey scheduled Admiral Turner's transports to make supply runs from Espiritu Santo to Guadalcanal on November 12. They would go in two separate groups. One group of transports would have as escorts the light antiaircraft cruiser *Atlanta* and three destroyers under Admiral Scott. A second group of transports would have as escorts the heavy cruisers *Pensacola*, *Portland*, and *San Francisco*; light cruiser *Helena*; light antiaircraft cruiser *Juneau*; and nine destroyers.[66] Admiral Turner would command this force personally, but the escorts would be commanded by Rear Admiral Daniel J. Callaghan.

At Nouméa was the carrier *Enterprise*, still being repaired from her close call at Santa Cruz. With her were the battleships *Washington* and *South Dakota*; heavy cruiser *Northampton*; light antiaircraft cruiser *San Diego*; and eight destroyers. They would set sail for Guadalcanal. If the *Enterprise* group could not get there in time, the battleships and four destroyers would be detached into their own task force under Admiral Lee and sent on ahead.

Supporting these efforts were Admiral Fitch's air assets at Espiritu Santo; the Cactus Air Force at Henderson Field; and 24 submarines in the Solomons, though, for reasons known only to the US Navy, not necessarily in The Slot, the most obvious and probable route of advance for the Japanese.

This, then, represented the commitment of practically all the operational surface assets of the US Pacific Fleet to the reinforcement of Guadalcanal and the defense thereof. Nevertheless, the US Pacific Fleet in this most important operation of the campaign, and perhaps the war, was badly outnumbered by the Imperial Japanese Navy's Combined Fleet.

That Imperial Japanese Navy pretty much stuck to the schedule *Magic* had intercepted, with heavy air attacks on November 11 and 12 against Henderson Field and the collection of ships trying to supply it. Admiral Turner had gotten information that a large Japanese surface force was to clear the way for the transports carrying infantry and supplies for Guadalcanal. He estimated its strength as two battleships, two to four heavy cruisers, two light cruisers, and ten to 12 destroyers.[67] Those two battleships were intent on making a sequel to "The Bombardment" of Henderson Field in October.

Admiral Turner had done the calculations. The only things standing between the approaching Japanese and their battleships on one end and Henderson Field and Turner's transports on the other end were the warships of Admiral Callaghan and Admiral Scott who were escorting him. Cruisers and destroyers attempting to stop battleships. More accurately, cruisers and destroyers whose guns could not normally penetrate the hull armor of battleships attempting to stop battleships. Not a pleasant prospect. Not a hopeful prospect. Not something for which they trained at the Naval Academy. But Turner saw no alternative.

Richmond Kelly Turner was many things, not all of them good, but no one questioned that two good things he had in abundance were intelligence and personal bravery. Both played roles in Turner's choice to strip his transports of almost all their escorting warships.

He and his transports would depart and, except for three destroyers and two minesweepers, leave all the warships behind to protect Henderson Field. Five cruisers and eight destroyers. After escorting the transports as far as Sealark Channel, those warships – heavy cruisers *San Francisco* and *Portland*; light cruiser *Helena*; light antiaircraft cruisers *Atlanta* and *Juneau*; and destroyers *Cushing, Laffey, Sterett, O'Bannon, Aaron Ward, Barton, Monssen*, and *Fletcher* would "return to Cactus tonight and strike enemy ships present."[68]

The final question for Admiral Turner was who was to command this hodgepodge slapped-together collection of warships. On hand was Admiral Scott, a night combat veteran whose conduct of the Battle of Cape Esperance in October was hardly perfect, but still enough to gain a US victory, rare enough in surface actions since the beginning of the war. He had studied the battle, especially the performance of SG surface search radar therein, and was willing to learn from his mistakes. He had resolutely drilled his crews in night combat and was comfortable fighting at night. In short, Admiral Scott was the perfect officer to command this force. Naturally, Turner did not choose him.[69]

Instead, in another one of Admiral Turner's vague decisions, he chose Admiral Callaghan. Callaghan had been Admiral Ghormley's chief of staff, "a task in which he had escaped distinction," to use Guadalcanal historian Richard Frank's description.[70] When Admiral Halsey took over for Ghormley, he sacked Ghormley's entire staff and brought his own, so Admiral Turner scooped up Callaghan. But Callaghan had recently spent most of his time in staff positions and had not been at sea in months. His only combat experience was the air attack of that afternoon.

In Turner's mind, what apparently made Admiral Callaghan better suited than Admiral Scott to command this force was the fact that he had been promoted to rear admiral two weeks before Scott and thus, in the Navy's rigid system, had seniority.[71] Callaghan was hard-working, conscientious, devoutly Roman Catholic, and well-respected by his colleagues and men under his command, but he had almost no combat experience, and he knew it. Nevertheless, Callaghan did not feel at liberty to turn down an order to take charge from a superior officer.[72]

Even so, while Admiral Callaghan certainly wanted a combat command, there were indications he did not want this particular assignment. He was observed endlessly pacing the flag bridge of the *San Francisco*, muttering that he was reluctant to carry out his orders, expressing his desire to talk things over directly with Admiral Halsey, admitting there was no time to do so, and telling the rattled officers and men around him that they were in for a rough night.[73] Callaghan was also seen arguing with Captain Cassin Young, the *San Francisco*'s new skipper of all of three days. According to one witness, Young, who had won the Medal of Honor for bravery at Pearl Harbor in the repair ship *Vestal* (which was parked next to the battleship *Arizona*), "was in an understandably agitated state, sometimes waving his arms, as he remarked: 'But this is suicide.' Callaghan replied, 'Yes, I know, but we have to do it.' He was calm, unemotional, resolute, and perhaps resigned to his fate."[74]

The rumors that they were going to fight battleships – and, Admiral Callaghan believed, lose – rapidly spread through the cruiser. "We were all prepared to die," recalled

Joseph Whitt, a Seaman 1st Class whose battle station was in Turret 1. "We could not survive against those battleships."[75] Not with guns. They could with torpedoes. But the US Navy had stupidly taken the torpedo tubes off its cruisers. The belief that they would not survive the night against the battleships did not prevent some from looking ahead. "It won't be long now," Lieutenant (jg) Sam Hollingsworth of the *Helena* reflected aloud, "before the Japs are forced to abandon Guadalcanal altogether. Then we'll be moving up through the Slot toward Bougainville, pounding the enemy's bases on New Georgia and Kolombangara." Sam liked to speculate and was more often right than wrong in his predictions. He had studied the charts of the Solomons area so often that every island, every coral reef and bay, was photographed in his mind. "Kula Gulf," he said, "is going to be a tough nut to crack. Very tricky proposition. A ship in Kula will be like a bug in a bottle."[76]

The bug was not in the bottle yet, but was instead facing a very big flyswatter. Admiral Callaghan put his ships in a column with four destroyers in front, the five cruisers in the middle, and five destroyers bringing up the rear. It was a simple formation for ships who had not worked or trained together before. It was symmetrical, which counts for something. Most naval warfare analysts have had little complimentary to say about the formation.

A formation that was thrown into confusion when, in the early hours of Friday, November 13, a speeding Japanese destroyer cut across the bow of the leading destroyer *Cushing*. The *Cushing* had to swerve to avoid a collision with the Japanese ship, while the American ships had to swerve to avoid the *Cushing*. The proverbial train wreck was avoided, oddly, when a searchlight from a battleship pinned the lead cruiser *Atlanta*, Admiral Scott's flagship, though Admiral Callaghan's formation had made Scott superfluous. The *Atlanta* opened fire on the searchlight, and the battle of Friday the 13th was on.

If Admiral Callaghan had a battle plan, he did not share it. Maybe he had planned it all along. Or maybe it was dumb luck. Whatever the reason, however it happened, the US Navy ships ended up in the midst of the Japanese formation, such as it was, mixed in with enemy ships. With American and Japanese ships "mingled like minnows in a bucket," to use Samuel Eliot Morison's phrase, Friday the 13th descended into general chaos, "a no-holds-barred barroom brawl, in which someone turned out the lights and everyone started swinging in every direction – only this was ten thousand times worse," in the famous words of Cal Calhoun.[77]

As a consequence of American and Japanese ships being mingled, whether by Admiral Callaghan's plan or by accident, the US Navy cruisers and destroyers were much, much closer to the Japanese battleships than they would have been if they had tried to stick to the naval warfare textbook. Normally, guns from cruisers and destroyers could not hurt battleships. Could not even reach the battleships, because the battleships' guns could outrange cruiser and destroyer guns, and the battleships screening cruisers and destroyers would keep the enemy away. But now, the American cruisers and destroyers were toe-to-toe with two Japanese battleships. The extremely close range meant there was at least a chance that the cruisers' 8-inch guns might penetrate the battleships' hull armor. Even if they could not, the guns of the cruisers and destroyers could still hurt the battleships. In short, Friday the 13th had developed into the one scenario in which battleships were vulnerable to the gunfire of cruisers and destroyers.

With the American sailors desperate to turn the Japanese battlewagons away from Guadalcanal, the Friday the 13th brawl largely centered on the leading Japanese battleship, later identified as the *Hiyei*, a more phonetic rendering of the name *Hiei* that was used postwar. The American formation disintegrated. The *Atlanta* was hit by a vicious blast from the battleship that likely killed Admiral Scott before a torpedo disabled the antiaircraft cruiser, which effectively cut off the leading four American destroyers from the ships behind them. The destroyers were too close to launch their torpedoes at the battleship, so they had every gun that would fire send a cyclone of hot shrapnel at the battleship's pagoda-like bridge tower. The *Hiei* simply cut through their little column, coming within a mere 20 feet of running over the *Laffey*. The battleship later came close to running over the destroyer *O'Bannon*. Friday the 13th was less Savo Island than it was Salamis.

With the *Hiei* so close to the destroyers that she could not depress her main guns to target them, she instead directed her main battery at the *San Francisco*. And vice versa. The ships were so close that the guns were firing directly, the barrels almost horizontal. The combination of the demonic destroyers in front of her and the spiteful *San Francisco* to starboard was akin to being pecked to death by ducks. With her superstructure in flames and barely making any headway, though she did not appear to have suffered damage to her hull, the *Hiei* slowly turned away to the north.

With, well, half of the battle won, the *San Francisco* switched targets to a destroyer, but as she did so she missed the disabled *Atlanta* drifting into her line of fire. The flagship's next 8-inch salvoes blasted the *Atlanta*. A horrified Admiral Callaghan yelled into the radio, "Cease firing, our ships."[78] He seems to have garbled a combination of two different ideas, ordering cease fire to the *San Francisco* because she was hitting American ("our") ships, and blurted it over the voice radio, which went to the entire task force. And while some of the American ships did cease fire, the Japanese did not. With ghastly consequences.

A plethora of searchlight beams met at the *San Francisco*, followed by very big shell splashes walking their way to the American flagship, presaging a frightful pounding. Sure enough, 14-inch shells from the *Hiei*'s sister ship *Kirishima*, largely untouched in the dark behind the Japanese flagship, walloped the *San Francisco*'s bridge, killing Admiral Callaghan and mortally wounding Captain Young. It was a parting gift from the battleship, who headed north with the rest of the Japanese force.

Dawn on November 13 revealed an Ironbottom Sound covered with oil, debris, bodies, parts of bodies, survivors, and wrecked ships. The US Navy destroyers *Laffey* and *Barton* had not survived the night. The *Cushing* and *Monssen* were disabled and afire; they would sink that afternoon. The *Aaron Ward* was disabled by a mysterious problem in her feed water system. The light antiaircraft cruiser *Atlanta* was wrecked and disabled, had a fractured keel, and was in danger of being boarded by Japanese on Guadalcanal. She was scuttled that night.

Nothing so fatal befell the heavy cruiser *Portland*, but not for lack of trying. A freakish torpedo hit left her able to steam only in circles. Somehow, in conjunction with a tug and a requisitioned civilian "yard patrol" boat, they managed to push, pull, shove, drag, coerce, cajole, browbeat, threaten, and bribe the *Portland* slowly toward the dubious safety of Tulagi. The safety was dubious enough because of the Japanese, but more because Tulagi was home to the precocious PT boats, who operated by the credo, "Shoot first and ask questions at the court martial. Maybe." As the *Portland* was about to enter the harbor, *PT-48* under the command of Lieutenant (jg) Tom Kendall, came out and, over the objections of the *Portland* and the assisting tug, actually launched four torpedoes at the helpless cruiser. It's unclear which is more embarrassing: that the US Navy PT boat fired four torpedoes at a helpless US Navy ship or that, having overestimated the helpless US Navy ship's speed, all the torpedoes missed. Angry *Portland* gunners fired back at the PTs, who acted offended.[79] The cruiser eventually made it back home for repairs.

With Admiral Callaghan and Admiral Scott killed the night before, command of the remaining US Navy ships fell to the skipper of the *Helena*, Captain Gilbert Hoover, a veteran commander on the fast track to flag rank. When Hoover gathered the remaining ambulatory ships to make the journey to the relative safety of Espiritu Santo, it was a pitiful harvest. While the *Helena* had suffered only superficial damage and the destroyer *Fletcher* none at all, witnesses counted no fewer than 26 holes in the charred hull of the *San Francisco*; a torpedo hit on the *Juneau* had fractured her keel, leaving her barely held together by her hull plating and bulkheads; and destroyer *Sterett* had damaged sound gear while the *O'Bannon* lost her sound gear altogether. Friday the 13th had been a strategic victory for the US Navy in driving the battleships away from Henderson Field, but even Pyrrhos of Epirus would have found the cost staggering.

It would only get higher on the trip back to Espiritu Santo. A torpedo from a Japanese submarine found its way into the torpedo hole made in the *Juneau* the night before. The result was catastrophic. In the words of one witness, "The *Juneau* didn't sink – she blew up with all the fury of an erupting volcano." He added, "Those who witnessed it called this terrible end of a gallant ship the most awesome spectacle of the battle."[80] Cal Calhoun, who was watching the *Juneau* and appreciating her beauty, said she simply "disintegrated."[81]

With an enemy submarine obviously in the area and no way to adequately protect his ships, Captain Hoover had the remaining ships speed away from the scene. It did not look like anyone could have survived such an explosion anyway. But Hoover did signal a passing B-17 of the loss of the *Juneau* so search planes could go over the area looking for any survivors. But the message got buried on someone's desk. The 100-odd survivors of the *Juneau* had to endure eight days of their own special hell, of which only ten survived to be rescued. As historian Eric Hammel put it so eloquently, "Every death was the culmination of intense agony and the most brutal mental and physical suffering imaginable."[82]

Captain Browning, Admiral Halsey's chief of staff and a brilliant man who has also been described as "brawling and ill-tempered" and "a psychotic misanthrope," harbored a grudge against Captain Hoover from their time at the Naval Academy.[83] Browning made sure the investigation and subsequent report put Hoover in the worst possible light. Admiral Halsey removed Hoover from command of the *Helena*. The decision devastated the crew of the cruiser. Halsey would later write that in that decision, "I was guilty of an injustice," admitting "Hoover's decision was in the best interests of victory."[84] Even a later court of inquiry that exonerated Hoover could not save his career.

Meanwhile, back in Ironbottom Sound, the dawn had revealed the Pyrrhic victory may have only been half right. Because though the *Hiei* had been relentlessly pecked by ducks, she was not quite dead yet, and instead was northwest of Savo, steaming in circles, trailing a large oil slick, and blackened like a charcoal briquette. Any battleship that close to Guadalcanal was a threat. The Cactus Air Force got to work on the wounded leviathan. They got a welcome surprise from the *Enterprise*, who had sailed into range and sent her attack planes to attack the *Hiei* as well, then stage into Henderson Field. The predicted Japanese carrier strikes never materialized, likely because the Japanese Zeros were trying to protect the *Hiei*. And failing. A day-long series of attacks by Marine Dauntlesses, *Enterprise* Dauntlesses, *Enterprise* TBF Avenger torpedo bombers, and Army Air Force B-17s added to the *Hiei*'s woes, but they could not put her under, and as the sun went down, the battleship was still afloat.

That night saw another bombardment of the Henderson Field complex by Japanese cruisers. Admiral Lee's battleships *Washington* and *South Dakota* were supposed to be detached from escorting the *Enterprise* to protecting the airfield, but, due to another miscommunication from Admiral Halsey, the *Enterprise* group was too far south for the battleships to make it in time. Nevertheless, the rain of 8-inch shells was shrugged off by the Americans on Guadalcanal as nothing compared to what they had avoided by the activities of Friday the 13th.

And as the sun came up on November 14, the *Hiei* was nowhere to be seen, a very large oil slick northwest of Savo marking where she had been. The Cactus Air Force took a few swipes at the Japanese cruisers who had cost them sleep, sinking one and damaging two others. But the real danger was not the cruisers. It was the giant Tokyo Express coming down through The Slot. Eleven transports packed full of supplies and Japanese troops, with a screening force of 11 destroyers. Again, the Cactus Air Force went to work. Again, Japanese Zeros did an inept job protecting their surface ships. With every strike a mixture of Marine, Army, and Navy aviators, the Cactus Air Force created an almost-assembly-line system for a day-long series of attacks on the transports: take off, attack, land, refuel and rearm, take off again. Lather, rinse, repeat. Two transports were hit by torpedoes and quickly sank. A third was damaged and went back to Shortland, where she was sunk by another air strike in relatively short order. Four more transports were hit by bombs, set afire, disabled, and abandoned. By the end of the day only four transports were still ambulatory and relatively on course for Guadalcanal.

That was still four transports too many. Having finally broken off from the *Enterprise* and holding a blocking position between the carrier and any potential Japanese surface force for most of the day, Admiral Lee moved into Ironbottom Sound with the battleships *Washington* and *South Dakota* and four destroyers. His mission was to make a nighttime sweep around Savo Island for enemy ships and deal with them. It was unusual and a violation of the US Navy playbook to use battleships in such restricted waters as Ironbottom Sound, but the *Washington* and *South Dakota* were simply all the Americans had left in terms of surface units, the only card they had left to play. Fortunately, though this was his first flag command, Lee was perhaps the foremost radar theoretician in the US Navy. He understood it, trusted it, and knew how to use it.

And he would need it. Because after Admiral Lee had to talk his way out of being attacked by those pesky US Navy PT boats, the Japanese showed up in numbers. Two Japanese light-cruiser-led destroyer flotillas stripped the American battleships of their escorting destroyers, with two sunk on the spot and a third mortally wounded. Then the *South Dakota* suffered an electrical failure that disabled her radar and her main guns. While it was quickly repaired, the battleship would have electrical issues for the rest of the night. Worse, she ended up in the crosshairs of two Japanese cruisers and one battleship, who used their guns to pound the *South Dakota*'s upperworks into a flaming shambles.

But pounding the *South Dakota* proved only a distraction from the bigger danger stalking the Japanese. Admiral Lee used all of his expertise in radar to determine that the big blip he saw on the *Washington*'s scope was a Japanese battleship. He opened fire with the *Washington*'s main guns. She scored with at least ten 16-inch shells on what was later identified as the *Hiei*'s sister ship *Kirishima*. At least two more shells appeared to have splashed short of the *Kirishima* but actually penetrated her hull below the water line. If the *Hiei* had been pecked to death by ducks, the *Kirishima* by comparison was being punched in the mouth. Hard. Over and over and over again.[85] She was never able to get a bead on the *Washington*. Her parting shot was directed at the *South Dakota*: a 14-inch shell that went through the main deck and bounced off the barbette of Turret 3 but did not penetrate the barbette or the magazine. It was the only hit that actually threatened the survival of the *South Dakota*.

Believing that he had delayed the bombardment of Henderson Field and thus the reinforcement convoy until at least daylight when the Cactus Air Force could handle it, and concerned about Japanese torpedoes, some of which had been observed detonating prematurely, Admiral Lee had his battleships skedaddle out of Ironbottom Sound. As he did so, he watched the radar blip of the *Kirishima* staggering into a circle from which she would never emerge. The *Kirishima* joined the *Hiei* on the bottom of Ironbottom Sound later that night.

Admiral Lee's calculations proved correct. The early patrols out of Henderson Field found the four remaining Japanese transports speeding for Guadalcanal. By the time the Cactus Air Force could show up with air strikes, all four had been run aground in the Tassafaronga area. Running the ships aground and then unloading was a tactic of desperation, sacrificing the transports themselves in the hope that once ashore *something* ould be unloaded. But most of what was unloaded did not last long. The Cactus Air Force completed the destruction of the transports themselves with whatever supplies they till held, then destroyed all the caches of supplies that had been unloaded on the beach and even in the jungle. Long streams of Japanese soldiers were seen leaving the beach and entering the jungle. They were machine gunned, but the destruction of almost all their supplies meant that, with the additional troops on Guadalcanal but no additional supplies for them, the Japanese were actually worse off than before the reinforcements arrived.

Shortly after the Naval Battles of Guadalcanal, Admiral King had stormed in to the Joint Chiefs of Staff "with his sword in his hand," in the words of Admiral William Leahy, newly appointed to the newly created office of Chairman of the Joint Chiefs of Staff to oversee the food fights that often resulted when Generals Marshall and Arnold got together with King to demand the transfer of ships from the Atlantic and Mediterranean to replace the losses in the Pacific.[86] It was not like the *Kriegsmarine* or the *Regia Marina* were much in the way of surface threats these days.

Admiral King won the immediate transfer of two cruisers, five destroyers, and three of those little escort carriers to the Guadalcanal area with more to follow. But it would take a while for them to arrive. In the meantime, Henderson Field was adding a mile-long strip so it could house B-17s and other heavy bombers. Since the naval battles of mid-November, the Cactus Air Force had increased in size from 85 aircraft to 188, including heavy bombers for that new airstrip as well as reconnaissance and antisubmarine aircraft.[87] It represented a critical mass of aircraft that could menace the Japanese up and down the Solomons.

They would be needed, because the Japanese did not appear to have given up on Guadalcanal. But they were back to the issue of supplying their troops on the island with, at the very least, food. The Japanese tried running submarines with supplies to the island, but, often forewarned by *Magic*, the Allies were able to send out PT boats or even the occasional destroyer to interdict those runs. When one of the precocious PT boats, *PT-59* under Lieutenant (jg) John M. Searles, plunked a fatal torpedo into one of those submarines in the wee hours of December 9, the sub runs seemed to stop. For a while, anyway.

Yet the Japanese were far from finished. They tried setting up supply points on New Georgia, from where they could make runs to Guadalcanal by hopping from island to island on barges. A few Allied air attacks took care of those efforts, but the Japanese were building something big on New Georgia in the area of Cape Munda. It was something to keep an eye on. For the moment, however, a big concentration of Japanese ships in the Shortlands suggested a major supply or reinforcement operation was in the offing. Fortunately for Halsey, now promoted to full admiral, and the Allies, American war assets were slowly but surely accumulating in the South Pacific. The headliner was the freshly repaired carrier *Saratoga* and her escorts, well on their way to the area, though not quite here yet, so the Allies still had to rely on the *Enterprise* with her jammed forward elevator. There was also a mass of cruisers: heavy cruisers *Minneapolis* and *New Orleans* and light cruiser *Honolulu* arrived at Espiritu Santo to join South Pacific veterans *Pensacola* and

Northampton. They would be sent to Guadalcanal with some destroyers to sweep Ironbottom Sound for the Japanese convoy they knew was coming. But who should command this force? With the deaths of Admirals Scott and Callaghan and the sacrifice of Captain Hoover to the gods of office and national politics, there were no flag officer experienced in handling surface forces at night. Admiral Kinkaid, having been recently replaced by Admiral Sherman as commander of the *Enterprise* task force, was available, so Halsey tabbed him to command this new force.

Admiral Kinkaid threw himself into his new command. He spent three days working up his general plan of battle, which was in general an excellent piece of careful consideration, self-reflection, and research. Naturally, after putting so much time and effort into preparing this tactical plan, Kinkaid was immediately reassigned. To the North Pacific to help retake from the Japanese those two Aleutian bastions of infinitesimal strategic value – Attu and Kiska. In fairness, Kinkaid felt like commanding a force of cruisers was a demotion from commanding a carrier battle group and wanted to be reassigned. His replacement would be Rear Admiral Carleton Wright. Wright had been Kinkaid's subordinate and was intimately involved in the development of the plan. Naturally, after taking command himself, Wright scrapped much of it.

Admiral Wright had no time to settle into his new command. On November 29, coded Japanese transmission was sent alerting the Japanese on Guadalcanal to what was going to be a supply operation. The transmission was promptly decoded by *Magic.*[8] Wright set sail with his cruisers and escorting destroyers. And during the night of November 30–December 1, he caught a force of Japanese destroyers off Tassafaronga in the midst of that operation.

When his leading destroyers requested permission to launch torpedoes, Admiral Wright hesitated for a few minutes because he was confused about the range. The hesitation ruined the torpedo attack, so Wright had his cruisers open fire with their main guns. Under radar control, Wright's cruisers threw a prodigious amount of explosive munition at the Japanese destroyers. One Japanese destroyer was buried under the avalanche of gunfire, and that because the ship had returned the gunfire. For the most part, the Americans' gunfire hit empty sea. The inexperienced radar operators in Wright's force did not understand that they were mostly targeting their own shell splashes. Nevertheless, the Japanese destroyers fled.

And that was when Admiral Wright learned the hard way that, as those destroyers were fleeing, they had launched torpedoes at the Americans. Wright's flagship *Minneapolis* had its bow blown off as far as the Number 1 turret. Behind her, the *New Orleans* had her bow blown off as far as the Number 2 turret. The severed bow floated down the *New Orleans* port side, banging against the hull as it did so, and making the *New Orleans* the only ship in US Navy history to have rammed herself.

That was not all. Behind the *New Orleans*, the *Pensacola* took a torpedo in a fuel tank, causing burning fuel to spew all over the ship, turning the cruiser into an inferno. Behind the *Pensacola*, light cruiser *Honolulu* swerved to avoid the rapidly decelerating ship in front of her. But behind the *Honolulu*, no amount of evasive action would save the *Northampton*. Hit near the stern, the veteran cruiser immediately started to list as, again, burning fuel spewed all over the ship, but now cooking off the ammunition. She would not survive the night. The *Minneapolis*, *New Orleans*, and *Pensacola* would, but their severe damage ensured they would be out of the war for months and months. This stinging defeat to an inferior force in his first battle ensured this would be the last battle for Admiral Wright. In a classy gesture, he absolved all the skippers under his command of responsibility for the defeat, taking the blame all on himself.

Just when you thought the Americans and Australians and Kiwis had turned the corner on the Guadalcanal Campaign, the Japanese gave them a bloody nose and two black eyes. The primary culprit was the torpedo. Specifically, the Japanese Type 93 "Long Lance" torpedo. Of Japanese torpedoes, Admiral Wright said:

> [T]he observed positions of the enemy surface vessels before and during the gun action make it improbable that torpedoes with speed-distance characteristics similar to our own could have reached the cruisers at the time they did if launched from any of the enemy destroyers or cruisers which were observed to be present.[89]

Wright surmised some of the torpedoes must have been launched by submarines; he could not conceive of the superiority of the Long Lance. Nor could Admiral Nimitz.

What Admiral Nimitz could admit was the superiority of Japanese torpedo technique, though he did not seem to grasp the substance of that superiority. As Morison commented, "American commanders of cruiser-destroyer task forces had the bad practice of tying their destroyers to a cruiser column instead of sending them off on an independent torpedo shoot before gunfire was opened."[90] In short, it was not just the torpedoes themselves, but how they were used.

Admiral Nimitz's solution to these problems was summed up by this phrase: "[T]raining, TRAINING and M-O-R-E T-R-A-I-N-I-N-G. Each commanding officer is called upon to do his share."[91] The second clause of this quote is often omitted, but it is important in understanding the philosophical foundation here.[92] In response to Nimitz's statement without the omitted clause, it has been suggested that it was the commanders who needed the training, much more than the men under their command. In fact, once the omitted clause is included, it becomes clear that training for commanders is part of what Nimitz was advocating. The commanders needed to break their habit of micromanaging their destroyers.

But Admiral Nimitz was careful to discuss the nature of the enemy Admiral Wright faced. Stating that Wright "led his force into action resolutely and intelligently and opened fire at a range that should have permitted avoiding surprise torpedo attack," he went on to note: "As in previous engagements, we are made painfully aware of the Japanese skill, both in night and day action, in the use of guns and torpedoes. To date there has been no reason to doubt his energy, persistence, and courage."[93]

The disaster at Tassafaronga left the Allies denuded of surface warships that could contest the waters off Guadalcanal, while the Tokyo Express kept coming. The Cactus Air Force tried to interdict these destroyer runs, but they were less than effective, with two attacks against two different convoys resulting in two damaged Japanese destroyers, not coming anywhere close to stopping the convoys. The only surface forces available to contest the convoys were those precocious PT boats. They would attack anything: enemy ships, friendly ships, neutral ships, ghost ships, warships, cruise ships, light ships. If it was a ship, they would attack it. It was hoped that with no friendly ships in The Slot or Ironbottom Sound the PTs would turn their torpedo tubes on more troubling targets.

It started out decently. The PTs attacked one convoy of destroyers – Japanese destroyers – on the night of December 7–8, and while none of the PTs' torpedo attacks were successful, they did scare off the convoy. On December 9, *PT-59* sank the submarine *I-3* as the Japanese boat tried to run in supplies. December 11 saw the PTs ambush another convoy of destroyers. The PTs lost one of their own, but Lieutenant (jg) Lester H. Gamble's *PT-45* bagged a big fish, the *Teruzuki*. In the cold calculus of war, exchanging a PT boat for a new destroyer was a victory for the US Navy and an exchange the Japanese could not afford to make.

A different kind of exchange was made on Guadalcanal. After being on the front lines of the Pacific War for four months, General Vandegrift and the 1st Marine Division was finally withdrawn during December 1942 and January 1943 for well-earned rest, recuperation, and refit. Combat operations on Guadalcanal were turned over to the US Army. The Americal Division under Major General Alexander M. Patch was to start the process of driving the Japanese from the island. Patch believed he needed a lot more troops to actually complete that process, but the Americal nevertheless began attacks to at least take Mount Austen, from which the Japanese had been watching, shelling, and generally causing problems for the Henderson Field complex.

This was where the US military began to see the dichotomy in the Imperial Japanese Army. Japanese army troops had mounted three major offensives to retake Henderson Field, and while one attack in September had come relatively close to succeeding, the attacks were mostly notable for their breathtaking ineptitude. The highlight of that ineptitude was, of course, the banzai charge, the human wave attack with bayonets and swords into defenses featuring machine guns, antitank guns, entrenchments, barbed wire, and artillery support; it became a Japanese trademark. There was far more to it, however, including poor coordination, a lack of artillery support, and an almost complete lack of initiative that would have been comical if lives, American and Japanese, had not been lost in the process. Courage was not lacking; competence was. But that was on the attack.

On the defense was another matter entirely. An example was a Japanese defense line west of Mount Austen that, for reasons known only to the Japanese, the Imperial Army troops nicknamed "Gifu" after a prefecture in the Home Islands. The line, held by some 600 troops, contained maybe 50 pillboxes, made of logs and dirt up to two feet thick, with only some three feet of pillbox projecting above the ground. Little short of a direct hit from a 105mm howitzer could hurt these things. The pillboxes were staggered, interconnected, mutually supporting, and very well camouflaged. Each of these positions contained several riflemen and one or two machine guns, usually Nambu Type 96 light machine guns. The entire position was supported by 81mm and 90mm mortars.[94]

The American's Lieutenant John B. George saw the fortifications and bunkers – "reception committee shelters" – at the troublesome Gifu firsthand. With tongue firmly in cheek, with an emphasis on the cheek, he described how these Japanese would welcome "visitors:"

These reception committee shelters were sighted [sic] with care so that there would be little or no chance of any visitor approaching unseen or unheard. The visitors would have to make their way through particularly inhospitable stretches of foliage before they approached their "hosts," clawing often at plant stems and turning now and then to remove the sticky, holding whip of a wait-a-minute vine from the cloth of a jacket or the flesh of a cheek or hand. The last few steps toward the waiting hosts would be in clearer, more open, spots in the jungle – not completely clear, but open as though these spots of ground had perhaps offered less appeal to roots of jungle weeds than had the surrounding area. And the first guests these hosts would receive in time-honored style would, at the moment of reception, be breathing thanks for a few feet of clear space in front of them.

But while the hosts were taking every step to prevent the guests from arriving unseen or unannounced, it was none the less their desire that the reception was to be in the nature of a surprise party. Along with the committee housing project there was also heavy effort under way to prevent the excavations from becoming an eyesore and smearing the pretty green landscape with unsightly mounds of yellow clay, framing the entrances to the committee chambers in a highly unartistic way – all out of keeping with the natural tropical garden atmosphere.

So, while some of the hosts dug with shovels and picks, others were busy with baskets woven from vines in which they carried away load after load of yellow dirt to a hidden place to the rear of the line of diggings. There the dirt was scattered around the roots of heavy brush where it would not change the garden picture of the "back yards," or else it was thrown into a little stream where it was washed away, yellowing the clean spring water. So thorough was this operation that scarcely one clod of yellow dirt was left to mar the perfect scene of green and dark shadow which surrounded the picturesque area.

After the rough line of shelters was finished, the sturdy, well muscled little builders got to work industriously upon a series of connecting tunnels, just large enough for the small and wiry bodies of the hosts to move through with comfort. These were artistically done, with the little bites of the shovels showing on their inside walls like adze marks on hewn logs. Roots were sharply and cleanly cut, cross-sections showing and oozing sap, mostly milk white and latex-bearing. And after the tunnels had been dug – a regular network of them to connect all of the individual larger shelters with each other – another project was begun. The chambers were enlarged and made more comfortable, and their roofs were built up solidly against the elements, with layer after layer of logs and pounded earth, which was now needed in such quantity at the building site that there was no need to carry it away. But the unsightly yellow of it was still not allowed to show. It was carefully covered over with sod, carefully matched to the local landscape. The hosts were still much concerned about the outside appearance of their dwellings. Each of the chambers had a small window, left open permanently, facing to the front. This was to serve the combined purposes of ventilator and living room window, permitting the host to breathe comfortably, see his front yard, and greet his guests. And the chambers were as near stormproof as structures could be. Any one of them would have made an absolutely safe hurricane shelter. The areas in front of the windows were sodded over carefully so that no dry leaves or other substance could be blown up into the chamber by a sudden gust of wind, and then the square outline of the window was artistically broken up by the bending and sometimes actual transplanting of pretty leaved plants, making the whole dome of the chamber-structure blend perfectly into the shadowy undergrowth.[95]

Lieutenant George would be compelled to admit:

[T]he Japanese were the most skilled fighters in the world as far as the Infantry aspects of sacrificial defense in jungle country are concerned. There are no other soldiers who would give them a run for their money in that type of fighting. Their excellence in that field was only part guts. A lot of it was due to their remarkable entrenching ability. The way they could build pillboxes and covered foxholes and organize them into clever, mutually supporting positions is perhaps their greatest defense asset. And their skill at camouflage was part of this remarkable entrenching skill.[96]

General MacArthur had already discovered the Japanese talent for camouflaged fortifications in his campaign to take Buna. Because of the need to rush reinforcements to Guadalcanal, the Japanese had halted their offensive from Buna down the Kokoda Trail to take Port Moresby and instead retrenched around Buna. In mid-November, MacArthur had begun his latest offensive in the now four-month-old campaign to correct the mistake. Leading the attack up the Kokoda Trail had been the 16th and 25th Brigades of the Australian 7th Division. As the Australian troops neared the northern coast of Papua, MacArthur brought in the 126th and 128th Infantry Regiments of the US 32nd Infantry Division. His plan called for the 7th to take Gona and Sanananda while the 32nd would take Buna. It sounded simple enough.

But, as in the Philippines, General MacArthur and his senior staff had badly misjudged the strength of the Japanese. MacArthur relied on his staff intelligence officer, Brigadier General Charles Willoughby, whom New Guinea Campaign historian Peter J. Dean says "demonstrated high levels of mediocrity" and was "one of the poorest, if not the worst, senior Allied intelligence officers of the war."[97] But he also had that sycophantic quality that was so important to MacArthur.[98] Willoughby had determined the Japanese had about 1,500–2,000 troops in the area of Buna and Gona, and that even these troops gave "little indication of an attempt to make a strong stand against the Allied advance."[99] Major General Edwin F. Harding, commander of the 32nd Infantry Division, had his own intelligence estimates and largely concurred with Willoughby and expected "easy pickings with only a shell of sacrifice troops left to defend [Buna]."[100]

Colonel Wills and the Australian intelligence staff, who "consistently proved more apt at analyzing Japanese strengths and intentions[,]" knew better.[101] But General MacArthur didn't listen to them. Because they were Australian and not American. In fact, the Japanese had some 6,500 fresh troops in the 11-mile-long coastal strip from Buna northwest to Gona. And they were very dug in, with a line of concealed bunkers made from coconut logs, some reinforced with steel, almost all with connecting trenches. Their fields of fire dominated the few trails leading from the swamps through which the Allied attackers would have to move.[102] General Sutherland "glibly" called these fortifications "hasty field entrenchments."[103] To top it off, the Australian 7th Division was badly under-strength, while General Harding's 32nd Infantry Division was half-trained, inexperienced, and under-equipped, consisting of Michigan and Wisconsin National Guardsmen who had never received jungle combat training.[104] General MacArthur ordered Harding to attack "regardless of cost."[105]

The offensive promptly stalled in the proverbial and literal quagmire. The swampland, as it was on Guadalcanal, was distinctly not healthy, providing the troops with malaria and dengue fever in generous quantities. Then the Japanese took their proverbial and literal pound of flesh. MacArthur accused the 32nd Division of a lack of "fight."[106]

On November 21, General MacArthur busted some heads. He summoned Lieutenant General Robert L. Eichelberger, commanding the 32nd's parent unit, the I Corps, to his headquarters.

"Bob," said General MacArthur in a grim voice, "I'm putting you in command at Buna. Relieve Harding. I am sending you in, Bob, and I want you to remove all officers who won't fight. Relieve regimental and battalion commanders; if necessary, put sergeants in charge of battalions and corporals in charge of companies – anyone who will fight. Time is of the essence; the Japs may land reinforcements any night."

The general said he had reports that American soldiers were throwing away their weapons and running from the enemy. Then he stopped and spoke with emphasis.

"Bob," he said, "I want you to take Buna, or not come back alive." He paused a moment and then, without looking at [Eichelberger's Chief of Staff, Brigadier General Clovis E.] Byers, pointed a finger. "And that goes for your chief of staff too. Do you understand?"

"Yes, sir," the corps commander answered.[107]

And General MacArthur meant it. Later in the campaign, when informed that General Eichelberger was risking his life at the front, MacArthur "cold-bloodedly" remarked, "I want him to die if he doesn't take Buna."[108]

But the Southwest Pacific commander was not above self-pity. At one point during his meeting with General Eichelberger, MacArthur had turned to him "with the memory of

Bataan in his eyes and a bitter query on his lips. 'Must I always,' he demanded, 'lead a forlorn hope?'"[109]

It was a sorry performance. Douglas MacArthur at his absolute worst. His self-pitying "bitter query" ignored his own role in making the Philippines situation exponentially worse, though whether that could have changed the final outcome of the campaign is doubtful, and his own role in making the Buna Campaign necessary by ignoring his competent intelligence people out of American chauvinism and neglecting the Buna sector until the Japanese took it for themselves. His arrogance and overconfidence had gotten him into trouble. Again. So now he drove his subordinates and his troops with a ruthlessness not usually seen outside the Imperial Japanese Army. All to correct his mistake.

Douglas MacArthur got his wish, more or less. Very aware that troops need to see their commander in combat, General Eichelberger indeed was risking his life at the front. After the I Corps commander arrived, he sacked General Harding and replaced him with the 32nd Division's artillery officer, Brigadier General Albert W. Waldron, who was promptly shot by a Japanese sniper and wounded. The division was then turned over to General Byers, who was promptly shot by the Japanese and wounded. Brigadier General Hanford MacNider had already been shot by the Japanese and wounded before Eichelberger had arrived. Three brigadier generals shot, all within 75 yards of the Japanese positions. All three would recover, though Waldron would be retired from the Army due to disability from his wound. As the only general left in the combat area, Eichelberger was compelled to take command of the 32nd Division himself in addition to commanding the I Corps.[110]

General Eichelberger gave his own description of the Japanese talent with concealed fortifications:

> The Japanese had had time enough to construct an excellent complex of bunkers and dugouts, and there were connecting trenches. Foot-wide coconut logs increased protection, so that small-arms fire made no impression, and, because the bunkers were so close to the ground, 25-pounders were often ineffective. Dense jungle and the camouflage of grasses and tree branches made these strongholds almost invisible in daylight.
>
> Clever concealment and thick vegetation made reconnaissance very difficult for our soldiers, and, also, very important. Not only the hard-pressed GI but experienced commanders frequently erred in estimating the strength of an enemy position. For one thing, the Japanese hesitated to deliver fire which might disclose a bunkers [sic] whereabouts and generally fired only when being actively attacked. Frequently the enemy allowed our troops to expose themselves unknowingly for hours without a trigger being pressed. This led casual observers to believe that few or no Japanese were present in areas where, in fact, they might be concentrated in force.
>
> [...]
>
> The invisibility of the Japanese gave a haunting and fearsome quality to any advance, and, indeed, even to a routine supply trip forward with rations. Every GI knew there were

snipers high in the trees, but he could not see them. And there seemed to him no rhyme or reason in their tactics. For three days a patrol might proceed forward and backward over a trail without molestation. On the fourth day enemy bullets would turn the swamp mud red, and our survivors would shoot angrily but unseeingly into the impenetrable green above. This was, of course, a calculated Japanese technique intended to mystify the Western soldier and to heighten that sense of insecurity which is inevitable in combat. I can say this: the technique worked.

[...]

The Japanese troops were not improvising. Over a period of many years expeditionary forces had been built up and trained for just that kind of fighting. They had been conditioned for it too. They could exist on short rations, and they could travel light. They could climb trees stealthily, and they were willing to live and die underground with surprising patience and unflagging courage.[111]

General Eichelberger elaborated on what he meant by "not improvising:"

[I]n strategy and tactics, the Japanese were rarely improvisers. They fought a battle just as they had been told to fight it; once the plan of a campaign had been drawn up, commanders in the field adhered adamantly to their book instructions – there was no flexibility of decision to meet unexpected situations.[112]

Due in part to the Japanese lack of improvisation and General Eichelberger's tireless (literally) efforts, on January 2, the Buna sector finally fell to General MacArthur's forces. After a campaign that was nothing short of brutal, far longer and costlier than it should have been. As Eichelberger described it, "The battle had to be fought through until, as one Australian writer phrased it, there was 'not one Japanese left who was capable of lifting a rifle.'"[113] Even so, upon the capture of Buna, from his forward headquarters in Port Moresby, General MacArthur proclaimed, "The utmost care was taken for the conservation of our forces, with the result that probably no campaign in history against a thoroughly prepared and trained army produced such complete and decisive results with so low an expenditure of life and resources."[114]

His troops were shocked. Several eminent historians have considered the claim "absurd" and "preposterous."[115] But there was no time to be offended because the campaign continued for another three weeks on Papua, as Gona and Sanananda were cleared. Though as far as General MacArthur was concerned, it was over. Having never visited the Buna sector even once, he flew back to Brisbane, telling the news media, "The Papuan campaign is in its final closing stage. The Sanananda position has now been completely enveloped. A remnant of the enemy's forces is entrenched there and faces certain destruction ... This can now be regarded as accomplished."[116] His troops were offended again. Nevertheless, General MacArthur may have privately chastened himself for the conduct of the Buna Campaign and his mistakes, not that he'd admit those mistakes to anyone. Even so, he promised, "No more Bunas." Maybe it was the Buna Campaign that made Douglas MacArthur remember that he was a much better general than he had been so far in this Pacific War. He had to be.

Indeed, MacArthur learned a lot from the campaign in Papua. As historian Alan Rems opined:

> Like a stereotypical World War I general seated far to the rear, he disparaged commanders and repeatedly ordered costly frontal attacks without full firsthand knowledge of battlefield conditions and regard for casualties. He would later avoid heavy enemy concentrations and protracted static fighting and would not initiate operations before establishing sound logistics. Also, from the experience of the 32nd Division, he gained an appreciation of the need for thorough troop training under realistic jungle conditions.[117]

MacArthur had just completely taken a major position from the Japanese, a first in this Pacific War. A first to which he had beaten the Marines and Army troops on Guadalcanal.

Or not. Because the general had some irons in the fire. After the mid-November naval battles around Guadalcanal, the general had figured, isn't Guadalcanal secured? If it is, then Phase One of *Pestilence* was complete and they could move on to Phases Two and Three, which, under the artfully titled "Joint Directive for Offensive Operations in the Southwest Pacific Area Agreed on by the United States Chiefs of Staff" (except for General Arnold) dated July 2, 1942, would place command under General MacArthur.

To that end, on December 1, 1942, General Marshall sent the draft of a directive to go ahead with Tasks Two and Three to Admiral King for comment. It was mostly the same as the "Joint Directive," but it did have some significant changes. It specified that the forces required would come from those already assigned to the South and Southwest Pacific Areas, subject to the approval of the Joint Chiefs. It reserved to the Joint Chiefs the right to withdraw naval units in the event of an emergency. Once again, it gave General MacArthur command over Tasks Two and Three.[118] Furthermore, it did circumscribe General MacArthur's command powers somewhat, specifying that direct control of the naval and amphibious phases of the campaign would be exercised by a naval officer. In essence, MacArthur's authority in these matters would be limited to selecting the objectives, allocating the forces, and fixing the timing and sequence of the operations.[119]

Admiral King had other ideas. The admiral started reconsidering the necessity and even the utility of proceeding up to Rabaul as he himself had originally suggested. King thought Tasks Two and Three – that is the remainder of the *Pestilence* offensive – might even be unnecessary. That he was considering canceling Tasks Two and Three just before the handover of those same Tasks Two and Three to General MacArthur was … probably just a coincidence. Admiral King doubled down on his very coincidental reconsideration. If the experience on Guadalcanal was any indication, a direct advance on Rabaul would fail or, more likely, bog down in a stalemate. Why not try to outflank Rabaul by just bypassing the Solomons and occupying the Admiralty Islands northwest of Rabaul instead?[120]

Though that idea was not nearly as preposterous as making a US Army general commander of the Pacific Ocean war, it was still preposterous. For reasons that Admiral Nimitz explained. The capture of Admiralties would not give the Allies control of the Solomons. The enemy's bases there, including the anchorage at Shortland and the new base at Munda, and in New Britain and New Ireland, he pointed out, were mutually supporting and there was no assurance that even the seizure of Rabaul would neutralize them or induce the garrisons to surrender. Furthermore, if the Japanese retained control of the sea lanes south and east of Rabaul, trying to bypass them would only expose Allied forces to a flanking attack therefrom, which could cut off whatever position the Allies held in the Admiralties. For these reasons, Nimitz concluded, the Allies must just accept a step-by-step slog up the Solomons – just as Admiral King had originally suggested – with the next objective Munda or Kahili, depending on the forces available and the state of the Japanese defenses.[121]

Otherwise, Admiral Nimitz and Admiral Halsey wondered, why Phases Two and Three were even under discussion when Phase One was not complete. In this view, Phase One would not be finished until air and naval bases had been established on Guadalcanal and the area firmly secured. Furthermore, it was impossible to start on Phase Two because the forces available in theater were not enough to complete the job. They needed reinforcements, those reinforcements that Generals Marshall and Arnold had throttled for so long. Finally, when the offensive was resumed it should be directed by Halsey, not MacArthur, declared Admiral Nimitz; because operations in the Solomons would require most of the surface forces of the Pacific Fleet, command should be vested in a flag officer.[122]

Both Admiral Halsey and General Harmon supported a step-by-step advance up the Solomons ladder as a prerequisite to the seizure of Rabaul. "To be able to attack the Bismarcks simultaneously from New Guinea and the Solomons," wrote Harmon, "would be ideal." But he admitted that for now the South Pacific naval forces could do little to support MacArthur's operations in New Guinea. "To send surface forces into the western areas of the Solomons Sea with the Jap air as heavily entrenched as it is," he told Marshall, "would be taking a risk beyond the gain to be anticipated even with the best of fortune."[123] In trying to mitigate this danger, Halsey suggested to General MacArthur taking Woodlark Island, between New Guinea and the Solomons, and building a new air base there. Admiral King was open to the idea and suggested alternatives including Kiriwina in the Trobriand Islands.[124]

General Marshall came back and turned Admiral Nimitz' argument for a step-by-step advance up the Solomons into another argument for a unified command under Douglas MacArthur. The Japanese positions in the Solomons and New Guinea, he pointed out, resembled an inverted "V" with the point aimed at Rabaul. Against each leg of the V the Allies had placed two strong but separate forces, one controlled by MacArthur and the other by Nimitz, thousands of miles away, and each independent of the other. "Skillful strategic direction, coordinating the employment of the two strong Allied forces available," Marshall insisted, "appears mandatory to offset the Japanese advantages of position and direction." Only in this way could the Allies exploit quickly success against either leg of the V and at the same time use their forces, especially the bombers with their strategic mobility, where they were most needed and where they could achieve the most decisive results.[125]

And so it went. Back and forth. Back and forth. The Army wanting a unified command under General MacArthur; the Navy agreeing to a unified command, but only under Admiral Nimitz.

The perils of the divided command in the Solomons and New Guinea – and, to be sure, there were many, such as the lack of naval support that General MacArthur had just experienced – were entirely the fault of the US Army leadership in Generals Marshall and Arnold, both for insisting on a US Army command for the entire oceanic Pacific theater, in addition to the European theater; to try to ram Douglas MacArthur down the throats of the US Navy in pushing for that command; and, failing to get MacArthur that command, insisting that in the alternative he get his own independent command.

Be that as it may, they were in a bureaucratic stalemate. The command arrangements for the South Pacific and the Southwest Pacific would stay as they were for the time being. Because while Douglas MacArthur and his partisans wanted Guadalcanal to have been secured so that Phase Two of *Pestilence* could kick in, the truth was that Guadalcanal was still contested.

Indeed, the Tokyo Express restarted its runs to Guadalcanal on January 2.[126] It was a test for a Henderson Field that was now a much larger, much more dangerous air base. A new airfield, called "Fighter 2" for now, "Kukum Field" later on, had been completed on January 1. It was meant to replace Fighter 1 and its intractable drainage issues, though in practice both airfields were used. The air base also now had Martin B-26 Marauders, the closest American analog to the torpedo-carrying Mitsubishi G3Ms and G4Ms, of the Army Air Force's 69th Medium Bombardment Squadron, though "Army Air Force" and "torpedoes" did not quite go together. Also based at the Henderson Field complex were the 12th Fighter Squadron of Bell P-39 Airacobras, the 44th Fighter Squadron with Curtiss P-40 Warhawks, and the 339th Fighter Squadron with Lockheed P-38 Lightnings.

Admiral Fitch commanded Aircraft South Pacific, but below him things were reorganized. The 13th Air Force was activated on January 13 and placed under the command of Brigadier General Nathan F. Twining, the brother of General Vandegrift's operations officer Colonel Merrill Twining. The 13th was parent of the veteran 11th and newer 5th Bombardment Groups with eight squadrons of B-17s. It also had two squadrons of B-26s, four fighter squadrons with P-39 Airacobras, one with P-38s, and one with P-40s; one reconnaissance squadron with modified P-38s; and one transport squadron.

Another Tokyo Express came down The Slot on January 10 in a seven-destroyer convoy. The convoy came with fighter cover from "clipped wing" Zeros, and it was timed so that when it passed coastwatcher Donald Kennedy on New Georgia, it was too late in the day for the Cactus Air Force to mount an air strike. With the PT boats the only surface assets available, the Cactus Air Force decided to use its new toy. In December the first elements of Patrol Squadron 12 under Commander Clarence O. Taff had arrived at Guadalcanal. Patrol Squadron 12 was equipped with Consolidated PBY-5A Catalina flying boats that had not just pontoons but the optional tricycle landing gear so they could take off from Henderson Field. They had that new-fangled airborne radar as well as new-fangled radio altimeter, which enabled precise measurements of altitude, which otherwise is dangerous guesswork at night.[127] The airborne radar and radio altimeter made night operations much more feasible.

For night camouflage these Catalinas were painted, oddly enough, black. "Black Cats" became the obvious nickname for Patrol Squadron 12, with the squadron insignia graded based on experience. For the first mission, a simple black cat could be painted on the Catalina's fuselage. After the second, eyes could be added to the black cat insignia. After the third, whiskers and teeth could be painted on. And after the fourth the pilot could add "anatomical insignia of a more personal nature."[128]

The Black Cats would shadow the Japanese ships in the dark and illuminate them with flares just as the Japanese had at places like Java Sea and Savo Island. Radioing their positions and vectoring in friends like PT boats. By themselves, the Black Cats represented something of a turning point. During the early part of the Pacific War, Japanese control of the skies meant their seaplanes had been ubiquitous. Especially during the Java Sea Campaign, the appearance of a Japanese seaplane was a harbinger of doom, impending an air or naval attack brought by the seaplane's contact report. In the Battle of the Java Sea, Japanese cruiser floatplanes kept the Allied task force under almost continuous surveillance, vectoring ships and spotting gunfire. Even at night, which shocked Allied sailors, most of whom had never heard of flying at night. The usually unflappable Allied commander Admiral Doorman was so frustrated by the Japanese floatplanes illuminating his ships and marking his course that he cursed them under his breath. Those seaplanes were, arguably, the difference in the battle. Then there was Savo Island, the worst defeat in US Navy history. Set up by seaplanes. Again. Cruiser floatplanes illuminated Allied ships while the Japanese remained hidden in the dark, setting up a decisive Japanese first punch. The Japanese owned the night, especially night aviation. That was then.

This was now. How times had changed. Now, it was not an Allied commander cursing the seaplanes. It was the Japanese. As designed by Admiral Tanaka, the Rat Transportation – the Tokyo Express – was to drop off troops and supplies on Guadalcanal and speed away from potential daylight air attacks from Henderson Field. Now they had to speed away from nighttime air attacks from Henderson Field as well. How Midway had changed everything. Japanese dominance was continuing its slow but steady erosion.

As January went on, the signs, as far as Allied intelligence analysts could tell, became more ominous. On January 14, radio direction finding located the *Zuikaku* and the *Zuiho* in the Home Islands. About a week later, they figured that at least the *Junyo* had reached

Truk. Intelligence then showed the *Junyo* sailed from Truk on January 23 with the carriers *Zuikaku* and *Zuiho* and the new superbattleship *Musashi*. Whatever it was, it was big. And as best the analysts could tell, the Japanese were calling it "Ke."[129]

To Admiral Nimitz, Admiral Halsey, Pacific Fleet intelligence, and everyone else, it looked like a new offensive:

> It is beginning to seem possible that the Japanese are shifting from [the] offensive to [the] strategic defensive in the New Guinea, New Britain, Solomon area; [the] accumulation of airfields would release [carriers] for operations elsewhere [and the] threat of raids may thus become more real in the next month or so.[130]

Giving some credence to the intelligence assessment was an attempted fighter sweep by Base Air Force on January 25, the first major raid since November. The Japanese attempted a night attack on January 27 with not so much Washing Machine Charlie as a full laundromat of at least 14 Mitsubishi G4Ms from the 751 Air Group arriving between 3:00 and 4:30am to wake up the Americans.[131] That was followed after dawn by air attacks from the Japanese Army Air Force, including nine Kawasaki Ki-48 Army Type 99 Twin-engined Light Bombers – the Allied reporting name for this aircraft was "Lily" – escorted by at least 74 Nakajima Ki-43 fighters – the official Allied reporting name for this aircraft was "Oscar," but most just assumed it was a Zero and called it an "Army Zero."[132] Both attacks were largely ineffective. On January 28, Japanese troops took over Baisen Island, one of the tiny islets in the Russell Island group northwest of Guadalcanal. It all pointed to a new offensive.

Admiral Halsey believed he could handle it. The naval forces of the South Pacific Command had increased markedly since the disaster at Tassafaronga. Halsey now had fleet carriers *Saratoga* and *Enterprise*, though the Big E's flight operations were still slowed by the elevator jammed at Santa Cruz. He also had six small escort carriers. Add to that three new, fast battleships, 13 cruisers, and 45 destroyers. By the standards of 1942 Ironbottom Sound, this was unheard-of wealth. And Halsey meant to make use of them for offensive action.

The South Pacific commander organized his ships into no fewer than six task forces. One was centered on the freshly repaired carrier *Saratoga*; with also freshly repaired light antiaircraft cruiser *San Juan*; and destroyers *Case*, *Maury*, *McCall*, and *Saufley*, all under Rear Admiral DeWitt C. Ramsey. Another carrier task force was under Rear Admiral Frederick C. Sherman, former skipper of the carrier *Lexington* at Coral Sea. Now he had the *Enterprise*; light antiaircraft cruiser *San Diego*; and destroyers *Ellet*, *Hughes*, *Morris*, *Mustin*, and *Russell*. There was the task force of three new fast battleships under Admiral Lee, with the *Washington*, *North Carolina*, and *Indiana*; and destroyers *Balch*, *Cummings*, *Dunlap*, and *Fanning*. There was also a task force of four old, slow battleships under Vice Admiral Herbert F. Leary, with the *New Mexico*, *Colorado*, *Mississippi*, and a freshly repaired *Maryland*; and destroyers *McCalla* and *Woodworth*.

There were now also two cruiser-destroyer task forces. Unheard of just one month earlier. One was under Rear Admiral Walden L. Ainsworth, with the heavy cruiser *Nashville*; light cruisers *Helena*, *Honolulu*, and *St Louis*; and destroyers *Drayton*, *Lamson*, *O'Bannon*, and *Reid*. And there was that second cruiser-destroyer task force that consisted of three heavy cruisers (*Wichita*, *Chicago*, and *Louisville*); three light cruisers (*Montpelier*, *Cleveland*, and *Columbia*); eight destroyers (*La Vallette*, *Waller*, *Conway*, *Frazier*, *Chevalier*, *Edwards*, *Taylor*, and *Meade*); and, in an interesting wrinkle, two escort carriers (*Chenango* and *Suwannee*). It was given the catchy title of "Task Force 18" and placed under the command of Rear Admiral Robert C. Giffen.

Because "Ike" Giffen, a veteran of the Atlantic and North Africa, was very new to the Pacific theater, Admiral Halsey wanted Giffen to "get his feet wet in the Pacific."[133] Which is perhaps not the best motivational phrase for someone commanding warships at sea. Late in the afternoon of January 27, 1943, the new admiral led his new task force out of Efate and headed for Guadalcanal. They would be looking for a fight.

And they got one, albeit not the one Admiral Giffen had expected. Giffen was obsessed with the threat of submarines, a remnant of his time in the Atlantic. He was also determined to make a scheduled rendezvous with the destroyers *Fletcher*, *De Haven*, *Nicholas*, and *Radford*, four destroyers of the so-called "Cactus Striking Force" under Captain Robert Briscoe, in a meet-and-sweep for Japanese ships in The Slot. In the process, Giffen ignored warnings and warning signs of a looming air attack, a much bigger and deadlier danger in the Pacific than in the Atlantic or Mediterranean, and did nothing to prepare for one. He proceeded to waltz into a twilight aerial ambush that put two torpedoes into the *Chicago*, leaving her disabled; the US Navy was lucky the score was not worse. The meet-and-sweep was canceled and Giffen was ordered to retreat. Efforts to tow the *Chicago* clear came to naught the next afternoon when a Japanese follow-up attack sank the cruiser with four more torpedo hits. Also plugged was the destroyer *La Vallette*, who suffered a 48-foot hole in her port side that flooded the forward engine and fire rooms, as well as a snapped keel.[134]

It would take much more damage control to save the career of Admiral Giffen. Admiral Nimitz's report to Admiral King said the loss of *Chicago* was "especially regrettable because it might have been prevented."[135] Nimitz knew Giffen was a favorite of King's, so he was circumspect. With his staff, however, Nimitz let loose a rare display of rage. He ordered that word of the cruiser's sinking be withheld from the public. He also vowed in a staff meeting, "If any man lets out the loss of the *Chicago*, I'll shoot him!"[136] Giffen was sacked, but, unlike the gallant Captain Hoover or the noble Admiral Wright, he would get another chance at a seagoing combat command. It was part of the unfairness of war that because of this one setback, there would be almost no Allied surface force standing between the Japanese and Guadalcanal.

Almost no Allied surface force. There was a tiny force that would have an effect out of all proportion to its size. While Admiral Giffen's force was disturbing a hornet's nest the night of January 29, 1943, the corvette *Kiwi* and her sister *Moa* of the Royal New Zealand

Navy were patrolling off Kamimbo. The *Kiwi* reported an Asdic contact and skipper Lieutenant Commander Gordon Bridson, certain they had detected a Japanese submarine, charged in, followed by the *Moa*. They had found the surfaced Japanese submarine *I-1* on a mole supply run to Guadalcanal.

A few depth charge attacks had damaged the *I-1*, forcing the boat to surface. The submarine was pinned against the Guadalcanal coast by the Kiwi corvettes, but the corvettes did not have the firepower to take on an enemy submarine on the surface. Lieutenant Commander Bridson resorted to the best tactic available under the circumstances: ramming. His *Kiwi* rammed the *I-1* three times, leaving the sub wrecked, aground, and half sunk.

But not wholly sunk. The senior survivor of the *I-1* was the torpedo officer Lieutenant Koreda Sadayoshi, who gave conflicting accounts of what he did with the top-secret materials remaining on board the boat. In one version, he took the top-secret code books that could not be allowed to fall into enemy hands, and, instead of burning or otherwise destroying them, he buried them on a beach in enemy territory. When you have nothing but bad options, you might as well pick the worst. His flabbergasted superiors in Rabaul ordered him to return to Guadalcanal to recover and destroy the top-secret materials.

What followed was nothing short of comedic. Lieutenant Koreda returned to the wreck with a demolition team, but their satchel charges failed to destroy the remnants of the *I-1*. Base Air Force sent a flight of nine dive bombers escorted by 28 Zeros to find and destroy the wreck. Only one of the nine bombers found it, and its bomb, though on target, again failed to destroy the submarine. Then the submarine *I-2* was sent in, with Lieutenant Koreda on board as guide, to destroy the wreck. But the *I-2* could not find it. When it tried a second time, US Navy PT boats were on hand to foil that effort. The Japanese gave up trying to destroy the submarine.

It was too late in any case. The *Moa* had already examined the wreck and recovered the probable log of *I-1* and some charts.[137] Divers from the submarine rescue vessel USS *Ortolan* recovered five code books and a list of call signs for ships and stations that dated from 1942. The documents were carefully dried out and then shipped to Pearl Harbor. By which time the documents were already out of date. The Japanese rightly concluded that their codes had been compromised and immediately issued new code books. A new additive table was also issued for the wartime code. New coding procedures were instituted as well.

But the haul was still a treasure trove of information for the Pacific Fleet's radio unit. The new Japanese countermeasures were already compromised by the *I-1* documents, which gave clues as to how the Japanese structured their code. And the Japanese did not bother to revise their strategic code book.

While *Magic* would remain the gift that kept on giving, the Pacific Fleet had more immediate concerns. Immediately after the sinking of the *Chicago*, Admiral Nimitz issued an all-hands warning of an enemy offensive. The intelligence bulletin that day was the first to put a time frame on the expected attack: between January 29 and February 12. The

Pacific Fleet intelligence summary released January 31 predicted the Japanese offensive would begin on February 3 or 4.[138]

After a Tokyo Express run the night of February 1–2, clearing Guadalcanal of Japanese became much more urgent. General Patch was making progress in that regard. The exhausted Americal Division was pulled back and the newly arrived 25th Infantry Division and 2nd Marine Division took over trying to secure Mount Austen and clear out the troublesome Gifu, which was completed after more than a month of fighting. General Patch turned his attention to clearing the Japanese troops positioned west of the Henderson Field complex. After a stumbling start, Patch's troops moved slowly and cautiously. Nevertheless, the combat got much easier. Too easy, almost the opposite of Gifu. The Japanese seemed to be pulling back, leaving a lot of equipment behind, and not putting up that much of a defense. Additionally, if these Tokyo Express runs were bringing in troops, where were they? They seemed to be doing a good job of hiding themselves. Maybe they were landing on the south coast of Guadalcanal. A mixed group of soldiers and Marines was sent to deal with that possibility, but at the cost of the destroyer *DeHaven*, literally obliterated by a curiously strong Japanese air attack.

The curious Japanese behavior continued with another Tokyo Express run the night of February 4–5. Air attacks and PT boats were not stopping them, nor even really inconveniencing them. It was February 6, when a few heretics within naval intelligence in Washington sent out a query to their compatriots at Pearl Harbor and in the South Pacific: "Are there any indications that recent Tokyo Expresses may have been for the purpose of evacuating Nip forces from Guadalcanal?"[139] By the time that possibility was seriously considered by the brass in Washington, Pearl Harbor, and Nouméa, the last Japanese evacuation convoy had returned to Shortland with the last load of troops.

At 4:25pm on February 9, organized combat on Guadalcanal ended.[140] This was victory on Guadalcanal. The first piece of Japanese-conquered territory had been finally wrestled back. General Patch sent a rather historic message to Admiral Halsey: "Total and complete defeat of Japanese forces on Guadalcanal effected 1625 today ... Am happy to report this kind of compliance with your orders ... because Tokyo Express no longer has terminus on Guadalcanal."[141]

Yet the victory came with something of a sour taste. They had let so many Japanese troops escape. Admiral Halsey had held back his major forces, General Patch had moved so cautiously, both expecting a major Japanese attack. When the Japanese were planning exactly the opposite. Operation *Ke* was, arguably, the best planned and executed Japanese operation of the war. Some 10,000–13,000 troops saved in the face of enemy air superiority at a cost of one destroyer sunk and a few others damaged. To call it a success is an understatement.

As disappointing a victory as it was without being Pyrrhic, the end of the Guadalcanal campaign ushered in a relative lull in the larger campaign for the Solomons. Lulls give bureaucracies a chance to bureaucratize, and there was considerable bureaucratizing here. On February 16, the Cactus Air Force, who had defended Guadalcanal from all manner of Japanese attacks in the toughest of environments with, on many occasions, only the slimmest of resources, passed into history. Rear Admiral Charles P. Mason, the former skipper of the *Hornet*, now promoted, arrived on Guadalcanal to take charge of a new organization incorporating the old Cactus Air Force. It would be called Air Command, Solomons, but would become better known by its disinfectant-sounding acronym "AirSols."

In the South Pacific chain of command AirSols still resided under Admiral Fitch's South Pacific Air Command, but the job of AirSols was to oversee all land-based aircraft in the Solomons, regardless of service or nationality. Formal commands, such as the Army's 13th Air Force and the Navy's 2nd Marine Air Wing, would not have operational authority in the Solomons, but would maintain administrative, training, and logistical responsibilities for aircraft, personnel, and materiel assigned to them.[142] AirSols had to be overarching, because when it was established, it commanded an eclectic array of air units. It would be difficult to mesh all these different air services and aircraft together into a coherent unit, but the Cactus Air Force had always done so. AirSols could be considered the Cactus Air Force writ large, a natural evolution from an informal to a formal organization.

To handle this eclectic array, AirSols would be divided into several component commands:

Fighter Command: The Army Air Force's 347th Fighter Group, composed of the 67th (Airacobras), 68th (Airacobras and Warhawks), 70th (Airacobras), and 339th (Lightnings) Fighter Squadrons, with detachments of the 12th (Airacobras) and 44th (Warhawks) Fighter Squadrons; US Navy's 2nd Marine Aircraft Wing (Wildcats and Corsairs), Marine Fighting 123 (Wildcats), and Fighting 72 (Wildcats). Fighter Command would handle air defense, ground support, and escort for air, naval, and some Command operations.

Bomber Command: The Army Air Force's 5th and 11th Bombardment Groups (Flying Fortresses) and the 69th and 70th Bombardment Squadrons (Marauders). Bomber Command would attack Japanese air, naval, and ground forces and bases.

Strike Command: US Navy's Marine Scout Bombing 131, 144, and 234 (all Dauntlesses); and Torpedo 11, 12, and 16 (all Avengers), who would attack Japanese surface units and airfields.

Search Command: The US Navy's Patrol Squadrons 12 and 51 (Catalinas); and the Royal New Zealand Air Force's No. 3 Squadron (Hudson), plus elements of Marine Scout Bombing 131, 144, and 234 when appropriate. Search Command's primary mission would be, oddly enough, searching, but would include both Dumbos and Black Cats.[143]

Admiral Halsey was looking for a way to "Keep pushing the Japs around," as he put it.[144] His goal, for this next phase of the Solomons Campaign, at any rate, was the capture of Munda. He did not have a lot with which to push, however. His infantry was pretty much exhausted after the Guadalcanal Campaign, with only the 43rd Infantry Division, assembled from various loose regiments lying around, available. It was also green and needed experience.

From a naval standpoint, the US Navy would not have anywhere close to superiority over the Japanese until the middle of 1943. Admiral Halsey had the carrier *Saratoga*, but the *Enterprise* was still dealing with the damage sustained at Santa Cruz, including that troublesome forward elevator. But Admiral Nimitz's plea to the Royal Navy for help was answered in the affirmative, in the form of the carrier HMS *Victorious* under the command of Captain L. D. MacIntosh. But she wasn't quite ready yet. Royal Navy carriers were (and are) very different from US Navy carriers, so she was being refitted at Norfolk. It would be some time before she arrived in the Pacific.

Admiral Halsey had air power, and that was pretty much it. And with air power you can attack, you can defend, and you can deny, but you cannot take. That pretty much ruled out Munda for a while. There was some proverbial low-hanging fruit, however, and Halsey decided to take it. So at 11:00pm on February 20 came the start of Operation *Cleanslate*: the capture of the Russell Islands, as amphibious forces left Guadalcanal. The combat portion of *Cleanslate* began at 6:00am on February 21, when the 43rd Infantry Division under Major General John Hester landed at Banika Island of the Russell group, while the 3rd Marine Raider Battalion landed on Pavuvu Island. It had been assumed that the Japanese would fight bitterly for the islands, as they had at Gifu, but this time including air and naval elements. There was very little combat, however, as the Japanese had just abandoned the islands, and there were no wild pigs, either. By February 26, the 579th Signal Company had set up an SCR 270 radar on the Lingata Peninsula of Banika Island, giving AirSols even more warning of approaching enemy aircraft. A PT boat base was quickly set up at Wernham Cove. The 33rd Seabees and the 118th Engineering Battalion immediately began construction of an airstrip.[145]

It would be a few weeks before the Japanese even noticed the occupation of the Russells. As they were not noticing, the center of action switched to New Guinea. On January 5, in what the Japanese called Operation *18*, five transports carrying the 102nd Regiment left Simpson Harbor for Lae, escorted by five destroyers.[146] Despite the Japanese having changed their codes on January 1, *Magic* was able to identify the convoy on January 9. The submarine command at the new base in Brisbane, Australia, led by US Navy Captain James Fife, vectored the submarines *Grampus* and *Argonaut* to intercept. Lieutenant General George Kenney, head of General MacArthur's 5th Air Force, had already found the convoy and mustered American Flying Fortresses, Liberators, and Marauders, joined by Australian and Kiwi Catalinas and Hudsons and supported by Lightnings and the venerable Warhawks, which included Australian Kittyhawks who were just renamed Warhawks, to hammer away at this convoy. Just not very well.

General Kenney's first effort occurred on January 5. Wanting "to try to see if we could break the movement up at the source," Kenney ordered the head of the 5th Bomber Command, Brigadier General Kenneth Walker, to conduct a "full-scale bomber attack" on Simpson Harbor at dawn on January 5, before the convoy had left. Walker counterproposed a noon attack, saying a dawn attack would have his bombers leaving in the pre-dawn darkness and make it too difficult for them to rendezvous. Moreover, Walker believed a noon attack would enable better concentration of defensive firepower and yield a tighter bombardment pattern. Kenney said he understood Walker's concerns, but Kenney was more concerned about his bombers being shot down than he was their staying in formation. As Kenney saw it, the Japanese fighters "were never up at dawn but at noon they would not only shoot up our bombers but would ruin our bombing accuracy. I would rather have the bombers not in formation for a dawn attack than in formation for a show at noon which was certain to be intercepted."[147]

With that, a massive spider web of intrigue and politics took on explosive qualities. There was a major dispute concerning air combat theory. It was something of an article of faith in the US Army Air Force that you were supposed to bomb targets from high altitude, beyond the reach of enemy antiaircraft fire. The Army Air Force used this tactic whether the target was on land, such as factories in Nazi Germany, or on the sea, such as Japanese task forces and convoys.[148] It was out of this philosophy that the Boeing B-17 Flying Fortress was developed. The idea was enunciated in the design in which the B-17 could "hit a pickle barrel from 20,000 feet." But what if that pickle barrel was moving?[149] This was the crux of the problem. Against moving ships at sea, bombing from high altitude simply didn't work. Bomber formations at high and even medium altitude would drop lots of bombs, but the results in terms of actual hits on the target were, in the words of one Army Air Force study, "less than satisfactory."[150] The Army Air Force had an answer to the problem of not hitting the target: add more bombers. If you have more bombers, you can basically carpet bomb the target, so missing would not be a problem.

Easy to say, but what if you don't have enough B-17s for the massed bombing Army Air Force doctrine demanded? Because you're, say, in New Guinea at the end of a very long supply line in a theater of war being starved for resources so everything could be used for the war against Nazi Germany.

As much as the Boeing B-17 Flying Fortress has become a symbol of Allied power in World War II, its performance in the early months was … less than satisfactory. The 19th Bombardment Group is but one example.

When the 19th Bombardment Group arrived in Australia in March 1942 after withdrawing from the Philippines, they continued to bomb from altitudes above 25,000 feet. According to one member of the 19th's 93rd Bombardment Squadron, "Most of our bombing during this period was done from 20,000 to 30,000 feet and we usually carried eight 600 pound demolition bombs."[151] The percentage of hits on Japanese shipping was less than one percent.[152]

General MacArthur was understandably not happy about the ineffectiveness of his Army Air forces. That was why he brought in General Kenney. According to Kenney:

[F]rom these altitudes everyone thought that was the thing to do – get up around 25 to 30,000 feet and do your bombing. Well, it didn't make any difference whether you had this marvelous Norden sight or what sight you had – you don't hit from that altitude. You don't hit moving targets or maneuvering targets like a ship, and so then everybody says, "Oh, let's go to pattern bombing. We'll get a whole formation and bunch them up together, and maybe out of all those bombs we drop, one of them will get on the deck." Well, I didn't have enough airplanes to do that kind of stuff. If I put 20 bombers over a target – why, that was a maximum effort there for almost the first year in the Pacific.[153]

And that ineffectiveness was obvious to the Japanese, as indicated by how they handled the placement of their ships and aircraft at Rabaul. "The placement of the vast number of ships also indicated little fear of bombing raids," Kenney believed.[154]

Kenney was one of the few Army Air officers who was willing to buck the prevailing philosophy. He didn't care about doctrine. He cared about results, particularly given the limited resources at his disposal. High-altitude bombing did not get results. Kenney was looking for something that did. He needed creativity, innovation.

If high-altitude bombing was ineffective, what about low-altitude bombing? It seemed kind of obvious, except to the Army Air Force brass, who refused to acknowledge a problem with their philosophy. That included General Walker. General Kenney said of Walker, "He was stubborn, oversensitive, and a prima donna, but he worked like a dog all the time."[155] Walker flew some 17 combat missions to gain experience of the problems facing the crews, which made him popular and respected by his men, though Kenney later grounded him to protect him from possible capture by the Japanese. Walker was good at talking with and listening to his men, regardless of rank. But Walker had a blind spot. He was a firm believer in existing Army Air Force doctrine and bombing from high altitude. In fact, he had written the book on strategic bombing tactics, which formed the basis of the doctrine. Walker and Kenney clashed over Walker's refusal to consider the evidence that high-level bombing was ineffective and Walker's insistence on continuing with high-level bombing until it worked. Walker did not appreciate General Kenney's objections to the prevailing Army Air Force wisdom, such as it was.[156]

So, for this January 5 "full-scale bomber attack" on Rabaul's Simpson Harbor, General Walker treated General Kenney's orders as what might be called "suggestions." Walker violated not one, not two, but a trifecta – three of General Kenney's orders. First, without telling Kenney, Walker ordered the takeoff time delayed until after dawn so the bombers would arrive over Rabaul at noon. Walker decided to conduct General Kenney's "full-scale bomber attack" without one full squadron, the 63rd, because Walker did not like the commander, who challenged the prevailing Army Air Force doctrine.[157] To top it off, General Kenney had a standing order for both General Walker and 5th Fighter Command head Brigadier General Ennis "The Menace" Whitehead that they not accompany combat missions. Walker was a valuable and popular officer and Kenney did not want him to take unnecessary risks. But Walker accompanied the mission anyway.[158]

After such a stellar period of preparation, it might be hard to believe the mission was less than a complete success. Yet here we are. Three B-17s of the 403rd took off ahead of the main strike in order to suppress the Lakunai airfield. One had to turn back. The remaining two, including that of Lieutenant Jean Jack, got to Rabaul at around 9:00am, but succeeded only in rousing the clipped-wing Zeros of the Navy's 582 Air Group and Oscars of the Army's 11th Air Regiment. The B-17s ended up dumping their bombs over Vunakanau. The Zeros and Oscars, which the crews mistook for German Messerschmitts, swarmed around Jack's Fortress, shredding it and compelling him to ditch off Urasi Island, east of Goodenough Island. He and his crew were rescued a few days later.[159]

This "full-scale bomber attack" ended up consisting of a dozen bombers. Unescorted.

Then for all of General Walker's desire that his bombers stay in formation, his formation broke up, with the Liberators moving ahead of the Fortresses and conducting their attacks ten minutes apart. The two groups ended up dropping 40 500lb demolition bombs and 24 1,000lb bombs from 8,500 feet. The 5,857-ton Imperial Army transport *Keifuku Maru* was indeed sunk, but the Japanese reported light damage to transports *Kagu* and *Seia Maru*s and destroyer *Tachikaze*.[160] Out of as many as 87 Japanese ships in Simpson Harbor. Only ten ships were involved in the convoy – and they had already moved out of Simpson Harbor two hours earlier.[161] It was, as one historian put it, "a total bust."[162]

And it got worse. The bomber in which General Walker was a passenger was shot down over water near Wide Bay. It is believed that two officers, neither of whom was Walker, bailed out over land and were captured and taken to a Japanese POW camp from which they ultimately disappeared. Otherwise, neither the plane, nor the rest of its crew, nor its passengers were ever seen again.[163]

Allied reconnaissance planes later found the convoy at sea headed for Lae. General Kenney's bomber crews began their usual high- and medium-altitude bombing attacks on the convoy, but with little effect. Except for the wee hours of January 7, when a Royal Australian Air Force PBY followed flares dropped by a B-17 that had been assigned to shadow the convoy and from 4,000 feet he released four 250lb bombs, two of which hit and fatally injured the *Nichiryu Maru*. Bad weather kept the Catalina from finding the Port Moresby air complex, and it ran out of fuel and crashed in the Gulf of Papua, killing all but three of its crew.[164]

General Kenney made a last-ditch effort to stop the convoy from reaching Lae. Five Royal Australian Air Force Douglas A-20 Bostons, what the Australians called the A-20 Havoc, attacked the runways at the Lae airfield to suppress fighter cover, while as many Flying Fortresses, Liberators, Mitchells, Marauders, and Havocs as Kenney could scrounge up went after the convoy as their escorting fighters tried to hold off defending Japanese fighters. The 9th Fighter Squadron's Lieutenant Richard I. Bong claimed three from the cockpit of his P-38. The bombers managed a few hits on the *Myoko Maru*, which had to be beached near Malahang outside of Lae; the other three successfully made port. Kenney then tried to bomb them all the next day as they were unloading. He succeeded in hitting the beached carcass of the *Myoko Maru*, but by then she had disembarked all her troops and much of her cargo.[165]

Though it had lost 40 percent of the transports on this run, the Tokyo Express managed to land some 4,000 troops at Lae with most of their supplies. The 5th, Royal Australian, and Royal New Zealand Air Forces were left bombing the supply dumps left behind and striking the empty retreating ships of the convoy on their way back to Rabaul, damaging the *Brazil Maru*.[166] One of the US Army Air Force bombers, its bomb racks empty, was over the convoy on January 10 when it saw what it thought was a hit on one of these escorting destroyers by a torpedo from a submarine. The destroyer was not hit and with some aerial guidance managed to find the offending submarine and dropped several depth charges. When the submarine's bow broached the surface at a steep angle, the bomber could only watch as now two destroyers blasted the submarine, later identified as the *Argonaut*, with 5-inch gunfire. After several minutes, the bow slid back beneath the waves, never to break the surface again.

The arrival of most of the Japanese troops and supplies in Lae was a major embarrassment to General Kenney, his 5th Air Force, and his Royal Australian Air Force units.[167] General MacArthur was not happy. But the convoy meant more than just a loss of face for the Southwest Pacific flyers. Because that 102nd Regiment was slated to help secure the Lae-Salamaua area by expanding the defense perimeter and moving southwest to capture the strategically-important-but-impossible-to-reach town of Wau.

The site of a gold rush in the 1920s and 1930s, Wau was at the south end of an almost completely isolated valley, accessible only by primitive tracks "through some of the wildest and most rugged country in the world – massive mountain ranges with peaks rising to 8,000 feet, more frequently than not covered in swirling cloud; precipitous gorges torn by rushing torrents, and dense rain forest, the whole drenched at frequent intervals by heavy tropical storms."[168] Wau's airfield, such as it was, consisted of one rough 3,100ft runway with a 10 percent slope heading directly for a mountain. Aircraft could approach only from the northeast – that is, from the direction of the Japanese – landing uphill and taking off downhill. The mountain prevented second attempts at landing as well as extension of the runway.[169]

Wau was a major problem because there were only some 400 Australian troops there, while the Japanese were approaching from Salamaua, much closer than Port Moresby, with some 4,000 troops. And it was almost impossible to rush in reinforcements. Until General Kenney arranged non-stop service to Wau by the US 347th Troop Carrier Group. A total of 244 sorties were flown in the four days between January 29 and February 1, bringing in supplies and reinforcements to bolster the Australian defenders. In some instances, C-47 transports had to circle the airfield while Australian troops drove back Japanese forces firing on the runway so the transports could land. The defenders of Wau soon numbered 3,166, with arms, equipment, ammunition, food, and other requirements all delivered by air.[170] The Japanese attack had been defeated.

For now. But Japanese reinforcements were coming, so they could try again. Two divisions of Imperial Japanese Army troops had moved into the area around Wewak. Another big troop convoy was set to arrive in Lae during the first week of March which the Allies found out thanks to *Magic*.

It was a Japanese message from February 21, intercepted, decoded, and forwarded by the US Navy. The message was from Base Air Force about a six-ship convoy intended to land the 51st Division on New Guinea about March 5.[171] As General Kenney explained it:

> [I]ndicat[ed] that a big Jap convoy was scheduled to arrive in Lae sometime early in March. Several cargo and transport vessels escorted by destroyers appeared to be coming from Rabaul and some others were coming from Palau. There might even be another increment from Truk. Both Madang and Lae were possibilities as unloading points for all or part of the convoy. The information was rather sketchy, but this was definitely to be on a much bigger scale than the convoy run into Lae on January 7th, which had consisted of five destroyers and five merchant ships. This looked as though it would be at least twice as large.

This was a major crisis. General MacArthur had just captured Buna and was planning to roll up Japanese strongpoints along the north coast of New Guinea, but the units he had used to take Buna, Gona, and Sanananda were pretty much exhausted and needed time to recover before undertaking any other major combat operations. A lot of Japanese troops running into Lae would complicate that tremendously. MacArthur had actually predicted such a Japanese move after he captured Buna. His own intelligence analyst General Willoughby warned on February 19 of "further troop movements to the Lae area."[172] MacArthur had been proven right. He believed that the Japanese planned to reinforce Lae with a full division, which would allow them to take the offensive in New Guinea. This convoy, MacArthur predicted, or convoys, would be composed of both troop and supply vessels, heavily escorted by surface craft and airplanes. He was mostly right.[173]

It was going to be a huge convoy. Eight transports and cargo ships with eight destroyers. It had to be stopped. The general did not have the naval forces to stop it, and his troops were too worn out to stand up to it on land. He did have heavy air forces. General Kenney sent a courier – a very fast courier – to General Whitehead, the deputy commander of the 5th Air Force, who not just ran the fighters of the 5th Fighter Command, but basically ran operations in New Guinea from what was known as the 5th Air Force, Advanced Echelon (with a painkiller-sounding acronym of "ADVON") in Port Moresby. Kenney passed along the information, if not the source, and ordered Whitehead to heavily patrol the Wewak-Admiralties-Kavieng-Rabaul area so they could locate the convoy early in its voyage. Kenney planned to pound the convoy relentlessly until it was sunk.[174]

But therein lay a few major problems. One was the weather. The forecasts indicated bad weather for the first three or four days of March along the north coast of New Britain.

The storm front would be the perfect cover for a troop convoy. General Kenney told General MacArthur he planned to find the enemy convoy as soon as possible and attack it with heavy bombers until it came into range of his medium and light bombers. And therein lay a second major problem, rearing its ugly head once again: the ineffectiveness of bombing ships at sea from high altitudes. Kenney's aircrews had been working on a solution, which was, basically, bombing ships at sea from low altitude.

One of the first ideas tried was called "skip bombing." Skip bombing involved the same concepts one uses when throwing a small rock across a lake and watching it bounce or skip across until its horizontal momentum and the upward pressure of the water are overcome by the rock's weight. Except instead of using a rock, you use a bomb. The idea was for a B-17 or similar bomber to not just go to low altitude, but really, really low altitude, as in between 200 and 250 feet. The bomber would release the bomb so it bounced a bit short of the target, with a perfect skip that would take the bomb the rest of the way to the ship. After some trial and error and fine tuning, Kenney's men got the concept to work.

A second tactic was low-altitude bombing. In fact, low-altitude bombing, also called masthead bombing because the bombers were often at the height of the top of the target's masts, evolved out of skip bombing. Instead of trying to get the bomb to skip, they would just aim for the hull of the target ship. The attack run would still be at low altitude – 2,000 feet or so – but not really, really low bombing as in skip bombing. At the end of a bombing run of about 20 seconds, the bomber or bombers, since it often worked better with two, but no more than that, would drop two to four bombs each, aimed at a reference point on the front of the aircraft used as a bomb sight. If anything, low-altitude bombing was even more effective than skip bombing.

Of course, low-altitude bombing – low-altitude anything – is dangerous, as pilots attempting to aim torpedoes at enemy ships had learned. Skip bombing and low-level bombing could be decent substitutes for those notoriously big, complicated, temperamental, expensive torpedoes. Bombs, at least dumb bombs, are cheap. But the dangers of low-level attacks remained. The big danger is from enemy antiaircraft fire. That was one reason the Army Air Force kept the high-altitude bombing theory, because it was well above antiaircraft fire. Low-level bombing and skip bombing added that variable back into the equation.

But where there's a will, there's a way. And there was a will among General Kenney's crews. One idea was to use a twin-engine bomber like the A-20 Havoc or the B-25 Mitchell, which were smaller, faster, more maneuverable, cheaper, and more plentiful than B-17s.

There had to be some way of minimizing that risk, however. One way was to suppress enemy antiaircraft fire by strafing the decks of the target ship, forcing the gunners to seek cover away from their guns. Enter one Major Paul Irvin "Pappy" Gunn, a popular officer with pretty much everyone except with inspectors. Major Gunn was a pilot, but when General Kenney met him in August, he was serving as a group engineering and maintenance officer – because he was an energetic, unorthodox mechanical genius. Gunn had taken A-20 Havoc light bombers that had been shipped to the war zone – without guns or bomb racks – and rebuilt the noses of the Havocs with a package mount of four .50cal. machine guns. Gunn even tested the design himself by flying a one-man attack at treetop level on a Japanese air base on the north coast of New Guinea. He managed to destroy several aircraft, set fire to a gasoline dump, and detonate parts of an ammunition dump. Not a bad job at all. Except he had not gotten permission for the aforementioned modifications. He rarely did, which would get him into trouble with the staff inspectors and the threat of court martial.[175]

That threat ended when General Kenney found him. Kenney found Gunn's style as unorthodox as his own, perhaps more so. Gunn's energy and enthusiasm was infectious. From the way Gunn talked, Kenney could tell he was highly intelligent, and his work showed he was creative, resourceful, and mechanically inclined. Kenney ordered him to report to Brisbane and put him in charge of "special projects."

Major Gunn's first "special project" was to take the 170-odd wrecked fighter planes sitting at an airfield west of Brisbane and get as many of them flying as possible – because General Kenney knew he was not going to be getting more in the way of aircraft from the US for a while. Gunn got more than 100 of them up and running. They were forwarded to New Guinea where they played a "vital part" in holding off the Japanese from taking the entire island.[176]

Next project for Major Gunn was skip bombing and low-level bombing, of which General Kenney was a longtime fan since at least the 1930s. But they faced the old problem of trying to suppress enemy antiaircraft fire.

According to General Kenney:

> I sent word to Pappy at Brisbane to pull the bomb sight, the bombardier, and the one 30-caliber gun out of the nose of a B-25 and fill the place full of as many 50-caliber guns as he could squeeze in there, with five hundred rounds of ammunition per gun. I suggested that he also strap a couple more guns on each side of the fuselage and about three more underneath. If, when he had made the installation, the airplane would still fly and the guns would shoot without tearing the airplane apart, I figured I'd have a skip bomber that could overwhelm the deck defences of a Jap vessel as the plane came in for the kill with its bombs.[177]

He had a few teething pains with adjusting the weight and the position of the guns, but eventually Major Gunn managed to put eight .50cal. machine guns in the nose of the B-25 Mitchell – four in the nose itself, and four more in blisters on either side.

By mid-December 1942, Pappy Gunn had turned the previously mediocre North American B-25 Mitchell medium bomber (the Doolittle Raid notwithstanding) into a strafing machine, a type of early gunship, or, what General Kenney preferred to call it, a "commerce destroyer."[178]

And thus strafing became an essential part of skip bombing and low-level bombing:

The added ability to strafe proved crucial to the success of the low-level mission against shipping. The firepower-laden aircraft negated the enemy's defensive fire: "The strafing attack is an essential element in minimum-altitude bombing of enemy vessels. To minimize losses from antiaircraft fire it is necessary to cover the enemy's decks with .50-caliber fire which will keep gunners away from their positions and greatly hamper the efforts of any gunners who do remain at their posts." These strafing attacks were carried out simply "by ruddering slightly during the bombing approach … [making] it possible to sweep the entire deck of an enemy vessel with machine-gun fire."[179]

By early February 1943 Pappy Gunn had modified enough B-25s to equip a squadron. Then came practice, practice, practice. With already-modified Havocs with their six .50cal. guns, and the Beaufighters with four 20mm cannons and six .303 machine guns.[180]

And practice made perfect. While heavy bombers had sunk one of the transports on March 2 in the Bismarck Sea, March 3 had been chosen for the ambush because the convoy would be in the Huon Gulf off Lae within range of light and medium bombers as well as heavy bombers. Arriving at the rendezvous for the air strikes off Cape Ward Hunt first was one squadron of B-25s of the 71st Squadron, 38th Bombardment Group, 28 P-38 Lightnings, 13 B-17 Flying Fortresses; two more squadrons of B-25 Mitchells – one of 13, the other of 12; 12 A-20 Havocs, and 13 Beaufighters who would lead off the strike by strafing the Japanese ship decks and gunners to force them to take cover. It might be just a few seconds, but those few seconds could be used by the following aircraft attacking at low altitude. Additionally, they were to attack the ships' bridges and thus cause maximum destruction and confusion in the ships' nerve centers.[181]

"The weather was near to perfect with only scattered clouds over the water," said the 39th Fighter Squadron's Captain King. "It was quite a sight for pilots who were accustomed to only small operations and who were almost constantly outnumbered in the air." It was a veritable layer cake of death, an aerial armada larger than anything the Allies had previously assembled in New Guinea, or, for that matter, the Pacific War.[182]

Though the attack started off very poorly. Not because of the low-level bombers but because of what happened to the B-17s bombing from medium-to-high altitude. All their bombs splashed into the water, and the P-38 Lightning escorts were not able to keep Japanese Zeros from the Flying Fortresses. Two B-17s were shredded but managed to stagger back to base. A third, that of the 65th Bombardment Squadron's Lieutenant Woodrow Moore, would not make it back to base, but would be the center of the day's outrage. A Zero came in under the wing and fired a burst of 20mm cannon upward into the fuselage. His Fortress crew saw an explosion in the cockpit and flames coming out of the bomb bay. Soon, flames were seen coming out of the bomb bay and "spouting from the windows and tail." Moore's B-17 began to lose altitude, its Number 3 engine and radio compartment ablaze. Its bombs tumbled out of the partially open bomb bay, followed by seven crewmen. Moore may have been trying to ditch the burning bomber, but just before it was to hit the water, the tail fell off and the plane disintegrated.[183] Of the seven crew who bailed out, one man was seen to fall out of his harness and plunge to his death. The remaining six opened their parachutes just long enough for three Zeros, from either the 204 or 253 Air Groups, to strafe them and riddle their canopies. Neither Moore nor any of the other crew was ever seen again.[184]

While the crews of the other Flying Fortresses seethed over what they considered a war crime, at lower altitudes their comrades in the Beaufighters, Havocs, and Mitchells were getting some appropriate revenge. The Japanese ships turning to present narrow profiles to what they thought were aerial torpedo attacks instead got stem-to-stern strafing runs by the Australian Beaufighters and their 20mm cannons, forcing antiaircraft gunners to dive for cover and shooting a torrent of white-hot metal into the bridges, shattering windows and thus adding even more shrapnel. According to the Royal Australian Air Force official history, "The attack had its intended effect of silencing many of the anti-aircraft gun crews, among whom the casualties, as torn and burning superstructure indicated, must have been considerable[.]"[185]

Then the Havocs and Mitchells got to work. The skip- and low-level bombings were being finely tuned in their first major mission. The typical attack would involve two aircraft, one to strafe the target ship from stem to stern, or vice versa, to suppress antiaircraft fire, and one to drop the bombs on the ship's beam.[186] The pilots would try for one direct hit and one near miss, the latter to have a mining effect on the hull.[187]

The result was a major victory for the Allies. All eight Japanese transports and cargo ships were sunk, along with four destroyers. The new low-level bombing tactics had been an unqualified success, though much of it was due to the coordinated nature of the attacks:

> Despite the phenomenal success of the mast-height attacks, it was clear to the aircrews who made them that "the success of the mission was due to the carefully planned coordinated attack. The high level bombers dispersed the convoy and attracted most of the anti-aircraft fire. Their hits and near misses prevented accurate fire from heavy guns while the Beaufighters must have knocked out a lot of the small caliber fire."[188]

But the victory came with a darker side. The bomber crews were thoroughly enraged by the deaths of Lieutenant Moore and his crew. Everyone focused on that one lost B-17, that of Lieutenant Moore. How the Japanese had machine-gunned the crewmen in their parachutes. Word of what was perceived as a war crime spread very, very quickly. Men who had never met Lieutenant Moore or any of the crew were suddenly gripped by a seething hatred for the Japanese. The crews were already aware of stories from around Buna and Kokoda of war crimes and even cannibalism. Vengeance was on everyone's mind.[189] As one aviator put it, "We were mad now. The Japanese had violated every rule including the unwritten rule of combat in the air. 'One never shoots at people when they eject from an aircraft.' The Japanese did it – in spades."[190]

112

Of course, unwritten rules are not worth the paper they're written on. The Japanese, both Navy and Army pilots, had been known to machine-gun parachuting airmen.[191] Sometimes there is a sense even among warring organizations of a certain shared brotherhood and mutual respect that reaches across the lines of war. This is true especially among pilots. By machine-gunning the survivors of Lieutenant Moore's crew, the Japanese – or at least these particular Japanese pilots – were saying they themselves were not a part of that brotherhood.

There was a new bloodlust for many members of the 5th Bomber Command. Making sure the crippled ships sink. And machine-gunning the survivors in the water. Lex McAulay, who has done more than anyone in piecing together the jumbled mess of reports that document the so-called "Battle of the Bismarck Sea," described the foundation of the bloodlust:

Only a year before it had been Japanese air forces which swept Pacific seas, beginning with the devastating attack on Pearl Harbor on a Sunday morning while their envoys supposedly held peace negotiations in Washington DC. [...] Then the Japanese rampaged southwards towards Australia, with aircraft ruthlessly sinking and strafing the ships fleeing Malaya, Singapore, Java, Sumatra and the Philippines. Stories from survivors of the ships had been preceded by others of Japanese behaviour in the war in Manchuria and China; tales of the Bataan Death March had leaked out; the Japanese caused many civilian casualties in bombing raids on Darwin and Broome.

[...] In the fighting across the Kokoda Track, and at Milne Bay, Buna, Gona, Guadalcanal, and other places in the Solomons, the Allies found evidence of what happened to prisoners taken by the Japanese: torture, brutality, beheadings, used for bayonet practice. A diary captured on Guadalcanal described experimental surgery (vivisection) carried out on two living Americans, who had been shot in the feet to prevent their escape. [...]

And added to that was Lieutenant Moore and his crew. Now the Japanese in the Bismarck Sea were to pay for all that.[192]

Most of the aforementioned atrocities were committed by the Imperial Japanese Army, whose members made up the bulk of the survivors now treading water or trying to escape sinking ships in the not-Bismarck Sea; what was coming now would be considered by some as "karma."

They went out "with blood in their eyes and revenge in their hearts."[193] Their orders were to bomb anything afloat. The gunners were to destroy any lifeboats or landing barges they saw. The bombers of the 5th Air Force spent the rest of the afternoon crisscrossing the oil- and debris-covered sea, dropping bombs on anything afloat, strafing any living thing they saw in the water.

Some of those living things managed to make it to shore. Numerous Imperial Army survivors from the convoy made it to Goodenough Island. One Australian patrol found eight Japanese soldiers who had landed in two boats. The Japanese were killed, and the boats examined. They were found to contain a lot of important-looking documents in sealed tins.

The documents were sent to General MacArthur's intelligence group in Brisbane, where even General Willoughby could see what they were. They included a list showing the names of all Japanese army officers and their units. Allied intelligence now had a complete and detailed picture of the order of battle of the Imperial Japanese Army. The list was disseminated to all Allied intelligence units in the war against Japan.[194]

It was 3:00am on March 4 when General Kenney woke up General MacArthur to give him the "final score" that had just come in from General Whitehead. "I had never seen him so jubilant," Kenney later wrote. MacArthur told Kenney to pass along a radio message to his men: "Please extend to all ranks my gratitude and felicitations on the magnificent victory which has been achieved. It cannot fail to go down in history as one of the most complete and annihilating combats of all time. My pride and satisfaction in you all is boundless. – MacArthur." Kenney dutifully forwarded the message with one of his own: "Congratulations on that stupendous success. Air Power has written some important history in the past three days. Tell the whole gang that I am so proud of them I am about to blow a fuze. – Kenney."[195]

With that military crisis out of the way, General MacArthur could go back to the political crisis. He had been busy. On February 12, MacArthur had completed development of a strategic framework he gave the name of a small Maryland town known for quickie marriages – "Elkton."

Elkton was basically a reworking of Phases Two and Three of *Pestilence*. Phase Two would involve capture of the central and upper Solomons concurrent with movements along the north coast of New Guinea to capture both Lae and Madang. Both advances would converge in the climactic Phase Three: the capture of Rabaul. Completion of these objectives would be in 1943 in order for General MacArthur to proceed with his real objective: a return to the Philippines, which he called Operation *Reno*.

General MacArthur wanted to advance against Rabaul with both axes in one continuous movement. In order to do so, MacArthur wanted to assemble all the necessary forces beforehand. That would be a tall order, because he had nowhere near the forces that he believed he needed. In both the South and Southwest Pacific Areas there were troops equivalent to 15 and two-thirds American, Australian, and New Zealand divisions. However, only five divisions plus several loose regiments could be considered ready for immediate deployment. The remainder were resting, recuperating, rebuilding, and refitting after extended combat in places like Guadalcanal, Papua, and the Middle East.[196] In terms of air power, both the Southwest and Southwest Pacific areas contained about 1,850 bombers, fighters, and cargo planes. That last category, obviously, was not considered combat-capable; then again, that last category had landed and taken off under fire at Wau, enabling the Allies to hold that isolated hamlet. This haul of aircraft came from the Army Air Force, Navy, and Marines of the US; the Royal Australian Air Force; and the Royal New Zealand Air Force.[197]

It was in naval strength that General MacArthur's Southwest Pacific was lacking, relatively speaking, much to his frustration. His naval forces had only cruisers, destroyers, and submarines – and not that many of the former two. He had little in the way of transports, cargo ship, and landing craft; and he had no aircraft carriers or battleships and little prospect that the US Navy would willingly give him direct command of either. The South Pacific area had not only those carriers and battleships, but the bulk of the Pacific Fleet.[198] The original *Pestilence* plan contemplated MacArthur at least having access to these naval assets.

Speaking of naval assets, the relative lull – emphasis on "relative" – in the South Pacific area allowed the reorganization of US forces in the South and Southwest Pacific to continue. Because, as previously noted, lulls give bureaucracies a chance to "bureaucratize." In this case, the bureaucracy was Admiral King himself.

Admiral King believed that part of the US Navy's "command difficulties" with the US Army was the result of what might be called "trademark infringement." Many of the Navy's groupings of ships, aircraft, and other assets were identified by the areas in which they were operating, such as Admiral Halsey's South Pacific Command and the Southwest Pacific Force. A US Army officer in command of an army grouping of troops, aircraft, and other assets might be identified by area descriptions that were the same as those for the US Navy. Thus, for instance, an Army officer in command of something called the "South Pacific Command" might conclude that he was also commanding Admiral Halsey's "South Pacific Command." This led to command disputes and attempts to limit these naval units to tasks specific to the Army units in that area and not the broader, more important mission to "maintain control of the sea," a mission specific to the US Navy.[199]

For that reason, Admiral King decided to do away with the geographic terminology and instead put all ships into fleets that were identified by numbers instead of area designations. On March 15, 1943, this new system went into effect. Fleets in the Atlantic and Mediterranean were assigned even numbers, fleets in the Pacific were assigned odd numbers. US naval forces based at Pearl Harbor and assigned to the Central Pacific were designated the 5th Fleet, while Admiral Halsey's South Pacific Command became the 3rd Fleet. This numbering went down to task forces, task groups, and task units. For instance, all South Pacific Command task forces and subdivisions would be designated by numbers beginning with the numeral 3. Task group and task unit numbers followed the task force number, but were separated by decimal points.[200] Now, the designation of every unit below fleet level looked like something out of a high school chemistry class. Despite this ordered change – or perhaps because of it – for some months to come, Admiral Halsey, now Commander 3rd Third Fleet, would continue to use his Commander South Pacific title.[201]

It went well beyond changing names to numbers and over-decimalization. General MacArthur had asked the Joint Chiefs for permission to send his chief of staff and several other officers to Washington to explain his *Elkton* and *Reno* plans. The Joint Chiefs approved but ordered that representatives from Admiral Halsey's and Admiral Nimitz's areas should also come for a general discussion of the Pacific situation. The delegates, so to speak, reached Washington on March 10. Two days later, Admiral King convened a set of meetings with the delegates that would become known as the Pacific Military Conference.

Army historian John Miller, Jr. would describe this conference as "an excellent example of the detailed and undramatic, but absolutely essential, spadework that had to precede major decisions affecting the course of the war in the Pacific."[202] And indeed they did. The acrimony, the arrogance, the suspicion that overshadowed earlier discussions was mostly gone, perhaps the reality of warfare having pushed everyone onto the same side.

General Sutherland, MacArthur's chief of staff, presented a revised *Elkton* plan. MacArthur had prepared it on the assumption that he would control both the Southwest and South Pacific forces for Phases Two and Three of *Pestilence*. That was the original plan, and Admiral Halsey, according to MacArthur, had already assented to *Elkton*.

The plan's intelligence estimate pointed out that the Japanese generally controlled the north coast of New Guinea northwest of Buna, as well as New Britain, New Ireland, and the Solomons northwest of Guadalcanal. Japanese defenses were concentrated, as were Allied holdings in the region, in the vicinity of airfields. Except for the perimeters around the airfields and naval bases, the land areas were mostly unoccupied.

Between 79,000 and 94,000 Japanese troops were thought to be stationed in the New Guinea-Bismarck Archipelago-Solomons area. Enemy air strength was estimated at 383 land-based planes, while four battleships, two aircraft carriers, 14 cruisers, 11 seaplane tenders, about 40 destroyers, numerous auxiliaries, and about 50 merchant ships of 3,000 tons or over were on hand for operations. It was expected that the Japanese, if attacked, could be immediately reinforced by 10,000 to 12,000 troops and about 250 planes as well as major portions of the Combined Fleet from the Netherlands Indies, Japanese home waters, and the Philippine Islands. In six months, 615 more aircraft could be committed, and ten or 15 divisions might be dispatched if shipping was available.

The execution of Phases Two and Three would require mutually supporting, coordinated advances along two lines: one, by Southwest Pacific forces in the west, from New Guinea to New Britain; the other, by South Pacific forces in the east, through the Solomons. *Elkton* broke Tasks Two and Three into five operations:

1. Seizure of airdromes on the Huon Peninsula of New Guinea to provide air support for operations against New Britain;
2. Seizure of Munda Point as well as other airdromes on New Georgia to cover operations against New Ireland in the Bismarck Archipelago and the remainder of the Solomons;
3. Seizure of airdromes on New Britain and Bougainville to support operations against Rabaul and Kavieng in New Ireland;
4. Capture of Kavieng and the isolation of Rabaul, although it was considered possible that Kavieng might be taken after Rabaul;
5. Capture of Rabaul.

The timing of these missions was not rigidly fixed, nor was there an estimate of the time required to carry them out.

The discussions of the conference can be boiled down to the necessity of replacing the July 2, 1942, directive with what became the March 28, 1943, directive in setting goals for 1943. The Joint Chiefs ordered General MacArthur and Admiral Halsey to establish airfields on Woodlark and Kiriwina, to seize the Lae-Salamaua-Finschhafen-Madang area of New Guinea and occupy western New Britain, and to seize and occupy the Solomon Islands as far as southern Bougainville. The operations were intended to inflict losses on the Japanese, to deny the target areas to the enemy, to contain Japanese forces in the Pacific by retaining the initiative, and to prepare for the ultimate seizure of the Bismarck Archipelago. The operations were to be under MacArthur's command. The advances in the Solomons were to be under the direct command of Halsey, who would operate under MacArthur's "strategic direction." Except for those units assigned by the Joint Chiefs of Staff to task forces engaged in these campaigns, all elements of the Pacific Ocean Areas would remain under Nimitz.

As historian Miller described it:

With this directive, the Joint Chiefs set the program for 1943 in the South and Southwest Pacific. There can be no doubt that they were disappointed by their inability to approach the goals set so freely at Casablanca, but the 28 March directive possessed the virtue of being based on assumptions that were realistic, even pessimistic. The defined objectives were believed to be surely attainable.

In essence, however, General MacArthur's direction over the Solomons Campaign would be nominal. He had his hands full in New Guinea, and he recognized that reality. To discuss their plans, Admiral Halsey requested an appointment with General MacArthur in Brisbane. Many waited for the fireworks to start. These were two strong-willed personalities used to getting their way.

But those looking for a spectacular display of verbal combat were to be disappointed. In Admiral Halsey's words:

Five minutes after I reported, I felt as if we were lifelong friends. I have seldom seen a man who makes a quicker, stronger, more favorable impression. He was then sixty-three years old, but he could have passed as fifty. His hair was jet black; his eyes were clear; his carriage was erect. If he had been wearing civilian clothes, I still would have known at once that he was a soldier.

The respect that I conceived for him that afternoon grew steadily during the war and continues to grow as I watch his masterly administration of surrendered Japan. I can recall no flaw in our relationship. We had arguments, but they always ended pleasantly. Not once did he, my superior officer, ever force his decisions upon me. On the few occasions when I disagreed with him, I told him so, and we discussed the issue until one of us changed his mind. My mental picture poses him against the background of these discussions; he is pacing his office, almost wearing a groove between his large, bare desk and the portrait of George Washington that faced it; his corncob pipe is in his hand (I rarely saw him smoke it); and he is making his points in a diction I have never heard surpassed.

He accepted my plan for the New Georgia operation, and L Day was set for May 15, to coincide with his own advances in New Guinea and his occupation of Woodlark and the Trobriand Islands. The combined operation on both fronts was known as ELKTON.[203]

But that name would be changed to something less ... infamous that would become more famous than the former plan's namesake Elkton or the original name *Pestilence*.

CHAPTER 3
I-GO

The catastrophe in the Bismarck Sea – well, just outside the Bismarck Sea in actuality, but everyone calls it the Battle of the Bismarck Sea – sent shockwaves across the sea, across the ocean, across the world. The Japanese struggled to make sense of it. The Army blamed the Navy for not protecting the Lae convoy because it was too focused on the Solomons, while the Navy blamed the Army for not committing enough of its fighters to protect the convoy.[1] More importantly, the Japanese struggled to figure out what could and should be done about it.

The issue was not just what had happened to the convoy, and not just how it happened, but the circumstances under which it happened. And not just for the Lae convoy but November's Guadalcanal convoy as well. The gigantic invasion convoys used in the Java Sea Campaign had been successful under complete Japanese aerial dominance with few major issues. The Japanese no longer had that dominance. That particular pendulum had been swinging in the Allies' favor since at least Midway. But the pendulum had not yet finished its swing. Imperial Japanese air power was still a force to be reckoned with. The Japanese could still contest the air. For now, at least. The Allies still did not have consistent aerial superiority, let alone the dominance the Japanese had during the Java Sea Campaign.

Yet that was hardly good news in the context of the destroyed Guadalcanal and Lae convoys. Both had been sent into waters under contested skies. The Guadalcanal reinforcement convoy had been sent to a destination with an enemy air base, which meant the enemy had local air superiority, albeit not dominance. Enemy air power was to have been suppressed by the *Hiei* and *Kirishima* bombarding the Lunga airfield, but US Navy ships arrived on scene and ultimately sank both battleships before the bombardment mission could be completed. Base Air Force provided fighter cover over the convoy from airfields at Rabaul and Buin, but the convoy destination was the furthest away from the Japanese airfields and the closest to the Allied-held Lunga airfield, which reduced the effectiveness of the Japanese fighters and acted as a force multiplier for the Allies. American air power based at the Lunga airfield sank six of the convoy's 11 transports and damaged a seventh so badly she was compelled to head back to Shortland, where she was quickly sunk by another air attack. The remaining four had to run themselves aground on Guadalcanal to make sure *something* reached the beleaguered Japanese there, though the transports themselves had to be written off and almost all the supplies were destroyed by more Allied air attacks.

On paper, the Lae convoy was different. While the Japanese were running these ships under contested skies, they were going to a major Japanese base with significant airfield facilities. Put another way, the closer the convoy got to Lae, the closer it got to a major Japanese air base. While that Japanese base was also the closest the convoy would get to the Allied bases in Port Moresby and Papua, those Allied bases were still much further away from the convoy than Lae. Fighter cover was provided by Base Air Force and the Imperial Army's 11th Air Regiment. In short, the Japanese should have aerial superiority, albeit not dominance, off Lae. But that Allied air power went straight into that area of Japanese air superiority, only about 80 miles from Lae, and sank all eight transports and cargo ships, plus four of the eight escorting destroyers. It turned out even worse than the Guadalcanal convoy.

In short, the Japanese had provided fighter protection for both convoys, yet Allied air attacks had still managed to completely destroy both convoys. The Lae convoy had made it to only 80 miles from the Lae airfields and Allied air attacks had *still* completely destroyed the convoy, along with half its escorting destroyers.

If the Japanese had looked at the details of both convoy operations, they might have realized the outcomes of both convoys were more nuanced than at first blush, which could have been both comforting and a sign of structural problems within the Imperial Japanese military. For instance, the Japanese had indeed provided air cover to both convoys. But that air cover usually consisted of maybe a dozen fighters operating in relays. Some of that is unavoidable when providing long-range fighter cover. The Japanese thought they had solved this problem in their first attempt to take Port Moresby, by landing troops there. The troops were in a convoy of transports escorted by the light carrier *Shoho*. But the Americans found the *Shoho* and sank her in spectacular fashion, complete with incredible photographs. Stripped of its air cover, the Port Moresby landing was aborted and the convoy returned to Rabaul.

That experience had been expensive, costing the Japanese a light aircraft carrier. And aircraft carriers weren't exactly growing on trees. But none of the transport ships were sunk. In both the November run to Guadalcanal and the March run to Lae, the Japanese had provided fighter protection from land bases, usually in groups of six or so operating in relays. Maybe that was defensible with the Guadalcanal convoy, when the Japanese believed they had sunk the last of the US Navy carriers in the Pacific. Even so, the Zeros showed an ability, amazing and annoying (to the Japanese, at least) in equal measure, to arrive just after enemy aircraft left and leave just before enemy aircraft arrived.

While the handling of the Guadalcanal convoy was defensible, if not correct, given what the Japanese wrongly believed at that time, the handling of the Lae convoy was flat-out inexcusable, especially after the experience with that Guadalcanal convoy. The Japanese had planned the Lae convoy to take advantage of a storm front. The tactic was effective, and the convoy was only located by long-range Liberators and Flying Fortresses, who sank one transport. Destroyers rescued the troops from it and ran them to Lae. A much better start than the Japanese had anticipated.

It was misleading. While the convoy was hidden by the storm, it was also outside the range of all but the longest-range Allied bombers, like the aforementioned Liberators and Flying Fortresses. It was the last day that had the Japanese the most concerned. The weather was predicted to be clear. The convoy was to be off Lae, close to the Imperial Army air bases there, but also within range of shorter-ranged Allied bombers such as the Mitchell and the Havoc (or Boston) and fighters.

For this most dangerous of days, the Japanese increased their fighter support to roughly a dozen, but otherwise stuck to their system. A dozen fighters providing protection and operating in relays from land bases, with Navy and Army fighters alternating shifts. It was a plan ridden with problems. A dozen fighters seemed like it might not be enough to deal with the expected multiple dozens of enemy aircraft. Worse, the initial wave of fighters were Zeros – Japanese Naval Air Force fighters operating out of Kavieng. In fairness, this arrangement was the product of tense negotiations between the Army and the Navy about the air cover. And, again in fairness, it appears that the fighters coming from Kavieng were to protect the convoy and then fly to Lae, where they would refuel and rearm.

Still, the local air superiority that should have been the result of being so close to the Lae air bases was nullified by having fighters fly in all the way from Kavieng on the other side of the Bismarck Sea. Complicating the fighter protection even more was communications, due to long-standing Japanese short-sightedness. The Japanese Army Air Force used radios that could not communicate with Japanese Naval Air Force radios. Complicating matters further was the fact that Japanese Zeros typically did not have radios. The pilots did not consider them reliable and usually removed them to save on weight and thus improve the Zero's airspeed. Some went so far as to saw the wooden antenna off to gain an extra knot of speed. The fighter pilots figured they could communicate with hand gestures or waggling their wings.

Leaving aside the fact that their use of wooden antennae might go far to explain the unreliability of their radios, the lack of radios crippled the operational responsiveness of the fighter arm of the Japanese Naval Air Force. Once the Zeros took off, that was it. No changes of plan, no new intelligence information could be communicated to the pilots. If the Zeros took off heading to the wrong place, that was tough. Information and communications are two interrelated factors that are always at a premium in any military engagement and are often deciding factors between success and failure, victory and defeat. And the Japanese, the Naval Air Force in particular, had thrown away their fighter communications. How bad was it? When the Allies started their thrashing of the Lae convoy, Imperial Army Major Taniguchi Masayoshi, executive officer of the 11th Air

Regiment and leader of 14 Ki-43s out of Rabaul who were to take over fighter cover from the Navy pilots, took two escorts and flew all the way to Lae to drop a message for the air base that the convoy was under attack and needed help.

In short, the Japanese had taken precautions. The precautions were not enough, in part because of structural issues within the Japanese military, in part because the numbers of enemy aircraft had turned against them, perhaps irrecoverably. The realization was chilling, its implications shocking for Imperial Army and Navy brass from Lae to Rabaul to Truk to Tokyo. How could the Japanese run troops and supplies into contested airspace? For that matter, could the Japanese run troops and supplies into contested airspace at all?

These shockwaves hit Imperial General Headquarters as it was debating which priority should get the aerial help available – New Guinea or the Solomon Islands. It was bizarre. In 1942, the Army had wanted to fight for Guadalcanal, but the Navy, especially Admiral Ugaki, thought New Guinea and Buna in particular were more important. Now, it was the reverse. The Navy, Admiral Yamamoto in particular, thought the Solomons were more important. Its islands had many more air bases than New Guinea, and if Bougainville fell, Rabaul would be endangered, and once Rabaul was neutralized, Truk, the major Japanese fortress in the Caroline Islands and current headquarters of the Combined Fleet, would be in danger. But the Army thought New Guinea was more important because, if it was lost, the Philippines and Java would be cut off.[2] The Army never did come up with an explanation as to why the loss of New Guinea would cut off Java, which was well to the west and had the Lesser Soenda Islands, Timor, and Celebes in between it and New Guinea; or the Philippines. But geographically challenged though they might have been, the Army generals ran the government and got what they wanted. With something of a catch.

In the midst of this debate, even before the Bismarck Sea debacle, the Emperor had suggested to Admiral Nagano Osami, the chief of the Naval General Staff, that they should bomb Guadalcanal from the new air bases on New Georgia and Kolombangara. This was more to the Navy's thinking than the Army's thinking. But as usual with such suggestions from the Emperor, Imperial General Headquarters took it as a directive and incorporated it into their plans. It was called "The Army-Navy Central Agreement of March 25." Which came out on, oddly enough, March 25, as part of what the Naval General Staff issued as "Directive No. 209." The order called for increased protection of convoys (like, say, Operation 81) and formalized what the West called the "Tokyo Express" system. Moreover, Directive No. 209 provided that "enemy fleets in advance bases will be raided and destroyed," and that the bulk of the Japanese Naval Air Force would be moved to the South Pacific to regain air superiority and destroy Allied strategic assets.[3]

That same day, the Naval General Staff issued Directive No. 213 directly to Admiral Yamamoto. It could not have made him happy. But it did typify the muddled, almost contradictory thinking at Imperial General Headquarters during this time, complicated by the Emperor's suggestion. Imperial General Headquarters wanted the Army and the Navy to work as one, which is impossible even in Western countries like the US and Great

Britain, let alone in Imperial Japan, where the Army and the Navy, based on ancient feuds in competing noble houses, held tremendous distrust, at best, for each other.

Be that as it may, Combined Fleet was to cooperate closely with the Imperial Army and concentrate their main effort in New Guinea. Army air forces were to relocate and operate there. The Navy would defend the islands and the Bismarck Archipelago with the ground forces allotted them. Combined Fleet would secure a network of transit bases and airfields from which the bases could be protected, and the Japanese Naval Air Force would resume mass air operations. Defense of the Solomons and Bismarcks would be divided, with the Army defending Bougainville, New Britain, and New Ireland, while the Navy would defend the Central Solomons such as New Georgia, Kolombangara, and Vella Lavella. Admiral Nagano's staff also alluded obliquely to a specific air campaign to consist of counterair missions, attacks on Allied transportation, interception of enemy attacks, and defense of communications lines.[4] This was the Emperor's suggestion given form.

The discussions behind these orders are unclear. The most reliable source for the internal workings of the Naval General Staff is the diary of Admiral Ugaki, but the entries for this time period are lost. What is known is that there was a long-standing dispute over the commitment of the carrier air groups. The carriers of *Kido Butai*, officially the 3rd Fleet, were either under repair or otherwise not involved in combat operations. Base Air Force needed aircraft, and Admiral Kusaka figured that if *Kido Butai* wasn't using its air groups, he wanted to borrow them for a while. And base them at Rabaul and other air bases.

Kido Butai had changed since the beginning of the Pacific War, not for the better, for the most part. But one way in which it was improved was in its commander. Admiral Nagumo may have led *Kido Butai* during its glory days at Pearl Harbor and in the Indian Ocean. But Nagumo only commanded *Kido Butai* because of the rigid seniority system in the Imperial Navy. Yamamoto had not wanted him in charge of the carrier force, and the two did not get along well. Nagumo's mediocre performance since the disaster at Midway was enough for Yamamoto to replace Nagumo with a highly respected officer who probably should have been commanding *Kido Butai* all along – Vice Admiral Ozawa Jisaburo.

Admiral Ozawa and the staff of *Kido Butai* argued against deploying their aviators to land bases. Their arguments were similar to those made by Admiral Fletcher after the *Enterprise* and *Saratoga* were put out of action: the carrier air groups were the best trained and most skilled aviators in the Navy, so their "integrity" – whatever that means – should not be compromised by taking them off the carriers and putting them at land bases for extended periods.[5] But Ozawa and *Kido Butai* had more substantive arguments as well. It was estimated that it would take three months to train new carrier aviators to replace the losses anticipated in this upcoming operation. Finally, Ozawa did not want his carrier planes commanded by a land-based air commander, which may have been a more diplomatic way of saying he could not entrust his carrier planes to someone who had no experience with carrier aviation. But if his carrier air groups took part, he would have to because Vice Admiral Kusaka had seniority over him.[6]

Also during this period, Commander Watanabe Yasuji, Admiral Yamamoto's operations officer, chess partner, and frequent ambassador, went to Tokyo. It has been speculated that he was carrying a proposed operational plan drawn up by Admiral Ugaki and the staffs of Combined Fleet and Base Air Force to present to Imperial General Headquarters.[7] What came out of Imperial General Headquarters was Operation "I" or, in Japanese, I-Go.

I-Go was basically going to be massed air attacks, utilizing every single aircraft of both Base Air Force and the air groups of Kido Butai in order to destroy Allied air power, bases, and shipping in Guadalcanal and Papua. The idea of maintaining the "integrity" of the carrier air groups was jettisoned, as it had been with the Pacific Fleet, for practical considerations, such as, "We need aircraft, and if the carriers are under repairs or just sitting around doing nothing – and they are – we might as well get some use out of the aircraft." Though the Army-Navy Agreement called for the focus on New Guinea, these mass air attacks, planned to be the largest since Midway, would strike Guadalcanal as well. Admiral Yamamoto wanted to strike the Solomons, and the Emperor did say he wanted to attack Guadalcanal from the new bases in the central Solomons.

There were other moves that were made perhaps to assuage an impatient Emperor. That's probably the best explanation for another of those shockwaves, this one reaching Rabaul and Truk. Admiral Mikawa, head of the 8th Fleet, was sacked. Why Mikawa would be blamed when he did not have command over the air forces on which Operation 81 depended is obscure, but that was the Imperial Navy's story and they were sticking to it. Mikawa was replaced as head of the 8th Fleet by Vice Admiral Baron Samejima Tomishige. This was apparently in many respects a political move. Before the previous October, when he had gone to Truk to head the 4th Fleet, Samejima had been Emperor Hirohito's senior naval aide. Working with Samejima at the Imperial Palace had been Captain Jyo Eiichiro, a naval aviator who became personally close to the Emperor. The selection of Samejima may have been an effort to placate the Emperor by giving him a set of eyes he trusted in the theater and letting Samejima experience the difficulties for himself. Samejima was also an Eta Jima classmate of Kusaka Jinichi's, which should help prevent the contradictory orders that had been a staple of relations between the 8th Fleet and what became the Southeast Area Fleet in the past. Plus, at Truk he had outranked Admiral Yamamoto's chief of staff Admiral Ugaki.[8]

But though the appointment may have been political, Admiral Samejima was a respected and capable officer. He had made a name for himself leading Special Naval Landing Force troops at Shanghai during a 1932 incident. He had been captain of, among other ships, the cruisers Mogami and Haguro and the battleship Nagato. He had even led an aircraft carrier division that included the Soryu and Ryujo. So Samejima would bring a wealth of experience and understanding in the relevant areas of carrier and torpedo warfare to the South Pacific area, even if that experience did not involve fighting the Americans.[9]

Nevertheless, the centerpiece of I-Go would be the air forces. In late March Admiral Kusaka repositioned Base Air Force for the operation. Rear Admiral Ichimaru Toshinosuke's 1st Air Attack Force (the operational name for the 21st Air Flotilla) moved its headquarters from Kavieng to Rabaul. Going with him were the 36 Zero fighters of the 253 Air Group. The headquarters of Rear Admiral Kosaka Kanae's 6th Air Attack Force (the operational name of the 26th Air Flotilla) moved from the Lakunai airfield to Buin. Also shifting to Buin would be the 45 Zeros of the 204 Air Group and the 27 Zeros and maybe 27 Aichi D3A carrier bombers of the composite 582 Air Group.[10] These air units were only brought up to something resembling their established strength by a reinforcement run on March 26.[11]

The reinforcements were needed because Admiral Kusaka and Base Air Force were slowly but surely losing control of the air. Guadalcanal was just the beginning. Its cancer had now spread to New Georgia and Kolombangara. The inability of the Imperial Army to take Port Moresby had allowed that cancer to spread to Buna, and now the Bismarck Sea catastrophe made clear that Lae was no longer safe. Even Rabaul and Kavieng were no longer safe. Since the Lae convoy disaster, the Rabaul area had been subject to four attacks by General Kenney's 5th Bomber Command – all at night. Since the death of General Walker, there had been no daytime attacks on Rabaul, but because the Japanese were well behind the Europeans and Americans in developing an effective night fighter system, Kenney put the lessons learned in Europe of bombing at night to use in the Southwest Pacific.

The first was the night of March 11–12 by Liberators of the 90th Bombardment Group. The following night it was eight B-17s (a ninth had to abort) of the 65th Bombardment Squadron. Neither attack seems to have been particularly effective or even mildly irritating to the Japanese, due in part to lousy weather. The third attack, the night of March 16–17, was different. The target this night for seven Flying Fortresses of the 64th Bombardment Squadron was Rapopo, a newly constructed airfield southeast of Rabaul also known as "Rabaul South" or "Rabaul No. 3." It was actually fairly distant from Rabaul, on New Britain's northeast coast but almost on the east coast. Rapopo was used mainly by the Japanese Army Air Force, especially the 14th and 45th Air Regiments. The former had some 36 Mitsubishi Ki-21 Type 97 heavy bombers, which the Allies eventually gave the reporting name "Sally," while the latter had those Ki-48 light bombers. More importantly for these B-17s, Rapopo was defended by 29 heavy, 21 medium, 13 light anti-aircraft guns, and five really bright searchlights.[12]

This time, the seven B-17s of the 64th Squadron encountered "perfect weather" in the Rabaul area. From altitudes of 5,500 to 7,000 feet, the Fortresses targeted both ends of the runway at Rapopo, where the Japanese bombers were dispersed, with 62 300lb bombs wrapped in barbed wire – "daisy cutters," these were called – and hundreds of 20lb and 30lb fragmentation bombs, along with 19 flares, four "photographic flares," and 21 bundles of propaganda leaflets.[13] How effective propaganda leaflets were supposed to be when they were dropped alongside bombs has never been explained.

Three of the Japanese searchlights snapped on, and the big antiaircraft guns barked. Just not very well. One bombardier wrote of the Japanese gunners, "They couldn't hit the ground with their hat."[14] Not much better was the twin-engine aircraft encountered by the

Fortress of 1st Lieutenant Charles A. Olson. It is believed to have been a Mitsubishi Ki-46 Type 100 Command Reconnaissance Aircraft – "Dinah", the Allies called it – modified to serve as a night fighter. Just not very well.[15]

On the opposite end of the spectrum, the 64th was bombing very well this night. They ended up hitting 23 Japanese bombers. An even dozen were those Kawasaki Ki-48 "Lily" bombers, continuing to live up to its reputation as "the plane most destroyed or damaged on the ground, by enemy air action [...] in the Pacific Theater." The remaining 11 were Sallys, including two that were completely burnt out. The operational strength of the 14th and 45th Air Regiments was reduced by at least a third, crippling their air operations in New Guinea for a few weeks.[16] Hence the need for the new aerial offensive ordered by Tokyo.

But by far the most ridiculous of the night raids was yet to come. At 11:45pm on March 22, nine B-17s of the 63rd Squadron and one from the 403rd took off from Jackson Field (7-Mile), Port Moresby. Most carried 24 100lb daisy cutters, but not all. Lieutenant Dieffenderfer carried four 500lb bombs with an early form of proximity fuse called the "advanced action fuse," designed to explode the bomb 300 feet above the ground. He also had four 500lb bombs fitted with fuses set to detonate 12 hours later, when the Japanese repair crews were active. The bomber of Captain Harry A. Staley carried eight 500lb proximity bombs and Major Jay P. Rousek, commander of the 403rd, carried four 1,000lb proximity bombs. They all managed to smash the searchlights at Lakunai and set several fires at and around the base.[17]

This particular night attack was the most ridiculous of all because of the B-17 of Major Carl A. Hustad. He carried two 2,000lb bombs – the heaviest in the 5th Air Force inventory – with 45-second delayed fuses. His job was to drop both bombs into the crater of the one of Rabaul's resident volcanos and, it was hoped, cause a volcanic eruption that would destroy Rabaul.[18] "Everyone hoped that the bombs could cause the lava to flow again," wrote Lieutenant Murphy. "That, of course, would necessitate the evacuation of the town as well as the runway and aircraft."[19]

What could be more stupid than trying to cause a volcanic eruption by dropping two giant bombs in an active volcano? Trying to cause a volcanic eruption by dropping two giant bombs in an active volcano and then dropping both giant bombs in the wrong volcano. According to the 63rd Squadron's war diary: "Major Hustad experimented on bombing Rabatana crater with 2 x 2000 demo bombs with 45 sec. delay fuses. The bombs fell within the crater but were not seen to explode."[20]

The slight problem is that there is no volcano in the Rabaul caldera known as "Rabatana." There is a volcano called "Rabalanakaia," one of the six (at least) volcanos on Crater Peninsula just southeast of Rabaul city. But that particular volcano is dormant. If you want to cause a volcanic eruption, drop the bombs in Tavurvur, the only active volcano on the Crater Peninsula and one of the most active in the world, and close to the Lakunai air base. In any event, the experiment failed, the bombs did not cause an eruption. In the words of one historian, "Afterwards, personnel realized how silly the idea was in the first place."[21]

In any event, joining the recently replenished Base Air Force would be the aviators of *Kido Butai*'s 1st Carrier Division, also called the 1st Air Flotilla (*Zuikaku* and *Zuiho*), and their commander Admiral Ozawa, who had taken a hand in the planning. Also joining were the aviators of the 2nd Carrier Division, also called the 2nd Air Flotilla (*Junyo* and *Hiyo*), and their commander, the fiery Admiral Kakuta Kakuji. The two carrier divisions added 103 Zeros and 81 carrier bombers and carrier attack planes.[22]

Remaining at Kavieng were 36 G4M land attack planes – called *Rikko* in Japanese – of the 751 Air Group and some of the fighters of the 253 Air Group. At Vunakanau were the 36 G4Ms of the 705 Air Group.[23] The G4Ms would not be involved in the Guadalcanal side of *I-Go*, but would be involved in the New Guinea side of it.

This was an impressive aerial armada: 339 aircraft, of which 184 came from *Kido Butai* and 155 from Base Air Force.[24] The largest aerial armada the Japanese Naval Air Force had assembled since Pearl Harbor. But this impressive number, much like the US Navy armada that landed on Guadalcanal the previous August 7, was misleading, masking the desperation of the Japanese situation. The swarm of aircraft that attacked Pearl Harbor had come from only part of the Japanese Naval Air Force, albeit the most skilled and effective part. The aerial fleet of April 1943 was everything the Japanese Naval Air Force could scrape together.

Lieutenant Commander Okumiya Masatake, Admiral Kakuta's air officer, was quite conscious of the grim reality:

[T]he total air power assembled by the admiral presented an alarming picture. His forces constituted the main strength of Japan's first-line air power after only eighteen months of war, during which time our Navy afforded aircraft construction its first priority. In other words, the Navy Air Force had not expanded. Indeed, we now had less combat airplanes than we did at the war's outset. This fact alone demonstrated dramatically the adverse conditions under which our Navy planes combated the enemy, for in this same time interval the Americans (as well as the English and the Australians) hurled ever-increasing numbers of fighters and bombers at us.[25]

The Japanese were now taking the protection of their aircraft and especially their aircrews more seriously than they had just a year earlier. Not that they still took it all that seriously. For reasons known only to Admiral Kusaka, on April 1 Base Air Force sent down the Guadal Highway two waves of Zeros; the first consisted of 32 Zeros (12 from the 204 Air Group and 20 from the 582), while the second had 26, all from the 253 Air Group.[26]

As usual, AirSols had warning from coastwatchers of their approach. And a suitable reception was arranged: six Lightnings from the 12th Fighter Squadron, eight Corsairs from Marine Fighting 124, 12 Wildcats from Marine Fighting 221, and 16 Wildcats from various units including the Navy's Fighting 27 and 28.[27] This reception committee met both waves over the Russell Islands and duked it out in an engagement lasting almost three hours. Five Wildcats and a Corsair were shot down (none from Marine Fighting 221, its war diary proudly points out, in the squadron's first combat), with three of the pilots recovered safely. The Japanese claimed they had fought 110 fighters, shooting down 53 of them, for losing nine of their own, including veterans Lieutenant (jg) Kawahara Shigeto and Flight Petty Officer 2nd Class Sugiyama Ei-Ichi of the 204 Air Group and Flight Petty Officer 2nd Class Ono Kiyoshi, Flight Petty Officer 1st Class Shimizu Hideo, Flight Leading Seaman Izumi Yoshiharu, and Flight Superior Seaman Sueo Mizuno of the 253 Air Group. Protecting their aircrews still did not involve making them wear parachutes.[28] A true samurai does not wear parachutes, apparently.

Following this pointless loss of more of the dwindling number of trained fighter pilots, arrangements were made to protect the aircraft and their aircrews – at least when they were on the ground and not needing parachutes. Generally, all the carrier aircraft would stay in the Rabaul area, then fly to one of the forward airfields the night before the attack to refuel, then take off the next morning. The biggest of these forward air bases was Buin, which was used by 32 Zeros, 27 carrier bombers, and four reconnaissance planes of Base Air Force and also nine carrier bombers of *Kido Butai*. Also used was Buka, which would house 54 Zeros from Base Air Force, while 45 carrier bombers of *Kido Butai* would shack up at the new Japanese air base in the Shortlands at Ballale, built through the backbreaking work of 517 British POWs from Singapore who, after the field was completed, were murdered by the 18th Naval Construction Unit.[29]

Joining this massive aerial army at Rabaul would be the Commander in Chief of the Combined Fleet of the Imperial Japanese Navy and architect of the attack on Pearl Harbor and the entire Centrifugal Offensive himself, Admiral Yamamoto Isoroku.

Though there would be a lot of admirals hanging around Rabaul and the northern Solomons – Kusaka, Ozawa, Kakuta, Samejima, even Mikawa was still here for a little while longer – there was no bigger indication of the importance of *I-Go* than the presence of Admiral Yamamoto and his staff. Never before had Combined Fleet headquarters been located ashore.[30] But it would be when Yamamoto arrived in Rabaul.

Lieutenant Commander Okumiya Masatake, Admiral Kakuta's air officer, described Admiral Yamamoto and how Yamamoto was viewed within the fleet:

As Commander in Chief of the Combined Fleets Admiral Isoroku Yamamoto held the unreserved respect and admiration of every man who served under him. Neither the debacle at Midway nor the shock of the Guadalcanal defeat marred the confidence of his men in the admiral. This was not merely the result of military conduct, but Yamamoto was afforded a personal loyalty which bordered on the fanatic. No other officer ever approached the immense popularity of this single man who, when confronted with the unexpected disasters in the Pacific, personally accepted the responsibility for failure, and at no time tolerated accusation of his subordinates.

Yamamoto was every inch the perfect military figure, and conducted himself on all occasions with military reserve and aplomb. [...] Yamamoto was not merely an admiral, he was the personification of the Navy.[31]

The commander in chief was aware of his effect on the morale of his sailors, soldiers, and aviators. Going to Rabaul, however, does not seem to have been his idea, but appears to have been the result of the command conundrum with Admirals Kusaka and Ozawa. Yamamoto settled the issue by taking over the operation himself.[32]

Not that Admiral Yamamoto was all that happy about going to Rabaul. The evening before he was to leave, Yamamoto said to his liaison officer, Commander Fujii Shigeru, "I shan't be seeing you for a while, so how about a game of shogi?" Shogi was a Japanese variant of chess. Fujii, who would be left behind in charge on the *Musashi* in the absence of Yamamoto and Admiral Ugaki, obviously could not refuse. Yamamoto won, two games to one. After they had finished, Commander Fujii said to Admiral Yamamoto, "So at last you're going right up to the front, sir."

"Yes," the commander in chief replied. "It seems there's a lot of talk at home lately about commanders leading their own troops into battle, but to tell the truth I'm not very keen on going to Rabaul. I'd be much happier if they were sending me back to Hashirajima.

"After all, do you think it's desirable, in terms of the overall situation, that our headquarters should allow itself to be drawn gradually closer to the enemy's front line? Admittedly, it's an admirable thing from the point of view of encouraging morale …"

It was indeed a big deal. At about the same time, his chief of staff, Admiral Ugaki, pointed out that sometimes risk cannot be avoided for a commander, and this was one of those times.[33]

The next morning, Saturday, April 3, the day before his 59th birthday, Admiral Yamamoto, along with Admiral Ugaki and other members of staff, took a launch to Truk's seaplane base, where they boarded a pair of four-engine Kawanishi H8K Navy Type 2 flying boats. Nothing but the best for the commander in chief and his staff. As was a standard precaution, Yamamoto and Ugaki rode in separate flying boats, so if one was shot down it would not take the entire staff of the Combined Fleet with it. Just in case.

The Kawanishis took off, circled the *Musashi* once as a farewell to their big, beautiful flagship of dubious utility, then with an escort of three Zeros, headed off to Rabaul. They touched down in Simpson Harbor at 1:30pm. Exactly on time. As was the commander in chief's habit.[34]

Greeting Yamamoto and his staff were Admiral Kusaka, Admiral Ozawa, and Admiral Mikawa.[35] Kusaka had not seen Admiral Yamamoto in six months. Kusaka was immediately struck by the commander in chief's appearance – his eyes were bloodshot and he just looked exhausted.[36] Yamamoto was getting vitamin C shots from his doctor to treat numbness in his hands. He was said to be changing shoes four or five times a day. This combination, medical experts who have studied the Combined Fleet head have speculated, suggests that he may have had a form of beriberi, a fairly common disease in the tropics caused by a deficiency in vitamin B1 (thiamine). Its symptoms include swelling of the lower legs, numbness of hands and feet, and possible mental impairments.[37] War has many ways to kill you. Not all of them involve weapons. Admiral Yamamoto would have hardly been alone in his suffering, however, even among the Combined Fleet brass. Admiral

Kusaka had been battling chronic diarrhea, a common ailment in Rabaul, another fact that did not make the tourism brochures. Now Kusaka was barely able to keep his food down.[38] That was life in the South Pacific.

If anyone thought the commander in chief was in Rabaul just for a visit and maybe a photo op, they quickly learned otherwise, which would have also boosted morale. Admiral Yamamoto's first stop was to Southeast Area Fleet headquarters, where they raised the commander in chief's flag. Now the headquarters of the Combined Fleet was officially ashore for the first time. Even more importantly, Yamamoto and Ugaki had brought with them their stewards and the fancy dishware, tablecloths, and silverware used to serve meals aboard flagship *Musashi*.[39] The men knew it was real when the brass brought out the fine china and dinnerware. Yamamoto was then shown his personal quarters, a cottage at Government House on Namanula Hill, "where the nights would be cool."[40] At least as cool as anything could be in Rabaul.

As if to welcome Admiral Yamamoto, the 43rd Bombardment Group of General MacArthur's 5th Air Force conducted a series of attacks on Kavieng. The Japanese had moved a number of their warships to Kavieng to make them more difficult for the 5th Air Force to attack, but all the same the 64th Squadron's Flying Fortresses brought to Kavieng a little skip bombing in the early morning dark of April 3. Not really the forte of the B-17, but, as Admiral King would say, you make the best of what you have.

And the best of what they had was particularly frustrating to the Japanese. One 500lb bomb skipped into the side of the newly repaired heavy cruiser *Aoba*. It's not clear who dropped the bomb, but its detonation very clearly caused two Type 93 torpedoes to explode, causing a major fire and venting out her hull below the waterline. Skipper Captain Yamamori Kamenosuke had to run the *Aoba* aground to keep her from sinking. The Fortresses also managed to sink the surprisingly resilient transport *Florida Maru* and damage the destroyer *Fumizuki* with a near miss. But the damage to the *Aoba* had to infuriate the Japanese; the cruiser had just returned following repair of the heavy damage she received at the Battle of Cape Esperance the previous October. It would take more than two weeks of emergency repairs to make the still-unnavigable heavy cruiser seaworthy enough to be towed to Truk by the light cruiser *Sendai*, escorted by two destroyers. The *Aoba* would be stuck at Truk for three more months of emergency repairs before she could sail back to Japan for still five more months of final repairs.[41] Once she was back in service, for all practical purposes, after her heavy damage at Cape Esperance, the *Aoba* would have been out of action for more than a year.

The next day, April 4, while the 5th Air Force's attacks on Kavieng continued, Admirals Yamamoto, Ozawa, and Kusaka went over the details of the first part of *I-Go*; a massive air attack on Guadalcanal scheduled for April 5. They gave it its own special menacing name: "Attack X." But a lot of planes and a name that sounded like the title of bad science fiction couldn't do everything. Like protect their pilots.

But perhaps the submarine *Ro-34* could. The *Ro-34* was vectored to a position east of the Russell Islands to act as Base Air Force's lookout as to the weather and to rescue downed pilots. She was operating on the surface at 2:00am on April 5, but her lookouts were apparently asleep. Literally. Because the *Ro-34* had missed the approach of Admiral Ainsworth's task force with the light cruisers *Honolulu*, *Nashville*, and *St Louis*; and the destroyers *Nicholas*, *Radford*, *Jenkins*, *Fletcher*, *Chevalier*, *O'Bannon*, and *Strong*. At 2:10am, the *O'Bannon* picked up a radar contact bearing 65 degrees True – east northeast – at a range of 7,000 yards. Three minutes later, the *Strong* picked up a similar contact. *O'Bannon* detected the unknown ship again at 2:25 at a bearing of 50 degrees True, almost directly northeast. The *O'Bannon* was ordered to investigate.

The destroyer approached and at 2:31 was able to make out a surfaced submarine. According to the official reports, the *O'Bannon* opened fire with her main battery. Skipper Lieutenant Commander MacDonald ordered battle stations and had the destroyer close to a range of 75 yards, with the submarine to port. The port side depth charge projectors were fired at the boat, which seemed to be not entirely under control. Continuing to launch her depth charges and now firing her machine guns, the *O'Bannon* opened the range a bit, but lost contact. When she regained contact at 3:17am, the submarine dove, though it was claimed she was in a sinking condition. MacDonald dropped a pattern of eight depth charges but could not regain the contact. Reportedly, there was a strong stench of oil.[42]

That is according to the official reports, but a story – a legend – emerged that was a bit different.

According to the story, after determining that it was a surfaced submarine, Lieutenant Commander MacDonald decided to ram it. The *O'Bannon* gunned its engines and headed straight for the boat. At the last minute, the officers on the destroyer's bridge decided it could be a mine-laying submarine. Ramming it could detonate the mines on board and blow up both the sub and the *O'Bannon*. MacDonald didn't like that. Not one bit. So, he ordered hard to starboard to avoid ramming the submarine he had planned to ram. Then-Radioman 2nd Class Ernest Adolph Herr tells the rest of the story:

At the last moment, the rudder was swung hard to avoid a collision and we found ourselves in a rather embarrassing situation as we sailed along side of the Japanese submarine.

On board the sub, Japanese sailors, wearing dark shorts and dinky blue hats, were sleeping out on deck. In what could be considered a rude awaking, they sat up to see an American destroyer sailing along side. Our ship however, was far too close to permit our guns lowered enough to fire and since no one on deck carried a gun, not a shot was heard. Ditto on the Japanese sub, no one there had a gun either. In this situation, no one seemed sure of the proper course of action and it probably would not have been covered in the manual anyway. Therefore everyone just stared more or less spellbound.

The submarine was equipped with a 3-inch deck gun and the sub's captain finally decided that now was probably a good time to make use of it. As the Japanese sailors ran toward their gun, our deck parties reached into storage bins that were located nearby, picked out some potatoes and threw them at the sailors on the deck of the sub. A potato battle ensued. Apparently the Japanese sailors thought the potatoes were hand grenades. This kept them very busy as they try [sic] to get rid of them by throwing them back at the *O'Bannon* or over the side of the sub. Thus occupied, they were too busy to man their deck gun which gave us sufficient time to put a little distance between our ship and the sub.

Finally we were far enough away to bring our guns to bear and firing commenced. One of our shells managed to hit the sub's conning tower but the sub managed to submerge anyway. At that time our ship was able to pass directly over the sub for a depth charge attack. Later information showed that the sub did sink.[43]

That was not the end of it. Not for the submarine, which was not sunk – yet – nor for the *O'Bannon*:

When the Association of Potato Growers of Maine heard of this strange episode, they sent a plaque to commemorate the event. The plaque was mounted in an appropriate place near the crew [sic] mess hall for the crew to see. [...]

The story was picked up by the papers back in the States and, shortly thereafter, a full blown account of the event was covered by a story in the READERS DIGEST.[44]

There is nothing in the official reports to corroborate the story. In fact, MacDonald himself later denied it. According to him, the ship's cook, who was on deck when the attack started, later told MacDonald that he thought he could have thrown potatoes at the boat. That was the extent of the potato involvement in the story. One remark.

"I've been trying to drive a stake through this story for years," MacDonald later claimed. He explained that even the crewmember with the best throwing arm could not have tossed a potato or anything else across the gap. "From that single remark has grown the entire legend of the use of Maine potatoes to sink a Japanese submarine."[45]

So it is considered largely apocryphal – then again, would you expect officers and official reports to confirm the use of potatoes in combat?

One of the multiple arguments against the truth of the story is the weather, which was battering Rabaul. A storm front settled over New Britain and drenched the dirt runways of the Japanese bases. The weather spiked Attack X, which had to be postponed one day to April 6. A frustrated Admiral Yamamoto tried to fill the time by visiting hospitals, touring workshops, listening to staff reports, and playing chess and cards.[46]

The commander in chief would play a lot of chess and cards, because the downpours continued on April 6. It would see Admiral Mikawa officially turn over the 8th Fleet to Admiral Samejima.[47] And the April 6 Attack X date turned over to April 7. In order to be ready for Attack X, many of the aircraft had to be staged to Buin and Ballale the evening before the attack, preferably after the last Allied photographic reconnaissance of the day over the Shortlands area was complete, but before dark. To this end, Admiral Kakuta and Lieutenant Commander Okumiya were to take off from Vunakanau in a G4M to lead some 45 Zeros of the 2nd Air Flotilla to Ballale.

Admiral Yamamoto rode with them from Rabaul to Vunakanau. Lieutenant Commander Okumiya was struck by how Yamamoto handled the weather:

The weather on the sixth was very bad. Constant heavy rains covered the airfield with volcanic ash, and there seemed little prospect for brighter skies. The ground crews worked ceaselessly to maintain our airplanes in readiness, despite the airfield's condition. The roads leading from the field to Rabaul became muddy quagmires, and travel by automobile was a risky affair. Despite the weather and the risk of becoming caught in the mud, Admiral Yamamoto drove to the field personally to see Admiral Kakuda off. The seventeen-mile trip to the field from Rabaul was a jolting, mud-splattered journey, yet Yamamoto appeared no more uncomfortable than if he were in his Tokyo headquarters.[48]

In his summer white uniform, Admiral Yamamoto climbed the steps to the veranda of a small building and spoke to the assembled aircrews. He told them to do their best in *I-Go*. "However difficult a time we are having, the enemy also has to be suffering," he said. "Now we must attack his precious carriers with Rabaul's great air strength and cut them down so they cannot escape. Our hopes go with you."[49]

"To the Japanese pilots, this was a great moment," wrote Okumiya. "They were fortified by Yamamoto's good wishes and no obstacle seemed too great to be overcome."[50]

Except when Admiral Kakuta and Lieutenant Commander Okumiya took off from Vunakanau like a mother duck followed by her Zero ducklings, they found their way blocked by "the black, boiling squall."[51] They searched for a way through but could find no route that would not be exceedingly dangerous to the following fighters. Kakuta and Okumiya were compelled to turn around and return to the mud of Vunakanau, where two of the Zeros got caught in the mud and were damaged on landing. Now the plans for Attack X had become more complicated, because now these Zeros had to fly from Vunakanau to Ballale in the morning to join the air strike later that day.[52] It would make for a long day for the Zero pilots and a delayed start to the operation.

But April 7 opened with a sunrise emitting bright rays that was reminiscent of the 16-ray Japanese battle flag, always believed by the Japanese to be a good omen. Admiral Yamamoto learned at his morning briefing that two Ki-46 Type 100 Command Reconnaissance Aircraft (one from the 204 Air Group, the other from the 253) reported 31–33 Allied warships and transports off Guadalcanal, including four cruisers, eight destroyers, and 14 transports.[53] Perfect for the opening day of Attack X.

Resplendent in his white dress uniform, Admiral Yamamoto went to the Lakunai airfield to see off the pilots.[54] It would be mostly a fighter sweep to gain air superiority. Mostly. Attack X would have two large waves, each with its own component waves. The first would be 20 Zeros from the 253 Air Group under Lieutenant (jg) Saito Saburo, immediately followed by 27 Zeros of the 204 Air Group under division officer Lieutenant

Miyano Zenjiro. Together they formed the "Air Control Unit" – Admiral Kusaka was very fond of air control units. The two units had moved to Buka, from which they took off at noon on April 7 to begin their "air control."[55]

Also taking off at noon from Ballale and Buin were 27 Zeros from the *Zuikaku* under Lieutenant Notomi Kenjiro and three from the *Zuiho* under Lieutenant Hidaka Saneyasu escorting 17 Type 99 carrier bombers from the two carriers commanded by the *Zuikaku*'s Lieutenant Takahashi Sadamu, with each bomber toting a 250kg (551lb) bomb, their preferred antiship weapon. Their attack would be immediately followed by the composite 582 Air Group, with 22 of its Zeros commanded by Lieutenant Suzuki Usaburo, along with four more from the *Zuiho*, escorting the 582's 18 Aichis, only about half of which were carrying the 250kg bomb; each Type 99 of the other half instead carried two 60kg (132lb) bombs, considered useless against ships, because of a lack of 250kg ordnance pylons. The 582's carrier bombers were led by Lieutenant Takahata Tatsuo. Together, all of this was the first wave.[56]

An hour later, the second wave would start with 24 Zeros from the *Hiyo* directed by Lieutenant Okajima Kiyokuma and six from the *Zuiho* under Warrant Officer Yamamoto Akira (no relation) escorting 17 dive bombers from the *Hiyo* commanded by Lieutenant Ikeda Toshimi. They would be immediately followed with the final sub wave of 23 Zeros commanded by Lieutenant Shigematsu Yasuhiro, division officer from the *Junyo* who had fought at Midway and Santa Cruz; and three more from the *Zuiho*, whose air group was sprinkled throughout this strike like salt – although they were not supposed to be – escorting 18 Type 99 dive bombers from the *Junyo* under Lieutenant Tsuda Toshio. All of the Type 99s from the carriers were armed with the 250kg bombs.[57]

It was not so much an armada of aircraft, the largest Guadalcanal would have seen since last year, as an ocean of aircraft. Wave after wave after wave after wave after wave after wave.

But would these waves break on the shores of Guadalcanal and its defending air force, or would they break through?

———————————— ◯ ————————————

Loitering off Guadalcanal this April 7, 1943, was the destroyer USS *Aaron Ward*. She had returned to duty in February after getting the damage she suffered in the Friday the 13th Battle repaired. The *Aaron Ward* spent most of her time escorting transports and supply ships in their various forms.

On this day, the *Aaron Ward* had escorted the destroyer-turned-high-speed transport *Ward* (no relation) and three tank landing craft from the Russell Islands to Savo Island. Then the destroyer sped on ahead toward Tulagi. The little convoy was moving slowly, and she wanted to arrange for air cover for it until they arrived in Tulagi, which was scheduled for about 2:00pm. That air cover became essential a little after noon, when she was informed that an air attack was on its way.[58]

Admiral Yamamoto's report was correct. The waters in and around Ironbottom Sound were filled with ships. At Lunga, four transports that had brought in the 145th Infantry Regiment of the 37th Infantry Division were loading the 132nd Infantry Regiment of the Americal Division, now withdrawing to Fiji after doing its part to drive the Japanese off Guadalcanal. It was almost ready to leave, too. Just one of the four transports remained to be loaded, the venerable *Hunter Liggett*. Five cargo ships were at various places; the oiler *Tappahannock* was pumping fuel into the underwater pipeline at Koli Point. Another oiler, the *Kanawha*, was in Tulagi Harbor waiting for permission to leave. Also at Tulagi were about 15 PT boats with their tender *Niagara*; the Royal New Zealand Navy corvette *Moa*, who had already punched well above her weight for the Allied cause, being fueled by the yard oiler *Erskine Phelps*, the 3,600-ton transport *Stratford*; minesweeper *Conflict*; net tenders *Butternut* and *Aloe*; New Zealand coaster *Awahou*; eight landing craft, six coastal transports, three tugs, and, one could almost imagine, a partridge in a pear tree.[59] Rear Admiral Ainsworth's task force was in Purvis Bay. And the *Aaron Ward* was trying to help take care of her charges.[60]

The coastwatcher Jack Read had a ringside seat at Teop Harbor on the northeast tip of Bougainville to the operations at the Buka airfield. He radioed warning of the Zeros' attack almost as soon as they took off.[61] It would be among the last warnings received from Read. The Japanese had won the support of the natives on Bougainville, who were now actively helping the Japanese root out Read and other coastwatchers. Read's warning about the Zeros headed for Guadalcanal was echoed by other coastwatchers down the lines of the Solomons.

The warnings were not entirely surprising. On April 2, Pearl Harbor intelligence warned of possible imminent attacks in the central Solomons. Two days later the fleet intelligence summary had advised "increased air activity expected soon," followed on April 6 by: "Large air action by land-based planes, possibly supplemented by carrier planes [is] expected within one week."[62]

Moreover, Japanese efforts to avoid Allied photo reconnaissance missions had not been completely successful. A flight by an unarmed modified P-38 Lightning of the 17th Photo Reconnaissance Squadron over the Buin complex on April 6 produced photos of 114 aircraft, where there had been 40 the day before. At Ballale, a land mass so small the runway extended the length of the island, a 17th Photo Reconnaissance Squadron Lightning found 95 Japanese planes; a day earlier the field had been empty.[63] To top it off, there had been the reappearance of the Washing Machine Charlie the previous night. The raid lasted nearly an hour, causing little damage but disrupting sleep, which was the whole point.[64]

But the AirSols staff was awake enough to be having lunch when Read's warning came in. AirSols was in the middle of an unplanned transition. Admiral Mason had come down with a deadly combination of malaria and pneumonia and had to be evacuated on April 1, to be replaced by Rear Admiral Marc Andrew "Pete" Mitscher.[65] The new AirSols commander, who would soon become a superstar with aircraft carriers, was not quite ready. Mitscher had received the intelligence warnings from Admiral Halsey, but it was only that morning when Halsey had given him a projected date for the Japanese attack – April 8, the following day. AirSols had planned to attack Kahili (the American name for the Buin air base) the following day, but in light of the warning, Halsey suggested they move it up by a day. So Mitscher was preparing five Fortresses and 24 Avengers to take off at 1:30pm for the attack. With the Japanese now coming a day early, that attack was now up in the air. So Mitscher got the B-17s and TBFs in the air, too, and had them circle east of Henderson Field to get them out of harm's way.[66]

At 12:20pm, Henderson Field issued a "Condition: Red" – basically warning of an imminent attack – and the sirens went off. The ships all tried to escape.[67] The veteran *Hunter Liggett* and the other troop transports raised anchor and headed east for the Solomon Sea. The cargo ships, escorted by the destroyer *Sterett*, soon followed, as did the *Tappahannock*. Admiral Ainsworth's task force, then northwest of Savo directly in the path of the attack, headed north and then east to loop around Florida Island and hide in some rain squalls. That left the frustrated *Kanawha* and the smaller craft at Tulagi, and several destroyers including the *Aaron Ward*.[68]

Henderson Field soon issued a "Condition: Very Red."[69] Royal New Zealand Air Force Radar Unit No. 52 began tracking the intruders with its British Ground Control Interception radar, which could track more accurately than its American equivalent, the SCR 270-B, and give altitude information as well. With tracking information being provided by the Kiwis, at 1:00pm AirSols Fighter Command started sending up the reception committee. It would consist of 89 fighters: 36 Wildcats from multiple squadrons including eight from Marine Fighting 214 and 17 from Marine Fighting 221; nine Corsairs from Marine Fighting 124; 13 Corsairs from Marine Fighting 213; 13 Airacobras, 12 Lightnings from the 12th and 70th Fighter Squadrons; and six Warhawks from the 68th Fighter Squadron.[70]

The American welcoming committee met the Japanese visitors at around 2:00pm near the Russell Islands. The result was a massive, wild melee involving 300 aircraft that was arguably the aerial version of the Friday the 13th Battle, sprawling from the Russell Islands all the way to Tulagi.

And it quickly became apparent that there were simply too many Zeros for the defenders to handle. At 2:59pm, Marine Fighting 214's Captain John Burnett saw a formation of Japanese aircraft emerge from behind a cloud and tersely reported, "There are Zeros and hawks all over me." Shortly thereafter, someone, maybe Burnett, shouted over his open microphone, "Holy Christ! There's millions of 'em."[71]

Not quite millions, but enough to keep the Americans away from the Vals, who made a beeline for Tulagi, likely hoping to catch Admiral Ainsworth's task force; but with him hiding safely in a squall, they had to settle for whatever was at Tulagi. The first wave of Vals from the *Zuikaku* and 582 Air Group apparently had some issues with dense clouds preventing them from finding "suitable targets."[72] They had more issues with one Lieutenant James E. Swett.

Marine Fighting 221's Lieutenant Swett had opened the day with the breakfast of champions: Spam and peanut butter. Now he found himself and his flight of Wildcats vectored to Tulagi. At about 15,000 feet, Swett raced ahead of his flight, which got jumped by Zeros, leaving Swett by himself. He saw the Vals start to go into their dives. Since he couldn't beat them, he decided to join them, and made a right turn to dive right along with them.[73]

He began to shoot them down one right after another, flaming three Vals. But he also saw bombs from other Vals scoring on a tanker and a destroyer. At very low altitude, he pulled out of his dive, taking a 40mm antiaircraft shell that bore a hole in his left wing, and headed north of Florida Island, where he shot down another four. Swett tried to add yet one more, but he got too close and the tail gunner got Swett's Wildcat, shattering the windshield and cutting the oil line. Swett used the last of his ammunition to kill the gunner and set the plane smoking.[74]

Though as of late many have questioned whether Lieutenant Swett even could have shot down so many Vals, he appears to have intercepted the attack by the Vals of the *Zuikaku* and 582 Air Group, "pretty well messing up the raid," in the words of the Marine Fighting 221 War Diary. Among those Swett is believed to have shot down is the commander of the 582, Lieutenant Takahata, whose D3A did not return to Buin; he survived and made it to Florida Island, only to killed by Melanesian natives.[75] And there went another Japanese veteran flight leader.

But more than a few would not be returning from this attack. Lieutenant Swett believed he had seen two ships hit by bombs. One was the oiler *Kanawha* under Lieutenant Commander Brainerd N. Bock. Admiral Halsey had ordered all ships away from Guadalcanal, specifically mentioning the *Kanawha*, "at the earliest practicable time in anticipation of Japanese air attacks." Bock wanted to leave Tulagi, but the senior Navy officer on Guadalcanal, Rear Admiral George H. Fort, considered the "earliest practicable time" only after the *Kanawha* had received an escort (preferably two) and fueled her first. So he ordered Bock to wait. Bock spent the time having his crew check their two 5-inch, two twin 40mm Bofors, and two twin 20mm Oerlikon antiaircraft guns; and covered the oil tanks with carbon dioxide. The destroyer *Taylor* from Admiral Ainsworth's force finally showed up, having already fueled at Tulagi from the *Erskine Phelps* and headed out to rejoin Admiral Ainsworth, only to be ordered back to escort the *Kanawha*.[76]

An exasperated Lieutenant Commander Bock finally got his ship under way, maneuvering to get out of Tulagi Harbor and join with the *Taylor*. But by then it was too late; the Japanese air strike was in sight. Waddling at 13 knots, Bock managed to get his ship out of the harbor, but several Vals headed straight as an arrow for the *Kanawha*. They plastered the old oiler. First hit was an oil tank under the bridge, which spewed burning fuel on the main deck, disabled the engines, and ruptured her hull in a number of places. After five Vals had left the *Kanawha* a burning wreck, the rest went to look for more undamaged prey. As burning oil spilled out of the oiler onto the sea, Bock ordered her abandoned while her momentum was still carrying her forward, thus reducing the danger to the crew from burning oil on the water. The *Taylor* fled from the burning *Kanawha* at 30 knots, claiming that her proximity to the shore made rescue efforts impossible. Other craft in the harbor disagreed, however, and moved to her aid.[77]

The other ship Lieutenant Swett saw hit was probably the Kiwi corvette *Moa*. For whatever reason, with everyone trying to flee the Lunga roadstead on a Condition: Very Red, the *Moa* never got the message and continued fueling from the *Erskine Phelps*. Fueling when enemy bombers arrive is a bad idea. Two bombs apparently intended for the *Erskine Phelps* hit the *Moa* instead. The corvette went down in four minutes, taking five men with her. Nevertheless, in her short wartime career, the *Moa* did far more damage to the Japanese cause than even her sinking could repay.[78]

That was the haul for the dive bombers from the *Zuikaku* and 582 Air Groups. When the dive bombers from the *Junyo* and *Hiyo* arrived, they were not hindered by low clouds and went after higher value targets.

The destroyer *Aaron Ward* had escorted the *Ward* and the landing craft to a spot near Tulagi when she was ordered to escort the *LST-449*, a landing craft packed with people that were being taken to Tulagi, among them one Lieutenant (jg) John F. Kennedy, who later on would gain some renown. The *Aaron Ward* escorted the *LST-449* toward the east. Tugs *Vireo* and *Ortolan* and several smaller craft took refuge under the destroyer's guns, and skipper Lieutenant Commander Becton tried to shepherd everyone out of the danger zone.

The *Aaron Ward's* lookouts saw dogfights in the direction of Savo Island and a group of Japanese planes approaching. Becton had his antiaircraft guns and main battery track this group. But usually it's not the ones you see; it's the ones you don't see.

And the *Aaron Ward* could not see a separate group of three Vals until they popped out of a cloud bank, after which the dive bombers put the sun behind them to blind the destroyer's gunners. Becton ordered flank speed and left full rudder. The *Aaron Ward's* 20mm guns opened up in the general direction of the attackers and the 5-inch guns swung around and opened fire. But it was no use.

The destroyer was hit by only one bomb; the second one dropped on her, but that one bomb was a direct hit in the after engine room, disabling her engines and causing her to lose power. Multiple bombs missed the ship by only about five yards, rupturing hull plates and causing more flooding, including both boiler rooms. The *Aaron Ward* drifted in a port turn until she lost momentum and came to a stop.

After about 90 minutes of this aerial onslaught, the Japanese headed back to their bases. The Americans were left assessing the damage and trying to save the *Kanawha* and the *Aaron Ward*. The *Ortolan* and the *Vireo* moved to the assistance of the *Aaron Ward*. Lieutenant Commander Becton reported the destroyer was sagging amidships, which suggests severe damage to her keel. In any event, the tugs tried to tow the *Aaron Ward* to Tulagi, but when the flooding continued and the destroyer took more and more of a starboard list, a desperate effort was made to beach her. But that effort was futile and at 9:35pm, just 600 yards from shoal water, the *Aaron Ward*, proud survivor of Pearl Harbor and the Friday the 13th Action, sank stern first, taking with her 27 of her crew.

The burning *Kanawha*, abandoned by her escorting destroyer *Taylor*, was not abandoned by tugs *Rail* and *Menominee*, minesweeper *Conflict*, and landing barges *LCT-58* and *-62*, all of whom came to her aid. Incredibly, a group of volunteers returned to the oiler and braved exploding ammunition to fight the fires and successfully put them out. The *Rail* towed her to the west side of Tulagi, where she was beached around midnight. Salvage efforts looked promising – until the *Kanawha* slid back into the water during the night and sank around dawn.[79]

Of the 76 fighters who moved to intercept the Japanese attackers, only 56 were able to make contact. Total Allied losses were seven aircraft and one pilot, Major Walden Williams, commander of the 70th Fighter Squadron, missing. Williams, flying the Airacobra because he was not yet familiar with the P-38, disappeared under mysterious circumstances, and was last seen diving toward the sea after jettisoning his external fuel tank for no apparent reason.[80] It could have been a lot worse. AirSols was very lucky to have been able to recover six pilots. In fact, it would not be unfair to say that given the resources Base Air Force put into Attack X, the return was underwhelming.

Not just underwhelmed but under water was Lieutenant Swett. With his oil line shot up, his engine froze. "That was the end of that," Swett recalled. "[O]ne blade of the propeller was standing straight up in front of me: the big finger."[81] He left it to the reader to figure out which finger.

He ditched his fighter, but it hit the water fairly hard, going some 20 feet under. Then Swett's parachute harness got caught on a hook behind the cockpit, and he struggled to get free and make it back to the surface. Seeing a picket boat in the distance, Swett fired a few tracers in the air.

Lieutenant Swett had been in the water only about 15 minutes by the time the boat reached him. Men with rifles looked suspiciously at Swett. One of them asked, "You an American?"

Swett shouted, "You're goddamn right I am!"

"Okay," the skipper said, "it's one of them smart-assed Marines. Pick him up."[82]

The mood in Rabaul was one of celebration.

Admiral Kusaka had sent an observation aircraft to watch the results of Attack X. When the observer's report was compared with the pilot reports, the Japanese determined that they had sunk ten transports, one cruiser, and one destroyer; and destroyed 41 aircraft. All for losses of seven D3As, with an eighth crashing on return, and 12 Zeros. The losses included another haul of veterans like Lieutenant Takahata of the 582 Air Group, Flight Leading Seaman Murata Makoto of the 204; Flight Leading Seaman Kanemitsu Yasuo of the 253; Flight Warrant Officer Matsuyama Tsuguo of the *Hiyo* but formerly of the *Hiryu* and 14th Air Groups; Flight Warrant Officer Katayama Shozo, formerly of the 12th Air Group; Flight Petty Officer 1st Class Yotsumoto Chiune, Flight Petty Officer 2nd Class

Ando Yuji, Flight Chief Petty Officer Kobayashi Matsutaro, Flight Leading Seaman Ninomiya Ippei, and Lieutenant (jg) Itesono Chiro, all from the *Junyo*. The proverbial baker's dozen aircraft had landed at Munda for the night. These results were forwarded to Imperial General Headquarters, who christened it the "Battle of Florida Island."[83] They were so happy.

The reports were inaccurate, as has been seen, but they provide yet another example, if one was already needed, of that distinctively Japanese habit of reporting combat damage inflicted on the enemy that was inversely proportional to the damage actually inflicted. To be sure, no military organization, including those of the US and Great Britain, is immune to overstating the damage inflicted on its foes, General Kenney being a case in point. But the Imperial Japanese military was in a class by itself. US Naval War College would later say the Japanese had "a tendency, which became more pronounced throughout the war, to make exaggerated claims concerning enemy damage without first making every effort to verify the truth."[84] That wasn't necessarily true here, because Admiral Kusaka had sent an observer specifically to assess battle damage, but the observer doesn't seem to have done any good in that regard. The reports of damage inflicted by Attack X were hardly an outlier. If anything, they were more conservative than usual. "Throughout the war the Japanese high command claimed to have inflicted losses on a scale and at a rate which even American ship yards could never have matched, and indeed Japanese claims were, by the least exacting of standards, fantastical," noted Pacific War historian H.P. Willmott in a devastating analysis of this trend. Indeed, to quote Willmot again, "Japanese claims seem almost to have been almost deliberately inversely related to reality."[85]

And the worst offender?

The Japanese naval air force was most certainly not alone among air services in consistently overstating its successes, but it seems alone in terms of the Second World War in the sheer scale and consistency of overstatement, not simply in terms of overestimation of whatever success it commanded but in turning abject failure into massive, overwhelming victory. …

What seems truly extraordinary about the Japanese situation … is what seems to be the usually uncritical acceptance of the most preposterous of claims on the part of higher authority, almost as if individual aircrew could not survive battle and report back to their superiors without having accounted for an enemy and their superiors being morally bound to believe them. […] various individual commanders seem to have entertained personal reservations which led them to discount the most extravagant claims but nonetheless still vastly overestimate the losses that had been inflicted on the Americans […][86]

Which describes Admiral Yamamoto, who determined that Attack X had achieved its objectives, so no further attacks were necessary at this time. Even though the Japanese side of the ledger was not yet complete.

Still to be entered was the submarine *Ro-34*, under the command of Lieutenant Tomita Rikichi. The *Ro-34* wasn't really doing anything; her mission was only to provide weather reports and rescue downed aviators. But she nevertheless kept attracting attention, and when she was on the surface she doesn't seem to have kept the good watch that was the norm in the Imperial Japanese Navy.

At a little before 10:00pm on April 7, the surfaced *Ro-34* was detected on radar – again – this time by the destroyer *Strong* of Admiral Ainsworth's task force at a distance of 9,350 yards. Just after 10:00pm, skipper Commander Joseph H. Wellings had the *Strong* pin the submarine with her searchlight and open fire with her main battery instead of potatoes. After being hit by at least three 5-inch shells, not the spud missiles she had experienced recently, the *RO-34* dove by the stern at a 10- to 15-degree angle. That was a bad sign for the submarine. Wellings had the *Strong* go over her position and drop two patterns of depth charges, which brought debris to the surface. That was a worse sign. The *Ro-34* and her crew were never seen again. The *Strong* was credited with a sinking, and Wellings received the Navy Cross.[87]

The Combined Fleet's commander in chief switched targets to New Guinea, the actual objective of the March 25 agreement, with an operation given the less sinister name "Attack Y." April 8 was spent analyzing the situation in New Guinea and preparing target lists for the next day. Except once April 9 arrived, the weather intervened again. A storm front had crossed from the Bismarcks to Papua. At the final briefing, Admirals Kusaka and Ozawa both requested delay, which Admiral Yamamoto granted. Admiral Ugaki visited the Lakunai and Vunakanau airfields while the G4Ms were readied for the attack. But concern remained for the "Type 1 cigars," as the G4Ms were nicknamed, and a second delay was approved to arrange for more fighter protection.[88]

Some one hundred aircraft from *Kido Butai*, to be less than precise, and none from Base Air Force, to be more precise. Their target was Oro Bay. Oro Bay was the location of Dobodura, a new air base complex that was being developed and expanded very rapidly. But the Japanese did not attack the air base, just the harbor itself. The first wave in this attack, which the Japanese called "Attack X-2," was a fighter sweep by 15 Zeros from the *Zuiho* led by Lieutenant Sato Masao. The Allies in New Guinea did not have quite the warning net that Guadalcanal had, and a fighter defense was somewhat late in positioning itself, and when it did, it did so poorly, so interception was only made in driblets. But rising to meet the intruders from *Kido Butai* were some 50 fighters, including 19 P-38s from the 9th Fighter Squadron and four from the 80th; and 16 Warhawks from the 7th and 12 from the 8th. The Japanese claimed they destroyed nine enemy aircraft.[89]

Next up were 27 Zeros under Lieutenant Notomi escorting 14 Aichi D3A dive bombers, all from the *Zuikaku*, with one Aichi aborting because of engine issues.[90] This was reported as "45 enemy dive bombers and fighters" in Allied circles. The fighter reception cost the Japanese two Zeros and three Vals. Finally came 21 fighters from the *Hiyo* under Lieutenant Okajima and nine from the *Junyo* under Lieutenant Okajima Koji, escorting eight *Hiyo* dive bombers commanded by Lieutenant Ikeda to Oro Bay. The *Junyo's* fighters managed to miss the fighting altogether for reasons that remain vague. One D3A was lost.[91]

These three waves of attack supposedly sank three transports and a destroyer. In actuality, they had sunk all of one 2,000-ton American cargo ship with two bomb hits. A second cargo ship was damaged enough that it had to be beached, while an Australian minesweeper was damaged as well.[92] General Kenney reported no Allied aircraft shot down but one Lightning crash landed at Dobudura.[93]

Kenney was "puzzled" by the Japanese attack on Oro Bay.[94] The nearby Dobodura airfield had more than 100 aircraft, but the Japanese neither hit it nor were scared off by it. Nor had the Japanese hit Milne Bay, on Papua's east coast, which was a far more lucrative target for attacking shipping. Kenney moved more fighters to Dobodura and Milne Bay and ordered seven B-17s from the 64th Squadron, six from the 65th, and one from the 403rd to conduct a moonlight air attack on Vunakanau, Lakunai, and Rapopo. The mission got off to a horrible start when Major McCullar's Fortress caught fire during takeoff. McCullar got to about 200 feet when his plane stalled, then banked left, and slammed into the ground nose first, after which the B-17 exploded, killing McCullar, a popular officer and early proponent of low-level attacks, and his crew. The cause of the crash was never conclusively determined, but the next morning a dead wallaby was found at the end of the runway. Not so much roadkill as runwaykill; the speculation was that McCullar had either hit the wallaby as it tried to cross the runway or he instinctively slammed on his brakes, which caused a fire in his hydraulics.[95] The crash badly delayed the mission and forced the B-17s to bomb Rabaul just after dawn on April 12, their first daylight raid on Rabaul since General Walker's death on January 5. But it also compelled hit-and-run tactics by the B-17s, who got out with no casualties but inflicted little damage on the air bases.[96]

They returned to Port Moresby just in time to experience the second day of *I-Go* air attacks on New Guinea, this time directed at the airfields around Port Moresby in what the Japanese called "Attack Y."[97] And it was a big one, the biggest one yet in the Southwest Pacific Area. It was the 106th Japanese air attack on Port Moresby, making it the Pacific version of the London Blitz.

In this attack the Mitsubishi G4Ms made their first appearance in *I-Go*, having been personally seen off by Admiral Yamamoto at Vunakanau. It would be the largest air attack on Port Moresby ever: 174 aircraft.[98] Lieutenant Commander Suzuki Masaichi, air officer of the 751 Air Group, led 17 G4Ms out of Kavieng. His escort was ludicrously large: 23 Zeros from the *Zuikaku* provided top cover, while just beneath them were 15 from the *Junyo* and 17 from the *Hiyo*; low cover came from 14 from the *Zuiho*; and 18 from the 253 Air Group provided close escort.[99] Behind them were 27 G4Ms of the 705 Air Group led by Lieutenant Commander Nakamura Tomomu, one of the executioners of the USS *Chicago*, escorted by a not quite as ridiculous 24 Zeros from the 204 Air Group and 20 from the 582. The overall strike was led by Commander Suzumoto Masahito of the 751, riding as "observer" in Suzuki's G4M.[100]

Radar warned Port Moresby of an incoming wave of Japanese aircraft. Almost all of Port Moresby's fighters had staged to Dobodura on the north side of the Owen Stanleys to intercept just such an attack. The Japanese appeared to be headed for Milne Bay, so the fighters were directed to make their stand near Goodenough Island.[101] According to General Kenney, however, the Japanese strike disappeared from radar, only to reappear over the Owen Stanleys headed for Port Moresby. He had guessed wrong and sent his swarm of defending fighters to the wrong place, where they were absolutely useless in defending Port Moresby. Those fighters were ordered to head toward Lae, where hopefully the Japanese would be refueling after this attack. In the meantime, the 5th Fighter Command was scrambling to scramble any fighters it had left to scramble. Kenney said all that was left to defend Port Moresby were eight Lightnings and 12 Airacobras. There seem to have been others, however, that showed up in driblets. Six Warhawks of the 8th Fighter Squadron, then two dozen Lightnings of the 9th, then three from the 80th, of which one had to abort because of engine trouble, only to be shot up by a Zero and have to make an emergency landing. The remaining two, led by Lieutenant Donald McGee, took a swipe at the Bettys, possibly shooting down one. Next up were six more Lightnings, these of the 39th, but one had to abort. These Lightnings, too, took a swipe at the incoming strike near the Owen Stanleys, but were unsuccessful. They were joined by 16 Airacobras of the 40th and 18 of the 41st. They were scrambled, but against 131 Japanese Zeros, they were outnumbered roughly 2 to 1.[102]

Nevertheless, the remaining P-38s quickly climbed to high altitude, roughly 18,000 to 20,000 feet, to engage the bombers when they arrived at 10:25am. Charging in line abreast almost like an old cavalry formation, the Lightnings took on the Bettys head on and quickly shot down three, passing through the formation. On orders from the 705 Air Group's Lieutenant Commander Nakamura, the G4Ms broke formation, released their bombs from high altitude, and turned away. The Lightnings then took on the second line of Bettys from the 751 Air Group, shooting down two before they, too, released their bombs. Airacobras mixed it up with the Zeros, allowing the 40th's Airacobras to swarm the G4M of the 751's Flight Petty Officer 2nd Class Minakoshi Koichi and bring it down.[103]

On the way back to Rabaul, however, an estimated 44 of the fighters General Kenney had sent to the wrong place, though low on fuel, joined and took one crack at the retreating Japanese. Lieutenant Richard Smith of the 39th kept slashing at the G4M of Flight Chief Petty Officer Nagamatsu Hiroshi, forcing it down into the side of Mount Albert Edward at 9,500 feet. They were joined by the Airacobras hacking away at the Bettys. Four Warhawks of the 8th Fighter Squadron found three straggling Bettys, believed to be those flown by Lieutenant Shimada Takuji and Flight Petty Officers 2nd Class Shirai Toshio and Iwasaki Shunji, over the water. None of the three returned to base. Though not necessarily too little, it was too late. For the day, the Japanese lost six G4Ms, all from the 751 Air Group, and two Zeros from the 253.[104]

On the ground, the Japanese drew their pound of flesh, in some cases literally, though it was not exactly the destruction of Cavite Navy Base, in part because the bombers divided their strength among the outlying airfields. Bombs hit runways at Ward ("5-Mile"), Berry

("12-Mile"), and Schwimmer ("14-Mile") airfields. Ward was also the site of a fuel dump that took a bomb hit, starting a nasty fire that killed a dozen men. One Beaufighter and three Mitchells were destroyed on the ground; 15 other aircraft were damaged. Additionally, two Airacobras had been shot down by the Japanese, though one pilot was able to return to Port Moresby safely, while two more Airacobras and two Lightnings had to be written off due to battle damage.[105]

Filling in for the regular fighter commander, General Ennis Whitehead, General Kenney had guessed wrong – twice – about this attack. He had guessed the Japanese were going to hit Milne Bay when they were actually going for Port Moresby, then he guessed they'd be returning to Lae when they were returning to Rabaul instead. Kenney knew he had had a bad day. "I got badly fooled and was lucky to get out of it as well as I did," he wrote. "What really burned me up was that, if I had guessed right, I would have had nearly a hundred fighters take on that Jap show and we would have made a killing worth writing home about."[106] But General Kenney apparently figured that if he kept guessing the Japanese would attack Milne Bay, he'd get it right. Eventually. "I gambled that the following day (April 13) they would hit Milne Bay with another big show if the weather was right."[107] Kenney gambled wrong. Again.

Back in Rabaul, Admiral Yamamoto was planning to spend April 13 planning the next attack, which would indeed be on Milne Bay – on April 14 – and mingling with his aviators. He could see the effect he had on their morale.

The mood in Rabaul was jubilant. The battle damage assessments performed after the April 12 attack indicated 28 enemy aircraft destroyed, with seven more damaged. Large fires were observed at 11 locations among the Port Moresby airfields, including three large explosions (one of which was the fuel dump at Ward), and one 7,000-ton transport was sunk in the harbor.[108] Their claims were exaggerated, of course, as the Japanese Naval Air Force's always were. For one thing, not only was no ship of any kind sunk in the harbor, no ship of any kind had even been attacked.

Admiral Yamamoto visited Admiral Ugaki in the hospital with his dengue fever the evening of April 12 to fill him in on how *I-Go* was going, which made his chief of staff very happy.[109] In fact, everyone seemed to be happy in Rabaul these days. Base Air Force, *Kido Butai*, the Imperial Army troops, 8th Base Force, even Tavurvur and Vulcan. Yamamoto was feeling better. Admiral Kusaka was feeling better. The happiness spread throughout the base complex, throughout the ranks. "The carrier-based pilots are all high-spirited," wrote Flight Petty Officer Igarashi Hisashi of the 705 Air Group on April 13. "They are a good stimulus to our land-based attack units as we tend to be in low spirits."[110]

So well were things going that Admiral Yamamoto decided to visit more of his aviators closer to the front, at the Shortlands complex on the southern tip of Bougainville, where the air crews had not had a chance to meet him yet. On April 13, the commander in chief announced his intention to visit the complex on the coming Sunday, April 18. Admiral Yamamoto detailed what he wanted to his longtime aide, friend, and shogi partner Commander Watanabe. That was all the commander needed. Watanabe knew his superior very well and was aware of his quirks, including his punctuality and his attention to detail. Watanabe checked distances, flight times, even tides. He planned out travel times, lunch, meetings, visits to the hospitals, bathroom breaks, smoke breaks, everything to the minute.

Only after all that was complete did Commander Watanabe draft the order:

To: Commander, 1st Base Flotilla
    Commander, 11th Air Flotilla
    Commander, 26th Air Flotilla
    Commander, 958th Air Detachment
    Chief, Ballalae Defense Unit
    From: C-in-C, 8th Fleet, South Eastern Area Fleet
    Information: C-in-C, Combined Fleet
    C-in-C, Combined Fleet, will inspect RXZ, RXE, and RXP on "Setsua" as follows:
    1. At 0600 leaves RR by "Chuko," a land based medium bomber (6 fighters escorting)
    At 0800 arrives at RXZ
    At 0840 arrives at RXE by subchaser (commander, 1st Base Force, will arrange one chase in advance)
    At 0945 leaves RXE by same subchaser
    At 1030 arrives at RXZ (at RXZ a "daihatsu" will be on hand and at RXE a "motor launch" for traffic)
    At 1100 leaves RXZ by "Chuko"
    At 1110 arrives at RXP
    Luncheon at HQ, 1st Base Force (attended by commandant, 26th Air Squadron, and senior staff officers)
    At 1400 leaves RXP by "Chuko"
    At 1540 arrives at RR
    2. Outline of plan after the verbal report on their present conditions briefly by each unit, unit members will be inspected (1st BF hospital will be visited).
    3. The commanding officer of each unit alone shall wear the naval landing party uniform with medal ribbons.
    4. In case of bad weather it will be postponed for one day.[111]

Watanabe took the document to 8th Fleet headquarters in Rabaul and requested that the orders be hand-delivered to the various commanders by courier. The communications staff told him it would be sent by radio instead. Watanabe was shocked and outraged, leaving the communications personnel dumbfounded by his reaction. They were going to send it in code, so what was the problem? Watanabe believed it did not matter if the code was unbreakable. Why take the chance that the enemy will be able to piece enough of it together to read it? "This code only went into effect on April first and cannot be broken," the communications staff assured him. Certainly not in that period of time.[112] Supposedly, even Admiral Ugaki rhetorically asked, "How could they possibly break the Japanese codes?"[113] Besides, it's not like Westerners can really understand Japanese.[114]

So, just before 6:00am on April 13, the itinerary for the visit to the front lines by the commander in chief of the Combined Fleet was radioed to all the appropriate commands. But at the insistence of a frustrated Commander Watanabe, the message was sent out in the Imperial Navy's most secure code, the D Code.

That's what the Imperial Japanese Navy called this encryption. Elsewhere, it was known by a very different name:

JN-25.[115]

CHAPTER 4
MAGIC IN THE AIR

General Kenney's dreams, so to speak, finally came true on April 14: Base Air Force finally attacked Milne Bay.

It was a planned two-pronged attack, designated Attack Y-1 and Attack Y-2. Lieutenant Commander Miyauchi Shichiso, who had the attacks on the *Prince of Wales* and *Repulse* on his resume, had just become the air officer of the 705 Air Group. Miyauchi knew *Rikko*; suave was his style. He would lead 26 G4Ms of the 705 and 17 of the 751 Air Groups in the Y-1 attack, which was to consist of high-altitude bombing. His escorts would be 21 Zeros from the 204 Air Group, 17 from the 253, and 20 from the 582 under Lieutenant Noguchi Yoshihito, though two had to abort.[1] The other attack, Y-2, would showcase the aviators of *Kido Butai* bombing from low altitudes: 23 D3A carrier bombers (12 from the *Junyo* led by Lieutenant Tsuda, but one had to abort; and 12 from the *Hiyo* under Captain Ikeuchi Toshimi) escorted by 75 Zeros (17 from the *Junyo* commanded by Lieutenant Fujimaki Hisa'aki, 20 from the *Hiyo* under division officer Lieutenant Fujita Iyozo, 23 from the *Zuikaku*, and 15 from the *Zuiho*). Their bombing objectives this day were split between the Milne Bay airfield, officially named Gurney Field and formerly called Fall River, and the ships in the harbor.[2]

The Milne Bay attack started off badly. Four G4Ms of the 751 Air Group had to turn back for various reasons. Two more collided in mid-air; one fell into the sea, killing its seven crew, while the other staggered back to Vunakanau and crash landed.[3] Then the strike flew over Kakakope, where the PT boat tender USS *Hilo* was anchored.[4] She reported the Bettys passing at 12:30pm flying at over 20,000 feet.[5] So much for surprise.

The Japanese caught a break with the weather, however; the Dobodura air base was fogged in, keeping 60 of General Kenney's fighters on the ground. Nevertheless, 17 Royal Australian Air Force P-40s from No. 75 Squadron under Squadron Leader Wilfred Arthur and another 19 from No. 77 Squadron led by Squadron Leader Richard Cresswell rose to meet the Japanese intruders. Cresswell and his pilots had been getting bored and wanted to get in on the action. Arthur was known for his energy and courage. However,

No. 75 Squadron had already scrambled for a false alarm, and thus was dangerously low on fuel.[6]

With fuel a problem and flying at high altitude dangerously limiting to the Kittyhawks' ability to maneuver, Squadron Leaders Cresswell and Arthur knew they would get only one go at the Bettys, so they formed their P-40s up line abreast and charged in like cavalry on the Japanese left, guns blazing. The typhoon of hot lead shredded two Bettys. One, flown by Flight Petty Officer 2nd Class Sagara Masao and commanded by Flight Chief Petty Officer Koike Yoshio, jettisoned its bombs and tried to stagger home, but was finished off by antiaircraft fire. The pilot of the second, Flight Chief Petty Officer O'Oe Yoshimi, was killed, but his co-pilot, Flight Chief Petty Officer Sagakawa Ryo, though wounded, managed to seize the controls and fly the G4M to a relatively gentle ditching off Fergusson Island.[7]

Completing their pass, the Australian aviators proceeded to run into the escorting Zeros from the *Zuikaku* and the 582 Air Group. But the result was only the briefest of tussles because the Kittyhawks were beyond dangerously low on fuel. They saw the Vals approaching below them and dove back in to try to disrupt their attacks in the second briefest of tussles before heading back to Gurney Field as best they could.[8]

Sergeant Lloyd Melrose of No. 77 Squadron was last seen under attack by two Zeros and headed out to sea. Sergeants Archibald Hall and J.R. White of No. 75 Squadron tried to land on the same runway at Gurney at the same time from opposite directions. It did not turn out well, but both pilots and planes eventually returned to service. Pilot Officer William Ward of No. 75 Squadron actually ran out of gas while in the landing circuit for Carney. Having priority because of his fuel – or lack of same – situation, Ward had to cut off a damaged P-38 to land, and in so doing overshot the end of the runway and crashed. Ward was fine but the Kittyhawk was a writeoff.[9]

Joining the Australians – more properly attempting to join the Australians – were eight P-38s led by Lieutenant William D. Sells from the US 9th Fighter Squadron, 49th Fighter Group. The P-38s took off, then were vectored by fighter control to meet the Japanese intruders near Goodenough Island. Three of the P-38s had to abort because of engine issues, the remainder found nothing near Goodenough. Sells and his wingmen descended to look for the enemy in the clouds at medium altitude, leaving only Lieutenants Richard Bong and Carl Planck.[10] Naturally, it was Bong and Planck who were in the way when the Bettys showed up. Naturally, it was this instant when one of Planck's engines chose to act up. So Bong had to face the remaining 35 Bettys and their close escort of 37 Zeros from the *Junyo* and *Hiyo* all by himself.[11]

No problem. At 12:35pm, Lieutenant Bong made one pass at the first wave of Bettys, those from the 751 Air Group, damaging two, one of which was written off after it force landed at Gasmata. Bong was chased off by six Zeros. The Zeros were flying close escort, however, and stuck with their charges. This discipline allowed Bong to recover and make one more pass, this at the 705 Air Group. He left one Betty's left engine smoking before two Zeros chased him off again, putting a 20mm shell in his elevator for his trouble. The G4M Bong hit was flown by Flight Petty Officer 1st Class Watanabe Tsuneo and commanded by Lieutenant Matsuoka Tatsu. The damaged land attack plane spun out of control and crashed into the sea some 20 miles southeast of the airfield, leaving no survivors. It was Bong's 10th aerial victory claim.[12]

In the interim, Lieutenant Sells and his wingmen had found Zeros from the *Junyo* and *Hiyo*. They broke off quickly to try to join the Kittyhawks in efforts to stop the Vals, but Sells' P-38 was shot up by Zeros, leaving his starboard engine damaged. Sells headed back to Carney with priority for landing due to his damage, but the starboard engine died, allowing him to be cut off by the P-40 of Pilot Officer Ward. Wells held up as long as he could, but when he touched down he also overshot the end of the runway and crashed in a ball of fire that killed Wells.[13]

Having fought through the energetic but badly outnumbered defenders to get to their targets, the land attack planes of the 751 and 705 Air Groups went on to do a thoroughly mediocre job of actually hitting their targets. Their bombs generally ran from a containment area of Gurney Field, where they did little damage, to the harbor, where their splashes momentarily hid the vessels therein and may have hit the empty 3,500-ton British steamer *Gorgon*, but otherwise seem to have done little harm.[14] Except for Lieutenant Commander Miyauchi, these were not the same aviators who had sunk the *Prince of Wales* and *Repulse* in the opening days of the Pacific War.

Kido Butai's D3A carrier bombers, though only armed with two 60kg bombs apiece, seem to have been a bit more productive than the land attack planes, but not by much. The carrier bombers are generally credited with hitting the *Gorgon* in the engine room, killing four Australian merchant sailors and almost all of her Javanese, Chinese, and Indian crew and starting a fire. The *Gorgon* sank in shallow water, which probably helped extinguish the fire, but was later refloated and returned to service. The Dutch merchant ships *Van Heemskerk* and *Balikpapan* and their escorting corvette HMAS *Kapunda* had just arrived at Milne Bay. The *Van Heemskerk* had unloaded her troops but not her cargo, which included ammunition and fuel. Four Vals made masthead attacks on her – imitation is the sincerest form of flattery – and hit her with multiple 60kg bombs, including one that exploded in the hold in a massive fireball. Now thoroughly ablaze, the *Van Heemskerk* was beached in a desperate effort to save the cargo, but the fires were too much. The corvette HMAS *Wagga* scuttled the wreck. For her part, the *Wagga* was slightly damaged by strafing, as was the *Kapunda*, in the only instances of Zeros strafing during *I-Go*. The Dutch steamer *Van Outhorn* was slightly damaged by two near misses from the Vals.[15]

That was pretty much it for the damage. Japanese combat losses for this attack were three land attack planes, three carrier bombers; and the Zero of the *Zuikaku*'s Warrant Officer Mitsumoto Jiro. For this, they reported sinking five transports and damaging eight or nine, while destroying 44 Allied aircraft. Actual Allied aircraft losses were one P-40 and one P-38. Four other P-40s were, in the words of General Kenney, "pretty badly shot up."[16] The actual results were not commensurate with the resources devoted to the attack. Nevertheless, Admiral Yamamoto received a congratulatory message from the Emperor, relayed through Imperial General Headquarters. "Please convey my satisfaction to the Commander in Chief, Combined Fleet," the message read, "and tell him to enlarge the war result more than ever."[17]

And with that, *I-Go* essentially came to a close. More attacks planned for April 16 were canceled when reconnaissance planes found no worthy targets. Admiral Yamamoto then declared *I-Go* a success and sent his precious carrier aviators back to *Kido Butai*.

That was in public. In private, Admiral Yamamoto was angered by the losses suffered by the Japanese Naval Air Force in what he considered to be an unnecessary and, indeed, stupid exercise. By Admiral Ugaki's count, of the 206 Zeros that had taken part in *I-Go*, 28 had been lost, or 12 percent. Of the 83 Mitsubishi G4M Type 1 land attack planes committed to the operation, 15 had been lost, a loss of 18 percent. By far the worst were the losses among the Aichi D3A Type 99 carrier bombers: of the 81 committed to *I-Go*, 21 had been lost, for losses of 26 percent.[18] A later report says the losses were eight land attack planes, 12 carrier bombers, and 17 Zeros; with another five land attack planes and two Zeros seriously damaged.[19] And what had they gained in exchange for these losses? They believed they had destroyed 134 Allied planes and damaged another 56. They had also sunk one cruiser, two destroyers, and 19–25 transports, with at least another 10–11 transports damaged.[20]

How much Admiral Yamamoto actually believed these estimates of damage inflicted on the enemy is unclear, but the air losses were a major topic of conversation during a study conference hosted that Saturday, April 17, by Admiral Ugaki, finally released from the hospital. Most of the top commanders were present, including Admiral Yamamoto, who preferred to listen to the discussions and said very little. The conference was basically a debriefing concerning *I-Go* and determining where to go from there. It does not appear to have been a happy meeting. The chief topic seems to have been the serious losses they suffered in *I-Go*, which was not commensurate with even the inflated damage reported by their aircrews. Lieutenant Commander Okumiya was present for the meeting and gave his own description:

> Our officers expressed great concern over the severe bomber losses we had experienced at the hands of the enemy fighter pilots, for only four missions had cost us fifty planes. No other action could have demonstrated so effectively the fact that the Americans were now matching and exceeding the performance of our own aircraft. The meeting concluded in a pessimistic air; we could anticipate only expanding enemy air strength and an ever-increasing drain of our own air power.[21]

A subset of that discussion was determining why Japanese aircraft caught fire so easily. It seemed that a Japanese Zero would explode even if you just looked at it wrong.

This was the fruit of the Japanese design philosophy that elevated combat performance above everything else, including the safety of the pilot. Almost exactly the opposite of the design philosophy in the West. As historian Bruce Gamble cheekily put it, "The Japanese were highly reluctant to admit that hundreds of aviators had been burnt to a crisp because the aircraft engineers scorned the weight penalty of protected fuel tanks."

Gamble further explained how it was treated:

[T]he Japanese typically accounted for their losses by applying reverse psychology: whenever one of their aircraft burst into flames or was otherwise shot down during combat, it wasn't entirely because the enemy had scored fatal hits; instead, the plane had merely been damaged, and its pilot decided to blow himself up (along with his crew, if applicable) as a symbolic act of suicide. The Japanese called this *jibaku*, which literally means to self-explode.[22]

This was bizarre for multiple reasons, not the least of which was that no Japanese aircraft is known to have included on its instrument panel a button for "self-explode." That some of the most educated people in the Japanese Empire – not just the aircrews themselves but even the top brass – believed this obvious garbage amounts to putting the collective head in the sand.

Yet it was Admiral Yamamoto's trip to the Shortlands that hung over the conference like another katana of Damocles. Everybody was distracted, concerned about the commander in chief going so close to the front.[23] Except for Admiral Ugaki. For a while he had wanted to visit the Shortlands, what with its bright sun, its palm trees, its white beaches, its blue waters, its air attacks, its war crimes…

There was heated debate over how many fighters should escort the commander in chief's aircraft. A compromise was reached in which it was decided that six Zeros from the 204 Air Group would accompany Admiral Yamamoto and his staff. Admiral Ozawa thought so few fighters protecting the commander in chief was stupid and offered to provide as many aircraft from *Kido Butai* as Yamamoto wanted. When he couldn't convince Yamamoto to accept that offer, Ozawa tried to go to Admiral Ugaki, telling senior staff officer Captain Kuroshima Kametgo, "If he insists on going, six fighters are nothing like enough. Tell the chief of staff that he can have as many of my planes as he likes." Kuroshima tried to, but Admiral Ugaki had been down with dengue fever since about April 13, when the itinerary was sent out, and upon his return had promptly held the senior officer conference. Kuroshima never got a chance to give him the message.[24]

Then it was the turn of General Inamura, probably Yamamoto's closest – maybe only – friend in the Imperial Army. Back on February 10, the general said, he had been flying to Buin when, about ten minutes before landing, he was ambushed by 30 enemy fighters, supposedly P-38 Lightnings. Inamura only escaped because his pilot was able to hide in a cloud. Admiral Yamamoto congratulated him on his narrow escape and praised the skill of Inamura's pilot, but he shrugged off the warning. The Japanese were strong in the central and northern Solomons, holding every major island north of Guadalcanal. All they had to do was look up to see approaching enemy planes. They'd send back the warning in plenty of time for the Buin and Ballale bases to put up a cloud of Zeros. Plus, while the occasional enemy bomber had come this far north, Allied fighters had not. So far.[25]

Joining in the warnings was Admiral Jojima of the R-Area Air Force. When he received Commander Watanabe's order with the itinerary the evening of April 13, he was furious. "What a damn fool thing to do, to send such a long and detailed message about the activities of the C-in-C so near the front! This kind of thing must stop," he told his staff. Jojima flew to Rabaul on April 17 to warn Yamamoto against the trip. Jojima, insisting that he knew the conditions at the front better than anyone else, argued, "Please, sir, this is dangerous." Do not go, he begged.[26] "This is no cause for concern," Yamamoto replied "I have to go. I've let them know, and they'll have got things ready for me. I'll leave tomorrow morning and be back by dusk." He added cheerily, "You must have dinner with me tomorrow night."[27] It was no use.

One small change was made to the commander in chief's itinerary, though it had little to do with security. The original travel plan had called for Admiral Yamamoto to fly first to the island of Ballale, then ride a subchaser to various island bases, ending at Buin. Now, instead of landing at Ballale, he would land at Buin.[28] The two airfields were so close together that it made no difference in the timeline, only in Yamamoto's comfort.

Sunday morning, April 18, arrived. Admiral Yamamoto showed up at Lakunai airfield in khakis. This was by design. Admiral Ugaki was trying to arrange a photo op for the commander in chief in khakis, but the photographer never showed. Would have to report him to the Kempeitai. Ugaki thought Yamamoto looked "a bit strange" in khakis. But as for himself, "I looked gallant."[29] There was a security element to the khakis, however Unlike the commander in chief's dress whites, khakis would not stand out and be noticed by an enemy sniper. Can never be too careful, you know. Except two of the staff, the fleet surgeon and the paymaster, showed up in white dress uniforms anyway. Evidently, they did not get the message. There was no way for them to change clothes now. But at least if there were any snipers about, maybe the snipers would target the surgeon or the paymaster instead of the commander in chief.[30]

The aircraft in which they would be riding were two brand-new Mitsubishi G4M Type 1 land attack planes from the 705 Air Group that had come over to Lakunai from their normal base at Vunakanau, where during the night they had been run through the plane wash and then detailed. Flight Warrant Officer Katani Takeo would fly the G4M numbered 323, carrying Admiral Yamamoto, his adjutant, the fleet surgeon, and one staff officer. Flight Petty Officer 1st Class Hayashi Hiroshi would be flying the second G4M numbered 326, carrying Admiral Ugaki, the fleet paymaster, the weather officer, and two staff officers. Each bomber carried an additional crew of six.[31] For security reasons, the air crews were not told of their mission until after they had turned in for the night, and then they were given detailed instructions verbally by Captain Konishi Yukie, commander of the 705 Air Group. It left Hayashi concerned – he had never landed at the Buin airfield.[32]

Escorting the commander in chief and his chief of staff was entrusted to six of the best fighter pilots. In Rabaul, at least. The fighters, all from the 204 Air Group, would operate in two groups of three. The first flight would be led by Lieutenant (jg) Morizaki Takeshi, who would command the entire escort. Morizaki's wingmen would be Flight Petty Officer 1st Class Tsujinoue Toyomitsu and Assistant Flight Petty Officer Sugita Shoichi. The second group would be led by Chief Petty Officer Hidaka Yoshimi, with Petty Officer 2nd Class Okazaki Yasuji and Assistant Flight Petty Officer Yanagiya Kenji on his wings. All the pilots were veterans. In fact, Sugita was considered one of the Imperial Navy's best pilots; a "Shoot-Down King," he was called. For his part, Yanagiya was veteran enough to wonder why more fighters had not been assigned to escort the admiral.[33]

Admiral Yamamoto was greeted at Lakunai by senior officers, including the 8th Fleet's Admiral Samejima. In celebration of the baron's appointment to head the 8th Fleet, the commander in chief handed Samejima a gift: two scrolls of Meiji poetry he had copied. Then the architect of the attack on Pearl Harbor climbed aboard his G4M with his staff. Admiral Ugaki did the same with his *Rikko*, suave in his khakis. The policy of not allowing the senior staff of the Combined Fleet to travel together in the same aircraft was in effect today. Because of the extra people on board, each of the G4Ms was in danger of being overweight. The pilots solved that problem by leaving behind extra drums of ammunition for the aircraft's defensive machine guns and 20mm cannon in the tail. They were not likely to need that extra ammunition.[34] And with that, Admiral Yamamoto's Type 1 roared down the runway of Lakunai into the air, followed by the Type 1 of Admiral Ugaki, and finally the six Zeros. At 6:00am Japan Standard Time, the flight formed up near Tavurvur, which Ugaki watched from his seat, and headed southeast.

Zero pilot Yanagiya Kenji checked the weather ahead. It was a nicer day than usual, with only intermittent clouds. He saw thunderstorms in the distance, but nothing that should interfere with this flight. Visibility was good, allowing him to see enemy aircraft long before they became a threat. The visibility was essential, because, once again, the Zeros lacked radios. If an attack developed, they would have to spot it, think quickly, and respond quickly. An attack would most likely come out of the sun to the east, into which the Zero pilots would be blind. And it would come from higher altitudes. The Americans in particular preferred to dive on their targets, making one pass and then running away. "Boom and zoom," they called it. They didn't want to dogfight Zeros.[35]

The flight reached the west side of Bougainville, keeping the mountains on the left so no aerial ambushes could come from that direction, though it didn't seem like any ambushes could come from any direction now.[36] They were close to landing. Admiral Ugaki was awakened by a crew member who handed him a note reading: "Our time of arrival at [Buin] is 0745 hours [8:45 local time]." The chief of staff looked at his watch. It was 7:30 Japan Standard Time. They'd be landing in 15 minutes.[37] They were right on time. As usual.

Yanagiya Kenji and the other Zero pilots were happy they would be landing in a few minutes. No planes had come out of the sun to attack them. They looked up, from where the Americans always, always, always, attack. Nothing. Buin should be coming into sight any second now …

Hayashi saw a Zero approach Admiral Yamamoto's G4M and "made movements," likely waggling its wings. The lead bomber immediately nosed downward, at maybe a 60-degree angle, and gunned its engine to 240 knots. That was strange. Hayashi tried to follow and stay in formation as he was supposed to, but his own G4M started to vibrate violently. Maybe a bolt or fastener had come loose. Hayashi eased the throttle to stop the bad vibration, and the commander in chief's plane pulled on ahead. Hayashi wondered, "What is going on?"

So did Admiral Ugaki. He asked the crew chief, who answered, "It looks as if we made a mistake, sir. We shouldn't have dived."

Hayashi thought the same thing.

Then he saw glowing red tracers shooting past him.

Flight Petty Officer Tanimoto Hiroaki, on this flight as an observer, slapped Hayashi on the shoulder shouting, "Enemy aircraft!"[38]

Hayashi looked up through the glass cockpit canopy. A fighter was right above him, almost sitting on top of him. Hayashi recognized it. It was impossible not to.

It was not a Zero.

It had the distinctive twin-fuselage silhouette of a Lockheed P-38 Lightning.[39]

The fighter pilot only a few feet over Hayashi's head was unaware that he had almost slammed into the top of the Betty, so focused was he on getting to that first bomber. He was tired, he was hot, he was scared, convinced that a Zero behind him was about to shoot a 20mm shell up his butt. But his only thought was to get that bomber. Even if he had to ram it.

It had already been a long day for this pilot, all these pilots flying the Lightnings. Though he was not aware of all the background, it had started at 5:55pm on April 13 (one day behind Rabaul, where it was April 14) when the naval radio station at Wahiawa, Hawaii, intercepted a coded Imperial Japanese Navy radio message. Though specifics of the message still needed deciphering, there were a large number of recipients. That was strange. It must be important. The message was forwarded to the Fleet Radio Unit, Pacific at Pearl Harbor.[40] The unit monitored Japanese radio transmissions and was the beating heart of *Magic*. The cryptanalysts got to work to strip the additives off the code groups. Their job was tougher in the last two weeks because the Japanese had changed their additive tables on April 1. Meanwhile, traffic analysts determined the address information and location designations. IBM mechanical card sorting machines ran text against known meanings in the JN-25 code.

The JN-25 code consisted of some 45,000 groups of digits, each representing a word or phrase, each designed to be put into a cypher of 100,000 "additives," also of five digits each.[41] The most recent version they had of the code, though not the most recent version the Japanese were using, was what the cryptanalysts called JN-25E14. Of which they had a code book, courtesy of the wrecked submarine *I-1* and her inept crew.[42]

The cryptanalysts managed to get several words: "On 18 April C-in-C Combined Fleet will [blank, blank] as follows [blank, blank] Ballale [blank, blank, blank]."[43] Then the message was handed to Marine linguist Lieutenant Colonel Alva Bryan "Red" Lasswell. Fluent in Japanese from having lived in Japan, with a history of service in radio intelligence in the Philippines and China before arriving at Pearl Harbor in May 1941, Lasswell immediately saw the words "C-in-C Combined Fleet" and knew the message he had just been handed was hot. But it was a dry heat, at least until he finished translating it. Understanding its importance, Lasswell called for help from cryptanalysts Lieutenant Commander Thomas Dyer and Lieutenant Commander Wesley "Ham" Wright.

They looked at some of those additives ... "RR" means Rabaul ... "RXZ" is Ballale ... "RXP" ... that's Kahili, right? "RXE" ... is that Shortland? ... Lasswell worked overnight translating it until ...

"*We've hit the jackpot!*" Colonel Lasswell yelled excitedly.

He had just translated the itinerary for a visit to the front line by Admiral Yamamoto, the commander in chief of the Japanese Combined Fleet. It had everything: time of departure, time of arrival, destination, activities, even the type of plane and the type of boat in which he would be traveling.[44] All known in advance. This translation was confirmed by General MacArthur's radio unit in Melbourne and Admiral King's radio unit in Washington.

As if to confirm Major Lasswell's translation, a second message, referencing the first, was intercepted. It was dated April 14, 1943, from the 8th Base Force, written in the less-secure JN-20H code. The radio unit had little trouble decoding it. The message discussed "the special visit of Yamamoto" with an order that the Ballale Base Unit should "act as heretofore."[45] Taken together, both messages gave a complete picture of Admiral Yamamoto's itinerary. Commander Watanabe had been right.

Major Lasswell handed the decoded message to Commander Edwin Layton, the Pacific Fleet's intelligence officer. Layton walked into Admiral Nimitz's office at 8:02am on April 14. Entering the inner office, Layton handed the dispatch to Nimitz. "Our old friend Yamamoto ..."[46] Admiral Nimitz took one look at the message and sat up bolt upright. He had to read it closely, carefully. It read: "The Commander in Chief Combined Fleet will inspect Ballale, Shortland, and Buin on April 18. ... 6am depart Rabaul in medium attack plane escorted by six fighters. ... 8am arrive Ballale. ..." The message continued with Admiral Yamamoto's itinerary for the day.

The commander in chief of the Pacific Fleet turned and studied the wall map. Admiral Yamamoto's tour would come within 300 miles of Henderson Field. Within range of American fighters – barely. The commander in chief of the Combined Fleet was (in)famous for his punctuality, so it was assumed he would follow the itinerary to the minute. Admiral Nimitz turned to Commander Layton. "What do you say?" the admiral asked. "Do we try to get him?"

It was not necessarily an easy question, and Admiral Nimitz and Commander Layton would hash out the possibilities. Most of them.

Layton replied:

Assuming that we have planes able to intercept him – it would have to be planes – you should first consider, I suppose, what would be gained by killing him.

He's unique among their people. He's the one Jap who thinks in bold strategic terms – in that way more American than Japanese. The younger officers and enlisted men idolize him. Aside from the Emperor, probably no man in Japan is so important to civilian morale. And if he's shot down, it would demoralize the fighting Navy. You know the Japanese psychology; it would stun the nation.[47]

"The one thing that concerns me," said Nimitz, "is whether they could find a more effective fleet commander." Well, not really. After a short discussion about the senior Japanese admirals, Layton concluded, "Yamamoto is head and shoulders above them all, as you know."

Then Layton paused. "You know, Admiral Nimitz," he added, "it would be just as if they shot you down. There isn't anybody to replace you."

Nimitz smiled at the compliment. "Yes, all right. Anything else?"

"No, sir. I'm sure it's sound doctrine to strike at the heart of the enemy, and I say this is a chance. I believe that's good Clausewitz.[48] Yamamoto is certainly a symbol of their first victories, here and Wake and the Dutch Indies and Burma."

"If we kill him," Nimitz wondered, "Would the Japs take some kind of revenge – put on more strikes?"

"We know they're straining harder every day," Layton answered. "They're scraping the bottom of the barrel for fighter pilots and all air group people. We've got them reacting to our attacks now. I can't see them putting on new offensives."

The commander in chief of the Pacific Fleet stared at the map of the South Pacific, lost in thought. "It wouldn't do our own morale any harm," he sighed. "Think of how it would cheer up Halsey and Mitscher. They took Pearl Harbor as a personal affront, and they've been living for the day they can pay 'em back in spades ..."

To put it mildly. While Admiral Yamamoto was, in the Japanese mind, a hero, a personification of the *Bushido* code of the samurai, in the American mind, at least, Yamamoto was a personification of the enemy, the man who had launched the attack on Pearl Harbor, as treacherous an act as had ever been committed. Admiral Yamamoto had been on the attack since then, with the blood of thousands of Americans, not to mention Australians, British, Dutch, Filipinos, and Indonesians, on his hands. Yamamoto had supposedly revealed his strategy when he said, "I shall not be content merely to capture Guam and the Philippines and occupy Hawaii and San Francisco. I am looking forward to dictating peace to the United States in the White House at Washington." Of course, he had not said that; no one could be that stupid and rise to a high command, unless, maybe, they were in the Imperial Japanese Army. What Yamamoto had said was, "Should hostilities breakout between Japan and the United States … To make victory certain, we would have to march into Washington and dictate the terms of peace in the White House. I wonder if our politicians … are prepared to make the necessary sacrifices."[49] It was not an arrogant threat or promise. It was a warning as to how long and hard the United States would fight, and the narrow, difficult path to a Japanese victory.

Both Layton and Nimitz knew Yamamoto, the former personally, and both respected him highly. They knew, even if the American people did not, that he was not nearly the villain he was made out to be. It was known that Yamamoto had opposed the war and bore little, if any, ill will toward the US. He fought out of a love of his homeland, Japan, not out of any hatred for the US or the West. In that regard, he was one of the few voices of reason, or at least one of the few voices of reason with influence, in senior Japanese government circles. Maybe Yamamoto could even help in ending the war.

Nimitz punted. "It's down in Halsey's bailiwick. If there's a way, he'll find it. All right, we'll try it." Then the admiral caught himself. "Is there a danger we'd compromise the [JN-25] code break with this one, and pay for it later on?"

"We shouldn't leave it to chance," Layton answered. "Why not have all the personnel involved briefed with a cover story? We could say it came from Australian coastwatchers around Rabaul. Everybody in the Pacific thinks they're miracle workers." Miracle workers, not omniscient deities.

Taking a pad, Nimitz wrote out a dispatch for Halsey, repeating Yamamoto's itinerary and suggesting, in order to protect the code break, that the information be attributed to Australian coastwatchers around Rabaul, which was, of course, nonsensical. Nimitz ended the message with, "If forces [in] your command have capability [to] shoot down Yamamoto and staff, you are hereby authorized initiate preliminary planning."

"Let's leave the details to Halsey," Nimitz said. "He'll have four days to get ready. He'll need 'em."

And so Admiral Nimitz did. That is about all that can be said with certainty as to the decision to ambush Admiral Yamamoto. Whether that decision went any higher than Nimitz remains murky. Nimitz is known to have sent a message to Navy Secretary Frank Knox, copied to Admiral King, about the possibilities of intercepting Admiral Yamamoto. There is no hard evidence of a reply from Knox or King, or President Roosevelt. That may be by design, however.

A story, perhaps better termed a scenario, developed over the years in which Deputy Chief of Naval Intelligence Captain Ellis M. Zacharias briefed Knox about the situation. Roosevelt, then on a trip to visit military bases – as Yamamoto was doing – in the south and west, was made aware of it by one of the White House communications personnel, Captain William Mott. Communications traffic went back and forth between Washington and the train on which Roosevelt was traveling, in which Zacharias talked to the Navy Judge Advocate General and a few intelligence personnel trying to figure out a way to convince Knox, who was balking at the decision for reasons unknown. This all supposedly led to a presidential order, signed by Knox, a version of which on blue tissue paper appeared on Guadalcanal on April 17. Historians Roger Pineau, who worked in the radio intelligence unit at Pearl Harbor and was involved in decrypting Yamamoto's itinerary, and John Prados have looked for a copy of the order (the reference to blue tissue paper suggests it was a carbon copy) or any communication of a decision by Roosevelt, Knox, or King communicated to Nimitz and found nothing – no copies of dispatches, communications of any kind, or any notes. As Yamamoto mission historian Burke Davis would later put it, communications between the offices of Secretary Knox and President Roosevelt "were deliberately omitted from the record." That said, White House communications specialist Captain Mott would later comment that, as far as he knew, Roosevelt took no active part in the decision, because "he left such things with the military." The most likely scenario, it would seem, is that after being informed of the possibility of ambushing Yamamoto, Roosevelt and Knox left the decision up to Admiral Nimitz and the officers on the scene. A decision was made on a military matter by a military professional depending on whether it was in the best interests of the United States. These days, that seems … quaint.[50]

Within two hours, Pearl Harbor passed the word to Admiral Halsey's headquarters. Naturally, Admiral Halsey wasn't there; he was meeting General MacArthur in Melbourne. Halsey's deputy, Rear Admiral Theodore Wilkinson, was in Nouméa. "Admiral Nimitz sent his best wishes, told us to go to it, and said he would take the responsibility for the security risk we were running," Wilkinson later recalled. Wilkinson forwarded it to Halsey. The South Pacific Commander ended his response with, "Talleyho x Let's get the bastard."[51]

Admiral Halsey determined the Yamamoto mission would fall under the purview of Admiral Mitscher and his antiseptically named AirSols, and so tossed the ball to him. Mitscher was up to the task. First question was, what American aircraft could handle the distance between Guadalcanal and Ballale and make it back? Not the Wildcats nor even the Corsairs, no. The only fighter that could make it, if it was fitted with drop tanks, was the P-38 Lightning. Which was not Navy or Marines, but Army, "much to the Navy's disappointment."[52] Many of the Navy air people on Guadalcanal had a low opinion of the Army Air Force's fighter pilots, considering them too timid. The P-38 was often derided as a "high altitude foxhole" because they were always given the high-altitude covering duties, and often failed to see things that happened below their altitude, often returning from major air battles without seeing any Zeros or any action at all.[53] Among those holding this opinion had been Marine Major John Condon, the operations officer for AirSols Fighter Command. Except Condon did not hold that opinion any more, seeing the pilots of the 339th and 12th Fighter Squadrons as among the best once they gained experience and confidence in their new Lockheed rigs. Admiral Mitscher agreed.

So Major John Mitchell, commander of the 339th, was chosen to lead this mission. He was the Army Air Force's leading ace on Guadalcanal, had extensive experience in the Solomons and knew them well, and was thorough in his preparation. Admiral Mitscher also chose four particularly aggressive pilots for what he called a "killer flight," who had the job of actually shooting down Admiral Yamamoto. They were Captain Thomas G. Lanphier, Jr., and Lieutenants Rex T. Barber, Jim McLanahan, and Joe Moore. The balance of the Lightnings would serve as their protection, to keep Zeros off their backs, because surely the Japanese were not going to escort Yamamoto Isoroku with a mere six Zeros. Presumably they'd have every fighter in Base Air Force and maybe every *Kido Butai* to guard him.

The afternoon of that Saturday, April 17, Lieutenant Colonel Henry Vicellio, newly promoted head of the 347th Fighter Group, popped his head into the 339th's headquarters tent, where Major Mitchell was catching a catnap. "Mitch, they want you over at the 'Opium Den' at Henderson," Vicellio said. The "Opium Den" was the pilots' nickname for the AirSols Fighter Command dugout and tent at Henderson Field, on account of the thick cloud of choking cigarette smoke inside the tent. "They've got something for you."[54]

Mitchell got into a Jeep with Vicellio, who told the pilots lounging around to skip the alcohol that night because they had a big mission tomorrow. Vicellio then picked up Captain Lou Kittel, commander of the 12th Fighter Squadron, who shared the 18 Lightnings on Guadalcanal with the 339th, flying them on alternating days. On the way to the tent, they saw Captain Lanphier. Vicellio asked him to come along, and the foursome continued to the Opium Den. When Major Mitchell, Captain Kittel, and Captain Lanphier walked into the tent, they quickly found themselves, if not like fish out of water, then landlubbers in a boat. The tent was filled with maybe 30 people, almost all US Navy and Marine, and all higher ranked – much higher ranked – than they were.

Major Condon walked over to them, a sheet of paper in his hand. His trembling hand, they noticed. What was going on here?

Condon gave the sheet to Major Mitchell. It was marked "top secret."[55] It must be important. It was:

> […] a radio message from Admiral Halsey. The message said that Admiral Yamamoto, commander in chief of the Combined Japanese fleet, was going to make a trip from Rabaul to one of their bases at the southern tip of Bougainville, a trip of 315 miles. It gave the exact time he was going to land at Ballale, a small island just off the southern tip of Bougainville, on the morning of the next day. He was going to visit his men there and travel to Shortland Island, a nearby troop base, by submarine chaser before returning to Rabaul. He would be flying in a medium bomber, probably a Betty, and be escorted by six Zeros. Known for his punctuality, there was no doubt that Yamamoto would be on time. Capt. William Morrison, an army officer, had lived in Japan and assured us that the admiral was widely known for holding to a precise schedule once it was set.[56]

Though Condon is not clear on this point, the message itself did not mention Yamamoto by name.[57] Someone at the meeting said it was Yamamoto. There was a slightly embarrassing moment when the name did not register with Major Mitchell. "Who's Yamamoto?" Captain Lanphier whispered, "Pearl Harbor."[58] Oh. That Yamamoto.

"We're going to get this bird," the Navy planners told Mitchell and Lanphier. "We mean for you to nail him if you have to ram him in the air. But he'll be taking off more than 635 miles away from here, and only good long-range flying will intercept him. Major Mitchell, that means Lightnings."[59] That seemed to be the end of the Army Air Force pilots' contribution to the meeting. The planners had talked about "ram[ming] him in the air" but they actually weren't so sure about that. The Navy and Marine fliers argued back and forth about how to get the Combined Fleet chief. Do they intercept Yamamoto's plane in the air? Do they bomb and strafe him on the submarine chaser? No one thought to ask the pilot who was going to be actually flying the mission. But he was only the leading ace on Guadalcanal. What did he know?

So the Navy and Marine people decided to bomb and strafe Yamamoto in the subchaser. They distributed strip maps that noted the directions for speeds and compass headings. Major Mitchell's patience was wearing thin when the Navy briefer told him that on the final leg of the flight to make the interception, the pilots would encounter a small to moderate wind off the port quarter.

Port quarter? "What the hell does that mean?" snapped Mitchell.[60] He had had enough.

"I don't know one boat from another, and even if we sink the boat, he could jump in the water in a life vest and survive. What if there are several boats? Which one would he be on?" He paused, swiveling his head to look around him at each officer who outranked him. There was fire in his eyes and in his voice. "We're fighter pilots. We should take him in the air."[61]

Mitchell later elaborated:

Being an air force type, I didn't know one boat from another, a subchaser from a sub. When I finally got a chance to put a word in, I told them that and added a second reason for not trying to get him on a boat: Even if we sank the boat, he might survive and take to a raft or swim to shore. Besides that, the Japs had seventy-five fighters only about fifteen miles from where Yamamoto was supposed to land. We would have to be over the target too long trying to get in trail to strafe a boat in the water. If they sent up fighters to escort the admiral, we'd be in a poor position to defend ourselves at such a low altitude and still get any hits on the target, assuming we could identify it in the first place.

The debate went on for a long time. I argued against the navy guys and gave my reasons for trying an air intercept. Lanphier backed me up. There was an obvious stalemate.[62]

It was left to Pete Mitscher. Always calm, cool, collected, seemed almost bored in combat. No ego, always brilliant. And practical. He hadn't said much, didn't say much, but what he did say always mattered. Here he had to play peacemaker, as he often did. They didn't have time for this.

"Since Mitchell's got to do the job," the head of AirSols said quietly, "let's let him do it his way." In other words, everyone shut up.

The admiral turned to Mitchell. "Where do you want to do it?"

"In the air, sir."

"You got it," the admiral said.

The designers of the mission, now called "Y" for the time being, informed Major Mitchell that 310-gallon drop tanks were being flown in from New Guinea to replace the 165-gallon drop tanks the Lightnings normally carried. There would not be enough to equip all the fighters with two of the tanks, but each would have at least one, mounted under one wing opposite the smaller 165-gallon tank under the other wing.

Major Mitchell was asked if there was anything else the Navy could do for him. Asking him for what he needed, which was a rarity at this briefing until Mitscher had intervened. Mitchell did have one request: "Get me a good compass. The fluxgate and the magnetic compasses in the P-38 aren't reliable and can't be trusted because they can't be swung properly. The only time we know if they're anywhere near accurate is when we line up for takeoff because we know the runway heading." Don't worry, Mitchell was told, a good Navy compass, the ones they use on ships, would be installed in his fighter. Mitchell was then given the latest intelligence information on Japanese forces in the Bougainville area: approximately 75 Zeros at Kahili, and a good many, perhaps all of them, could be counted on to escort Admiral Yamamoto in. Then he was given the weather forecast for April 18: clear with haze limiting visibility to a few miles over the water.

That was it. Except it wasn't.

This was going to be an extremely difficult mission, the longest fighter intercept in history. He was expected to find another specific plane. In midair. Without radar. Like hitting a bullet with a bullet. "At that time, I figured the odds at about a thousand to one that we could make a successful intercept at that distance," Mitchell recalled.[63]

Major Condon had given him a strip map with course headings, speed, distance, and time figures. Good job, good effort, but it was not enough. Condon and his people were not fighter pilots and did not know the P-38 Lightning. By Major Mitchell's calculations, Condon's instructions left him about 50 miles short of the intercept point. Mitchell tossed Condon's plan aside.

Major Mitchell went to the 339th Squadron's operations tent, spread out a map of the Solomons on a table, and, with the assistance of Navy intelligence officer Lieutenant Joseph E. McGuigan and Army intelligence officer Captain Morrison, from the briefing – who had lived in Japan – they started working out a new plan from scratch ...

It was 4:30 on Sunday morning when Major Mitchell woke up. Paranoid as anyone would be before a big mission, presentation, test, argument, he checked the flight plan he had developed one more time. Then Mitchell ate a small breakfast. He did not want stomach or bladder issues on this flight. He swallowed an antimalarial tablet and headed to the operations tent.

He assembled his pilots, who had been ordered to wake at 5:00am, eat breakfast, and attend the mission briefing at 6:00am. Even though it was before dawn, the briefing had maybe 100 people there. The rumor was out that something big was up. Everyone wanted to be in on the mission. Every one of the some 40 pilots available.

Major Mitchell pulled aside the curtain to reveal a mission board with the names of the pilots he and Captain Kittel had selected for the mission. The "kill group" was led by Captain Lanphier (70th, but attached to the 339th) with Lieutenant Rex Barber (339th) as his wingman, and Lieutenant Joseph Moore (70th but attached to the 339th) with wingman Lieutenant Jim McLanahan (339th).[64] Just as Admiral Mitscher wanted. Mitchell called them "Four of the best men we had." All four had been due to leave Guadalcanal the next day for a rest period but were held over specifically for this operation.[65] The remaining 14 pilots would provide fighter protection for the kill group and could be asked to replace any member of the kill group who had to drop out. The first flight consisted of Major Mitchell (339th), with wingman Lieutenant Julius Jacobson (339th), leading the strike; and Lieutenant Doug Canning (339th) with wingman Lieutenant Delton Goerke (339th), all from the 347th Fighter Group. From the 19th Fighter Group, Captain Louis Kittel (12th) led the first flight with wingman 2nd Lieutenant Gordon Whittiker (12th); and Lieutenant Roger Ames (12th) with wingman Lieutenant Lawrence Graebner (12th). The second flight had Lieutenant Everett Anglin (12th), with wingman Lieutenant William Smith (12th); while Lieutenant Eldon Stratton (12th) would have as wingman Lieutenant Albert "Huey" Long (12th). There would be a reserve flight of two: Lieutenants Besby F. Holmes (339th) and Raymond K. Hine (339th), who would move up in the formation if anyone, especially from the kill group, had to drop out.[66]

"I told them it was to be an all-volunteer mission and, as I expected, everyone kept asking if they could go," Mitchell later recalled. As it was, the selection caused a fistfight or two.[67]

Major Mitchell revealed the basics of the mission. "Yamamoto's supposed to be coming to Bougainville [this] morning." A murmur ran through the assembled men. Everyone knew who Yamamoto was – except Mitchell, apparently – and knew what he had done. Payback for Pearl Harbor was on everyone's mind. Mitchell continued, "We figure he'll land at 9:45. We're going to jump him there, to the west, 10 minutes before that."[68] Then he got into the specifics of his plan to surprise and ambush the Japanese commander in chief:

> I told them the strategy I was going to follow and the dogleg route we would follow entirely out of sight of land. When we made landfall at Bougainville, we would skin off our drop tanks and a killer section of four aircraft would seek out the bomber and the six fighters. The rest of us would climb rapidly to altitude to be top cover for the killer section and also be ready to bounce any of the seventy-five to one hundred Zeros based at Kahili near Buin. I really expected them to send up at least fifty of those fighters [...] I anticipated a real turkey shoot [...]
>
> I briefed the pilots on the routes out and said we would come back direct to Guadalcanal when the job was done. We wouldn't linger because we wouldn't have the fuel.[69]

The trip out was going to be extremely difficult. To avoid any possible detection by the Japanese, Major Mitchell could not lead his flight on the direct route through the Solomons to Bougainville for the very reasons Admiral Yamamoto expressed: The Japanese would see them and send up the warning. So Mitchell plotted a course of four doglegs looping around to the south of the Solomons, well out of sight of land. Just the featureless waters of the Coral Sea. They would have to navigate by dead reckoning – that is, just use the compass and track their speed and the time they had been flying on a particular course. Or, as Mitchell told his pilots, "Just follow me."[70] Worse, to avoid giving any kind of radar signature, they would have to hug the water, altitudes of maybe 50 feet. They had to pay attention the entire time or else they could find themselves cartwheeling into the Coral Sea. And, it almost went without saying, there would be radio silence. "No one was to touch that mike button from the time we took off until we engaged the enemy planes."

"I cautioned them about strict radio silence on the trip out and told them I would use the usual signals of kicking my rudders to fishtail my plane when I wanted the formation to spread out and wagging my wings to bring them in close. I would use hand signals otherwise."[71] In other words, like a Zero. This mission would be a test of physical, mental, and intellectual endurance. Mitchell warned his pilots:

> There's a tendency to daydream and get sleepy on a trip like this. You're going to be hot and it's going to be boring. Don't stare at the water. Your depth perception goes to hell down low like that and you're going to bust your butt if you get careless.[72]

Historian Donald Davis described the challenges facing the pilots:

> The course for the first leg would take them west on a heading of 265 degrees for exactly fifty-five minutes at an airspeed of 210 miles per hour. That would take them precisely 183 miles to a point between the sun and the sea with no land in sight. Just follow me, Mitchell said, and his southern drawl made it sound easy.
>
> The pilots studied the course. Just getting there was going to be a problem. Staying awake out over the water for so long, flying low, being trapped in the cockpit and broiled by the sun, would be grueling, and dozens of other hazards ran through their minds. A lot of things could go wrong, and, in fact, something already had: They were heading to the wrong place.[73]

Indeed, they were. According to *Magic*, Admiral Yamamoto was supposed to land at Ballale, one of the Shortland Islands off the southeastern coast of Bougainville. But the plan had been changed locally without going through the radio transmissions that could be decrypted by *Magic*. In fact, Yamamoto was supposed to land at Buin, what the Allies called Kahili, on Bougainville itself near that southeastern coast. The two airfields were close together as the Zero flies, but with timing so critical on this mission, the difference could be catching Yamamoto or not.

Major Mitchell and the pilots headed out to their planes readied at Fighter 2, some trying to formalize it as "Kukum Field." Eighteen Lockheed P-38 Lightning heavy fighters.

Each with one 20mm cannon and four .50-caliber machine guns. Each with one 165-gallon drop tank under one wing and one 310-gallon tank under the other. The 310-gallon tanks had been flown up from Port Moresby by B-24 Liberators of the 90th Bombardment Group.[74] Mechanics had labored all night in a thunderstorm to get the tanks attached, with the last tank fitted as dawn broke. The P-38 was seen as strong enough to withstand the weight imbalance. The mechanics also had to install that "good mariner's compass" in Mitchell's P-38. There was also the usual to fill all the ammunition trays, patch every hole, fix every circuit, make certain each Lightning was ready to fly. The mechanics could not help but notice the intense interest of high-ranking officers in their work.[75]

Admiral Mitscher sat in a Jeep watching Major Mitchell's P-38 Lightnings take off at 7:10am. It had been exactly one year since he had watched B-25 Mitchells – without Pappy Gunn's modifications – take off from his carrier *Hornet* to bomb Japan in a small if embarrassing blow against the military establishment there. Today, if successful, would be a much, much bigger blow. But already it was going wrong. Lieutenant McLanahan was roaring down the runway when he blew a tire on a jagged edge of some Marston matting. Cursing up a storm, McLanahan drove his P-38 off the runway and shut down the engines. That was one member of the killer flight gone.[76]

The Lightnings took to the air and circled the Henderson Field complex to form up, and perhaps soak in the moment. Admiral Mitscher saluted them. Then Major Mitchell led them west in a gradual descent toward sea level. Which is when Lieutenant Moore discovered his drop tank was not feeding fuel to the engine. He would not have the fuel to make it to Bougainville. He used hand signals to inform Mitchell, then disgustedly headed back to Henderson Field. That was two members of the killer flight gone. Lieutenants Holmes and Hine were tabbed to replace them. One catch: though a very experienced fighter pilot, Hine had never flown a P-38 on a mission before.[77]

Executing the flight plan he himself had designed, Major Mitchell had the flight descend to about 50 feet, then they spread out. Each had to keep at least one other Lightning in view, because if anyone got lost out here in the middle of the featureless Coral Sea, it might be permanent. But Mitchell did not want any midair collisions.[78]

Now, the drudgery, the boredom of the mission flight set in. No radio … no co-pilot … sun beating down on the cockpit … water, water … in every direction.

Don't fall asleep. … Check the airspeed. … Check the heading. … Look for your Lightning-mates. … Mile after mile. … Minute after minute. … Second after second. … So hot in this cockpit. … How long have we been flying …? Don't fall asleep!

After 55 minutes, Major Mitchell led his fighters to course 290 degrees. Everyone followed. Then they settled back. Major Mitchell watched in horror as the propeller of one of the Lightnings caught the water. Fortunately, miraculously, all it did was spray the cockpit, and the aircraft was soon under control. "I know damn well that woke him up," Mitchell recalled. "He had to clean off his windshield when he got back. I think that's the only thing he had to clean up but word got back to me later that he wasn't able to get back to sleep for a couple of days."[79]

After 27 minutes, Major Mitchell led the fighters to course 305 degrees. They all turned and settled in once again. The boredom started to release its hold, thanks in part to showtime getting closer and closer, in part to a cornucopia of sea creatures now visible beneath them including sharks – Lieutenant Canning counted 48 of them … it was almost like counting sheep …[80]

"[I]t was kind of a dull flight, really," Mitchell remembered.[81]

"It was hot as hell in those cockpits and I dozed off a couple of times but I got a light tap on my shoulder from the Man upstairs and caught myself," Mitchell later remembered.[82]

After 38 minutes, Major Mitchell led his fighters to course 20 degrees True. Yes, they were coming at Bougainville from the south and slightly to the west. It was 9:45am. Mitchell signaled for the fighters to wake up and tighten up. Except … They couldn't see any land. Water, water everywhere, and not a drop of land. Major Mitchell started to panic:

> Could I have been so far off that we weren't near land at all – any kind of land? I was really getting itchy because I hadn't seen a single checkpoint from the time we left. There are some pretty high hills on Bougainville and I couldn't see anything ahead in the haze and sunlight.
>
> I glanced once more at my strip map and then ahead. Out of the haze I saw a beach and there we were just about where I wanted us to be off the southwest corner of Bougainville. It was 0934 – a minute ahead of our scheduled time.[83]

Crisis averted. They had flown 494 miles, barely above the water, without a checkpoint, by dead reckoning. And they were exactly where they were supposed to be. One minute early. It was already a major achievement. For the pilots, and especially for Major Mitchell. "Mitchell laid out the course, speeds, gas mixture settings, and finger-to-the-wind estimates of what the weather elements would be the next day," Captain Kittel remembered years later. "All the credit for the planning should stop with Mitchell."[84] But they didn't care about that. They had a completely different achievement in mind.

The flight started ascending. They would go to 10,000 feet and wait if they had to.

They didn't have to. The radio finally came to life. If they were following Major Mitchell's orders, as they should, that could mean only one thing. Lieutenant Canning confirmed it.

"Bogeys. Ten o'clock high."

Major Mitchell looked up and quickly found them. About five miles away, their course almost perpendicular to his own. "Roger," he replied. "I got 'em."[85]

But there were two bombers. No one said anything about two bombers. Is this Yamamoto's flight?

Then he spotted six Zeros … six? … only six? … about 1,000 feet above the two bombers.

"Skin off your tanks," Mitchell ordered. And the drop tanks were, appropriately enough, dropped. Except for two. The Lightnings lurched upward. They were even with the bombers in a few minutes.

Major Mitchell radioed Captain Lanphier, "All right, Tom. Go get 'im. He's your meat." "Roger," Lanphier replied.[86]

But the party was not yet all ready. The two drop tanks of Lieutenant Besby Holmes would not release. Yet another problem with the killer flight.

Holmes radioed Lanphier, "Hold it a second, Tom. I can't drop my tanks. I'll tear them off." So Holmes headed back over the water and went down into a violent, spinning power dive. "I put my nose down at 350 miles per hour, pulling such high Gs [multiples of the force of gravity]… that I almost blacked out, then I kicked the rudder," Besby remembered. "No external stores will stay on an airplane at those forces," he said.[87]

And they didn't. The forces ripped the drop tanks away. That was the good news. The bad news was that he had lost sight of the flight, except for Lieutenant Hine. Hine had followed the rule of a wingman and stayed with his leader. It was instinct, but it was the worst news: Holmes had now taken two – half – of the killer flight out of the battle.

That left two P-38s to deal with two bombers.

As Major Mitchell led the rest of the flight to 18,000 feet to deal with whatever reinforcements came out of Kahili, Captain Lanphier did not "hold it a second," as Lieutenant Holmes had requested, but kept going toward the bombers, climbing at 2,200 feet per minute, racing at 200 knots with Lieutenant Barber alongside.

When they were only one mile away from the bombers, three of the Zeros caught sight of the Lightnings, dropped their own external fuel tanks, and dove toward them. Lanphier and Barber were roughly perpendicular to the bombers' course. With three Zeros approaching, Lanphier turned toward the prospective attackers, ready to take them on head on with his 20mm cannon and four .50-cal. machine guns. That's what he had been taught, and that was his instinct, to turn into them.

Major Mitchell was helplessly watching these developments from above. He was just livid. "Leave the Zeros, Tom," Mitchell shouted over the radio. "Bore in on the bombers! Get the bombers! Damn it all, the bombers!"[88]

This was the plan: you fly up there, shoot down that plane, kill the admiral. What could be simpler?

Allegedly, no one heard Major Mitchell's cursing missive over the radio. But maybe Rex Barber did.

The 339th had one rule that was inviolate: "Formation flying is vital." "We fought the Japs all over Guadalcanal and the Solomons for months, and I can't remember a time when we weren't badly outnumbered. You can meet that kind of opposition in one way only, by sticking together. You must stay together, at least in pairs," Mitchell explained.[89]

Except, today, if Lieutenant Barber followed his leader, the mission would fail. "My primary job, as I saw it," Barber later recalled, "was to get that bomber."[90]

Going against everything in his training and his instinct, this wingman did not follow his leader Captain Lanphier. One could argue that he left Lanphier out to dry by having him take on three Zeros by himself. But the mission ultimately was to get the bombers.

Except Lieutenant Barber was coming on too fast. He would overtake the bombers, and it would be hard to shoot them down if he was in front of them, if he did not slow down. Of course, if he did slow down, he would be a prime target for the Zeros. A bit of a dilemma whose solution was more than obvious; Barber did a hard right turn. As his aircraft banked, he lost sight of both bombers.

But as the P-38 leveled once more, Lieutenant Barber found himself behind the first Betty. Where the second Betty was, he had no idea. No idea that he was almost literally sitting on the second Betty's cockpit.

They were only about 1,000 feet above the ground. The bomber sharpened its dive, trying to get away. It was not going to outrun a P-38; even at reduced speed Lieutenant Barber's Lightning would overtake the Betty in a matter of seconds. But for now, Barber found himself slightly to the left of the bomber, about 50 yards behind.[91]

And well within range of the Betty's rear 20mm cannon. It could start firing at him any second now.

Lieutenant Barber positioned the aiming reticle across the opposite side of the bomber's fuselage over the right engine.

He tightened his grip on the Lightning's control stick and pressed the firing triggers.

One minute Flight Petty Officer Yanagiya was getting ready to cover Admiral Yamamoto's landing on the Buin runway, almost in sight. The next, he saw his flight leader waggle his wings and then dive. Without the use of a radio, that was the signal they were under attack.[92]

Yanagiya was confused. We're under attack? From where? He scanned the sky above him. There was nothing. Nothing that he could see, anyway. Then he looked down ...

They were difficult to see against the forest below, because they had jungle camouflage. But he saw them nonetheless. A flight of those fork-tailed devils, the P-38 Lightnings. In attack formation. Already close to the bombers. Attacking from below.

Attacking from *below*? Can they *do* that?

Yanagiya released his drop tank and followed his section leader into a dive. Their immediate goal for the moment was remarkably restrained for the Japanese. They were not looking to shoot the P-38s down. Not yet, anyway. They wanted to repel the Lightnings' attack and drive them away from the bombers. To that end, the Zeros opened fire, not on the P-38s themselves, but in their flight path. It seemed to work, some. One of the Lightnings turned toward them.

But another did not. It went straight for the bombers.

On board Admiral Ugaki's plane, the chief of staff was shouting at pilot Hayashi, "Follow Plane Number 1! Follow Plane Number 1!"[93] Hayashi opened the throttle as far as it would go and dove for the treetops. As soon as it had leveled off from its dive, the crew went to battle stations. The three gunners readied the defensive machine guns.

Glancing out the window, Admiral Ugaki caught a glimpse of Admiral Yamamoto's plane, now about four kilometers away. The sight gripped him in horror … The G4M was trailing black smoke, with flames gushing from the engines, starting to engulf the fuselage. The bomber carrying the commander in chief of the Combined Fleet was losing speed and altitude, now barely skimming over the treetops …

"My God!"[94]

Lieutenant Barber had fired his 20mm cannon and his .50cal. machine guns at Admiral Yamamoto's right engine. The bullets and shells tore into the cowling, sending pieces of it flying off. He then slid in directly behind the bomber, walking his gunfire to the left toward the Betty's vertical stabilizer and chewing off bits of the rudder. He aimed back at the right engine – for a Type 1 cigar, it certainly was not lighting very easily – but it did now. The shells tore into the engine, and thick black smoke started streaming from around the cowling.

Maybe 100 feet behind the bomber, Lieutenant Barber continued to fire, curious the entire time as to why the rear 20mm gun had not fired back at him. Barber walked his guns back left toward the right wing connection and the fuselage, all the way over to the left engine. The G4M was convulsing under the pounding. Without warning, the bomber suddenly "snapped" left. Had he hit the pilot?

The Betty rapidly slowed, and Barber had to dodge the right wing. He saw the plane, its right wing vertical, its right engine enveloped in black smoke, plummeting toward the ground.[95]

Lieutenant Barber never saw the bomber again.

But he did see three angry Zeros behind him.

"Look at the commander in chief's plane!" Admiral Ugaki shouted as he grabbed the shoulder of staff officer Lieutenant Commander Muroi Suteji and pointed at Admiral Yamamoto's *Rikko*.

The chief of staff could not point long, however, because Hayashi threw the bomber in a downward spin to the left, then looped back, toward the water, a turn of as much as 270 degrees.

Ugaki waited impatiently for another chance to see the commander in chief's plane. But he never saw it again. It had been only about 20 seconds since the attack began.

The next time Ugaki got a look at where the G4M should have been, it was gone. It its place was a column of black smoke boiling up from the jungle. "Oh! Everything [is] over now," Ugaki lamented.[96]

Not exactly. Because the Lightnings had been so focused on Admiral Yamamoto's plane, they had pretty much ignored Admiral Ugaki's. Until now. With the commander in chief's bomber gone, the Americans could now all focus on the one remaining bomber – Ugaki's.

Hayashi could see the Buin runway in the distance, but he knew he would never make it. He dove to the water and raised the throttle as much as he dared, but he still picked up a Lightning on his tail. The gunner manning the 20mm cannon in the tail tried to keep the Lockheed at bay, but Ugaki saw tracers on both sides of the aircraft and felt impacts on the hull. The 20mm cannon went silent. Ugaki looked over and saw Lieutenant Commander Muroi sprawled on a table, motionless. He noticed he could no longer hear the aircraft commander, either. Ugaki thought about how many must have been killed. "Now we are hopeless," he thought.

Hayashi felt the right wing and engine taking hits and knew he could not stay aloft much longer. He tried to use a down rudder to smoothly ditch the plane in the water, but Hayashi lost control at the end – he later blamed damage to the elevator – and as the G4M hit the water it flipped to the left and sat in the water upside down.[97]

The chief of staff was thrown about the passenger compartment. "This is the end of Ugaki," he thought in the third person.

And then Admiral Ugaki's world went black.[98]

Major Mitchell continued looking down on the action from high altitude. He was waiting for the swarm of Zeros from Kahili to show up. Where were they? There had to be more Zeros out there. Had to be. The Japanese wouldn't guard their commander in chief with only six of them. They couldn't be that stupid.

As he looked down he heard a call for help from Captain Lanphier. While Lieutenant Barber had continued on toward the bombers, Lanphier had turned toward those three Zeros. And in the process he had probably kept them away from Barber long enough for Barber to shoot down the first Betty.

Captain Lanphier would later claim he had shot down the middle Zero of the three and passed between the two wingmen. Then he allegedly flipped his Lightning over and looked at the world upside down. At which time he saw a bomber. Lanphier said he cut his speed and dropped his flaps to slow down as he came up on the bomber from a near-perfect right angle. With Zeros approaching him, he felt he had time for only one shot, so he fired his 20mm cannon and .50cal. machine guns in one long burst from almost a full deflection angle of 70–90 degrees – the most difficult shot possible – into the bomber's line of flight, tearing into the right wing and setting the right engine on fire. The Betty's rear 20mm cannon was firing at him, until the right wing snapped off and the bomber plowed into the floor of the jungle.

No one could corroborate his story. No one saw him shoot the plane down.

Captain Lanphier then hit the deck and redlined his engine to get away from the Zeros. That was when Major Mitchell and his wingman Lieutenant Jacobson showed up to chase the Zeros off. Lanphier was free – only to find that he was at the edge of the Kahili airfield. With Zeros now scrambling. Flight Petty Officer Yanagiya had flown over the base at low altitude and fired a burst from his machine guns – the signal that Admiral Yamamoto's flight was in trouble. The vigilant Buin air base managed to miss the signal completely.

With the airfield's antiaircraft guns opening fire on him and, as far as he could tell, its Zeros taking off, Captain Lanphier put his P-38 in a climb no aircraft could match. Up, up, and away.

Lieutenant Barber had caught a glimpse of a column of black smoke rising from the jungle, but he was more concerned at the moment about the Zeros on his tail. He had headed toward the coast of Bougainville to try to shake them. That was where he found the other bomber, going so low that its propellers kicked up spray.

And that is where Lieutenant Holmes and Lieutenant Hine found Lieutenant Barber. It was the odd sight of three Zeros chasing a Lightning chasing a Betty. Holmes and Hine barrel-rolled down in behind the Zeros. So now it was the curious sight of two Lightnings chasing three Zeros chasing one Lightning chasing one Betty.

Lieutenant Holmes told Lieutenant Hine to take the Zero on Lieutenant Barber's right wing while Holmes would take the two on the left. They proceeded to shoot down all three Zeros – or so they thought. Then Lieutenant Holmes took on the bomber – "a sitting duck as far as I was concerned," recalled Holmes.[99]

But a duck with a stinger on its tail. The Betty's rear 20mm cannon was firing at Holmes, as were the bomber's other machine guns. Holmes used his .50cal. machine guns:

[…] to get the proper deflection and check the range. There was no need to be in a hurry. There was still sufficient time to shoot the bomber down in my own way. The next burst of fifties kicked up the water just short of the bomber.

"Next time," I said aloud […]

Holmes positioned the targeting reticle further ahead of the Betty: "Now!"

I touched the trigger. The fifties chattered and vibrated, shaking the whole airplane. Bullets tore into the Betty, showing me that my range and deflection were perfect. I pressed the button to fire my 20mm cannon […][100]

A few shells from that cannon quieted the Betty's own 20mm cannon. Lieutenant Holmes slid in behind the bomber, aimed for the right engine, and unleashed his guns:

The bullets tore into the engine and wing root and I could see little tongues of flame leap out. But the Betty wouldn't go down!

I heard myself yelling, "Go down! Go down! Go down or blow up, dammit! What do I have to do to make you go down?"[101]

These alleged "Type 1 cigars" were certainly not living up to that reputation today.

I continued to squeeze the triggers and sent a long burst into the engine. A huge puff of smoke, followed by orange flame, burst from the engine cowling. I stopped yelling and quickly came to my senses just as I found myself about to ram the Betty's tail. In my haste and eagerness I had forgotten how fast I was going in comparison to the speed of the bomber. It almost ended the scrap for me right there.[102]

Lieutenant Holmes ended up passing the Betty – whether he went above or below it is disputed – but when he looked back he saw the bomber crash into the water. It had been Lieutenant Barber who finished the work Holmes had started:

Holmes started firing. His initial bullets hit the water behind the bomber, then walked up and through the right engine. A white vapor started trailing behind the right engine. [...]
    I dropped in behind the Betty and as I closed in to less than fifty yards, I opened fire, aiming at the right engine. Almost immediately, the bomber exploded. As I flew through the black smoke and debris, a large chunk of the Betty hit my right wing, cutting out my turbo supercharger intercooler. Another large piece hit the underside of my gondola, making a very large dent in it.[103]

The bomber crashed into the water.
    The entire engagement had taken less than ten minutes. Which was good, because they did not have enough fuel to wait around.
    Major Mitchell gave the universal signal for going home:
    "Let's get the hell out of here."[104]

While this air battle was going on maybe ten miles away, the Buin air base was peaceful, expectant. Many were standing in the heat and humidity at attention in their dress uniforms along the runway, ready, excited even, for the arrival of the commander in chief. That excitement was tempered a bit when a curious telegram from Rabaul was delivered. It contained one simple question: "Has C-in-C plane arrived?"[105]
    Admiral Kusaka had expected to have received a confirmation message of his arrival by now – 49 minutes after he was supposed to arrive. He was always so punctual. Yet they had heard nothing from Buin about Admiral Yamamoto's plane.

But the Buin air base had received no messages, no indication that anything had gone wrong. So, the base commandant sent back the reply that Admiral Yamamoto's flight had not yet landed.[106]

Not on the runway, at least. But soon, landing on said runway were five Zeros of Admiral Yamamoto's fighter escort. And ... nothing else.

The commander of Admiral Yamamoto's escorting fighters, Lieutenant Morizaki, jumped out of his Zero and immediately rushed to Admiral Kosaka, commander of the 6th Air Attack Force in Buin.[107] The Navy and Army personnel standing at attention in dress uniforms watched bemusedly. Then they saw the officers' reactions. And word leaked out.

The last of the escorting fighters to land was Flight Petty Officer Yanagiya. He was delayed because he had chased one of the P-38s to the vicinity of Shortland, shooting at it until smoke came out of one of the engines, but he lost track of it and made his way to Buin.[108] What happened after he landed was disclosed in a small book published by the Naval Air Group 204 Association:

> He got down from the plane with tottering steps and a blank expression, just like a sleepwalker's. As if the officers could not believe the report given by the previously arrived members, they called Yanagiya and asked, "Was Admiral Yamamoto really killed?" The faces of the commanders were pale. Yanagiya could not say that the Admiral had died. He was hesitant to give further blows to the dismayed officers and push them too far. On top of that, he did not have the face to say, "Yes. He is dead," while the six escort planes had no real damage.
>
> Yanagiya answered in a roundabout way, "Because the Admiral made an emergency landing in such a fierce fire, he may not have survived. However, I cannot be assertive because I myself did not see him."[109]

He was badly shaken, probably in some form of psychological shock, and very suspicious, even angry. But Yanagiya kept some semblance of his wits about him, which considering the circumstances is saying something.

Yanagiya could do math. Those P-38 Lightnings went straight for the bombers. "They knew who was flying in the plane," he said. "It was deliberate. It was not an accident." But no one talked to him, no one debriefed him.[110] He was just a lowly, enlisted fighter pilot who had failed to protect the commander in chief of the Combined Fleet. It wasn't his fault, wasn't his flight-mates' fault, of course, that the number of escorts assigned to this mission was pitifully small. Everyone, including Yanagiya, believed he should have gone down with the G4M. No one cared what he thought.

Meanwhile, outside of Yanagiya's view, things were happening on Bougainville. After the war, Lieutenant Shimizu Yasuo revealed he was part of a flight of 14 floatplanes whose mission was "to intercept and 'guard' Admiral Yamamoto as he came in over Bougainville." Ten of these floatplanes were two-seaters, probably Type 0 Observation Seaplanes, while the remaining four were three-seaters, probably Type 0 Reconnaissance Seaplanes, which had to be confusing. Shimizu said that he saw the P-38s intercepting the G4Ms, but was unable to intervene, either because he was too far away or the Japanese floatplanes were not considered fighters and could not handle the P-38 Lightning. Of course, that last factor had never stopped the Japanese from sending up hopelessly overmatched floatplanes before. It has been speculated that this flight of 14 floatplanes "had to be north of Empress Augusta Bay in the Cape Torokina area." These would have been from the 958 Air Group operating out of Shortland and, as seaplanes, would have been part of the R-Area Air Force under the command of Admiral Jojima, who was so passionate in his pleas to Yamamoto that he scrub his trip to Bougainville. The combination of floatplanes from Jojima's command in the air but far away from Yamamoto's flight – the Americans never saw these floatplanes – brings up the possibility that Jojima, unable to convince Yamamoto to nix the visit, sent up what aircraft he could as an "honor guard," far enough away that they would not interfere with Yamamoto's flight but close enough to intervene if trouble arose. In that last part, they failed; if he meant them to intervene, it's curious that Jojima did not assign the Nakajima A6M2-N Navy Type 2 Interceptor/Fighter-Bomber, which was the "float Zero," a Zero fighter with float pontoons bolted on. Then again, that might have been a bit too obvious.[111]

Admiral Jojima may not have been the only one sending up some unauthorized escort, either. There have been consistent reports that at least 16 and as many as 30 Zeros were scrambled from Buin. The circumstances under which they were supposedly launched remain murky. They were either an impromptu and locally organized escort or honor guard for Admiral Yamamoto's arrival, or a belated and futile attempt to catch the American assassins. Operating from Buin were Zeros from the 201, 204, and composite 582 Air Groups, as well as the carrier *Ryuho*. All except those from the *Ryuho* were from Base Air Force and thus normally answered to Admiral Kusaka, but those from the *Ryuho* would normally have answered to Admiral Ozawa, who also was emphatic that Yamamoto should have a bigger escort. It's possible that he ordered the *Ryuho* fighters aloft as another distant "honor guard" in case trouble arose. It's also possible that these reports are nothing more than garbled recollections of that flight of 14 floatplanes.[112]

Be that as it may, Admiral Kitamura, the paymaster, Hayashi, the pilot, and Admiral Ugaki had been picked up by Army forces and taken to the Buin base medical facility. Kitamura had a hole in his throat and was blinded in one eye. Ugaki was by far the worst injured. Still struggling to recover from dengue fever, Ugaki had now been dunked in the ocean, thrown from a plane, and suffered a compound wrist fracture and lacerations of his right bicep, right eye area, and both thighs.[113]

At 11:08, Admiral Kosaka sent a cable to Admiral Kusaka, commander of Base Air Force in Rabaul, with the highly unusual heading "Highest Priority, Confidential." It was coded with the "top secret" Ro-3 encryption:

1. Two *Rikko* carrying C-in-C, Combined Fleet, and his party engaged in aerial combat with over 10 P-38s at about 0740. Second plane was forced down into the sea off Moira

Point [sic]. Chief of Staff, Chief Paymaster (both wounded), one pilot rescued. First plane in flames seemed to have plunged at a slight angle into the jungle about 11 miles west of RXP. Searching underway.

2. Two direct-escorting planes shot down six hostile planes (of which three planes were forced landing; certain). No damage to our side.[114]

As crazy as it sounded to the American pilots when they found out later on, none of the escorting Zeros had been shot down, though one had to make an emergency landing on Shortland Island.

But they were damaged. Not damage you could see. It was far worse.

Two hours after they landed, the Zero pilots were ordered to return to Rabaul.[115]

───────────── ⬤ ─────────────

Near the south coast of New Georgia flew a PBY Catalina of Patrol Squadron 44 piloted by Lieutenant (jg) Harry Metke. Metke and his crew had two missions for this day. The first was to deliver some supplies to coastwatchers on New Georgia. After that, they were to play the role of "Dumbo," picking up downed airmen.[116] But Lieutenant (jg) Metke and his crew were to fly Dumbo for a specific Army Air Force mission of "unknown purpose and destination."

Metke and his crew were at about 500 feet off the water when they saw more than a dozen P-38 Lightnings flying *below* them. At wavetop level. That was strange. They were heading west northwest, toward Bougainville. What was that all about?

The Catalina delivered the supplies and took off again to resume its Dumbo patrol. Suddenly, the radio crackled with a lot of talk, chatter, yelling … an air battle of some sort. Involving those P-38s they had just passed. Then they heard an announcement that the mission had been accomplished and the fighters were headed back to base.

Lieutenant (jg) Metke turned the Catalina toward Espiritu Santo, his own base, figuring the Lightnings would overtake his lumbering PBY. One Lightning did. Aviation Machinist's Mate 1st Class Charles Marsh was in the waist hatch when he saw a P-38 making a sweeping turn before eventually pulling even with the Catalina to starboard at 700 feet altitude.

The P-38 was having serious issues. The left engine was stopped, with the propeller feathered and bullet holes evident in the engine cowling. Marsh pointed it out to Metke, who radioed the Lightning pilot and asked if he was OK. After a pause the pilot said he thought so. Metke then asked about the other engine, and the pilot replied that it appeared to be OK, and that he had enough fuel to get back to base. Metke advised him that if he wanted to ditch, the PBY could easily pick him up. That's what he was out there to do. The Lightning pilot hesitated and made another sweeping turn about a mile out. He then asked for a compass heading for Guadalcanal and said he thought he could make it back, and then flew ahead and disappeared in the distance.

Over a half century later, Metke recalled, "I had no knowledge of the plans to attack Yamamoto, nor of the P-38 squadron that was in the area while we were there. When the news came out about the Yamamoto ambush, I realized it was an amazing coincidence that we were in the area at the time."

The pilot, who does not seem to have identified himself to Lieutenant (jg) Metke, was Lieutenant Ray Hine. His Lightning was shot up by Petty Officer Yanagiya and possibly Petty Officer Sugita; this exchange suggests Hine may have been wounded as well.

Neither Hine nor his P-38 Lightning were ever seen again. He would be the only casualty of this mission, later called Operation *Vengeance*.[117]

At Fighter 2, the maintenance crews and operations staff had set up a powerful radio receiver. They wanted to hear the play-by-play and color commentary from Bougainville. Of course, for the first few hours, there was nothing but silence.[118] Well, not quite silence. Static.

Then they caught snippets of chatter. Combat talk. The Lightnings were wrestling with Zeros. Much of it was unintelligible and they could not tell what was happening. Then the silence returned. For the most part, anyway. But the static seemed to increase a bit, cracking even …

"I got Yamamoto! I got the son of a bitch! He won't dictate peace terms in the White House now!" The voice was that of Captain Tom Lanphier.[119]

So much for secrecy.

The celebration began. At Fighter 2 and elsewhere on Guadalcanal.

But not everyone was so jubilant. Flying somewhere behind Captain Lanphier was a horrified Lieutenant Graebner. "Oh my God," he thought. "What are you doing?" "I can still remember how upset I was when Tom Lanphier made his statement over the open mike," Lieutenant Ames later recalled.[120] Lanphier was the only one who celebrated on the radio.

But the pilots were nevertheless in a celebratory mood. The returning Lightnings put on an impromptu celebratory air show, with multiple barrel rolls and some "widowmaker" landings, a prohibited maneuver in which the pilot banks around sharply, cuts his throttles, and lowers his flaps and wheels, with one wing pointed at the ground. The returning Lightning pilots "tore the place up."[121] When they landed, they were welcomed by cheering mechanics and operations personnel. They were heroes. They had gotten Public Enemy Number 1.

Well, not "they" in the mind of one of them. As Captain Lanphier landed he was met by Lieutenant Joseph Young, who remembered, "From the aircraft he claimed victory over Admiral Yamamoto in no uncertain terms. His reaction was astounding to me and appeared to be irrational. He was visibly shaken, but very adamant about his victory."[122]

As the party continued, everyone saw Captain Lanphier standing in the back of a Jeep parading down the runway like he was Julius Caeasar in a triumphant chariot on the way to the Temple of Jovis Capitolinus. Lanphier was shouting, "I got him! I got that son of a bitch! I got Yamamoto!"

Lieutenant Barber returned to Fighter 2 and left the flight mechanics in awe. His Lightning had 104 holes in it. The Zeros had shot his P-38 to pieces. It should not have made it back, but somehow it did. Or, more properly, somehow Barber had brought it back. As he usually did.

Barber went to the joyful headquarters tent and sat down at a table. He was well within earshot of Captain Lanphier and his triumphant shouts of "I got Yamamoto! I got Yamamoto!"

Lieutenant Barber was dumbfounded. He had flown out on Captain Lanphier's wing, had seen him peel away from the bombers to meet the approaching Zeros. He had seen no more of Lanphier. But he had seen both Bettys, he shot down one and saw it fall toward the jungle, then he finished off an already damaged second that had been tagged by Holmes and Hine. Barber did not know if Yamamoto was on either of them. Lanphier was nowhere to be seen during that time. The next time Barber saw Lanphier was back on Guadalcanal.

Captain Lanphier was a braggart, to be sure, and was usually taken with a shaker of salt. But this was too much. "How in the hell do you know you got Yamamoto?" Barber asked.

"You're a damned liar! You're a damned liar!" Lanphier shot back.

"But I haven't made a statement," Barber responded. "I just asked a question." He was right. Rather than argue further, he walked out of the tent. Barber and Lanphier were longtime friends. No longer.

And so began a controversy that continues to this day:

Who shot down Admiral Yamamoto?

───────○───────

That afternoon, the bigger controversy was how to inform Admiral Halsey of the news of the mission's success. Admiral Mitscher had his deputy chief of staff, Commander Stanhope C. Ring, and assistant chief of staff Commander William A. "Gus" Read draft a message. Read suggested using slang, a favorite tactic of Halsey's to confuse any enemy versions of *Magic*. He asked, "How about 'Pop goes the Weasel'?"

"That's good," Ring answered. And so a coded transmission went out to Admiral Halsey, with Admiral Nimitz copied:

P 38s led by Major J. William Mitchel [sic] USAAF visited Kahili area. About 0930L 18 shot down two bombers escorted by 6 Zeros flying close formation. 1 other bomber shot down believed on test flight. 3 Zeros added to the score sums total 6. 1 P 38 failed return. April 18 seems to be our day.[123]

It made no mention of Yamamoto, thus keeping *Magic* secure. In theory, anyway. The last sentence was a personal reminder from Mitscher to Halsey that it was the first anniversary of the day they launched the Doolittle raiders toward Tokyo.

Admiral Halsey responded, "Congratulations to you and Major Mitchell and his hunters. Sounds as though one of the ducks in their bag was a peacock."[124] Not exactly preserving the secret, either, was he.

But Halsey was more gruff the next day, acting not quite as happy as Admiral Nimitz had expected. At the daily staff meeting the next morning in Nouméa, Admiral Turner whooped it up when the shoot-down was announced. Admiral Halsey, privately exulting, chose to tease Turner.

"Hold on, Kelly! What's so good about it?" the Bull groused. "I'd hoped to lead that scoundrel up Pennsylvania Avenue in chains."[125]

Almost frantic, Commander Watanabe had tried to fly to Buin as soon as he heard Admiral Yamamoto's plane was down. No aircraft was immediately available for him, however, and before Base Air Force could get one ready, a storm moved in and blocked the route. Watanabe was delayed until the morning of April 19.

Accompanied by the chief medical officer of the Southeast Area Fleet, Commander Watanabe went immediately to the officers' medical quarters, where he sought out Admiral Ugaki. The chief of staff was in an ... odd state. Not only was he badly injured and sick, but he had been injected multiple times with painkillers and drugs to prevent infection, at which time he joked that they would probably "cure his [gonorrhea]."[126] Too much information, admiral. But when he saw Commander Watanabe, his eyes welled. All Admiral Ugaki could do is say, "The C in C's 4.5 miles northeast of Point Camau! Get there quickly! Quickly!" Over and over and over again.

Commander Watanabe snagged an older Kawanishi E7K Type 94 Reconnaissance Seaplane – the Allies would call this alien-looking aircraft the "Alf" – and took to the air. "Camau" is actually on the southern coast of Indochina; it is today part of Vietnam and considered something of a tourist destination. Whether Watanabe remembered his conversation with Admiral Ugaki incorrectly or Ugaki just uttered Camau out of his feverish delirium, the commander managed to locate the crash site inland of Point Moila. It was not hard to find; a cleared area ringed with burned trees stood out against the green background of the jungle. Watanabe had the biplane circle low over the site. The G4M's fuselage was broken just ahead of the *hinomaru*, the Rising Sun emblem. He could see no bodies or signs of movement.

A highly intelligent and resourceful type, Commander Watanabe had commandeered maybe 15 rubber balls. He had cut each of them open and inserted into each a slip of paper that read, "This is Watanabe. Please wave your handkerchiefs." He dropped them from the Type 94 at the site, hoping that they didn't strike anyone in the head. The rubber balls bounced around, as rubber balls tend to do, and came to rest. There was no immediate response. Watanabe had the biplane circle several more times in case survivors were hidden by trees or wreckage, but after dropping the balls he saw no further signs of movement.

As he had previously arranged, Commander Watanabe had the E7K land on water off Point Moila beside minesweeper *W-15*, where a search party of members of the ship's crew was waiting for him. Watanabe took charge, and everyone took a boat that had been loaded with emergency supplies up a small river believed to be the Wamai. The river proved unnavigable, however, and they continued moving on foot. They ended up stymied late in the day on April 19 and made camp.[127]

At the same time they were making camp, ironically, an Imperial Japanese Army search party had finally reached the site, more than 24 hours after the crash.[128] Troops at Ako plantation (local spelling: "Aku"), about 18 miles west of Buin, under the command of 2nd Lieutenant Hamasuna Tsuyoshi, had been overseeing a road crew of locals on April 18 when the aerial battle started. Hamasuna and his men were cheering encouragement to the Japanese pilots. When they saw a large, dense black cloud rising from the jungle, they celebrated what they thought was the destruction of an enemy fighter. A few hours later a runner arrived from the regimental headquarters about one-third of a mile away. He passed along a verbal order to Hamasuna: "A plane carrying top navy brass has crashed. You are to organize a search party and go to look for it. You were watching, so you'll know roughly where it crashed."

Lieutenant Hamasuna tabbed a sergeant and nine men from his own platoon and set off to hack and slash their way through the steaming jungle with all of one compass to guide them. With the foliage so thick that it darkened the jungle floor and removed any semblance of landmarks, Hamasuna's party took to notching trees to mark their path, if they wanted to be able to find their way back. They didn't find the plane by the end of the day and so returned to Ako, where headquarters told them to try again tomorrow.

So the next day, April 19, they again set off to hack and slash their way through the steaming jungle with only one compass to aid them – again. At one point they saw a Japanese plane circling, apparently that of Commander Watanabe. They signaled him. The plane dropped a message tube asking if they had found the wrecked plane, but they had not. Not yet.

It was late afternoon and the search party was about to call it a day when one of the soldiers thought he smelled gasoline. Soon everyone could smell it, then they followed their noses until they came to what looked like an embankment, actually the tail of a crashed plane. They followed it into a clearing.

The clearing was not natural. It was ringed by scorched trees and stank of smoke, gasoline, and … worse. The remnants of the clearing's creator remained: a Navy Mitsubishi G4M Type 1 land attack plane. It had the number "323" stenciled in white on the tail section. Its fuselage was broken just forward of the *hinomaru*. The forward section of its passenger compartment was a gutted, "burnt-out hulk." Lieutenant Hamasuna and his team had hoped to look for survivors, but it was obvious there would not be any. This was an unhappy but necessary recovery effort.

Eleven sets of human remains were recovered from the wreckage and the area around it. Not all of them recognizable. Several of the burnt corpses seem to have been in a pile. The Japanese troops respectfully laid the bodies in a clearing. One of the bodies was that of an older man in an unbuttoned white uniform, which was found spread-eagled on his back with no visible injuries. It seemed to have been thrown clear of the fuselage and the burned area, to the left of the fuselage. The body was later identified as Chief Fleet Surgeon Rear Admiral Takata Rokuro.

Only three feet away from Takata was a second curious corpse. He was sitting up in his seat, still strapped in. It had not yet been attacked by maggots. The officer's left hand was still clutching his katana, with his right hand laying on top. He was hanging his head, as if meditating – except he was missing his lower jaw, probably much of his face, and part of his left shoulder. That was the story, anyway. Lieutenant Hamasuna vaguely recognized the body, like he should know it but couldn't quite place it.

In the clearing, the bodies were searched for identification. Most were so badly burned that they had to be identified by their boots, on which their names were written. But that guy who was still sitting ... he had a lot of medals and ribbons on his chest. But what really got the lieutenant's attention was the body's left hand. It was covered with a white glove, with two of the fingers tied back. Because that left hand was missing those two fingers. That was a famous injury on a famous officer. Now Lieutenant Hamasuna recognized him. And shuddered at the realization. A diary found in his pocket confirmed it.

The body had to be that of Admiral Yamamoto Isoroku, Commander in Chief of the Combined Fleet of the Imperial Japanese Navy.[129]

Lieutenant Hamasuna and his team left the recovered bodies in a small shelter they had built and started to head back to Ako, only to bump into a search party of the 6th Sasebo Special Naval Landing Force sent out from Buin. They both made camp with the intention of returning to the site in the morning. Before they did so, Buin sent a top-secret message, "Ko Report No. 4," up the chain of command: "None alive aboard Plane A. Corpses are being picked up."[130] That was it. It was now official.

In the morning, the army and naval infantry did indeed return. They each made their own (inaccurate) sketches about the state of the aircraft. In actuality, the left wing had been sheared off by impact with the trees and ended up some 150 feet behind the main wreck. The right wing remained with the plane, damaged by clipping treetops, and ultimately separated on impact. Both engines had been flung forward. Subsequent inspections showed bullet holes primarily in the tail area going forward – as if the bomber had been attacked from behind.

Commander Watanabe had still not made it to the site. His efforts were stymied by thick jungle and giant mosquitos that so thoroughly chomped on Watanabe and his men that their faces were grotesquely swollen; Watanabe was already coming down with dengue fever. An aircraft had signaled to him that the wreck had been found and bodies recovered.

He retraced his steps down the Wamai River to the coast, where he met the naval search party carrying the stretchers. Here Watanabe made the formal identification of Yamamoto and ordered everyone to silence about this until Tokyo figured out what to do. Together they loaded the bodies on the *W-15*, where the bodies were placed under a tent built on the forepart of the main deck to keep the sun off.

It was here that the chief medical officer of the Southeast Area Fleet, one Captain Okubo, conducted a preliminary examination. The admiral's watch stopped at 7:45, which suggested that was the time the aircraft hit the ground. Regarding the bullet that entered Yamamoto's jaw and exited through his temple, Okubo commented, "This alone would have killed him outright."[131]

The *W-15* made its way to Buin, where an autopsy was conducted on April 20 by Lieutenant Commander Tabuchi Jisaburo, Chief Medical Officer of the 1st Base Force.[132] Four other officers observed: Commander Watanabe; Captain Okubo; Captain Uchino, chief medical officer of the 8th Fleet; and Rear Admiral Itagaki Sakan, commander of the 1st Base Force. According to Tabuchi's official report, Yamamoto suffered from two significant wounds:

1. Almost center part of left shoulder blade, there was a wound the size of the tip of a little finger. The wound towards inside and up.
2. A shot hole at left side of lower jaw. Outlet of upper part of right eye, size fingerprint by thumb.[133]

That would be the "official story." As for the other bodies, the major curiosity was with that of Admiral Takada, the fleet surgeon. The "official report" would state "burns on the upper half of the body and signs of a violent blow to the head were noted, from which it is concluded that a broken neck led to the occlusion of the vital organs and instant death."[134] This is at variance with what Lieutenant Hamasuna's search party saw of the fleet surgeon's corpse and, for that matter, what Dr Tabuchi saw during his autopsy, which agreed with the search party. "[The fleet surgeon] was also completely free from apparent injury," Tabuchi later said, "so much so that one wonders how he could have died."[135]

There were several of what one might call "irregularities" in the Imperial Navy's handling of the autopsies of Admiral Yamamoto and his party. Yamamoto biographer Agawa Hiroyuki would flat out say the autopsies "were tampered with on orders from above, in order to make things look better."[136] It would spark considerable speculation after the war that Dr Takada had staged Yamamoto's body, perhaps still alive if mortally wounded, in a last service to the admiral before taking his own life. But it would, it could, always be only speculation.[137]

After the autopsies were completed, the bodies were taken to the 6th Sasebo Special Naval Landing Force's base outside Buin, where they were placed in pits and cremated. Admiral Yamamoto's body was cremated separately, in a separate pit. His ashes were collected by Commander Watanabe and placed in a special box lined with papaya leaves.

The other sets of ashes were collected as well. Now in the grip of dengue fever, Commander Watanabe the next day took them back to Rabaul, accompanied by Admiral Ugaki, Captain Okubo, and others. A wake was held for the commander in chief there, a very small wake in order to keep his death secret, even from the personnel in Rabaul.

The following day Watanabe flew them back to Truk, where he took a portion of Admiral Yamamoto's ashes, put them in an urn, and placed the urn in a small shrine in his quarters on the *Musashi*. Then Watanabe collapsed from the dengue fever and remained bed-ridden for the next two weeks.

On the bridge of the carrier *Hiyo*, watching Admiral Yamamoto's flag being ceremonially lowered from the *Musashi*'s mast, were Admiral Kakuta and Lieutenant Commander Okumiya. The fiery, combative Kakuta had been struck speechless when he received the news of Yamamoto's death. As he watched the flag being lowered, Okumiya thought to himself:

> Those who so strongly insisted upon war with the United States and England may still be dreaming of success, although victory slips further and further from our grasp. Perhaps, however, we who are carrying the fight to the enemy, as we are ordered to do, may still survive this conflict. It is impossible for me, or any other man, to express in words the mixed emotions which must have been experienced by the admiral who so long ago realized the dark future of our country should we be forced by those in power to launch this war. Despite his apprehensions, as the Commander in Chief, Yamamoto was obliged to serve his country to the best of his ability. This he did, but with his command went the feeling of guilt that he had failed in his efforts to convince his government and its ruling hierarchy that war could bring only disaster.
>
> Whatever history will decide, the admiral now can rest peacefully in his grave. At least his death came in a plane of the Naval Air Force for which he was directly responsible. His unflagging efforts had given his country the most powerful naval air arm in the world.[138]

And it was. For a time. But perhaps therein lay the seeds for Admiral Yamamoto's death. The Sea Eagles had become so powerful that they started a cancer within the Combined Fleet. Arrogant. Overconfident. Sloppy. Yamamoto was the consummate gambler, it is true, but he was best – his operations were best – when he was careful, when he tried to minimize danger and events left to chance, whether it was Pearl Harbor, the Centrifugal Offensive, or *Ke*. When he wasn't, the results were catastrophic. Midway. Operation *Vengeance*, as the interception of Yamamoto would become known, when he insisted on going to the front with an escort of only six fighters.

The same day, Tokyo dispatched a coded message to the commanders of the Combined Fleet, the Southeastern Area Fleet, the Southwestern Area Fleet, and the 2nd, 3rd, 4th, 5th, 6th, and 8th Fleets: "Koga appointed by His Majesty C-in-C, Combined Fleet on 21 April. Further, this matter is being kept top secret even within navy beside Combined Fleet to say nothing of outside the Navy until special further orders."[139]

"Koga" was Admiral Koga Mineichi, then the commander of the China Area Fleet and not part of Combined Fleet. Nevertheless, in 1941, Yamamoto had written a secret memorandum discussing officers who could succeed him. Koga's name was at the top of that list. The respect was mutual, and the two were known to be close. Koga was also well-respected within the Imperial Navy. Ten men had seniority over Koga, but Yamamoto's recommendation and Koga's relationship with the royal family carried the day.[140]

Admiral Koga was nevertheless humbled by his appointment. He said, "There was only one Yamamoto and no one can replace him."[141]

CHAPTER 5

WHERE SEA EAGLES DARE

It's not normally difficult to cross a strait or any body of water. The Japanese would send ships out to bring supplies and troops to their bases in the central Solomons. Several of them never arrived. It left them fumbling for options to get reinforcements and supplies to Munda and Vila-Stanmore. It did not seem hard, since these were islands, after all. If you could not reach them from The Slot to the north, just reach them from the south.

Except, well, it was complicated. The Japanese had chosen the Munda site well for their next airfield. In terms of climate and environment, pretty much everything that has been said about Guadalcanal can be said about New Georgia.[1] Looks like Paradise, is more like Paradise Lost, thanks to the rain, mosquitos, malaria, rot, and kunai grass, to name just some of the difficulties.

Like Guadalcanal, New Georgia is in the southern line of the double-line of the Solomon Islands. Unlike Guadalcanal, New Georgia is not at the end of that line, but in the center – 180 miles from Guadalcanal, 110 miles from Bougainville. It is not just an island, but an island group – a group of three large islands, maybe nine smaller islands, and countless islets forming an archipelago some 150 miles long and 40 miles wide that is more of a maze, isolated from the rest of the Solomons and the Pacific at large by an outline of islets and coral reefs. This description is a gross oversimplification, to be sure, which will be addressed shortly.

The star of this particular island show is New Georgia proper, shaped like a fat comma tipped over onto its concave side, some 45 miles long and 20 miles wide. Covered with dark, dense, primordial jungle, of course, and disfigured with a ridge, featuring two 2,000-plus-foot volcanic peaks.

The Japanese had chosen the site of the Munda air base well, at least tactically. Like the beautiful woman at the party, New Georgia is more or less unapproachable. The island's southern coast is shielded by a reef for almost 20 miles. Between the reef and the coast is a body of water varying from one to three miles in width called Roviana Lagoon. Deep draught ships cannot get through the reef; only small boats can, if they're careful. Southeast of Roviana is an actual harbor, Viru, accessible by a narrow, twisting channel.

The entirety of the east coast of the island is outlined with another reef. So is the north coast, all the way to Visuvisu Point, the entrance to Kula Gulf. On the Kula Gulf side, New Georgia has three harbors, fed by rivers flowing down from the volcanic mountains. Two of them, Rice Anchorage and Enogai Inlet, are small, lined with mangrove swamps being pushed by the omnipresent primordial jungle. The third, Bairoko Harbor, is deeper and longer, but also is partially blocked by more of those pesky coral reefs.

To complete the circumnavigation of New Georgia, to the south of Bairoko is Hathorn Strait, which separates New Georgia from Arundel. Hathorn Strait tapers to its south to become Diamond Narrows, 224 feet wide at its narrowest point, only navigable by small boats. The narrows take you back to Munda and Roviana Lagoon. If the island had a convention and visitors bureau, it could have a great tourism slogan, "New Georgia: You can't get there from here," which may explain why it does not.

But the Japanese had managed to get there. Slowly, to be sure, picking their way through the islands, islets, rocks, and reefs. And now they would do so again. The Blackett Strait was mostly between Kolombangara and a concentric reef that ran from Arundel Island, just across the strait from Vila, south and southwest of Kolombangara to a tiny islet with the improbable name of Plum Pudding Island and from there west northwest to Gizo. The only opening in this reef was southwest of Kolombangara through a poorly charted break called Ferguson Passage. Because going north of Vella Lavella through Vella Gulf or Kula Gulf was now too dangerous, the Japanese decided to go south of Vella Lavella and enter the Blackett Strait through Ferguson Passage to go to Vila, then return to Shortland the same way.

The new route was to be used by Guadalcanal veterans now returning to the Solomons: Destroyer Division 15 under Captain Mutaguchi Kakuro. His destroyers *Oyashio*, *Kuroshio*, and *Kagero* were rat run veterans. *Kagero* and *Oyashio* had escorted Admiral Tanaka's ill-fated transport convoy to Guadalcanal, and even undertook torpedo attacks on the battleship *Washington*. All three were heavily involved in the Battle of Tassafaronga. These were veteran destroyers who knew how to make the dangerous rat runs and fight their way out, if necessary.

These tin cans of Destroyer Division 15 had just finished a refit at Kure naval base and had sailed down from Truk on April 24 to return to action in the Solomons. Captain Mutaguchi and his ships had stopped at Rabaul for supplies and orders, and were back in the Shortlands on April 29. That night, they ran to Vila with food, ammunition, and 24 barges – and evacuated 289 troops. Then on May 3 they brought in 350 troops and 14 tons of supplies.[2]

The plan was for Destroyer Division 15 to alternate the rat runs to Vila and Munda with another force made up of destroyers *Umikaze* and *Hagikaze*, who made runs to Vila on April 30 and May 4. On May 7, it was the turn of Destroyer Division 15 again. Captain Mutaguchi's destroyers embarked some 300-odd soldiers of the 3rd Battalion of the 13th Infantry Regiment, and 18 tons of munitions at Buin. Then, at 5:20pm, he had his *Oyashio* lead his tin cans out of the Shortlands back toward Vila.[3]

And into a dark and stormy night. Stormy nights are certainly not the best time for going through the treacherous Ferguson Passage and Blackett Strait. Captain Mutaguchi's destroyers struggled with the rain, the heavy winds from the southwest, and low visibility. The lookouts could not find the tiny islets that formed the entrance to Ferguson Passage, or any other navigational markers for it. The *Oyashio* snapped on her searchlight in the rain to get her bearings, and Destroyer Division 15 inched through the passage into Blackett Strait.[4] They arrived at Vila safely, but very late – at about 3:30am. The delay had been enough to convince those manning the barges at Vila waiting to transport the supplies and personnel to stop waiting for the destroyers offshore and head back to base. Having to call them back out delayed the mission further. Delays, delays. No mission is perfect.[5] Nevertheless, Captain Mutaguchi's destroyers dropped off the 18 tons of supplies and the 3rd Battalion. Then, as planned, he embarked some 300 troops of the 3rd Battalion of the 66th Infantry Regiment.

Captain Mutaguchi had his *Oyashio* lead the other destroyers out of Vila and back the way they had come. They crept along a bit, but after about an hour, as the Blackett Strait opened up, they worked their speed up to 18 knots or so.[6] They were late and dawn was breaking, but they were close enough to Buin that they felt relatively safe from air attack.

Until one minute before 6:00am. Then the *Oyashio* suffered an underwater explosion aft. The engine rooms quickly flooded, and the destroyer went dead in the water. The *Kagero* and *Kuroshio* immediately took up antisubmarine positions as the *Oyashio*'s crew took up damage control. Then the *Kagero* suffered her own underwater explosion and went dead in the water. Just seven minutes after the *Oyashio*. The *Kuroshio* was left to circle her division-mates as the *Kagero*'s and *Oyashio*'s crews took up damage control. The *Oyashio*, in particular, was having major problems as her crew spaces had flooded, her boiler rooms were taking on water, and she was starting to settle by the stern.

Then, at 7:00am, the *Kuroshio* exploded. Multiple times, it would seem. She didn't last long, sinking "in seconds" along with 83 of her crew.[7] Clearly, this was one busy submarine.

Or not. Less than 24 hours earlier, on the night of May 6–7, the US Navy destroyer *Radford* used her radar to lead in rainy weather three old destroyer-turned-minelayers, the *Preble*, *Gamble*, and *Breese*, in laying three lines of a total of more than 250 mines "as neat as a cabbage patch," according to Samuel Eliot Morison, across the Blackett Strait bisecting the Ferguson Passage to within 1,000 yards of the Kolombangara shore.[8] Admiral Halsey had been aware of the change in Japanese logistical arrangements; these three lines of cabbage patch balls were his response.

A response that was more than okay with Royal Australian Navy coastwatcher Sub-Lieutenant Arthur Reginald Evans, operating from Hiruka on Kolombangara. His scouts had awakened him to report the searchlight sweeping the entrance to Ferguson Passage. Evans knew exactly what that was and radioed it in, then went back to bed. He woke up at dawn with an interesting view from his hilltop observation post – two disabled Japanese destroyers in Blackett Strait.[9] Two of the three destroyers that had forced him to wake up in the middle of the night. Evans radioed Guadalcanal of the destroyers' predicament.

Commodore Mutaguchi had also gotten off a radio call for help, and the *Umikaze* and the *Hamikaze* were on their way to tow the disabled destroyers to Shortland. By this time, despite the dubious safety of his own command ship, Mutaguchi ordered boats sent out to rescue survivors of the *Kuroshio*. The powerless *Oyashio* continued her drift and at around 9:10am crunched to a halt on the reefs forming the east side of Ferguson Passage on the west side of Anuin Island.[10] The inclement weather from the previous night had, if anything, worsened, with a cloud ceiling at 900 feet. The weather gave the Japanese hope as they tried to firewall the flooding. But at 11:17am their problems got much worse when the Japanese lookouts reported 50 aircraft incoming.

The aircraft were from AirSols: three Avengers, 19 Dauntlesses, eight Kittyhawks from the Royal New Zealand Air Force's No. 15 Squadron, and 32 Corsairs (16 from Marine Fighting 112 and 16 from Marine Fighting 213). The TBFs and four of the Corsairs from Marine Fighting 213 could not find the destroyers in the murk and truncated their mission to bomb and strafe Munda.[11]

But while the remaining Corsairs patrolled for enemy fighters and the Kittyhawks under Squadron Leader M.J. Herrick strafed the destroyers to suppress the antiaircraft fire, the SBDs from Bombing 11 found a hole in the overcast and glide bombed from 4,500 feet. Glide bombing, however, is not nearly as accurate or effective as dive bombing. They managed a number of near misses on the *Oyashio* but did get two direct hits, one on the bridge, the other on the Number 2 5-inch mount.[12]

After a little more than a half hour, the AirSols strike headed back, and the Japanese were left to their own devices: trying to control the relentless flooding on both ships, especially the *Oyashio*, whose stern was dragging lower and lower in the water; and using boats to rescue the survivors of the *Kuroshio* and shuttle them to Kolombangara. Very soon, however, the *Oyashio* and the *Kagero* would need the boats for themselves.

Because at 4:30pm came a second AirSols strike. And this was a big one – 14 Avengers, 17 Dauntlesses, six Flying Fortresses, 32 Wildcats, 21 Corsairs (12 from Marine Fighting 213 and 11 from Marine Fighting 112, but two aborted), 12 Lightnings, and 18 Kittyhawks and Airacobras. Of which all but three Wildcats from Fighting 11 could not find the destroyers. The fighter pilots of Marine Fighting 112 acidly commented that maybe the B-17s could have found the targets if they had gone down below an altitude of 10,000 feet. So it ended up being a very tiny air strike. All they could manage to do was strafe the *Oyashio*, but it was enough.[13]

At 7:45pm, the destroyer suddenly heeled over to starboard. That was the end. The order to abandon ship was given, and ten minutes later the *Oyashio* rolled over and sank onto the reef. The *Kagero* outlasted her by a scant 22 minutes. The former took 91 dead with her, the latter 18. The survivors made their way to Kolombangara, from where they were recovered. Among the survivors were Captain Mutaguchi; the *Oyashio*'s skipper Lieutenant Commander Higashi Hideo; the *Kagero*'s skipper Commander Arimoto Terumichi; and the *Kuroshio*'s skipper Commander Sugitani Nagahide, who had been her skipper for less than three months.[14]

So, for the expense of some 250 mines and one SBD Dauntless of Bombing 11 lost to navigational error (the crew recovered), AirSols had just destroyed one of the best, most experienced divisions of Japanese destroyers with three of the most modern destroyers. Not bad for 20 dozen cabbage patch balls.

It was largely a one-off, however. The Japanese were now very aware of the possibility of mines in their sea lanes and made a habit of regularly sweeping for them. This motivated Admiral Halsey, Admiral Mitscher, and AirSols to get more creative. Their solution was what might be called the "mine raid."

The mine raid had first been tried the night of March 19–20. A flight of 18 Flying Fortresses and Liberators dropped fragmentation bombs on the runways and revetments at Kahili. The bombing was merely a distraction, because while it was going on, 42 Navy and Marine TBF Avengers, each carrying a 1,600lb Mark 12 magnetic mine, flew over the Shortlands anchorage. The Avengers descended to 800–1,300 feet and released their spiky balls by parachute into the water, albeit not as neat as a cabbage patch. Not one plane was lost, due in no small part to a Kiwi Hudson from the No. 3 Squadron near Vella Lavella dropping flares in the dark to help guide them back to base. The next night, it was 18 bombers covering for 40 Avengers dropping mines, again guided back by a Hudson. While the Japanese were good at sweeping up the mines laid by the minelayers, their efforts at even detecting, let alone removing, aerial mines seem to have been much less effective. One of the Avengers' mines damaged the destroyer *Kazagumo* on April 3. One cargo ship hit a mine and sank on April 18, almost a full month after the mine raids.[15]

After the wipeout of Destroyer Division 15, Admiral Halsey went back to more conventional attacks for a bit, such as a dusk air attack by six Avengers from Marine Scout Bombing 143 (four with bombs and two with flares) on the Shortlands on May 14 that forced the cargo ship *Houn Maru* aground of Tonolei, a total loss.[16] But he eventually did try the mine raids again, with the same *modus operandi*. During the night of May 19–20, four AirSols Flying Fortresses and two Liberators bombed Ballale and Kahili as cover for 30 Avengers from Torpedo 11 and Marine Scout Bombing 143 dropping mines off Kahili. Two Torpedo 11 TBFs failed to return for reasons indeterminate; the rest made it back safely, thanks again to a Kiwi Hudson. The effort was repeated the following night, dropping mines off Shortland, and the night of May 23–24, when the Kahili area was mined again. A total of 80 mines were released into the Shortlands anchorage during these three mine raids.[17] But it took weeks after the first series of attacks for results to show, and it would take time again.

It was a small thing, one the Japanese were slow to grasp, but they understood the overall trend. Their adversary was getting stronger, more nimble, and more creative. While their own capabilities were declining. With no end to that decline in sight. The difficulty of crossing a strait could easily become the difficulty of crossing the Pacific if they could not find a way to stop that decline.

Stepping from a launch onto the *Argonne*, the flagship of Admiral Halsey sitting in the harbor of Nouméa, were Lieutenant Rex Barber, Captain Thomas Lanphier, and Brigadier General Dean C. "Doc" Strother, operations officer of the 13th Fighter Command. They had been sent to New Zealand for leave after the shootdown of Admiral Yamamoto. But after considerable golfing, they returned to Nouméa to find a note ordering them to report to the South Pacific commander.

So, here they were. Being escorted to Admiral Halsey's cabin on the main deck by an aide who seemed oddly stern. The Army Air Force officers were shown in. Lying on an oak table were recommendations Admiral Mitscher had submitted for them to be awarded Medals of Honor. The letters contained phrases like "high courage," "beyond the call of duty," and "superlative gallantry and intrepidity in action," calling the mission a "masterpiece." The mission was so important, so high profile, that it was hardly surprising the South Pacific commander would want to see them.

Lieutenant Barber, Captain Lanphier, and General Strother entered the cabin and raised their hands to their foreheads in salute. Admiral Halsey ... did not respond. Did not salute them back. "He just stared at us," Barber recalled. There was a long, uncomfortable moment of frozen silence. A silence that was broken only when the admiral barked, "Hands down!" But he kept them at attention.

"I was scared to death," Barber remembered. "He kept staring at us and we didn't know what to do.

"Then he started in on a tirade of profanity the like of which I had never heard before."

Lieutenant Barber, Captain Lanphier, and General Strother did not know that on May 11, J. Norman Lodge, senior war correspondent for the Associated Press in the theater, had submitted an article to the censors about the ambush of Admiral Yamamoto. "Sarge," as Lodge was nicknamed, was well-known in the South Pacific and had close contacts in Halsey's headquarters. After he had heard about the Yamamoto ambush, Lodge had flown to Auckland in search of more information. Barber, Lanphier, and Strother were playing golf almost every day. Lodge soon made the threesome a foursome.

The war correspondent poked around for information, but seemed to know everything about the mission already. Mostly the Army Air Force officers confirmed things for him.

It seemed okay to them. The mission was no big secret on Guadalcanal, nor was the fact that the genesis of the mission was an intercepted radio message. They knew nothing could get past the censors. According to General Strother, they had met Lodge, who:

> … was already in possession of the salient facts as far as I knew them and I discussed the mission with him. Mr Lodge wanted to get the story released by [Admiral Halsey], and I explained to him that this mission was not a story and probably would not be released for security reasons. I gave him no authority to quote any member of my command or myself and no authority to submit the results of our discussion as an interview.[18]

The mission was a huge story. A huge story that could compromise the war effort in the Pacific, especially the part that Lodge had written about how "intelligence had trailed Yamamoto for five days."[19] Lodge could just sit on the story, but that's lousy journalism.[20] Democracy may die in darkness, but Yamamoto would not if Lodge had his way.

A full investigation was in the offing, but Admiral Halsey had already decided who was guilty:

> He accused us of everything he could think of from being traitors to our country to being so stupid that we had no right to wear the American uniform. He said we were horrible examples of pilots of the Army Air Force, that we should be court-martialed, reduced to privates, and jailed for talking to Lodge about the Yamamoto mission. He raved on about security and officer responsibility about security matters.
>
> He paced back and forth while he shouted profanely, waving his fists and declaring that we were the sorriest trio of Americans he had ever seen. I knew he had been nicknamed "Bull" Halsey by the press and now I understood why. He asked no questions and would not give any of us the opportunity to say a word or answer his charges. It was the worst "chewing out" I ever received.

That wasn't even the worst part.

> When Halsey's rage tapered off, he turned to a large oak table nearby and fingered through five pieces of paper on his desk.
>
> "Know what these are?" he asked rhetorically. "These are recommendations for Mitchell, Lanphier, Barber, Holmes, and Hine to get the Medal of Honor. As far as I'm concerned, none of you deserve even the Air Medal for what you did. You ought to face a court-martial, but because of the importance of the mission, I'm reducing these citations to the Navy Cross."
>
> With a curt wave of his hand toward the door, we all saluted but, again, he did not return the courtesy. We about-faced and left. We were shocked by this encounter and really didn't know what to make of it. We had been tried and judged guilty.[21]

As Admiral Halsey later explained it:

> We bottled up the story, of course. One obvious reason was that we didn't want the Japs to know that we had broken their code. The other reason was for Lanphier's personal sake. His brother was a prisoner of war, and if the Japs had learned who had shot down Yamamoto, what they might have done to the brother is something I prefer not to think about. [...]
>
> Unfortunately, somebody took the story to Australia, whence it leaked into the papers, and no doubt eventually into Japan. (The usual route was via a broadcast from South America.) But the Japs evidently did not realize the implication any more than did the tattletale; we continued to break their codes, and Lanphier's brother received only routine mistreatment.[22]

Admiral Halsey's reasoning was understandable. His methods were an abject disgrace. He had apparently learned nothing from his experience sanctioning the *Helena*'s Captain Hoover after the *Juneau* affair.

Lieutenant Barber was at a loss:

> I have felt bad about this episode ever since. Not for myself or Lanphier because we should not have talked to Lodge at all, even though he had all or most of the information. I feel sorry for John Mitchell who did such a superb job of planning and leading the mission and had nothing to do with the Lodge episode. He should have received the Medal of Honor, just as Jimmy Doolittle did for leading his famous raid on Japan. I wish I could do something about this injustice.[23]

Not to mention Lieutenant Hine, whom Lodge could not reach for comment. But Halsey never rectified the injustice. Not the injustice he had committed against Captain Hoover, nor the injustice he committed here.

The secret of the Yamamoto mission was an open secret, at least on Guadalcanal, it was later determined. It was not difficult for such a secret to get out among all the people – operations personnel, mechanics, traffic control, everyone – who had to work to make the mission a success. That said, Guadalcanal was and is relatively isolated, to put it mildly. It's not easy for information to leave that theater. After all, Lodge had not learned about the mission on Guadalcanal. He had learned about the mission in Nouméa – from Admiral Halsey's own headquarters – from where he had flown to Auckland to find Barber, Lanphier, and Strother.

"Secure and seal" the story in a safe, Admiral Nimitz ordered Halsey. Get all copies and all notes and warn Lodge and anyone else knowing about the mission to "maintain complete silence."[24]

But though Lodge may have been the only journalist arrogant, selfish, and stupid enough to actually write a story about it, he was not the only one to learn of it. Correspondent Bob Miller of the United Press had also heard about Yamamoto being shot down. The popular Miller had worked extensively under fire on Guadalcanal, to the point where the Marines had almost adopted him. When Miller went poking around the intelligence people off the record, he was surprised at the anger over the death of Yamamoto. Miller recalled that instead of a unanimous decision to carry out the mission, some officers in "navy intelligence had argued in vain" against it. "They said that the Japanese would deduce from the attack on Yamamoto's plane that their codes had been broken and would act quickly to change them. That, they argued, would be a military intelligence disaster far outweighing any possible gains accruing from the admiral's death."[25] A valid concern, to be sure.

But it went beyond the exposure of *Magic*. There were also members of the intelligence community who wanted Admiral Yamamoto to stay alive. Because he could stand up to General Tojo and the Imperial Army in arguing that the war was lost and help convince Japan to seek peace. "Because of the respect and admiration with which he was held by both the Palace and the populace, Yamamoto was the one man with enough clout to force the bitter pill of defeat down the throats of the Japanese," Miller's sources said.[26] It was an argument that had occurred to Admiral Nimitz and his people. It was also likely wishful thinking, basing policy on what someone might do as to what they had shown they were capable of doing.

Unlike Lodge, Miller would not report on the story, because his sources had sworn him to secrecy. "This macho-military blunder, motivated solely by pique, eliminated the one Japanese who might have shortened the Pacific war," Miller believed. For someone who had been all over the Pacific and had even worked under fire on Guadalcanal, Miller seems to have understood very little about the Pacific War and the nature of the enemy. As if the fact that Yamamoto was the Imperial Navy's demonstrably best commander was unimportant, secondary to something good he might do in the future. That said, he understood the danger in writing such a story, that perhaps there was something more important than getting the story. Unlike Lodge.

But Lodge was hardly the only one who wanted to get the story out. There were certain people even within the Allied military establishment who wanted the story public. The story Lodge had submitted looked identical in numerous spots to the official report submitted of the Yamamoto ambush. Lodge had not seen that report, but he had talked to the person who had written it – Thomas Lanphier.

A report that credited Thomas Lanphier, albeit not by name, for single-handedly shooting down Admiral Yamamoto's bomber. As a result of that report:

He was thus crowned. Tom Lanphier, the brilliant pilot with seventy missions and 175 combat hours, an ace in the air and a pal to the guys in the squadron, had shot down Admiral Yamamoto. Tom Lanphier, the politically ambitious, media-friendly, and well-connected son of a ranking officer on the general staff, had shot down Admiral Yamamoto. Tom Lanphier, the killer flight leader who broke away from the chase, violated radio silence, stood in a jeep to cheer his self-proclaimed victory, wrote the after-action report, and talked openly to a reporter about the secret mission, had shot down Admiral Yamamoto.[27]

To be sure, Lanphier was a hero, just as all the other pilots on the mission were heroes. Moreover, without Lanphier turning toward the three Zeros and thus keeping them off Barber's back as he went after Yamamoto's plane, Yamamoto might well have escaped. Lanphier's act enabled the mission to succeed. He was a hero, just not the hero he wanted to be.

But that wasn't good enough for Lanphier. "Lanphier was the one pilot who was rightly in hot water, but he had a four-star angel and a bunch of lesser lights protecting him."[28]

Lanphier was also handsome and gregarious, making friends – and allies – easily. Barber was much more reserved.

Officially, until the end of the war, the record had the mission shooting down three bombers and three Zeros. Lanphier was given credit for shooting down Yamamoto's bomber. Lieutenant Barber was credited for shooting down a second bomber. Lieutenant Holmes and Lieutenant Hine were nowhere to be found.

***

Magic was, many have argued, the difference between victory and defeat in the Pacific. Its list of accomplishments was impressive – Midway, Bismarck Sea, Admiral Yamamoto's ambush.

But *Magic* was not omniscient. It was not an entity unto itself. It was a tool, and only a tool. In the hands of a skilled craftsman, it could be extremely useful. Otherwise, it could actually be dangerous to its users.

Submarine operations in the middle and upper Solomon Islands as well as the Bismarck Sea area were under the jurisdiction of the Southwest Pacific Fleet's Task Force 42 under Captain James Fife, Jr. Fife was an experienced submariner, had started the war in Manila on the staff of the Asiatic Fleet's submarines, where he had seen the excessive caution on the part of submarine skippers and the torpedo issues on the part of the Mark 14 that crippled American undersea operations during that dark time. In commanding Task Force 42, Fife had taken those lessons to heart. Maybe too much.

What normally happened was a submarine would head out – usually from Brisbane on the east coast of Australia, where Captain Fife was building a giant submarine base – to patrol a designated area. Headquarters would send out updates and orders. Perhaps too many. As the respected submarine historian Clay Blair, Jr, put it:

Fife believed the generally poor showing of US submarines basing in Brisbane up to then was due to overcaution. When he had his feet firmly planted beneath his desk, he abandoned caution. Each of his skippers would give a good account of himself or else he would be summarily relieved.

Up to then, most of the skippers had been assigned an area to patrol and left pretty much on their own. Before the Japanese changed the codes in February, there was a steady flow of information from the codebreakers about Japanese maritime forces reinforcing the

Solomons from Palau and Truk. Fife believed the submarine force could better capitalize on this information if the boats were more tightly controlled from Brisbane and shifted about frequently as targets became known. He believed he should take a direct – and firm – hand in the shifting – or as he told his staff, "playing checkers" with submarines.[29]

Using information provided by *Magic* as a guide, Fife would frequently order his boats moved about the Solomons and the Bismarck Sea. It meant a lot of messages sent out to his submarines. And a lot of acknowledgments and other messages back, which the boat could send and receive only when it surfaced, usually at night so its batteries could recharge. As a result, while surface ships and aircraft could usually radio a message when they encountered the enemy before they entered combat, a submarine usually could not. Headquarters regularly learned about submarine combat only after the fact, sometimes long after the fact, and other times not even then. If the submarine was sunk while submerged, unable to call for help, unable to abandon ship, the only ones outside the submarine who would have any idea it was sunk would be enemy.

Headquarters could be receiving a submarine's radio reports regularly, if at uneven intervals. And then ... silence. One day someone in fleet submarine operations realizes the submarine hasn't checked in and radios a request for acknowledgment, only to be met with ... silence. An order to end the patrol and return home is met with ... silence. As far as headquarters knows, the boat just vanished. All attempts to contact it are met with silence. Frustrating, ominous silence.

Submarine operations in the Task Force 42 area were even more dangerous than usual in the first three months of 1943. Recall how, on January 9, *Magic* had identified a Japanese convoy headed for Lae. Despite the Japanese having changed their codes on January 1, *Magic* was able to identify the convoy on January 9. Captain Fife vectored the submarines *Grampus* and *Argonaut* to intercept. After losing two ships to air attack, the convoy did reach Lae, then headed back with its empty ships. The *Argonaut* moved in to attack, but was detected and, in full view of a US Army Air Force bomber with empty bomb racks, was first pinned by a Val of the 582 Air Group and then blasted so badly by the destroyer *Maikaze* that the submarine's bow poked through the surface and hung there while the *Maikaze* and *Isokaze* pounded her with 5-inch gunfire until she slid back into the sea, leaving some gruesome debris. According to the Japanese, the "destroyed top of the sub floated."[30]

It was an unnecessary loss, almost self-inflicted. The largest submarine in the US Navy inventory, the *Argonaut* was, in the words of respected submarine historian Clay Blair, "[a]ncient and clumsy." She had been extensively refitted to serve as a Marine transport, the only one in the South Pacific.[31] But the same size that made her useful as an undersea transport made her unsuitable for major combat. Commander Richard H. O'Kane, who had served aboard the *Argonaut* for four years before becoming skipper of the *Tang*, said of her fighting capability, "If a fleet boat were stripped of one battery, two engines, six torpedo tubes, and could use no more than 15 degrees of rudder, she would still have greater torpedo attack and evasion ability than *Argonaut*."[32] Even historian Kent G. Budge, editor of *The Pacific War Online Encyclopedia*, went so far as to say the *Argonaut* "really had no business making a regular war patrol [...]."[33] For reasons known only to Captain Fife, he sent this cumbersome and lightly armed boat to intercept a heavily defended convoy of empty ships on her first and last war patrol.

The *Argonaut*, however, was only the start of what seemed like open season on US Navy submarines, at least those in the Task Force 42 zone. Recall that in the dark days of October 1942, after "The Bombardment" by the *Kongo* and *Haruna* had left the Cactus Air Force almost bereft of aviation fuel, the submarine *Amberjack* made an emergency run to Guadalcanal loaded with the stuff. She continued to be a very active submarine. Skippered by Lieutenant Commander John A. Bole, Jr, the *Amberjack* had left Brisbane on January 26, 1943, for her third patrol of the Solomon Islands area. She became an even more active submarine, thanks to Captain Fife. In a brilliantly written account, Clay Blair probably best described the *Amberjack*'s trek:

> Fife controlled these boats strictly, repeatedly moving them around on his checkerboard. *Amberjack*, for example, was first moved from west of New Guinea to west of Shortlands, then to west of Buka. She was next ordered west of Vella Lavella. En route, she was ordered west of Ganonnga Island. A few days later she was ordered north to cover traffic to the Shortlands. Then she was ordered farther north, and subsequently to the area between New Ireland and Bougainville. She was then shifted north of New Ireland, then ordered to a position west of New Hanover. Her last position was west of Cape Lambert.[34]

On February 3, Lieutenant Commander Bole sent his first radio report, claiming to have made contact with a Japanese submarine 14 miles southeast of Treasury Island on February 1 and sunk a two-masted schooner by gunfire 20 miles from Buka the afternoon of February 3. On Valentine's Day 1943, Bole reported the *Amberjack* had been forced down the night before by two destroyers after having fished an enemy aviator out of the water. The *Amberjack* was never heard from again.

Next was the *Grampus*, who had been very active in her own right. In October she had landed Australian coastwatchers and supplies on Vella Lavella and Choiseul. Back in January she had been vectored along with the *Argonaut* to attack that Japanese convoy bound for Lae. More recently, under skipper Lieutenant Commander John R. Craig, she had left an exercise target off Brisbane on February 12 for her sixth war patrol and a series of movements dictated by Captain Fife on his checkerboard.

On Valentine's Day 1943, the *Grampus* was ordered to patrol the area west of Shortland and south of latitude 06 degrees 30 minutes South, then the entire Rabaul, Buka, and Shortlands area, splitting the area with the submarine *Triton*, who was to cover the southern part of the zone. Six days later, Brisbane sent out orders for the *Grampus* to patrol north of latitude 04 degrees 30 minutes South until dawn on February 21, and then to patrol east of Buka and Bougainville. On March 2 she was told to round Cape Henpan, proceed down the west coast of Bougainville, south of the Treasury Islands, north of Vella Lavella, and arrive in the Vella Gulf on the afternoon of March 5, when the *Grampus* was to join the submarine *Grayback* in patrolling the Vella Gulf to catch Japanese ships trying to escape Admiral Merrill's advancing cruiser force through the Blackett Strait. These orders went out to both submarines and made each aware of the other's assignment. The *Grayback* acknowledged the order but the *Grampus* did not, just as she had not acknowledged any of the other orders she had received – had apparently not communicated at all with anyone – since she left on February 12.

After she left Brisbane, the *Grampus* was never heard from again.

Like the *Amberjack* and *Grampus*, the *Triton* had been a very active submarine. Under skipper Lieutenant Commander George Kenneth MacKenzie, Jr, the *Triton* left Brisbane on February 16 for her sixth war patrol. She would pass through the Rabaul-Buka-Shortlands area, the *Grampus*' patrol area, on the way northward to her own patrol zone. At around noon on March 6, in the adjacent patrol zone of the submarine *Trigger*, the *Triton* engaged a Japanese convoy of five ships – the destroyer *Yuzuki* escorting the freighters *Kiriha*, *Mito*, *Nagano*, and *Ryuzan Marus*. MacKenzie managed to plunk a torpedo into the stern of the 3,057-ton *Kiriha Maru*, killing four of the ship's crew as well as the ship itself. Another torpedo apparently thunked into the side of the *Mito Maru*, not exploding but leaving an unsightly dent. A third torpedo of the *Triton*'s made that special torpedo maneuver seemingly unique to American torpedoes – the Circular Torpedo Run, in which the torpedo is launched and, instead of heading for the target on the assigned gyro angle, it circles around threatening to hit the submarine that launched it. The *Triton* had to dive deep to avoid her own munitions. It also gave the *Yuzuki* the chance to drop depth charges on her, albeit without damage.[35]

Lieutenant Commander MacKenzie reported this action in messages of March 7 and 8. The *Triton* later tried two night attacks, one at dawn, and one in the afternoon, all without success. She started heading back to her area, but not before making one more night attack on a convoy. MacKenzie claimed five hits out of eight torpedoes fired, sinking two freighters, although he could not confirm results because an escorting destroyer charged in and forced the *Triton* to go deep.[36]

On March 11, Captain Fife's headquarters received a message from the *Triton*: "Two groups of smokes (funnel smoke from a ship's stack), 5 or more ships each, plus escorts ... Am chasing." In response, Fife ordered the *Triton* to stay south of the Equator and reminded her that the submarine *Trigger* was in an adjacent patrol area.[37] Two days later, a warning was sent out that three Japanese destroyers had been sighted heading northward in the general direction of her patrol area, probably on a submarine hunt or a convoy cover who had missed contact with their charges. Her patrol zone was moved slightly to the east on March 16. Finally, on March 25 the *Triton* was ordered back to Brisbane. But after the submarine's March 11 update, all messages sent to the *Triton* were met with silence.

The *Triton* was never heard from again.

On March 22, the US Navy listed the *Amberjack* and *Grampus* as overdue and presumed lost, beginning the process of notifying the crew's families. On April 10, the same determination was made for the *Triton*. Public announcements were made on June 12 and July 22, respectively.

Four boats lost within two months. As Clay Blair put it, "In peacetime, the loss of four submarines in so short a time would ordinarily prompt an extensive investigation to determine blame: heads would roll."[38] Of course, in peacetime, no enemy would be trying to sink the submarines, so the loss of four submarines in so short a time would be much more cause for concern.

The Navy investigated the loss of each of the submarines, but until they had access to Japanese records – and at this time the Japanese were being less than completely cooperative – they had very little to go on. After the war, it … didn't improve much.

Part of the problem was that the *Amberjack* and the *Grampus* were lost in the same area at almost the same time. To further complicate matters, there was considerable submarine and antisubmarine activity in that area, any one or more of which could have involved the *Amberjack* and the *Grampus*. Investigators found a number of clues to sort out.

According to Japanese records, at 10:00am on February 16, a convoy consisting of the torpedo boat *Hiyodori* and the submarine chaser *Ch-18* escorting the transport *Noshiro Maru*, with air cover provided by a seaplane, probably an Aichi E13A Type 0 reconnaissance seaplane from the 958 Air Group, left Rabaul for Kolombangara. They were off Cape St George when, at 3:28 that afternoon, they spotted four torpedo tracks off the starboard beam, 4,000 meters away. The torpedoes were successfully avoided.

About six minutes later, the seaplane located the attacking submarine and dropped several depth charges. At 3:40, the *Hiyodori* arrived on site and dropped nine depth charges on the submarine's suspected location. Some five minutes later, the *Ch-18* got a fix on the boat and dropped six depth charges. This last attack brought oil welling to the surface. As the oil slick expanded, in the middle of it a conning tower appeared, its upper section bursting through the surface. That's generally a bad sign for the submarine. Before the Japanese could train their guns on it, however, the tower disappeared back into the oil slick.

Smelling blood or at least oil in the water, *Ch-18* dropped three more depth charges, and would have dropped still more except "parts of the hull" floated to the surface. That was it for the combat. The Japanese milled around looking for more debris. At 4:42pm, the *Hiyodori* recovered several items, including a life raft printed with the words "Philadelphia Navy Yard." Debris in the water is usually a good indication of a sinking. The Japanese certainly thought so and recorded it as such.

The next day, February 17, the Japanese made two submarine sightings, both times apparently catching the same submarine. Which would soon make a nuisance of itself. On February 18, the armed auxiliary aircraft transport *Keiyo Maru* took a submarine torpedo and was "lightly damaged." This was not the result for which the boat's skipper had been hoping, so she came back for Round 2 on February 19. This time the results were "unknown," but the *Keiyo Maru* remained afloat and operational. Another proud performance for the Mark 14 torpedo.

Two attacks in two days by the same submarine on the same ship, resulting in, at best, light damage. That was embarrassing. For both the Americans and the Japanese. The Japanese were having none of it. The 958 Air Group sent out several seaplanes, probably Aichi E13A Type 0 reconnaissance seaplanes again, to bother the bothersome boat.[39] They found a submarine southeast of New Britain, probably at periscope depth, and proceeded to bomb it. They reported one direct hit on the conning tower. The next day two patrol boats returned to the area and found a large oil slick.[40] The Japanese considered that evidence of a sinking and, again, recorded it as such.

But, well, it may not have been. The Japanese reported another submarine sighting on February 24. And recall that on February 27, in the aftermath of an American air attack on a convoy off Kolombangara that heavily damaged the transport *Kirikawa Maru* and forced her scuttling, the escorting minesweeper *W-22* was the recipient of an ineffective submarine attack.

The antisubmarine attack on February 16 was in the *Amberjack's* patrol area, though the recipient could have been the *Grampus* if she had strayed into that area tracking a particular target. All the submarine sightings and attacks, as well as the antisubmarine attacks after February 16 referenced above, were in the patrol area of the *Grampus* as it shifted on Captain Fife's checkerboard. There was one further sighting of a submarine in the *Grampus'* patrol area. On the night of March 5–6, when the *Grampus* and *Grayback* were assigned to hold blocking positions in Vella Gulf, the *Grayback* heard propellers and sighted a dark shape moving in the area assigned to the *Grampus*. The *Grayback's* skipper Lieutenant Commander Stephan assumed it was the *Grampus*, but he could not confirm it because his boat's SJ radar, by which those signals would have been transmitted and received, was malfunctioning.[41]

The *Minegumo* and *Murasame* had passed through the Vella Gulf and the Blackett Strait, but aside from their destruction at the hands of Admiral Merrill's cruisers, the *Grayback* saw nothing else of note that night.

That was the last reported sighting of anything that could have been a submarine in the patrol zone assigned to the *Grampus*. The next afternoon, a scout plane from Guadalcanal, probably a Kiwi Hudson from No. 3 Squadron, reported an oil slick southeast of Kolombangara, suggesting damage incurred the previous night, presumably in some sort of combat action.[42] The *Grampus* was ordered to check in on March 7, then again on March 8. No reply from the submarine was received.

The above factors – sightings of a submarine in patrol areas assigned to the *Grampus*, the presence of two enemy destroyers in her area the night of March 5–6, the oil slick reported the next day, the lack of any communication with or sighting of the *Grampus* after March 6 – have led to the conclusion that the *Grampus* was sunk the night of March 5–6 by the Japanese destroyers *Minegumo* and *Murasame*, whose own sinking a few hours later accounts for the lack of records of their attack on the submarine. It is a sound, logical conclusion based on the available information. Naturally, it is wrong.

The destroyer *Minegumo* had 122 survivors, including the gunnery officer Lieutenant Tokuno. The *Marusame* had 53 survivors, including Captain Tachibana, skipper Lieutenant Commander Tanegashima Youji, and gunnery officer Lieutenant Kayama. At no time did any of these senior officers, or any other survivors of the two destroyers, mention conducting any kind of antisubmarine or surface action before they landed at Vila. For that matter, the timeline of their approach to Vila does not leave room for an antisubmarine attack. The sighting of the unidentified shadow submarine in the *Grampus'* patrol area of Vella Gulf may have even been after the two destroyers had passed into the Blackett Strait. For the record, the Vella Gulf has never been a hotbed of maritime activity.

Further complicating matters are silence on two major questions. A scout plane from Guadalcanal reported an oil slick "SE (of) Kolombangara" the afternoon of March 6. This would seem to reference the source of the "oil slick reported in Blackett Strait" on March 6 that so many histories mention, but the wording of the report leaves open the possibility that the slick may not have been in Blackett Strait but in Kula Gulf, expanding the already significant possibility that it is not related to the loss of the *Grampus*. More frustratingly for investigators and historians, there was no communication at all from the *Grampus* after she left a practice target off Brisbane on February 12. This major wild card, oddly, does not get a lot of attention from historians. The fact that the *Grampus* made no radio communication since what was effectively the beginning of her war patrol suggests she developed a problem early on with her radio suite that prevented her from sending messages, a problem she perhaps did not detect for some time. At the same time, however, the sighting of submarines in the patrol area of the *Grampus* as that patrol area shifted with Captain Fife's orders suggests she was able to receive messages.

In short, it seems that the submarine *Grampus* survived until at least March 5–6. At some point during that night or afterwards, the submarine sank for reasons unknown. What is known is the 958 Air Group reported making antisubmarine attacks on March 15 and 16 while covering a sea truck en route to Bairoko Harbor, New Georgia.[43] Also of possible interest is the record of the Royal Australian Air Force's No. 71 Squadron, who was responsible for antisubmarine patrols off Brisbane, the main base of submarine Task Force 42. On March 17, a patrol plane dropped a 250lb bomb on a suspected submarine. Eleven days later, another scout plane reported being fired on by a similar vessel.[44] Any of these incidents, or the US Navy's Circular Torpedo Run or other operational accident, could have caused the end of the *Grampus*. Without more information, all that can be said is that the *Grampus* went down with all hands no earlier than March 5–6, 1943, time, place, and cause unknown.

Which brings up the even more complicated case of the submarine *Triton*. On March 11, the *Triton* reported that she had sighted "Two groups of smokes, five or more ships each, plus escorts ... Am chasing." That was the last definite time anyone heard from the *Triton*. The US Navy's official position:

Information available now that the war is over shows that *Triton* was, without a doubt, sunk by the enemy destroyers of which she was given information on 13 March. Enemy reports show that these ships made an attack on 15 March at 0°-09'N, 144°-55'E. This position was slightly north and west of *Triton's* area, but she undoubtedly left her area to attack the destroyers or the convoy they were escorting. The report of the attack [by] the destroyers leaves little doubt as to whether a kill was made, since they saw "a great quantity of oil, pieces of wood, corks and manufactured goods bearing the mark 'Made in U.S.A.'" In addition, *Trigger*, in whose area this attack occurred, reported that on 15 March she made two attacks on a convoy of five freighters with two escorts at 0°N, 145° E. At this time she was depth charged, but not seriously, and she heard distant depth charging for an hour after the escorts had stopped attacking her. Since she was only about ten miles from the reported Japanese attack cited above, it presumed that she heard the attack which sank *Triton*. Apparently by this time the destroyers had joined their convoy.[45]

The US Navy's official position tries to wrap everything up with a nice bow, but the wrapping paper isn't quite taped down. Submarine historians Clay Blair, Jr and Ed Howard, and *Imperial Japanese Navy Page* historian Allyn Nevitt have all found the Navy's position lacking in specifics and unconvincing. Blair wrote, "After the war, US naval authorities made an intensive hunt in Japanese records to determine the causes for each loss [i.e., *Triton*, *Grampus*, and *Amberjack*]. There were clues, giving rise to various speculations, but nothing positive was ever learned about any of them."[46] Howard was more blunt:

> The only thing that can be said with certitude is that *Triton* was never heard from again after March 11, 1943. At that time, she reported being in pursuit of two groups of enemy vessels, each having five or more ships with escorts. We know that the Navy was under a lot of pressure after the war to find explanations for the losses of the *Amberjack*, the *Grampus*, and the *Triton*. The final report they published on the *Triton's* loss in 1946 does not bring final closure to the issue. Research published since its publication casts doubt on most of the explanations presented in the Navy's report and renders it speculative, at best. The *Triton's* loss remains an unsolved mystery.[47]

Meanwhile, Nevitt performed a thoroughly thorough analysis of the movements of 35 Japanese destroyers in the South Pacific in the time period around March 15, 1943, the date of the *Triton's* reported sinking. Nevitt could not identify the "three destroyers" allegedly responsible for the sinking, but suggests the origin and identity of these mysterious "three destroyers."[48]

It will be recalled that March 11 saw the last message ever received from the *Triton*, reporting that she had sighted "Two groups of smokes, five or more ships each, plus escorts ... Am chasing." The *Triton* appears to have been chasing the convoy designated "Hansa No. 1," with seven transports carrying elements of the 20th Division to, oddly enough, Hansa Bay, eastern New Guinea. It left Palau on March 6 with the escort of destroyers *Kazagumo*, carrying the commander of Destroyer Division 10, Captain Yoshimura Matake; *Yugumo*, *Satsuki*, *Akigumo*, and *Samidare*. It was while escorting this convoy that on March 11 the *Satsuki* dropped six depth charges on a suspected submarine, with "results unknown."[49]

The convoy arrived at Hansa Bay on March 12. Offloading was completed in a day. Captain Yoshimura was ordered to take the *Kazagumo*, *Yugumo*, and *Satsuki* to Rabaul, where they were to make supply runs in the Solomons, so they headed out together. The *Akigumo* and *Samidare* got the privilege of escorting the transports back to Palau. But on their way out, at about 6:30pm on March 13, they were caught by five B-17s from the 5th Air Force's 63rd Bombardment Squadron, 43rd Bombardment Group, who managed to hit the *Momoyama Maru*, killing nine and leaving the transport disabled. The *Akigumo* took survivors on board and scuttled the derelict with one torpedo.[50] This convoy was the likely genesis for the warning of "three destroyers heading north" toward the *Triton*'s patrol area. Those three destroyers were the *Kazagumo*, *Yugumo*, and *Satsuki* heading to Rabaul. Either the B-17s or the submarine *Greenling*, who had witnessed the attack on the *Momoyama Maru*, probably saw Captain Yoshimura's three destroyers in the distance and called it in.[51]

At around the same time, a second convoy left Rabaul on March 12, 1943, bound for Palau. The convoy consisted of seven merchant ships with an escort of the old destroyer *Mochizuki* and the repair vessel *Nagaura*.[52] Not part of the convoy were the subchasers *Ch-23* and *Ch-24*, but they left Rabaul the same day to meet an incoming convoy for escort.[53]

The trip was uneventful until March 15, when at 12:15pm the *Momoha Maru* was hit by a torpedo in the engine room and lost power. The torpedo was courtesy of the stern tubes of the submarine *Trigger* under Lieutenant Commander Roy S. Benson. Two minutes later, he fired three bow tubes at a second target at an angle almost right on the bow, a "down-the-throat shot," and promptly dove so his target would not ram his boat. Benson heard what he thought were hits, as well as the sounds of a ship breaking up from the direction of her first target. This would have been the *Momoha Maru*, who sank with no casualties five minutes after she was hit.[54] The *Nagaura* was detailed to pick up survivors.

About two hours later, the escorts were transferring the *Momoha Maru*'s survivors to the *Florida Maru* when, at 2:55pm, the *Florida Maru* took a torpedo and was disabled. Subchaser *Ch-23*, though not part of the convoy, was directed to pick up her survivors.[55] At the same time, the *Trigger* was lurking underneath the waves, looking for another opportunity to attack. It was shortly after this time that the *Trigger* heard distant depth charging, which Lieutenant Commander Benson assumed was from aircraft, that lasted about an hour. Closer to evening, the *Trigger* came back to periscope depth and took a look around. Benson saw a ship that looked like his second target, now inching along with the help of another ship, both of which were protected by a pair of small escorts. What

Benson saw now was the damaged *Florida Maru*, moving very slowly, possibly with the current. Not unreasonably, Benson thought the *Florida Maru* was wallowing in the water as a result of his earlier attack. More interesting here are the three ships around the staggering transport. Two were "small destroyers or corvettes," which is a description consistent with a subchaser. The *Ch-23* had been assigned to help the *Florida Maru*. Benson made two attacks after dark, neither of which was successful. The *Trigger* was later given credit for sinking one ship, the *Momoha Maru*, and damaging a second, the *Florida Maru*.

However, awarding the *Florida Maru* damage to the *Trigger* was erroneous. Lieutenant Commander Benson launched the torpedoes for his second attack only about two minutes after his first attack that sank the *Momoha Maru*. Japanese records are specific in that survivors of the *Momoha Maru* were being transferred to the *Florida Maru* when the latter took a torpedo, which was a little more than two-and-a-half hours after the first attack. While Benson's belief that his boat had torpedoed the *Florida Maru* was reasonable at the time, when his timeline is placed against that of the Japanese, it becomes clear that the *Trigger* could not have torpedoed the *Florida Maru*. It would seem that Benson's torpedoes had detonated prematurely; ask the *Argonaut* how that happens.

Nevertheless, it is quite obvious that *someone* torpedoed the *Florida Maru*. That someone had to be the *Triton*, who was known to be operating in the area of the *Trigger*. While the *Trigger* was submerged after her first two attacks, the *Triton* attacked the *Florida Maru* and scored one disabling hit. Lieutenant Commander Benson and his crew heard the aftermath of this attack: the depth charging of the *Triton*. Who did the depth charging is open to debate: the most likely culprits are the Japanese subchasers *Ch-24* and *Ch-22*.[56]

The *Triton* was never heard from again after this. If the US Navy's version is to be believed, the Japanese reported the water where she went down was covered in "a great quantity of oil, pieces of wood, corks and manufactured goods bearing the mark 'Made in U.S.A.'"

The ambush of Admiral Yamamoto changed little in the Solomons Campaign. The holding pattern that had been in place since the occupation of the Russell Islands after securing Guadalcanal remained. Both sides continued trying to rotate some units in and out while building up others for the next round of fighting that was sure to come. It was during this time that the Pacific War settled back into its normal routine – not the big battles like Midway and Friday the 13th, but smaller scale air attacks, fighter sweeps, clashes of patrol planes, one-off bombing attacks on isolated enemy ships; a nick here, a cut there, a bruise someplace else. These little wounds, as always, would add up.

The night after the death of Admiral Yamamoto, ten G4Ms of the 705 Air Group took off from Buka for a nighttime air attack on Guadalcanal. Only nine returned, because the Type 1 of Flight Chief Petty Officer Furaya Sadao was shot down (to the cheers of thousands of watching troops on the ground) by Captain Earl Bennett and his radar operator Corporal Edwin Tomlinson from the 6th Night Fighter Squadron.[57] The 6th was a new organization that had been in Guadalcanal since early March, but teething pains such as too short a runway and a lack of ground control interception equipment or a compatible ground radar station had prevented it from becoming fully functional until late March. Bennett and the other members of the squadron flew the P-70 Nighthawk, which was only an A-20 Havoc modified to act as a night fighter. Although these Havocs had not been modified by Pappy Gunn to become heavily armed commerce destroyers, they were heavily armed enough: four 20mm cannons, two .50-cal. machine guns firing forward, a third .50-cal. machine gun firing below and aft; and two .30-cal. machine guns firing above and aft. More importantly, each Nighthawk had SCR-540 airborne interception radar, an American copy of the British Mark IV airborne interception radar.[58]

This night, it paid off with the first night fighter victory by the US Army Air Force, for which Bennett and Tomlinson had to be proud.[59] It was not the first, nor the last, loss of a veteran Sea Eagle pilot and air crew, and a night-trained crew at that. That was enough to get the 705 yanked back to Tinian for some training and R and R, or at least as much R and R as was possible on Tinian.[60] Conversely, it had taken about three months, but the Americans now had a counter for Japanese attacks such as the one that sank the *Chicago*. And while the Nighthawk was very flawed as a fighter – for example, its operating ceiling was too low to engage high-altitude targets, and the radar overloaded its electrical system – the Americans now had a little bleach for Washing Machine Charlie and insecticide for Louie the Louse.

It was part of the program to reinforce the Henderson Field complex as well as rotate its units. As the Yamamoto mission was being prepared, the US Army Air Force's 18th Fighter Group started to Guadalcanal, joining the 347th Fighter Group. The 12th, 40th, and 70th Fighter Squadrons were transferred to the 18th from the 347th, which retained the 67th, 68th, and 339th Fighter Squadrons.[61]

For his part, Admiral Kusaka was planning to rotate his own air units. Already dissolved back in April was Admiral Jojima's 11th Seaplane Tender Division and with it the cryptically named R-Area Air Force.[62] The 25th Air Flotilla under the command of Rear Admiral Ueno Keizo was set to return to the Solomons to relieve Admiral Ichimaru's 21st Air Flotilla, which would return to Japan for some R and R. Similarly, Admiral Kosaka's 26th Air Flotilla was to be relieved by the 24th Air Flotilla, coming down from Saipan.[63]

But the Americans threw a monkey wrench into the works. Or, more precisely, the Japanese response to American actions threw a monkey wrench into the works. On May 11, US Army troops landed on Attu, one of the two Aleutian islands captured by the Japanese during the Midway operation in June 1942. While the landing threatened a Japanese-held position, to be sure, the response by Imperial

General Headquarters to the American landing was out of all proportion to the island's infinitesimal strategic value.

The first response was by the Naval General Staff, who activated the 12th Air Fleet. Now Combined Fleet had two land-based air forces, Admiral Kusaka's 11th Air Fleet and this new 12th Air Fleet. The 11th Air Fleet had been "Base Air Force," because it was an air force that flew from a base. Now there were two air forces that flew from bases, so the 11th became "1st Base Air Force" and the 12th became "2nd Base Air Force." Adding the ordinals reduced the coolness factor of the name "Base Air Force," especially since both the 1st Base Air Force and the 2nd Base Air Force together did not match up in terms of combat strength with the original Base Air Force. Sequels are rarely as good as the original.

But, far worse, the Japanese were now pulling some of the units Admiral Kusaka had planned to rotate into Rabaul to fill the new 2nd Base Air Force and deal with the Aleutians situation. Instead of rotating with the 26th Air Flotilla, the 24th Air Flotilla was packaged with the 27th Air Flotilla in 2nd Base Air Force. Admiral Kosaka and his pilots would get no relief. Admiral Ichimaru's 21st Air Flotilla was still pulled out, but instead of going to Japan it was sent to Saipan, which may not have been the rest the aircrews had been hoping for.

Admiral Ueno's 25th Air Flotilla's happy return to the mosquitos, malaria, and volcanoes of Rabaul came off on May 10 as planned, but without its 801 Air Group, which was sent to the Marshall Islands. That left the 25th with only two air groups, but both were formidable. The 251 had 60 Zeros and ten of the new Nakajima J1N Navy Type 2 Reconnaissance Planes. The Allies would call this plane the "Irving," but the Japanese would call it the *Gekko* ("Moonlight"). The Gekko would be their insurance against enemy nighttime attacks by serving as a night fighter. Night fighting would become the primary mission of the 251. The 25th's other air group was the 702, which had 47 G4Ms at Vunakanau by May 14.[64]

Just after the American landing on Attu, on the night of May 12–13 Admiral Ainsworth came up with four light cruisers (*Nashville, St Louis, Helena,* and flagship *Honolulu*) and seven destroyers (*Strong, Chevalier, Nicholas, Jenkins, Fletcher, Taylor,* and *O'Bannon*) to bombard Munda and Vila once again.[65] The combination of this bombardment and the invasion of Attu convinced Admiral Kusaka and General Inamura that a move against New Guinea was imminent. The Japanese could not accept that other militaries did not share their passion for division, diversion, and distraction. In fact, Ainsworth's bombardment was only a cover for laying another minefield. Admiral Halsey wanted the Ferguson Passage mined because the Japanese could use it to enter the Blackett Strait and get to Vila. They already had, actually; and it was just luck that they had still sailed into the minefield Lieutenant Commander Romoser and his minelayers had laid. So Romoser once again had his destroyer *Radford* lead the *Preble, Gamble,* and *Breese* in laying another minefield, this time blocking the Ferguson Passage instead of bisecting it, under the bombardment's cover.

Very expensive cover, as it turned out. The light cruiser *Nashville* suffered an explosion in her Number 3 6-inch turret that necessitated her return to the US for repairs, while a powder cartridge in the destroyer *Nicholas* cooked off, wrecking the mount. The *Chevalier* suffered a mount explosion of her own and was lucky to avoid colliding with the destroyer *Strong*, whose steering engine had broken down. The anchor of the light cruiser *St Louis* was swept away and punched a hole in her bow. To top off this Wile E. Coyote operation, the Japanese quickly swept up the mines, so ultimately the operation brought little benefit to the Allies.[66]

Be that as it may, on May 13 Admiral Kusaka tried to counter this supposed operation against New Guinea by launching two air operations. The first had a cast of 22 Zeros from the 204 Air Group, 18 from the 582, and 14 from the 253, all there to sweep over the airfields on the Russells and Guadalcanal. In response, AirSols sent up a swarm of 102 fighters, including Marine Fighting Squadrons 112 and 124 with their Corsairs, and the Army Air Force's 70th Fighter Squadron with its Lightnings, along with its usual eclectic assortment of Wildcats, Airacobras, Warhawks, and Kittyhawks.[67]

It promised to be a chaotic battle royal, and it was, albeit not in the way either side intended. As it always did, AirSols had problems directing its usual eclectic assortment of Corsairs, Lightnings, Wildcats, Airacobras, Warhawks, and Kittyhawks, so only about a third of the interceptors reached the Japanese, giving the Japanese a numerical advantage. Four Corsairs, including one flown by veteran Marine Fighting 124 commanding officer Captain William Gise, whose body was never recovered, and one Lightning, were lost. For their part, the Japanese lost four fighters with their pilots, including veterans Flight Warrant Officer Noda Hayato and Flight Petty Officer 2nd Class Kariya Yuki of the 204 Air Group and Flight Petty Officer 2nd Class Sasaki Shogo of the 582, with five planes damaged.[68]

The fighter sweep may have been cover for Admiral Kusaka's second operation against Guadalcanal, which itself had to be juggled with the ever-present need to keep the pressure up in New Guinea. The operation ostensibly consisted of two parts. In the first, the 702 and 705 Air Groups were tasked with the destruction of enemy shipping southeast of San Cristobal. Generally, a reconnaissance plane would scout ahead to find targets for a following formation of maybe six to 12 G4Ms from Vunakanau. Both the scouts and the follow-up strikes had to fly routes north of the Solomons, then turn south to get to the target areas without alerting those meddling coastwatchers. The second part was a series of nighttime attacks on the airfields on Guadalcanal and in the Russell Islands.[69]

If this sounds like a prescription for wearing out the bombers' crews, that's because it was. And that was far from all, as the need to keep the pressure on New Guinea poked its head in again. The 751 Air Group was supposed to be pulled back to Tinian for some of the R and R that only Tinian could offer. But it was called upon to perform just one last mission. It's always just one last mission.

This mission was to be a daylight attack on Oro Bay in New Guinea on May 14. Lieutenant Commander Nishioka Kazuo, a savvy veteran who had led the *coup de grace* of the *Chicago*, led 18 G4Ms out of Kavieng to Rabaul, where they were joined by an escort of 33 Zeros from the 251 Air Group out of Lakunai. They arrived at the north coast of New Guinea around 10:20am, but any hopes the Japanese had of surprise were foiled by the inopportune appearance of a Japanese Army Air Force Mitsubishi Ki-46 reconnaissance plane. Two American P-38s of the 9th Fighter Squadron were vectored to investigate it. Lieutenant Martin "Pete" Alger sighted the Dinah heading for Oro Bay. He described it:

> I saw the enemy aeroplane at "nine o'clock" at about 28,000ft. I called Lt Finberg and told him the position, but he could not see it, so he told me to chase it. I turned toward the enemy and gave chase. I was indicating 250mph at 28,000ft, and caught him after about five minutes. I made an attack from the left rear and set the left engine alight. I passed under him and turned back for a rear attack from the right. On this pass I set his right engine smoking. I then sat behind him and continued to fire until he blew up, the aircraft continuing to burn all the way down. I saw one half-opened parachute following the flaming ship, and it hit the water about 100 yards behind the bomber. I claim one enemy bomber, type "Dinah."[70]

Alger shot the Dinah down by the shore of Cape Ward Hunt at 9:35am.[71] The incident seemed to alert the 9th that something was up, so they were ready when the incoming bombers were detected on radar.

As a result, all three squadrons from the 49th Fighter Group – 13 Lightnings of the 9th Fighter Squadron; 16 Warhawks of the 8th; and eight Warhawks from the 7th, all from the Dobodura air complex – were in the air when the Japanese arrived. While four Warhawks from the 8th received garbled information and never engaged the Japanese, the rest jumped the Japanese strike south of Oro Bay, resulting in a brutal 45-minute melee that for the most part saw the Lightnings tangle with the Zeros and the Warhawks hit the Bettys. The 9th's 2nd Lieutenant Arthur Bauhoff was caught in a crossfire by a pair of 251 Air Group veterans and had to parachute from his falling fighter into the sea; a rescue boat later sent to recover him found only a school of sharks. Bauhoff was the only pilot lost, though one P-40 had to be written off after landing. How many Japanese aircraft were lost is subject to some dispute. American sources state that officially 11 Bettys and ten Zeros did not return to base. Japanese sources insist all their aircraft returned except for six G4Ms: three were shot down and three were so badly damaged they had to ditch on the way back. Among those who ditched was Nishioka. Japanese submarines managed to recover two of the downed aircrews, but not Nishioka, who joined the *Chicago* at the bottom of the sea.[72] That one last mission had been one last mission too many, costing another of the dwindling number of veteran Sea Eagles, an expense the Japanese Naval Air Force could not afford.

The expense increased the next day, as a dozen 251 Air Group Zeros escorted G4Ms on a mission searching for Lieutenant Commander Nishioka and the other missing bomber crews. The Japanese stumbled across six of General Kenney's B-25 Mitchells near

Gasmata. In the brief melee that followed, the Mitchells appear to have kept a strong defensive formation, with their gunners shooting down three Zeros, killing two fighter pilots. The Japanese claimed one B-25 shot down and one probable, though in actuality they had shot down no one.[73]

In the meantime, Admiral Kusaka was going ahead with his daily day-night doubleheader of attacks by (1st) Base Air Force. Four daytime attacks were made on Allied shipping, but only one had any semblance of success. On May 23 at 11:35am, the advance scout passed over the PT boat tender *Niagara* and a flock of six PT boats of Motor Torpedo Boat Division 23 some 200 miles southeast of Lunga.[74] The *Niagara* had been leading her boats on a feint toward Espiritu Santo until outside the range of Japanese air attacks, then making the run to her real destination: Milne Bay. That effort was moot now: the Japanese had found her.

The *Niagara*'s skipper, Lieutenant Commander David B. Coleman, ordered battle stations and flank speed, and had the boats assume a wide circular formation around the ship. For all the good that did. The aircraft turned around and roared back, dropping four bombs in an effort to hit the *Niagara*. Coleman had the ship in a hard starboard turn, but once the bombs started falling, he swung the rudder back to center. The evasive maneuvers worked, sort of. No bombs hit, but three were near misses to starboard and one to port. The concussions disabled the sound gear and jammed one of the 3-inch guns in train. Worse, the *Niagara* lost rudder control. Still, like so many other instances in this war, it could have been worse.

And it soon was: 30 minutes later, to be precise. Helm control had been restored, but six Bettys of the 702 Air Group came from the north at 12,000 feet, well above the range of the *Niagara*'s sole remaining operational 3-inch gun, let alone her 20mm guns.[75] Even so, the multiple calm, cool passes over defenseless Cavite Navy Yard this was not. The G4Ms made one pass over the *Niagara*, dropping 12 to 18 bombs. They got one hit, on the forecastle, and several damaging near misses whose towering water columns hid the tender from the view of her surrounding PT boats.

When she reappeared, it seemed that this meager score for the 702 Air Group was enough. Thick white smoke boiled from a fire near the bow caused by the hit. A near miss caused a 14-inch hole six feet below the waterline that flooded two storerooms and a passageway, causing the *Niagara* to quickly develop a port list. Ultimately, because the *Niagara* was an old, converted yacht and very poorly compartmentalized, the hull rupture caused flooding in the engine room. All power went out and the *Niagara* stumbled to a halt. Power and helm control were restored within seven minutes after the attack. But Lieutenant Commander Coleman struggled to correct or even stabilize the list to port, while damage control was having difficulties controlling the blaze near the bow. With the fire approaching the *Niagara*'s gasoline storage tanks, Coleman ordered the PT tender abandoned.

Lieutenant Charles H. Jackson, head of Motor Torpedo Boat Division 23, brought his *PT-146* to the port side of the *Niagara*'s stern, while Lieutenant William E. Stedman brought *PT-147* to the starboard side of the stern. Both commenced evacuating the wounded and other crewmen; still others went over the side to be rescued by other PT boats. By this time the fire in the bow had spread all the way to the bridge, cooking off the ammunition in the ready service boxes, with no end in sight to the advancing conflagration.

One PT boat historian admits that the *Niagara* "might have stayed afloat for an hour or more," but with the PT boats now deprived of their fuel source, Lieutenant Commander Coleman wanted to free them as soon as he could, so he ordered the *Niagara* scuttled. Lieutenant Stedman had the *PT-147* launch one torpedo that hit the gasoline tanks, sending a fireball 300 feet into the sky and the *Niagara* down to the depths in less than 60 seconds.

It was an outcome that pleased neither side. The idea that the *Niagara* "might have stayed afloat for an hour or more" seems to have gotten back to Admiral Nimitz, who thought Lieutenant Commander Coleman's decision to scuttle the tender, "seem[ed] precipitate," meaning hasty or not completely thought out. But Nimitz did allow, "Details regarding the *Niagara* are insufficient for judgment."[76] By that same token, sinking a motor torpedo boat tender was not exactly the strategic coup for which Admiral Kusaka had so hoped with his antishipping attacks.

The admiral's attacks on Guadalcanal and the Russells did not go much better. The first night attack, made by six G4Ms the evening of May 13, ran into Lightnings from the 12th Fighter Squadron, whose Lieutenant William Smith claimed one Betty shot down and another pinned in searchlight beams damaged. The Japanese recorded all land attack planes returned to base, but the attack damaged little.[77]

The next of the night attacks took place on May 18–19, with six G4Ms attacking the Russell Islands and Guadalcanal's Fighter 1 for three hours, but, again, doing little damage. That whole bombing-a-dirt-airfield thing. The following night came the biggest raid of Admiral Kusaka's mini campaign: nine G4Ms in four separate attacks, this time killing 14 and wounding 20 on the ground. But there would be a price for Base Air Force, because the Type 1s faced a bunch of P-38 Lightnings, seven of which were sent up in four relays, so one was always ready to intercept. This night, that one was often Louis Kittel, now a major with the 70th Fighter Squadron. He would orbit at high altitude in his P-38 and watch for the Bettys showing up in searchlights or for pinpoints of fire from the Bettys' exhausts. When Kittel saw these signs, he would pounce, shooting down one Betty at 9:02pm and a second at 11:16.[78] Kittel had made himself an innovator in the field of night interception, particularly night visual interception. He volunteered for eight night-interception missions for a total of ten hours during May 13–23. Kittel intercepted three and shot down the aforementioned two. His efforts earned him the Distinguished Flying Cross.[79]

The results of the night aerial Japanese offensive were underwhelming and costly. First was the material damage. The 705 Air Group suffered so many damaged G4Ms that repair crews had to be flown from Rabaul to its forward base at Ballale to make repairs.[80] And the missions were costing the Japanese Naval Air Force more aviators that it did not have. The shortage had reached critical proportions in the bomber units. After the 751 Air Group was withdrawn to Tinian, without its veteran air officer Lieutenant Commander Nishioka, it was compelled to reorganize its G4M crews, and not in a good way. The standard complement was reduced from seven to five; one of the positions eliminated was that of the co-pilot. So, if the pilot was killed, wounded, or otherwise incapacitated, good luck to the rest of the crew. It was a practice that eventually found its way into the other land attack plane units, contributing to the loss of even more experienced air crews.[81]

The results were not up to Admiral Kusaka's expectations or hopes. But he was willing to give it another *I-Go*. Kusaka believed it would "buy time to increase the defensive force in the Central Solomons." That it was needed so soon after the first *I-Go* suggested that the first operation had not bought that much time, a conclusion that does not seem to have occurred to the admiral. So in late May, Kusaka proposed another *I-Go* to Admiral Koga using aircraft from both 1st Base Air Force and *Kido Butai*. Koga nixed the idea of using *Kido Butai* because he was going to move the carriers to Truk so they would be ready for that decisive battle with the Pacific Fleet, whenever that happened. But Kusaka, Koga said, could attack with his Base Air Force on his own if he wished. Kusaka must have been thrilled.[82]

Base Air Force began its planning. The G4Ms of the 702 and 705 Air Groups would not be used, presumably because they had been chewed up and worn out performing those day-night doubleheaders a few weeks prior, which were evidently considered so effective that they would repeat those day-night doubleheaders during the current operation.[83]

Base Air Force had 105 Zeros and 25 D3A dive bombers to conduct this effort, which was scheduled for June 5–16. It would have two phases. In the first phase, called *So-Go*, the fighters would conduct their standard fighter sweeps, but some of the Zeros would carry an improvised explosive device filled with gasoline which they would drop on the airfields to … do something. It was a creation of the 204 Air Group and they were sticking to it. Once air superiority was regained, the second phase, *Se-Go*, would commence, which involved the Aichis bombing Allied shipping off Lunga, which seemed to be increasing of late.[84]

While this preparation was going on, the Allies tried some air attacks of their own to keep 1st Base Air Force occupied. On June 5, AirSols Strike Command sent 26 Warhawks and six Lightnings ahead on a fighter sweep of the Shortlands. They were preparation for a dozen TBF Avengers and 18 SBD Dauntlesses, escorted by 21 new Corsairs of Marine Fighting 112 and 124, to attack the harbor off Kahili.

The Zeros of the composite 582 Air Group scrambled to intercept, along with some A6M2-N float Zeros and F1M float biplanes from the 938 Air Group, totaling some two-dozen aircraft. The Japanese mostly ignored the fighter sweep to focus on the Navy and Marine planes. The Allied bombers scored hits on two corvettes and a cargo ship, leaving them afire, at a cost of two Dauntlesses and two Avengers. The cost would have been higher but for the actions of the 44th Fighter Squadron's Lieutenant Jack Bade. He saw four unescorted bombers near Shortland with maybe ten Zeros on their tails. Suffering from a head wound, his Warhawk shot up, his guns jammed, Bade nevertheless flew several Thach Weave scissoring maneuvers to bluff the Zeros off until they ran low on fuel and turned back near Vella Lavella. For his efforts, Base was awarded the Air Medal. Bade was very lucky, far luckier than the 44th's Lieutenant Ralph Sooter, who did not return to base, his precise fate unknown. Nevertheless, the Japanese lost three Zeros with their pilots.[85] On the eve of their own operation.

The next day, the 251 Air Group staged into Buka while the 204 Air Group moved to Buin. The movement was apparently not observed by Allied intelligence. The next morning, June 7, veteran Lieutenant Commander Shindo Saburo of the 582 Air Group led 81 Zeros – 21 from Shindo's own 582, 24 from the 204 (eight carrying those gasoline bombs), and 32 from the 251 – down the Guadal Highway. They had barely gotten on the on-ramp when, over Gatukai, the 582 Air Group's Zeros and others ran into eight US Navy Wildcats from Fighting 11, a unit that had staged to Guadalcanal because its previous intended destination, the carrier *Hornet*, had been sunk at Santa Cruz. With odds of 9-to-1 – it would have been 10-to-1, but eight of the Zeros were carrying those gasoline bombs – the Wildcats were lucky to lose only three of their own, with all three pilots rescued by scouts working for coastwatcher Donald Kennedy.[86]

The odds evened up somewhat over the Russells. AirSols sent up 104 fighters, keeping half of them in a blocking position over Savo Island to protect the shipping in the Lunga roadstead and leaving half to face the Japanese. The defending fighters included a dozen Warhawks of the 44th Fighter Squadron, nine Lightnings of the 339th, a dozen Kittyhawks of the Kiwi No. 15 Squadron, 12 Corsairs of Marine Fighting 112, and eight Corsairs from Marine Fighting 124. Still almost 2-to-1 in favor of the Japanese. Except it appears the Kiwis rushed out ahead of the main formation and bit off more than their guns could chew. They ended up forming a defensive circle, just as Joe Foss' pilots had done some six months earlier, but apparently without the effectiveness of Joe Foss' pilots; they quickly had four of their own damaged and another two ended up crash landing on the Russell airstrip. Lightnings of the 339th dove in to help the harried hawks. Then the Corsairs charged in, and the driblets added up until a massive free-for-all began.[87]

And with it the craziness, as evidenced by Marine Fighting 112's 2nd Lieutenant Sam Logan. Logan was trying to aid a Kiwi Kittyhawk when his own plane was hit and set afire, so he bailed out at 18,000 feet. Logan pulled his rip cord and the white parachute opened, attracting the attention of a Zero. The unidentified Japanese pilot tried a replay of the mid-air massacre of the 65th Bombardment Squadron's Lieutenant Woodrow Moore and his crew off Lae. Except his aim was not as good – or perhaps his aim was not as good as it had been off Lae – and all his rounds missed.[88] Now he was out of ammunition. No matter. The Sea Eagle still had his propeller. Rather than targeting Logan's parachute canopy, which Moore was trying to collapse until he fell below the combat zone, the pilot tried to fly through Logan himself. On the first pass Logan managed to pull his legs up and the propeller missed, but the second time the Zero's propeller cut off parts of both of

Logan's feet. This was not going in a good direction for Logan, but fortunately the Kiwi pilot whom Logan had helped, Squadron Leader Herrick, was, and he occupied the Zero's attention long enough for Logan to parachute to relative safety in the water. Logan was later rescued and returned to flight status.[89]

This was a day of Japanese machine-gunning parachuting pilots. The 44th Squadron's Lieutenant Henry Matson chose to dogfight a Zero and, after not making a hit on his first two passes, detonated the Zero on his third.[90] That was the good news. The bad news was that Matson was in turn targeted by another Zero. Matson turned toward his new opponent and set him afire with a machine gun burst at close range – too close range. Matson could not completely avoid his flaming target, his propeller cutting into the Zero's wing, and soon Matson's Warhawk was burning as well. Time to bail out.

Lieutenant Matson did so at 18,000 feet. With burns to his head and hands, Matson pulled the rip cord and his parachute opened, and immediately attracted the attention of three Zeros, who moved toward him. Thinking quickly while slowly floating down in his harness, Matson bowed, saluted, and waved to the Zeros. Smart move. In so doing, he convinced the Japanese pilots he was one of them. They waved and flew away. Matson splashed down, inflated his rubber boat, injected himself with morphine, and settled into blissful numbness while waiting for rescue that came two hours later.

It was a very curious coincidence that of the major instances of machine-gunning parachuting aviators – Lieutenant Moore's B-17 during the Bismarck Sea action and this day – during this time period, the only common denominator was the involvement of the Japanese Naval Air Force's 204 Air Group, suggesting that the same unit was involved both times. Not among the common denominators was the reaction of the Americans to these incidents. The deliberate targeting of Lieutenant Moore's crewmates brought out a visceral rage from the 5th Bomber Command that resulted in machine gunning survivors of the Bismarck Sea action while they were struggling in the water. Conversely, the reaction by AirSols was muted at best. Perhaps after almost a year of fighting in the Solomons, their aviators were used to Japanese atrocities.

On a positive note, Marine Fighting 112's Lieutenant Gilbert Percy had been entangled in the same dogfight as Lieutenant Logan when he took 20mm shrapnel in both legs and an arm. Percy's Corsair was in even worse shape, compelling him to bail out at 2,000 feet. Percy pulled the rip cord and was treated to that awful feeling of the parachute not opening; the canopy was entangled in the lines and had become a "streamer." What to do? He kept his legs and feet tightly together, hoping to minimize the impact and therefore make it survivable. It worked, with only a cracked pelvis and a pair of sprained ankles. After inflating his life vest, Percy swam for three hours to a reef. He was rescued the next morning by friendly Melanesian natives, who turned him over to a fishing boat. After a year of hospitalization and therapy, Percy returned to duty.[91] Miracles do happen.

Ultimately, this high drama accomplished little except attrition, which favored one side. And it was not the Japanese. AirSols lost four Corsairs, three Wildcats, six Kittyhawks, and Lieutenant Matson's Warhawk. The 204 Air Group dropped its gasoline bombs on the Russell

Islands runways, but, again, at a major cost. Six pilots from the 251 Air Group were lost. The 582 Air Group apparently suffered no losses, but also hardly made contact with the enemy. From the 204 itself, three Zeros failed to return, two of which were flown by Petty Officer 2nd Class Okazaki and Chief Petty Officer Hidaka, both veterans of the Yamamoto escort mission. Three more "force landed" at Munda and Vila. Among those "force-landing" at Munda was a badly wounded Flight Petty Officer Yanagiya, another veteran of the Yamamoto mission. Yanagiya had been jumped by American fighters, who sent a stream of hot metal crashing through his windshield and against his control stick. He sustained massive injuries to his right hand and right leg. In severe pain and somewhat reminiscent of Sakai Saburo's legendary, semiconscious flight back to Rabaul after a bullet had gone through his eye into his brain, Yanagiya had to fly his damaged Zero using only his left hand. He got to Munda, where he crash-landed and was knocked unconscious. While he was out, the medical staff stuffed cotton in his mouth and three sailors held him down while his hand was amputated – without anesthetic. The pain was so intense that it brought him back to consciousness, at which point he likely wished he were out again.[92] The amputation saved his life.

Tit-for-tat was not quite the result for which Admiral Kusaka had hoped. Not that anyone told him. At a conference the next morning, Kusaka's staff determined they had shot down 41 enemy fighters. They had not, of course, but it was an Imperial Japanese Navy thing. Kusaka may have been highly intelligent, respected by his men, creative and flexible in ways not normally seen in the Japanese military, and another one of the "good guys" in that military – one commentator compared his personality to that of the late actor Alec Guinness – without even an accusation of ordering a war crime to his name, but he was Imperial Japanese Navy through and through.[93] Good enough to proceed with the second attack of *So Go* – if that second attack was delayed until June 12 so that the 251 and 582 Air Group Zeros could practice using four-plane groupings that the 204 had been using. And so that maintenance could be performed on the Zeros. The five-day interval suggested that both were pressing issues.[94]

In the interim, June 10 saw an Allied convoy of five transports (*McCawley, President Hayes, President Jackson, President Adams,* and *LaSalle*) and six destroyers (*Farenholt, McCalla, Ralph Talbot, Buchanan, Converse,* and *Taylor*) approaching the Solomons from Espiritu Santo. So did a G4M, scouting ahead for a ministrike of three more G4Ms. This convoy was a little hamstrung, because Admiral Turner, long a maestro at handling ships in the face of air attack, was supposed to be commanding it from the *McCawley,* but he had come down with malaria and dengue fever and was (forcibly) taken to a hospital ship in Nouméa, so the convoy was commanded by Captain Paul Theiss in the *President Jackson.* Coastwatchers reported the Bettys approaching, so AirSols set up an ambush with four Marine Fighting 124 Corsairs patrolling between Malaita and Santa Ysabel and four Lightnings from the 339th Fighter Squadron patrolling over Ndai Island. The intercept was complicated by extremely bad weather, but the Americans sprang their trap northeast of Malaita. The Japanese aborted their air strike, but not before two of their number were shot down. The scouting G4M was left loitering around the convoy waiting for help that didn't come until near dusk, when seven G4Ms arrived in a twilight strike. Theiss had his slow transports undergo radical maneuvering "in the best Turner tradition," and none of the bombs scored. The seven Bettys were followed by an actual moonlight strike of apparently 11 more land attack planes that was mostly about dropping flares that did not flare for bombers that did not bomb. After some six hours of harassment, the Bettys broke off and the convoy eventually reached Guadalcanal safely.[95]

This less-than-successful attack did not stop the second attack of *So-Go* from going ahead on June 12 as planned. This time, it was veteran Lieutenant Miyano leading 24 Zeros of his own 204 Air Group, 32 of the 251 Air Group, and 21 of the 582 in a fighter sweep of the Russells.[96] The usual eclectic AirSols assortment met them near Vella Lavella. Leading off at 10:48am were eight Kiwi Kittyhawks of No. 14 Squadron, four Warhawks of the 44th Fighter Squadron, and one Airacobra of the 68th. As usual, the arriving driblets – this time including the Corsairs of Marine Fighting 121, newly arrived at Guadalcanal, as well as the Wildcats of Fighting 11 and the Lightnings of the 339th – led to a free-for-all headed for the Russells and Guadalcanal.[97]

It was, in fact, the very first scramble for the Corsairs of Marine Fighting 121 and combat was a shock. For that matter, the prospect of combat was a shock. All the training in the world just creates muscle memory. It does not totally prepare you for what combat is like, what the imminence of combat is like, as squadron flight officer Captain R. Bruce Porter quickly learned:

> For all the long months of practice and performance in Samoa and at Turtle Bay, I did not have a calm cell in my body. It is unusual to sweat at altitude, even in the tropics, but bodily fluids were running off me in rivulets. I was even concerned that my canopy would fog up from so much moisture. I had no fear, but my bloodstream had an overabundance of adrenalin and, I'm sure, other life preserving substances that gave off a rank odor and copious amounts of perspiration. In a way, my discomfort shielded me from dwelling too much on the possible consequences of the onrushing confrontation.
>
> I do not think I was ever as exhilarated as I was during that flight.[98]

And then the combat actually started when he saw a Zero engage his Corsairs:

> All the best training in the world could not abate the instant of sheer surprise when my eyes locked onto a target of their own. [...]
>
> I never consciously pressed my gun-button knob. I had practiced this encounter a thousand times, and I seemed to know enough to allow my instincts to prevail over my mind. My guns were bore-sighted to converge in a cone about 300 yards ahead of my Corsair's propeller spinner. Anything within that cone would be hit by a stream of half-inch steel-jacketed bullets.
>
> My Corsair shuddered slightly as all guns fired, and I saw my tracer passing just over the Zero's long birdcage canopy. Then he was past me.[99]

After some high-pressure maneuvering and a chase, Porter finally got the Zero in his sights:

> I squeezed the gun-button knob beneath my right index finger. The eerie silence in my cockpit was broken by the steady roar of my machine guns.
>
> The Zero never had a chance. It flew directly into the cone of deadly half-inch bullets. I was easily able to stay on it as the stream of tracer sawed into the leading edge of the left wing. I saw little pieces of metal fly away from the impact area. [...] The stream of tracer worked its way to the cockpit. I clearly saw the glass canopy shatter, but there was so much glinting, roiling glass and debris that I could not see the pilot. The Zero wobbled, and my tracer fell into first one wing root, then the other, striking the enemy's unprotected fuel tanks.
>
> The Zero suddenly blew up, evaporated.[100]

The exchange took a lot out of Captain Porter. As he was returning, he realized his flight suit was soaked, he had a pounding headache, his breathing was shallow, and he felt faint. A few draughts of oxygen from his mask and he felt better. After one more exchange in which his wingman shot down a Zero, Porter returned to Guadalcanal.

> I had not only weathered first combat, I had scored my first kill. I had been baptized. I had won my spurs.
>
> It did not dawn on me until late that night that I had also killed a man.[101]

Better for this to dawn late at night than in the midst of combat, where such a dawning and the hesitation it brings could be deadly.

Captain Porter may have killed a man, but not from Lieutenant Miyano's 204 Air Group, which headed back with all its Zeros intact, just one damaged. The 251 lost four aircraft and three pilots, while the 582 lost three pilots of its own.[102]

The Japanese claimed 24 Allied aircraft shot down. An impressive showing, if true. A photographic reconnaissance of the Guadalcanal-Russells area showing some 250 Allied aircraft at the various airfields perhaps should have suggested that maybe the Sea Eagles were overstating their success, far more than fighter pilots normally do. In fact, they had actually shot down six – five Wildcats, four of whose pilots were later rescued, and one Kiwi Kittyhawk. The numbers revealed in those photos had to give Admiral Kusaka pause. Not a kamikaze type, Kusaka cared deeply for the men under his command and took their well-being personally, which was one reason he was so popular. Even so, Kusaka approved going ahead with the second phase of the operation, *Se-Go*, attacking the increasing Allied shipping with dive bombers.[103] With 250 enemy aircraft nearby. What could go wrong?

So-Go passed into history and *Se-Go* commenced on June 16. The centerpiece of the attack would be 24 Aichi D3As of the 582 Air Group. Their 70 escorting fighters – 16 from the 582 Air Group, 24 from the 204 and 30 from the 251 – would be arrayed on both sides and in the rear, and with one group, apparently that of the 582, slightly ahead, Lieutenant Commander Shindo was leading this attack once again, but the 204's Lieutenant Miyano had a major hand in the planning. He had noticed that most of the losses among the Aichis came after they had released their bombs, so Miyano suggested keeping a group of fighters at low altitude to defend the D3As. Shindo approved it, and off they went.[104]

Lieutenant Commander Shindo's approach plan called for passing south of the Russells, turning north at Guadalcanal's Beaufort Bay, and approaching the Lunga roadstead from the south. It was an unusual route. Nevertheless, it was detected, mostly. Just after noon, a coastwatcher on Vella Lavella reported 38 Zeros flying to the southwest. Then a coastwatcher on Kolombangara reported that 50 Vals and 30 Zeros were inbound. Marine Fighting 121 Corsairs in the Russells were scrambled, but they never made contact with the Japanese. The reason why was revealed at 1:09pm, when the Japanese finally showed up on radar, well south of their normal route.[105]

One minute later, AirSols Fighter Command scrambled 16 fighters to defend the ships off Lunga, which at that time were destroyers *O'Bannon*, *Nicholas*, and *Strong*; destroyer-transports *Waters* and *Schley*; minesweeper *Skylark*; cargo ships *Celeno*, *Aludra*, and *Deimos*; oiler *Monongahela*; liberty ship *Nathaniel Currier*; and several landing ships and patrol boats. Then, just to be safe, it scrambled 88 more over the next hour, during which time it declared a "Condition: Red" but, fortunately, not a "Condition: Very Red." First off were a dozen P-38s of the 339th, then the Wildcats of Fighting 11. Two of the Lightnings had to turn back with mechanical issues, but the remainder made first contact with the incoming Japanese at 1:47pm, likely with the Zeros of the 582 Air Group, at 27,000 feet over Beaufort Bay. As they did so, the tough Navy Wildcats started hacking their way through to the Vals at 15,000 feet.[106]

This chaotic creation drifted northward into the main AirSols fighter defense, which included the Corsairs of Marine Fighting 122, 124, and, later, 121; Wildcats of Fighting 11; 21 Warhawks of the 44th Fighter Squadron, eight Airacobras from the 68th, 12 Lightnings from the 339th; and eight Kittyhawks from the Royal New Zealand Air Force's No. 14 Squadron, though one had to abort. It drifted over the Henderson Field complex and the Lunga roadstead, meaning antiaircraft fire was added to the equation. To the satisfaction of AirSols Fighter Command, 74 of the defending interceptors made contact with the enemy.[107]

The result was perhaps the craziest air battle of the Pacific War. So crazy that it became impossible to track its progress or who shot down whom and when – so impossible that not even the talented James Grace, who sorted out the Friday the 13th mess, could figure it out. As a different historian put it, "It is virtually impossible to disentangle the details of the battle on 16 June."[108] It thus became a combat engagement better told through stories and emotion than a tactical analysis.

A Warhawk pilot of the 44th Fighter Squadron reported that he "saw a large dog fight going on 5 miles SE of Savo. I came down in a dive and saw a Grumman and a P-40 collide close to the water. They were making opposite passes on a Zero." They weren't the only ones. A Navy pilot from Fighting 11 saw two of his squadron-mates collide and fall into the water. It's amazing such collisions didn't happen more often in aerial engagements. Three Wildcats were lost this day, all due to collisions.[109]

But there were even crazier events. According to one Airacobra pilot, "One P-38 and an F4F were scissoring together like they had been training for it all of their life [sic]," he reported. "I saw two F4Us and a P-40 working together as a perfect combat team. I saw many other weird combinations. Weird but they work." Meanwhile, the 68th's Lieutenant William Wells used the guns of his Airacobra to set a Val on fire. As the dive bomber plunged downward, the rear gunner kept firing at Wells and firing and firing and firing, and when it splashed into the water and sank, the gunner was still firing. A pilot from Marine Fighting 121, arriving late from the Russells, reported that as he climbed to engage, "one flaming Zero almost fell on his plane." It's amazing that didn't happen more often.[110]

The craziness came in all shapes, sizes, and colors. The 339th's 2nd Lieutenant Bill Harris managed to set one Zero on fire before his machine guns jammed. He used his cannons to set a second on fire, then came in for a landing. But while he was on his approach, a Zero made a strafing run on his P-38 Lightning nicknamed *Hattie*. Harris managed to land safely, but that just wouldn't do. *No one* puts bullet holes in *Hattie!* Thoroughly enraged, Harris jumped out of his cockpit and commandeered another P-38 so he could perform some vigilantism on the vandal. Harris roared down the runway in his lent Lightning – and blew a tire.[111] How disappointing. And somewhat anticlimactic.

The star of this day, however, was one of Harris' squadron-mates, 2nd Lieutenant Murray Shubin. Shubin had already been credited with shooting down a Zero and a float Zero. He led a flight into the initial engagement over Beaufort Bay and claimed shooting down two Zeros. About 15 minutes later, he sighted a formation of six more Zeros, probably from the 251 Air Group, below him near Savo Island. All by himself, Shubin charged at them. Shubin claimed to have shot down one Zero on his initial pass, which seemed to have left the others somewhat bemused. The Zeros could not mount a coordinated response – that whole not-having-radios thing making itself felt once again – so Shubin started individual dogfights to pick them off one by one. After he landed, according to Shubin, "Col Aaron Tyler, my group CO, told me that Capt F.P. Mueller, G Company, 35th Infantry, witnessed, through binoculars, the Esperance-Savo part of the long battle and definitely established that I had shot down three of the five Zeros, it made me feel damn good to know that I has [sic] sent five Tojos to the showers and given the sixth joker an afternoon he probably won't tell his grandchildren about."[112]

Shubin was credited for the day with shooting down five Zeros, with one more probable. His five kills or more qualified him as a fighter ace, while having five kills in one day qualified him as an "Ace in a Day," the 13th Air Force's first. He was not the only one to achieve ace status this day. Indianapolis-native Lieutenant William F. Fiedler, Jr of the

68th shot down two Vals with only his .30-cal. wing guns to become the only Army Air Force ace to score all of his victories while flying the much-maligned P-39 Airacobra.[113]

Keeping fighter pilots like Lieutenant Fiedler off the D3As was why Lieutenant Miyano had kept the 204 Air Group's Zeros at low altitude, to cut down on the number of Aichis shot down as they pulled out of their dives. But this was not *Kido Butai* at an almost undefended Darwin. The dive bomber pilots of the 582 were not *Kido Butai*, and the Henderson Field complex and its Lunga anchorage were far from undefended; in fact, the Japanese were outnumbered. Just getting into their dives proved to be a problem, as the Navy Wildcats were able to hack through the 582 Air Group escorts and wreak havoc on the Vals. The disruption was manifested in over-targeting.

For example, the tank landing ship *LST-340* was reportedly the target of nine Vals, an exceedingly large number of bombers for such a limited value target. Three of the planes attacked the ship immediately, dropping nine bombs in sticks of three. One dive bomber that came in from port got two 300lb bombs to splash about 50 feet off the landing ship's starboard side and one direct hit on the main deck. Another plane, perhaps one of Lieutenant Miyano's Zeros, roared in from the port bow on a strafing run, leaving over 100 holes in her port side.[114]

But the *LST-340* had far bigger problems than antiaircraft fire. Landing ships had little in the way of armor, so the single bomb hit was very damaging. The explosion killed one gun crew member and nine Army passengers and wounded four sailors. It also wrecked the main deck, knocked out the electrical system, disabled communications, and left a fire in the officers' quarters and a second, more dangerous fire fed by fuel in the engine room. The *LST-340* was abandoned by all but a skeleton crew.[115]

Also earning Japanese ire was the cargo ship *Celeno*. Unloading cargo off Lunga, the *Celeno* was attacked by "a swarm" of Vals. The cargo ship opened up with her 3-inch and 5-inch antiaircraft guns, of which she had one each, and her machine guns. She was repaid with a trio of near-misses before a hit to the quarterdeck disabled the 5-incher and jammed the rudder. A second hit started fires in two of the cargo ship's holds, while a near miss ignited her deck cargo of diesel oil and gasoline. The *Celeno* was left an inferno, circling helplessly, with 15 dead and 19 wounded.[116]

By 2:30pm, the D3As started making for base, with the 204 Air Group's Zeros trying to screen off any trouble. The 204 considered staying at low altitude a success, claiming 14 victories, including six shared and one probable. Perhaps the suppression of antiaircraft fire was another objective Lieutenant Miyano had in staying at low altitude for the Aichis. In any event, he paid for his new tactic with his life – Miyano never returned from Guadalcanal, nor did Lieutenant (jg) Morizaki, who had led the Yamamoto escort mission, nor did two other pilots from the 204, while three more "force-landed." The pilots of the 251 Air Group claimed nine shot down and one probable, but lost six of its own, including two Zeros seen to be hit by antiaircraft fire; a seventh ditched on the way back. The composite 582 Air Group was simply shredded: of the 24 Aichi D3As, at least 13 did not return, along with four of the 16 Zeros. That would be 28 aircraft lost to Base Air Force, including the veterans Miyano and Morizaki. All for what the Japanese claimed were 28 enemy aircraft shot down, at least four midsized cargo ships, one large transport, and one destroyer sunk, with damage to four large transports in this "Air Battle of Lunga."[117]

It was a disastrous exchange for the Japanese even assuming the Japanese damage claims were true. They weren't. AirSols lost six fighters, four of which collided with each other, and five pilots. Two Warhawks crash-landed with damage. On the ground and water, 25 men had been killed, 29 wounded, and 22 missing. While Allied intelligence expressed admiration for the determination of the Val pilots – "The Jap dive bombers again showed their doggedness in pressing home their bombing runs" – the Vals had managed to seriously hit only two ships, the *Celeno* and *LST-340*. And both were salvaged. The *LST-340* was run aground on Tenaru Beach and, with the assistance of *LST-398*, her fires were brought under control some four hours later. Despite her jammed rudder, the *Celeno* was somehow also run aground, this time at Lunga Point, where her fires were extinguished. Both ships were ultimately repaired and returned to service.[118]

In short, the *Se-Go* attack, at an extreme cost, had inflicted little damage on the enemy. Admiral Kusaka could not believe so few of his aircraft had returned. Initially, he convinced himself many of them had made emergency landings instead. Aerial searches the next day of Santa Ysabel, Choiseul, and the south coast of New Georgia found nothing. Kusaka probably also had radio inquiries made of Munda and Vila as well, but aside from two D3As and three Zeros who had "force-landed" at Vila, they brought no solace.[119]

Admiral Kusaka was horrified. *Se-Go* had been an abject disaster. His Base Air Force held a second evaluation meeting for *So-* and *Se-Go*, which was a far more somber affair than the first. It took this meeting with all these Japanese brass and their staff officers to determine that Allied fighter performance had improved. Beyond such astute observations – and such avoided observations such as the decline in the skill of Japanese pilots – it was also determined that the Aichi D3A Type 99 Carrier Bomber was now so outclassed that it could no longer make daylight attacks on the Guadalcanal base complex, which, since the G4Ms were also restricted from attacking Guadalcanal during daylight, meant that Base Air Force could no longer attack Guadalcanal during daylight.[120] It was a humbling, perhaps humiliating admission from the famed Sea Eagles.

But all would be fixed, though, when the new carrier bomber entered service.[121] That would be the Yokosuka D4Y Carrier Bomber. Called the "*Suisei*" ("Comet"), the D4Y was supposed to have the bombing capacity of a D3A and the speed – and armor, and fuel tank protection – of a Zero. In fact, the Suisei was supposed to have replaced the Aichi D3A already, except during test flights it showed a marked tendency to flap its wings. Sort of like a bird, except that in the case of an airplane it's more like an oscillation, in which the vibration of the wings matches the aircraft's natural frequency. If the oscillation is not properly damped, the oscillations could continue increasing in amplitude – making the wings flap, which in aeronautical terms is called "flutter" – until the wings finally break off. Which, when an aircraft is in flight, can be a very bad thing. While the Japanese were trying to fix that whole flapping wings thing, they had pressed the few Suiseis available into service as the Type 2 Reconnaissance Plane, which had so far displayed a healthy tendency for finding enemy carriers and an equally healthy tendency for being unable to report its finding of enemy carriers until it had landed and the battle had been decided.

With more than a little urgency, Admiral Kusaka requested immediate reinforcements. Combined Fleet responded that Base Air Force's 5th Air Attack Force would get the 201 and 501 Air Groups. But there was a catch; these days there was always a catch. The 201 would not come until mid-July and the 501 was still training, so it would arrive ... whenever it was finished training. The 582 Air Group's losses in dive bombers would be replaced by the dive bombers of the light carrier *Ryuho*, with arrival set for July 1.[122]

In contrast, AirSols' Admiral Mitscher wrote of the June 16 action, "hard to believe, but this was a Roman holiday on Jap airplanes."[123] Whatever that means. But while his staff's conclusion that AirSols could "look forward to continued superiority in planes" was correct, there would be no triumph of legionaries with Admiral Mitscher riding in a chariot heading to the temple of Jupiter Capitolinus.[124] Chariots were in short supply on Guadalcanal. The war was still going on.

The attrition was often caused by American submarines, attacking Japanese supply ships, thus supply lines, and thus supplies. The veteran Japanese seaplane tender *Kamikawa Maru* was north of Kavieng on a run from Rabaul to Palau at about 10:00am on May 28 when she was found by a B-24 Liberator. She and her escorts, subchasers *Ch-12* and *Ch-37*, drove the bomber off without suffering damage, but the bomber had to have friends, so the *Kamikawa Maru* was probably happy when she found a convenient heavy squall to hide in. She found out the bomber's friends were not all of the aerial variety at 1:03pm when she was hit by three US Navy Mark 14 torpedoes that actually detonated not prematurely, but in her starboard side, the first in the Number 1 hold, the second in the engine room (always a very bad place), and the third in the Number 4 hold. Just her luck. The *Kamikawa Maru* lost power and started to settle by the stern. Much of the day appears to have been spent trying to tow the seaplane tender, but those efforts failed. The *Kamikawa Maru* was ordered abandoned and the crew took to the lifeboats. But the seaplane tender was not sinking quickly enough for her undersea assailant, Lieutenant Commander Walter G. Ebert's USS *Scamp*. After midnight on May 29, Ebert attacked again, working to send another torpedo into the Number 2 hold from the port side at 1:14am. About five minutes later, the *Kamikawa Maru* rolled over to port and sank, taking with her 39 sailors, including her master Captain Hara Seitaro, who had been called out of retirement to command her, and three Army civilian employees. The *Scamp* survived a vengeful counterattack and escaped.[125]

The morning of June 17, transport *Myoko Maru* was on a run from Truk to Rabaul with the *Yuri Maru* and ancient destroyer *Asanagi*.[126] Just before 7:00am, two US Navy Mark 14s explosively tunneled themselves into her stern. The *Myoko Maru* quickly heeled over to port and sank, taking 34 passengers and one crewman with her. These rare, fully functional Mark 14s came compliments of Lieutenant Commander Bernard F. McMahon's submarine USS *Drum*, which escaped a retaliatory aerial depth charge attack while the *Asanagi* rescued survivors.[127]

Unlike American submarine operations, Japanese submarine operations were not strategic, but tactical, with an emphasis on attacking warships and not noncombatants. This came with its own dangers, such as when the *Ro-102* disappeared southeast of Milne Bay sometime in mid-May.[128] But there's always an exception, and the eastern coast of Australia was one big exception during this time period, as Japanese submarine operations in the area had been intensifying during the first half. Every plane, every ship the Australian military assigned to antisubmarine duties off the east coast was one less plane, one less ship for General MacArthur's war in New Guinea. Can't have that.

Until the middle of May, that is. May 15, 1943, to be precise. At 10:40 that morning, an Avro Anson, a patrol plane used for antisubmarine operations despite being obsolete and underarmed, took off from Lowood to provide antisubmarine protection for a mini convoy consisting of the big Kiwi freighter *Sussex* escorted by the Guadalcanal veteran destroyer USS *Mugford*. For three hours Flying Officer O.K. Crewes and navigator Flying Officer J.W. Keith of No. 71 Squadron kept the Anson near the convoy, usually ahead of it. No enemy was sighted, so they headed home.

Only then, at about 2:00pm, did they sight something. Not a submarine. It was "a ship's life-boat containing 30 live persons." Certainly better than the alternative. But no ships had been reported sunk. Where did it come from? Crewes returned to the convoy and signaled, "Rescue survivors in water ahead." He circled twice and dropped a smoke marker, then, short of fuel, returned to Lowood.[129]

The *Mugford*'s veteran skipper Lieutenant Commander Howard Grant Corey radioed for air cover for the *Sussex* and told the freighter to proceed alone while he went to pick up survivors. The destroyer carefully maneuvered toward the boat and a group of rafts and floating debris "amidst the usual flurry of reported 'periscopes,' 'disturbed water,' 'torpedo wakes.' Although none proved authentic, minimum time was spent stopped." Corey reported the survivors were:

> in two large groups plus three smaller groups in about a two mile radius of oil slick, wreckage and debris. Regular gas drum rafts, hatch tops, cabin tops, gratings, large shelf structures, and one wrecked lifeboat (awash) had been used by the survivors, many lightly clothed, some naked, some injured and burned, and about half with life jackets. One other lifeboat, bottom up, was seen.[130]

The *Mugford* ultimately picked up 63 men and one woman, a nurse, all of whom had been in the water for some 36 hours. Additional searches found no more survivors. The destroyer provided them medical care before turning them over to Australian authorities at Brisbane that evening. These survivors told a tragic and thoroughly enraging story.

They were from the *Centaur*, an Australian hospital ship, designated by the Red Cross and so marked and illuminated. On May 14, the *Centaur* had been heading north at 12 knots. A bit after 4:00am, she was 23 miles off Point Lookout lighthouse on North Stradbroke Island when she suffered an underwater explosion on her port side, near her fuel bunkers. As had been the case when the USS *Wasp* was torpedoed, the fuel ignited, and the hospital ship was soon an inferno. She sank within two minutes, so quickly that there was no time to send a distress call or launch lifeboats, though two broke free as she sank. Moreover, most of those aboard had been asleep. There was no time, no chance for those 268 souls to escape.[131] This was a major maritime disaster, the biggest individual loss from a Japanese torpedo suffered in Australian waters during the war.[132]

And a war crime. Attacking a legally marked hospital ship is a violation of the Geneva Convention and, thus, the laws of war. But the Japanese had previously shown a lack of respect for hospital ships. During the Java Sea Campaign, for example, the Japanese bombed the Dutch hospital ship *Op ten Noort* – twice – and later seized her when she was attempting to rescue survivors of the Battle of the Java Sea.

Now the Japanese had done it again. It seemed obvious that the *Centaur* had been hit by a torpedo from a submarine. Survivors reported hearing and even seeing a submarine in the area after the sinking. A Japanese submarine, one of several known to be operating off Australia's east coast.[133]

When the story of the sinking of the hospital ship *Centaur* broke on May 20, it was front-page news that sparked outrage. General MacArthur spoke of the enemy's "limitless savagery" and Australian Prime Minister John Curtin announced that an immediate and strong protest was being addressed to the Japanese Government.[134] That'll show 'em.

Amidst all the very justified anger directed at Japan for this latest atrocity was considerable anger over Australia's conduct of antisubmarine operations. One magazine asked why it took 36 hours to even discover the sinking and the survivors. The article declared, "Circumstances surrounding the loss of the hospital ship *Centaur* on May 14 reflect no credit upon Australian naval and air administration … losses on the coast recently have been heavy. They have got to be stopped."[135]

The criticism was by no means entirely external. At the next Advisory War Council meeting on June 3, former Australian prime minister William Morris "Billy" Hughes, in a "damning statement," detailed "deficiencies in present methods" of antisubmarine warfare and gave suggestions as to how they might be improved. Hughes apparently had access to expert, inside information, the implication of which being that the Royal Australian Navy had not devoted enough attention or resources to antisubmarine warfare.[136] It hadn't. Neither had anyone else. Not the US, not Britain, not Japan, not Germany …

Not the Royal Australian Air Force. That same month, the Royal Australian Air Force Command's "Tactical Bulletin" made a startling admission:

Few RAAF crews have ever had any great experience with enemy submarines. Indeed very few have ever even seen one of our own at sea. This is regrettable but unavoidable and until such time as we are allotted submarines for training purposes little can be done.[137]

Not entirely. The limited training and experience was indeed a problem, and is why there is some suspicion that the US Navy submarines *Triton* and *Grampus* were victims of friendly fire off Brisbane. However, the problem could only be solved by additional organization, such as an antisubmarine warfare command, which was established in May; adding new equipment such as radar and asdic (the European version of sonar); and, especially, additional resources such as aircraft and ships. Like Admiral Kusaka and his Suisei dive bombers, the Australians were counting on more advanced weaponry coming on line in the immediate future, especially a new line of frigates.

Suffice it to say, despite the fact that the *Centaur* should never have been attacked in the first place, there was a lot of pressure on Australian authorities after the *Centaur* disaster to improve antisubmarine performance. They were given an assist by the Japanese themselves, whose submarines seemed to disappear for a few weeks after the *Centaur* attack; when they returned, their attempts at attritional warfire misfired as their torpedoes had a habit of avoiding their targets.

At around 4:30am on May 28, an actual bomber, a Bristol Beaufort from No. 32 Squadron out of Bundaberg, picked up an unknown ship on her radar at a range of 8,000 yards. The Beaufort went to 1,800 feet and was able to close to maybe 800 yards, where they could make out a submarine. Which promptly crash dived. So much for that. On May 29, the corvette *Mildura*, escorting a 17-ship convoy, reported sighting torpedo wakes at 9:18pm when she was 35 miles north-northeast of Cape Howe. Some 90 minutes later, a pair of torpedoes missed the US Navy Liberty ship *Sheldon Jackson* some 150 miles north-northeast of Sydney. On June 1 just before noon, four torpedoes missed the American ship *Point San Pedro*. Though only 40 miles from Cape Moreton, it took almost two and a half hours for a No. 71 Squadron Anson from Lowood to arrive on scene, and once it did, it could not find the submarine.[138] A pattern was developing.

Mostly. On June 4, it was not torpedoes but gunfire. Some 30 miles southeast of Cape Moreton, the US Army transport *Edward Chambers* was astonished when a little before 11:00am it saw a submarine surface *in broad daylight*. To this insult the submarine tried adding injury when the boat opened fire with its 12mm deck gun at a range of about 12,000 yards. The *Edward Chambers* fired back with her aft 3-inch gun. Maybe five minutes later, after nine 120mm and a dozen 3-inch failed to hit the target, the submarine receded back into the water from whence it came.[139]

During the engagement, the *Edward Chambers* had sent a distress call, which was picked up by convoy *GP53* then only 11 miles to the northeast. The convoy was diverted 15 miles to seaward to avoid the submarine, while the corvette *Bendigo* was detached to investigate. She could not find the submarine.[140]

Surfacing in broad daylight was a slap in the face of the Royal Australian Air Force. No more Mr Nice Bloke. Bring on the bombers: Bristol Beauforts of No. 32 Squadron from Camden. They searched until dawn on June 5. They could not find the submarine. Then they were relieved by five Ansons from No. 71 Squadron out of Lowood, following a creeping-line-ahead search. They still could not find the submarine.

Finding the submarine was the Liberty ship *John Bartram*. At dawn on June 7, four torpedoes were seen approaching the freighter. Two missed ahead. Three of the torpedoes exploded, but the *John Bartram* was not hit and made Sydney that day as scheduled.[141]

This submarine had crossed from annoying to insulting to just plain obnoxious. It was just dumb luck no one had been hurt yet in this latest attritional phase. But it's never good to depend on the enemy's inaccuracy. It wouldn't last forever. The Australians knew it and so they kept hunting the slippery submersibles off the east coast.

But they couldn't catch a break. Around midnight on June 15, a No. 32 Squadron Beaufort out of Coffs Harbor detected an unidentified contact on her radar. Moving in to investigate, the Beaufort sighted a wake that appeared to be from a vessel heading north. Both the wake and the radar return disappeared within one minute. The Beaufort dropped a bomb without result. About a half hour later, the contact reappeared. After another bombing attempt, the contact disappeared and was not detected again that day.[142] The inability to sink, damage, hold down, or even find this submarine would now carry a price.

At 8:45am on June 15, the convoy *GP55* left Sydney headed for Brisbane, comprising ten merchant ships and three US Navy tank landing ships escorted by five corvettes with some of the most colorful names any smaller combatant ever had: *Warrnambool*, *Deloraine*, *Kalgoorlie*, *Cootamundra*, and *Bundaberg*, all of the *Bathurst* class that had been criticized as too slow. Even so, they surrounded the convoy, which was in a rather weird formation: five columns abreast, with two ships in each of the two flanking columns and three each in the middle three columns. The second ship in the fourth column from port was the American transport *Portmar*, who had a bit of a storied history. She had been in the anchorage at Darwin on February 19, 1942, when the Sea Eagles of *Kido Butai*, in all their glory, attacked and largely destroyed the practically undefended port. The *Portmar* had been badly hit and was run aground to prevent her sinking. Towed to Sydney, she was repaired and returned to service. Just behind the *Portmar* was one of the tank landing ships, the *LST-469*. Four Ansons of the Royal Australian Air Force's No. 71 Squadron were to provide aerial antisubmarine protection.[143]

Not for long, however. The *Portmar* was struggling to stay in formation and was slipping behind. The *LST-469* maneuvered to give the *Portmar* room to pass and retake her position. By dusk on June 16, when the convoy was 35 miles east of Smoky Cape, the *Portmar* was passing the *LST-469* to port. Her bow was in line with the landing ship's stern.[144] At least, that's how it appeared in the submarine's periscope.

The sun had been below the horizon for about a half hour when at 5:21pm a big ball of fire, this one accompanied by a towering plume of water, erupted from the *LST-469*'s starboard quarter.[145] The *Portmar* saw the explosion – and another torpedo coming straight for her. A hard port turn was ordered, but there was no time …

Another big ball of fire erupted from the *Portmar* as a torpedo burrowed through the starboard side into the Number 1 hold. And sent up an even bigger ball of fire from the freighter's cargo – ammunition and gasoline. Completely ablaze, the *Portmar* sank in about ten minutes. Two of her crew were killed; the Australian corvette *Deloraine* picked up 71 survivors.

Meanwhile, the impact of the torpedo and the concussion of its detonation had swung the *LST-469* to starboard. She began to settle by the stern and take a starboard list. The landing ship's damage was severe. Her steering gear was wrecked. Three of her Army passengers were killed and two wounded; of her crew, 15 were killed, 13 wounded, and eight missing. Nevertheless, the list was corrected, and she was eventually towed to Sydney, repaired, and returned to service. Eventually. But very soon, the loss of the use of *LST-469* would be felt.[146]

And right now, the depth charges of the escorting Australian corvettes were felt. While the lone remaining Anson had seen no submarine and was returning to base for lack of fuel and the *Deloraine* was picking up survivors from the *Portmar*, the corvettes reversed course to sweep back in line abreast over the submarine's presumed position. All according to plan. Except, the savvy *Warrnambool* decided to look behind the convoy – and, less than a half hour after the attack, made an asdic contact at 2,700 yards. The *Kalgoorlie* then joined the *Warrnambool* in a hunt for the submarine, making four depth charge attacks. They lost contact a little less than two hours later, but not before they smelled oil.[147] That was a good sign. It could mean they had sunk the submarine. Finally.

Or not. That night two Beauforts from Bundaberg and one from Coffs Harbor, all from No. 32 Squadron, headed back to the convoy. One led the convoy out of the area while the other two combed an 80-mile box southeast of Coffs Harbor. They could not find the submarine. Nor, ominously, could they find evidence it had sunk. Ansons were sent out the next day. They too could not find the submarine.[148]

This was ridiculous and would be comedic if not for the deaths involved. All the King's horses, all the King's men, all his sailors and his airmen, could not find the submarine again. It would attack now and then, but all the King's sailors knew not when. Australian frustration had to be boiling by midnight on June 18. Three Beauforts from No. 32 Squadron out of Coffs Harbor went on another line ahead search. Just after midnight, Pilot Officer A.L. Harrison picked up an unidentified contact on his radar. Turning to investigate he found … lo and behold … a surfaced submarine.[149] Had they finally found their tormentor?

From an altitude of 30 to 50 feet, Harrison dropped three depth charges, each filled with 250lbs of Torpex, which sounds like a prescription drug about which you should ask your doctor, but was actually an enhanced blend of TNT, "Torpex" being short for "torpedo explosive." Yet Harrison's crew saw no explosion. Inexperience, once again. Depth charges don't always or even usually have an explosion on the surface. But a depth charge detonation does have one characteristic: *For an instant, the water seems to freeze and turn white.*

Harrison's crew did see the submarine submerge to conning tower depth. It was a weird maneuver. Harrison dropped a fourth depth charge, maybe half-a-submarine length ahead of it. The submarine fully surfaced after this attack and seemed to be trailing oil, a slick about two miles long and a quarter-mile wide. Believing he had damaged the submarine, Harrison hung onto the submarine like a leech, dropping flares to illuminate it and attract the attention of surface ships and aircraft.

Pilot Officer Harrison and his crew were relieved by another Beaufort flown by Flying Officer D.L.G. Cushway, who had followed Harrison's flares all the way to the site. The submarine was moving on the surface at a speed of 10 to 12 knots. Cushway went on the attack, dropping four depth charges from an altitude of about 200 feet. Four times. All overshot the submarine by about 40 feet.

Cushway went back to the convoy, then about six miles away, and tried to point out the submarine to the escorting corvette *Deloraine*. That didn't work. So Cushway went back to the submarine and machine-gunned it, hoping to attract the *Deloraine*'s attention that way. That didn't work, either. He machine-gunned the submarine again. This time the boat machine-gunned him back. It didn't hit him, though, and the *Deloraine* remained oblivious to the entire exchange.

Between the oil slick and the submarine not diving in the face of the air attacks, it seemed that she had been damaged. Flying Officer Cushway had to return to base, but was relieved on site by a third Beaufort, who could not find the submarine.

Someone seems to have hit the *Deloraine* over the head, or at least the pilothouse, because she – eventually – came on site with the *Kalgoorlie* to conduct a careful antisubmarine search. In this they were joined by the destroyer HMAS *Vendetta*, specially modified for convoy escort duties, including extra depth charge chutes and throwers. Such was the priority attached to this search that a dozen Ansons maintained a continuous search. Strike aircraft including No. 23 Squadron's first two Vultee Vengeance dive bombers at Lowood and four Vengeances from No. 24 Squadron at Bankstown were ready with engines warmed up to take off as soon as the submarine was found. After all this preparation, all this build up, naturally, the submarine was never seen again. A sample of the oil slick was recovered and tested. It was found to be burnt, which suggested it was from the *Portmar*.

The disappointment was beyond bitter. This had been the first "organised co-operative hunt" by the Royal Australian Navy and Air Force. Its failure to destroy what appeared to be a damaged enemy submarine was yet another embarrassment and resulted in a Board of Enquiry. It determined that the breakdown in communications had been the principal cause of the failure.[150]

But was it a failure? The lack of a specific reference to an identified Japanese submarine likely stands out to the reader. The reason is that to this day, which submarine was doing what off the east coast of Australia during this period has not been conclusively determined. What is known is that one particular submarine, the *I-174* under the very talented Lieutenant Nanbu Nobukiyo, was responsible for most of the trouble.[151] Japanese records show it was the *I-174* who had attacked the *Point San Pedro*, *Edward Chambers*, and *John Bartram*. Most importantly, it was Nanbu's submarine that had attacked the convoy GP55, sinking the *Portmar* and damaging the *LST-469*. The antisubmarine counterattack by the

Warrnambool and *Kalgoorlie*, despite the stench of oil afterwards, did not sink the submarine. Nanbu reported some damage, "but nothing to impede easy combat sailing." On June 20, the *I-174* was ordered to return to Truk, where she arrived on July 1.[152]

That leaves several other attacks made by submarines yet to be identified, including, critically, the attack on the hospital ship *Centaur*. The *I-174* is not among them, as the day the *Centaur* was attacked, May 14, Lieutenant Nanbu's submarine was still sitting in Truk Harbor. The candidates for the attack on the *Centaur* generally boil down to the *I-177* under Commander Nakagawa Hajime and the *I-178* under Commander Utsugi Hidejiro. The general consensus seems to be that it was the *I-177*. It is disputed whether or not Nakagawa denied the sinking, but he was convicted of a war crime in machine gunning merchant survivors in the Indian Ocean, so he was certainly guilty of something.[153]

The *I-178*, however, would seem to be a bit of a wild card, because she never returned from her war patrol off the east coast of Australia. US Navy sources claim that on May 29 the submarine was depth charged and sunk by the subchaser *SC-699* 30 miles west of Espiritu Santo. This claim would seem to be in some doubt given that the *I-178* had submitted a routine report to 6th Fleet, the Japanese submarine force, on June 17. Some Australian sources state that on August 25, the submarine was sunk southeast of the Solomons by the US destroyer *Patterson*. This claim, too, would seem to be in some doubt given that the aforementioned June 17 message was the last message received from the *I-178*.[154]

The last message received from the *I-178* was only hours before No. 32 Squadron's Pilot Officer Harrison found a submarine on the surface and, with Flying Officer Cushway, attacked it, leaving it apparently damaged enough to leak oil and be unable to dive. That submarine was never seen again. It was the *I-178*. The Australians had indeed sunk a Japanese submarine. Just not the one causing almost all the trouble off the east coast. Though the *I-178* had caused some trouble, to be sure. On April 27, she had sunk the Liberty ship *Lydia M. Childs* off Newcastle. Sinking nothing after that could have caused enough frustration to build that Commander Utsugi took it out on the misnamed *Centaur*. It will always remain a mystery.

That would be the end of Japanese submarine attacks off the east coast of Australia. Japanese submarine operations continued in and around the Solomons, including more attritional attacks. The morning of June 23 saw a convoy of destroyer *O'Bannon*, old destroyer-turned-transport *Ward*, which literally fired the first American shots of the Pacific War, hitting and sinking a Japanese midget submarine with two shells just before the Pearl Harbor attack; and minesweeper *Skylark*, escorting a convoy of cargo ships *Aludra* and *Deimos* and liberty ship *Nathaniel Currier* heading back after making the run to Guadalcanal. More of that Allied shipping about which Admiral Kusaka had been so concerned.

Not for long, however. At 4:44am, some 50 miles south of the eastern tip of San Cristobal, the *Aludra* suffered an underwater explosion on her port side. So did the *Deimos*. Both were from torpedoes that came compliments of Lieutenant Ichimura Rikinosuke's submarine *Ro-103*. With two dead and 12 wounded, the *Aludra* sank a little less than five hours later. The *Deimos* lingered on, but was irreparably damaged, so she was evacuated and scuttled by gunfire from the *O'Bannon*.[155]

Lieutenant Ichimura's *Ro-103* was a busy boat. After sunset on June 29, she was off New Georgia recharging her batteries when she saw seven enemy ships south of Gatukai. Ichimura dutifully reported it.[156] Probably yet another enemy bombardment of Munda, right?

Not exactly.

CHAPTER 6
PARTHIAN SHOTS

In many ways, the American English language makes little sense. We have things like "horseback riding," as opposed to "horse riding," even though there is no place to ride a horse other than on its back. A military commander can be seen as "ruthless," even though we have no antonym like "ruthful." A person can be "overwhelmed" or "underwhelmed," but not, it would seem, just plain "whelmed."

Along those same veins, we can have an "unexpected surprise." Isn't a surprise by definition "unexpected"? Well, maybe not, because the summer of 1943 was the "Summer of the Expected Surprise." Back in the European Theater, after the encirclement and destruction of the German 6th Army at Stalingrad, the Soviets staged their normal winter counteroffensive and drove the Germans back, recapturing the industrial city of Kharkov (Kharkiv) in eastern Ukraine. The brilliant German Field Marshal Erich von Manstein pulled back and let the Red Army outrun its supply lines, at which point he staged another of his superbly planned operations, smashing the Soviet spearheads and recapturing Kharkov.

Then the eastern front stabilized, from Leningrad (St Petersburg) in the north to the Kerch Strait in the south, a long, diagonal, relatively straight line – except for a very prominent Soviet-held bulge. Called in military terms a "salient," this bulge into the German lines was just north of Kharkov around the city of Kursk.

Salients can be very tricky. The German 6th Army in Stalingrad had been in something of a salient, one whose flanks were secured, if you could call it that, by two Romanian field armies. The Romanian troops broke down under Red Army assault, allowing the Soviets to drive through both Romanian armies, leaving both German flanks hanging in the air. The Red Army troops linked up in the German rear, cutting off – permanently, as it turned out – the 6th Army and part of the 4th Panzer Army.

That was the danger of a salient. Unless you held it with a lot of troops, what forces were in the salient were in danger of being cut off. Salients often attracted enemy attacks as a result. Pinch off the salient, and you have a lot of bad guys in the bag. The reverse side of that coin: while you try to pinch off the salient, your pincers are themselves in danger of being cut off and surrounded.

So, with the Soviets holding a big salient around Kursk, the question was not whether the Germans would attack it and try to pinch it off – though why the Germans would attack the single most obvious place to attack is a question only Hitler can answer – but when. Early July, as it turned out. An expected surprise.

Far to the southwest, the Americans and British had just driven the Germans out of North Africa, finally securing the port of Tunis, near ancient Carthage. As the Carthaginians had known, and as the Romans under Marcus Atilius Regulus and Publius Cornelius Scipio Africanus Major had learned, it's not hard to cross from Sicily to North Africa.[1] And, more importantly for the purposes of World War II, vice versa. So the question was not whether the Allies would land in Sicily, but when. Early July, as it turned out. Yet another expected surprise would come in the South Pacific. But just before both Kursk and Sicily.

The Japanese had built the air base at Munda on New Georgia, too late to save or even make a contest of Guadalcanal. But, unlike Guadalcanal, they would not leave that airfield practically undefended.

By the end of June 1943, the Japanese had dumped some 10,500 unfortunate troops, mostly at Munda and at the satellite base at Vila-Stanmore, across the Kula Gulf on Kolombangara, but others at smaller, even less desirable positions around both islands.

The land defenses were largely the responsibility of the "Southeast Detachment," administratively the 38th Infantry Group, under Major General Sasaki Minoru.[2] The Imperial Japanese Army had placed all of two regiments under Sasaki. One, the 13th under Colonel Tomonari Satoshi, was from the 6th Kumamoto Division, veterans of the Rape of Nanking. Charming. They were all based around Vila. The other, a reconstituted 229th under Colonel Hirata Genjiro, was from the 38th Nagoya Division, Guadalcanal veterans, if you could call them that. They were scattered across New Georgia. The understrength 1st Battalion was at Wickham on the east coast of Vangunu across from Gatukai, and at Viru on New Georgia proper. The 2nd was at Munda itself, while the 3rd, full of green replacements, was sharing Vila with the 6th Division.[3]

But the Imperial Army was not the only one with troops guarding New Georgia. So was the Imperial Navy, through its Special Naval Landing Force troops, in this case the 8th Combined Special Naval Landing Force. Unlike most units of the Special Naval Landing Force, this unit was not named after the city in which it was formed, because it was actually two naval infantry units – the 6th Kure, with 2,000 troops under Commander Okumura Saburo, guarding Bairoko, Enogai, and Munda Point; and the 7th Yokosuka, with 2,000 troops under Commander Takeda Kashin, based in Vila. These naval troops were led by Rear Admiral Ota Minoru.[4] Largely. No one was ever sure of exactly who was in charge of Japanese defenses, either land or naval or both.

Which is why, as part of those interservice agreements concluded back in March 1943, some command responsibilities were laid out with specificity but with flexibility as well. Again, the Imperial Army would defend the upper Solomons and the Imperial Navy the central Solomons, but it was also agreed that some Army units would be placed under navy command according to agreements between the local commanders in Rabaul. That is, Admiral Kusaka and General Inamura. The agreement effectively committed the Army to the defense of New Georgia.[5]

It would not be that much of an issue, due in large part to the relationship between Kusaka and Inamura, who were longtime friends. They enforced the agreement on relatively pleasant terms that filtered down to Admiral Ota and General Sasaki. The result was the "Navy/Army Agreement on Defense in the New Georgia Area," which set up a joint command for what was called the "New Georgia Defense Unit." Generally, in all areas of the island, the senior officer present regardless of service would be in charge, including on New Georgia proper, and by date of commission the senior officer was Sasaki.

That said, Sasaki would handle the defense of the all-important Munda area personally, while Ota would oversee the northern sector, including the region of Enogai and Bairoko. Sasaki would be responsible for all land operations, while Ota would handle coastal artillery, communications with rear areas, and barge operations; the Japanese were big on barges. Both would handle antiaircraft defense. "It was a ground breaking development," the official Japanese army historians wrote, "for the Imperial Army to be placed under the Navy from the early stages of operations preparation and to assign roles that maximized the strength of both the Army and the Navy."[6] Groundbreaking for Imperial Japan, at any rate.

While he was no General Yamashita, General Sasaki was also not one of the arrogant sadists, rapists, and thugs that infested the Imperial Japanese Army. Sasaki was an intelligent, thoughtful commander. He took stock of the situation when he arrived on New Georgia. What he found was not encouraging. Communications, one of the two most important commodities in any military operation, were almost nonexistent, with nothing in the way of telephone or telegraph lines, no roads, and the few trails across the island regularly washed out by rain. Navy radio centers were placed in underground bunkers, which is why Admiral Ota remained in charge of communications. The terrain posed major problems inasmuch as his troops struggled to dig into the coral for trenches and communications lines. The 6th Kure Special Naval Landing Force had placed four 140mm guns at Enogai, but there was next to nothing at Bairoko. The 7th Yokosuka Special Naval Landing Force had placed a section of 120mm guns on the tip of Baanga Island just off the western shore of Munda.[7]

General Sasaki attacked these problems as best as he could, using a fairly accurate assessment of the threat facing him. Unlike his superiors in Rabaul, who believed the Allies would attack in late July or early August, Sasaki believed the attack everyone knew was coming would be in late June. But from where? That was the ¥64,000 question, and Sasaki was flailing. He believed the Americans could land at Munda directly – exactly how was a question the Japanese never answered – which he heavily fortified. Sasaki solved the entrenchment problem by building bunkers and other fortifications with blocks of coral, eventually building two-tier log and coral pillboxes that could withstand anything except a direct hit by heavy artillery. Sasaki considered the possibilities of attacks from everywhere from Roviana to Rendova to Bairoko. The air attacks on Vila got the Japanese thinking the Americans would land there. "The enemy objective seems to be Kolombangara Island rather than Munda," a mid-June intelligence report concluded. "It is thought that this may be part of the enemy's plan to cut off our rear." In short, the Japanese had no idea where the Americans would land, and Sasaki was compelled to keep his limited Army and Navy forces spread thin.[8]

And, as General Sasaki was finding out, the Imperial Army and the Imperial Navy were not the only ones with troops guarding New Georgia. Someone else was there, too. Someone or something near Segi Point. The area had long been a problem for the Japanese on New Georgia. Every patrol sent to the Segi area had simply vanished. Not killed. Vanished. There were no bodies, nothing. They were just ... gone.

General Sasaki was aware of a coastwatcher in the area, Donald Kennedy, who had caused the Japanese no shortage of headaches. Sasaki directed Major Hara Masao, the new commander of the 1st Battalion, 229th Regiment, to apply some aspirin to this particular headache.

The major's first effort involved taking barges down Blanche Channel to Nono. The Japanese troops found no indication of enemy activity, so they went back to Viru Harbor. A second effort that came hacking through the jungle from Viru was ambushed in their bivouac near Nono. The survivors fled back to Viru without having fired a shot. A third effort involved 25 men from the 229th Regiment's 4th Company, who were moving out of Viru Harbor. They were bivouacked near Nazareth village, maybe five miles west of Segi, when on June 16 they were attacked by what they reported to be 50 Melanesian guerillas led by a Caucasian. All of the Japanese had escaped, but in the process left behind all their equipment and documents. What was the deal with the Japanese inability to secure their secret documents? Whether it was Colonel Ichiki's patrol or General Kawaguchi's base on Guadalcanal or the submarine *I-1*, when crisis came the Japanese displayed a consistent inability to either destroy secret documents or carry them away to prevent them from falling into enemy hands.

General Sasaki had his confirmation as to the nature of the problem at Segi: the coastwatcher Donald Kennedy. Sasaki directed Major Hara "to settle things." Hara took the 3rd Company of the 1st Battalion and a machine gun platoon to Viru Harbor and began to slowly scour the area. Hara knew where Kennedy was and he would take the arrogant westerner down. Slowly and methodically.

Unless something intervened. Like, say, enemy invasion transports showing up, which they did in the early hours of June 21, as reported by Japanese lookouts near Wickham. Admiral Kusaka's communications staff had noticed an increase in Allied radio traffic. Now they were seeing transports. This was it. At Munda, General Sasaki positioned his guns to cover a frontal assault; the Japanese went into a defensive crouch. At Rabaul, Kusaka immediately put Southeast Fleet on alert, ordered submarines to the area, and ordered Base Air Force to concentrate around Buin, to where he flew with some staffers. They would be ready to counterstrike ...[9]

Except scout planes reported no additional activity around New Georgia. And the volume of radio traffic went back down as well. It was just as well. Admiral Kusaka and General Inamura continued to believe there would be no invasion of New Georgia until at least late July or early August, conveniently after Kusaka had received his aerial reinforcements. This was just confirmation of that timetable.[10]

So, with nothing going on as far as he could tell, Admiral Kusaka ordered Base Air Force back to its dispersal bases and canceled the alert on June 27.[11]

Three days too early.

Admiral Kusaka's instincts had been right. Those high-speed transports were, in fact, a presage of the long-awaited Allied invasion of New Georgia.

Marine Raiders had been on New Georgia, off and on, since March 3, when a batch of them, including Captain Clay Boyd of the 1st Marine Raiders and naval intelligence officer Lieutenant William P. Coultas, who had been to the Solomons on a scientific expedition before the war, knew the jungle, understood the locals, and even spoke some of the local language, landed in the Segi area, where they met up with coastwatcher Donald Kennedy and his scouts. They were hoping to find a suitable beach for landing troops from which they could sweep northwest across the island and capture Munda.[12] What could be simpler?

Except nothing in the Solomons is simple. Not even for the indigenous population, some of which served as Kennedy's scouts and troops protecting his coastwatching operation against the periodic Japanese attempts to rid themselves of the headache he represented. The New Georgia jungle was, if anything, even worse than Guadalcanal. While the Melanesian locals on Guadalcanal could and did make their way through the jungle, the locals on New Georgia preferred to not deal with it if they didn't have to. They had given up the old ways of headhunting in favor of farming, trading, and especially fishing and as such knew the coasts and waterways of New Georgia and its maze of islands, islets, reefs, and just plain rocks intimately. But the inland jungle? They knew *of* it. The Marine Raiders ended up agreeing with the Melanesians. The beach at Segi was too small, and the coastal terrain impassable for any large body of marching troops.[13] They'd have to find a different way to attack New Georgia which was just as good. Recall the Joint Chiefs Directive of March 28, 1943, which set the goals for 1943 for General MacArthur and Admiral Halsey. First, they were to set up airfields on Woodlark and Kiriwina, two sizable island groups north of Milne Bay. The second objective was to seize the Huon Peninsula – Lae, Salamaua, Finschhafen, and Madang – of New Guinea and occupy western New Britain. Third was to seize and occupy the Solomon Islands as far as southern Bougainville.

Subsequent to this directive, Admiral Halsey went to meet with General MacArthur on April 15. The two hit it off and were able to smooth out a few bumps in the Joint Chiefs plan. Originally, Halsey was not to move up the Solomons until MacArthur had taken Lae and Salamaua. That was not scheduled to take place until September, meaning Halsey's 3rd Fleet naval forces would be twiddling their thumbs and growing barnacles for six months. That wasn't acceptable to Halsey or to Admiral King, for that matter. Halsey suggested that he move simultaneously with MacArthur's occupation of Woodlark and Kiriwina, provided Halsey would not get himself into such a mess that he needed MacArthur's help to clean it up. The general was agreeable to it. Once Halsey's ideas were incorporated, MacArthur's original plan, code-named *Elkton*, was re-issued on April 26, re-code-named *Cartwheel*: your simple plan for conquering Rabaul in only 13 easy steps.[14]

Generally, it would work as follows. The next phase, as the Joint Chiefs had planned, would involve General MacArthur taking Woodlark and Kiriwina. It should be relatively simple, since both were unoccupied, but, then again, part of the initial opposition on Guadalcanal involved wild pigs. While that was going on, Admiral Halsey would move into New Georgia. It was predicted that five months would be required to finish the New Georgia group. While that was going on, MacArthur would start taking the Huon Peninsula. By the time that was finished, Halsey would be in the Shortlands and on Bougainville. The plan would come together with MacArthur landing on Cape Gloucester on the southwest coast of New Britain across from the Huon Peninsula while Halsey captured Kieta and neutralized Buka.[15] These would be two mutually supporting advances, both aimed at Rabaul. It would drive the Japanese nuts trying to figure out which one was the main advance.

In turn, it would drive the Allies nuts trying to figure out when those advances would start. *Cartwheel* was supposed to start rolling on May 15 – "L-Day." But, well, General MacArthur needed more time to prepare to capture those two unoccupied islands. L-Day was ultimately pushed back to June 30. That was OK with Admiral Halsey because he was struggling to find a place to land on New Georgia from which his forces could approach the Munda air base. He even considered bypassing New Georgia altogether and landing on Kolombangara instead. Another scout team of Marine Raiders nixed that idea. First, there were few beaches suitable for a landing, so few that they were easily defended and would cause heavy casualties in an amphibious assault. More significantly, the Vila airfield site could not be expanded to meet AirSols' needs.[16]

Eventually, Admiral Halsey settled for a "simple" four-part operation, one that he named "*Toenails*," inside one part of the simple 13-part *Cartwheel*. This plan to capture Munda, issued on June 3, involved four simultaneous landings, none of which would actually capture Munda. Each landing site had not just a tactical objective, but an operational and perhaps even strategic objective as well. One landing would be at the aforementioned Segi Point, which was suitable for an airfield. If the Japanese were going to have an airfield on New Georgia, the Allies were going to have one, too. It was just the principle of the thing. A second landing site would be the aforementioned Wickham Anchorage, between

Vangunu and Gatukai, which could be a useful base for PT boats, landing craft, and other small craft. Ditto for a third landing site, Viru Harbor, on New Georgia proper.[17]

The most significant and important of the landing sites would be the fourth: Rendova, the sizable island across the Blanche Channel from Munda Point. Rendova would be the staging point for troops to be shuttled to New Georgia proper for the attack on Munda. Additionally, Rendova was only five miles or so from the runways at Munda, and so would be able to shell the runways, far more effectively than "Pistol Pete" or "Millimeter Mike" had done to Henderson Field, and make them unusable. Really the centerpiece of *Toenails*, Rendova would be the fungus that spread to Munda.

Toenails was promising to be the biggest amphibious operation since *Watchtower* – and a lot more complicated. For all practical purposes, *Watchtower* had two landings: Guadalcanal and Tulagi, though to be sure Tulagi had a few sublandings like Gavutu and Tanambogo. *Toenails* involved landings at four widely divergent locations. It would require a master of organization to pull off. Fortunately, Rear Admiral Richmond Kelly Turner was just such a master of organization. Like pretty much everyone else on the Allied side, Turner had learned a lot from the *Watchtower* landings, which was good, since his (for the next few weeks) South Pacific Amphibious Force, designated Task Force 31, would be the big little piggy in *Toenails*.

And thanks to the division into two forces in *Watchtower*, *Toenails* was ingrown with a division into two forces. There was an Eastern Force under Rear Admiral George H. Fort. This Eastern Group would include the Viru Harbor (minesweeper *Hopkins*, fast destroyer transports *Kilty* and *Crosby*; eight tank landing craft, and two "small coastal transports" that were 103-foot wooden-hulled things of about 258 tons that could make 10 knots with the wind at their backs); Segi Point (four "small coastal transports"; two tank landing ships, five infantry landing craft; and 12 tank landing craft), and Wickham Anchorage (minesweeper *Trever*; fast destroyer transports *McKean* and *Schley*; seven infantry landing craft, 16 tank landing craft, and four "small coastal transports") occupation groups; all supported by a dozen PT boats from the Russells.[18]

The other force, the Western Force, was the big one and thus Admiral Turner commanded that himself with the exception of the tip of the spear. This was the Onaiavisi Occupation Unit featuring the fast destroyer transport *Talbot* and minesweeper *Zane* bringing in two companies of the 169th Infantry Regiment; and the Rendova Advance Unit, with the fast destroyer transports *Waters* and *Dent* bringing in two companies of the 172nd Infantry Regiment. But Turner commanded at least most of the spearhead behind the tip.[19]

The heart of Admiral Turner's force was the Transport Division under Captain Theiss that featured Turner's traditional flagship *McCawley*; three other "attack transports" in the *President Jackson*, *President Adams*, and *President Hayes*; and two "attack cargo ships" – a military euphemism if there ever was one – in the *Algorab* and *Libra*. Screening this tip of the spear were eight destroyers under Captain Ryan: four (*Ralph Talbot*, *Buchanan*, *McCalla*, and flagship *Farenholt*) providing gunfire support under Ryan's direct command;

the other four (*Gwin*, *Radford*, *Jenkins*, and *Woodworth*) under Commander J.M. Higgins providing antisubmarine protection. Additionally, there was a squadron of a dozen PT boats, always useful for running errands, under Lieutenant Commander Robert B. Kelly. Behind all this were ten tank landing ships, 11 infantry landing craft, another dozen PT boats, and tugs *Rail* and the veteran *Vireo*.[20]

All of these various fast destroyer transports, "attack transports," tank landing ships, infantry landing craft, and "small coastal transports" would be carrying the appropriately named New Georgia Occupation Force. It included the US Army's 43rd Infantry Division and the 136th Field Artillery Battalion of 155mm howitzers from the 37th Infantry Division; the US Marines' 1st Marine Raider Regiment, except for two battalions; the 9th Defense Battalion with its own unit of 155mm artillery; the US Navy's "Acorn 7," built around the 47th Construction Battalion; the 24th Construction Battalion and one section from the 20th, plus base and communications units; and the 1st Fiji Infantry.[21] All would be under the authority of the 43rd's commander, Major General John H. Hester.

Behind all this was Task Force 36, which consisted of all the combat ships necessary to fight a major surface or air battle. It was under the direct command of Admiral Halsey, so sailors and Marines could feel confident there would be no repeat of Admiral Fletcher's abandonment of the Marines in Guadalcanal from the previous August. Nor would there be a repeat of the Japanese sortie that led to the disastrous Savo Island battle, not if Halsey or Admiral Turner had their way.

That was the thinking behind designating certain subgroups of Task Force 36 as "support groups." Designated "Support Group A" was Admiral Ainsworth and his flagship light cruiser *Honolulu* followed by light cruisers *Helena* and *St Louis*; and destroyers *O'Bannon*, *Chevalier*, *Nicholas*, and *Strong*.[22] Designated "Support Group B" was Admiral Merrill with his flagship light cruiser *Montpelier* followed by fellow light cruisers *Cleveland*, *Columbia*, and *Denver*; destroyers *Pringle*, *Waller*, *Renshaw*, *Saufley*, and *Philip*; and those spunky destroyer minelayers *Preble*, *Gamble*, and *Breese*.[23] Available to provide air support if necessary was a group designated "Support Group C," in which Rear Admiral DeWitt C. Ramsey had his flagship carrier *Saratoga* and the Royal Navy aircraft carrier *Victorious*, plus light antiaircraft cruisers *San Juan*, freshly repaired after the bomb damage at Santa Cruz, and *San Diego*; and destroyers *Fanning*, *Dunlap*, *Cummings*, *Case*, *Maury*, *Gridley*, and *Craven*. Glenn Davis, now a rear admiral after his experience off Guadalcanal, commanded not one but three battleships – *Massachusetts*, *Indiana*, and *North Carolina*, with destroyers *Claxton*, *Dyson*, *Stanly*, and *Converse*. The *North Carolina* would provide fire support for the landings if necessary.[24]

It was hoped the carriers would not be needed, that all the necessary air support could be provided by Admiral Fitch's South Pacific land-based air, designated Task Force 33. Running point for Task Force 33 was Admiral Mitscher's AirSols, but Fitch worried that Guadalcanal and the Russells were too far from New Georgia to adjust to changing conditions there. For that reason, Fitch created something called either the "New Georgia Air Force" or "Air Command New Georgia," or both, or both at the same time. It sounded at once both confusing and more grandiose than it actually was, comprising Brigadier General Francis P. Mulcahy, his 2nd Marine Air Wing staff, and something called "Argus 11," which consisted of one advanced base fighter direction unit with one New Zealand and two American radar units. The aircraft of the "New Georgia Air Force" were simply AirSols aircraft on missions to New Georgia; as soon as they took off, they came under Mulcahy's authority.[25]

Toenails was painted and polished with a mostly unspoken color of "No new Guadalcanals." *Watchtower* had a timid theater commander; *Toenails* had General MacArthur. *Watchtower* had a carrier commander haunted by losing two aircraft carriers spooked because he saw an enemy bomber; *Toenails* had Admiral Halsey, a carrier commander who had only lost one aircraft carrier instead of two. *Watchtower* had the 1st Marine Division stranded on Guadalcanal without adequate supplies because the cargo ships had fled to far off Espiritu Santo or, worse, Nouméa; *Toenails*, thanks to a sustained supply buildup called operation *Drygoods*, had 54,274 tons of supplies, 13,085 tons of assorted gear, 23,775 drums of fuel and lubricants, and various vehicles available on Guadalcanal and the Russells.[26] *Watchtower* had had no aircraft ready for the Guadalcanal airfield for almost two weeks after it was captured and operational; *Toenails* had aircraft ready before the invasion. *Watchtower* had a Japanese naval sortie that destroyed the warships screening the invasion transports; *Toenails* would reverse that, they hoped. They would not make the same mistakes they had made at Guadalcanal. Instead, they would make all new mistakes.

Watchtower had invaded its targets, Guadalcanal and Tulagi, all at once. *Toenails*? Well, it was complicated. For one thing, *Toenails* added in mid-June a fifth landing site, this one at Rice Anchorage on Kula Gulf. Landing here, it was hoped, would cut off any Japanese reinforcement through that quarter, plus enable an advance toward Munda through Enogai and Bairoko. Problem was that all the forces available had been allocated to the other four landings, so the Rice Anchorage landing would have to take place a few days after the initial landings.

Of course, that depended on a very particular definition of "initial landings," because certain landings had already taken place in the New Georgia area. On June 13, a Catalina flying boat brought Captain Boyd back to Segi, now leading seven Marine Raiders specially trained in reconnaissance. They had very specific assignments: preparing the landing beaches, collecting canoes, cutting paths from Rice Anchorage toward Enogai.[27]

These were advance teams, going in ahead to the main landing to help prepare the way. Technically, they were not the famous Pathfinders, who would go in ahead of the main force to set up and mark drop zones for parachuting troops, but that's basically what they were, except they were pathfinders for amphibious landing troops. Guided by Donald Kennedy's scouts, these pathfinders in all but name split up and traveled by canoe to their various assigned areas: Viru Harbor; Oloana Bay on Vangunu two miles west of Wickham Anchorage; Rendova; and, of course, the aforementioned Rice Anchorage. Some would stay at Rendova and Oloana Bay to man beacon lights to guide in the landing craft, with the landings being at night. A coastwatcher, Flight Officer J. A. Corrigan, and a party of local Melanesian escorts, would be waiting at Rice.

The necessity of the Melanesian escorts became apparent soon enough. Donald Kennedy may have been a coastwatcher whose assignment was just to watch the Japanese and report what they were doing, but his hobby was running his own small guerilla group. They were the reason Japanese patrols kept disappearing near Segi Point. However, Hara and Sasaki were using fairly intelligent tactics and bringing their superiority in men and materiel to bear. Kennedy soon realized that Hara was far more formidable than his predecessors.

Kennedy's June 16 ambush of the 25-man Japanese patrol – by a dozen Melanesian guerillas, not the 50 reported by the Japanese – seems to have been the watershed moment and a massive warning. In reviewing the trove of documents captured from the patrol, Kennedy saw that Major Hara had located Kennedy's headquarters – and was moving toward it from three directions.[28]

That wasn't good. No way did Kennedy and his Melanesian scouts have the men or weapons to even mount a defense. Kennedy radioed the *Ferdinand* base on Guadalcanal that he needed help fast or else he would have to abandon Segi Point.[29]

Ask and ye shall receive. Just before 6:00 the next morning, June 21, the old destroyer-turned-"high-speed" transports *Dent* and *Waters* – the transports seen by the Japanese lookouts at Wickham – were off Segi Point, and 400 members of the 4th Marine Raider Battalion under Colonel Michael S. Currin were coming ashore in landing boats where Kennedy had lit beacons for their approach. They were greeted by Kennedy himself. They had beaten Major Hara to Segi Point, in part because Hara's troops were still burning the village of Regi three miles away.[30]

Even though beleaguered with malaria and dengue fever that kept him hospitalized in Nouméa, Admiral Turner had determined that the airfield site at Segi was just too important to risk losing it even before the invasion, and not just losing it, but watching the Japanese reinforce it. Turner authorized the immediate transport of Colonel Currin's Marines. And then a reinforcement the following morning by two companies of the 103rd Infantry Regiment, as well as Admiral Fitch's colorful engineer Commander Wilfred L. Painter and his party. After all, if they were going to Segi anyway, might as well get started building the airfield. And the first step in building the airfield is surveying the airfield site.[31]

So that was where things stood late on June 29 into the wee hours of June 30, when the "No new Guadalcanals" theme was going to start being tested. Admiral Merrill's "Support Group B" was working its way up The Slot toward Shortland. The destroyers *Waller* and *Renshaw* were detached at 5:45pm to bombard Vila-Stanmore. That would give the Japanese something to think about. The two destroyers returned to the formation a little after midnight. A half hour or so later the *Pringle* left with the three minelayers.

Shortly afterward, Admiral Merrill and his ships were introduced to the theme for the day: rain. And lots of it. A deluge that reduced visibility to almost nothing. But Merrill would keep playing. He didn't think the heavy stuff would come down for quite a while. The admiral had his ships turn to the southwest and pass close to Poporang Island, one of the Shortland Islands just southeast of Shortland proper, and proceeded to blast it with his guns. That would give the Japanese something else to think about.

And while the Japanese were thinking about that, they would not be thinking about what the *Pringle*, *Preble*, *Gamble*, and *Breese* were doing, which was, according to the *Pringle*'s war diary, "taking the mining force under Tojo's nose closer than any previous operation," laying the "standard three-row minefield" between Fauro and Shortland "200 yards closer to the entrance (to the Shortlands anchorage) than anticipated . . . completely undetected."[32] Everyone returned safely with no casualties.

In the meantime, on this night, Japanese lookouts at Nassau Bay, 15 miles southeast of Salamaua in New Guinea, in the words of Samuel Eliot Morison, "reported a large scale invasion in progress and, as the 300-man garrison had not been ordered to stand and die, it turned and ran."[33] At least it kept a reputation for never surrendering intact. This was the start of General MacArthur's part of the operation. A little different than had been originally planned, but, then, no plans survive contact with the enemy anyway.

The Japanese might have stood and fought if they had known just how fouled up the operation already was. The Nassau Bay landing was thrown together on the fly as part of something called Operation *Doublet*, and it showed. Some three dozen landing craft, each capable of maybe 8 knots at the fastest, in three waves, each wave led by a PT boat, moving 25 knots at the slowest, meant that opposites did not necessarily attract in keeping the escorts and the escorted together in efforts to land the heavily reinforced 1st Battalion of the 162nd Regiment from the 41st Infantry Division. Taking Nassau Bay was primarily about logistics. The Australian 7th Division, facing the Japanese 51st Division, had to have supplies flown into Wau — recall that Wau was not easy to supply under the best circumstances — and then carried in backpacks by local porters some 25 miles to the 7th's supply depots. There was simply no way to get sufficient supplies, especially artillery shells, to the 7th in this manner. A fully seaborne supply line through Nassau Bay could solve that problem. A landing at Nassau Bay could also have the effect of diverting the attention of General Inamura and the 8th Area Army away from New Georgia.[34]

Best laid plans and all that. But these were not the best laid plans; they were slapped together. And even the best laid plans would have had trouble on this night. Like it was off Shortland, the weather was stormy with low visibility. The improvised convoy had to go into the teeth of a wicked southeast wind that made raindrops feel like bullets. *PT-68*, serving as the convoy's lone escort and not carrying any troops, got lost and just sort of wandered around. *PT-142*, leading the first wave of landing craft, missed Nassau Bay in the murk, so she turned around and doubled back. And ran into the second wave and its leader, *PT-143*. The first wave's assault boats scattered in the dark, and *PT-142* was compelled to round them up and point them toward Nassau Bay, where the second wave was already landing. In the 12-foot-high surf, the only way to land the troops was for the landing barges to run at full speed onto the beach, which they did. And onto each other in the overcrowded conditions. The surf drove them higher onto the beach and into each other, wrecking the boats. Others broached – a nautical term meaning the boat has made an unplanned turn so it faces the waves – causing the boat to roll and take on water or even capsize. The result: of the 24 boats that reached the beach, 23 were wrecked. The third wave didn't try to land and just sheltered in a cove until the seas calmed. One cheeky observer called it a "shipwreck landing," albeit a shipwreck landing with no casualties. Lieutenant D.B. Burke, leading one of the teams placing beacons to guide the boats in, later wrote, "It was a great effort on the part of the troops and the inexperienced navigators in the landing craft, that they ever managed to reach the beach in one piece." It wasn't pretty, but they landed most of the troops. More would be landed in the next few days.[35]

It was 5:00am when the Japanese in Rabaul received word of the landing at Nassau Bay. That was their first indication that something big was going on. It was only seven hours or so after Lieutenant Ichimura in the submarine *Ro-103* had reported seven enemy ships south of Gatukai. That message does not seem to have gotten through to Admiral Kusaka or anyone in authority. So their first warning was a misdirection, just as the Allies had intended. And it worked. For about 90 minutes.[36]

Toenails supposedly took in all the lessons of Guadalcanal. One of those lessons, as explained by General Vandegrift, was that "landings should not be attempted in the face of organized resistance, if, by any combination of march or maneuver, it is possible to land unopposed and undetected."[37] In short, hit 'em where they ain't. If it seems kind of obvious, that's because it is.

Four landings, all intended to land at points unopposed, if not necessarily undetected. In theory. It didn't quite work out that way. It never does. Almost the entirety of New Georgia Island is separated from the South Pacific by a series of reefs and islets that make approaching the island by deep-draught ship dangerous, if not impossible. The only breaks in the reef were on the island's south side near Munda. Two miles east of the eastern end of the Munda runway is Ilangana Point, which forms the western end of the 25-mile-long Roviana Lagoon. Roviana Lagoon is separated to the south from the Blanche Strait, which itself separates New Georgia from Rendova Island, by more of those islets and reefs. But there is a break in those reefs called Onaiavisi Passage, between the little islets of Dume and Baraulu.[38] Since Onaiavisi Passage was one of the few routes through the reefs to Munda, controlling it became a high priority.

To that end, another old destroyer-turned-"high-speed" transport *Talbot* and the old destroyer-turned-minesweeper *Zane* each picked up a company of the 169th Infantry Regiment and a landing barge in the Russells on June 29. Beginning at about 2:30am on June 30, they landed their troops on Dume and Baraulu Islands. Without opposition, at least from the Japanese. They had opposition from other quarters however. During the heavy rain at around 3:00am, the *Zane* ran aground forward. The former four-piper huffed and puffed and was finally able to back herself off at 5:23 – only to almost immediately run aground aft. This time the *Zane* could not free herself and had to be hauled off by the tug *Rail* nine hours later. The aft grounding had damaged the *Zane*'s propellers, so she had to be towed all the way back to Tulagi.[39] But the little *Talbot* and *Zane* had successfully, if inelegantly in the case of the *Zane*, completed their mission. The troops were landed in the right place and on time.

In other places, not so much. The *Waters* and the *Dent* had been detailed to drop off two companies of the US Army's 172nd Infantry Regiment. These troops were specially trained for the jungle and had earned the nickname "Barracudas," a somewhat bizarre choice considering that barracudas live in water and not in jungles. The plan was for the *Waters* and *Dent* to land them at a beach on Rendova that pathfinders had marked with a light. The troops were supposed to hit the beach at dawn, but for reasons unknown did not land until after 6:00am. But when they landed, they landed in the wrong place; the rains had washed out the landing beacons placed by the pathfinders. At least they landed the troops; they got that part right. But the Barracudas' assignment was to take out any Japanese opposition to the later landing, and now they could not.

Waddling into the waters off Rendova were Admiral Turner's flagship transport *McCawley*, carrying not just their not-entirely-recovered fearless leader but the 3rd Fleet's own fearless leader Admiral Halsey, leading veteran transports *President Jackson*, *President Adams*, and *President Hayes*; and cargo ships *Algorab* and *Libra*. Escorting them were Captain Ryan's eight destroyers.

The troops piled into the landing craft to storm the beaches for their first objective. And then at 6:46am they heard Admiral Turner's voice over the loud speakers: "You are the first to land, you are the first to land. Expect opposition."[40]

Initially, there wasn't. The Japanese had built this nice airfield at Munda and stuffed it with troops, but did not bother to guard the controlling approaches. Though General Sasaki had considered the possibility of an enemy landing on Rendova, within shelling distance of the Munda airfield, he had posted only about 140 troops, half from the 229th Infantry Regiment and half the 6th Kure Special Naval Landing Force. One Japanese wrote in his diary, "I can't understand why Headquarters does not reinforce troops on Rendova which is a good landing place. A sad case!"[41] Smart guy. And in a nice replay of the initial landings on Guadalcanal, the few troops they did post were taken completely by surprise.

Both Imperial Army and Navy troops were thoroughly demoralized. The individual in command of this Rendova garrison, Lieutenant Suzuki Toshio of the 229th, was not even on hand; he was across the water at Munda, down with malaria. Lieutenant (jg) Niyake Naoto Niyake, a young naval doctor, noted that Allied planes were overhead almost constantly, with no Japanese fighters to oppose them. In his diary he compared himself to "a lonely candle standing in the midst of a fierce wind." He would make millions out of that quote, if only he could wait 40 years to sell the licensing rights to certain singers. But he didn't have 40 years, or even 40 days, and he knew it. "I know I shall really feel helpless when the enemy lands," Niyake wrote in his diary on June 25. "Our reactions now are slow, just like that."[42]

Just like that, the enemy had landed. And just like that, the Japanese reactions were slow. They had been awakened by a false alarm earlier that morning and went back to snoozing. By the time they had been alerted again, the Americans were on the beach, having overrun the beach defense positions without a fight. The Japanese tried to stand and fight, but the muddy ground waterlogged from the heavy rains meant their entrenchments were useless. The commander of the local naval infantry stopped a machine gun burst with his face. They could not ask for help or warn Munda because the batteries of their radio were dead. The best they could do was shoot four blue flares into the air and signal Munda by Aldis lamp. The Special Naval Landing Force troops had a reputation for never surrendering, and, just as at Guadalcanal, they didn't – they fled into the jungle.

So, there wasn't much opposition, not on Rendova, at any rate. There was elsewhere, however. The eastern force had been left to Admiral Turner's second-in-command, Rear Admiral George Fort. Fort's main claim to fame so far in this Pacific War was providing one of the few successes of *I-Go* when, as senior Navy officer on Guadalcanal, he needlessly delayed the departure of the US Navy oiler *Kanawha* in the face of an imminent Japanese air attack that prevented her escape and ultimately sank the ship. And, no, Fort had not improved much since then. He personally directed the Wickham anchorage landings, which did not actually take place in Wickham anchorage. Wickham had a small beach patrolled by Japanese. Oloana Bay (or Oleana Bay), on the other hand, had a big beach not patrolled by Japanese. Landing at Oloana and marching on Wickham made sense. You would have done it, too.

But maybe not in the weather of July 30, 1943, in the Solomons. The storms, heavy rain, winds, and choppy seas convinced Admiral Fort, in his flagship, the destroyer-minesweeper *Trever* (chosen, it is generally believed, because the *Trever* was the only ship available to him that had radar), to delay landing his units until dawn, but he could not get the word out. So the *Trever* and the destroyer-transports *Schley* and *McKean*, carrying N and P companies of the 4th Marine Raider Battalion, stopped off Oloana Bay in the dark and rain at about 2:30am. In the stoic language and 24-hour time of the US Navy, the *Schley*'s log described what happened next:

0256. Heavy seas running, making embarkation of Marines extremely difficult.
0303. Sighted light on beach.
0316. Launched all boats.
[...]
0434. Landing made at wrong beach – about 6000 yards northwest of western end of Oleana Bay.
0435. Commenced steering various courses and speeds proceeding to Oleana Bay. Boat #3 and LCV following ship; unable to contact other boats.[43]

So the transports started landing the Raiders and then realized they were at the wrong beach, some three miles west of the right beach. It's not like they could stop and ask for directions. As they started moving toward the right beach, they could not contact all of the Marines that had already started to land. Once they got back into the area of the right beach, the landing craft carrying Lieutenant Colonel Brown's troops had started to arrive, which meant the Raiders' ships and landing boats had to avoid colliding with the Army landing craft, and vice versa. The result was, in the words of one historian, "The assault wave of marines landed in impressive disorganization." They were strewn over a seven-mile stretch of the island, including one platoon stranded on a reef. Six landing boats were smashed by the surf upon the rocks.

For their part, the Army landing craft, arriving closer to sunrise, had some daylight available and were able to find the right beach. Nevertheless, the 2nd Battalion's operations officer described it as, "a screwed-up mess." Pathfinders Lieutenants James Lamb, Ellis Satterthwaite, and Frederick Burnaby had endured weeks of danger and privation to blaze the trail for the landing and set up the landing beacon, but it was almost undone because Lamb's watch was five or ten minutes fast, so the beacon flashed too soon and the landing craft commanders missed it, leaving them confused as to where to go. While they were trying to figure it out, the landing craft roiled and pitched in the surf. They made it to the beach, but they were all seasick – nausea, vomiting, crushing headaches, barely able to stand. All this and, yet, no casualties.[44] Unless one counts the seasickness.

When Lieutenant Colonel Brown made it ashore, he was greeted by Lieutenants Lamb, Satterthwaite, and Burnaby, who gave him the fresh intelligence that the Japanese, long thought to have been concentrated at the village of Vura to the east, had now moved further east to Kairuku. Once his artillery had landed, Brown led his nauseous, vomiting troops in staggering eastward through the pouring rain on a muddy, slippery jungle trail cut by Kennedy's scouts.

The Japanese troops in the Wickham area that morning consisted of the 2nd Rifle Company of the 6th Kure Special Naval Landing Force, camped on the south bank of the Kairuku River, and one platoon from the 229th Regiment, occupying Vura, with a 37mm gun and mortars set up at Seke Point. All were under the command of Lieutenant Yamamoto Kazuo. At around 10:00am, General Sasaki ordered Yamamoto to pull his troops back to the northern coast of New Georgia. It appears that Yamamoto neither received this order nor was informed of the Oloana Bay landing; he had not even attempted to position his troops for combat.

The Americans took advantage. One company scattered the Japanese troops at Vura and took positions to support the more difficult attack on Kairuku. Lieutenant Colonel Brown began his attack on Kairuku village from the north side of the Kairuku River at 2:05pm, but without planned 81mm mortar support because communications – notice a theme here – were down as a result of the rain. Brown's assault pushed the Japanese back, but incurred 22 killed (12 Marines and ten soldiers) from the Nambu machine guns and could not clear the town. Brown was able to establish positions at the mouth of the Kairuku River, overlooking the bay. It was from this position that at 2:00am on July 1 they ambushed three Japanese barges approaching the town, killing 109 Japanese troops. Three Americans were killed.

After dawn, Lieutenant Colonel Brown sent out patrols to locate the Japanese positions. Finding out they were mostly concentrated around Seke Point on the coast, Brown decided to withdraw his troops to Vura. From there he could defend the artillery and Seabees, while that same artillery and air support could finish off the Japanese at Kairuku, with much less risk of American casualties than a second attack.

It sounded good in theory, and the 105mm howitzers at Vura began bombarding Seke Point on July 2, joined by the 3-inch guns of the *Trever*. But a mixup in communications – that word again – delayed the arrival of air support until July 3, when 18 Dauntlesses plastered Seke Point with 1,000lb bombs. After that, Kairuku village was occupied without a fight and Seke Point was taken with minimal opposition. But the Americans found only seven Japanese corpses; the Japanese troops had disappeared. Prisoners revealed they had been evacuated the night before, made possible by the Americans pulling back from their Kairuku Harbor positions. Nevertheless, the Americans would find Japanese stragglers in this part of New Georgia throughout 1943.

While not exactly smooth, the Wickham operation had gone roughly according to plan. The Viru Harbor operation, not so much. The landing at Viru had been unintentionally complicated by Donald Kennedy's activities.[45] Major Hara's movement of troops into the area swelled the number of potential defenders to about 300. Despite the presence of Kennedy and the June 21 pre-emptive landing that was meant to save his coastwatcher cell from Hara's advance, Allied intelligence was strangely unaware of the presence of Hara's troops. Lieutenant Colonel Currin was ordered to lead his Marine raiders west from Segi Point to attack two Japanese bivouacs guarding the entrance to Viru Harbor. The entrance to the harbor was narrow – maybe 300 yards wide – bracketed by sheer cliffs about 100 feet tall topped by thick foliage. If the entrance was defended, entering it would be next to impossible. Currin took one company by boat to a village west of Nono and then started overland, only to run into a swamp that delayed his advance. To make matters worse, a brush with a Japanese patrol nibbled away at his rear guard, leaving five Marines dead and one wounded, with 18 dead Japanese. The Raiders camped for the night at the Choi River, then split up, one party headed to the east side of the entrance, the other, led by Currin, to the western side, and resumed the trudge toward their targets.

Lieutenant Colonel Currin had no working radio, so he sent two of Kennedy's scouts back with word that he would be delayed. That information never reached the transports, however. Communications again. Commander Stanley Leith arrived off the entrance to Viru Harbor at about 6:10am in the destroyer-minesweeper *Hopkins*, leading the fast destroyer transports *Kilty* and *Crosby*, all of which were carrying B Company of the 103rd Infantry Regiment. Having had no communications with Currin's unit and not sure of what he was facing, Leith cautiously inched his ships toward the entrance.

This slow advance went on until 7:10am, about 15 minutes after sunrise, when a big splash announced someone was shooting at them. Specifically, an old British-made 3-inch naval gun the Japanese had deployed at the west side of the harbor entrance near the village of Tetemara. Protecting it from air attack were four 80mm antiaircraft guns. The *Kilty* and *Crosby* shot back with their own 3-inch guns. The *Crosby* reported seeing an explosion near the Japanese position after the 10th round. Both sides ceased fire and Commander Leith moved his ships out of range of the Japanese gun to await developments with Currin's advance party. Major Hara reported that his troops had repulsed a landing. In response, General Sasaki ordered him to withdraw to Munda, where he was concentrating Japanese troops.

Meanwhile, the American air liaison officer at Segi Point requested an air strike on the troublesome Japanese gun, and at 9:00am, 17 Dauntlesses arrived and dropped 1,000lb bombs on the gun, missing the gun but convincing its crew that their talents were needed elsewhere. Currin's Raiders began their attack on the western side of the entrance about 90 minutes later; the eastern side had already been cleared. By early afternoon, Admiral Fort had ordered Leith to land his troops at the Choi River, where the Raiders had spent the previous night. Leith treated his orders as suggestions and landed his troops all the way back at Segi Point at 4:30pm, about the same time Currin had cleared the western side of the entrance. Major Hara and 160 survivors withdrew westward into the jungle.

In comparison to the other landing sites, there was remarkably little combat involved in the Allied landing at Segi Point. Which is a good thing since Segi Point was already held by Allied forces. But given the already mentioned communications issues on this day, it is a minor miracle that no Allied force was unaware of the fact that Segi Point had already been in the hands of Allied forces for nine days, and thus a friendly fire incident was avoided. Nevertheless, the landing craft did encounter resistance – from the reefs in the area, and several ran aground. Even so, Acorn 7 landed at 10:10am, and in less than three hours the Seabees were working on the new airfield.[46]

By a trickle of reports, the news of the landing had gotten to Rabaul. At 6:50am, the 8th Combined Special Naval Landing Force had reported sighting Admiral Turner's screen. The Japanese submarine *Ro-101* under Lieutenant Commander Orita Zenji had also reported the landing to Rabaul. According to Lieutenant Commander Hanami Kohei, skipper of the destroyer *Amagiri*, "The information created a tumult at Rabaul Base."[47] According to one Japanese history, "the landing on Rendova Island completely baffled our forces."[48] Among them were Admiral Kusaka and General Inamura, who were both taken completely by surprise – and completely unprepared. Base Air Force had fewer than 30 Zeros available at Buin. The battered dive bombers of the 582 Air Group were at Kavieng, on the opposite side of Rabaul from Buin. The 8th Fleet was now little more than the 3rd Destroyer Flotilla, and much of that unit was scattered between Rabaul and Shortland.[49] They would respond, but it would take time to get together.

In the interim, Rabaul had responded to *Ro-101*'s report of the landing with an order to attack the beachhead. But Admiral Turner had anticipated such an action and positioned a flock of motor torpedo boats – PTs *118, 151, 153, 154, 155, 156, 157, 158, 159, 160, 161,* and *162* under Lieutenant Commander Robert B. Kelly – to counter it, and the submarine got nowhere.[50]

More problematic for the Americans was Japanese artillery from across the strait. That battery of 120mm artillery from the 7th Yokosuka Special Naval Landing Force on Baanga Island opened fire on the western section of destroyers. One shell hit the engine room of the *Gwin* a little after 7:00am, killing four and injuring seven. The *Farenholt* and the *Jenkins* reported near misses. The *Buchanan* was ordered to take out the guns, and so she held herself out as bait. The Japanese battery fired sporadically throughout the morning, causing no additional damage or deaths, but after the destroyer lobbed 64 5-inch shells onto the island, the shelling ceased.[51]

Still more problematic was the threat of air attacks. The Guadalcanal landings had been most fortunate inasmuch as the American fighter direction in the face of multiple attacks by Base Air Force had been ineffective, to put it mildly, but the Japanese attacks had been even more ineffective. Now, AirSols – well, the "New Georgia Air Force" – had a plan; the "Argus 11" fighter control team on board the destroyer *Jenkins* would direct what was called a "Rendova Patrol" of 32 fighters maintained over the landing areas. Orbiting in a 10-mile circle, stacked at various altitudes, these 32 fighters were to be maintained in relays, changed on visual contact, until 4:30pm, when 16 fighters would stay overhead for the final half hour of patrols.[52]

They would be needed. At 8:56am, a false alarm of an air attack cost about an hour that could have been spent unloading troops and supplies, but the alarm that came at about 11:00am was the real thing. It was a housewarming party from the original Base Air Force of 15 Zeros from the 582 Air Group and 12 from the 204. Of these 27 Zeros, 14 carried bombs. Dangerous though it was, it was barely a shadow of the old days of *Kido Butai*, Clark Field, and Force Z. The 204 had been so shredded by losses that it had no officer aviators remaining and was led by Chief Petty Officer Watanabe Hideo.[53]

And the decline showed. The Sea Eagles had swung around to attack Rendova from the southwest, but they ran into a buzzsaw of 16 Corsairs from Marine Fighting 121 and 16 Wildcats from Fighting 21. The Japanese ended up dropping none of their bombs and losing four Zeros, with two pilots killed, for their trouble. But they claimed 24 American fighters shot down, with six probables. Actual American losses were, roughly, zero.[54]

Once that enemy attack thing was handled, the 6,300 American troops continued making their way ashore, where it soon became apparent that those lessons from Guadalcanal had not quite been digested. For all the talk about "combat loading" invasion transports, these transports were loaded for peacetime, so that while they were unloaded in fairly short order, the supplies got piled up on the extremely muddy beach. The 24th Construction Battalion described the area behind the landing zone as a "marsh." For all the miracles the Seabees were usually able to work, they had difficulty building roads and fortifications in the wetlands, difficulty compounded by their equipment being buried in the holds of the cargo ships. Marine observers were critical. Lieutenant Colonel W.J. McNenny reported that "equipment and stores carried in the New Georgia operation were excessive. It appears the forward base must be considered as an assembly area for launching the assault." Colonel George W. McHenry wrote in his notes, "Believe too much gear for initial landing. Stress what [is] necessary to fight and eat. Bring other up after secure."[55]

Even so, almost all of the supplies were landed; all but 50 tons. As a point of comparison, during the *Watchtower* landings, more than one transport skipper had to leave the anchorage with more than 50 tons of unloaded supplies in his hold. In his command post on a hill maybe two miles north of the Munda runway, General Sasaki had watched most of the landing of troops and unloading of supplies, completely mesmerized by the spectacle.[56] According to one Japanese history, "The speedy disembarkation of the enemy was absolutely miraculous. The convoy sailed after completing debarkation within two and a half hours after arrival in port."[57]

Something of an exaggeration, but it was quick, because Admiral Turner wanted to get out of there; at some point, Admiral Turner had said, "The Japanese will attack – their planes will come in around three o'clock." He was wrong; it was 3:45.[58] The 702 Air Group's Lieutenant Commander Nakamura Genzo led 17 G4Ms from the 702 and nine from the 705, all armed with torpedoes. Their escort consisted of 24 Zeros of the 251 Air Group led by Lieutenant Mukai Ichiro, a rising star among the Sea Eagles.[59]

The *Rikko* were not in a diamond, but in a big "V" formation of little three-plane Vs. They circled over Roviana Island and approached the port side of Admiral Turner's convoy, now heading out of Blanche Channel. Turner was an old pro at this; he had his convoy in an antiaircraft formation, the transports in two columns, the destroyers on the outside.

For some reason, it is considered good practice to attack something when its guards are changing shifts. This attack showed why such a practice is stupid. The Rendova Patrol was changing shifts, and now instead of the 32 fighters it usually had overhead it had some 48 – Corsairs from Marine Fighting 213 and 221 and Wildcats from Fighting 21. Their radios crackled with the voice of Rendova Fighter Control on the *Jenkins*, "Go get em, boys."[60] In the words of Marine Fighting 221's war diary, "Twenty seven [sic] Bettys in a Vee of Vees began to get hell."[61]

Not quite fast enough. The malicious Mitsubishis roared over the water at altitudes as low as 50 feet, as they had done against the *Prince of Wales* and *Repulse* of Force Z in those first days of the Pacific War. And they pressed home their attacks in the face of brutal antiaircraft fire, to the admiration of many of their opponents. Admiral Turner, again, was an old hand at this, and he swung his ships hard to starboard, to present their narrow stern profiles to the Bettys.

Not narrow enough, it would seem. General Harmon was watching the proceedings from the *McCawley*:

I was standing on the port wing of the bridge and at about this time [3:55–4:00pm] observed torpedo release against the AP [transport] just astern of *McCawley* in our column. It looked like a perfect attack and I was anxiously awaiting the subsequent detonation when someone said "Here it comes." I glanced out to port, saw the approaching track and soon realized that it was going to be a hit – I thought just aft of the bridge. Glancing back at the next ship in line, I saw she had apparently not been hit, ducked away from the rail, crouched down with a yeoman-like grip on a stanchion and awaited the explosion. It came after a longer interval than I had anticipated; the ship gave quite a lurch, something big went over the port side from high above (maybe the top of the funnel) together with some odd bits and pieces and we listed quickly and sharply to port. Instinctively I moved starboard direction and heard the command "Trim Ship." On reaching the starboard rail a torpedo track was running about forty feet out at a slight converging angle to our bow and across our bow. It cleared us handily and missed the ship ahead though it looked bad for a moment or two.[62]

The Japanese managed to hit one ship, but, of course, it was the flagship of the invasion the old transport unaffectionately known as "Wacky Mac" and Admiral Turner's flagship since those early Guadalcanal days. The *McCawley* had been hit in the engine room, killing 15, and leaving her dead in the water. And like those early Guadalcanal days, the Japanese managed one torpedo hit – well, two, but the torpedo that hit the *Farenholt* just left an unsightly dent and did not explode – at a cost so brutal it bordered on the absurd.[63] Of the 17 G4Ms of the 702 Air Group, only three, including Lieutenant Commander Nakamura's returned to Vunakanau; a fourth was forced to ditch, its crew recovered. Of the nine G4Ms of the 705, only five returned, one of those crashing on landing.[64] That's 19 out of 26 bombers, and 17 out of 26 crews, gone. The losses among the escorting Zeros were not nearly as bad, but they were bad enough. Eight shot down, their pilots killed, including the formerly rising ace Lieutenant Mukai as well as yet another of the rapidly dwindling number of officers, Lieutenant (jg) Ohno Takeyoshi.[65] They managed to shoot down four Wildcats.[66]

That was not quite the end of the air attacks. At around 5:30pm came one last attack that seems to have been slapped together. The centerpiece was ten Aichi D3As of the composite 582 Air Group, escorted by 24 Zeros from the 582 and 204 Air Groups, all led by Lieutenant (jg) Suzuki Usaburo. They were joined by 13 F1M Type 0 float biplanes from the 938 Air Group because … why not?[67] The Japanese were always willing to add seaplanes to any operation, no matter how pointless and stupid it was. It was just the principle of the thing.

And it indeed was pointless and stupid sending them against 16 Curtiss P-40 Warhawks of the Army Air Force's 44th Fighter Squadron (though some were flown by pilots from the 70th). The Vals carried out their attacks but made no hits and took no loss. The Zeros seem to have shied away from fighter opposition, leaving the Petes to the tender mercies of the Warhawks. After seven of the float biplanes were shot down, the F1Ms called it a day and headed back.[68]

Once again, it had been a brutal day for Base Air Force. At a cost of eight fighter pilots, 17 bomber crews, and seven floatplane crews, they had managed one detonating torpedo hit on one transport, and taken out 14 AirSols fighters, including seven Wildcats, and seven pilots.[69]

That one exploding torpedo was a doozy, however, hitting the invasion flagship *McCawley* and the only transport with radar as it did, though, fortunately, not until after the transport had completed unloading its troops and supplies. Within minutes of the hit, destroyers *Ralph Talbot* and *McCalla* moved in to assist. Admiral Turner had ordered the cargo ship *Libra* to tow the *McCawley* while he and his staff borrowed the *Ralph Talbot* to help quickly shift his flag to the *Farenholt*. Admiral Wilkinson, scheduled to take over the South Pacific Amphibious Force from Turner when Turner moved to the Central Pacific, was left to head salvage efforts.[70]

But the salvage efforts were losing. The *McCawley* kept sinking lower and lower into the water. The tow was eventually transferred to the tug *Pawnee*, but she lost the tow at about 8:00pm. About 20 minutes later, the *McCawley* was hit by two torpedoes. At the same time, two more torpedoes were spotted heading toward the *McCalla*, though she managed to comb them. The *McCawley* could not, obviously, and quickly sank by the stern.[71]

Admiral Wilkinson promptly commenced a search for the culprit, assumed to be a submarine. In fact, the culprit was a PT boat. You never knew what they were going to do next, and, likely, neither did they. Lieutenant Commander Kelly's charges had swarmed the prospective targets and unloaded on them with torpedoes. It seems to have been either *PT-153* or *PT-118* who finished off the *McCawley*. Three other motor torpedo boats managed to miss with their torpedoes. That's the problem with friendly fire – it never ends well. You either hit it and hurt or kill a friendly unit, or you reveal to the world that your aim stinks.[72]

That was the end of the first day on New Georgia, albeit not the end of the first day elsewhere in the *Cartwheel* universe. General MacArthur was still carrying out his part of the plan in occupying Woodlark and Kiriwina Islands, an operation that he called "*Chronicle*." The planning for *Chronicle* had been going on since May at the headquarters of "Alamo Force," the operational name of the US 6th Army under Lieutenant General Walter Krueger, which was a lot of time to plan an unopposed amphibious landing on islands that are not occupied by the enemy. But *Chronicle* would be the first major amphibious operation in MacArthur's area, so the pressure was on.[73]

Scouting and engineering parties from Alamo Force had been poking around Woodlark and Kiriwina since May. Just after midnight on June 23, the destroyer-transports *Brooks* and *Humphreys* had landed on Woodlark members of the 112th Cavalry Regiment, which were among the forces Admiral Halsey had lent to General MacArthur for this operation. They were to perform advance work for the invasion, more involved than pathfinders, what with no enemy opposition and all. No enemy opposition, but almost some friendly opposition. No one had bothered to warn the Australian coastwatcher on Woodlark about the 112th's arrival. He and his scouts had formed a defense line and only stood down when they heard the invaders speaking American English. The *Brooks* and *Humphreys* dropped off a similar advance team from the 158th Infantry Regiment on Kiriwina the following night.[74]

All in preparation for the landings that were to take place on June 30, in conjunction with *Toenails*. And they did, mostly. Some 2,600 troops from the 112th Cavalry Regiment, the 134th Field Artillery Battalion, and the 12th Marine Defense Battalion, all borrowed from Admiral Halsey's command, started landing on Woodlark at 9:00pm on June 30. The follow-up echelons landed the following day, and construction of defenses and an air base began. The landings on Woodlark went relatively smoothly, at least in contrast to Kiriwina. The landing craft with the 158th Infantry Regiment, the 148th Field Artillery Battalion of 105mm howitzers, and additional 155mm guns, engineers, and assorted units, struggled with both the weather and the coral reefs that surround Kiriwina. Their landing went slowly, but was completed nonetheless, and they began to build defenses and their air base. Two islands so strategically important that the Japanese neither defended them nor even monitored them. *Chronicle*, and thus General MacArthur's part in *Toenails*, was complete on *Toenails'* first day.[75]

A grim first day for the Japanese, a grimy first day for the Americans. Admiral Kusaka was left scrambling to replace his losses. He ordered the 21st Air Flotilla at Saipan to send down the 1st Squadron of a dozen G4Ms from the 751 Air Group under Lieutenant Motozu Masao.[76] Ordered down from the Aleutians area were two squadrons with a total of 21 G4Ms from the 752 Air Group under Lieutenant Nonaka Goro. Kusaka asked for more reinforcements from Combined Fleet, assuming that the bombers he was borrowing from the *Ryuho* were not going to be enough. And he talked his friend General Inamura to commit the Japanese Army Air Force's 6th Air Division.[77] Kusaka hoped all this duct tape would be enough to hold Base Air Force together.

But it was still just duct tape, not the structural help Base Air Force – the Imperial Japanese Naval Air Force – needed. The next day, Kusaka sent up from Buin all of six D3As from the 582 Air Group, with an escort of 34 Zeros – 12 from the 582 Air Group, 12 from the 204, who were still under Chief Petty Officer Watanabe, and ten from the 251. The Aichis' targets were barges landing the 3rd Battalion, 103rd Infantry Regiment, on the west coast of Rendova at Poko. Arriving between 10:15 and 11:00am, the Japanese found waiting for them 20 Warhawks and Wildcats of the 44th Fighter Squadron and Fighting 27 and 28. The result was a small but intense brawl resulting in three Vals, five Zeros, and five Warhawks shot down before the fight broke up at 11:40am or so.[78]

For General Sasaki, the ineffectiveness of Base Air Force's air attacks was not helping a situation that was already discouraging. Ordered to sit and defend the airfield, Sasaki had ordered all of the outlying units, army and navy, to converge on the Munda air base for its defense. But watching the continued consolidation of the Allied positions on Rendova, he realized all the units he had on the island would not be enough to defend the airfield against so many troops. Not if the enemy used his troops properly, at any rate. On July 1, he ordered 3rd Battalion, 229th Infantry Regiment, into defensive positions at Munda, watching the coast specifically. "Maintain alerted conditions throughout the night and guard against enemy landings," Sasaki instructed. "If the enemy commences to land, destroy him at the water's edge."[79]

Yet Base Air Force's attack that General Sasaki had witnessed on July 1, ineffective as it was, wasn't even an appetizer. By contrast, July 2 was an all-you-can-eat buffet. Admiral

Kusaka and General Inamura had managed to get their respective air services together without forming a mass banzai charge. Not yet, anyway. But the day was young. An Army major, Endo Masao, would open the attack with 18 Mitsubishi Ki-21 Type 97 – the Allies would call it the "Sally" – bombers from the 14th Air Regiment escorted by 23 fighters – Nakajima Ki-43s and newly arrived Kawasaki Ki-61 Army Type 3s – the Allies would call the latter the "Tony" – operating out of Rapopo. The Imperial Naval Air Force apparently chipped in with 20 newly arrived fighters from the 253 Air Group and the carrier *Ryuho*.[80]

In contrast, AirSols had ordered – three times, uncoded – the Rendova Patrol to withdraw due to worsening weather. The portable SCR-602 radar went down for an oil change, while a longer-range SCR 270-D was limited in its effectiveness because it was sitting disassembled in a crate on the beach with the notation "some assembly required." As a final complication for the Allies, Major Endo was savvy enough to loop around a hill to approach the Rendova landing area from the east and use a cloud bank for maximum cover until the last moment. As a result, Endo's bombers not only had no aerial opposition, they also gave almost no warning of their approach until they were right over the invasion beaches at 1:30pm.[81]

The result was most unpleasant for the US Marines and Army troops in the landing area. Around 1:30pm, Major Endo's Ki-21s dropped 50 bombs in the midst of the landing craft in Rendova Harbor, that area partially enclosed by the islands of Bau, Korkorana, and Rendova. The attack killed 59 and wounded 77. Casualties were especially heavy in the 2nd Battalion of the 172nd Infantry Regiment, the 24th Construction Battalion, the 9th Defense Battalion, and staff officers of the various headquarters. Many of the supplies still on the beach were destroyed, including much of the personal baggage, ammunition for the Marine 155mm guns, medical supplies, and three bulldozers. Admiral Mitscher was embarrassed by the surprise attack and promised to never let it happen again. The Japanese lost three of the new Ki-61s from the 68th Air Group not to antiaircraft fire but to "a navigational error."[82] Army pilots flying over water and all that. Not an auspicious debut for the Ki-61.

But the Japanese were not done for this July 2. In the afternoon, a dozen Zeros from the 204 Air Group and another dozen from the 582 returned to try a fighter sweep. The Japanese fighters were apparently trying to copy Major Endo's tactic of approaching the Rendova area from the east. Except east of Rendova they ran into seven Corsairs from Marine Fighting 121. It did not go well for the Marines. Three of the F4Us were shot down, with one pilot, Lieutenant C.A. Barker, killed. However, this little firefight convinced the Zeros to head back to base without adding to the damage on the ground.[83]

But the Japanese were still not done for this July 2. The first of Admiral Kusaka's aerial reinforcements from the carrier *Ryuho*, 11 fighters and 13 dive bombers, arrived; they would all be in place by July 5.[84] And with that, Base Air Force finally called it a day.

AirSols had not, however. After an initial botched rendezvous attempt, four Corsairs from Marine Fighting 213 escorted four B-25s from the 42nd Bombardment Group to the area north of Munda along Kula Gulf shore. Their goal was to attack a reported

Japanese transport that was hidden and camouflaged along the jungle shoreline. The Mitchells could not find the ship, but the Marine fighters could and did. A few strafing runs was all it took to reveal the "perfectly camouflaged" ship, which the Corsairs then circled a bit to help mark it for the Army Air Force aviators, though the smoke and fire caused by the Marines' strafing and the ship's own antiaircraft fire certainly helped in that effort. After a few bombing runs by the Mitchells and a few more strafing runs, the Marine pilots could see "great fires and explosions coming from the ship." After one more strafing run by the Corsairs, the fire went out and the ship seemed to disappear. Indeed, one of the bomb hits had blown out the hull below the waterline and the ship, actually the auxiliary minelayer and cargo ship *Kashi Maru* (or *Kasi Maru*), who had been offloading fuel and vehicles at Bairoko, had sunk.[85]

The Japanese still hoped to repeat the success of Admiral Mikawa in his attack off Savo Island in the first days of *Watchtower*. Admiral Samejima ordered Rear Admiral Akiyama Teruo, commanding the 3rd Destroyer Flotilla, to attack the Rendova invasion area, similar to Admiral Mikawa's Savo Island operation the previous August, without actually following the successful elements of that operation: without the ships, for the most part, and without Admiral Mikawa himself.

Oh, well, details. For reasons known only to Admiral Koga and the naval general staff, the American attack on Attu was seen as an existential threat to the Japanese homeland. As a consequence, Admiral Samejima's 8th Fleet had been starved of ships and reduced to basically just the 3rd Destroyer Flotilla. New antiaircraft destroyer *Niizuki*, sister to Admiral Tanaka's sunken *Teruzuki*, had just arrived at Rabaul to serve as the squadron's flagship, replacing the light cruiser *Yubari* in that role. She was assisted by a rather elderly contingent of other warships: 20-year-old *Yubari*, herself a veteran of Admiral Mikawa's Savo Island victory; Destroyer Division 11's *Amagiri* and *Hatsuyuki*, themselves over a dozen years old, which by Pacific War standards was apparently elderly; five still older destroyers of the ancient *Mutsuki* class (*Nagatsuki*, *Minazuki*, and *Satsuki* of Destroyer Division 22, and the *Mikazuki* and *Mochizuki* of Destroyer Division 30); and the practically prehistoric *Yunagi*, another veteran of Mikawa's Savo Island victory.[86]

Toenails had caught the Japanese destroyers in the midst of supply and reinforcement runs, with the 3rd Destroyer Flotilla strewn from Rabaul to Buin.[87] One such mission had the destroyers *Nagatsuki*, *Minazuki*, and *Mikazuki* running to Kolombangara the night of June 29–30, but the mission was aborted, reportedly because of air attack, and the destroyers returned to Buin.[88] The *Amagiri* and *Hatsuyuki* had just completed a run to Buka.[89] At Rabaul were the *Niizuki*, *Yubari*, *Satsuki*, *Mochizuki*, and *Yunagi*.

Despite the disassembly of his fleet, Admiral Samejima still hoped to get in a quick counterattack. On June 30, he had Admiral Akiyama order destroyers *Amagiri* and *Hatsuyuki* to move up from Buka and rendezvous with the *Nagatsuki*, *Mikazuki*, and *Minazuki*, then at Buin. They would then sail to Rendova and wreak havoc. Except it was the weather that wrought havoc, on the Japanese as it had on the Americans, and the simple rendezvous itself was a struggle. According to the *Amagiri*'s skipper Lieutenant

Commander Hanami, the force moved out "in full strength with determination to blast the enemy on the sea but efforts to locate him finally ended fruitlessly."[90] They returned to Shortland.

There, Admiral Samejima was concentrating Admiral Akiyama's ships. The *Niizuki* and her friends had moved up from Rabaul to the Shortlands so the entire 3rd Destroyer Flotilla (except for the *Minazuki*, who had returned to Rabaul, and two destroyers being refitted back in Japan) could strike.[91] This time, the plan called for the *Yubari* and destroyers *Yunagi* and *Mikazuki* to act as a diversion.[92] The Japanese loved to include diversions in their plans, never noticing that they usually did better when they operated straight up. Anyway, while the *Yubari* was making a mess south of the Treasury Islands, Akiyama would take six destroyers and go to Rendova to shoot up the invasion ships in the harbor.[93]

The same bad weather that prevented the Americans from providing air cover to the Rendova anchorage gave cover to the Japanese. Nevertheless, a Navy Liberator spotted Admiral Akiyama's little force, which may have persuaded Akiyama that the diversion was indeed a stupid idea, because the *Yubari* and her friends stayed with the main force, which now was the *Yubari* and destroyers *Niizuki, Mikazuki, Yunagi, Mochizuki, Nagatsuki, Hatsuyuki, Satsuki,* and *Amagiri*. Two strikes by AirSols – one by Liberators, the other by Mitchells – did not find the Japanese ships; a third strike by Dauntlesses and Avengers was grounded by the bad weather.

So Admiral Akiyama got to Rendova and started shelling … something. The Japanese don't know what their munitions hit and neither do the Americans.[94] It is believed they landed in the jungle somewhere. If a shell explodes in the forest and no one is there to hear it, does it make a sound?

The admiral was not alone in his ineffectiveness. A Black Cat from Navy Patrol Squadron 54 had found Admiral Akiyama's ships and proceeded to hang onto them like a leech, dropping the occasional bomb without scoring a hit. The Black Cat radioed some friends in the form of PT boats, who were always ready, willing, and able to shoot first and ask questions later.

Lieutenant Commander Kelly had taken *PTs -156, -157,* and *-161* to patrol off Baniata Point, the westernmost tip of Rendova, and wait for possible intruders. Via his base, he received the Black Cat's report of enemy ships at around midnight. About an hour later, he saw gunflashes to the northwest. Those were the enemy ships.

Or were they? Lieutenant Commander Kelly was still smarting from his boats torpedoing Admiral Turner's flagship, so to say he was sensitive to the issue of target identification is a bit of an understatement. The weather did his boats no favors, as the night was so dark that the PTs passed completely through the Japanese formation without identifying any of the ships as enemy or friendly. This gave Admiral Akiyama's destroyers the upper hand, and they exploited it in an action that lasted only about ten minutes. Lieutenant Commander Kelly's PTs struggled against the main battery fire to even launch their torpedoes, which resulted in no hits. The engaged boats successfully escaped, as did the Japanese destroyers, but two US Navy PTs who were not engaged, *PTs -153* and *-158*, ran aground and had to be abandoned.[95]

It had not been a good day for the Americans, but the next day, July 3, was not good for the Japanese. The Americans had continued landing troops on Rendova, and had brought in the 155mm howitzers of the 192nd Field Artillery Battalion and the 155mm guns of Battery A, 9th Marine Defense Battalion. The big guns unlimbered on Rendova and surrounding islets and began bombarding the Munda airfield across the Blanche Strait. The Japanese may have still held the airfield, but the shelling rendered it useless.

Far worse for the Japanese was what they noticed some six miles east of Munda on New Georgia proper: American troops. Specifically, the 1st Battalion of the 172nd Infantry Regiment, 43rd Infantry Division was at Zanana Beach.

Admiral Halsey and his staff had set several conditions which needed to be met before the troops at Rendova could begin the move to New Georgia proper:

1. The Rendova base had to be sufficiently established to support the New Georgia Occupation Force; it was, manned by at least one full battalion, plus artillery.
2. The Japanese could not hold any of the preselected New Georgia beachhead sites in any strength; Army scouts examining the shores of Roviana Lagoon reported that Laiana beach, two miles from the Munda airstrip, was heavily defended, but Zanana, more than three miles further east, was not.
3. Segi, Viru, and Vangunu had to be secured in order to block any Japanese counterstrokes from those areas; they were.
4. Local air and naval tactical superiority had to be assured; it was, even before the invasion.
5. Ground superiority at the beachhead on New Georgia had to be in favor of the 43rd Infantry Division by least two to one during the initial landing phase; the four or five infantry battalions that would be sent to New Georgia would immediately outnumber available Japanese ground units by more than two to one.[96]

With the conditions met, on July 2 Admiral Halsey had ordered Admiral Turner to begin moving against Munda itself. It was a little early in the New Georgia plan, but it wasn't like the Japanese had put up much of a fight so far.[97]

Remembering General Vandegrift's advice to land where there wasn't enemy resistance, during the night of July 2–3, local guides led members of the 1st Battalion in landing craft through the Onaiavisi Passage and the maze of rocks and islets in the Roviana Lagoon to Zanana Beach. Again, no Japanese resistance developed, and the 1st Battalion was able to set up an 800-yard-wide defense perimeter secured with barbed wire, machine guns, 37mm antitank guns, and antiaircraft guns. The artillery on Rendova had an enfilading field of fire for any Japanese defense. Brigadier General Leonard F. Wing, assistant commander of the 43rd, set up a command post. Over the next three days, the remainder of the 172nd came in, along with the 169th Infantry Regiment.[98] General Hester was reportedly "well satisfied" with the setup at Zanana.[99] They were set to advance. Only six miles of dense jungle and a few rivers and creeks stood between them and Munda. How hard could it be?

Despite the lack of Japanese resistance, General Sasaki had noticed the landing and dutifully reported it to his superiors. Admiral Kusaka responded with a fighter sweep of 48 Zeros – the 204, 251, and 582 Air Groups each supplied 16 – which was pretty much all Base Air Force had left. AirSols sent up 16 Lightnings of the 339th Fighter Squadron, which in two flights of eight lunged into the mass of Zeros northwest of Rendova. This short engagement was another tale full of sound and fury signifying nothing, as the Japanese did not reach Rendova and neither side shot down anyone. Three Lightnings, those of Lieutenants Richard Baker, Robert Sylvester, and Howard Silvers, failed to return, but it is believed they got lost in a fast-developing storm and crashed when they ran out of fuel.[100] A tragic reminder that the Japanese were not the Allies' only enemy in the Solomons.

And perhaps not the most dangerous enemy, for the time being at least. The ineffectiveness of the Japanese response to the New Georgia landings had not been lost on General Sasaki. From his headquarters on Kokengola Hill, Sasaki could only watch in frustration as the shells from the 155s hit the Munda runway, rendering takeoffs and landings impossibly dangerous and dangerously impossible. He had proposed a counterlanding on Rendova, and, in fact, Allied planners were concerned about the possibility of a Japanese counterlanding operation and had arranged their defenses in preparation for it. But Admiral Kusaka and General Inamura believed a counterlanding was not possible because the air and naval forces necessary were not available. Sasaki's frustration boiled to the point where, at a strategy meeting around midnight on July 3, he suggested having Colonel Tomonari's 13th Infantry Regiment use Admiral Ota's barges to mix in with the American barges shuttling troops from Rendova to New Georgia. In Sasaki's view, even if half the force were lost, the attack would be worth it because … well, he was a little vague on that. It would not be worth it to Ota because those barges were needed to bring in the reinforcements from Vila where they were scheduled to land on July 4 and 5. A "visibly upset" Sasaki adjourned the meeting and left the room. Ota went after him and brought him back, agreeing to help Sasaki work on plans for the counterlanding. Rabaul quashed the plans, as Ota likely knew they would. Sasaki could only sit on Kokengola Hill and fume as the American buildup east of Munda commenced.[101]

While General Sasaki was compelled to inaction by his orders, Major Endo was not. On July 4, Endo led a second combined Japanese Army and Naval Air Force strike, this one of 17 Ki-21 bombers, 17 Ki-43 and Ki-61 fighters, and 49 Zeros. His target was the area around Roviana Island, but this mission had issues from the start. Endo had to mark time near Kolombangara because AirSols was bombing the Munda airfield with 18 Avengers and 20 Dauntlesses; evidently, the 155mm shells were just not good enough. Because of warning by coastwatchers and Endo's delay, 32 Navy Wildcats from Fighting 21 and 28 were able to take a quick swipe at the Sallys. Once the Munda strike had left, Endo resumed his trek toward Roviana, only to find nothing of interest there. Maybe 20 of Endo's fighters moved to engage the Wildcats while his Ki-21s looped around to head for Rendova from the east. Despite their superiority in numbers, the Japanese fighters could not keep the Wildcats off the Sallys. When Endo's bombers got over the harbor at 2:10pm, things got even worse, with the heavy antiaircraft guns of the 9th Defense Battalion now fully set up and at least 20 landing craft firing their guns as well. The Ki-21s slightly damaged two landing craft, killed five and wounded 14, at a price of six bombers shot down, with two more damaged. Additionally, three Ki-43s and one 251 Air Group Zero were lost with their pilots.[102]

General Inamura decided he had taken enough losses in New Georgia and pulled the 6th Air Division out of the campaign. He needed it to defend Salamaua, and Base Air Force was starting to receive reinforcements, such as the aircraft from the *Ryuho* and the 1st Air Attack Force, necessary to keep the pressure on without help from the 6th. For his part, Kusaka was now turning his aerial attention to the American positions east of Munda. He quickly had yet another area grab those aerial attentions.

With General Hester "well satisfied" with the Zanana Beach situation, Admiral Halsey ordered Admiral Turner to go ahead with the final landing of *Toenails*: Rice Anchorage. The idea behind the Rice Anchorage landing was simple: cut off the Munda air base from reinforcement or retreat. The Japanese supply line landed on New Georgia through the area of Bairoko Harbor and Enogai Inlet, which was heavily defended. Rice was about five miles to the north on the Wharton River. Again, following General Vandegrift's advice.

Landing 2,600 men, to be precise, under US Marine Colonel Harry B. Liversedge. Three battalions: the 3rd Battalion of the 145th Regiment; the 3rd Battalion of the 148th Regiment, all from the 37th Infantry Division; and the 1st Marine Raider Battalion. The 4th Marine Raider Battalion was originally slated to take part, but it was tied up at Segi Point and Wickham Anchorage, so the 3rd Battalion of the 145th was substituted. As the presence of the Raiders suggests, this was to be a very lightly armed landing; in order to facilitate movement through the jungle and swamps of New Georgia, the heaviest weapons taken along were machine guns and mortars.

And since they were lightly armed, the Marines and soldiers could be transported by those fast converted destroyer transports. The transport unit for the Rice landing was a hodgepodge of destroyers (*McCalla*, *Ralph Talbot*, and *Woodworth*), destroyer transports (*Dent*, *Talbot*, *McKean*, *Waters*, *Kilty*, *Crosby*, and *Schley*), and destroyer minesweepers (*Hopkins* and *Trever*), with close escort by the destroyers *Radford* and *Gwin*. Providing surface protection and gunfire support was Admiral Ainsworth's "Support Group A," with the light cruisers *Honolulu*, *Helena*, and *St Louis*; and destroyers *O'Bannon*, *Chevalier*, *Nicholas*, and *Strong*.

The Rice operation was getting off to somewhat of a rocky start. Minesweeper *Zane* was supposed to transport troops here, but the damage from her (repeated) grounding forced her to the sidelines, to be replaced as transport by the destroyer *Woodworth*, reducing the close screen by one destroyer. The transport unit also had a *Talbot* and a *Ralph Talbot*, two different ships, two different ship types, two very similar names. Always a bad sign.

The opening of *Toenails* featured a *McCawley* and a *McCalla*, and you see what happened there. It was just asking for trouble.

But this was something Admiral Ainsworth and his ships had done before. His orders were to bombard Bairoko to suppress the Japanese artillery there, and to bombard Vila because it was there. Ainsworth wanted to bombard Enogai as well, but Ainsworth and his staff "were talked out of this by [Admiral Turner]," who said that their photos and reconnaissance showed no guns at Enogai, though Ainsworth recalled receiving fire from Enogai previously. Besides, that ammunition might be needed for other purposes. From *Magic* decrypts, Pearl Harbor had determined that the Japanese planned a reinforcement run to Vila. That information was forwarded to Turner, who forwarded it to Ainsworth with the note, "This may give you a real target."[103]

Admiral Ainsworth's flotilla led the transport force up The Slot. As they did so, the *Ralph Talbot*, carrying 210 soldiers from I Company and the headquarters of the 3rd Battalion, 148th Infantry, treated the Army passengers like honored guests:

> The battle weary veterans were given the best treatment the *RT* was capable of providing. The men had been living off C and K-rations for months. As the *Ralph Talbot* raced up the slot the cooks loaded the mess hall tables with chicken, ham, beef and all the trimmings the food locker could provide. The invasion troops were showered with luxury unknown to them in the infested swamps on Guadalcanal.[104]

For the transit, Admiral Ainsworth's cruisers were in a column led by Ainsworth's flagship *Honolulu*, followed by the *Helena* and *St Louis*, in that order. The destroyers were positioned in a circular antisubmarine screen around the cruisers.[105] Behind them, the transport unit under Commander Leith was divided into two columns. The starboard column was led by the *Hopkins*, Leith's command ship, followed by the *Trever*, *Woodworth*, *Ralph Talbot*, *Schley*, and *McCalla*. The port column was supposed to be led by the *Dent*, though she seems to have had trouble keeping station, followed by the *Talbot*, *Waters*, *McKean*, *Kilty*, and *Crosby*.[106]

General quarters was issued on Admiral Ainsworth's ships at 10:00pm. A little less than 90 minutes later, they reached Visuvisu Point, the northwestern tip of New Georgia marking the entrance to Kula Gulf, and turned to port to 215 degrees True – roughly southwest – to hug the coast of New Georgia. Commander Leith's transport group turned inside Ainsworth's cruisers, even closer to the coast. Five minutes after midnight on July 5, Ainsworth turned to starboard to 255 degrees True – roughly west southwest – and went further into the Kula Gulf.[107] This move to first hug the New Georgia coast then dart toward Kolombangara was necessary to avoid the minefield of cabbage patch balls off Kolombangara that the US Navy had laid back in May. Ainsworth had no way of knowing that the Japanese had already swept up all the mines.

Things started getting real at 12:19am, when the cruiser force turned to course 190 degrees True – just west of south – and shifted from its antisubmarine formation to its column battle formation. The destroyer *Nicholas* led, followed by the *Strong*. Ainsworth had instructed these two destroyers not to take part in the shelling of Vila, unless targets of opportunity presented themselves, but to instead watch for enemy ships and submarines. Behind the *Strong* was Ainsworth's flagship *Honolulu*, followed by the *Helena* and *St Louis*, in that order. Behind the light cruisers was the veteran destroyer *O'Bannon* and, bringing up the rear, the destroyer *Chevalier*.[108]

The *Nicholas* and *Strong* did their searching and detected nothing on their SG radars, except for one bogey that was determined to be a Black Cat, flying close to Vila to aid Admiral Ainsworth's ships in spotting. No enemy ships, aircraft, or submarines, as far as they could tell. The Americans had come in undetected.

At 12:26am, four minutes ahead of schedule, the *Honolulu* unloaded her 6-inch guns on the Vila air base. Each of the three light cruisers proceeded to lob about 1,000 6-inch high-capacity shells, using, for some reason, a newly developed flashless powder. The *O'Bannon* and *Chevalier* added in a lot of 5-inch high-explosive shells, also with flashless powder, all aimed at the beach areas. The *Strong* joined in for ten salvos when she thought shore batteries were firing back at the US Navy ships; in reality, it was just the cruiser shells exploding.[109] The "high sustained bombardment fire on this leg was extremely accurate," Ainsworth wrote. For what that was worth. Dirt airfields and all that.

While that was going on, the destroyer *Ralph Talbot*, not to be confused with the *Talbot*, was using her search radar, which the *Talbot* did not have, to shepherd the transport ships into their landing position. She gave them bearings for Rice Point and Wharton Point, which bracketed the anchorage and basically marked the coast area in which the transports were to unload. In their two columns, the "fast" transports rounded Visuvisu Point and plodded into the Kula Gulf at 12:30am.[110]

Strangely at 12:31am, the *Ralph Talbot's* radar detected two contacts about five miles away bearing 290 degrees True – west northwest – heading course 315 degrees True – north northwest – out of Kula Gulf at a brisk 25 knots. Someone was leaving Kula Gulf in a big hurry. Why would they do that? The contacts disappeared from the screen four minutes later. The *Ralph Talbot* let the other ships know via voice radio.[111]

The *Nicholas* had already led Admiral Ainsworth's cruiser column on a port turn to course 90 degrees – dead east – for the New Georgia coast. They had completed their shelling of Vila and at 12:32am starting shelling Bairoko to starboard. All seven lobbed shells in succession at Bairoko, again using flashless powder.[112]

On this night, the US Navy ships were big believers that it was far better to give than to receive. At 12:39am, the lead destroyer *Nicholas*, having given her assigned contribution of high-explosive shells to Bairoko, turned to course 000 degrees True – due north – and moved to exit the Kula Gulf.[113]

Admiral Ainsworth radioed Captain Francis X. McInerney, commanding Destroyer Squadron 21 on the *Nicholas*, "Any trouble ahead?" Quickly, McInerney responded, "Everything clear ahead."[114]

About 1,500 yards behind her on the *Strong*, gunnery officer Lieutenant (jg) James A. "Al" Curran had just finished watching his guns give the destroyer's entire assigned contribution of high-explosive shells to Bairoko.

At 12:40am, the *Strong* swung to port to course 000 degrees True to follow the *Nicholas* out of the Kula Gulf. As the destroyer's bow slowly swung to the left, Lieutenant Curran swiveled his head to the left as well … and "saw a thin phosphorescent wake about 3,000 yards in length" rapidly approaching the *Strong*.[115]

Curran quickly switched to the skipper's circuit on the sound-powered telephone and shouted, "Left …" No one heard the rest of his order.[116]

On the *Nicholas*, Captain McInerney noticed the radar showed the *Strong* no longer in formation. It must have been a mechanical breakdown, probably steering, everyone assumed.[117] McInerney quickly radioed his wayward destroyer, "Are you all right? Come in please." Silence.[118]

The commodore notified Admiral Ainsworth, who was asking the *Ralph Talbot* about that fleeting radar contact, but the admiral had already noticed on radar that his column was missing a ship. McInerney then ordered the *Chevalier*, at the back of the column, to try her hand at raising the *Strong*. No luck.

The column continued moving north. As the US Navy ships headed out, one lookout on the flagship *Honolulu* thought he glimpsed the missing destroyer in the dark, "sharp on starboard bow, damaged and smoking, dead in the water and on opposite heading."[119] He was the only one who saw it. The new flashless powder Ainsworth's ships were using generated a lot more smoke than the smokeless powder they normally used. The US Navy did not think the smoke would be a big issue because of radar. With the cruisers bathed in their own smoke, no one else saw the disappearing destroyer.[120]

The *Chevalier* and veteran *O'Bannon*, at the rear of the column, were ordered to locate the *Strong*. It did not take them long. They found her dead in the water about two miles west of Rice Anchorage. The *Chevalier* pulled alongside the stricken *Strong* and quickly signaled Admiral Ainsworth, "*Strong* needs aid." "Care to be more specific?" the admiral responded. The *Chevalier* answered: "*Strong* is sinking."[121]

Admiral Ainsworth was perplexed. What happened? He radioed the *Chevalier*, "As soon as you can, find out and let me know how she got hurt." A moment later he emphasized it, "Was it torpedo or gunfire? Must know whether it was gunfire or torpedo." The *Chevalier* answered, "Hit by torpedo."[122] That was bad. His ships were in grave danger.

Before he could consider the question of from where the torpedo could have possibly come, Ainsworth had to get his ships out of danger. He sped his cruisers out of the gulf as fast as he could, before turning around and making a radar sweep toward Kolombangara.[123] What could have launched that torpedo? And where was it?

The explosion that had drowned out Lieutenant Curran's order had been "terrific," knocking skipper Commander Joseph H. "Gus" Wellings, standing on the navigation bridge, to his knees.[124] Destroyers don't normally get along well with even a single enemy torpedo, but this one was unusually devastating, burying itself so deep into the *Strong's* port side Number 1 boiler room that it punched completely through the ship. So, though the *Strong* had been hit on the port side, the destroyer quickly heeled over 15 degrees to starboard, a heel that turned into a quickly increasing list.[125] That was a bad sign.

But not the worst, not even close. The boiler room and an engine room were flooded, knocking out power and killing nearly everyone in those two compartments. "The cries and moans of my men, for a split second or two before their almost instant death, haunted me for years," Commander Wellings later admitted.[126]

The port side of the deck house superstructure collapsed onto the torpedo mount and main deck. There was a giant hole in the port side and main deck, as though the Lernaean Hydra had risen up and taken a good-sized chomp at the ship. The starboard side had ruptured plating of its own. The deck plates buckled, revealing a sag in the ship that evinced a broken keel. The *Strong* was doomed. On the good side, though, emergency power quickly kicked in and her internal communications were in good order.[127]

As the destroyer slowly heeled over to a 30-degree list to starboard, there was no panic among her crew. Damage control teams went to work as best they could on the tilted decks. The engineers methodically shut down the remaining boiler and engine room to set the ship up for towing, in theory. Commander Wellings ordered preparations to abandon ship, but kept everyone on board, believing a friendly ship would come to rescue them in short order. Admiral Ainsworth had promised to aid any of his destroyers should they get into trouble.[128]

And aid did come, though perhaps in not quite the way Commander Wellings had intended. "I was horrified but still most thankful at [1:13am], to see the destroyer *Chevalier* appear out of the darkness steaming at about ten knots and crash into our port side at an angle of about thirty degrees."[129] Assigned to take off the *Strong*'s crew, the rescue destroyer was perhaps a bit too cavalier in her approach. "I thought the *Strong* would roll over from the crash. Fortunately, the ship did not roll over but the list to starboard increased to about fifty degrees. The *Chevalier* stopped with her bow just forward of our bridge."[130]

But perhaps the approach had not been so cavalier. The destroyer *O'Bannon*, also assigned to aid in the evacuation, could not pull up to the starboard side of the *Strong* as planned because the *Strong*'s starboard deck railing was already awash. So, the *O'Bannon* just loitered around for a while. Until someone on the *Chevalier* noticed the *O'Bannon* rapidly overtaking the *Chevalier* from astern. The *Chevalier*'s executive officer, Lieutenant Commander George R. Wilson, ordered emergency full speed to get out of the *O'Bannon*'s way. The *O'Bannon* grazed the *Chevalier*, knocking out the latter's starboard depth charge rack and smoke screen generator. The cost of reducing the *O'Bannon* collision to a grazing blow was a more serious collision with the *Strong*.[131]

Admiral Ainsworth had told the *Chevalier* and the *O'Bannon*, "Take your time. Get everybody and rejoin outside." The *Chevalier*'s skipper, Commander Ephraim Rankin McLean, Jr, had determined that they didn't have any time to take. The *Strong*'s situation was so desperate that to get the crew off he had to bring his ship's bow alongside the *Strong* with some force, but perhaps not this much force. Commander Wellings sent his executive officer Lieutenant Commander Frederick W. Purdy to the port bow area to assist with the evacuation. As Purdy started down the ladder to the main deck, Wellings admonished, "Fred, be sure to get aboard *Chevalier* before she casts off from alongside." Purdy smiled and responded, "Don't worry about me, Captain."[132]

Nevertheless, the collision had a side effect that was fortunate. With the *Chevalier's* bow tied to the *Strong's* bow and the *Chevalier's* engines holding the ships fast together, as McLean had intended, many of the *Strong's* crew were able to just walk over onto the *Chevalier's* bow embedded just aft of the *Strong's* Number 2 5-inch mount. The *Chevalier* also tossed cargo nets and mooring lines over the side so crewmen who could not just cross over on the bow could use them to climb aboard. It sped up evacuation considerably.[133]

This was important because the *Strong's* rapidly increasing submergence was soon joined by a second problem. Admiral Turner was not on hand to explain why if, as he had insisted, there were no Japanese artillery in Enogai, the *Strong* now found herself in the midst of shell splashes. Splashes that looked suspiciously like what would be produced by a 140mm gun, the kind the Japanese 6th Kure Special Naval Landing Force did not have at Enogai, according to Turner. They were soon joined by smaller Japanese batteries around Bairoko Harbor that had remained quiet during the American bombardment. The Japanese couldn't just let the *Strong* sink; they had to hasten it along. There was no quarter in this Pacific War. A Japanese floatplane showed up to drop flares and illuminate the destroyers for the Imperial Army and Navy gunners.

Rescue operations continued while the first Japanese salvos straddled the *Strong*, but things got more serious when a dud shell hit the *Strong*. Commander Wellings was slightly injured when shell fragments struck his right wrist and lower right leg. Though Captain McInerney would later describe the shelling as "[s]pasmodic and ineffective," it was enough for the *O'Bannon* to move off and fire her own 5-inch guns at the Japanese harassers. The *Chevalier* also fired her own aft 5-inchers at Enogai. The Japanese floatplane made an even bigger nuisance of itself by dropping a stick of four or five bombs some 75–100 yards off the *Chevalier's* port quarter, shaking the destroyer violently and splitting open hull seams near the stern.[134]

The continuing attacks convinced Commander McLean the area was getting too hot. The *Strong* was now listing 30–40 degrees and, in the colorful words of Morison, "settling like a punctured beer can." From the starboard wing of the *Chevalier's* bridge, McLean shouted through a megaphone to Commander Wellings, "Gus, I think everyone who was topside is either aboard, or in the water alongside. I better cast off and get out of here in a minute or two, before I am hit and crippled with all of your men on board." Wellings sadly agreed. The *Chevalier* had rescued seven officers and 234 men from the *Strong* in seven minutes.[135]

Commander Wellings went back to make sure no one was left aboard the *Strong*. At 1:22am, maybe two minutes after Commander McLean suspended the rescue efforts, the *Chevalier* backed away from the *Strong* with a 2-by-10-foot gash in her bow maybe 6 to 8 feet above the waterline from the collision. Wellings and his Chief Quartermaster Maurice A. Rodrigos, who refused to leave the captain, only had to step off the bridge into the water. Within a minute, the *Strong's* stern, sticking in the air, broke off and completed its roll. Both parts of the *Strong* slid beneath the waves.[136]

But those immutable laws of the Solomon Islands, "No good deed goes unpunished" and 'Always add injury to injury," manifested themselves once again. Though they had been set on "safe" so they would not explode, several of the *Strong's* depth charges exploded in the water. When abandoning ship, the crew would always check to make sure the depth charges were set on "safe," then when the ship finally sank, the depth charges would explode anyway. It happened so often during the Pacific War that it's fair to ask what the point was in setting them to "safe," or if it would have been safer not to do so. As it was, depth charges exploding in the water are intended to sink submarines, so imagine what they do to people in the water, like Commander Wellings and Chief Rodrigos, who suffered severe internal injuries as a result.[137]

As if that was not enough, the depth charges exploded under the *Chevalier's* bow. "The ship appeared to be lifted out of the water and then settled down with a shudder," Commander McLean reported. The shock knocked out the *Chevalier's* radars, sound gear, and radios. Even worse, the shock detonated a 5-inch shell jammed in Mount 3, demolishing it and starting a fire, which was put out within five minutes.[138]

The transports had stopped in the landing area and commenced landing operations at 1:25am.[139] Under fire from Bairoko and Enogai, illuminated by flares, leaking both fore and aft, the *Chevalier* decided to call it a day and head back to Purvis Bay, but as she did so she crept among the transports and came across their screening destroyers *Gwin* and *Radford*, who themselves spent some 1,100 rounds of 5-inch ammunition dueling the Japanese batteries at Enogai that Admiral Turner insisted weren't there. The *Chevalier* signaled, "*Strong* went down. You know where we were. I suffered injuries myself. Have picked up large number of survivors. Some still in water. Please pick them up."[140]

The *Chevalier* sped off as fast as her now-flooded bow would allow, joined by the *Jenkins* on her way to Purvis Bay, and Commander McLean sped off for the Navy Cross that his actions on this night had earned. The *Gwin* and *Radford* did indeed look for survivors; it was the *Gwin* who rescued Commander Wellings, Chief Rodrigos, and three others. The *Ralph Talbot* also picked up a boat full of survivors that included Lieutenant Donald A. Regan, the officer of the deck when the torpedo hit, whose activities in evacuating the *Strong* included rescuing a badly injured engineer from a dark, flooded engine room. Not included in the survivors picked up was wounded machine gun officer Lieutenant Hugh B. Miller, who ended up on Arundel Island as a one-man guerrilla group for the next month-and-a-half before he was rescued. Lieutenant Commander Purdy did not make it to the *Chevalier* before she pulled away, having returned to the main deck to help an injured sailor. Purdy was later seen in a float net with other survivors. A Japanese boat later entered the area and began shooting survivors; Purdy is believed to have been one of the people killed. His body washed up on Kolombangara.[141]

The landing itself was proceeding, first the "fast" destroyer transports, then the actual destroyers, and finally the destroyer-minesweepers, albeit not smoothly. Flight Officer

Corrigan and a team of native Melanesians had activated a light to act as a landing beacon at 2:00am – right on schedule, but 15 minutes after the landing boats had left for the beach, which left the boats fumbling in the dark. There was a reef between the transports and the landing beach, and some of the landing boats were so loaded that they could not clear the reef and were grounded. So boats had to come in with lighter loads, which increased the number of trips necessary between the transports and the beach. The beach itself was too small, able to accommodate only four boats at once, which was a problem when there were 28 boats shuttling between the transports and the beach.[142]

Because Admiral Turner was concerned about a Japanese air attack on his transports, he had ordered them to be clear of the Kula Gulf by 7:00am. With the landing of all but 72 troops and two percent of the supplies completed, Colonel Liversedge gave orders to halt the landing operation and for the transports to leave, so the entire transport force hauled anchor and left. Very hurriedly, which caused a few issues. A dozen landing boats with 200 to 300 men of the 3rd Battalion, 148th Regiment were left in the water unsure of where to go. The Japanese batteries at Enogai started targeting the boats, so they had to get out of the water fast. Captain Charles A. Henne took charge and landed the men at Kobukobu Inlet, north of Rice Anchorage by about 3,000 yards – 3,000 yards of dense jungle. A separate, but just as serious issue was among the two percent of supplies left aboard the fleeing transports – a US Navy TCS radio that Liversedge had specifically requested because of its long range.[143]

So, the landing at Rice Anchorage, and with it *Toenails*, was complete. They had been attacked by an unknown force. They had landed troops in the wrong place. They had landed troops on a beach that was too small and blocked by a sand bar. They had completely missed a battery of Japanese heavy artillery at Enogai. And they had not landed a long-range radio that the commander considered mission-critical. Information and communications, those two most precious commodities in any military operation, were already lacking.

Admiral Ainsworth was aware of that lack of information as he raced back to Purvis Bay. He was very much bothered by the torpedoing of the destroyer *Strong*, as any commander would be. Ainsworth could not make sense of it. The *Strong* had been hit by a torpedo on the port side, the side facing away from New Georgia and toward Kolombangara. It had to come from waters off of Vila. Except immediately before the *Strong* was hit, his ships had passed through those same waters and had detected nothing – no submarines, no surface ships.

Well, that last part wasn't quite true. The radar on the destroyer *Ralph Talbot* got a fleeting glimpse of ... something ... heading away from Kula Gulf, far to the northwest. Admiral Ainsworth thought that contact was a surfaced submarine, a submarine that submerged, approached undetected, and launched the torpedo that sank the *Strong*. Captain McInerney disagreed. Referring to the two radar contacts, the commodore wrote, "It is believed that these contacts were two destroyers which left the gulf at a high speed. Either or both of these ships could have fired torpedoes from long range."[144] But the only surface contact their radar had picked up was ... whatever it was the *Ralph Talbot* had detected. The torpedo couldn't have come from those ships, not from that location, anyway. They were some 12,000 yards away. A torpedo couldn't travel that far, Ainsworth figured. Could it?

Too many questions. Too many unknowns. They were very disquieting, especially when Admiral Ainsworth and his force had yet to face Japanese warships in this campaign.

Or had they?

For all of the power, grandeur, and innovation of ancient Rome, it certainly had its dark side. One was a sense of greed far beyond what is often experienced today. And few if anyone in Rome could match the outright avarice of one Marcus Licinius Crassus.

With commendable initiative if not ethics, Crassus became the richest man and largest landowner in Rome through means that included falsely listing people whose property he wanted as "enemies of the state" so their property would be forfeit to the state and he could buy it cheaply. He also had his own private fire department that would show up at a fire (that Crassus' people had often set) and not put out the fire until the property owner had sold him the property. The original "fire sale." But Crassus never attained political power commensurate with his wealth. He did become a member of the First Triumvirate with Gaius Julius Caesar and Gnaeus Pompeius Magnus (Pompey the Great).[145] It made sense. Caesar was the politician, Pompey was the general, and Crassus the financier.

Crassus was never popular, mainly because his military abilities, always important in Rome, were mediocre at best. So, he decided to do something about it. With commendable initiative if not competence, he led a massive Roman army of heavy infantry on an invasion of Parthia, which had an army known for its heavy cavalry and horse archers. After marching through the desert, Crassus and his army encountered the enemy near the town of Carrhae (now Harran, Turkey).

Where Crassus quickly discovered that slow heavy infantry are perhaps not the best way to deal with fast horse archers. Worse, the Roman cavalry could not deal with the horse archers, either because the horse archers had a very annoying habit of swiveling their torsos around, facing behind the horses that were still running away, and shooting arrows at their pursuers. With deadly accuracy. That is how being shot by a fleeing enemy, usually at long range, became known as "Parthian shot." Those Parthian horse archers surrounded Crassus' heavy infantry and buried them in a shower of arrows. Crassus ended up dead – killed, some say, when the Parthians poured molten gold down his throat. And the term "Parthian shot" entered the Western lexicon.

The Japanese had been doing a lot of running away of late, and not just the Special Naval Landing Force troops which would flee into the jungle so they could preserve their reputation of never surrendering. Imperial General Headquarters, and especially the naval general staff, did not want to run any more. They were drawing the line at New Georgia. Even the Imperial Army agreed with the Navy that the island group had to be held "at all osts," and were even chipping in 4,000 troops to make that happen.[146] The trick was getting them to New Georgia.

The Japanese used to have a veteran admiral who could run troops and supplies in and out under difficult conditions, who did it again and again and again. Sometimes even, against the odds, delivering a bloody nose to the hated Americans in the process. Like at Tassafaronga, when his fleeing destroyers sent their Parthian shots of Long Lances into four US Navy cruisers, sinking one and causing severe damage to the other three. But Tanaka Raizo didn't live there anymore.

But Akiyama Teruo did. Akiyama was a new flag officer, having been promoted just the previous November. He was not exactly a grizzled veteran; Akiyama had held mostly staff and shore positions since the beginning of the war, so he had almost no combat experience. Naturally, Combined Fleet chose to put Akiyama in charge of the 3rd Destroyer Flotilla, in the hottest naval combat area in the Pacific, as well as the Transportation Unit formerly headed by the outspoken, cynical, and unpopular but very successful Admiral Tanaka.

Admiral Akiyama's first combat had actually been on the night of July 2–3, that bombardment that landed somewhere in the rain forest with no one there to hear it, followed by that ten-minute affair against US Navy PT boats. Akiyama was not present for what the Japanese were calling the "4th July Night Battle of Kula Gulf."[147]

The title was accurate. That day, Admiral Akiyama had ordered Captain Kanaoka Kunizo, Commander of Destroyer Division 22, to make a reinforcement run to Vila.[148] For this run, Kanaoka had his own command destroyer *Nagatsuki* and his other destroyer *Satsuki*, but was also given old *Yunagi* and the *Niizuki*. Though the *Niizuki* had been sent down specifically to be Akiyama's flagship, Akiyama would not go on this operation. He would stay behind and . . . plan future operations.

Another one of those big antiaircraft destroyers of the *Akizuki* class, the *Niizuki* was brand new. More importantly, the *Niizuki* was state-of-the-art – for the Japanese at any rate. Like all *Akizuki*s, the main battery of the *Niizuki* was based on the Type 98 3.9-inch gun. Though smaller than the typical 5-inch guns, it was a true dual-purpose gun, and could thus be used for both antisurface and especially antiaircraft combat. The gun was reliable with a high rate of fire, good penetrating power, and actually better range than the American 5-inchers. The *Akizuki*s had eight Type-98s in four dual high-angle mounts, two forward and two aft, with the middle two superfiring.[149] Naturally, the *Akizuki*s each had torpedo tubes, albeit only four, to launch the deadly Type 93 torpedoes. Finally, the *Niizuki* was among the first Japanese ships built with a full radar suite. Specifically, a Type 21 general purpose radar that was designed primarily as an air search system but proved (sort of) useful in surface search as well.[150] Combined Fleet wanted to see how the new *Akizuki*s functioned as flotilla leaders. Captain Kanaoka would get to try the *Niizuki* on this mission.[151] A bit like driving the boss's car – don't scratch it . . .

At 4:40pm, Captain Kanaoka's destroyers left the Shortlands carrying 1,300 troops and 15 bargeloads of supplies to take to Vila.[152] He arranged his destroyers in a column, with apparently the *Niizuki* in the lead because of her radar, probably followed by the division command ship *Nagatsuki*, her divisionmate *Satsuki*, and last the *Yunagi*.[153] His only support would be the Japanese submarine *I-38*, whom Admiral Kusaka had sen ahead to harass the Americans who, in turn, were harassing the Japanese supply runs.[15] If everything went all right, Kanaoka's ships would land the troops and supplies in Vila that night.

The sea that night was calm under an overcast sky with scattered squalls. The plan wa for the column to make for Choiseul Island, then hug its southern coast until they reached a position almost directly north of Kolombangara. They would then dash across The Slot enter Kula Gulf, and hug the coast of Kolombangara all the way to Vila-Stanmore. Afte unloading their troops and cargo, the destroyers would quickly return before dawn to the Shortlands.[155]

But as Captain Kanaoka led his destroyers around Tuki Point on Kolombangara aroun 12:15am, the new-fangled Japanese radar on the *Niizuki* detected something. A bunch o enemy ships, some of which appeared to be even bigger than the *Niizuki*. Cruisers, maybe Four cruisers and four destroyers, they were guessing.[156] Very efficient performance for the Japanese newcomers to radar, far better than their American counterparts at an equivalen time, the Battle of Savo Island, though that's not saying much. For that matter, it was fa better than their veteran American counterparts on this night.

The efficient performance of the Japanese radar quickly indicated that this superio enemy force was moving away from them. The efficient performance of the Japanes lookouts quickly indicated gun flashes and explosions in the general area of their destinatio – Vila-Stanmore. These efficient performances convinced the commodore his fou destroyers were in over their heads, figuratively speaking, but soon to be literally speaking if they did not get out. He ordered the mission aborted and his ships to reverse course.[157]

The *Niizuki* led the column of destroyers in a column turn to head back to the Shortlands. As she did so, however, she launched four Type 93 torpedoes at 12:28am. And as she followed, the *Nagatsuki* fired six Type 93s. And as she followed, the *Satsuki* fired zer Type 93s, for reasons that remain a mystery; and as she turned the *Yunagi* fired four of the older 21-inch torpedoes.[158] It was basically a shot in the dark – there had been no chanc to develop a proper firing solution. That ancient Japanese credo: *When in doubt, launc torpedoes.*

It was Captain Kanaoka's retreating ships that the radar on the *Ralph Talbot* ha detected. It was a torpedo from Kanaoka's retreating ships that had shattered the *Stron* not a submarine. At a range of 11 miles, believed to be the longest successful torped attack in this war, and perhaps any war. A true Parthian shot. Who exactly fired the fata fish remains unclear, though the extreme range and devastating damage suggest the culpri was one of the ten Type 93s from the *Nagatsuki* and *Niizuki*.

So, unbeknownst to Admiral Ainsworth, he had indeed been in a surface engagemen that July 4 night. And lost. The only problem from the Japanese standpoint was that whe the danger reared its ugly head, Captain Kanaoka turned his tail and fled, meaning nothing had been landed on Vila. They would have to make a double run on July 5.

And July 5 was getting off to a bad start. As light cruiser *Yubari* was arriving at Buin, she struck a mine, generally believed to have been one of the Mark 12 aerial mines dropped back in May, but given that Admiral Merrill had just laid that minefield between Shortland and Faisi, there is a chance she struck one of those. The *Yubari*'s forward food store and freshwater tank were flooded and her speed was limited to 22 knots, with 26 of her men wounded.[159] No high-speed runs for her; if anyone had planned to use her on the double run, now they couldn't.

Things got better, relatively speaking. With word of the landing in Rice Anchorage, Base Air Force sent a strike of seven D3As escorted by 48 Zeros to attack enemy shipping off the landing beach. Except, thanks to Admiral Turner's orders, the shipping had all left. So, the pitifully few Aichis left, too, and went back. So did some of the Zeros. But maybe 16 of them remained to tangle with about a dozen Warhawks of the 44th Fighter Squadron. The Warhawks lost one of their own, the pilot recovered, but claimed two Zeros; Base Air Force admitted losing roughly zero Zeros, but claimed 13 enemy fighters destroyed and three more probables.[160]

Which left the double run for the Japanese on this July 5. A bigger run meant bigger brass, so Admiral Akiyama would personally lead this reinforcement from his flagship *Niizuki*, taking it back from Captain Kanaoka. In typical Japanese fashion, Akiyama divided his swollen force three ways, with a covering force and two transport units carrying a total of 2,400 troops and 180 tons of supplies. The First Transport Unit would have the destroyers *Mochizuki*, *Mikazuki*, and *Hamakaze* of Destroyer Division 30 under Captain Orita Tsuneo, while the Second Transport Unit would have the destroyers *Amagiri*, *Hatsuyuki*, *Nagatsuki*, and *Satsuki* of Destroyer Division 11 under Captain Yamashiro Katsumori.[161] All were older destroyers and would be burdened with troops and supplies. Perhaps that's why Akiyama divided them into two groups even though they were all going to the same place, Vila. Or maybe he did it just because he could.

Burdened with troops and supplies as they would be, the Transport Units needed a combat-ready force to cover them and watch for trouble. This was the Support Force, featuring the destroyers *Suzukaze* and *Tanikaze* and Admiral Akiyama's own flagship *Niizuki*, the only state-of-the-art destroyer in the bunch.

It was Admiral Akiyama's Support Force that led the Japanese transport units out of the Shortlands at 5:00pm and down The Slot.[162] Akiyama may not have been experienced, but he was intelligent, and he did not see the utility in having the transports lead the combat ships as other Japanese admirals did. The trip down to Kula Gulf was uneventful, though the destroyer *Mochizuki* lagged behind the others due to a damaged port propeller, caused by either a reef or an entangled barge tow cable.[163] Because of inclement weather, Akiyama did not have to deal with curious Catalinas or bothersome bombers. So he had that going for him, which was nice.

Hugging the Kolombangara coast, at 12:26am on July 6 Admiral Akiyama sent Captain Orita's First Transport Unit off to Vila. The remainder of his destroyer force continued southward at 21 knots to sweep the base of the Kula Gulf while the first group of destroyers were unloading.[164]

It was during this time that at 1:06am Admiral Akiyama's flagship *Niizuki* detected … something.[165] Sources are divided on the nature of this contact. Some call it a radar contact that petered out; others hold that what the destroyer picked up were radar waves, meaning the *Niizuki*'s radar suite included a radar detection unit of some sort.[166] It concerned the admiral enough to, at 1:18am, order the Support Force and the following Second Transport Unit to turn back by column turn to investigate the contact.[167] Concerned or not, however, Admiral Akiyama was unable to determine what if anything it was; the ephemeral nature of this contact suggests it was probably radar waves. And, as Admiral Kusaka had hammered home, his first priority was getting the troops to Vila.[168] So at 1:42am he radioed the Second Transport Unit, "Proceed to Vila."[169] The transport destroyers split off while his Support Force continued heading north to keep a blocking position.

It took only five minutes for the admiral to regret giving that order. At 1:47, the lookouts on the *Niizuki* spotted shadows approaching out of the dark eight miles away.[170] His three destroyers were about to be outnumbered by these shadows, some of which looked big. Bigger than destroyers. Admiral Akiyama radioed Captain Yamashiro to have the Second Transport Unit turn around again and return to him. Despite the fact that the Second Transport Unit's destroyers had Imperial Army troops and supplies including ammunition unprotected on their decks. The destroyers' guns and, especially, torpedoes were necessary to help even the odds. Akiyama ordered battle stations and increased speed to 30 knots, throwing the helm over 40 degrees to port.[171]

Everyone in the force knew what the admiral had in mind. The *Niizuki* led the *Suzukaze* and *Tanikaze* to course 320 degrees True – west by northwest, paralleling the interlopers' course but staying ahead of them.[172] The torpedo tubes swung outward. The targets came into the firing arcs, the firing solutions were calculated. It took maybe ten minutes, but finally all was ready. Admiral Akiyama just needed to give the order …

The maelstrom of molten metal that came at about this time rudely brought any thought of offensive action to a screeching halt. Like a speeding train hitting a stalled car. A galling gale of gunfire. Seemingly all directed at the *Niizuki*. Seemingly all hitting the *Niizuki* at the same time.

The effect of multiple body blows all at once was numbing. The lifespans of Admiral Akiyama, skipper Commander Kaneda Kiyoshi, and everyone on the bridge were now measured in minutes – at most. The *Niizuki* was hit very early and very, very often. So hard and so fast – Japanese survivors marveled at the Americans' "6-inch machine guns" – that it's not clear precisely when and where each hit took place and what damage each hit caused, with a few exceptions.[173] At some point, Akiyama had gotten his order out: launch torpedoes.[174] The torpedoes had left their tubes, which were already trained in and in the midst of a reload. Nevertheless, in all likelihood it was the last order Akiyama would give. By some accounts, Akiyama was killed by the very first American salvo, which "almost entirely leveled and demolished" the *Niizuki's* bridge, leaving it "look[ing] almost like a giant's foot ha[d] stepped on it."[175]

It was clearly a very big salvo, because it smashed a lot more than the bridge of the big destroyer. Also known to be hit was the *Niizuki's* steering gear, which seems to have been demolished. Other hits included her engine and boiler rooms, causing the destroyer to lose power. Maybe one of her twin 3.9-inch dual-purpose mounts was hit as well. Behind her the *Suzukaze* and *Tanikaze* watched in horror as the *Niizuki* reeled under the pummeling, slowing to a crawl, and drunkenly staggering out of line to port, a blazing jumble of metal barely recognizable as the state-of-the-art warship she had been only five minutes earlier, now "non-operational."[176]

There was no time for the *Suzukaze* and *Tanikaze* to indulge their horror, let alone stop and aid their stricken flagship. Even if they had time, they couldn't help her, nothing could help her now. The *Suzukaze* led the *Tanikaze* on a wide turn to port to avoid the *Niizuki*, stay out of the glare of her fires, and keep those fires from silhouetting them.

Their admiral was gone. But as they sped on past the dying flagship, the *Suzukaze's* skipper Lieutenant Commander Yamashita Masao and the *Tanikaze's* Commander Maeda Shinichirou knew the drill. They had received their admiral's last order. They knew what their admiral had been planning. They resolved to carry out that plan themselves.

And they had found a target: one of the attacking cruisers stood out with the prominent flash of her guns. She made a nice target.

All in line, they knew, with that ancient Japanese credo: *When in doubt, launch torpedoes.*

While Admiral Akiyama was confirming his reservation for Yasukuni Shrine, Admiral Ainsworth was watching the search radar scope for the results of his cruisers pouring some 1,500 6-inch shells into the three targets showing on the radar. The targets appeared to be dead in the water, and Ainsworth declared this group "practically obliterated," feeling very satisfied with how this engagement was opening.[177]

As had been done in so many battles before, such as Java Sea, Guadalcanal, and Tassafaronga, Admiral Ainsworth's force had been slapped together on the fly. Just 24 hours earlier, his cruisers and destroyers had been leaving Kula Gulf, pondering the loss of the *Strong*, and looking forward to some down time when the men could rest. These night bombardments were very hard on crews. As *Helena* Seaman 1st Class Edwin Rick described it, "You don't get a whole lot of sleep and the next day you have to stand watches."[178]

The crews needed rest and the ships needed maintenance. The *Helena*, for example, was having issues with her main battery. The shell hoist for the left gun of Turret 5 had malfunctioned and Turret 2 was having recurring issues with powder cases jamming the gun barrels.[179] While the flotilla headed for a refueling rendezvous off Santa Ysabel, the *Helena's* very experienced and efficient crew took care of both problems.

It was late in the afternoon when the crews started making some rather uncomfortable observations. "I looked out the bunkroom door and saw the *Honolulu* turning one eight (180 degrees) and with signal hoisted for speed 29 knots," remembered *Helena* Lieutenant (j.g.) William McKeckney. "That seemed to indicate that we were going back on another business trip."[180] After the refueling was aborted, rumors started circulating to that effect.

Rumors that would prove to be true. It was 3:00pm on July 5 when Admiral Ainsworth informed his skippers of the message he had received from Admiral Halsey: "Cancel refueling. Proceed high speed to Kula Gulf to intercept a Tokyo Express run midnight. If no contact made by [2:00am], retire."[181] A coastwatcher had reported ten Japanese destroyers leaving the Shortlands headed down The Slot at a speed of 30 knots.[182] With so many destroyers, it was an obvious supply run. Halsey and his staff had calculated that the ships would arrive in Kula Gulf just after midnight.[183]

So much for a day of semi-rest. Admiral Ainsworth, still unaware he had been in a surface battle the night before and had actually turned away a Japanese reinforcement convoy, wearily turned his tired force around and entered The Slot between Florida and Santa Ysabel Islands. He set speed for 29 knots, which, due to engineering issues, was the fastest the *St Louis* could go.[184]

Admiral Ainsworth had a few other nagging issues besides the *St Louis'* engines. One was fuel. Due to the new orders, the planned refueling of his ships had been aborted. The cruisers had enough fuel to make the run and back, but two of his destroyers, *Nicholas* and *O'Bannon*, were running seriously low. Destroyers were and are notorious fuel hogs. Their high speed and relatively small fuel bunkers meant they were always thirsty. Ainsworth and his staff calculated that the *Nicholas* and *O'Bannon* had enough to make it to Kula Gulf and back, barely. So, unable to completely quench their thirst, their combat operations would be somewhat limited.

The situation was even worse for Ainsworth's other two destroyers. One, the *Strong*, was sunk, which would seem to preclude her inclusion in this latest effort. The other, *Chevalier*, was packed with survivors from the *Strong* and had a hole in her bow. They had to be replaced. Destroyers *Radford* and *Jenkins* were transferred from Admiral Turner's command to Ainsworth's task force.

At that time, the *Radford* was at Purvis Bay, in the Florida Islands southeast of Tulagi, refueling from the oiler *Erskine Phelps*, which she completed at 4:47pm.[185] When she received her new orders, skipper Commander William K. Romoser ordered her into Tulagi itself and anchored at 5:21pm.[186] Though the *Radford's* fuel bunkers were now filled to the brim, her counterbattery fire from the night before meant she was now critically low on ammunition for her 5-inch main battery. Romoser sent out an urgent request for 5-inch ammunition. The *Jenkins* had followed the *Radford* over from Purvis Bay and moored alongside, where she passed 300 rounds by hand in the amazingly short time of 22 minutes.[187] The *Jenkins* sped off to join Ainsworth.[188]

Commander Romoser then put in a request to the *Chevalier*, who had just docked. The damaged destroyer passed 200 rounds of 5-inch ammunition to the *Radford*.[189] Tulagi's port manager sent over a barge with even more rounds, but Romoser had to respond with a hearty "No, thank you." There was simply no time. Leaving at 6:37pm, the *Radford* was already late and would struggle even at full speed to catch up with Ainsworth's force. As it was, Admiral Turner felt compelled to radio Admiral Halsey that the *Radford* would not be able to join Ainsworth's squadron. The *Radford* picked up Turner's message, however, as she rounded the western end of Florida Island to head north to join the formation.[190] An indignant Rosomer had no intention of missing the battle, and poured on even more speed. Finally reaching the line of sight required for the Talk Between Ships voice radio, Rosomer cited Turner's message in requesting permission to join the force, which was granted by a pleasantly surprised Ainsworth.[191]

As the *Radford* joined the group at around 8:25pm, the American ships moved into a "night antiaircraft cruising" formation.[192] Not antisubmarine – antiaircraft. The costly lessons of the Rennell Island affair had a significant impact on US Navy thinking in the South Pacific, if perhaps not on the man most responsible for that affair. The cruisers were in what was known as "Column Open Order," in which ships would sail just off the flagship's wake in order to more easily keep their position in the column.[193] The flagship *Honolulu* led the *Helena* followed by the *St Louis* at 1,000-yard intervals. Destroyer *Nicholas* was some 3,000 yards ahead off the *Honolulu*'s starboard bow, the *O'Bannon* a similar distance off the port bow. Newly arrived *Radford* was some 2,500 yards off the *St Louis*' starboard quarter, the *Jenkins* a similar distance off the port quarter.[194] This transit formation would make it easy to switch to a column formation for night combat.

The addition of the *Radford* and *Jenkins* at the last minute conjured up images of another disaster, that of Tassafaronga the past December. Admiral Ainsworth had a different battle in mind: Vila-Stanmore, in which Admiral Merrill's force surprised the Japanese destroyers *Murasame* and *Minegumo*, swamping them with gunfire and the Japanese barely even getting a shot off. That was the thinking behind his battle plan, given the catchy title of "Night Battle Plan A."

Night Battle Plan A was based on US Navy doctrine, intelligence information, and the hard lessons of battles like Savo Island, Cape Esperance, Guadalcanal, and Tassafaronga. It had two major assumptions: that the Japanese might have search radar, but it would not be as accurate as American search radar. As a corollary, the American fire-control radar was a potentially decisive advantage that could and should be exploited. Second, pretty much all Japanese surface warships carried torpedoes, which, naval intelligence believed, had an effective range of 6,000 yards.[195] Obviously unfamiliar with the true capabilities of the Japanese Long Lance.

Admiral Ainsworth wanted another Vila-Stanmore, needed another Vila-Stanmore, where he could overwhelm the enemy quickly. His plan was to have the 6-inch-gunned cruisers surprise the enemy by opening fire under full radar control at a range of 8,000–

10,000 yards, "beyond the maximum range of (nighttime) visibility," he said.[196] Clearly, he didn't know the Japanese capabilities very well either, but it was even worse than that. Ainsworth needed to quickly overwhelm the enemy with gunfire because his supply of the flashless gunpowder – long a Japanese monopoly but now appearing in US stocks – was almost out. For reasons known only to Ainsworth, his cruisers had used almost their entire supply of it the night before in the shore bombardments against targets that did not have the range to respond to the cruisers' 6-inch guns. The *Honolulu* and *St Louis* had enough left for about three or four salvos; the *Helena* allegedly 50 per turret. After that, the cruisers' positions would be more easily pinpointed by their gun flashes.

The cruisers and their rapid-fire 6-inch guns were the centerpiece of Night Battle Plan A. Destroyers were free to use their guns and torpedoes only after the cruisers had finished their barrage, mostly to finish crippled ships. Maneuvers would be by simultaneous turn so the force could be kept concentrated and minimize the danger of friendly fire. Night Battle Plan A was a carefully considered plan relying on the best intelligence information available and seeking to maximize American advantages and minimize Japanese advantages. As such, it represented the apex in tactical planning of what the finest minds in American intelligence and tactical thinking could devise. And it was wrong.

By midnight, when Admiral Ainsworth ordered battle stations, his force was 28 miles from Visuvisu Point, marking the eastern end of the entrance to Kula Gulf.[197] The night was dark, as nights tend to be, only more so. No moon, overcast, intermittent showers. Visibility was about two miles, though sporadic storms reduced that visibility further.[198] Ainsworth ordered battle stations. He cut speed to 27 knots. The aborted refueling was making itself felt, as Ainsworth described fuel supplies as "running pretty low."[199] A half hour later he cut speed again, to 25 knots, and turned to starboard to 292 degrees True – west northwest – to sweep across the mouth of Kula Gulf.[200]

It was 1:36am when the search radar operators on the *Honolulu* saw something seem to break off from the mass of Kolombangara that dominated the screen. The operators reported it: "Enemy ships bearing 218 degrees True, range 26,500 yards."[201] With the radar room next to his flag plot, Admiral Ainsworth was able to check the contact himself. It was blurry, but definitely separate from the island by about 5,000 yards.[202] It was a column of three or four ships, heading northwest.

That the ships were heading northwest – heading out of Kula Gulf – was disappointing. Admiral Ainsworth and undoubtedly Admiral Halsey had been hoping to prevent the reinforcement. If the ships were leaving Kula Gulf, the reinforcement had likely already taken place. Too late to stop the reinforcement, Ainsworth wanted to at least make it painful.

Without even reporting the contact to his ships, he radioed his ships, "Form for attack. Prepare to attack in battle plan Able (Battle Plan A)."[203] Since Ainsworth had not reported the contacts to his ships, this was the first indication they had that enemy ships had been detected; skippers began checking their own radars to get an idea of what their admiral may have seen. The *Radford* detected the Japanese at 224 degrees True, range 24,700 yards.[204] The *O'Bannon* picked them up as they got within 18,000 yards.[205] The *Honolulu* was now tracking the ships with her fire control radar, showing them on a bearing of 208 degrees True, distance 19,700 yards. The Japanese group was zigzagging at 21 knots on a base course of 355 degrees True, northwest by north.[206] A little slow for combat, Ainsworth thought, so, as best as he could tell, they had yet not detected his ships.[207] He wanted to strike before they did. To do that, he needed to quickly get closer.

At 1:42am – one minute after ordering combat formation, according to the admiral – Ainsworth ordered, "Turn left 60 degrees to course 232 degrees True to close hostile ships."[208] All the ships would turn simultaneously and head toward the enemy in something resembling an echelon formation. Once they had gotten close enough, the US Navy ships would turn back into a column formation. Sounded simple enough. The three cruisers, already in column, each simply turned in place to the new course.

But the turn, coming only a minute after the admiral had ordered the column formation, put his destroyers in a difficult spot because they had not yet assumed their positions in the column. Once the simultaneous turn was completed, destroyer O'Bannon, who had been on the port bow of the formation, found herself directly ahead of the Honolulu. She was supposed to be ahead of the Honolulu, but behind the Nicholas, Commodore McInerney's command ship. And the Nicholas, who had been on the starboard bow, was nowhere to be seen. "We were not astern of the Nicholas as yet," reported the O'Bannon's skipper Lieutenant Commander Donald J. MacDonald, "and this turn sort of complicated matters somewhat due to inability to follow leader [sic] in the dark."[209] The O'Bannon had to run around looking for her squadron leader, who was gunning her engines to take her station as column leader. Meanwhile, the Jenkins, which had been on the port quarter, slowed to take her position, while the Radford, which had been off the starboard quarter, was, like the Nicholas, left gunning her engines trying to catch up to the column.[210]

While the destroyers were struggling to take their spots, the Helena's skipper Captain Charles Cecil announced over the radio, "I have a surface radar contact distance nine miles." "Who reported that?" Ainsworth asked. "Me," Cecil radioed back. Then the Helena's captain repeated the contact and added it was bearing 214 degrees True.[211] After another moment, Cecil reported that there appeared to be three or four enemy ships.[212] In those days, radar was in the eye of the beholder. "Normal fire distribution," Admiral Ainsworth ordered, meaning each cruiser was to engage its opposite number in the enemy battle line.[213] The cruisers' main and secondary batteries were loaded; their fire-control radars started tracking their targets and developing firing solutions.

And finding out that things were getting more complicated. At 1:44am, St Louis reported, "Radar contact – seven ships – bearing 202 degrees True, 17,000 yards."[214] A second group of ships had appeared, maybe 6,000 yards south of the first.[215] The group appeared to be three or four "heavier" ships.[216] Cruisers, maybe. Hugging the coast of Kolombangara. "At this time the radar screen indicated that there were two distinct groups of ships," Captain McInerney reported, "the first group consisting of about four or five 'pips,' which appeared to be smaller 'pips' than those of the second group of about three ships."[217] The distance between the second group and the first seemed to be increasing.[218]

Before dealing with that wrinkle, Admiral Ainsworth had to make sure his ships did not close the range too much. At 1:50am, he ordered, "Ships will turn simultaneously to 292 degrees True."[219] This simultaneous turn reformed the column, at least as far as the cruisers were concerned, and brought them broadsides to the enemy, enabling them to fire all 45 of their 6-inch guns. The turn helped the destroyers a bit, too, except for the *Radford*. The leading destroyers *Nicholas* and *O'Bannon* were now 4,000 yards slightly on the *Honolulu*'s starboard bow, roughly where they were supposed to be. The rear destroyers were still having difficulties getting into their assigned positions. The *Jenkins* continued pushing it to take her spot behind the *St Louis*, but the *Radford* was still way behind the *Jenkins* and not making much progress catching up.[220]

Seemingly oblivious to the problems facing his destroyers, Admiral Ainsworth now busied himself figuring how to deal with the two groups of enemy ships. Would it be possible to hit both at the same time? The cruisers and the two rear destroyers could take on the second group, which seemed to have cruisers of its own, while his destroyers in front could take on the first group, which seemed to have only destroyers.[221] With a little luck, he could knock out both before his cruisers ran out of flashless powder. The admiral radioed Captain McInerney at 1:54, "Take first target, 8,000 yards. Cruisers will take heavy ships."[222]

By now, the range to the first group had dwindled to 9,000 yards on a bearing of 225 degrees True – southwest. The Americans were about to cross the Japanese "T." Three minutes later, the range was 7,050 yards. Getting close to the range of Japanese torpedoes, or so the admiral thought. Neither he nor anyone else on the American side had any idea that they were well inside the range of Japanese torpedoes, that the simultaneous turn Ainsworth had ordered at 1:50am had probably saved his ships, because the *Niizuki*'s torpedoes were in the water, that the simultaneous turn had ruined the *Niizuki*'s firing solution. What Ainsworth and his men did know was, they were out of time.

So Admiral Ainsworth gave the long-awaited order: "Commence firing."[223]

Or not. Within seconds, Captain McInerney radioed back, "Gunfire or [torpedoes]?"[224] As the always-entertaining historian C.W. Kilpatrick opined on this directive, "An order to open fire should *never* require a question and an explanation."[225] No, it should not.

And, yet, here we are. "Gunfire first," the admiral answered. Then he added the kicker, "But hold everything."[226] Such decisive leadership can make all the difference in a tight battle. Everyone was so thoroughly confused that no one had opened fire on anyone.

None more confused than Captain McInerney. With very good reason. Admiral Ainsworth had just ordered everyone – cruisers and destroyers – to open fire at the same time. An order that contradicted his previous order to implement the aforementioned Battle Plan A, under which the cruisers were to open fire first, while the destroyers were supposed to hold their fire until the cruisers were done, at which time the destroyers would go to work with their guns and torpedoes. So which order was McInerney and his destroyers supposed to follow?

Admiral Ainsworth's newly hatched battle plan to take on two groups of ships at once had other, more severe issues as well. Dividing his combat power between the two groups

Admiral Yamamoto Isoroku (left, in white) addresses Japanese fighter pilots at Lakunai airbase, Rabaul, during *I-Go*, April 1942. Vice Admiral Kusaka Jinichi (center, facing the pilots), commander of Base Air Force, looks on. (ullstein bild/ullstein bild via Getty Images)

P-38 Lightning "Miss Virginia" piloted by Lieutenant Rex Barber. It was badly shot up after the Yamamoto mission but was in service for another month. Here it is shown after a belly-landing that subsequently forced it to be scrapped. (NARA)

Last salvo of US light cruiser *Helena* in Kula Gulf, just before she was torpedoed in the wee hours of July 6, 1943. The next ship astern is USS *St Louis*. Photographed from USS *Honolulu*. (Naval History and Heritage Command)

Right • Josef Lörks (Joseph Loerks), German national and "The Fighting Bishop" of the Roman Catholic Vicariate Apostolic of Central New Guinea, one of 62 Christian missionaries and lay people murdered aboard the Japanese destroyer *Akikaze* on March 17, 1943.
(Robert M. Myers Archive, Chicago Province of the Society of the Divine Word)

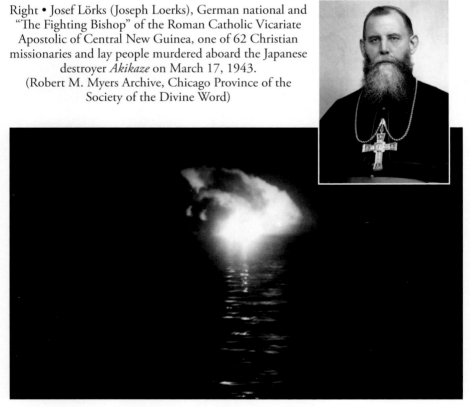

Japanese destroyer *Niizuki* burns in Kula Gulf the early hours of July 6, 1943. Photographed from USS *Nicholas*. (Naval History and Heritage Command)

A photograph of a Japanese *daihatsu* run aground on a New Georgia beach in July 1943. (Marine Corps History Division)

The wreck of Japanese destroyer *Nagatsuki*, grounded and wrecked off Bambari Harbor, Kolombangara, after the Battle of Kula Gulf on July 6, 1943. (Naval History and Heritage Command)

The light cruiser USS *St Louis* showing torpedo damage received during the Battle of Kolombangara on July 13, 1943. The photo was taken while the ship was under repair at Tulagi on July 20, 1943. The bow of the repair ship USS *Vestal*, which was alongside the USS *Arizona* during the Pearl Harbor attack, is visible at left center. (Naval History and Heritage Command)

A view of the USS *Honolulu*'s collapsed bow at Tulagi on July 20, 1943.
(Naval History and Heritage Command)

Japanese destroyer *Mikazuki* (sometimes rendered *Mikatsuki*) aground and under attack
by B-25s of the 3rd Bombardment Group, 5th Air Force off Cape Gloucester,
New Britain, on July 28, 1943. The *Mikazuki* has a fire forward of the bridge.
(Naval History and Heritage Command)

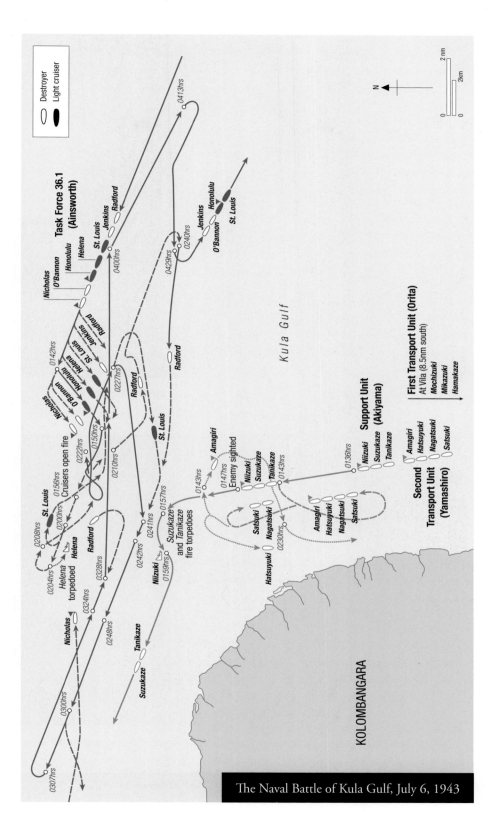

The Naval Battle of Kula Gulf, July 6, 1943

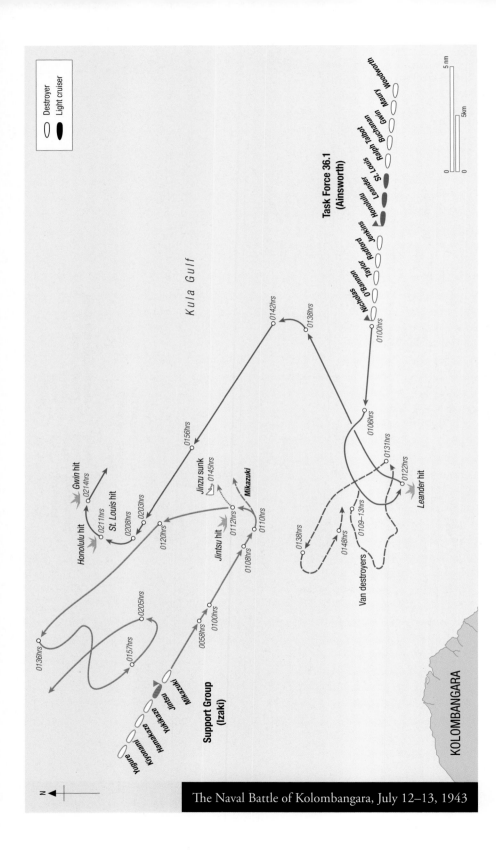

Destroyer

Light cruiser

Kula Gulf

Task Force 36.1
(Ainsworth)

Woodworth
Maury
Buchanan
Gwin
Ralph Talbot
St. Louis
Leander
Honolulu
Jenkins
Radford
O'Bannon
Taylor
Nicholas

0100hrs
0106hrs
0131hrs
0122hrs
Leander hit
0109–13hrs
0148hrs
0138hrs

Van destroyers

0138hrs
0142hrs

0156hrs

Jinzu sunk
0145hrs
Mikazuki
0112hrs
0110hrs
Jintsu hit
0120hrs
0203hrs
0208hrs
St. Louis hit
0211hrs
Honolulu hit
Gwin hit
0214hrs

0108hrs
0100hrs
0058hrs
0205hrs
0157hrs
0136hrs

Mikazuki
Jinzu
Yukikaze
Hamakaze
Kiyonami
Yugure

Support Group
(Izaki)

KOLOMBANGARA

N

5 nm
5km

The Naval Battle of Kolombangara, July 12–13, 1943

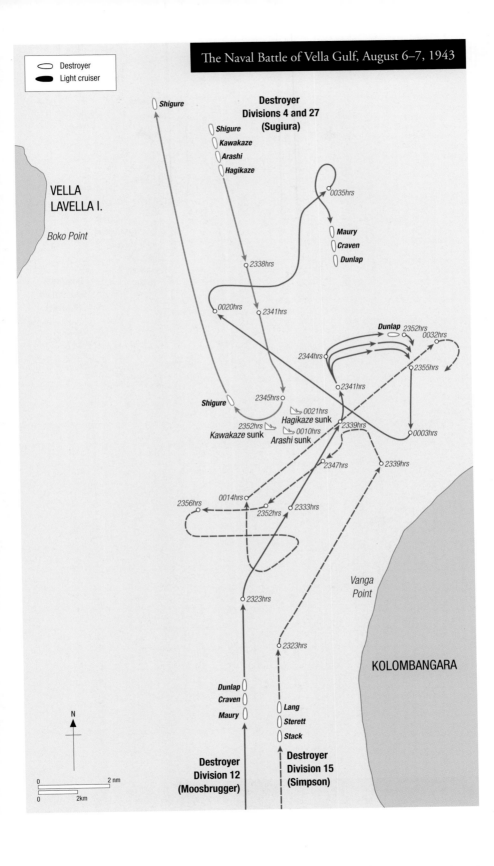

The Naval Battle of Vella Gulf, August 6–7, 1943

Destroyer
Light cruiser

VELLA
LAVELLA I.

Boko Point

Destroyer
Divisions 4 and 27
(Sugiura)

Shigure

Shigure
Kawakaze
Arashi
Hagikaze

0035hrs

Maury
Craven
Dunlap

2338hrs

0020hrs   2341hrs

Dunlap 2352hrs
0032hrs

2344hrs

2355hrs

2341hrs

0003hrs

Shigure   2345hrs

0021hrs
Hagikaze sunk

2352hrs
Kawakaze sunk   0010hrs
Arashi sunk

2339hrs

2347hrs   2339hrs

2356hrs   0014hrs

2352hrs   2333hrs

Vanga
Point

2323hrs

2323hrs

KOLOMBANGARA

N

Dunlap
Craven
Maury

Lang
Sterett
Stack

Destroyer
Division 12
(Moosbrugger)

Destroyer
Division 15
(Simpson)

0   2 nm
0   2km

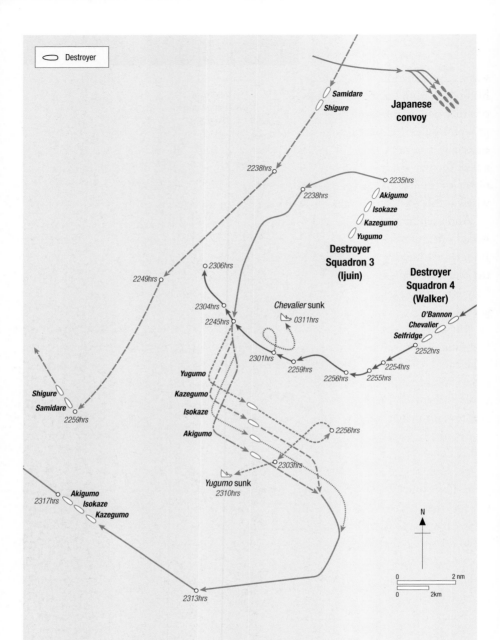

Destroyer

Samidare
Shigure

**Japanese
convoy**

2238hrs

2235hrs

2238hrs

Akigumo
Isokaze
Kazegumo
Yugumo

**Destroyer
Squadron 3
(Ijuin)**

**Destroyer
Squadron 4
(Walker)**

O'Bannon
Chevalier
Selfridge

2249hrs

2306hrs

2304hrs

Chevalier sunk

2245hrs

0311hrs

2301hrs

2259hrs

2256hrs   2255hrs

2252hrs

2254hrs

Shigure

Samidare

2259hrs

Yugumo

Kazegumo

Isokaze

Akigumo

2256hrs

2303hrs

Yugumo sunk
2310hrs

2317hrs   Akigumo

Isokaze

Kazegumo

2313hrs

N

0   2 nm

0   2km

The Naval Battle of Vella Lavella, October 6–7, 1943

was a clear violation of the combat principle of concentration of force. By concentrating his firepower on one of the enemy groups, he could give his ships the best shot at wiping out that one group. By dividing his firepower, he increased the risk that each of his own groups would not have the firepower to deal with its assigned enemy group. This was especially true of Captain McInerney's destroyers. Having the *Nicholas* and *O'Bannon* attack the first enemy group meant pitting two American destroyers against three or four of their Japanese counterparts. Which was, at best, not ideal. Ainsworth quickly – and wisely – thought better of it.

And even more quickly radioed a new plan, which was like Battle Plan A. The cruisers would open fire first, targeting the first group of ships, now only some 7,000 yards away. It increased the risk that the second group would just turn around and run southward to the Blackett Strait and relative safety, but that just couldn't be helped. Ainsworth explained, "My intention is to blast this group first, reach ahead, then make a simultaneous turn and get the others on the reverse course."[227]

The admiral checked in with each cruiser individually to make sure each was ready. He had time to be careful, Ainsworth figured, since the Japanese had not seen his ships. As far as he could tell, anyway. The *Honolulu* and *St Louis* had quickly switched targets to the first group, as ordered – the *St Louis* to the nearest ship – and reported they were ready.[228] The *Helena* asked, "Wait" and took maybe 30 seconds longer to acquire her new target, but she, too, ultimately answered as ready.[229]

So, finally – again – at 1:57am, Admiral Ainsworth gave the even-longer awaited, now coded signal, "Execute dog."[230]

No animals were harmed in the effecting of this command, but numerous Japanese were. Early and often. Opening fire under full radar control, Ainsworth's three cruisers opened that five-minute, 1,500-shell maelstrom of molten metal at the first Japanese group of ships – Admiral Akiyama's Support Group with the flagship *Niizuki* and the older *Suzukaze* and *Tanikaze*.[231] *Honolulu* fired on a target bearing 198 degrees True, range 6,650 yards. *Helena*'s main battery opened fire on a target at a range of 7,050 yards, while her secondary battery took on the ship in column behind the main battery's target. *St Louis* opened fire with main battery at target 204 degrees True, range 6,800 yards; and secondary battery at target 210 degrees True, range 8,500 yards.[232]

The destroyer *Nicholas*, with Captain McInerney on board, also opened fire with her 5-inch guns. Behind her, the *O'Bannon*'s Lieutenant Commander MacDonald was looking for an opportunity to launch his torpedoes. And he had one, with a perfect firing solution – except the enemy ships were on the wrong side, the port side. The *Nicholas* and *O'Bannon* were still off the *Honolulu*'s starboard bow. MacDonald feared that if he launched his torpedoes to port, he could be endangering his flagship. So he contented himself with three minutes of gunfire. Which was more than the rear destroyers managed to do. The *Jenkins* did nothing at all, while the *Radford* was so far out of position off the *Jenkins*' starboard quarter that the *Jenkins* fouled her line of fire, requiring Commander Romoser's destroyer to keep quiet as well.

Admiral Akiyama's ships were caught between Admiral Ainsworth's ships and the coast of Kolombangara. In times past, Japanese ships caught against a shore, while having little room to maneuver, were able to use that shore for visual and radar camouflage – Admiral Mikawa at Savo Island, Admiral Kimura at Guadalcanal, Admiral Tanaka at Tassafaronga. Admiral Akiyama was not Mikawa, Kimura, or Tanaka. This was his first major combat action. And his last.

"Both cruisers and destroyers had demonstrated in several radar controlled target practices that they do not miss at ranges less than 7,000 yards," Ainsworth later wrote.[233] And, he believed, this action showed it. After two minutes of rapid fire, the *Honolulu* saw her target burning and switched to the ship right behind it.[234] The flagship's gunnery officer Lieutenant Commander Francis Alvin McKee reported setting her second target afire and at 2:01 switched to a third target, stopping only after watching that target's radar return disappear three minutes later.[235]

Meanwhile, the *Helena's* guns were at "continuous fire in complete automatic," in the words of Captain Cecil, until about 2:00. In the words of Ensign Chick Morris, the *Helena's* radio officer:

> The Japs in one of their communiques had accused the *Helena* of using "new secret weapons 6-inch machine-guns!" Now those "6-inch machine-guns" spoke with a bellow that shook the night apart and sent thunder racing on giant feet over the islands. All up and down the line our ships were hammering the enemy. [...]
>
> Just thirty seconds after the first defiant bellow, a report reached us from the bridge. "One down!" To the men topside, the death of that Jap was an unforgettable spectacle. She was a light cruiser following the destroyers which were leading the enemy line, and when smothered under an avalanche of 6-inch shells, she was torn apart as though made of paper, exploding with a blinding burst of light that shot a thousand feet into the sky. While we swung to targets behind and ahead of her, she exploded again and again, and chunks of her superstructure went shrieking through the smoke of battle.[236]

Both her fire control and her search radars reported the target, not a light cruiser but the big destroyer *Niizuki*, disappearing from radar, at which point her main battery switched to the secondary battery's target. The *Helena* quickly exhausted her remaining flashless powder, forcing her to switch to ... flashful powder. Her continuous-firing guns were now also continuous-flashing beacons in the darkness, fouling her crew's night vision and continuously giving away her position.

But Ensign Morris wasn't worried:

> Our fire was continuous. Other ships in our force loosed their shells in salvos, pausing briefly for breath, but for nine minutes not a heartbeat of silence interrupted the bellowing of the *Helena's* guns, and the Japs were torn apart as though caught in a hurricane.

"Two down! There goes another!" came the word from the bridge. The speaker might have been watching workmen fell trees in a forest. But to the men on deck it was an awesome sight. The guns of our force had halted the enemy in his tracks and thrown him into confusion. He fired back wildly. Some of the shells from Jap ships at the end of the line probably fell on Jap ships at the head of it. Nearly all the shells that screamed at us fell short, hurling up columns of water.

The *Helena* had sunk one cruiser. Our second victim, a destroyer, had sped from the destructive fire of our secondary batteries and was blown up as she led. A third Jap exploded as though by spontaneous combustion when our tornado of fire fell across her. In nine minutes the *Helena*'s veteran gun crews had fired more than 1000 rounds, an all-time record, and the devastation was unbelievable.[237]

While the *Helena* had too much visibility, the *Honolulu* and the *St Louis* had the opposite problem: the flashless powder they were still using had the side effect of producing an excess of dense smoke. The smoke streamed from the cruisers' gun barrels like a cigarette smoker's exhale and completely enveloped the cruisers. They could see very little beyond what radar showed them.

The radar now showed them "all remaining pips were dead in the water," leaving Admiral Ainsworth "no hesitancy in expressing the firm opinion that this first group of enemy vessels were [sic] practically obliterated by the end of five minutes[.]"[238] A good beginning, the admiral thought.

But radar also showed them the second group of Japanese ships was reversing course, information which Admiral Ainsworth passed on to his ships. "Are we reversing course?" the *O'Bannon*'s Lieutenant Commander MacDonald asked. "Negative, not yet," was the admiral's response.

But through the smoke they did see a little something: shell splashes from Japanese guns. From the perspective of the flagship *Honolulu*, Japanese gunfire was "relatively light and ineffectual. Numerous salvos were observed to fall short and astern, a few were reported to have landed over. A few shell fragments fell on deck."[239]

The *St Louis* was not so dismissive. By now, she had switched to a second target, bearing 187 degrees True, 7,500 yards. But at 2:03am she saw a four-gun salvo that "appeared to be from 4[-inch]" or 5[-inch]" guns fall 1,200 yards short, but in line with the ship. The next salvo was 700 yards short, still in line with the ship. The next one, which detonated upon hitting the water, was only 300 yards short, still in line with the ship.[240] The enemy's correction of his aim was getting rather uncomfortable as the *St Louis*' lookouts contemplated the next incoming salvo ...

Peering through the thick smoke, the *St Louis*' lookouts could see shell splashes about 10 degrees off the port bow between her and the *Helena* just ahead. The *St Louis*' skipper Captain Colin Campbell caught a glimpse of what looked like the *Helena* being hit and starting to slow.[241] Campbell decided to swerve to port to avoid crashing into the *Helena* and instead pass her to starboard ...

"Execute Turn 18." This order, shorthand for "Ships turn 180 degrees to starboard," came from the admiral at 2:03am, less than one minute after he had told the *O'Bannon* they were not reversing course.[242] This was a simultaneous turn, as contemplated in Battle Plan A. All three cruisers would turn to reverse course to starboard at the same time, and literally countermarch. The last shall be first and the first shall be last, as the *St Louis* would now lead the cruiser column and the flagship *Honolulu* would be at the back. For that matter, the *Radford* and *Jenkins* were now the lead destroyers and the *Nicholas* and *O'Bannon* were in back. In so doing, the column would become the cross for a second "T," this one capping the second group of Japanese ships who had just been observed on radar reversing course.

The reason for the simultaneous turn instead of the follow-the-leader column turn was to avoid the cruisers' fouling each other's line of fire while the turn was in motion. The order came at a perfect time for Captain Campbell, solving his dilemma over how to avoid the *Helena*. He would just turn to starboard and leave the *Helena* to port.[243] Easy.

Or not. As the *St Louis* settled on her new course of 112 degrees True (southeast) some 1,000 yards from her previous course, her search radar went out. The concussions from the guns had jarred it offline. This was not an uncommon problem during the war. While her crew was repairing it, they experienced another not-uncommon problem. *Time* magazine war correspondent Duncan Norton-Taylor, aboard the light cruiser, watched "a thick white finger coming straight at us like a chalk line drawn across a blackboard." A signalman shouted a warning and everyone braced, but all they got was an uncomfortable THUNK! just aft of Turret 3. It was a Japanese torpedo that hit the hull and did not explode, though it did leave an unsightly dent like a giant door ding that would just buff right out.[244]

While the ships were turning, Admiral Ainsworth took the opportunity to ask his destroyers if they had launched their torpedoes. All the destroyer skippers had wanted to fire torpedoes before firing their guns, but only one had: the *Jenkins* had launched three from her Number 2 mount with a 2-degree spread on a bearing of 249 degrees. It was a low-percentage shot, a stern chase of the first group of ships who were sailing away, and all three torpedoes missed.[245] Worse, she had fouled the *Radford*'s line of fire, so Commander Romoser could not get a shot off, shell or torpedo.[246]

With the course reversal, Admiral Ainsworth's cruisers had to reacquire their targets. Wanting no misunderstandings, Ainsworth ordered, "[*Helena*] and [*St Louis*], open fire as soon as you have target [sic]."[247] The *St Louis* dutifully acknowledged.

Trying to keep the optimum firing position for his 45 6-inch guns, at 2:07am, Admiral Ainsworth ordered, "Ships turn right 30 degrees to course 142 degrees True."[248] The flagship continued firing to starboard, now on her fourth target, ceasing fire at 2:12 after seeing explosions on the target. She then switched to her fifth target, joined shortly thereafter by the *St Louis*, who with her radar out was keying on the *Honolulu*'s targets.[249]

As the cruisers were firing shells as fast as they could, Captain McInerney's destroyers were struggling. It was 2:10am before the *Radford* had a clear field of fire and was able to launch four torpedoes to starboard, set for a mean firing track of 252 degrees True (west southwest), speed of 27 knots, with the targets estimated going at a speed of 15 knots on a course of 280 degrees True (west northwest). Commander Romoser had badly underestimated the speed of the targets, which were fleeing the area, and the torpedoes had a hopeless stern chase. Romoser was finally able to open fire with his guns two minutes later.[250]

Trying to get his destroyers in the game, Captain McInerney ordered the *Nicholas* and *O'Bannon* to launch five torpedoes each. The *Nicholas* replied that she didn't have a target. Lieutenant Commander MacDonald on the *O'Bannon* answered that he had, at 2:14am, just launched five torpedoes, at what were those same targets, believed to be two destroyers heading away to the northwest, at a bearing of 240 degrees True, distance 9,000 yards, of the *Radford*'s torpedoes. It was another hopeless stern chase.[251]

Admiral Ainsworth would keep going back and forth across the mouth of Kula Gulf to stay as crossed on that "T" as possible. At 2:15am, he ordered, "Ships turn left 60 degrees to 082 degrees (True). *Helena* and *St Louis* acknowledge."[252] Captain Campbell on the *St Louis* answered with a "Wilco."[253] They were on a roll. At 2:17am, the *Honolulu* opened fire on her sixth target, which she "observed optically to be a three-stack cruiser." The flagship's "[f]irst salvo hit; target on fire[,]" so she stopped shooting. Two minutes later her lookouts reported the target exploded, broke up, and sank. The flagship switched to her seventh target. To Admiral Ainsworth and the *Honolulu*, this war was a snap.

To others, not so much. Like the *St Louis*. The light cruiser continued keying on the *Honolulu*'s targets and joined in the fusillade on the flagship's seventh target, which appeared to be having issues of its own. The radar contact seemed to just stop. To the radar operators on the *Honolulu*, it looked like she had run aground on Kolombangara.[254]

While the *St Louis* had her radar issues, the *Radford* was having radar issues as well. At 2:20am, she had to swerve to port to avoid "what appeared to be a 2100-ton destroyer close aboard on starboard bow. Ship plainly visible but radar could not establish its presence."[255] Captain McInerney was still trying to get his destroyers involved, and repeated his order to the *Nicholas* and *O'Bannon* to launch five torpedoes (a half salvo). This time the admiral interjected that he wanted them to launch the torpedoes "12,000 yards due south of us" at "heavy ships" headed "this way."[256]

Admiral Ainsworth ordered, "Turn Buggy," apparently a reference to a 30-degree turn, at 2:19am. "[*Helena*], [*St Louis*] acknowledge." That elicited a "Roger" from the *St Louis*' Captain Campbell. It had just dawned on the admiral that he had not heard a peep from the *Helena* in some 15 minutes. Was she having radio issues? Not unheard of when firing the main battery. "*Helena*, did you get that message?"[257] The order was rebroadcast over all voice radio circuits and flashed with Aldis lamp forward and aft.[258]

But the admiral had no time to worry. He still had a battle to fight. The *O'Bannon* launched her torpedoes at 2:22am as ordered, but she had trouble acquiring a target – she had one or two that were south-ish 10,000 yards away, but their radar returns were only intermittent – so Lieutenant Commander MacDonald just sent the torpedoes into their general vicinity. If the ships kept coming, the torpedoes had a chance to hit. The ships didn't, so the torpedoes didn't.[259]

"Execute turn 15 [150 degree turn to starboard.]" The order came from the *Honolulu* at 2:27am. Whatever the *Helena*'s issues, the admiral's order gave the *Radford* maneuvering issues. She was supposed to turn to starboard to course 263 degrees True – almost due west. But if the *Radford* turned to starboard, she would run afoul of that strangely radar-resistant destroyer she had just sighted off her starboard bow.[260] *What is that ship, anyway?* Commander Romoser wondered. *Is it one of ours?*

"Are all our people accounted for?" Commander Romoser radioed Captain McInerney on the *Nicholas*.[261] Funny he should ask. The admiral interjected, "Coming to course 263." McInerney acknowledged, as did the *O'Bannon*. But the *O'Bannon*'s Lieutenant Commander MacDonald did not want Romoser's question to be missed and go unanswered, so he repeated it. "Are all our people accounted for?" The admiral responded, "Yes. All except [*Helena*]. Possible radio gear out."[262]

Was the mysterious ship off the *Radford*'s starboard bow the *Helena*? It couldn't be. The shadow was too small to be the *Helena*. Commander Romoser later determined the unknown ship off the *Radford*'s starboard bow was a "phantom ship." Perhaps recalling Plato's allegory of the cave, the phantom was most likely a silhouette of the *Radford*, the negative space of the backlighting gunfire of the cruisers reflected off low-hanging clouds or drifting smoke.[263]

That solved that mystery. But that phantom had very real effects in preventing the *Radford* from turning with the other US Navy ships. She had to keep her course. Now Commander Romoser's ship was more than 8,000 yards astern of her assigned battle position. As was typical of nighttime engagements, the formation was fraying badly.

The *St Louis* had managed to repair her SG radar, which Captain Campbell reported to Admiral Ainsworth at 2:32am. The admiral still couldn't raise the *Helena* and, rather more disturbingly, couldn't see her, either. But Ainsworth wisely did not completely trust what he was seeing or not seeing. It was night, a night combat engagement with all its accompanying smoke and flashes that ruined night vision. At night, you can't see things that are right in front of your face – ask the destroyer *Blue* – and you can see things that aren't there – ask the *Radford*. Wanting a second set of eyes, Ainsworth asked the *St Louis* about the *Helena*.

"Can you see [*Helena*]?"

"Believe she is on our port quarter," Campbell answered.

The admiral pressed him, "Does [*Helena*] seem all right?"

"Appears to be all right."[264]

That was a load off Admiral Ainsworth's mind, somewhat. The *Helena* must be having issues with her radio. Likely the concussion of her guns had knocked her voice radio offline, like the concussion of the *St Louis*' guns had knocked her search radar offline.

With no contacts appearing on the radar, Admiral Ainsworth decided the engagement was over. At 2:35am, the word was passed, "Unload all guns through muzzle!"[265] Any shells remaining in the barrels were fired, and the guns left unloaded.

In theory. Several of the ships fired starshells to illuminate the area. Also at 2:35am, the *Nicholas* picked up one ship on the port bow, course 120 degrees, speed 12 knots. Seven minutes later, Captain McInerney had skipper Lieutenant Commander Andrew J. Hill fire a half salvo of five torpedoes and open fire with guns at a range of 5,000 yards. The target, likely the hulk of the *Niizuki*, disappeared from radar.[266]

Well aware of how the Japanese in the past had used the dark background of the coast to hide their ships, Admiral Ainsworth had crept up on the coast of Kolombangara to see if any had tried to hide there. Finding nothing, at 2:41am, he ordered a 30-degree (actually a 29-degree) turn to starboard, ending up on a course of 292 degrees True – west northwest – so he could poke in the direction of Shortland. They found nothing. The only enemy ship of which they were aware was one that appeared to have run aground in the vicinity of Waugh Rock, off Kolombangara. Its return showed up on radar and it was reported by a Black Cat flying overhead.[267] They would have AirSols take care of it.

The battle appeared to be finished. At 2:54am, Admiral Ainsworth ordered "Cease firing."[268] Well, except the *Jenkins*, apparently. At 2:58am, she fired two torpedoes at … something. An intermittent contact she had on her radar. Just in case it was enemy.[269] The destroyer had carefully followed every order she was given, but she hadn't fired her guns once all night and she had fired her torpedoes only on low-percentage shots.[270]

The admiral was conscientious and thoughtful. His ships had fought an almost-perfect action, Ainsworth believed. Sunk at least six enemy ships and left one more beached.[271] Sure, the Japanese had landed their troops and supplies, but at a disastrous cost for them. For the Americans, the cost was … nothing but ammunition and fuel. As far as Ainsworth could tell.

But due diligence and all that. Finding nothing there, at 3:05am Admiral Ainsworth aimed most of his ships for home.[272] With a few exceptions. He ordered Captain McInerney and the *Nicholas*, "Put on speed. Make sweep of Vella Gulf. Report."[273] After an obviously very thorough radar sweep, McInerney came back within a minute: "See no targets ahead."[274]

Ainsworth similarly ordered the *Radford*, "Make sweep [of] Kula Gulf. See if there any targets left." About 15 minutes later, Commander Romoser reported, "Results of sweep were negative."[275]

But the admiral was not convinced. "Make a triple radar sweep to see if you can see enemy anywhere."[276] Not just any radar sweep; a triple radar sweep. Admiral Ainsworth meant business, so the *Radford* made her radar sweeps again. And reported at 3:18am: "I smell a skunk 80 degrees True range 5,000."[277] "Skunk" was an unidentified radar surface contact, and it didn't actually smell, usually. The news seemed to catch the admiral off guard. After what was apparently a moment of silence, Commander Romoser asked, "Do you hear me?"[278]

"Open up on target," Ainsworth responded. When you don't know what it is?

Commander Romoser clarified, "It appears to be a small but good pip. Do you desire me to investigate it?"[279] Ainsworth caught himself. "Close in, illuminate it, and see if it is the *Helena*." At 3:24, the *Radford* came back with the ominous news, "My skunk is the bow of a ship sticking vertically out of the water." The admiral ordered Romoser, "Turn the searchlight on it. Try to identify it." Ainsworth then spoke to Captain McInerney and all of his destroyers: "This is the Admiral. Illuminate anything you see. We still cannot find the *Helena*, the same thing for all destroyers."[280]

Captain Campbell on the *St Louis* chimed in: "Think we see two digit number on the bow [*Radford*] is illuminating."[281] "Go up and see if it is [*Helena*]," the admiral ordered.[282] "I will go up and investigate it," Commander Romoser answered. "If it is [*Helena*], I will pick up survivors."[283] Everyone waited.

At 3:33am came the news everyone dreaded: "I have closed the hulk. I am sorry to report that the number '50' is visible on the bow. I am afraid it's [*Helena*]."[284]

The admiral's heart sank. "Understood," Ainsworth replied. This was crushing. His "perfect battle" now had a large blemish and, much more importantly, an even larger loss of life. The *Helena* was hit and sunk, and no one saw it happen? How was that possible?

But Admiral Ainsworth had a responsibility to the men of the *Helena* and he knew it. "Keep your searchlight on, pick up survivors," he ordered Commander Romoser, right before ordering Captain McInerney in the *Nicholas*, "Join [*Radford*]." Ainsworth added, "When you are sure you can do no more, sink hulk and rejoin."[285]

It was with a heavy heart that Admiral Ainsworth, his two remaining cruisers, and two of his destroyers headed back down The Slot. With an even heavier heart was the destroyer *O'Bannon*. The destroyer's crew had forged tight bonds with the *Helena*'s crew. Not only had they participated in the infamous Friday the 13th Battle together, as well as several other actions, their crews had often hung out together at Tulagi, Espiritu Santo, and Nouméa. The men of the *O'Bannon* proudly wore the nickname "Little *Helena*," bestowed on them by officers and enlisted in the South Pacific, and some of the crew considered the cruiser an honorary member of their destroyer squadron.[286] The *O'Bannon*'s sailors took the sinking of the *Helena* hard.

One of those sailors approached Lieutenant Commander MacDonald on the bridge. "Captain," the man said, "we want to go back after the men of the *Helena*. They are our buddies. They've always taken care of us." Several others made similar requests. The skipper addressed the crew over the ship's loudspeakers, explaining the dangers of remaining in Japanese-controlled waters, and asked if they were certain they wanted to risk their lives to rescue *Helena* crewmen. The crew shouted its approval. MacDonald signaled Ainsworth: "The officers and men of the *O'Bannon*, with full awareness of the hazard, request permission to return to pick up survivors of the *Helena*." Ainsworth turned them down. Not unreasonably; the *O'Bannon* was almost out of ammunition, and the cruisers still needed antisubmarine protection for the trip back. MacDonald's disappointment was limited; he was so proud of his men for even making the request of their own volition. "It was a happy moment of my life," he later wrote. "Men have to be great to be willing to lay down their lives for their fellow men."[287]

It would be left to the *Nicholas* and *Radford* to rescue these fellow men from the *Helena*. And it would be left to Admiral Ainsworth to figure out how the cruiser had been hit. Just like the loss of the *Strong* the night before, the admiral couldn't make sense of it. What had happened? How had the Japanese done this?

Nevertheless, Admiral Ainsworth knew he and his sailors had pummeled the Japanese with their rapid-fire 6-inch guns. They had sunk at least six ships and run one aground. They had still won a major victory.

Hadn't they?

___

Sitting alone in the spotlight of the *Radford's* shining searchlight was something that looked more like the blade of a meat cleaver. Or a fire axe, hacking its way through the surface of the water, a premonition of coming death.

It was mute testimony, but testimony nonetheless, to the truth of the statement by her Lieutenant (jg) Hollingsworth back in November before the Friday the 13th Action. "It won't be long now," Hollingsworth declared on the eve of the Friday the 13th Action, "before the Japs are forced to abandon Guadalcanal altogether. Then we'll be moving up through the Slot toward Bougainville, pounding the enemy's bases on New Georgia and Kolombangara." "Kula Gulf," he said, "is going to be a tough nut to crack. Very tricky proposition. A ship in Kula will be like a bug in a bottle."[288]

Like many, though not all or even most of his crewmates, Lieutenant (jg) Hollingsworth was floating somewhere in the Kula Gulf and not on board the *Helena*.

Sailors are, by nature, a superstitious lot. They notice things, things that mere landlubbers might not. On February 28, 1942, the Australian light cruiser *Perth* saw its portrait of the Duchess of Kent, who had renamed the ship for the Royal Australian Navy, crash from the wardroom bulkhead to the floor. While in port that same day, the ship's cat mascot tried to escape – three times. That same day, the cat mascot of the US Navy heavy cruiser *Houston* tried to escape as well. Her sailors recalled that when they passed through the Soenda Strait heading north, they heard the sound of a gate clanging shut, its origin a mystery. Less than 24 hours later, both ships were at the bottom of Bantam Bay, sunk in their attempt to escape doomed Java south through the Soenda Strait.

The *Helena* had her own unhappy history; she was damaged during the Pearl Harbor attack, after all. But she had been a happy ship. And the *Helena* had made it through the Guadalcanal Campaign's most vicious actions – Cape Esperance, the Friday the 13th Battle, the submarine ambush on the way home from the Friday the 13th Battle – with nary a scratch. She had trekked up The Slot numerous times in support of actions against Japanese. All without a scratch.

But not this time, as Lieutenant Hollingsworth had obliquely predicted. What he had not predicted, obliquely or otherwise, was the effect of the "flashful" powder.

The *Helena* had just used her rapid gunfire to sink her first two targets, she believed. But in the process she had used up the last of that flashless powder. She had used up almost all of the flashless powder against the Japanese guns of Vila and Bairoko, which had little ability to hurt her, so when she faced ships that had great ability to sink her with torpedoes, she was almost all out. Her rapid gunfire revealed her position and served as a great point of aim. At 2:03am, as she switched to her third target, her crew topside saw a large flash, followed by a towering column of water that crashed down behind Turret 1 on the superstructure, drenching those in the forward main battery director. According to the plotting officer Lieutenant (jg) Ray J. Casten, "the *Helena* reared up as though striking a solid rock ledge. I was pitched forward off my navigational stool[...] "[289] Others were knocked to the deck, like Ensign Morris:

> In a heap on the deck of the shack I looked about in total bewilderment unable to believe we had been hit. I reached for my headphones; they had been jolted to the deck. The ship had leaped into the air and dropped again and now was trembling a curious, muttering tremble, almost dainty, like that of a young girl frightened in the dark.
>
> But her guns were still blazing. The destroyer which had rushed in to plant the fish in us was ablaze and sinking.
>
> I picked myself up slowly, and so did the others, piled atop of one another in a fantastic heap under books and papers. The *Helena* at last ceased firing and the silence was a smothering thing that made breathing difficult. In that whole room there was but one sound: the soft and stealthy settling of dust disturbed by the torpedo's impact.[290]

A torpedo had hit on the port side, maybe 150 feet from the bow. But after shaking a bit, the *Helena* kept going.[291] The *Helena*'s engineering officer Lieutenant Commander Charles Cook, Jr, was in the after engine room. "A quick glance at the gauge board showed steam pressure normal in both plants," he later wrote of the moment. "The after engines continued making turns for 25 knots."[292] Though she seemed to be running harder, like the water was resisting her movement or something, her engines were fine and she could still move.

Until two minutes later. Then she suffered another explosion that sent up another towering column of water, this time amidships, crashing down on the stacks. Another torpedo hit. In the after engine room, Lieutenant Commander Charles Cook, Jr "saw the main steam gauges, which show the pressures in each plant, drop rapidly."[293] Power and locomotion immediately went out. As Captain Cecil later described it, "It struck in the one position where it is possible, in a single stroke, to render inoperative all of the main propelling machinery. That is, it caused serious damage in both plants by striking close to bulkhead 82."[294]

On the *St Louis*-class (or "improved" *Brooklyn*-class) light cruisers like the *Helena*, bulkhead 82 was the dividing line – dividing wall, really – between the forward and after propulsion plants. Basically, a "propulsion plant" on a ship consisted of the engines and the boilers that powered the engines. The ship's propellers might be under the stern, but the engines that turn those propellers are in both the forward and after parts of the ships. The *Helena* had four propellers, each attached to an engine. Propellers 1 and 4 were driven by engines 1 and 4 in the forward engine room. Both engines were powered by boilers 1, 2, 3, and 4, just forward of the forward engine room in one large compartment consisting of two boiler rooms and one operating station. Propellers 2 and 3 were connected to engines 2 and 3, which were in the after engine room. These two engines were powered by boilers 5, 6, 7, and 8, located just forward of the after engine room and just aft of the forward engine room in one large compartment consisting of two boiler rooms and one operating station.[295]

"The engineering plant was split, as had been the invariable rule since the war commenced," Lieutenant Commander Cook reported. "The forward boilers and main engines and their auxiliaries were running absolutely independently of the after boilers, main engines, and auxiliaries, so that the possibility of damage in the forward plant affecting the after plant and vice versa, would be minimized."[296]

In theory. But the forward propulsion plant and the after propulsion plant were not entirely independent, because they did share one very important thing: a bulkhead. Specifically, bulkhead 82. The dividing bulkhead between the forward engine room and the boilers that service the after engine room – the dividing bulkhead between the forward and after propulsion plants – was bulkhead 82.[297]

The Type 93 torpedo had lanced into the *Helena*'s port side and exploded right at bulkhead 82, some ten feet below the waterline, and below the armor belt. Lieutenant Commander Cook knew immediately what had happened. The sudden drop in steam pressure "indicated that a torpedo had struck in the vicinity of bulkhead 82, the dividing line between the forward and after plants, and had put both plants out of commission, most probably by rupturing bulkhead 82 and flooding forward engine room and number three fire room."[298] Captain Cecil had also concluded that as a result of the hit, bulkhead 82, in the technical language, "ruptured." A more accurate term might be bulkhead 82 was demolished. The forward engine room flooded, killing everyone inside, and the after boiler rooms flooded, killing or mortally injuring all but three. Consequently, both the forward and after propulsion plants – all four of the *Helena*'s engines – were disabled in one shot.

Though water was leaking into it, the after engine room and its engines 2 and 3 were still functional. So were the forward boilers. The torpedo hit caused her to vomit much of her fuel into the water, but she still had some to use. As part of basic damage control, you could cross-connect those forward boilers to the after engine room so the *Helena* could still move and have power. The problem was that the cross-connecting valves were located at bulkhead 82. The cutouts all went through bulkhead 82. All of them were now under water and probably too damaged to use anyway.[299]

The Long Lance struck in exactly the wrong place. Captain Cecil was brutally honest in his assessment: "Hit number two was in the Achilles Heel of this class of cruiser."[300] A better term might be "design flaw." Other warship designs try to avoid just such an Achille heel by keeping the forward and after propulsion plants separated by a compartment.

The *Helena* would never again move under her own power. To have any hope of saving her, she would have to be towed to port. This was already catastrophic damage, withou even considering the effect on the *Helena's* structural integrity and buoyancy. Which wer negatively impacted, to put it mildly.

And if they had not been negatively impacted enough, then the third torpedo hit coming at 2:06am, about a minute after the second, took care of that. This third hit wa just aft of the second, and overlapped it in effects. According to Ensign Morris, the secon and third torpedoes overlapped in time:

> They struck as one, so close together that the sound was a single shuddering blast. The explosion slammed us to the deck again in the same grotesque heap. But no one cried out.
>
> The lights died. The shock had smashed our generators and blown out the communication circuits. For a moment we struggled in darkness to extricate ourselves. Then the battle lights came on, a dim, weird glow through which the shaken dust swam redly in space.
>
> The *Helena* was done for. I knew it. We all knew it.[301]

She was. Her damage was far, far worse than anyone realized, though they had hints Lieutenant (jg) Casten noticed, "[T]he ship seemed to buckle as if the keel gave way."[30] The *Helena* was hogging amidships, a sign that, like the *Juneau* after Friday the 13th, he keel had snapped. In fact, like the *Atlanta*, much of the midships bottom of the *Helena* wa simply gone. The second and third torpedoes pretty much disemboweled the light cruiser In the words of the Bureau of Ships, "The effects of the two hits amidships were combined in about the worst possible manner from the standpoint of maximum damage to the ship girder."[303]

"About two minutes after the third torpedo hit orders were given by word of mouth to man abandon ship stations," Captain Cecil later wrote, "followed a minute or two later by the order to abandon ship."[304] It was not a hard decision. The *Helena* was flooding, dead in the water, with no power, no communications, and a broken keel.

Ensign Morris soon discovered the damage went well beyond the broken keel:

> The ship was sinking midships, her bow and stern high, belly sagging, but there was no hurry. I stood at the rail, gazing at the eerie display of fireworks over there across the gulf, and the echoing thunder of the guns made me feel better about the *Helena*. We were giving the Japs a beating.
>
> "There's time enough," I thought, "to go to your room for the papers you want." They were valuable papers to me, at any rate and there was all the time in the world now. The ship herself had said so. She was not trembling. "Go ahead," she said.
>
> [...]

My room was at the bottom of the ladder, forward of number two turret. That is, it had been. I reached for the ladder and caught myself just in time, lurched backward and stood shaking, cold and frightened again. Another step and I should have fallen into the sea, headlong.

Because nothing was there now. The *Helena's* bow had been blown apart just where my room had been. The torpedo had gone through the room. "This is how you feel," I thought, "when you come home one night and find only a heap of ashes where the house had stood." And I thought of the times we had sat in that room [...] discussing what might happen if ever a torpedo came through the gray steel bulkheads. Well, a torpedo had come through them. And now I lost that foolish feeling of security. "Get off the ship!" I thought frantically. "Get off now!"[305]

That first torpedo hit may not have damaged the *Helena's* engines, but it had detonated the magazine for 6-inch Turret 1. The flash people saw was an explosion both fast and cataclysmic. As far as anyone could tell, it had literally blown the bow off the ship as far as just forward of the barbette of 6-inch Turret 2. Turret 1 was completely destroyed, blown off the ship. The severed bow, no longer slicing through the water but pushing it, was why the *Helena* had started running harder after the first hit. The bulkhead beneath Turret 2 ruptured and flooded compartments beneath.[306]

Somehow, pretty much everyone (everyone not on or in the bow) had missed that the bow and Turret 1 were missing. "Gun flashes were blinding and, through this volume of fire, no person in a position to observe the forward part of the ship was able to do so, and the fact that turret one had been lost and no fire was coming from that turret escaped our notice," Captain Cecil later wrote.[307] Sounds reasonable. Except, it seems, none of the forward 6-inch turrets, the still-functioning Turret 3, the damaged Turret 2, and the blown-off-the-ship Turret 1 fired after the first torpedo hit.[308]

With all communications out, the order to abandon ship was passed by word of mouth. On the bridge, Chief Signalman Charles Flood flashed a distress message on an Aldis lamp. None of the other ships saw it. Admiral Ainsworth's 180-degree turn, made right when the *Helena* was hit, had taken the American ships maybe a kilometer north of the *Helena*. Swathed in smoke, glued to radar screens, none of the eyes on the other ships saw the *Helena* in her agony. As historian Vincent P. O'Hara put it, "the American ships seemed unaware of anything beyond their radar scopes[.]"[309]

Though the keel was broken and the *Helena* was gradually jackknifing in the middle, the process of sinking, as Ensign Morris indicated, was so slow that the evacuation was conducted in a very orderly fashion. Lieutenant Commander John L. "Jack" Chew, the *Helena's* combat information center officer and assistant gunnery officer, and Lieutenant Commander Warren Boles, the gunnery officer, and Major Bernard T. Kelly, commanding the ship's 42-man Marine Detachment, checked the main deck to make sure no one was left behind. "Practically all rafts were successfully launched and it is believed that practically all surviving personnel succeeded in abandoning ship," Captain Cecil later declared.[310]

The process of sinking was slow, especially for a ship in the condition of the *Helena*, but it had to end soon. With the keel broken, the remnants of the ship's internal bulkheads and girders simply could not hold the ship together. The collapsing bulkheads and girders were audible, and made a loud death rattle as the middle of the ship sank lower and lower, the stern and what was left of the bow pointing higher and higher. Finally, the *Helena* broke in two. The stern rose up almost vertically. The shattered forward part heeled over 45 degrees. Both were only maybe 30 degrees from the vertical. Then they both slid into the depths. The time was 2:25am. The *Helena* was gone.

Or was she? Ensign Morris was in the oily water with a group of survivors:

There were hundreds of us somewhere in that crowded, night-black sea, clinging to rafts or bits of debris, floating in life belts or swimming aimlessly in the dark. Our little group clung to the overturned raft and looked at the place where the *Helena* had vanished, and felt alone, deserted, and it was the end of all the world.

And then the sea began bubbling, boiling, above the grave of our ship. We watched it, wide-eyed and alarmed. Up from the depths lurched a strange, awesome shape, a metal island all wet and gleaming, the sea pouring from its sides as it emerged. It rolled as though shaking its head; it shuddered and shook the water from its brow and at last, sure of itself, settled down to a gentle swaying. Fifteen feet high, this gleaming thing loomed above the sea in the dark, while the sea rocked it and the waves from its resurrection rolled out to bring us its message.

It was the *Helena*'s bow, her white "50" proudly standing out against the wet gray steel. Down there on the floor of Kula Gulf, under forty or more fathoms, our ship had broken in two. [Three, actually] The strakes or keel holding her together midships had let go. This much of her, a ship's spirit proudly encased in steel and bravely holding aloft her identifying numerals, had returned to comfort us.

We were not alone.

Those of us who still clung to the raft gazed at her in silence. Here was something no man could fail to feel, whatever his faith. It was not a question of religion. I have talked to some of those men since, to be sure of that. By recalling lessons in ship design and compartmentation, one can explain readily why she came up. But there in the darkness of Kula Gulf, surrounded by death and loneliness and fear, such material explanations were inadequate. The *Helena* had risen in her death agonies to be sure that we were not left alone to face our fate.

It was with a sense of gratitude and humiliation that we pushed and paddled our raft toward the risen remains of the ship. Other rafts, too, sought security in the *Helena*'s presence, and soon there were several of us.

We could hope now. When the battle ended, the *Helena* would be missed. Our destroyers would surely come seeking her. And when that happened, this fifteen-foot monument of comforting steel would be more easily spotted than a scattered fleet of life rafts.[311]

A poetic, even romantic notion, to be sure. And all true. The *Helena*'s bow had apparently not been blown completely off the ship, but had still been connected underwater at the bottom of the hull, which had acted as a hinge of sorts as the rest of the bow hung below it. As the cruiser plunged to the depths, for whatever reason, the bow broke free from the rest of the hull, and had retained enough air and buoyancy to float back to the surface.

It was a miracle that helped save the *Helena*'s men because the bow showed up on radar. That is how the *Radford* found her. "We are in midst of survivors now," Commander Romoser reported at 3:43am. Captain McInerney acknowledged the news and at almost the same time joined her in the *Nicholas* in conducting rescue operations.[312] The two destroyers slowly and carefully picked their way through the survivors. "In the white light they looked like a school of black fish thrashing around in the phosphorescence," Romoser explained to *Time* magazine reporter Duncan Norton-Taylor. "They gave us a cheer and I ordered two boats lowered and they began swarming into them. Many of them had knives in their teeth. They were not certain of our identity and they were prepared to fight for their lives if my ship had turned out to be a Jap."[313]

But there was a complication. As Captain McInerney noticed, the bow was "6½ miles northeast of the northeast shore of Kolombangara and almost directly in the track of any enemy which would leave Kula Gulf to retire northward to their bases in [the Shortlands]."[314] In short, the *Helena*'s bow and all the survivors who had congregated around her were in a very dangerous place. The *Radford* and *Nicholas* put cargo nets over the sides so survivors in the water could grab a hold of them and climb aboard. Putting boats in the water to recover survivors was too dangerous in this environment.

As became apparent at 4:03am, when the *Nicholas*' radar picked up two contacts, almost due west, at 16,000 yards.[315] Coming around the tip of Kolombangara, it seemed. Both US Navy destroyers moved to investigate the unexpected visitors at 30 knots after telling the *Helena* survivors in the water, "We'll be back for you."

Which was a very common thought right about now. Commander Romoser informed Admiral Ainsworth of the dual interlopers, leaving the admiral alarmed. "We are coming back to help you," Ainsworth radioed.

The admiral was more concerned than Captain McInerney. At 4:06, the commodore ordered the *Radford* to resume the rescue work while the *Nicholas* assumed a blocking position between the *Helena* survivors and the pair of ships.[316] Probably because by that time, the pair of ships had turned around and were heading away from Kula Gulf.

The pair of ships were the Japanese destroyers *Suzukaze* and *Tanikaze* from Admiral Akiyama's first group of ships. This was the group of three ships Admiral Ainsworth described as "practically obliterated by the end of five minutes." Of these three ships, the *Niizuki* had been practically obliterated. Behind her, the *Suzukaze* had taken four hits, which jammed her forward 5-inch mount, destroyed a searchlight, and started a fire in the machine gun ammunition locker. The *Tanikaze* had been hit by one American shell, which did not explode.

When the *Suzukaze* and *Tanikaze* had disappeared from US radar, it had not been because they had sunk but because they had fled to the northwest. They had launched their torpedoes at the Americans; it was their tin fish that had hit the *Helena*. Another Parthian shot. Their flight had been tactical, merely to reload their torpedo tubes, which normally took 20 to 30 minutes. Tonight, it had taken almost 90 minutes, because the torpedomen on the *Suzukaze* handling these very large, explosive objects had lost their "presence of mind and calmness" working below the fire in the ammunition locker, at least according to a report written by someone who had never had to handle very large, explosive objects below a fire in an ammunition locker.[317] Both destroyers "could not find the *Niizuki* nor enemy ships, so they returned to port."[318] It was one of the few instances – so far – of the Americans seeing the Japanese without vice versa.

The *Nicholas* and *Radford* went back to their rescue work, which was by its nature slow. Now they resorted to stopping and lowering boats to fish survivors out of the water. There were just too many survivors who were too injured or lacked the strength to climb up the cargo nets. They needed people to help them out of the water. But the danger in stopping was soon revisited. At 5:19am another contact appeared on radar.[319] It was Captain Yamashiro's command destroyer *Amagiri*.

Back when the battle was just starting, Captain Yamashiro had followed Admiral Akiyama's order for the Second Transport Unit to come up and assist his badly outnumbered support group. He arrived too late to help Akiyama, but just in time to have the American cruisers cross his "T." Seeing the hailstorm of 6-inch gunfire coming at him, Yamashiro had the *Amagiri* lay a smokescreen and turn around hard to starboard behind its protection. The wily destroyer was hit five times – all by duds – that, very importantly, prevented her from launching her deadly torpedoes.[320]

Behind her was the *Hatsuyuki*. Seeing the unpleasant welcoming committee ahead of him, skipper Lieutenant Commander Sugihara Yoshiro had the *Hatsuyuki* turn around hard to port. Even so, she took three hits that damaged the gun director, knocked out her communications, and disabled helm control from the bridge, forcing her to go to manual steering aft; cracked a boiler and a main feedline, twisted a torpedo mount, wrecked three of her spare torpedoes, killed six, and, very importantly, prevented her from launching her torpedoes. It was fairly significant damage – that would have been far worse if any of the three shells had exploded.[321] On this night, the Americans were being let down by their equipment. Again.

Japanese destroyers, with their Type 93 torpedoes to equalize any unfavorable odds, tended to be rather fearless creatures in the face of the enemy. Understandably, they also tended to be rather less so when their decks were packed with Imperial Army or Special Naval Landing Force troops and supplies. The last two destroyers in Captain Yamashiro's unit, the *Nagatsuki* and the *Satsuki*, decided their job was to land troops. No one had said anything about fighting US Navy cruisers. After *Nagatsuki* took one 6-inch hit, they turned around to starboard inside the *Amagiri's* track, heading for the shadow of the shoreline, and sped back south, heading for Vila to land their troops.[322]

Having unloaded her troops at Vila around 4:00am, the *Amagiri* had been heading back to Shortland, hugging the coast of Kolombangara and hoping to go unnoticed, when at 5:15am she heard shouting from the water. They were survivors from the dearly departed *Niizuki*, struggling in the midst of an oil slick. Captain Yamashiro had the destroyer stop to pick them up.

Only to have the destroyer go to full speed northwest. Her lookouts had spotted the *Nicholas* and *Radford* some 15,000 yards away. At the same time the *Amagiri* had found the survivors of the *Niizuki*, the *Radford* had found the *Amagiri* on radar. Before the Japanese destroyer had even stopped to pick up the survivors of Admiral Akiyama's flagship, Captain McInerney had his destroyers suspend their own rescue operations to take care of this latest threat. During the rescue of the *Helena's* men, the two US Navy destroyers had drifted so close together that they had to use their engines to keep from colliding.[323] But they had kept their engines going so, in case of combat, they could in theory get moving fairly quickly.

But before they did so, the *Nicholas'* skipper Lieutenant Commander Hill suggested to Captain McInerney that they launch torpedoes while the destroyer was stopped so the torpedoes' gyros (always troublesome things) would not be disturbed by the *Nicholas'* movements. The commodore agreed, and at 5:22am, when the range to the *Amagiri* had closed to just under 8,000 yards, the *Nicholas* launched five torpedoes at the Japanese destroyer. Then Hill ordered full speed ahead and sped to the northeast.[324] At 5:30, the *Radford* launched four torpedoes of her own. The *Amagiri* was struggling to even find a target, but at 5:53 she loosed five torpedoes in the general direction of the *Nicholas* and *Radford*, who by the time the Japanese torpedoes arrived had changed course to the northwest to parallel the *Amagiri*. Even so, one Type 93 passed 15 feet astern of the *Radford*, while Captain Yamashiro watched American Mark 15s pass both in front of and behind the *Amagiri*.

The *Nicholas* shot up some starshells that backlit the *Amagiri*, and the Japanese and Americans started a gun duel. It ended quickly and rather anticlimactically when at 5:35, the *Amagiri* took a 5-inch shell hit in her radio room, killing ten and knocking out communications and fire control. Captain Yamashiro had the destroyer swing hard to port and withdraw under cover of a smokescreen.[325] The *Nicholas* and *Radford* went back to their rescue work.

Or tried to. Because they had just gotten back to the *Helena's* sea of survivors when the two US Navy destroyers got yet another radar contact coming out of Kula Gulf. Captain McInerney had to be frustrated by now. How many ships did the Japanese have in Kula Gulf? Hadn't six been sunk? He must have thought. No, actually. For all of Admiral Ainsworth's and the US Navy's belief in the combat power of the rapid-fire guns, on this night they had sunk only one ship, the *Niizuki*. A big ship, the most modern ship, and the flagship, to be sure, but just one ship nonetheless. Lieutenant Commander Hill was certainly frustrated, growling, "If the son-of-a-bitch wants a fight, I'll give him a fight."[326]

The son-of-a-bitch was the destroyer *Mochizuki*. She had been part of the First Transport Unit and had not taken part in combat. The other two destroyers of the unit, the *Mikazuki* and *Hamakaze*, had dropped off their troops and departed through the Blackett Strait according to plan. The *Mochizuki* had taken much longer to unload her troops and supplies and did not end up shoving off until 6:00am or so. Since it was so close to dawn, her skipper Lieutenant (sg) Ikunaga Kunio figured there would be no enemy ships in Kula Gulf so he could take that route back to base instead of the narrow, twisting Blackett Strait.

Now began yet another gun battle, in which both sides could, to a degree, see each other at a range of about 5 miles. And yet it was still relatively ineffective. The *Mochizuki* got no hits, and after she took two hits, one to her torpedo tubes and another to her Number 1 4.7-inch mount, Lieutenant Ikunaga called it a day and withdrew under a smokescreen, launching one torpedo to discourage any pursuers.[327]

Captain McInerney was about to call it a day as well. Dawn was breaking and that meant air attacks. His destroyers could not stop and pick up survivors during the daylight, especially so close to Japanese bases. He never received the message that Admiral Ainsworth had requested long-range air cover for him to continue the rescue work. For that matter, he never received the message that Ainsworth had turned around and was coming back to help him deal with the seemingly never-ending succession of Japanese destroyers coming out of Kula Gulf. With the *Nicholas* and *Radford* packed with some 739 survivors of the *Helena*, McInerney left four boats manned by volunteers behind to look for more survivors, then at 6:17am high-tailed it back to Tulagi.[328]

It would be up to AirSols to clean up after this action, known as "the Battle of Kula Gulf." Starting at 7:43am, July 6, a Lockheed Hudson of the Royal New Zealand Air Force's redoubtable No. 13 Squadron, performing its normal morning patrol, flew over Kula Gulf. It reported a large number of survivors in the water and on rafts.[329] Which there were, though the breakdown by this point is a bit suspect. How many Japanese from the *Niizuki* were left at this time is unknown. After the *Amagiri* left, none of them was ever recovered.

But there were still a large number of *Helena* survivors in the water, divided generally into two groups. One, the group the Hudson saw, was maybe 200 men congregated around the bow. The other group was smaller, 88 men, including Captain Cecil, mostly in whaleboats. Cecil led them to Visuvisu Point, where they were picked up the next morning by two destroyers.[330]

The other group was not nearly so lucky. Around noon, it was spotted by a Bombing 101 PB4Y Liberator piloted by Lieutenant James C. Nolan. Nolan and his crew came in low, dropped four packaged rubber lifeboats and all its life preservers, and radioed request that Catalina flying boats be sent to pick up the survivors.[331]

With good flying weather, AirSols was in action. At 8:00am a scheduled air strike hit Enogai. At 10:10am came another AirSols strike, 11 Dauntlesses and ten Avengers escorted by 18 Wildcats. This time their target was not Enogai, but the Japanese ships Admiral

Ainsworth had reported were damaged during the night. They were especially going after the Japanese destroyer that was reported to have run aground off Waugh Rock. The aircraft went to Waugh Rock and found nothing there.[332]

But they did find something else, near Bambari Harbor. A destroyer that had run aground. Was it the same ship? They looked it over very carefully for about a half hour, then decided the destroyer was indeed Japanese.[333] Waugh Rock, Bambari Harbor, close enough.

The destroyer was the *Nagatsuki*, Captain Kanaoka's command ship. The erstwhile member of the Second Transport Unit had decided her mission was to land her troops, not have it out with American cruisers, so she and her sister *Satsuki*, along with the *Hatsuyuki* and Captain Yamashiro' *Amagiri*, withdrew from Admiral Ainsworth's onslaught to drop off their troops and supplies at Vila.

But the *Nagatsuki* never made it to Vila. It seems a sandbar just jumped in front of her five miles short of her intended destination, and she ran aground off Bambari Harbor, still carrying her troops and supplies. She disgorged her Imperial Army troops – Major Hara Hidetome's 2nd Independent Quick-Fire Battalion, with 37mm and 47mm guns – as fast as she could under the circumstances; coastwatchers reported 14 boatloads had left the destroyer by 7:15am. But the sandbar would not disgorge the *Nagatsuki*, still upright but with a decided list to port, so easily. The *Hatsuyuki* stood guard while Captain Kanaoka transferred to the *Satsuki*, then the *Satsuki* passed lines to the grounded destroyer. But though the *Satsuki* huffed and puffed, she could not pull the *Nagatsuki* off that dastardly meddling sandbar. She gave up at 4:00am, and with the *Hatsuyuki* headed south for Blackett Strait, missed combat altogether.[334] Captain Yamashiro's *Amagiri* went north through Kula Gulf, and you saw how that worked out.

The crew of the stranded destroyer dreaded the daylight, knowing what it would bring. And it did, once the AirSols strike found the immobile man-of-war and figured out it was Japanese. Admiral Kusaka had not given up completely on saving the *Nagatsuki*, as Base Air Force sent seven Zeros to try to defend her. But the Wildcats of Fighting 11 had no trouble keeping the Zeros off the Dauntlesses and Avengers, shooting down four in the process. The *Nagatsuki* still had a skeleton crew manning her guns, but she had no luck keeping the bombers off her, either. Then the bombers had no luck finishing her off. It was left to Mitchells of the 42nd Bombardment Group, escorted by four P-38s of the 339th Fighter Squadron, arriving at 2:27pm, to administer the *coup de grâce*. At least one bomb from the B-25s hit the *Nagatsuki*, evidently forward of the bridge. The bomb apparently went through the destroyer's main deck and exploded near the forward magazines, which in turn set off a devastating explosion that blew off almost all of the *Nagatsuki*'s bow and left a 3,000-foot column of smoke over the destroyer.[335] The *Nagatsuki* was a total loss; the lone bright spot for the Japanese was that she lost only eight dead and 13 wounded; the survivors made their way to the Vila-Stanmore base.[336]

Still, it was mission accomplished. At the cost of his life, his new destroyer flagship, and the *Nagatsuki*, Admiral Akiyama had indeed accomplished most of his mission. Out of 2,600 men and 180 tons of supplies loaded at Buin, he had landed 1,600 troops, including the 1st Battalion of the 13th Infantry Regiment, and 90 tons of supplies.[337]

But the situation was so serious that Admiral Kusaka moved his headquarters down to Buin so he could keep a closer watch on the situation and maintain closer command of Base Air Force. Kusaka also asked Combined Fleet for reinforcements. Admiral Koga sent him Admiral Tanaka's old 2nd Destroyer Flotilla, now commanded by Rear Admiral Izaki Shunji, and the 7th Cruiser Division with the heavy cruisers *Kumano* and *Suzuya* under Rear Admiral Nishimura.[338]

Admiral Ainsworth and the Americans had entered the Battle of Kula Gulf confident in their gunpower, confident in their radar, confident they would win, and win easily. And despite the loss of the *Helena*, they were confident they had won at least a tactical victory.

They were wrong.

It was a sign of things to come.

Communications and information. Those two twin towers – intertwined twin towers – of any military operation. This narrative has hit the theme time and again that without one or both of those towers, any military operation is in dire peril.

On July 8, three days after landing Colonel Liversedge and his troops at Rice Anchorage, Admiral Turner sent a message to General Hester: "What is Liversedge's situation?"

The next day, General Hester responded, "No contact with Liversedge."

To be sure, Colonel Liversedge and his troops were not the modern day Roman 9th Legion *Hispana*, disappearing into the trees with no trace, no explanation, and no eagles. But after leaving three companies of the 145th Regiment to guard the Rice area, Liversedge was going through the jungle without that important radio that had been left on board the transports.[339]

Colonel Liversedge, the 1st Marine Raider Battalion; the 3rd Battalion, 148th Infantry Regiment; and K and L Companies of the 145th Infantry started out for their ultimate objective: Dragons Peninsula, the piece of land lying between Enogai Inlet and Bairoko Harbour. They advanced on three parallel tracks, of which two were newly cut by local guides. In the lead were the Marine Raiders, now commanded by Lieutenant Colonel Griffith.[340]

Heading for their first waypoint, the Giza Giza River, was a miserable experience, as Lieutenant Colonel Griffith later explained:

> The terrain over which we marched on 5 July from Rice to the Giza Giza River was difficult
> and even the nature lovers found the beauties of the New Georgia "rain forest" beginning to
> pall after four or five hours in turkish [sic] bath humidity while we alternately stumbled up
> one side of a hill and slipped and slid down the other. In the afternoon the battalion arrived
> at the Giza Giza and without opposition secured a bridgehead on the west bank to cover the

crossing in the morning. An all-round defense was set up, fox holes were dug, and we bivouacked. The rain again began to fall torrentially. The men ate cold K rations and huddled under their ponchos in a vain effort to keep themselves and their weapons dry.[341]

There they spent the night. Getting to their next waypoint, Tamakau River, should be easier. Because, as Lieutenant Colonel Griffith happily explained, it was less than a mile from the Giza Giza to the Tamakau "as the crow flies." To which one astute Marine Raider observed, "That may be, Colonel, but we ain't crows."[342]

It doesn't matter if your destination is five feet in front of you if it takes you five miles of walking to get to it. Lieutenant Colonel Griffith learned this the hard way:

The narrow trail wandered more or less aimlessly through swamp that was nowhere less than calf deep and, in many places, knee deep. During most of the morning while we progressed through the swamp, the battalion actually extended in a slow-moving column of files from the Tamakau River back to the Giza Giza. With such terrain in the backyard, we could understand why we had not yet encountered any Japanese patrols from the garrisons on Dragons Peninsula.[343]

Nevertheless, the Raiders advanced, and that morning one company gained a crossing over the Tamakau. Sort of. The incessant rain had flooded the river and they had neither the time nor the equipment to build a bridge or ferry across. They took to pushing a giant log over the river and everyone had to cross this one rotting slippery log over a tiny but raging river. The crossing took the rest of the day.[344]

This was New Georgia, this was Guadalcanal, this was the Solomon Islands, at their finest. Swamp, rain, rot, mud, mosquitos, malaria, and thick, thick jungle. So thick that radio had trouble penetrating it, which is why the far superior radio left aboard the transports was such a serious loss.

To be sure, Colonel Liversedge had some radios. Just not the good one he needed, specifically requested, and had left behind on the transports. But he did have some less effective radios, one of which was promptly crushed by a falling tree.[345] It should be no surprise that Liversedge was out of touch with command.

It should also be no surprise that he was falling behind schedule, which was a more serious matter than usual. To speed the advance, the Marines and Army troops were traveling light – as in, with enough food for only three days. The idea had been to capture Enogai Point in those three days, which meant capturing it by July 8. In those three days they had only advanced seven miles to the village of Triri on the west side of Enogai Inlet. There, they had clashed with a small Japanese working party, killing two, but the remaining three escaped. Figuring his troops had been discovered, Colonel Liversedge ordered Lieutenant Colonel Griffith to secure and prepare defensive positions at Triri with his Marines and US Army troops. As a Marine demolition platoon was coming up, they ran into another, much stronger Japanese patrol from the 6th Kure Special Naval Landing

Force. After one Marine company outflanked the Japanese, the naval infantry fled. The Marines suffered three killed and four wounded. The Japanese lost almost a dozen killed, including a platoon commander carrying maps of the Bairoko and Enogai defenses and those annoying guns at Enogai Point.[346] But none of the Special Naval Landing Force troops surrendered, and that was at least as important as some trivial issue like operational security. At least it was to the Japanese.

At Triri, the Americans had come to a fork in the road. Colonel Liversedge decided to take it. One prong headed toward Enogai Point. Lieutenant Colonel Griffith led the Raiders down that prong. For a bit less than two miles, at which point the track ended in an impassible mangrove swamp. Griffith called it "one of the disheartening episodes of the operation." Well, he had not yet seen the disaster that was developing at Munda. Griffith turned his troops around and headed back to Triri, then under attack by about one company of Imperial Army Major Obashi Takeo's 2nd Battalion of the 13th Regiment, which General Sasaki had rushed to the Dragons Peninsula area to reinforce the Special Naval Landing Force troops and, apparently, to take command. Marine Raiders moved around the Japanese left into their rear and scattered Major Obashi's troops. The Japanese left behind 20 dead and two of their Nambu machine guns; the defenders, one company of the 3rd Battalion, 145th Infantry suffered four wounded, including company commander Captain Donald Fouse. While that was going on, 17 Dauntlesses of Marine Scout Bombing 144 hit the Japanese positions at Enogai Point at 4:20pm.[347]

July 9 opened with Colonel Liversedge's troops desperately short of food and now rationing their rations. Lieutenant Colonel Griffith set out again early that morning, following a track to the west of the one used the previous day that ended in the swamp and apparently unknown to the Japanese. As he did so, 18 Dauntlesses from Marine Scout Bombing 132 came in from the southeast, split up, and hit both Enogai and Bairoko with 1,000lb bombs. Griffith made very good time, for once, due to this very good trail. He was in sight of Leland Lagoon, between Engoai and Bairoko, by 11:00am. It was around 3:00pm when Griffith's troops made first contact with Enogai Point's Japanese defenders, a platoon of the 2nd Battalion, 13th Regiment, along with an indeterminate number of naval infantry from the 6th Kure Special Naval Landing Force. Griffith and his men hunkered down for the night, their food gone, to perform more scouting on the Enogai positions.

The next morning, Lieutenant Colonel Griffith and his Marines and soldiers moved on Enogai Point. With support from the Marines' 60mm mortars, the American right punched through the Japanese line and swept across the Japanese line to Enogai. By 1:00pm the Japanese were seen fleeing across a spit of land on the north side of Leland Lagoon, where they were subject to enfilading machine gun fire. Unlike their compatriots near Munda, Major Obashi's Imperial Army troops had not had the time to set up fortifications like Gifu and the naval infantry simply had not done so. The Marines lost 47 killed, 74 wounded, and four missing. Raider casualties were 47 killed, 80 wounded, and four missing. The Japanese said that 81 members of the 6th Kure and "a platoon" of army troops "died honorably." The Marines had captured three .50cal. antiaircraft machine guns, four heavy and 14 light machine guns, a searchlight, rifles, mortars, ammunition, two tractors, some stores and documents, and those four 140mm guns that had harassed the *Strong*, *Chevalier*, *O'Bannon*, and the landing at Rice. The Japanese naval gunners had disabled the guns by removing their breech blocks, and then, with the deep ocean being right in front of them, chose to bury the blocks at Enogai. The blocks were quickly recovered by US Marines while digging foxholes. Evidently, the lack of common sense so prevalent in the Imperial Japanese Army also was present in the Special Naval Landing Force. The 140mm guns were now used by the Americans to defend the hard-won prize, now named "Camp Cain," in honor of a distinguished Corporal William Cain, killed in action on July 9. And – finally – supplies were brought up at around 3:00pm and Griffith's men were able to eat.[348]

Admiral Kusaka was ready with retaliatory air strikes. Around noon on July 11 came nine G4Ms of the 705 Air Group with an escort of 47 Zeros. The Rendova Patrol was on hand, but because of "communication problems" at Rendova Fighter Control, as well as some mechanical issues, only five Corsairs of Marine Fighting 221 were left to face the Japanese. A ratio of 5-to-47 is not generally favorable, but the Marines nevertheless charged in. Three dove out of the sun at the Bettys, shooting down one, damaging three more, and harassing others into dropping their bombs into the water uselessly. But enough of the G4Ms were able to drop their bombs on target to kill three Raiders and wound nine more. Zeros from the 253 Air Group and the *Ryuho* quickly flocked around the three F4Us. One Corsair, that of Lieutenant William E. Sage, was never seen again; the other two made it back, but one of the pilots was injured. As the Japanese headed out, the two remaining Corsairs attempted an intercept, but at 2-to-47 odds, it did not go well. Both were badly shot up, one crashing in The Slot, the other crashing off Segi. Both pilots were rescued.[349]

That wasn't it for Base Air Force on this day. Later that afternoon came eight Zeros escorted by 15 more. This time, the Rendova Patrol and Rendova Fighter control were ready. Eight 68th Fighter Squadron Airacobras flown by pilots from the 339th Fighter Squadron were vectored in to Rice Anchorage, but were driven off by the Zero escorts. The P-39s had friends however, including Corsairs from Marine Fighting 213 and 214. None of the Japanese got through to inflict any damage on Rice or Enogai, but they drew blood nonetheless. Two Corsairs were shot down, both pilots recovered, as well as one Airacobra, flown by First Lieutenant Edward B. Whitman. Whitman bailed out of his damaged P-39 and parachuted, but not to safety. When his parachute opened, his harness snapped against his face, breaking bones in his cheek. When he landed, his canopy got caught in a 100ft-tall tree. As he was climbing down, while he was still 25 feet off the jungle floor, he fell and broke his arm. Whitman had to gingerly move his way through the jungle, hiding from Japanese patrols, until he ran into two survivors from the destroyer *Strong*, Radarman 2nd Class Sigmund "Siggy" Butler and Fireman 1st Class Robert McGee, both already injured and dead tired. They found a raft and, in order to avoid a Japanese patrol, paddled out into Kula Gulf, where they were spotted by a Corsair who directed them toward the American lines, where they were later rescued. For the day, the Japanese lost one G4M and three Zeros, one each from the *Ryuho* and the 251 and 582 Air Groups.[350]

It had moved forward in fits and starts, but Lieutenant Colonel Griffith's capture of annoying Enogai was a well-oiled, finely tuned machine compared to what the Americans were doing elsewhere on New Georgia. Back at Zanana Beach, General Hester, who had heard nothing from Colonel Liversedge, was getting ready to start his drive on Munda proper.

The general's plan was as follows: with the 169th and 172nd Regiments, he would march maybe three miles from Zanana to the Barike River, then deploy for combat and attack west starting on July 7 to capture the Munda base. They based their movement orders on a map drawn from aerial photography that showed the coast and the airfield, but, well, nothing else accurately. US troops were frequently unable to even locate their own position on the map, let alone that of the enemy.[351] Back on Guadalcanal, General Kawaguchi had tried to attack the airfield using a hydrographic map of the north coast of Guadalcanal that did not show his attack route. General Hester was trying to one-up him in the useless map department.

Indeed, the entire Allied experience was starting to resemble the Japanese experience on Guadalcanal. Landing at different places. Not knowing the terrain. Underestimating the effect of the jungle. Not having enough food. Having to hack your way through the bush toward an enemy airfield. The enemy having interior lines and thus able to redeploy forces to any threatened sector. No new Guadalcanals? New Georgia was Guadalcanal inverted. The Allies were the Japanese and vice versa.

Just as Colonel Ichiki's and General Kawaguchi's doomed attacks could not even get to their starting points without coming out on the losing end of encounters with Americans with guns, so General Hester's troops could not even reach the Barike River starting positions without coming out second in a contest with Japanese troops, in this case Lieutenant Yamamoto Yoshio's 11th Company from the 229th Regiment holding a blocking position on the upper Barike. They killed six and wounded 30 of Lieutenant Colonel William Stebbins' 3rd Battalion of the 169th Regiment.[352]

The Americans on and around Zanana Beach were strung out. The men of the 43rd Infantry Division were green; their first actual combat had been the invasion of Rendova. And they seem to have been taken by surprise by both the nature of the island and the Japanese. A barrage of grenades by Japanese knee mortars – a spring activated grenade launcher – sent so many men from one company of the 172nd panicking and running away that First Lieutenant Ben Sportsman threatened to shoot the next man to break ranks and flee. After his troops camped for the night, loud screams were heard coming from somewhere in the jungle, their source a mystery. Few of the troops slept.[353]

A lack of sleep is always a theme during war, but it became a major theme for the 43rd Infantry Division at Zanana Beach. The Japanese, mostly from Captain Yamamoto's 11th Company, would use night harassing tactics – moving around, shouting, and occasionally shooting – and letting the imaginations of the green, sleepless American soldiers do the rest. A favorite target became Lieutenant Colonel Stebbins' battalion. His green troops had not set up proper camp perimeter defenses or lookouts for their camp, so the Japanese were able to creep up to within shouting distance of the camp and begin trash-talking. The Connecticut troops heard words out of the darkness telling them their training days were long over and that life would be changing – a lot – presumably not for the better. The exclamation point on the taunts was the last: a specific challenge directed to a "First Lieutenant Marr, commanding I Company." The commander of I Company of the 169th Regiment was First Lieutenant Samuel Auburn Marr. At that point, the Japanese faded back into the darkness, letting that bit of information hang in the air. Others approached the aforementioned I Company as well, calling, in English, the code names of the companies of the 3rd Battalion and such standard fare as "come out and fight."[354]

It had the desired effect. The green Americans thought the Japanese were all around them, infiltrating their perimeter with ease. In their minds, the phosphorescence of rotten logs became Japanese signals. The smell of the jungle became poison gas; some men reported that the Japanese were using a gas which, when inhaled, caused men to jump up in their foxholes. The crawling of the numerous land crabs was interpreted as the sound of approaching Japanese. The Japanese were said to have specific nocturnal raiders who wore long black robes. Some even came with hooks and ropes to drag Americans from their foxholes.[355]

These sound like stories parents tell to misbehaving children, but they were all too real to the men of the 3rd Battalion. They slept little, if at all; were on edge all night. Some fired their guns at imaginary targets. It got to the point where some threw grenades blindly in the dark. Some of the grenades hit trees, bounced back, and exploded among the Americans. In the morning no trace remained of Japanese, no corpses, no wounded. But there were American casualties. Some wounded by knives, some even stabbed to death. Others were wounded by grenades – American grenades.[356]

In the realm of "getting a bad feeling about this" was Colonel George W. McHenry of the 3rd Marine Regiment, as he wrote in his diary:

Believe advance will bog down due to loss of momentum and drive and that fresh troops will have to be thrown in to keep moving toward Munda. Looks like a week's job at the present rate and believe troops will be exhausted before then. They need a few "first down[s]" to bolster their spirits. Night harassing tactics are taking a lot out of them. They do not regain their nerves until about 0900. Maybe some limited night movement would help and restore confidence. Seems pretty low and haggard. They probably scare each other with their haggard look and tired eyes. Most all losing weight and are tired.[357]

These were inexperienced troops. They had no idea what they were getting themselves into. The official Army Air Force history gives a snapshot:

> Here on Munda the enemy enjoyed shorter lines of supply than at Guadalcanal; his strong Bougainville bases were closer, his naval forces were at hand, and he had organized an ingenious and thorough defense system based upon numerous mutually supporting pillboxes and log dugouts, all well concealed and powerfully constructed. Even his military tactics had improved. His troops, physically fit and well fed and equipped, seemingly had access to an inexhaustible supply of ammunition, and they were prepared to die rather than yield.
>
> New Georgia's terrain provided the enemy with a powerful ally. It is characterized by dense jungle with thick, almost impenetrable undergrowth and low ridge lines, possessing no well-defined spurs or landmarks, nor any open country such as exists on the north coast of Guadalcanal. For the ground forces all this meant jungle warfare of a type even more vicious than that encountered in the first campaign; here there were severe restrictions upon freedom of movement and visibility often was limited to a few feet.[358]

General Hester was compelled to delay the start of the attack by one day, to July 8, just because the troops were not in position. Then it took another day to reduce that Japanese roadblock in the upper Barike. With the 172nd and 169th Regiments finally in position on the Barike, the big offensive to take Munda started on July 9.

With lots of explosives. At 5:00am, Brigadier General Harold R. Barker's artillery, comprising the 105mm howitzers of the 103rd and 169th Field Artillery Battalions, the 155mm howitzers of the 136th Field Artillery Battalion, and the 155mm guns of the 9th Marine Defense Battalion, deployed on Rendova and the islets marking the Onaiavisi Passage and began the hour of power, dumping 5,800 high-explosive rounds on Japanese rear areas, lines of communication, suspected bivouac areas and command posts, and suspected centers of resistance. As if that was not enough, in that same hour Captain Ryan's destroyers *Farenholt*, *Buchanan*, *McCalla*, and *Ralph Talbot* lobbed 2,344 5-inch rounds onto the Munda base. The Japanese reported that the area was lit up as if it were daytime.[359] All to soften the defenders and the ground for the long-awaited attack to take Munda set to begin at 6:30am. The big moment came and ...

Nothing happened. Nobody moved. Nobody stepped off to begin the attack. And nobody knows why.[360]

At 8:30 came a pre-planned air attack by AirSols. One hundred and seven Dauntlesses and Avengers dumped 79 tons of bombs on Munda, Enogai, and Bairoko.[361] That seemed to get things moving a bit, and at 9:00am the 172nd Regiment finally started crossing the Barike. By 2:00pm, it had advanced more than 1,000 yards, encountering no opposition from the Japanese, only from the jungle and the terrain.

The 169th barely moved, and seems to have been haunted by the Japanese taunting and night harassment tactics, especially the 3rd Battalion, which again did not move at all. General Wing resorted to sacking Lieutenant Colonel Stebbins and replacing him with Colonel Frederick G. Reincke.[362]

The performance of the troops, especially the 169th, was getting to be embarrassing. Though, to be sure, some historians have tried to explain it:

> The inertia of the troops must be explained in terms of a hundred variations of simple personal rationalizations – or else a bogged-down advance by 4,000 men against a mere handful of defenders would seem more absurd than it really was. The terrain was difficult, certainly, but the crux of the difficulty lay in the minds of men.[363]

In fairness, the jungle has that effect on its own, but the Japanese night harassment of the 169th was paying dividends. Though perhaps not for much longer. The night of July 9–10 brought the normal harassment of shouts and shots in the dark. The Americans were jumping, even shooting, at anything or nothing at all. Restless, obviously. Scared beyond the ability to function. Quietly panicking. The men were on the verge of having their own firefight against themselves.

Then, from somewhere out in the darkness of the nighttime jungle, came an extremely loud Tarzan call.

The Americans all stopped, processing what they had just heard. Then Sergeant Ernie Squatrito of K Company, 3rd Battalion, jumped to his feet, pounded his chest, and let out another Tarzan call. The men of K Company started laughing. The laughter spread throughout the camp, with many, many others making their own Tarzan calls. That seemed to break the panic, for the 3rd Battalion, at least. It remained to be seen whether the battalion that could yell like Tarzan could also fight like Tarzan.[364]

The 43rd Infantry Division's lethargy in even beginning the advance had aided General Sasaki and he made good use of it. First, in order to get reinforcements. On July 9, the destroyer *Satsuki* led fellow destroyers *Mikazuki*, *Matsukaze*, and *Yunagi* out of the Shortlands with 1,200 troops and 85 tons of supplies. Destination: Vila. Expecting a fight, Admiral Samejima assigned the transport destroyers a heavy escort: heavy cruiser *Chokai*, probably the most powerful ship in the Solomons; light cruiser *Sendai*; and destroyers *Yugure*, *Yukikaze* with her radar detector, *Tanikaze*, and *Hamakaze*. Scouting ahead of this force was submarine *I-38* in Kula Gulf and the seaplanes of the 938 Air Group. A Black Cat spotted the force off Visuvisu Point, and at 2:45am, five US Navy PB4Y Liberators from Bombing 101 and 102 came in with a nighttime bombing attack, claiming one hit but actually getting none. The force made Vila, dropped off their troops and supplies, and returned to the Shortlands.[365] A far cry from Admiral Akiyama's experience.

Second, the delays had given General Sasaki time to shift his troops around. Those interior lines and all that. From Vila, Sasaki sent 1,300 troops of the 13th Regiment by barge to Bairoko. He also moved Major Kojima Bunzo's 3rd Battalion of the 229th Regiment to the Munda area. It had already made itself felt with Captain Yamamoto's roadblock. He would be heard from again, as Kojima's troops were now in position facing the American offensive.[366]

An offensive which ground to a halt on July 10. The 169th was held up by heavy machine gun fire from one of Major Kojima's roadblocks. That night, Captain Yamamoto was back to harass the men of the 169th and deny them sleep again – and cause them more self-inflicted casualties. Now General Wing sacked the 169th's commander, Colonel John D. Eason, and replaced him with Colonel Temple G. Holland from the 145th Infantry Regiment of the 37th Infantry Division. This was looking like ancient Carthage, with commanders being removed left and right. New Georgia was turning into the death knell of careers, albeit, unlike ancient Carthage, not necessarily death itself. At least Colonel Eason and Lieutenant Colonel Stebbins did not have to face crucifixion for their failures, real or perceived.

And though they did have failures, to be sure – the lack of adequate camp security is how the entire panic mess had started – it was not entirely their fault. This green 43rd Infantry Division had been sent into action against basically Gifu II, lines of camouflaged self- and mutually supporting bunkers made of coral and logs. Hidden within these bunkers were light and heavy machine guns, including the dreaded Nambu, and 57mm and 75mm guns. If necessary, they could call upon 90mm mortars in the rear for fire support.[367] It was no wonder the offensive had ground to a halt.

The offensive ground to a halt because the combat power of the 43rd Infantry Division was weakened by two major issues. First, the right flank of the 43rd, more precisely the right flank of the 169th Regiment, was in the air. If the Japanese could find the end of the 169th's line, they could just go around it and attack the Americans from the rear. Moreover, despite the minimal gains, the troops had outrun – perhaps "outrun" is too strong a word; maybe "outwalked" or "outhacked"? – their supply lines. The engineers were trying to build a road through the jungle from Zanana to the front for jeeps and trucks to carry supplies, but they could not build the road quickly enough. There was a large gap between the end of the road and the front. As a result, about half the combat troops were required to carry forward ammunition, food, water, and other supplies, and to evacuate casualties. Allied cargo planes were used to parachute supplies to the infantry at the front, but there were never enough planes to keep up with the demand. The troops at the front were running out of all kinds of supplies, especially food.[368]

Never fear, for General Hester had a solution: have the 172nd disengage the Japanese on the American left, and head south and then west to seize Laiana beach and use it as beachhead, because it was indeed a beach, to bring in supplies. The 3rd Battalion of the 103rd Infantry Regiment would land once the beach was secured.[369] Once consolidated with the Zanana Beach positions, the flanks could then be anchored on the coast.

US Navy historian Samuel Eliot Morison's assessment of this idea is simply brutal:

This was perhaps the worst blunder in the most unintelligently waged land campaign of the Pacific war [...]. Laiana should have been chosen as the initial beachhead; if it was now required, the 172nd should have been withdrawn from Zanana and landed at Laiana under naval gunfire and air support. Or Hester might have made the landing with his reserves then waiting at Rendova.[370]

In fairness, it should be recalled General Vandegrift's lesson of the Guadalcanal landings, which amounted to "Hit 'em where they ain't." It could have been legitimately said that "They ain't at Zanana and they ain't ... at Laiana." Which was Vandegrift's whole point, a point reiterated by Admiral Turner.[371]

Contrary to Morison, historian Eric Hammel detailed General Hester's rationale:

General Hester might well have landed his infantry regiments at Laiana to begin with. Or, once the road to Laiana from Zanana was seen to be impossibly long, he might simply have halted the land drive, withdrawn a regiment or more from the Zanana front or Rendova and the barrier islands, and undertaken a direct amphibious assault at Laiana. But Hester did not see his options in those terms at the time. What he did see was that he had two infantry regiments that were just penetrating a built-up zone of defense from which they could not be easily withdrawn; he had, at best, barely acclimated combat troops on his front lines who might interpret a withdrawal for any reason as being a defeat at the hands of the enemy they might just be learning to overcome; he was still awaiting some sort of counterthrust by an enemy whose options were open, so he had to keep his reserves – the 103rd Infantry – in reserve; and he had sufficient reason to believe that a frontal amphibious operation against Laiana would be met at the beach by a determined defending force of considerable size. In the end, Hester seems to have made the only decision warranted by the information he then had.[372]

Be that as it may, at 10:00am on July 11, the 172nd duly pulled out of line and swung to the south, under a barrage of Japanese mortars, marching through knee-deep mud.[373] It was the literal quagmire, but not the proverbial quagmire. Yet.

After the 172nd had camped for the night, Admiral Merrill came in with his cruiser force – flagship light cruiser *Montpelier*; light cruisers *Columbia*, *Cleveland*, and *Denver*; and destroyers *Waller*, *Renshaw*, *Saufley*, *Philip*, *Pringle*, *Farenholt*, *Buchanan*, *Gwin*, *Ralph Talbot* and *Maury* – to bombard Munda.[374] It was a much larger destroyer screen than usual, because Merrill was required to do his shooting parallel to and one mile west of the lines of the 43rd Infantry Division, so his shells would avoid hitting the American troops. This requirement meant that his ships would be in the confined waters of the Blanche Channel, which magnified the threat from submarines. So, Merrill and his ships came in, tossed 3,204 6-inch and 5,470 5-inch shells at Munda, and left.[375] The effect on the Japanese was questionable. The effect on the 172nd was definite: another night without sleep.[376]

While that was going on, at 1:20am on July 12, the fast destroyer-transports *Kilty*, *Crosby*, and *Schley*, escorted by destroyers *Woodworth* and *Taylor*, arrived off Rice Anchorage bearing gifts, or at least reinforcements and supplies. Except, as Commander Leith reported:

There has been no challenge from the beach, no boats to meet us, no signs of life whatever. [...] Boats had difficulty in finding channel and some ran aground. [... Boat officer] reports that our arrival was totally unexpected and the first boats were nearly fired upon. He reports great difficulties in unloading. [...] There is room for only four boats to unload at a time. [...] All unloading will have to be done by such troops as we brought with us plus boat crews and personnel sent by ships. Unloading proceeding more slowly as boats become damaged and more seriously grounded. [...] Many ships' boats have not returned. [...] Have arrived at the decision to leave at 0430 regardless of the boat situation, primarily to get down into air support area by dawn. [...] All personnel have been disembarked and eighty five percent of the cargo. [...][377]

That whole communication thing again. For the lack of that state-of-the-art radio that Colonel Liversedge had requested. And received, only for it to be left in a cargo hold.

Admiral Ainsworth was guarding the convoy from surface interference. He still had his flagship *Honolulu* and the *St Louis*, with destroyers *Jenkins*, *Nicholas*, *O'Bannon*, and *Radford*. Joining the group to replace the *Helena* was the light cruiser *Leander* of the Royal New Zealand Navy.[378] They ended up with little to do except watch the flashes from Admiral Merrill's cruisers bombarding Munda. Again.

Though perhaps they should have had something to do. At 4:45am, as the convoy was leaving, the destroyer *Taylor* picked up a contact on her radar and sonar at a range of 6,800 yards. Nine minutes later, the destroyer's lookouts sighted a conning tower some 2,500 feet away. No US or Allied submarines were known to be in this area, so it must be Japanese. Just to be sure, skipper Commander Benjamin Katz had the searchlight snap open and pin the target.[379]

It was a Japanese submarine, all right. The *Ro-101* under veteran skipper Lieutenant Commander Orita Zenji. She had sighted the invasion convoy headed for New Georgia back on July 30. She had missed this convoy entirely. She paid the price for her lack of vigilance when the *Taylor* opened fire, reportedly scoring four hits on the submarine, killing torpedo officer Lieutenant Tokugawa Hiromu and two lookouts, who had not lived up to the standard established by earlier lookouts at places like Savo Island. Lieutenant Commander Orita had to drag their bodies away before he could get back into the conning tower and close the upper hatch so the submarine could dive.[380]

And dive she did. To 460 feet, almost twice her maximum depth. Orita had to blow the main tanks to halt the descent before the *Ro-101* was crushed or cracked. The *Taylor* dropped a pattern of nine depth charges at 5:04am and dropped two more six minutes later. The *Ro-101* no longer appeared on radar or sonar, and Commander Katz "[c] onsidered submarine definitely sunk by gunfire attack, possibly helped by depth charges."[381]

The *Taylor* had to end her attack regardless, because daylight was coming and with it a Japanese air attack. The Japanese had spotted Admiral Ainsworth's force and wanted a crack at it. Base Air Force sent 13 D3A dive bombers escorted by 47 Zeros from the 582 and 251 Air Groups. For some reason, they seem to have thought that Ainsworth would still be off Visuvisu Point. Though why he and his light cruisers and destroyers would have been hanging out there for half the day or so in the face of air attacks for no apparent reason is unclear.[382]

In an effort to draw the defending AirSols fighters away from the Aichis, some of the Zeros staged a fake dogfight over Kolombangara. It was a stupid idea and it didn't work. For their part, the D3As didn't find Admiral Ainsworth's force, because it wasn't there, so they instead targeted shore facilities at Rice Anchorage, where they did little damage. Eight Warhawks of the 44th Fighter Squadron moved to intercept, followed by Corsairs of Marine Fighting 122. One major dogfight later, four Zeros (two each from the 251 and 582 Air Groups), one Corsair, and one Warhawk were shot down, with one D3A forced to ditch short of Ballale. The P-40 was flown by 2nd Lieutenant William Ehrenmann. Wounded in the leg, Ehrenmann had managed to crash land. Then he spent two days and one night on a log floating down a river through Japanese-held territory until he ended up at the American lines. He was flown out for medical care.[383]

Meanwhile, the 172nd Regiment had resumed its slog through the mud. Colonel David M.N. Ross, commanding the 172nd, hoped to get to Laiana before dark. Ross reported that the carrying parties, who were trying to get supplies to the front and get out the wounded, equaled the strength of three-and-one-half rifle companies – almost a full battalion, unable to fight, because it was committed to supply. And those supply efforts were failing; they had not gotten any supplies in two days, and they were out of food and water. Nevertheless, the troops trudged on through the mud and jungle until late afternoon. The leading elements were just 500 yards from Laiana when they were stopped by machine gun and mortar fire. Scouts reported pillboxes containing machine guns and supported by mortars. The bunkers were connected by trenches that ran northwest from Ilangana, which was about 500 yards beyond Laiana.[384]

Colonel Ross' desperately hungry and especially thirsty troops had to camp for a very uncomfortable night. He was aware that Japanese patrols had cut into the rear of the 172nd, between it and the 169th and the rest of the 43rd Infantry Division. American roving patrols were keeping them at bay, but it was only a matter of time. The 172nd was essentially without a line of communications. The troops could hear the Japanese cutting down trees, presumably to clear fields of fire for the machine guns in those pillboxes. Japanese mortars "registered" (basically zeroed in) on the 172nd's camp, in preparation for the next day, July 13. The day the 172nd simply had to clear Laiana.[385]

Because the supplies weren't coming any faster and the going wasn't getting any easier. The Japanese were getting reinforcements. On June 12, the first of 52 Zeros of the 201

Air Group arrived in Rabaul. Commander Chujiro Nakano, head of the 201, rated the abilities of his pilots at this time as eight who were skilled, 20 who were competent, and 24 who were "inexperienced." Well, you have to get that experience sometime. The US Army's 43rd Infantry Division was getting badly needed experience on the battlefield, and you see how well that was working out. Also arriving in Rabaul were the elements of the *Junyo's* air group.[386]

That Base Air Force workhorse, the composite 582 Air Group, was now in for major changes. It had been sort of grandfathered in when the Japanese Naval Air Force reorganized in November 1942. No longer. The 582 was stripped of its fighter component. Many of the pilots were transferred to other fighter units, but 13 were kept, merely transferred to the 204 Air Group so air operations in the Solomons would not suffer.[387] Not much, anyway.

General Sasaki was due for some reinforcements as well. Some 1,200 troops were due to land at Vila that night. He had figured out what the Americans were doing. And he had a plan for dealing with it, one that quickly got approval from General Inamura and Admiral Samejima. In the aftermath of the fall of Enogai, Sasaki had sent two companies of the 13th Regiment to reinforce the 6th Kure Special Landing Force troops at Bairoko. Now he ordered Colonel Tomonari, the 13th's commander, to move his 1st and 3rd Battalions by barge to Bairoko and overland from there to the Zieta. The chess pieces were moving into place.[388]

As evening approached, in the Kula Gulf, a submarine surfaced, its hull dented in numerous places, its Number 1 periscope disabled. It was the *Ro-101*, the same boat that the *Taylor* had attacked the night before and believed it had sunk. The effects of the attack were visible on the submarine, as Lieutenant Commander Orita and the crew noticed when they checked the submarine for damage, but she was not sunk. Orita had the *Ro-101* head to the coast of Kolombangara to make some repairs.[389]

But it would not be a peaceful night for Lieutenant Commander Orita or his crew. After sunset, while they were surfaced making repairs, from out in the dark in the Kula Gulf came the low growl of gunfire and lots of it. They could see searchlight beams sweeping the darkness.[390]

What was going on?

The Japanese used to have a veteran admiral who could run troops and supplies in and out under difficult conditions. Who did it again and again and again. Sometimes even, against the odds, delivering a bloody nose to the hated Americans in the process. Like at Tassafaronga, when his fleeing destroyers sent their Parthian shots of Long Lances into four US Navy cruisers, sinking one and causing severe damage to the other three. But Tanaka Raizo didn't live here anymore. His replacement as head of the Transportation Unit, Akiyama Teruo, was dead.

In war it's always next man up. Now it was Rear Admiral Izaki Shunji, Admiral Tanaka's replacement as commander of the 2nd Destroyer Flotilla, now back with its traditional light cruiser flagship *Jintsu*.[391] Like Tanaka, Izaki had skippered the *Jintsu*, though only for a few weeks at the end of 1939.[392] Izaki had also commanded at various times the *Sendai*, *Maya*, and *Mogami*. You can never really get over commanding the *Mogami*.

At 5:00am on July 12, this latest Japanese supply run left Simpson Harbor. In the lead were five destroyers of the 2nd Destroyer Flotilla, *Yukikaze*, *Hamikaze*, *Yugure*, *Mikazuki*, and *Kiyonami*. Following them were four destroyers serving as transports: *Satsuki*, *Minazuki*, *Yunagi*, and *Matsukaze*, all under Captain Kanaoka, carrying some 1,200 troops of the 2nd Battalion of the 45th Infantry Regiment of the 6th Kumamoto Division under Major Yamada Tadaichi to be landed at Ariel, a new barge base on the southwest coast of Kolombangara. Pulling up the rear was the 2nd's traditional flagship, light cruiser *Jintsu*, flying Admiral Izaki's flag.[393]

The movement did not go unnoticed, and at about noon a coastwatcher near Shortland relayed word to Guadalcanal and to Admiral Halsey. An hour later, the *Honolulu* and *St Louis*, south of Guadalcanal and heading for Espiritu Santo, received an urgent message from Halsey, "Reverse course. Proceed to Kula Gulf at high speed."[394] Kula Gulf? Again? "Must be something big," Admiral Ainsworth commented. "Kelly Turner never lets go of anything if he can help it."[395]

There would be some differences this time. No *Helena*, obviously. Next man up, or in this case next ship. That next ship was the New Zealand light cruiser *Leander*. The Kiwis aboard her were anxious to finally get involved in this Pacific War doing something other than escorting convoys and sitting around. As one crewman remembered, "Day after day we lay at single anchor in Santos with little to do but look forward to the evening films ... American cruisers and destroyer flotillas went out daily to return on most occasions depleted in number, and this was destroying our moral[e]."[396] In response to the admiral's signal of welcome on July 11, *Leander* skipper Captain C.A.L. Mansergh answered, "Hope to help you avenge the loss of *Helena* and *Strong*."[397]

This would be *Leander*'s second appearance in this Pacific War, sort of. On August 9, during the disastrous Battle of Savo Island, the Japanese spotted a damaged ship creeping through the western end of Ironbottom Sound headed for the Coral Sea. They thought it was the *Leander*, and the next day Base Air Force sent G4Ms out to sink the damaged ship. They did sink the ship, but it was not the *Leander*; it was the unfortunate destroyer *Jarvis*.

In that sense, the *Leander* was lucky. Like the *Helena* had been. Until she wasn't. But the *Leander* was not the *Helena*. She did not have the *Helena*'s 15 rapid-fire 6-inch guns. She only had eight 6-inch guns, and they were not rapid-fire. But the Royal Navy had not stupidly removed the torpedo tubes from its cruisers like the US Navy had, and the *Leander* had eight of them. They could add a dimension to the surface force to which the US Navy was not accustomed.

But the US Navy was accustomed to – well, more like tolerated – what Admiral Halsey was doing now. Halsey ordered Admiral Turner to give Admiral Ainsworth all the additional ships that he could. Turner promptly told Captain Thomas J. Ryan to report to Ainsworth with his Destroyer Squadron 12. Ryan's ships had never worked with Ainsworth's ships before and had no idea of the battle plan or Ainsworth's communications protocols. This was another instance of putting onto the battlefield the best force they could slap together. It had not worked very well before, most recently at Tassafaronga. Even Captain McInerney, after Kula Gulf, had warned, "It would be better to leave destroyers in port, rather than to fill in at the last hour in squadrons or divisions with which they have never operated – they become a liability, and are apt to be sunk by own ships, rather than an asset."[398] But what did he know? Halsey, who "fully appreciated the situation, felt that the advantages to be gained justified the risks involved."[399] If you say so.

Admiral Ainsworth quickly got back to Tulagi and just before 4:00pm sent a boat to pick up Commodore Ryan to take him to the *Honolulu* for a conference. Like a late-night study session before a big midterm, for 20 minutes in *Honolulu's* Flag Plot, Ainsworth and his staff tried to cram all the necessary instructions and information into Ryan's brain. Ainsworth's formations and battle plan were not particularly unusual or difficult. In fact, Ainsworth was going to copy his "Night Battle Plan A" from the Kula Gulf Action.[400] But in terms of communications, one of the two most important factors in any operation, the voice codes and call signs were completely unfamiliar to Ryan and his skippers.[401] And combat is not the place where you want to be stopping to figure out what your call sign is or what the code is for what.

Captain Ryan returned to his ship *Fahrenholt* to find his available destroyer skippers already waiting for him to brief them. Ryan had all of five minutes before Admiral Ainsworth's *Honolulu* signaled for all ships to get under way. To top it off, the *Fahrenholt's* skipper told Ryan that the ship had engineering issues and could only make 25 knots. The commodore had to quickly switch his flag to the destroyer *Ralph Talbot* and take off at 5:30pm with the destroyers *Buchanan*, *Woodworth*, *Gwin*, and *Maury* to catch up to Ainsworth.[402]

As it was, Commodore Ryan's ships weren't fully ready. *Ralph Talbot* and *Buchanan* had engineering issues of their own that, while not as bad as those of the *Fahrenholt*, did limit their speed to 30 knots. The *Woodworth* and *Gwin* did not have SG radar. *Gwin* was still dealing with damage from the Rendova landings. The *Maury* had only been in the force for three days. Ryan looked at his ships in the back of the formation and shook his head.[403] It was the best force they could slap together. A group of damaged and worn ships that had never worked together before. What could go wrong? Remember the Battle of the Java Sea?

At least Captain Ryan could take comfort that his ships were not the only newcomers here. The *Jenkins* had a new skipper. At Kula Gulf, the destroyer had carefully followed every order she was given, but she hadn't fired her guns once all night and she had fired her torpedoes only on low-percentage shots. After that, Commander Harry F. Miller, who had skippered the *Jenkins* since her commissioning in July 1942, was quickly replaced by Lieutenant Commander Madison Hall.[404]

So, once again the force headed up The Slot, again with the cruisers in column open order, with destroyers forward and behind in a 3,000-yard circle.[405] At 10:00pm, Admiral Ainsworth ordered Battle Stations.[406] An hour later, the formation was 25 miles east of Visuvisu Point, the northern tip of New Georgia. Which is where a Japanese scout, likely a floatplane launched by the *Jintsu* at 10:16pm, found the force before it was chased off by gunfire.[407] So much for catching the Japanese by surprise.

But the Japanese were not going to be surprised anyway. Admiral Izaki may not have had radar, but both the *Jintsu* and *Yukikaze* did have those new-fangled radar detectors. Copied from the German Metox design, the E27 radar detectors were designed to warn of radar transmissions coming from Allied ships. On this night, they worked perfectly. Admiral Izaki's ships sped through the Solomons without being stopped once. He turned southeast to enter Kula Gulf at a speed of 30 knots.

Captain Shimai Yoshima in the destroyer *Yukikaze* as head of Destroyer Division 16 later said, "We positively determined the presence of the enemy two hours before we met him. Right up to our meeting with him we were aware of the changes in our relative positions and were able to verify the remarkable effectiveness of this instrument which gave us ample confidence in our ability to gain prior knowledge ...."[408] Though it's not clear from his statement, Shimai was likely referring to the floatplane's report of enemy ships coming in roughly two hours before visual contact.[409] After detaching the four transport destroyers to make for Vila, Izaki switched from a cruising formation to an "alert cruising disposition," a column with the *Mikazuki* in front, followed by the flagship *Jintsu*, *Yukikaze*, *Hamakaze*, *Kiyonami*, and *Yugure*, in that order.[410]

At 12:42am, a Black Cat PBY with *Honolulu* gunnery spotter Lieutenant M.E. Barnett aboard radioed, "Six enemy ships northwest of you. Course southeast toward Kula Gulf at high speed."[411] Admiral Ainsworth radioed, "Enemy estimated six vessels, bearing 310, distance 20 miles. [Destroyers] form column ahead and astern."[412] This would be the battle formation, which because of the lack of time for preparation had to be a simple column – four miles long.[413] Captain McInerney's *Nicholas* and destroyers *Radford*, *O'Bannon*, *Jenkins*, and *Taylor* formed in the lead easily enough; they had done this before with Ainsworth. But Captain Ryan's ships struggled. The correct order of his destroyers would have been his own *Ralph Talbot*, then *Buchanan*, *Maury*, *Woodworth*, and *Gwin*, in that order. Except, somehow, the *Buchanan*, the planned second destroyer in the rear of the column, ended up on the starboard quarter of the *Woodworth*.[414] The battle had not even started yet and the Allied formation was already beginning to fray.

Two minutes later, at 12:49, Ainsworth ordered speed increased to 28 knots. He also radioed McInerney, "Bend on some knots and reach ahead."[415] But the admiral wanted to stay hidden for the moment and did not want the Japanese to see his ships. They would not be seeing the *Radford* for a bit anyway. Water in her fuel lines caused two boilers to go out, and she lost speed and fell behind her destroyer-mates, slipping down the column on its starboard hand.[416] It was 1:00am before she could regain steam pressure, and by then the *Radford* was focused on getting out of the way of the maneuvering Allied cruisers.[417]

At 12:52, a second report came in from Barnett's Black Cat, "Enemy is 5 destroyers, one cruiser in column. Cruiser is second in column."[418] At 12:59, radar on board the *Honolulu* detected the incoming ships, bearing 297 degrees True, distance 30,200 yards. McInerney's destroyers, except for the *Radford*, were racing ahead at 32 knots to get a better radar picture. One minute later McInerney radioed, "I smell a skunk"; bearing 300 degrees True, distance 12 miles.[419]

It was more than just a skunk at 1:03, when the *Nicholas* reported, "We have enemy visually." Admiral Ainsworth was still hoping to take the Japanese by surprise, a surprise that would be ruined if they saw Captain McInerney's destroyers too soon. Ainsworth hurriedly instructed McInerney, "Bear off to the left. Keep him out of visual contact." Which brings up the question of why exactly Ainsworth sent them ahead if he wasn't willing to risk their being seen. McInerney led his ships left on course 260 degrees True, reporting the enemy now at 317 degrees True, range 16,500 yards.[420]

Even though he had radar, Admiral Ainsworth was having some difficulty visualizing the setup. He asked Captain McInerney, "Then you are across his bow. Is that correct?"

"That is correct."[421]

Just as he had at Kula Gulf, Admiral Ainsworth decided to quickly close the range, so at 1:07 he ordered, "Turn Three," a 30-degree line turn to starboard, to settle on a course of 305 degrees True. The *Honolulu* was now charging directly at the enemy. Well, Ainsworth did want to close the range. A minute later, McInerney reported his range to the enemy was down to 12,000 yards. Just as he had at Kula Gulf, Ainsworth ordered, "Prepare to attack in accordance with Battle Plan Able!"[422] When McInerney radioed that he was in torpedo range at 1:09, the admiral ordered, "Execute William one half."[423] "William" was the code for launching torpedoes.

At the same time, the admiral ordered, "Three turn," a 30-degree turn to port.[424] All the ships complied except the destroyer *Jenkins*, who mistakenly turned to starboard.[425] New skipper and all that. Ainsworth ordered another "Three turn" to bring his ships to course 245 degrees True.[426]

The intention had been to unmask the main batteries for the cruisers. But it also settled for Captain Ryan the question of how to launch his torpedoes: to starboard. Ryan radioed the flagship, "We are going in to let him have it!" The commodore instructed his ships to fire torpedoes "as soon as ready," adding, "Good luck, boys."[427]

Beginning at 1:10, the *Nicholas* launched five torpedoes, the *Taylor* nine, and the *Radford* five.[428] It was, perhaps, the best executed torpedo attack by US Navy surface ships so far in the Pacific War. Naturally, all the torpedoes missed. Admiral Izaki had his column execute a sharp 80-degree port turn that put the American torpedoes in a stern chase they had no chance to win.[429]

At 1:11, the shutters of a searchlight on the *Jintsu* snapped open. The Japanese did love their searchlights. The beam swept the darkness and fell on the destroyer *Jenkins*, whose mistaken turn to starboard had made her the closest American ship. The *Jenkins'* new skipper, Lieutenant Commander Hall, did not enjoy his ship's time in the spotlight. She quickly shot off two torpedoes, then scampered away from the Japanese.

Given that most of their success in night surface engagements came from surprise and attacking from positions of concealment, the Japanese fixation on searchlights was curious. At the November 13 naval battle of Guadalcanal, Commander Chihaya's impeccable logic in ordering the use of searchlights was that if you use searchlights in the dark, you can see things, which is, of course, true. Also true is that if you use searchlights in the dark, things can see you, too.

As the *Jenkins* skedaddled back to the relative protection of the American formation, she was covered by gunfire from the *O'Bannon* and *Taylor* directed at the *Jintsu's* searchlight.[430] That was about the time when Admiral Ainsworth radioed the cruisers "Commence firing."[431] They were quickly joined by the *Honolulu*. The *Leander*, *St Louis*, and *Jenkins* soon joined in shooting at that searchlight. The Kiwi cruiser added four torpedoes from her starboard quadruple tubes, the *Jenkins* added two, and the *Buchanan* five to the barrage of hot lead aimed at the source of that beam of light.[432]

Like the *Hiei* and *Akatsuki* in the November 13 battle, the *Jintsu* took one for the team. Like the *Niizuki* a week earlier, a veritable maelstrom of molten metal came down on the light cruiser. Like a speeding train hitting a stalled car. A galling gale of gunfire, 2,630 rounds.[433] Seemingly all directed at the *Jintsu*. Seemingly all hitting the *Jintsu*. And seemingly all hitting the *Jintsu* at the same time.

The *Jintsu* was hit very early and very, very often. So hard and so fast that it's not clear precisely when and where each hit took place and what damage each hit caused, with a few exceptions. According to the Japanese, the *Jintsu* was "exposed to a concentrated fire, so, together with the [*Mikazuki*], she ducked into a squall and disappeared to the eastward."[434] She tried to, anyway, but an early shell is known to have hit the rudder and knocked out the *Jintsu's* steering gear at 1:17.[435] The light cruiser's boiler rooms took what the Japanese described as "more than ten" hits.[436] As the *Jintsu* skewed to starboard and lost momentum, her bridge was smashed by multiple shell hits, killing pretty much everyone there, including Admiral Izaki and his staff, skipper Captain Sato Torajiro, and Executive Officer Commander Kondo Issei.[437] A torpedo from either Captain McInerney's destroyers or *Leander* buried itself in the starboard side in the aft engine room. The *Jinstu* drunkenly staggered to starboard and finally stopped, a blazing jumble of metal barely recognizable as the flotilla flagship she had been only five minutes earlier.[438]

Admiral Ainsworth was running the same playbook he had used at Kula Gulf page by page, and the battle so far was going almost exactly as it had at Kula Gulf, page by page, right down to disabling the largest enemy ship early on by an overconcentration of gunfire. He hoped the similarities would end there. At 1:14, the admiral ordered, "Execute to follow, one eight turn."[439] This was to be a simultaneous 180-degree turn to the east northeast. The admiral received an acknowledgment from the *St Louis*, so at 1:16 he followed up with "Execute one eight turn."[440] Most ships reversed course as ordered.

But all was not well. The *Honolulu*'s forward voice radio, the one in use on the flag bridge, had a blind spot aft, and the concussions from firing the main battery had knocked the transmitters around a bit, so several ships did not receive the full series of orders.[441] Captain Ryan's destroyers had received nothing, except for the *Ralph Talbot*, who had received the "execute" order but no preparatory order, so a minute later, Ryan asked, "Did you execute one eight turn?" The seconds seemed like hours as the *Ralph Talbot* headed into the beam of the last cruiser when the voice radio finally came back "Affirmative." The *Ralph Talbot* had to use full rudder to avoid a collision with the cruiser and "back full, maneuver radically, and use whistle signals to narrowly avoid collision with rear destroyers [that] were standing on at 30 knots," who had received neither the preparatory nor the execute orders.[442]

That was not all. The *St Louis* had acknowledged the order, but the *Leander* had not, and as the *Honolulu* turned, the *Leander* suddenly appeared in her path. Both ships ceased firing, and the *Leander* veered hard to port.[443] The *Honolulu* eventually fell in behind the *St Louis*.[444]

Naturally, it was during this time of confusion and milling around, not knowing what was going on and what one was supposed to be doing, that torpedoes started appearing all around the Allied ships. Because that's the way it always works. At 1:08am, before the Allied ships had started firing guns or torpedoes, Admiral Izaki had invoked the ancient Japanese credo: *when in doubt, launch torpedoes*. Before she was reduced to a dumpster fire, the *Jintsu* and her destroyers had launched 31 Type 93 torpedoes at Admiral Ainsworth's ships.[445] So they would arrive now. At the worst possible time.

The *Ralph Talbot* narrowly avoided three that passed within 25 yards of her stern. The *Leander* was not that lucky. The cruisers were badly bunched at the turn and, almost as soon as the *Leander* had just settled behind the *St Louis* on the new course, she suffered an underwater explosion on the port side amidships in the Number 1 boiler room. The concussion whipped her mainmast back and forth and popped her own searchlight's shutters, sending an unwanted beam of light into the sky like a Hollywood opening night. Captain Mansergh immediately ordered the engines stopped to ascertain the damage, especially the condition of the engines.

The torpedo had been unusually damaging, blowing a 20-by-30-foot hole, with distortion of armor, plating, and frames, including cracks in the ship's hull and lower deck, extending more than 50 feet fore and aft. The *Leander* quickly listed to port 10 degrees.

The Number 1 boiler room was wrecked and all inside it were killed. The blast threw up a giant column of water which came crashing down on the after part of the cruiser and swept several men overboard. Blast pressure vented up a boiler-room vent and blew seven members of a 4-inch-gun's crew overboard as well. The port quadruple torpedo-tube mounting was lifted bodily aft for several feet, leaving the torpedoes lolling dangerously over the ship's side. Main steam failed to the two after engines that powered the inner propeller shafts, and soon steam was lost to the port forward engine due to the evacuation of the Number 2 boiler room. Electric power was cut off everywhere forward of the Number 3 boiler room, plunging the ship into complete darkness and knocking offline all communications, except the very limited number of sound-powered telephones, and all gunnery fire-control and radio equipment. Five fuel-oil tanks were wrecked and two others badly contaminated with sea water.[446]

There was no way the *Leander* could continue fighting in this condition. Her first surface combat engagement since 1941, a chance her crew had long awaited, and she was out of the fight early on, with 28 dead. "The curtailment of *Leander's* part in the operations was a bitter disappointment to me and to everyone on board," wrote Captain Mansergh in his report of the action. "There was but a fleeting opportunity for the ship to demonstrate her weapon efficiency, but the conduct and bearing of all hands during the action and the trying passage back to harbour were a source of extreme pride and gratification to me. All behaved like veterans. In particular, the work of the engine-room, damage control, and medical personnel call for very high commendation."[447]

The battle was going on without the *Leander*. The destroyer *Taylor* had to veer hard to port to avoid the slowing Kiwi cruiser, while the *Jenkins* noticed men in the water that she believed were from the *Leander* and had to veer hard to port herself so she wouldn't run over them.[448] Admiral Ainsworth noticed the *Leander* had fallen out of formation and ordered *Radford*, "Stand by *Leander*, who is out of formation."[449] On the flip side, Captain Shimai of Destroyer Division 16 had taken over control of the remainder of the Japanese force in the absence of the fallen Admiral Izaki and had his *Yukikaze* lead the *Hamakaze*, *Kiyonami*, and *Yugure* into a rain squall. Radar can generally see through rain, but this squall was apparently special and Admiral Ainsworth's ships were not able to continue tracking the Japanese destroyers. The only ships they could find were the burning *Jinstu* and the destroyer *Mikazuki*, which was standing by her. But the Black Cat with the *Honolulu's* Lieutenant Barnett on board tracked down Shimai's four destroyers. At 1:32am, Admiral Ainsworth radioed Captain McInerney: "Go get 'em! ... Go get 'em!" McInerney responded, "We four are on course 325 chasing enemy. Don't throw anything at us!" Ainsworth replied, "Wouldn't do it for the world. Go to it and get the bastards! Good luck!"[450] The commodore herded his wayward destroyers and pointed them in the general direction of the Japanese.

Admiral Ainsworth was very much willing to throw anything and everything at the *Mikazuki* and *Jintsu*. The *Honolulu*, heading northeast, took both under fire, and the *Mikazuki* scampered off to the north. The *Honolulu* ceased fire at 1:31.[451] Four minutes later, the *Radford* radioed, "*Leander* reports torpedo hit forward. I am with him. Will report more later."[452]

Captain McInerney's destroyers chased to the northwest at 30 knots for five minutes, but never saw what they were supposed to be chasing. The commodore turned his ships left into a column to pass about 5,000 yards from the burning *Jintsu*, firing starshells to light the area. With nothing better to do, at 1:35am the *O'Bannon* fired one torpedo at the derelict. Three minutes later the *Nicholas* fired three more. McInerney then turned his ships 90 degrees to port to put the enemy astern, ran out 3,000 yards, then turned 90 degrees to port again, putting the *Jintsu* on his port hand. At 1:44, the *Taylor* launched her last torpedo at another ship she saw just to the right of the light cruiser. By now, the *Mikazuki* had left, so it's not clear what the destroyer saw. In any event, McInerney's other ships fired more starshells to illuminate the area and pumped more 5-inch shells into the *Jintsu*'s hulk.[453] At 1:48, the wrecked light cruiser suffered a massive explosion in the forward part of the ship, an explosion the Japanese believed was caused by a torpedo, which suggests it was the *Taylor*'s torpedo. The spectacular blast tore her in two.[454] According to the Japanese, the *Jintsu* "achieved a heroic end, with the admiral, his staff, the commanding officer and all but a very few witnesses heroically killed."[455] The total of those heroically killed on the *Jintsu* was 482.[456] With the *Jintsu* torn asunder, she disappeared from radar. Captain McInerney ordered, "Cease firing. Unload all guns through the muzzle." With his four ships now in a column, he headed east.[457]

Meanwhile, the *Honolulu*'s radar was showing nothing except the burning derelict *Jintsu*. Admiral Ainsworth did some deduction. Coastwatchers had reported ten Japanese ships approaching. He had just sent Captain McInerney after four. After some complicated math, the admiral calculated he had sunk six Japanese ships. That wasn't enough. He wanted all of them. At 1:38 Ainsworth ordered *St Louis*, "Zero Zero Zero Corpen" – turn to course 000 degrees True, which is due north, and ordered *Honolulu* to follow her.[458]

Captain Ryan's destroyers were now thoroughly confused, more so because Ryan's *Ralph Talbot* had gotten separated from them. On board the *Gwin* was Commander John M. Higgins, commander of Destroyer Division 23. His *Gwin* now led a column of herself, *Woodworth*, and *Maury*, with *Buchanan* catching up from astern. Higgins asked Ryan for instructions. Ryan replied that *Ralph Talbot* was out of position and told Higgins to take charge until he could catch up. Higgins ordered the *Gwin*'s skipper Lieutenant Commander John B. Fellows to increase speed to 35 knots and parallel the cruisers, signaling his other destroyers to "follow me."[459] Admiral Karel Doorman's famous signal from the Battle of the Java Sea. This was becoming more and more like the Battle of the Java Sea. And not in a good way.

As if to confuse Captain Ryan's discombobulated destroyers further, at 1:42, Admiral Ainsworth ordered, "Six Turn," which was a 60-degree turn to port to course 300 degrees True, roughly northwest, making a steady 30 knots. Commander Higgins now found his ships on the port quarter of the cruisers. But he continued to push ahead with his speed advantage of 5 knots and gradually drew abreast of the larger ships. As he stood to the northwest, Ainsworth could see nothing on the radar scope where he estimated *Leander* should be and asked Radford for a report on the New Zealander. Radford replied, "*Leander* is able to make 10 knots and proceeding with me and I am screening." Ainsworth instructed Ryan to send one of his ships to assist Radford. Ryan passed the task to Higgins, and Higgins had to decide which ship to send. Since neither *Woodworth* nor *Buchanan* had SG radars, he decided to keep them with him and send *Maury*. At 1:50, Higgins ordered the *Maury*, "Stand by *Leander*."[460]

That meant a major shift of gears for the *Maury*, going from trying to overtake Admiral Ainsworth's two cruisers to poking around in the dark somewhere to port for the disabled cruiser. Skipper Commander Gelzer L. Sims asked, "Can you give me any idea where we can find the *Leander*?" to which Ryan came in with "Wait one moment." To expedite things, Sims started the *Maury* on a turn to port, passing astern of the *Buchanan*, and asked the combat information center, the centralized location where among other things the radar screens were watched, where the *Leander* was. It was a surprisingly difficult question:

> Our PPI was cluttered with pips. The enemy ship, which had turned on its searchlight, had been smothered with gunfire and probably hit by torpedoes. She was a flaming shambles but still returned a strong echo. The other enemy ships had disappeared from the PPI, and rain clutter blanked large segments of the scope. I guessed a group of pips at the edge of the PPI to the southwest might be McInerney's destroyers, but there were many dozens of pips nearer the center of the PPI. They could be ships or they could be sea return, reflected from high-speed wakes. The line-of-bearing formation, so useful for ship identification at the beginning of the battle, no longer existed. Here was I, in CIC with the fabulous SG radar in front of me, and I could only tell Captain Sims that I didn't know which pip was *Leander*, or even, for sure, which was flagship *Honolulu*![461]

Fortunately, after about two minutes, Captain Ryan provided the *Maury* with a bearing for the *Leander* of 240 degrees True – roughly southwest. Commander Sims saw a ship in that direction, but it wasn't disabled and was instead "going like hell." The *Maury* moved in closer, and Sims identified her not as the *Leander* but as Ryan's *Ralph Talbot*.[462]

Perhaps frustrated with the inability of anyone in Captain Ryan's group to find the *Leander*, Admiral Ainsworth radioed the *Jenkins* from Captain McInerney's group, "Assist *Leander*, who cannot steer."[463] This led to an exchange between Ryan and McInerney trying to figure out where the *Leander* was and who exactly was supposed to be standing by her.[464] In the midst of this borderline comical interlude in the midst of battle, Commander Sims decided to catch up to Ainsworth's cruisers. The *Maury* was now seven miles behind them.[465]

Meanwhile, after sailing to the northwest-by-west for 14 minutes, at 1:56 the *Honolulu*'s radar detected a column of four ships to the west northwest at a range of 20,000 yards. Admiral Ainsworth later called it "a confusing picture."[466] What were they? Captain McInerney's destroyers? The Flag Plot had lost both radar and radio contact with them. Nevertheless, "[t]he general belief in CIC and Flag Plot was that those ships were our van destroyers returning from their mission against the cripples."[467]

There was a lot of chatter on the "Talk Between Ships" voice radio channel. Too much. A lot of it coming from . . . whichever were the ships standing by the *Leander*. Communications and information, those two most critical commodities in any military operation, were absent. At 1:58, frustrated with the inability to determine where his ships were while using the overcrowded voice radio channel, Admiral Ainsworth barked at his destroyers, "You little boys get off this circuit awhile."[468] As they had been doing much of the night when the forward voice radio went on the fritz, the flagship *Honolulu* had the destroyer *O'Bannon* relay the admiral's messages, this time queries to Captain McInerney. They were able to determine that McInerney's radar showed no enemy contacts. Ainsworth's own plot showed that the unidentified ships had changed course and were now closing rapidly.[469] It looked like an attack? Was it?

Admiral Ainsworth was "practically certain that these were not McInerney's destroyers."[470] But he wanted to be definitely certain. He ordered the *Honolulu* and *St Louis* to fire starshells to illuminate the contacts, but not to open fire on them yet. The starshells burst and started falling, backlighting two of the ships in the process. They were "identified as two-stack destroyers similar in appearance to ours."[471] That didn't help much. Whatever they were, they seemed to be turning away from the Americans ... as if they had just launched ...

"Execute turn six," roared the admiral. It was 2:06am. And it was too late.

"Torpedo just passed us!" came a shout from the *Honolulu*'s bridge. Torpedoes were seen approaching on the port beam. Captain Robert W. Hayler kept her rudder in a full starboard turn. That didn't help the *St Louis*. The destroyer *Woodworth* reported seeing at 2:08 "a dull red flash accompanied briefly by a shower of sparks in the vicinity of her bow."[472] A Type 93 had lanced the cruiser at bulkhead 6 in her anchor windlass, so far forward that damage control admitted it was not clear if the torpedo had come from port or starboard.[473] Her speed was knocked down to 8 knots.[474]

Captain Hayler continued the *Honolulu*'s starboard turn, with three torpedoes passing ahead of her, one went under the stern, and two more missed the stern by about 100 yards. As the *Honolulu* finally settled on a course of 90 degrees True – due east – torpedoes were sighted coming from the starboard quarter. Hayler swung back to port to try to comb them. It was almost enough. One torpedo hit the starboard bow at about bulkhead 9 and bit off a chunk of the bow, but the concussion of the hit was "not great."[475] Another torpedo climbed up the ship's wake and struck the stern at the centerline, leaving a 2-foot-by-2-foot hole, but it did not explode, and once its propulsion exhausted it dropped off into the sea.[476]

While this was going on, another torpedo whacked Commander Higgins' destroyer *Gwin*, who had been ahead of the *Honolulu*. The Type 93 buried itself in the after engine room where it exploded in horrifically spectacular fashion, blowing the after deck house and the Number 4 5-inch mount overboard, and starting an intense fire that set off 40mm ammunition and fuel hoses that had been secured to the aft deck house, sending up a column of black smoke 300–400 feet into the air.[477]

The chaos did not conclude there. Right behind the *Gwin* was the *Woodworth*. Her skipper Commander Virgil F. Gordinier saw the *Gwin* get hit and turned slightly toward her before thinking better of it and turned to port to comb any other incoming torpedoes. When he thought all torpedoes had passed, he continued around in a 360-degree turn to start circling the *Gwin*.

Further back in Captain Ryan's discombobulated destroyer dance, the *Buchanan* took a wide turn around the cripples and ended up blinded inside a squall. When the *Buchanan* emerged from the squall, she sighted the *Maury*, who was screening the damaged *Honolulu*, ahead at short range moving from starboard to port. *Buchanan* skipper Lieutenant Commander Floyd B.T. Myhre ordered hard to starboard to avoid the *Maury*. He succeeded, only to find the *Woodworth* some 2,000 yards off the starboard bow on a reciprocal course. They would pass starboard-to-starboard, Myhre thought. The *Woodworth*'s Commander Gordinier disagreed – he thought they were on a collision course, with the *Buchanan* on his port bow. To avoid the collision he thought was coming, Gordinier had the *Woodworth* turned hard to port, which came across the *Buchanan*'s bow. Myhre ordered, "All engines back full" and "Right full rudder," causing his ship to skid to a stop. The *Woodworth*'s stern scraped against the *Buchanan*'s bow, tearing off her own port propeller guard, nicking her port propeller, and ripping off her port depth charge rack, dumping all the depth charges contained therein into the water. Though set on "safe," one of the depth charges detonated under the *Buchanan*'s bow, leaving her all shook up but causing no additional damage.[478] Captains Myhre and Gordinier later papered over the incompatibility of their descriptions of the accident in their after action reports by blaming it on the lack of SG radar.[479] Diplomacy.

All of that from a simple massed torpedo attack by Captain Shimai and his destroyers. Like Admiral Izaki, Shimai remembered that ancient Japanese credo: *when in doubt, launch torpedoes.* And he also remembered its corollary, little known in the West: *when in doubt, launch torpedoes again.* The Japanese were the only navy that could have that corollary because the Japanese were the only major navy that had reloads for their torpedo tubes, which was another nasty surprise for the Allies in the Pacific. During Shimai's tactical retreat, his ships had hidden in that convenient rain squall and reloaded their torpedo tubes in 18 minutes.[480] He had his destroyers turn around, and execute Hara Tameichi's famous hyperbola in the middle of which they emptied their tubes. Then they laid a smokescreen and skedaddled up toward the Shortlands, out of the reach of Admiral Ainsworth's ships. Yet another set of Parthian shots.

Captain Shimai's ambush might not have worked if Admiral Ainsworth had been informed only a few minutes earlier that the aft radar on his own *Honolulu* had identified the incoming ships as enemy. No uncertainty, no indecision. But that information didn't make it to the admiral in time. Everyone had assumed he already had it.[481] Now it was too late. The only response they could muster was at 2:13, when Captain Ryan's *Ralph Talbot* launched a half salvo at what her plot showed was the broadside of the Japanese destroyers. But a quick turn by the destroyers left the torpedoes in another hopeless stern chase.[482]

Realizing his cruisers were now vulnerable, especially to air attack, Admiral Ainsworth radioed, "Need small boys to come to [*Honolulu*'s] assistance."[483] Captain McInerney informed Captain Ryan of the order and asked him to relay it to the destroyers guarding the *Leander*. Then he brought the *Nicholas*, *O'Bannon*, and *Taylor* to join the flagship.[484]

This got the admiral concerned over who was standing by the *Leander*. He did not need an international incident of Americans abandoning Kiwis in a chaotic retreat. "Where is [*Leander*]? Who is standing by her and what speed can she make?"[485] This in turn brought out the earlier confusion over who was supposed to be with the *Leander*. Captain Ryan answered Admiral Ainsworth, "[*Maury*] and [*Radford*] are standing by [*Leander*]. Have not seen them for about an hour."

At which point the *Radford* chimed in, "[*Maury*] did not show up."

Commander Sims was not going to let that just sit there. "We are closing in on you[,]" he chimed in to the *Radford*.[486]

By this point, Admiral Ainsworth was wondering where all his destroyers were. He radioed Captain McInerney, "Check on your little boys."

The commodore was ready for that one, "My little boys pursued the enemy and sunk one ship."

The *Taylor*'s skipper Lieutenant Commander Benjamin Katz did issue one clarification. "*Gwin* went to the Happy Hunting Ground. I saw him."[487]

Not quite. The *Taylor*'s captain was premature. The *Woodworth* was even receiving signals from the *Gwin*. Admiral Ainsworth ordered one destroyer dispatched to look for her. Captain Ryan volunteered and, after getting some directions from the *Taylor*, took the *Ralph Talbot* to find her.

Captain Ryan located the *Gwin* and exchanged recognition signals with her at 4:10am. The destroyer was in deep distress. The *Gwin*'s main deck was awash due to a stern trim and her rudder was jammed hard to port, but her starboard engine was functional. The *Ralph Talbot* moored to the starboard side to try to counteract the jammed port rudder and began towing the *Gwin* at 5:25. The tow lasted 15 minutes until steering problems developed, compelling the *Ralph Talbot* to move to the port side while the *Maury*, who had just arrived, took station ahead.[488]

But it was a losing battle. The *Gwin* continued settling by the stern, and by 9:30 the forefoot was out of the water while the stern was under 10 feet of it. The *Maury* resorted to taking the crew off and Captain Ryan had the *Ralph Talbot* send one torpedo into the *Gwin*, taking only 15 seconds to send her to the Happy Hunting Ground.[489]

And with that, Admiral Ainsworth's force headed back to Tulagi in three separate groups. The *Leander* had started down The Slot with *Jenkins* and *Radford*.

The Japanese had managed two Parthian shots within one hour. The first, on orders from Admiral Izaki, hit the *Leander* badly. The second, ordered by Captain Shimai, damaged the *Honolulu*, *St Louis*, and *Gwin*, the last fatally. Twice in the same battle, twice within one hour. And indirectly damaged the *Woodworth* and *Buchanan*. On top of that, the Japanese transport destroyers had successfully landed Major Yamada's 1,200 troops at Ariel, completing their work at 3:40am and heading back to Shortland after a search in vain for survivors of the *Jintsu*.[490] While Admiral Ainsworth thought he had sunk six Japanese ships, in reality all he had done was sink the *Jintsu*.

Samuel Eliot Morison gave the performance of the Japanese the highest praise:

> Rear Admiral Izaki may be said to have lived up to the fine squadron traditions established by Tanaka. He had lost his flagship and his life, but had carried out his mission, sunk a destroyer and knocked out three cruisers – two for several months and one for the rest of the war.[491]

It was a major defeat for the Allies, the third in the last four engagements. And it followed the same pattern:

1. Japanese reinforcement run, supply run or both;
2. Allied cruisers come in to intercept;
3. Sometimes the Japanese land their troops and supplies, sometimes they don't;
4. The Allied ships put out an impressive amount of munitions in overconcentrating their gunfire on the biggest target that appears on radar – the *Takinami* at Tassafaronga; the *Niizuki* at Kula Gulf; and the *Jintsu* at Kolombangara – and sinking it;
5. Allied gunfire after sinking that first ship is inaccurate and no other enemy ships are sunk or even seriously damaged;
6. The Japanese launch torpedoes and flee the area, sometimes twice – the Parthian shots;
7. The Allies blunder into the torpedoes – the *Minneapolis*, *New Orleans*, *Pensacola*, and *Northampton* at Tassafaronga; the *Strong* the first night of Kula Gulf, the *Helena* the second night; the *Leander* first at Kolombangara, then the *Honolulu*, *St Louis*, and *Gwin*.[492]

Admiral Wright had produced Tassafaronga; Admiral Ainsworth had basically produced a second Tassafaronga. The only exception to this pattern was the engagement off Vila-Stanmore on March 6, when Admiral Merrill's cruisers ambushed and sank the Japanese destroyers *Murasame* and *Minegumo*.

While the Japanese could not afford to lose modern ships like the *Takinami* or especially the *Niizuki*, or flag officers like Akiyama Teruo and Izaki Shunji, for the US Navy trading multiple cruisers for extended periods of repair – or permanently in the case of the *Northampton* and *Helena* – was still a very expensive exchange, one that was not sustainable in the short term. And Admiral Nimitz was taking notice.[493]

Consequently, with all these cruisers out of action, the US Navy would have to oppose Japanese reinforcement efforts with only destroyers.

CHAPTER 7
QUAGMIRE

Whether South Pacific Command or 3rd Fleet, the Allied South Pacific organization was not good about responding to radio calls for help concerning survivors of sunken warships. This appalling deficiency was evinced by the tragic story of the survivors of the *Juneau*. Maybe the *Juneau* experience had taught them something. Maybe not, because another *Juneau* story was in the making up The Slot.

Some 200 survivors of the light cruiser *Helena* had been clustered around the still-floating bow around noon on July 6. That was when Lieutenant Nolan's Liberator spotted them. Nolan dropped down low so his crew could drop out all the aircraft's life vests and four packaged lifeboats. Nolan then radioed the sighting in and asked for Catalinas to be sent to pick up the survivors.[1]

Four inflatable lifeboats were hardly adequate for 200 men – it was the best a single PB4Y could do – and became even less adequate when one of the boats refused to inflate and instead sank. Three lifeboats for 200 men. Each boat could hold four. The most seriously wounded were placed on board the boats, while the ambulatory clustered around the boats, and everyone waited for rescue.[2]

It never came. For whatever reason, no Catalinas, no aircraft of any kind came for the survivors. No Allied aircraft, at least. Japanese Zeros showed up. The apprehension built among the men of the *Helena*. Watching them approach, Major Kelly recalled the Battle of the Bismarck Sea, and how the Japanese had strafed and killed parachuting airmen from a B-17, in response to which Allied aircraft strafed the Japanese survivors in rafts and in the water after sinking their transports. There was little Kelly and his fellow survivors could do but tread water and brace for the worst.

The Zeros flew over. The nearest pilot pulled back his canopy and looked at them, trying to determine who they were. The fighters circled and made a second pass. As they circled again, they fired a few short machine gun bursts. They came in very low, almost touching the water and ... the lead pilot smiled, waved, waggled his wings, and led the fighters away. The *Helena* survivors were grateful but bemused, wondering why the brutal

Japanese had not strafed them. The best guess was that the survivors were so coated with oil that the pilots could not tell if they were American or Japanese or what. It should be noted that they were in the area where not just the *Helena* but the *Niizuki* had sunk.[3]

Lieutenant Commander Chew organized the survivors and took charge. As much as he could, anyway. The group was completely at the mercy of the wind and the current, and in the Solomons, the prevailing wind, the bane of US Navy carrier operations during the Guadalcanal Campaign, was from the southeast. So the survivors, their oil slick, and their debris field, were blown to the northwest. That is, further up The Slot into Japanese-controlled waters. The passing Zeros were a reminder and a warning. If they didn't do something, they'd be blown all the way to Shortland. That would not be a good thing.

So, Lieutenant Commander Chew decided to get clear of the *Helena*'s bow, which finally sank toward evening, and make for Kolombangara. Two rafts tied together, wounded on board, the able men in the water holding on to the rafts, kicking and pushing to provide propulsion. Imagine that. Kicking and kicking for hour after endless hour in water topped with oil, especially, and debris.

It was exhausting. Lieutenant Commander Chew tried to rotate the people in the water, but all he could do was arrange for a 10-minute break every two hours. There could be no other breaks, not even for sleep. And the men were desperately tired. The night was miserable. But fall asleep in the water and you could drown. Some did, letting go of the raft and disappearing into the depths. Major Kelly nodded off twice. The second time he was awakened close to dawn by a mouthful of salt water, with the other survivors nowhere to be seen. One of the injured died aboard a raft.

After morning on June 7 arrived, it soon became clear that they were not going to make Kolombangara; their kicking would not overcome the viscosity of the oil in the water or the current. And they passed the island. Their best hope was the next island, Vella Lavella, which was visible and close to their path. It was occupied by the Japanese, but Lieutenant Commander Chew had heard the locals were friendly – and it was probably their last chance for landing before the Shortlands. They started kicking again. A crate of potatoes drifted their way, and they had something to eat. Major Kelly, having found a raft, rejoined the group, as did five others from the *Helena*'s Marine detachment after swimming for 30 hours in a supreme example of the toughness of US Marines.

But dusk on June 7 saw them still far away from Vella Lavella. It meant a second night in the water, and a murderous second night it was. Ten men disappeared into the darkness. Falling asleep, giving up, both. Others started hallucinating. The group became more scattered, ultimately breaking up into two groups.

Dawn on July 8 saw Vella Lavella only one mile away, but it was a mile too far. Discipline collapsed completely. The able-bodied men on the rafts refused to rotate with the men in the water. Lieutenant Commander Chew could not enforce his orders. That was it, and Chew knew it. A strong swimmer, at 7:00am, Chew, Lieutenant Commander Boles, and two others made the break for Vella Lavella. They were dead tired, hungry, thirsty, with stiffening muscles and burning skin. All four drifted apart and lost track of each other.

The strongest swimmer of the four was Lieutenant Commander Boles. And Boles seemed to have possessed the most field awareness remaining. He headed for a beach that looked good. Upon reaching it, he found a coconut in the sand, and cracked it open for a drink of coconut water and probably some meat. Then he crawled under a bush and went to sleep.

Lieutenant Commander Chew was well behind Lieutenant Commander Boles, and by 4:00pm had reached the end of his endurance. But he still possessed enough of his field awareness to see the canoe approaching with two Melanesian locals. They came alongside, and asked the obvious question:

"You American?"

"You betcha!" And they sort of rolled Chew into the canoe. Once they reached land, they explained that they would hide him. They asked if he could walk. Certainly, Chew replied – and immediately collapsed.

These were scenes repeated over a 10-mile stretch of coast, except for the collapsing, which was sporadic. Melanesians went out in canoes to fish men out of the water or tow rafts in. Some swimmers and rafts made it to the beaches, stumbling ashore as darkness began to close on the island. A few, like Major Kelly, barely made it to the trees before a flight of Japanese Vals roared over at about 500 feet.

Meanwhile, one of the locals, a scout for veteran coastwatcher Henry Josselyn, ran up to Toupalando, a tiny village tucked on a hill deep in the jungle of Vella Lavella. It was also the base of Josselyn, who had guided US Marines during the Tulagi landings. Josselyn was out at the moment, but the scout found his assistant, Sub-Lieutenant Robert Firth. The scout gasped "plenty Americans" coming in from the sea. He held up some dog tags as proof.

Firth wasn't going to just take his word for it, not because he didn't trust the scout, but you just didn't know what devilment the Japanese were capable of. Firth radioed Guadalcanal with the information on the dog tags. An hour later, Guadalcanal came back with the confirmation: the dog tags were from crewmen of the *Helena*, sunk on July 6.

Firth contacted Josselyn, who agreed that it appeared to be "something big." This meant all hands on deck. The survivors seemed to have congregated in two groups, one landing near Paraso Bay, on Vella Lavella's northeast coast; the other near Lambu Lambu, set in the middle of the east coast at almost its easternmost point. And both places with Japanese camps.

They had to get everyone off the beaches and away from the coasts. Josselyn sent a runner to find the local chief in the area, called Bamboo, and ask him to send out canoes to pick up any men still in the water, post sentries to watch for Japanese patrols, and help on food and housing. Bamboo and his people came through in a big way. Josselyn sent another runner to get word to another coastwatcher, Methodist minister Reverend

A.W.E. Silvester, one of the few men of the cloth who were also taking sides in this war; the Japanese 2nd Special Base Force might have taken an interest in him. Silvester would take charge of the *Helena* men near Lambu Lambu. A Melanesian known as Mickey did a fine job in organizing the survivors and leading them inland to a shanty owned by a Chinese trader named Sam Chung, who graciously offered it up to the arriving Americans. Those who couldn't walk, like Lieutenant Commander Chew, were carried on litters. That evening Reverend Silvester arrived. Now they had a whole village of *Helena* survivors. Chew started setting up the new village for defense, including a force of Marines, petty officers, and Melanesians under Major Kelly that earned the nickname "Kelly's Irregulars."

While Chew and his group were enjoying their first night on Kolombangara, about 12 miles away, Henry Josselyn was walking all night to get to the Paraso Bay area, arriving at dawn the next morning, July 9. Josselyn led these *Helena* survivors deep inland to another camp protected by trees. Now there were two villages of *Helena* survivors. To house, to feed, to clothe, to provide medical care to. But most importantly to hide. Deep in Japanese territory. Practically unarmed. And they had to stay that way until help arrived.

The local Melanesians put themselves and their extremely limited supply of food at the disposal of the men of the *Helena*. So did Josselyn and Silvester, the latter especially helpful with his mission's supply of medicine. Silvester helped organize foraging parties. They produced a grab bag of potatoes, tapioca, yams, pau pau, taro root and bananas, much of which was tossed in a giant pot with fish and a few pieces of Spam found on the beach. Two cooks from the *Helena* turned it into a watery stew that was occasionally purple. Sometimes pink, at other times white and perhaps most alarming, on some occasions, black. But it kept the men, who had had little or no food since they evacuated the *Helena*, alive.

Speaking of alive, they took one prisoner alive. A patrol of four Japanese came close to the camp. The Melanesian scouts killed three of them, but the fourth was captured. With not quite enough food to even feed themselves, the island crawling with Japanese, and the prisoner having seen way too much, Lieutenant Commander Chew decided it was too dangerous to have the prisoner around and had him executed. He wasn't proud of it, though Reverend Silvester agreed with the decision. Sticklers for the Geneva Convention would not agree. Then again, they have never been trapped behind enemy lines with barely enough food to stay alive.

The firefight was another sign of just how precarious a position they were in. Another came when a 20-man Japanese patrol approached the camp, only to turn around and run back to the beach after a Corsair came low on a strafing run and blew up their barge. Perhaps a victim of Corsairs was a Zero pilot brought in to Henry Josselyn's camp by Melanesian scouts. The decision was made to execute him, too, but no one could bring themselves to do so. It was a miracle for the pilot, because the men were tense and Josselyn was big on security, moving his camp every night.

Josselyn knew the clock was ticking. The Japanese were closing in. He had to get these men off the island. There were 50 with him, 104 with Lieutenant Commander Chew, and 11 more at a separate camp. He had been in contact with Guadalcanal, and had arranged a pickup on July 12, bringing the men to the beaches and everything – they were to be picked up in two groups, one at Lambu Lambu, the other at Paraso Bay – but the Battle of Kolombangara got in the way and they had to go back. The rescue was postponed to July 13, then July 14, and finally July 15. Actually, 2:00am on July 16.

The survivors of the *Helena* were led to the coast again, arriving just before dark. Lieutenant Commander Chew assigned Lieutenant Commander Boles, who had learned sailing as a kid in Marblehead, Massachusetts, to guide the rescue ships in. It would be a bit of a challenge. Boles was in a native canoe paddled by a single Melanesian who couldn't speak English and didn't understand any instructions. The moon provided some light, but that was more than canceled out by the shadows of the jungle that hid the coastline. Melanesians were standing in the water to mark navigational waypoints, though in the darkness, as historian Walter Lord put it, "[I]t was debatable whether they were more a help than a hazard."

He and the Melanesians must have done all right, because they got to The Slot and waited for the rescuers. And waited and waited and waited. They heard ships going by at high speed, and saw a few flares and explosions. That wasn't encouraging.

Now they were off the mouth of the river, bobbing in the waters of The Slot. Here they waited and waited for some sign of the rescue ships. Once they heard the whine of destroyer blowers and vessels going by at high speed then a few flares and explosions. Japanese ships were apparently on the prowl, sniffing trouble. Then it was dark again, and the wait continued.

Henry Josselyn also had the job of guiding in the rescue ships. At midnight he took off in a large canoe with three locals and Chief Warrant Officer William Dupay, one of the *Helena*'s gunners. They settled in about a mile off shore and waited and waited.

They spotted dark shapes approaching them. At 2:00am. Right on time. Josselyn took out a light and flashed a series of "Rs" – the recognition signal.

A signalman yelled, "Captain, there's a light."

The skipper went out to the wing of the bridge and saw a canoe approaching. Someone in the canoe shouted, "I am the gunner of the *Helena*!"

Just what he, Commander John D. Sweeney, was looking for. The commodore had his ship, the fast destroyer-transport *Dent*, and her sister ship *Waters* lower boats into the water to start shuttling the survivors of the *Helena* over.[4]

As Admiral Turner explained, "It means a lot to know that if the worst happens and you get blown off your ship and washed ashore somewhere, the Navy isn't going to forget you."

And the Navy did not forget. Both Admirals Turner and Ainsworth were determined to rescue all the *Helena*'s survivors – all 165. The problem was that rescuing 165 men trapped behind enemy lines is a huge job. A PBY Catalina – even all the PBY Catalinas they had – would not be enough to pick up all 165. Nor would PT boats. They needed ships. Specifically, those very useful, very versatile, very expendable converted four-piper transports.

They arranged a very unique rescue mission. Two fast destroyer-transports under Commander Sweeney, *Dent* and *Waters*, would race up The Slot, pick up all 165 *Helena* survivors, and race back. They would be escorted by Captain Ryan's destroyers *Taylor*, *Maury*, *Gridley*, and *Ellet*. Positioned further out to cover everybody would be Captain McInerney's destroyers *Nicholas*, *Radford*, *Jenkins*, and *O'Bannon*.[5] The *O'Bannon*, ordered not to take part in the original mission to rescue the *Helena*'s survivors, did not need to be ordered to join this second rescue mission. "Our job was tough," said *O'Bannon*'s skipper Lieutenant Commander MacDonald, "but the *O'Bannon* was willing to do anything to get those boys back."[6]

With apparently no opportunity for a conference, Captain McInerney, who was senior officer in this operation, sent Commander Sweeney over to Captain Ryan's command destroyer *Taylor* with a memorandum outlining McInerney's intentions for his covering force and offering suggestions for how Ryan could handle the transport force. McInerney made clear that these suggestions were not orders, but Ryan found the suggestions to be very good and incorporated all of them into his own plan. Ryan told McInerney as much in what might be called a "thank-you dispatch" while the ships were en route. It was an example of coordination and cooperation between sections of a divided force, another concept that had been painfully learned at Savo Island 11 months earlier.[7]

At noon on July 15, Captain Ryan's destroyers and Commander Sweeney's destroyer-transports left Guadalcanal. They were to proceed south of the New Georgia group and pass through the treacherous Gizo Strait, which no US Navy ship had yet transited – to the Vella Gulf, at which point they would continue moving north by hugging the Vella Lavella coast.[8]

Three hours after Captain Ryan's ships left Guadalcanal, Captain McInerney's destroyers left Tulagi on a course completely different from Ryan's, headed up The Slot at 25 knots for a point ten miles north of Vella Lavella.[9] Lieutenant Commander MacDonald addressed his crew: "Tonight we are going on a mission that might be called dangerous. I hope we will not see any action tonight. This is one night we are not looking for any trouble." But trouble found them: those ever-annoying Japanese seaplanes. "We had to maneuver nearly all night in a black sea," MacDonald recalled, "while Japanese airplanes overhead circled us like vultures, dropping bomb after bomb. They are great pyrotechnicians and their flares made us visible again and again." It was this exchange that Lieutenant Commander Boles had witnessed. MacDonald called it "the worst night we ever spent, because we couldn't do much about the attack." Despite those risks, his men "stayed through that night like steel."[10]

In a way, as the men knew, the Japanese snoopers harassing the *O'Bannon* and Commodore McInerney's other ships were a good thing. It meant they were not harassing the more important group of ships under Captain Ryan. When Ryan's transport group reached Paraso Bay at about 1:30am on July 16, the *Maury*, *Ellet*, and *Gridley* stood watch while the *Taylor* led the *Dent* and *Waters* poking their way toward the reef-lined coast.

With contact established, the canoe went alongside the *Dent* and Josselyn and Dupay went aboard. Josselyn served as a pilot for the boats going to and from the shore to pick up the survivors, but they were all brought aboard quickly. At 3:30am, Commander Sweeney signaled "finished."[11]

Commander Sweeney's destroyer transports moved off. Josselyn told him that these were less than half the survivors, the other half being at Lambu Lambu. Sweeney seems to have had some concerns about going to Lambu Lambu. He did not know the coast, and dawn was approaching. But Josselyn knew the coast very well and would act as guide. Sweeney informed Ryan's guarding destroyers what was happening, and he made his way to Lambu Lambu.[12]

Where Lieutenant Commander Boles was waiting very nervously. Around 4:00am, he saw ships coming into the cove, but from the wrong direction. He had been expecting them to come in from the south and Tulagi, and these were coming in from the north and Shortland. No one had told him the ships were stopping at Paraso Bay first. Which was OK, since no one had told Commander Sweeney the ships were stopping at Lambu Lambu.

Lieutenant Commander Boles flashed out the recognition signal, the number "50," the *Helena*'s hull number. Boles didn't see a response. That was not encouraging.

From somewhere in the dark came the growl of engines, gradually getting louder and louder. Then a voice with an English accent calling out: "Hello there!" It was the Englishman Henry Josselyn, guiding the first of the boats from the *Dent*. Lieutenant Commander Boles had missed the responsive recognition signal, a long red light, but the boat was there nonetheless. Boles was injured and struggled to board Josselyn's boat, but he did so, and guided the other boats in to pick up Lieutenant Commander Chew's village of survivors, along with a downed P-38 pilot, Lieutenant Eli Ciunguin, who had been helping Sub-Lieutenant Firth man the radio; and 16 Chinese, mainly Sam Chung and his relatives.

While the *Dent* and *Waters* were taking on the survivors at Lambu Lambu, a Japanese plane flew directly over them. Many a breath was held, but the plane appears to have missed the destroyer-transports altogether, as well as the covering destroyers further out. Hugging the coast of Vella Lavella had paid off.[13]

The Melanesian scouts were given profuse thanks and numerous presents. The transfer was completed at around 4:50am, and the US Navy ships sped away to safety. Captain McInerney would later call this "a most daring and skillful rescue operation, which, though fraught with danger, turned out to be a simple routine operation thanks to the skill with which it was executed."[14] Part of that skillful execution was on the part of the coastwatchers, Silvester and Josselyn, who now disappeared back into the jungle from whence they came. Vella Lavella was quiet again.

For now.

———————————⬤———————————

Quagmire. It conjures up images of brown mud. When you step in it, it sucks your foot down and keeps sucking your foot down until you commit the extra energy required to pull your foot out to pick it up again for the next step. Every. Single. Step. In the modern vernacular, in the United States and elsewhere, "quagmire" has been used to describe overseas military operations – any overseas military operation. Whether it's Vietnam, Grenada, Lebanon, Panama, Iraq, Somalia, the former Yugoslavia, Afghanistan, Iraq (again).

We can get in. Will we be able to get out? And, if so, how?

A quagmire was what Imperial Japan had found in China. The war in China was costing Japan the equivalent of $5 million per day. Japan had committed the bulk of the Imperial Army to China, beaten the forces of Chinese nationalist leader Chiang Kai-shek in battle time and again, and had taken every city, port, industrial, and agricultural area of value in China. Yet it could not inflict a final defeat and impose terms on the Chinese, because Chiang had retreated up the Yangtze River to Chungking (Chongqing), a very defensible position beyond the logistical reach of the Japanese, and would not surrender. For her part, Japan could not just … leave. That would be embarrassing, and a loss of "face." The major reason behind the Pacific War was to seize the resources necessary to bring the war in China to a close. Not necessarily a victory.

A quagmire is also what the Allies were finding on New Georgia. With the objective of taking the Japanese airfield at Munda Point, the Allies invaded New Georgia at five different locations, none of which seriously threatened Munda. The Allied invasion force was centered on the US Army's 43rd Infantry Division, a trained but inexperienced unit. That in and of itself is not necessarily a crippling blow. The 1st Marine Division was inexperienced before the invasion of Guadalcanal. The Marines gained that experience relatively quickly. But there was another element the planners of *Toenails* had not considered, but probably should have after the experiences at Guadalcanal. That element was the jungle.

Maybe the experience of the 1st Marine Division on Guadalcanal blinded the Allied planners to the issue of the jungle. When the Marines landed on Guadalcanal, it was presented with a completely alien jungle environment. Before their first major engagement with the Japanese in late August, the Marines had a few weeks to adjust to that environment and its sounds, smells, and activity and what it meant, which they did, albeit not exactly pleasantly. When the just-as-inexperienced US Army 43rd Infantry Division landed on New Georgia proper, just a few days after landing on Rendova, it was faced with combat almost immediately. Unlike the 1st Marine Division, it had to adjust to both the jungle and combat at the same time.

It was a tremendous strain to put on the men of the 43rd Infantry Division. Perhaps too much. Major General Oscar W. Griswold, who had succeeded General Patch as commander of the XIV Corps, of which the 43rd Infantry Division was a part, saw as much when he arrived at Zanana Beach on July 12. Griswold had arrived at the front line in expectation of setting up his XIV Corps headquarters to prepare to move on Vila as soon as Munda had fallen. But he quickly saw that Munda was not going to fall any time soon, at least not with the forces currently committed. As Griswold recorded in his diary, "Many wounded coming back. Losses heavy. Men look all [worn] out. Bewildered look of horror on many faces. Troops impress me as not having been mentally prepared or well trained. Impress me as not doing job very effectively. Enemy resistance however is very stiff."[15]

It was not complimentary of the work done by General Hester preparing the troops for the rigors of combat in the jungle. In fairness, Hester had taken steps to train and prepare the troops for the jungle, but those steps seem to have been ineffective. He had them practice attacking bunkers, but those bunkers were set up in fields in New Zealand, not in a jungle. The 43rd had been exposed to the jungle on Guadalcanal for a little bit, but not enough to acclimate it, in part because while the Guadalcanal jungle is similar to New Georgia, there were significant differences. New Georgia was like the "New Improved Guadalcanal: Twice the jungle! Twice the mountains! Twice the mud!" The jungle on New Georgia was much thicker than on Guadalcanal, so thick that the indigenous population stuck to the coasts. Admiral Halsey himself described it as "so thick that it isolated every man from the man beside him."[16] The soil had much more coral, which made digging entrenchments more difficult. To top it off, the 43rd was not defending a set piece of ground like Henderson Field, but was moving through those thick, muddy jungles. All these stresses added up.

Added up to, in the words of one historian, "[t]he [43rd] division bec[oming] a mental basket case, prominent in the annals of the Army's medical histories." Taking up most of that basket was a "mental disturbance" that was called "war neurosis." From 50 to 100 men each day were leaving the front line due to this war neurosis. Medic Captain Joseph Risman of the 169th Regiment described sufferers of war neurosis as men "who had not changed clothes or had two continuous hours of sleep [... A]ll had the same expression. Their hair was matted and muddy, and beards were ½ inch in length, eyes were sunk in, dark, and had a strained expression. Gait was plodding and methodical, no spring or bounce. When they stopped walking they fell in their tracks, until it was time to proceed again."[17] It sounds like another version of what is now called "combat stress reaction." But the XIV Corps surgeon, Colonel Franklin T. Hallam, thought that description was overbroad.

Colonel Hallam visited the front on July 14. From his observations, Hallam determined "war neurosis" was a "misnomer in most instances," because men suffering simply from physical exhaustion "were erroneously directed or gravitated through medical channels along with the true psychoneurotic and those suffering with a temporary mental disturbance currently termed 'war neurosis.'"[18]

He would detail it:

At least 50% of these individuals requiring medical attention or entering medical installations were the picture of utter exhaustion, face expressionless, knees sagging, body bent forward, arms slightly flexed and hanging loosely, hands with palms slightly cupped, marked coarse tremor of fingers ... feet dragging, and an over-all appearance of apathy and physical exhaustion. About 20% of the total group were highly excited, crying, wringing their hands, mumbling incoherently, an expression of utter fright or fear, trembling all over, startled at the least sound or unusual commotion, having the appearance of trying to escape impending disaster. Another 15% showed manifestations of the various types of true psychoneurotic complexes. The remaining 15% included the anxiety states, and those with various bizarre somatic disturbances. These were the individuals whose symptoms were of insidious onset, starting with insomnia, vague digestive symptoms, bad dreams, frequency of urination, irritability, diminished ability to concentrate, and a generally reduced efficiency in the performance of assigned duties.[19]

"[A] generally reduced efficiency in the performance of assigned duties" was an apt description of the American troops in the Munda sector of New Georgia so far. Of course, it's not necessarily the troops' fault. As Admiral Halsey put it, "[T]he 43rd was not only unblooded, but certain units were feebly led."[20] Leadership. Already, as seen earlier, one regimental and one battalion commander had been sacked. Training, as General Griswold mentioned, which included the ineffective camp security. There was also the matter of their numbers, as in, whether enough troops had been committed to the capture of New Georgia.

Just after he reached Zanana Beach, well before the 43rd Infantry Division's troops had even begun their offensive, General Hester had recognized the difficulty his troops were facing and requested reinforcements. Admiral Turner, commanding the New Georgia Occupation Force, General Harmon, now commanding all Army units in the South Pacific, and General Griswold met on July 5 and agreed to send most of the 37th Infantry Division. Two battalions of the 145th Infantry Regiment – the third battalion was with Colonel Liversedge – began moving to Rendova.

That set up a command conundrum. The overall New Georgia Occupation Force was under the command of Admiral Turner, even though the naval operations connected to the invasion were completed. The land operations were under the command of General Hester, who commanded the 43rd Division. If the 37th Division was also to be committed, that meant more than one division would be in combat, so they both should be commanded by a corps commander – specifically, General Griswold, commander of the XIV Corps, of which both the 43rd and the 37th were part.

Having a corps commander on hand suggested that maybe, with most of the operations now taking place on land, an army commander should be in charge of the New Georgia Occupation Force instead of a naval commander. To be sure, Admiral Turner, in charge of the operations of the invasion itself, which were his area of expertise, was supposed to hand over command to the army at some point. That point was left ... undefined in the planning for *Toenails*.

Perhaps the most famous instance of naval commanders leading land troops, as Turner was trying to do, was the Athenian invasion of Sicily, which ended with all of the aforementioned admirals and their troops either dead or enslaved in salt mines near Syracuse. General Vandegrift, General Patch, and the soldiers and Marines on Guadalcanal resented Turner's meddling in their operations. General Harmon, General Griswold, and General Hester did as well. Harmon later explained that Turner was "inclined more and more to take active control of land operations."[21]

That's not what he told Admiral Halsey at this time, however. Diplomatic and mindful of interservice relations, General Harmon radioed Halsey that he thought General Griswold's XIV Corps headquarters staff should go to New Georgia to operate under General Hester in preparation for taking over supply, administration, and planning, because Hester's staff was too small to perform those tasks. Admiral Halsey responded to General Harmon's message the next day, telling him to augment Hester's staff however he wished, but to wait on having General Griswold take over until they could discuss it further. That same day, however, Halsey ordered Admiral Turner to get with General Hester and begin planning the invasion of Kolombangara and its Vila-Stanmore base.

This wasn't a case of crossing the bridge before getting to it so much as crossing the bridge before it's even built. They could do nothing with Vila until they captured Munda. And it didn't look like they were going to capture Munda any time soon, which was accentuated when General Hester delayed the start of the 43rd Division's attack because the troops had not yet reached their starting points.

For his part, Admiral Turner showed his rarely if ever seen diplomatic side. Turner regretted having to disagree with General Harmon, Turner said, but General Hester, in his view, should keep command – which, of course, meant Turner keeping command. While General Griswold and his staff were excellent, Hester was conducting operations "in a manner much to be admired." Superseding him would hamper the operation "by inducing a severe blow to morale."

Given the war neurosis of many of the men of the 169th Regiment, how much worse morale could get was an open question. The delay in the 43rd Division's attack spurred General Harmon to fly to Nouméa to discuss the matter with Admiral Halsey personally. Harmon's presentation seems to have been effective, because on July 9 Halsey sent a message to Admiral Turner:

[O]n orders of COMSOPAC (Admiral Halsey), all ground forces, including naval units attached to the forces of occupation, will pass from the Command of CTF 31 (Admiral Turner) to the Corps Commander (General Griswold) who will assume the title of COMGEN New Georgia.[22]

That was what prompted General Griswold to head to New Georgia, where, he quickly saw, the troops were "not doing [the] job very effectively." There was some ray of hope on July 13. Colonel Reincke's 3rd Battalion of Colonel Holland's 169th Regiment finally managed to chisel some territory away from the Japanese in the form of a ridge that dominated the strategic intersection of the Munda and Lambeti trails, a ridge the men named "Reincke Ridge" after their commander and, probably, because of alliteration. At the same time, the 172nd Regiment managed to capture the Laiana beach against oddly passive opposition. That was the good news.

The bad news was that now, instead of one beachhead defended by two regiments, the Allies had two beachheads, each defended by one regiment, that were neither connected nor mutually supporting of each other. This was an example of the questionable work performed by General Hester and his staff. And General Griswold saw it firsthand. Late on July 13, Griswold reported, "Things are going badly. Forty Third Division about to fold up. My opinion is that they will never take Munda. Enemy resistance to date not great." They would need reinforcements from not only the 37th Infantry Division, but the 25th Infantry Division as well.[23]

A similar report was coming from Colonel Henry D. Linscott, Admiral Turner's acting chief of staff, whom Turner had sent to check on the situation. Admiral Turner was loath to give up command, but he was first and foremost a patriot, and he would not jeopardize the operation for his career. He radioed Admiral Halsey, "I regret that I am compelled to agree with Griswold. From my own private advices received today from my staff officers returning from Rendova. [...] Recommend immediate transfer of New Georgia Occupation Force to Griswold." At the same time, Rear Admiral Turner advised Major General Griswold: "I agree with you and have so told Halsey. Request you take command as soon as you are able to exercise it."[24]

So, there was not so much a change of command as there was a supersedence of command. That was very messy and would only get messier. For some time, Admiral King and Admiral Nimitz had wanted Admiral Turner to take charge of putting together a new amphibious force for the Central Pacific area, the US Navy's 5th Fleet, in preparation for advancing into the Japanese-held Marshall, Gilbert, and Caroline Islands. But the transfer had to be put on hold while *Toenails* was going. Now, the landing part of *Toenails* was over, so Turner was scheduled to turn over to Admiral Wilkinson on July 15 the South Pacific amphibious force that he had put together from scratch.

Except the New Georgia operation was not going well. Wilkinson, in Halsey's opinion, was "ill-fitted by experience and knowledge" for the job.[25] Admiral Turner sent a message to Admiral Halsey, "In fairness to Wilkinson and me, recommend that I retain command of this operation until affairs are again going smoothly." *Again* going smoothly? Had they ever gone smoothly in this operation? And yet the landing part was completed, and successfully so. Halsey denied the request: "Your relief by Wilkinson will be effected on 15 July as planned in view of [Admiral Nimitz'] requirement for your services."[26]

General Griswold would take over the New Georgia Occupation Force, with General Hester reverting to command of only the 43rd Infantry Division and answering to Griswold. Admiral Wilkinson would take over the amphibious force and answer to Griswold, who set up his corps headquarters in the mud of Rendova directing his two isolated, regimental-sized pockets. With one new regimental commander and one new battalion commander. It was a command mess that would take time to straighten out.

Naturally, this is the time General Sasaki launched his counteroffensive.

While the Allied men on the ground had been having a miserable time on New Georgia, the Allied brass had viewed the Japanese activities in defense of New Georgia as being unusually passive. The Japanese had harassed the Americans at night by creeping up to their camps and taunting them, provoking them to shoot among themselves, even occasionally launching very limited attacks. Japanese troops in their defensive bunkers had weathered Allied shooting, shelling, and bombing with little in the way of a response. This behavior was very different from what the Americans had seen on Guadalcanal, and the Allied brass worried that it was the proverbial calm before the storm.[27]

It was. Again, unlike most of the officers in the Imperial Japanese Army, General Sasaki was a careful, thoughtful commander not given to impulsive, reckless, or arrogant actions. He had spent these first few weeks of the Allied offensive trying to group his forces, but mostly just observing. He knew the Americans' ultimate objective would be the Munda airfield, but he was watching to see where their axes of advance developed. By July 8, Sasaki was comfortable that he had an accurate picture of the Americans' plan. The primary push, he believed, would come from the Barike River area northeast of the Munda perimeter. A secondary push was coming from the north. It was likely intended to prevent reinforcement of the Munda defenses, either by pinning down Japanese troops or even cutting off the line to Kolombangara. This effort had stalled for the time being. Sasaki had also figured out that this Allied force in the north had no artillery.[28]

General Sasaki's plan was for Colonel Tomonari's 13th Infantry Regiment in the form of its 1st and 3rd Battalions to assemble in the upper Barike, on the Allies' right flank, from where the Japanese would attack the flank and rear, drive to the Zanana beaches, and cut off and destroy the entire Allied invasion force. To prevent the Allied troops from repositioning themselves to meet this threat, elements of Colonel Hirata's 229th Regiment would attack the American front line facing the Munda perimeter, thus tying those units down. Not particularly creative, perhaps, but not a bad plan at all. It was certainly better than anything the Imperial Army had used on Guadalcanal, where mindless banzai charges into heavily prepared enemy defenses and diversionary attacks that were impossible to coordinate in the thick jungle were the norm. All told, it was the best plan that could be done under the circumstances. Because he would need reinforcements to bolster the Bairoko sector he was stripping for this operation, Sasaki had to get approval from Admiral Samejima and General Inamura to carry out the plan. Their approval came in short order.[29]

In much shorter order than the counterattack itself. General Sasaki hoped to make the attack around July 13 or so. For that to happen, Colonel Tomonari's 13th Regiment had to move quickly. But moving quickly through a jungle is almost an oxymoron for even the best units. The 13th had gotten to Bairoko all right on the night of July 9. But you know how those things are. On July 10, Tomonari's trek from Bairoko to Zieta ran into a trail block thrown up by the 3rd Battalion of the US Army's 148th Infantry Regiment. No matter how careful General Sasaki was, he could not overcome the extreme arrogance that was endemic in the Imperial Japanese Army. Tomonari and his men believed themselves an elite unit, and as such they should have no problem sweeping these impudent Americans aside. Moreover, while it had been at Rabaul, the 13th had been taught American tactics, based on the lessons the Japanese learned at Guadalcanal. They were the wrong lessons. Maybe 48 hours and 100 casualties later, Tomonari decided to bypass the trail block, and on July 12, he and his troops stumbled into Zieta, where the 6th Kure Special Naval Landing Force had set up a farm to prevent the starvation that had become Japan's number one enemy on Guadalcanal.[30]

The next day, General Sasaki's chief of staff, Lieutenant Colonel Kamiya Hoshiharu, met Colonel Tomonari with orders for the counterattack. "The 13th Regiment will immediately maneuver in the area of the upper reaches of the Barike River," they read, "seek out the flank and rear of the main body of the enemy who landed on the beach east of the Barike River, and attack, annihilating them on the coast."[31] To aid Tomonari and his troops, Sasaki attached a platoon of engineers, a radio squad, and a reserve artillery detachment to man any captured artillery. Sasaki had thought of everything. Except a map.[32]

Oh, well, details. They did have someone from the 229th to guide them, so presumably they were set. With about six companies, Colonel Tomonari and his troops left Zieta on July 14 bound for the upper Barike and disappeared into the jungle. In more ways than one. On July 16, having heard absolutely nothing from Tomonari despite the specially assigned radio squad, a concerned General Sasaki sent out a patrol to find the 13th Regiment. He heard nothing until about 4:00pm on July 17, and then only a radio message that "the regiment is attacking the opponents near Zanana." Then silence once more. To this day, no one is quite sure what these two battalions from the 13th Regiment actually did.[33]

This radio message occurred at about the same time that a party taking wounded from the US Army's 169th Infantry to the medical stations was ambushed on the Munda Trail near one of the Barike bridges. The attack was so fierce that a platoon from the 169th had to dig in and await relief.[34] The details of what happened after this are murky, It seems that as they waited in vain all night and the next day, the Americans collected numerous wounded inside their very makeshift perimeter, stuck in a tense standoff with the Japanese. The following night the Japanese swept the bivouac, killing most of the litter patients, two medics and one soldier. After that, the west bridge was christened "Butcher's Bridge."

Much of the Imperial Army's activities on New Georgia during this period remain vague or even completely unknown. This ambush is the latter, inasmuch as it is unknown who launched it. Though Japanese records do not indicate what the Japanese 13th Regiment was doing during this period, it has generally been assumed that it was the offending party here. The problem with that assumption is that Colonel Tomonari was trying to conceal his presence, having undertaken this slow, painstaking, and dangerous flank march to launch a surprise attack around the right flank and into the rear of the Americans. As far as he and his men knew, they had a good chance of surprising the Americans. Giving away your presence early to ambush a litter party seems like a massive waste of such an opportunity. But if not Tomonari's troops, then who?

In what might be an utterly bizarre coincidence that would throw another agent of chaos in a place and at a time with too many already, Major Hara Masao and some 160 survivors of the 1st Battalion, 229th Regiment, are believed to have blundered into the Barike area trying to make their way back to Japanese lines from Viru. They had been thrashing through the jungle for more than two weeks with no communication with anybody and thus no idea a major Japanese counterattack was ramping up in the same area they were apparently crossing. There is considerable belief that Hara's troops had infiltrated the American positions from the American rear and, quite possibly, were responsible for this ambush near the Barike bridges. Hara's men were probably involved in other shenanigans as well, but all that is known of their activities is that they did return to Japanese lines, such as they were, on July 18 or 19, at Munda or the 6th Kure Special Landing Force's farm near Zieta.[35]

Not so helpless were the 43rd Cavalry Reconnaissance Troop and the 1st Fiji Commandos, who had been patrolling the Americans' open right flank. They reported that some 200–300 "fresh-looking" Japanese infantry were heading into the rear of the division in the Zanana sector. A single platoon of the reconnaissance troop tried to set up an ambush, but was unable to position itself in time.[36]

The news of the Japanese move was received with extreme consternation in the 43rd's advance command post, which was on Zanana Beach and thus directly threatened. That same afternoon, apparently just after this report came in, General Hester received orders from General Griswold. "Hold your present position. Make no more attacks," the orders read. "Conduct active patrolling. Rest your tired troops. Make every effort to complete [the] road from Laiana. Prepare plans for a coordinated attack along your entire front using troops of the 37th Division. Target date about July 21. Until further orders, all troops in [the] Munda area [are] under your command."[37]

And would be commanded from that forward command post of maybe 125 troops that, along with some water points, supply dumps, the camps of a medical company and two companies of engineers, was in serious danger.[38] The Allied troops were, in the words of historian Eric Hammel:

> ... not in the best of defensive deployments. Security forces covering the right flank were inadequate, as evidenced by the necessity of employing a single reconnaissance platoon

against nearly 300 Japanese. The meandering, broken front of the 169th Infantry was particularly vulnerable to flank and rear assault. But this was nothing compared to the predicament of the rear-area troops. Aside from a few small combat units, such as the 43rd Reconnaissance Troop, there were virtually no organized armed units. The men behind the lines were mainly clerks, gunners, medical personnel, service and supply troops, communicators, technicians, and ordnancemen.[39]

These men were all that stood in the way of a potential catastrophe. These men were all that stood in the way of the Japanese capture of Zanana Beach, thus cutting off the troops on New Georgia from supplies or reinforcement, and possibly ending the New Georgia campaign in a major defeat for the Allies. While maintaining lines in jungle terrain is always difficult, that this campaign was hanging by the proverbial thread because the enemy had found an open flank and was moving against the invasion beach that, though essential to the campaign, was relatively poorly defended and not ready for combat of any kind is an indictment of how this campaign had been conducted so far.

But ready or not, here they came. That evening of July 17, Colonel Tomonari began his "more or less coordinated assault."[40] Closer to the less side of that equation. With the 13th Infantry's 1st Battalion on the left and 3rd Battalion on the right. Well, the 13th Infantry's 1st Battalion on the left, at any rate; where the 3rd Battalion was and what it was doing is anybody's guess. The 1st Battalion headed toward the 43rd Division's rear area, maybe a mile from the beach.[41]

The only combat units around Zanana were one platoon of the 43rd Cavalry Reconnaissance Troop and 70 men of the second section of the 1st Fiji Commandos, who had just landed at Zanana and were rushed up the road to the 43rd's defense perimeter, such as it was.[42] By themselves, they were nowhere near enough to stop the Japanese onslaught.

Though perhaps "onslaught" might be too strong a word. This was not the usual big human wave banzai charge assault, though there were still shouts of "Banzai!" However, the attack splintered into numerous smaller actions. Though this was in part due to the fact that there was no main defense line – there rarely is in a jungle – but instead scattered camps and outposts, this may have been by design as well. Colonel Tomonari divided his force into small groups operating semi-independently; there is some belief that he did so on orders from General Sasaki.[43] With the result that the fighting became confused.

For instance, as historian Ronnie Day pointed out, "One report said the Japanese briefly penetrated the perimeter and destroyed communications equipment; other accounts claimed the perimeter was not breached."[44] The US Army's history says the attacks against the engineer and medical camps "were easily beaten off," but that depends on what is meant by "easily."[45] The medics and doctors who "fought like demons" to protect their wounded patients might not agree with that description. In the medical bivouacs, the Japanese bayoneted helpless patients and anyone who tried to defend them.[46]

As brutal as these incidents were, none of them was the main event this night. That was reserved for the desperate combat around the 43rd's forward command post. It was 8:30pm when General Griswold received a message from General Hester: "Force estimated to be 75 to 200 Japs approaching command post on north flank about 800 yards distant."[47]

It was around this forward headquarters that the battle ultimately focused. General Hester was not at the headquarters, but General Wing, the assistant division commander; Lieutenant Colonel Elmer Watson, the division operations officer; and Brigadier General Harold Barker, the division artillery commander, were. As the Japanese moved to surround the post, some 100 troops – remnants of the 43rd Cavalry Reconnaissance, the 1st Fiji Commandos (known for being excellent jungle fighters), and basically anyone who could hold a rifle – took positions in hastily dug foxholes, stiffened by two machine guns scrounged from Jeeps.

However tenaciously the Americans and the Fijians fought – and they did fight tenaciously – this perimeter does not seem to have been enough to stop the Japanese. Before leaving China, all the battalion commanders of the 6th Kumamoto Division had been briefed by a staff officer from Imperial General Headquarters about American artillery fire, which he described as "tremendously fierce and concentrated."[48] Thus prepared, Colonel Tomonari's troops broke through the line and knew exactly where to go: for the thick communications cables lying on the ground linking the 43rd's command post with the divisional artillery back on the islands off the coast. But they were not prepared enough; Colonel Tomonari's troops were not given any cutting tools, so they had to use their swords and bayonets to hack away at those cables. Nevertheless, one by one the phone lines went dead. Ultimately, the Imperial Army troops reached the division switchboard and smashed that, too.[49]

But they missed one. It's always the one you miss. One phone line was laid over a different route than the others and did not pass through the division switchboard. This line went from General Barker to the Division Artillery Fire Direction Center on Baraulu Island. And Barker, acting as a high-ranking forward observer, used it.[50]

General Barker knew artillery, which was a good thing since he headed the 43rd Division's artillery. He, Captain James R. Ruhlin, and a private identified only as "F. Chamberlain" manned the fire control phone from a foxhole on the perimeter. Because it was impossible to rely on sight detection of targets, Captain Ruhlin expertly corrected the guns by sound alone – a method normally of dubious accuracy that is used only in desperate circumstances, which these were.[51]

The results were nothing short of impressive. After cutting down some trees that had blocked their line of fire, the 155mm howitzers of the 136th Field Artillery Battalion (technically part of the 37th Infantry Division but attached to the 43rd for the New Georgia landings) laid a box of fire around the command post. General Barker would say this artillery support "saved the personnel of the division [command post] from possible annihilation." He tactfully did not mention that one of the personnel saved was himself.[52] According to the US Marine history:

General Barker's 43d Division guns responded magnificently. With the general himself acting as one of the forward observers, the artillerymen planted heavy shells 100 to 500 yards from the edge of the camp. Barker called in box barrages at irregular intervals for the remainder of the night to prevent the enemy from organizing a banzai. Of the great number of rounds fired that night only one fell short, and that a single shot fired during registration.[53]

US Marine observer Colonel George McHenry described it as "beautiful." The Japanese description was less complimentary, calling it so devastating that they feared 1st Battalion would be destroyed.[54]

Nevertheless, the danger was ongoing. At 3:00am, the 43rd Division Artillery relayed a message to XIV Corps Headquarters that the 43rd Division forward command post had sent over that one remaining phone line: "Division [command post] under attack. Request one infantry battalion [on the] beach [at] daylight. Medics and engineers in grave danger."[55]

The grave danger went well beyond the 43rd's command post. While the US Marines were present at the command post in the form of observers like Colonel McHenry, who would be in combat soon enough, on Zanana Beach the US Marines were present in full battle array, or at least as close to full battle array as they could manage. Marine First Lieutenant John R. Wismer normally commanded the 3rd Platoon, Battery G, 9th Defense Battalion, but these days he was commanding elements of that and other units grouped into a "Special Weapons Group" of 52 men who were manning four 40mm antiaircraft guns and four .50cal. machine guns whose job was to give Zanana Beach antiaircraft and anti-boat defense.[56] But now he needed to give Zanana Beach anti-infantry defense as well. And Wismer had only a "handful of combat troops," not nearly enough to stop the Japanese.

The senior officer in the vicinity was Army Major Charles C. Cox, but he was actually a lawyer and a member of the Judge Advocate General's Department, meaning his brand of combat was not what was necessary right now, so he wisely let combat-trained Lieutenant Wismer run the show. Refusing to destroy his weapons to keep them out of Japanese hands should his ad hoc unit be overrun, Wismer decided to half-man his guns and had the rest of his men occupy a knoll. From the XIV Corps salvage dump nearby the Marines obtained two light .30cal. machine guns, which they made operable by cannibalizing other damaged weapons. Wismer set up the newly acquired machine guns to fire down – well, up, actually – the trail from the beach, and turned the machine guns over to Corporal Maier J. Rothschild and Private John J. Wantuck.[57]

According to Lieutenant Wismer:

At about nine o'clock at night approximately 100 Japanese came into the draw and started to set up mortars. We held our fire until the last moment before they started firing in order that the greatest concentration of enemy troops would be present. Upon opening fire, we drove back the Japanese into the jungle. They regrouped and made a banzai charge. The forward positions were overrun and individually we made our way back to the gun positions on the beach, where we prepared to defend against the next charge. To our surprise, it did not materialize.[58]

Elsewhere, on the Japanese side, attempts at a coordinated operation in the jungle, as usual, had failed, as Colonel Hirata's 229th Regiment launched its attacks to tie down possible reinforcements at nowhere near the time of Colonel Tomonari's attack. The 2nd Battalion under Major Sato Giichi, at the southern end of the Japanese line, launched its attack against Colonel Ross' 172nd Regiment at the beach. When we last left Ross and his men, they had just captured the Laiana Beach and were thus close to opening a seaborne supply line from Rendova and the barrier islands. Nevertheless, Ross and his men still had some serious problems, the biggest of which was they were largely cut off from their neighboring 169th Infantry to the northeast because Japanese troops had managed to slip into the gap.

Those problems multiplied at the rather odd time of 4:30pm, just before sunset, when Major Sato's troops attacked the Laiana Beach positions of the 3rd Battalion, 103rd Infantry Regiment, a battalion which had been sent forward and attached to the 172nd Regiment as a reinforcement. The Japanese attack, which seems to have been rather perfunctory, was beaten back in about an hour, but not before Colonel Ross got a call from the 43rd Division's forward command post saying it was under attack and needed reinforcements. Ross replied that he was under attack himself and had no help to send, which was the purpose of Sato's effort. Believing his lines were too thin, Ross ordered his troops to firm up their lines, even if they had to fall back, in preparation for another Japanese attack. But no attack came.[59]

While Major Sato's 2nd Battalion of the 229th Regiment attacked too early, Major Kojima's 3rd Battalion of the 229th attacked too late and under a set of self-defeating circumstances. In order to begin the offensive, the 3rd had to regroup in a staging area behind the front line. To move to that staging area, Kojima's troops had to pull back from their fortified positions on a hill facing the Americans. The US Army's 1st Battalion, 169th Infantry Regiment, under Major Joseph E. Zimmer, quickly took the hill, with all of its formerly Japanese defenses and more than a few Japanese weapons. A patrol from the 229th investigating noise heard from the hill blundered into the new American positions. The subsequent skirmish drew Japanese artillery fire onto the hill, killing 14, including US Army 2nd Lieutenant John R. Kelley, in whose honor the hill was named.[60] Kojima's assignment in this Japanese offensive would be to retake the hill he had just abandoned in order to take part in this offensive. Kojima Bunzo had to be just thrilled. It made little sense to abandon fortified positions on a strategic position like a hill in order to regroup for an attack to retake that same hill. Yet, here we are.

At 15 minutes past midnight on July 18 – well after Colonel Tomonari's troops had begun their attack – Japanese machine guns began raking the hill with covering fire for

Major Kojima's infantry trying to scale the hill's western slope.[61] Though the defending Americans had outrun their supply lines in taking the hill, they had a cornucopia of captured Japanese equipment to make up for it, including a large cache of Japanese ammunition and grenades and two Japanese machine guns. With help from mortars from the 3rd Battalion on Reincke Ridge, the American defense held. The Japanese troops went streaming back down the hill. Major Kojima pulled the survivors together and berated them for a lack of heart. And the Japanese troops went back up, this time on the north slope, this time with perhaps less enthusiasm. They were sent streaming back down the hill, where, again, a very irritated Kojima awaited them.[62]

Again, they went back up the hill, this time with definitely less enthusiasm. But this time was different. They had found a natural "dead zone" in a hollow close to the American line where the American machine guns could not depress enough to hit them. The Japanese troops crawled into this hollow and started tossing grenades up into the American entrenchments. It's generally a bad idea to toss a grenade up at something, but it went well for a while. Until the mortars from Reincke Ridge found the range to hit the Japanese packed into this little gully and turned what had been a sleepy hollow into a slaughter hollow. Down the Japanese troops streamed again, and no amount of berating from Major Kojima could convince them to go back.[63]

The back of the Japanese attack, their best chance for driving the Allies away from Munda and maybe off New Georgia, had been broken, achieving approximately none of its objectives. The last diehards of Colonel Tomonari's troops pulled back at around 4:00am as dawn approached.[64]

The morning light revealed the carnage around the US Army positions. Around Kelley Hill, Major Zimmer's men counted 102 Japanese corpses.[65] Around the 43rd Division's forward command post, maybe 75 Japanese corpses were counted; among them were two who, before they were cut down by machine gunfire, had gotten within 10 yards of the foxhole where General Barker and Captain Ruhlin were calling down the offshore artillery that had saved their lives. Captain Ruhlin was awarded the Legion of Merit for exceptionally meritorious conduct during this attack.[66]

The dawn also revealed the reason why a second charge against the Zanana Beach positions had not taken place. Lieutenant Wismer led a patrol back to the hill where Corporal Rothschild and Private Wantuck had been cut off with their machine guns. Wismer found their position was surrounded by Japanese – more than 100 of them, all dead. Wantuck's body was found beside his gun, its magazines empty. A slightly wounded Rothschild was found hiding under some brush in a nearby gully.[67]

As the US Marine history opined, "These two men alone may well have saved Zanana Beach for the XIV Corps."[68] They may very well have saved New Georgia for the Allies. General Hester recommended both for the Medal of Honor.[69]

The most dangerous phase of the land campaign on New Georgia was over. What General Sasaki thought of this defeat is not recorded, but he immediately ordered Colonel Tomonari to keep his troops in the area and to prepare for another attack on the American northern flank. Indeed, Tomonari's men did stay in the area and seem to have taken over for Major Hara's troops in harassing the Barike bridge zone, where medical litter parties had dug in to protect themselves. Again, what happened in this area remains unclear, but what is known is the Japanese, often drunk on whiskey looted from the 43rd's supply dumps, killed most of the litter patients along with two medics and one soldier. As a result, the west bridge over the Barike was christened "Butcher's Bridge."[70] What the Japanese troops themselves thought, however, was indeed recorded: "13th Infantry Regiment members realized in the past several days that things were really different from what they were in China."[71] It was a lesson the Imperial Japanese Army had learned the hard way for the past 11 months.

General Griswold ordered a battery of artillerymen and a battalion of infantry – the 1st Battalion of the 148th Infantry Regiment was later chosen – to move to Zanana at dawn.[72]

After all, the Americans had to prepare to launch an offensive of their own.

When we last saw that master of hyperbola and hyperbole, Hara Tameichi, he was trying to coax his destroyer *Amatsukaze*, with her rudder jammed and her main battery disabled in the Friday the 13th Action, back to Truk for emergency repairs. It was considered a miracle that he was able to bring the ship in, and Hara entertained a constant stream of visitors to show off her damage. That constant stream of visitors, who included Combined Fleet staff officers, never asked Hara for his opinion or recommendations. Hara found this lack of curiosity, especially official curiosity, disconcerting.[73] After a week, the *Amatsukaze* was seaworthy enough to sail back to Japan, where she arrived on December 1, 1943. With the destroyer in the drydock, Hara Tameichi was relieved as her skipper. In early March 1943, Hara was given command of not one destroyer but four of them.[74] In US Navy terms, this made Hara a commodore, an officer who commanded more than one ship but was not of flag rank. It was common for destroyer division commanders.

Commodore Hara was not entirely pleased with his new assignment, however. His new command was Destroyer Division 27, which had issues. The 27th consisted of the *Shigure*, *Shiratsuyu*, *Ariake*, and *Yugure*, whom Hara described as "four old 1,700-ton destroyers whose best speed was 30 knots. Their crews, strictly second class, were the object of derision to men of other ships."[75] When he went to his command ship, the destroyer *Shigure*, Hara thought her crew "looked like an ill-disciplined bunch of landlubbers."[76] The *Shigure* herself was not much better. Hara found her "quite decrepit," specifically, "old, sadly in need of maintenance, and, worst of all, she could do no better than 33 knots."[77] But Hara was confident he could whip the crew of the *Shigure* into shape.

The *Shigure* headed for the South Pacific through Truk, where Captain Hara stopped to report to Admiral Kondo, commander of the 2nd Fleet, aboard his flagship *Atago*. Kondo had earned a reputation for being a dapper gentleman, but Hara was shocked by his "haggard appearance." Kondo's voice was even worse: "hoarse and low and he spoke slowly as if with great effort." The admiral's words were not exactly out of Leonidas: "Hara, you have all my sympathy in your new assignment. It is a tough one. I can only say, take care of yourself. Use every possible caution."[78] Then Admiral Kondo explained how Captain Hara's new gig came with a caveat: "Although you are a division commander, we are so short of ships that three of yours are being used by other commanders. It may be months before you have your full division under your command."[79]

It meant that, for now at least, Captain Hara currently commanded a division of destroyers that had only one destroyer, the *Shigure*. But driven by his own South Pacific experiences Hara spent the next few months rigorously training the crew of the *Shigure*.

It was on July 20 that Captain Hara finally got orders formally placing Destroyer Division 27 in the 2nd Destroyer Flotilla of the 2nd Fleet and sending the *Shigure* toward the front. To Rabaul, specifically, from where his destroyers *Yugure* and *Ariake* were operating. After some four months of intensive training, the crew was actually excited to be going to the front, especially where their division-mate *Yugure* had just taken part in the victory off Kolombangara.[80]

That victory was good for morale in Admiral Samejima's 8th Fleet, because elsewhere the pattern of nicks and cuts had been continuing. On July 15, the light cruiser *Nagara*, having just escorted carrier *Junyo* on an aircraft ferrying mission, was attempting to dock at Kavieng shortly before 4:00pm when she struck a mine, laid either by Royal Australian Air Force PBY Catalinas in a night attack or the US submarine *Silversides*, who laid 24 mines off Kavieng more than a month earlier on June 4. The mine slightly damaged the *Nagara's* bottom under the stern, but she was able to continue operations.[81]

Of course, nicks and cuts work both ways. Dawn of July 16 saw the US Coast Guard cutter-turned-seaplane tender USS *Chincoteague* hanging out alone in Saboe Bay of Vanikoro Island in the Santa Cruz group way at the other end of the South Pacific theater. Japanese scout planes found the *Chincoteague* on July 14 and again on July 15, and decided this state of affairs was highly objectionable.[82]

The *Chincoteague* was given a taste of what the seaplane tenders *William B. Preston* and *Langley* had experienced during the Java Sea Campaign: all alone under Japanese air attack with no help available. At 7:17am on July 16, five Japanese bombers (from which unit is unknown) attacked the *Chincoteague* from 8,000 feet, but all their bombs landed in the jungle nearby. At 11:10am it was nine bombers, who arrogantly made several practice runs on *Chincoteague*, as they had done with the *Langley*. After almost a half hour of this, the aircraft finally released their bombs, earning misses astern and on the port quarter. Then the planes left and the *Chincoteague* went back to her duties of preparing PBY Catalinas for a night bombing mission. That bombing mission took place without a hitch and the last of the Catalinas landed at 7:25am on July 17.

At which time the *Chincoteague* was straddled by towering splashes from a stick of Japanese bombs. Five "twin-engined bombers" – evidently Mitsubishi G4M "Betty" land attack planes whose unit is unknown – had followed the Catalinas back to their base and proceeded with a bombing run. All the bombs missed, and the *Chincoteague* got under way for the open sea. The Bettys made a second run, which was also ineffective. No matter; the Bettys made a third attack, and got two misses about 50 feet off the *Chincoteague's* starboard side, perforating the hull and causing minor flooding.

By this time, the *Chincoteague* had reached the open sea. So did four Japanese bombers, who attacked at 8:05, but all the bombs missed. The Japanese planes headed back to their base and the *Chincoteague* headed back to her bay to service her seaplanes. By 10:20am, her duties were completed and the *Chincoteague* left the bay once more. But an hour later, the Japanese returned and made an unsuccessful bombing run at 11:45. Five minutes later came another bombing run, and this one would hurt.

The *Chincoteague* was hit by a 140lb Type 99, No. 6 general purpose bomb that passed through three decks to detonate in the after engine room just forward of and between the two diesel main engines. Though the outer hull had not been pierced, the engine room was completely flooded by an 8-inch suction line that usually supplied cooling water to the engines. The *Chincoteague* staggered onwards at 10 knots using her forward engines, but she started settling by the stern and a starboard list developed from poorly plugged holes caused by the earlier near misses. Those holes had created a free-surface effect on the partially flooded second deck, and the *Chincoteague* began to roll dangerously.

Curiously, with all the commotion and available targets around strategically important New Georgia, the Japanese seemed determined to bury this one little seaplane tender alone in her corner of the South Pacific. At 2:20pm came yet another attack, this by three bombers. They got no hits, but they might as well have. One bomb detonated about 15 feet from the port side, denting a large area of the hull, though not penetrating it. The explosion sent up a towering column of water that crashed down on the main deck. The concussion broke electrical equipment and gauges in the forward engine room – and stopped the forward engines.

Now the *Chincoteague* was flooding, listing, and dead in the water with no power. But dead in the water is not dead. A half hour later came yet another attack, this by a single aircraft. All of the plane's bombs missed by 200 yards. At about 6:00pm came yet one more attack – the eleventh, by the US Navy's determination – but it was driven off by fighter cover that had showed up in the interim. The Japanese finally called it a day.

The *Chincoteague* wished she could call it a day, but she could not. With no power, her crew had to use bucket brigades and gasoline hand billy pumps to try to keep the flooding at bay. But it was not enough. Then someone managed to get the forward engines started again, returning power to the ship's big pumps. At 11:50pm, the *Chincoteague* got under way again, headed for Espiritu Santo.

By that time, the converted destroyer-seaplane tender *Thornton* had arrived on the scene to render assistance. She transferred three hand billy pumps and one electric submersible pump to the *Chincoteague* and stayed with the stricken seaplane tender.[83] This proved prescient. A little after 2:30am, the Number 2 forward engine began to overheat.

Efforts to investigate the problem backfired – literally – when the engine began to speed up out of control. Shutting the engine down had no effect, and the engine raced to a dangerously high speed, starting a fire. The Number 1 engine had to be shut down and the engine room abandoned. With the *Chincoteague* now without power once again, the *Thornton* came alongside to provide some power and firefighting facilities, but after three hours of dumping the entire supply of firefighting foam into the engine room, the fire continued to smolder.

The *Thornton* started towing the *Chincoteague* and, except for a two-hour break for investigation of a sonar contact, continued doing so until 12:17pm, when the flooding had become so bad that a tow was dangerous for both ships. Orders to lighten the *Chincoteague* were passed, and torpedoes, heavy machinery, winches, and other gear on the starboard side were jettisoned. Nevertheless, the *Chincoteague* reported that the fire had flared back up and was out of control, the flooding was increasing again, and she "was losing [her] fight to stay afloat."[84]

The *Thornton* pulled up to the *Chincoteague* again to provide power to the electric submersible pumps. A seaplane from Espiritu Santo set down at 1:06pm bearing gifts: four electric submersible pumps and two hand-billy pumps.[85] Later that afternoon the destroyer *Jenkins* showed up, with an aerial battle between three Japanese bombers and four US Marine Corsairs taking place above her. At 6:20pm the destroyer-minesweeper *Trever* joined the group.[86] It was a dangerous situation. The *Chincoteague* was dead in the water, the *Trevor* was stopped alongside to provide power; they would be nice targets for a Japanese submarine. The *Jenkins* and *Trever* were badly needed to provide some semblance of an antisubmarine screen, which they did.[87]

The wind increased, the *Chincoteague* started rolling again, battering the topside of the *Thornton*. Nevertheless, the brave *Thornton* stayed alongside throughout the night. The pumps appear to have been used first to drain the second deck and end the dangerous free surface effect there. By midnight on July 18, the flooding and fire were reportedly under control. The *Thornton* took wounded from the *Chincoteague* for treatment and at 10:21am was compelled by heavy seas to pull away from the *Chincoteague* and join the antisubmarine screen with the *Jenkins* and *Trever*. By that time, the tug *Sonoma* was in sight. She passed over even more pumping equipment and at 12:30pm took the *Chincoteague* in tow.[88] They arrived at Espiritu Santo at 8:25am on July 21. The *Chincoteague* was in bad shape, but she was alive and she would fight again.

This was a description only partially applicable to the Japanese destroyer *Hatsuyuki*. This survivor of the Battle of Kula Gulf had had her slight damage repaired at Rabaul and was sent out again on July 16 as the *Chincoteague* drama was just starting to run troops to the Shortlands. The next day, while the aerial battering of the *Chincoteague* was continuing, the *Hatsuyuki* was docked at the pier at Kahili unloading her passengers when AirSols showed up. Taking off just before 9:30am were 36 US Navy and Marine Dauntlesses (18 each from Bombing 11 and Marine Scout Bombing 132) and 35 Navy Avengers (from Torpedo 11 and 21), escorted by Marine Corsairs (from four squadrons including 16 from

Marine Fighting 122, several from Marine Fighting 211, 15 from Marine Fighting 213, and eight from Marine Fighting 221). They were joined by seven 13th Bomber Command US Army Air Force Liberators (at least one of which was from the 370th Bombardment Squadron, 307th Bombardment Group); and ten Army Air Force Lightnings of the 339th Fighter Squadron, as well as Army Air Force Warhawks; eight Kittyhawks from the Royal New Zealand Air Force's No. 14 Squadron; and Army Air Force Airacobras. This conglomerate of an air strike, totaling 81 bombers and 114 fighters overall – showed up over the Shortlands.[89]

Showing up at various points to meet them were 18 Zeros from the 204 Air Group; three from the 251 Air Group; eight from the *Ryuho*; and 19 from the *Junyo* who just happened to be flying in from Rabaul. What followed was an airborne brawl over Buin. But no matter how many fighters you send up, you do not want to be tied up at a pier during an air attack, like the *Hatsuyuki* was. One bomb (it's unclear from whom) exploding in her after magazine later, the *Hatsuyuki* was no longer docked at the pier, but was sunk in shallow water. The explosion left 120 dead, including 38 passengers, and 36 wounded; skipper Lieutenant Commander Sugihara Yoshiro was among the survivors, and went on to command the destroyer *Samidare*. The old destroyer *Yunagi* suffered "medium" damage to her hull and armament from a near miss. American aviators claimed a total of 52 Japanese aircraft shot down; the actual number was 12, including veteran Lieutenant (jg) Fujimaki Hisa-aki, Chief Petty Officer Moriyama Kenji, and Petty Officers 1st Class Kojima Kiyoshi and Takezawa Hideya from the *Junyo*; Chief Petty Officer Hiramoto Masaharu and Petty Officer 2nd Class Nakazono Yoshio from the *Ryuho*; and Lieutenant (jg) Koshida Kisaku from the 204 Air Group. Japanese aviators claimed 22; the actual number was five (including the SBD of Marine Scout Bombing 132's Lieutenant (jg) Edward Henry Hughes; the F4U of Marine Fighting 213's Lieutenant Foy Ray Garrison; and the P-38s of Lieutenant James W. Hoyle and 2nd Lieutenant Benjamin H. King, who was rescued. Considering the large number of AirSols aircraft committed to the attack, the return of one destroyer sunk and one damaged out of 23 ships present had to be very disappointing.[90]

But if the Allies didn't like that result, they would like the next day's result even less. The largest escort of the war so far (134 fighters, including pilots from Fighting 21, 26, 27, and 28; Marine Fighting 122 and 213; and the 70th Fighter Squadron) joined 36 Dauntlesses (including 18 from Marine Scout Bombing 132); 35 Avengers from Torpedo 11 and ... "Composite" Squadron 26, and 21 Liberators (from the 370th and 424th Bombardment Squadrons of the 307th Bombardment Group) in another attack on the Shortlands area. The Liberators mostly focused on the Buin airfield while the SBDs and TBFs hit shipping in the anchorage. They were met by 18 Zeros from the 204 Air Group; eight from the *Ryuho*; and 11 from the *Junyo*. The Japanese reportedly operated in two groups making quick, long-range passes that were described as "unsuccessful." Not that unsuccessful. AirSols losses were heavy: six Wildcats (including Fighting 26's Lieutenant (jg) James H. Waring and Ensign John Pierson; and Fighting

27's Lieutenant John S. Dalton and Ensigns John R. Landis, Jr. and James M. Lewis); three Corsairs (including Marine Fighting 121's Lieutenant (jg) William C. Rhodes; Marine Fighting 213's Lieutenant Charles C. Winnia; and Marine Fighting 122's Lieutenant Ernest A. Powell, who disappeared just three days after achieving ace status); and the Avenger of Composite 26's Ensign Joe David Mitchell. Only one fighter pilot, Lieutenant S.O. Hall of Marine Fighting 213, was rescued; ultimately, so was the crew of Mitchell's TBF. The return was: three Zeros, damage to the airfield and light damage to the destroyer *Mochizuki*.[91]

The Japanese gave little good news to the Allies in the Pacific on July 18. The submarine *Ro-106* under new skipper Lieutenant Nakamura Motoo was hanging around off Rendova seeing what trouble she could cause. Nakamura caused that trouble in the form of a torpedo into the eight-month-old *LST-342*. The tank landing ship was blown in two, with the stern sinking immediately and the bow remaining afloat. The bow was eventually towed to Purvis Bay, where she was beached, stripped of any usable equipment, and abandoned. The bow remains beached there to this day.[92]

That July 18 had been an unhappy one for the Allies. The next few days would be unhappy for the Japanese. It started out encouragingly enough, with another morale boost, albeit a small one, this from the imminent arrival of the *Shigure*. The feeling was mutual, mostly. There was a feeling of anticipation aboard the *Shigure* when she arrived in Simpson Harbor on July 23. Captain Hara reported to the headquarters and was promptly handed a report concerning his destroyer *Yugure*.[93]

The *Yugure* had been part of what was called the "Night Battle Force" on the night of July 19–20. For this mission, a transport force consisting of the destroyers *Mikazuki*, *Minazuki*, and *Matsukaze* under Captain Orita Tsuneo, the commodore of Destroyer Division 30, was to deliver a small reinforcement to Ariel, a barge base on the southwest coast of Kolombangara. This reinforcement had an unusually large escort. There was the "Main Body" with the heavy cruisers *Kumano*, *Suzuya*, and *Chokai* under Admiral Nishimura, commander of the 7th Cruiser Division and this expedition. Also taking part as escort was the 3rd Destroyer Flotilla, with the light cruiser *Sendai* and destroyers *Yukikaze*, *Hamakaze*, *Kiyonami*, and *Yugure* under Baron Ijuin Matsuji, the former skipper of Admiral Kondo's flagship *Atago* and now in the process of being promoted to rear admiral.[94]

If this force seems light on the reinforcement and heavy on the escort, that's because it was. The reinforcement was only part of the mission and not the main part. Allied forces centered on light cruisers had recently challenged Japanese reinforcement efforts like this, which resulted in the engagements at Kula Gulf and Kolombangara. It was thought – hoped, really – that the Allies would show up to contest this reinforcement as well. Because if they did, Admiral Nishimura would have three heavy cruisers to more than match the three Allied light cruisers and an entire destroyer flotilla to handle everything else.

The Japanese got part of their wish; the Allies did show up. Admiral Nishimura's force apparently repelled without damage an air attack of an indeterminate nature at a little after 9:00pm. It convinced Nishimura that his reinforcement would face opposition, just as he wanted. But no enemy surface forces were found. The transport destroyers were ordered to move in and deliver their men and materiel to Ariel as planned. Then a flare appeared over the transport destroyers. That had to mean combat was imminent, Nishimura believed, and he ordered the Night Battle Force to prepare for gun and torpedo action. But, again, no enemy ships were found. Disappointed, Nishimura had his ships turn around and head back toward Shortland to get out of range of the Lunga airfield by daylight.[95]

Daylight wasn't the issue, however. That flare was. And this is where incomplete and contradictory records start to muddy the waters of what actually happened. The flare was apparently dropped by a "Black Cat" PBY, who reported Nishimura's ships headed for Vella Lavella on a course of 150 degrees True, speed 12 knots. About an hour later came six TBF Avengers of US Navy Torpedo Squadron 21. Not armed with torpedoes, this time, but extra heavy 2,000lb bombs that had a 4.5 second delay each. By this time, the Night Battle Force was heading northwest of Vella Lavella in The Slot heading northwest. The Avengers proceeded to make radar-assisted attacks using moonlight to help guide them. Despite intense Japanese antiaircraft fire, about five minutes into the attack, the *Yugure*, on the starboard flank of the formation, was hit by a bomb amidships. There was, as one might expect from a one-ton bomb, a very large explosion, "completely demolishing [the *Yugure*]." The destroyer sank immediately.[96]

Japanese efforts to rescue the *Yugure*'s crew were delayed as the attack by the Navy Avengers continued for over an hour. Another one of the giant bombs detonated just off the stern of the *Kumano* with an explosion so large the Japanese thought the cruiser had been hit by a torpedo. She had not, but the bomb had ruptured her aft hull plates, necessitating a two-month repair job. Nishimura shifted his flag to sister ship *Suzuya*. Nishimura's mission was ultimately aborted.[97]

About an hour later came another five Avengers of Torpedo 21, this time armed, oddly enough, with torpedoes. They appear to have gone after Captain Orita's transport destroyers specifically. Not effectively, however. In fact, their torpedoes "were seen to malfunction and sink." The heavy antiaircraft fire shot down two TBFs.

At some point during the night, the destroyer *Kiyonami* was dispatched to look for survivors of the *Yugure*. She managed to fish maybe 20 crew members out of the water, but her rescue efforts were cut short.[98] It is known that during the night eight North American B-25 Mitchells of the 69th Bombardment Squadron, 42nd Bombardment Group, were vectored in to engage the Night Battle Force in a night battle. Among their claimed results was "one light cruiser left burning and dead in the water," at a cost of one B-25 shot down, its crew eventually rescued.[99]

After dawn came one more attack by Mitchells, specifically eight from the 390th Bombardment Squadron, also of the 42nd Bombardment Group, "found the cruiser damaged in the previous night's action creeping to friendly waters at a speed of 2 knots."[100] It was no cruiser, but instead the destroyer *Kiyonami*, and it is unclear if she was in fact damaged during the first B-25 attack. What is clear is that she would be damaged now. Making bombing runs at masthead height, the B-25s started off with at least one hit aft, which left the *Kiyonami* disabled. There quickly followed three or four more bomb hits, the last of which was reportedly dropped by the B-25 piloted by 2nd Lieutenant William G. Schauffler and exploded in the *Kiyonami*'s magazine. And the *Kiyonami* followed the *Yugure* to the depths, leaving some 60 survivors in the water.[101]

But no ship would stop to rescue them. The danger was too great. The *Kiyonami* had stopped to pick up the *Yugure*'s survivors and you see what happened to her. As it was, Admiral Nishimura had to worry about the damaged cruiser *Kumano* and also the destroyer *Minazuki*, who at some uncertain point suffered a cracked turbine foundation that reduced her speed to 18 knots.[102] Instead, the Japanese put the word out: "Personnel from our ships are adrift in the vicinity of position bearing 265 degrees 24 miles from Base Ko 3. Proceed at once to carry out search over a wide area in this vicinity and rescue these men. (You may temporarily unload any cargo)."[103] On August 5, a single survivor of the *Kiyonami* was rescued. Of the rest, 228 in *Yugure* and 240 in *Kiyonami*, none was ever recovered.[104] When Captain Hara told the crew of the *Shigure* the news, they sat in stunned silence.[105]

The day was not a complete victory for the Allies, however. Captain Orita, whose mission was not canceled, delivered 582 men, 102 tons of ammunition and supplies, and 60 drums of fuel to Ariel. That was not the tragedy for the Americans, however.[106]

That same morning of July 20, three US Navy PT boats *PT-164, -166,* and *-168* were just south of Ferguson Passage returning from their patrol when they were strafed by four US Army Air Force Mitchells, possibly returning from the strike on the *Kiyonami*. All three boats were hit. But no one knew friendly fire better than the US Navy's motor torpedo boats in the South Pacific, though most of their experience had come from initiating that friendly fire, not receiving it. Skipper Lieutenant Edward Macauley III restrained his *PT-168* from returning fire. On the other two no order was given to fire, but some of the gunners, who were still green, panicked and did fire back. "I got confused," one gunner said, "and thought it was a Jap plane with our insignia." It just complicated matters. *PT-166* caught fire; all of its crew, some of them wounded, were able to evacuate before the boat exploded; they were all rescued by *PT-164*. Though his boat was burning, Macauley took his *PT-168* to the crashed bomber. As the PT's crew extinguished the fire, three survivors from the Mitchell, all wounded, were fished out of the water. They had been told no friendly ships were in the area. The tally for this incident was one PT and one B-25 lost; three of the B-25's crew dead; three more were wounded, as were one officer and ten men from the PTs. Given how the Battle of the Bismarck Sea had shown just how devastating strafing from modified Mitchells could be, the US Navy and Army Air Force were very fortunate the cost was not higher.[107]

The next day, July 21, was one of those perfect tangles of service branches. It began with another of the foul-ups and blunders that had become so common on the American side during the New Georgia operations. At 1:00am on July 18, the fast destroyer-transports

Ward, Kilty, McKean, and *Waters* had arrived off Enogai and debarked Lieutenant Colonel Michael Currin and 35 officers and 666 enlisted men of his 4th Marine Raider Battalion. Also dropped off were five units of fire, 15 days' rations, and 40 tons of other supplies.[108]

While that was going on, the fast-destroyer transports' escorts had a more exciting night than was warranted. The escorts were the destroyers *Waller, Saufley, Pringle, Lang,* and *Stack* under the command of Captain William Cooke, commodore of Destroyer Squadron 22. At 1:17am, the *Pringle* picked up a message from a Black Cat giving the position of "[T]hree enemy destroyers [near Vanga Point off the northwest coast of Kolombangara], speed zero, dead in water, course 040 degrees." An opportunity but also a threat. Cooke set out to investigate. After about 20 minutes, Cooke himself sighted three targets about 20,000 yards ahead, hardly dead in the water but instead speeding toward the coast of Kolombangara when they turned toward Cooke's destroyers. After another ten minutes or so, the range had closed to about 12,000 yards, and the commodore had his own destroyer *Waller* open fire. He was compelled to order a hard to starboard upon a report of torpedoes to port, but it was a false alarm and Cooke had his ships turn back toward the targets, who had disappeared behind a pall of smoke. Knowing US Navy PT boats who could handle these targets were further to the south, Cooke turned back toward Enogai. His targets had actually been *PT-159, -157,* and *-160,* who had strayed north of their patrol area. Believing the ship firing at them was enemy, they did launch torpedoes, which missed. No harm no foul.[109]

With the arrival of the 4th Battalion on July 18, Colonel Liversedge believed he was strong enough to take Bairoko. Except for artillery. He had almost no mortars and absolutely no artillery. But Liversedge knew he needed some heavy preparation before trying to take Bairoko, his final objective. He decided to try what the Wehrmacht called the "flying artillery" – air attacks. So, at 5:00pm, he sent a message to AirSols requesting a heavy air strike on Bairoko before 9:00 the next morning, July 21.[110]

Colonel Liversedge started his troops' advance at 8:00am. As they moved, they noticed something not quite right. At 9:00am, the 4th Raider Battalion noted, "Heavy air strike failed to materialize."[111] It turned out that his request for those heavy air attacks reached Admiral Mitscher too late on July 19 for such strikes to be launched on July 20.[112] Colonel Liversedge decided to continue. With lightly armed troops attacking fortified positions with no prior preparation of those positions, no artillery support, no armor support, and no air support. What could go wrong?

Colonel Liversedge had in fact stuck his men's heads into the mouth of the tiger. While Japanese troops on the attack had been nothing short of inept on Guadalcanal and elsewhere since the Centrifugal Offensive, on defense, they were geniuses. The Gifu positions on Guadalcanal had also found their way to the Buna sector of New Guinea and now New Georgia. These bunkers could not be taken out with small arms. Nevertheless, they pushed deeper into this Gifu-like web of concealed bunkers against increasing fire and with increasing casualties, especially from devastating 90mm mortars, before being stopped cold. Liversedge and his commanders realized that they needed heavier weapons.

So, the attack was called off; Colonel Liversedge would pull his men back to Enogai. But to do so, he needed to extract their heads from the mouth of the tiger. To do that, he requested massive air strikes the morning of July 21 on both sides of Bairoko Harbor. At 7:00pm, he sent the request to Enogai, who relayed it to AirSols on Guadalcanal: "Request all available planes strike both sides Bairoko Harbor beginning 0900. You are covering our withdrawal."[113]

After a nocturnal Japanese probing attack against the 1st Raider Battalion that was repulsed at a cost of one man killed and nine wounded, at 6:00am, the Marines and soldiers began their withdrawal. Not exactly Napoleon retreating from Moscow, or Hitler retreating from Stalingrad, but bad enough. The Japanese made no attempt to interfere. But at 10:00am – an hour later than Colonel Liversedge had requested – he finally got his air strike. As historian and Marine Reserve Major John Rentz said, "Apparently the last sentence of the message – 'You are covering our withdrawal' – had worked like magic."[114] Albeit not like *Magic*.

Major Rentz would continue:

Practically everything in the South Pacific Area that could fly (including OS2U's, landbased [sic] patrol planes) began a series of sorties over Bairoko and continued their attacks until dusk. Over 133 tons of bombs were dropped that day, to record the heaviest air strike – over 250 sorties – thus far in the New Georgia campaign.[115]

Well, maybe not the OS2Us, the Vought Kingfisher observation floatplane that by this time was obsolete by a generation. And maybe not 250 aircraft in the air at the same time. But it was big enough. It was actually a little before 10:00am – Major Rentz must have rounded his times – when the first strike of 24 Dauntlesses (probably from Bombing 11 and 21 and Marine Scout Bombing 144) and 25 Avengers arrived.[116] A half hour later came eight Mitchells from the 42nd Bombardment Group. At noon it was 37 TBFs and six B-25s; at 4:00pm it was 48 SBDs and 22 TBFs; and at 5:00pm it was eight B-25s. They were covered by 50 fighters – Navy Wildcats, Marine Corsairs, and New Zealand Kittyhawks. When the Mitchells had finished dropping their bombs, they returned for a strafing run, their pilots reporting their .50cal. machine guns cut down trees. Pappy Gunn would be proud. The fighters also made strafing runs as soon as their charges had finished bombing. Some 130 tons of bombs hit Bairoko, along with around 24,000 rounds of machine-gun fire.[117] Liversedge and his men reached Enogai safely.

But this was when the trouble began. As those last eight Mitchells were arriving, and, critically, just after the last AirSols fighter cover over Rendova had retired, nine Japanese D3A dive bombers (probably from the 582 Air Group) also arrived, along with their escort of 58 Zeros, including 15 from the 201 Air Group in their first offensive mission since the unit's arrival in the South Pacific. Rendova was not completely defenseless, as there were the Corsairs who had escorted the Mitchells in as well as Fighting 21, who had staged into Segi Point for just this possibility. AirSols claimed two Zeros against one

F4F lost, but the bigger loss was on the ground, or, more accurately, in the water, where one Val got a direct hit on the bridge of *LST-343*, which wounded several men and killed Pacific Fleet Medical Officer Captain Elphege Alfred M. Gendreau, who was a close friend of Admiral Nimitz. It was a personal loss deeply felt by the Pacific Fleet commander.[118]

All of these engagements were merely the undercard to the main event, at least as big a main event as can be without capital ships or even heavy cruisers. For the Combined Fleet, it would be bad enough.

Like any good flag officer, Admiral Koga tried to think several moves ahead. Like any bad flag officer, most of Koga's thoughts as to what those moves might be were wrong. This time, Koga believed that with New Georgia slipping away, the next target for Allied might would be the Shortlands. He decided it needed heavy reinforcements. Fast.

For this job, Admiral Koga chose a veteran of many reinforcement runs in the Solomons, the seaplane carrier *Nisshin*. Koga had her packed with 630 troops of the 4th South Seas Guard Unit, 22 tanks, eight field guns, eight mortars, food, and gasoline. Escorted by the destroyers *Arashi* and *Hagikaze*, the *Nisshin* left Kure on July 10. After a stop at Truk, where she picked up extra escorts in heavy-cruiser–seaplane-carrier thing *Mogami*, newly built light cruisers *Agano* and *Oyodo*, and destroyer *Isokaze*, she arrived in Rabaul on July 21.[119]

Admiral Kusaka was anxious to get the *Nisshin* to the Shortlands and back to minimize the danger of air attack. Each of the three destroyers took on 250 additional troops, giving the convoy a total of some 1,380 troops to take to Buin. So important was this reinforcement that Rear Admiral Osugi Morikazu, commander of the 10th Destroyer Flotilla, shifted his flag from the *Agano* to the *Hagikaze* to personally lead it. Late that evening, after a layover shorter than most modern airlines have, the *Nisshin* and the three destroyers steamed out of Simpson Harbor into the night.

A night that was neither as dark nor as peaceful as Admiral Osugi and Admiral Kusaka had hoped. At 11:00pm, enemy aircraft were spotted. Had they discovered the reinforcement mission? Did it matter? Osugi thought not and pressed on. At 1:30am, course was changed to 140 degrees True – southeast – and the destroyers arranged themselves in a triangular formation with the *Nisshin* at center three kilometers from each of the destroyers. Flagship *Hagikaze* was on the seaplane carrier's starboard bow, *Arashi* was off the port beam, and *Isokaze* was in back. They settled in at flank speed and held their breaths as dawn approached.

The sun came up, and the tension went up as well. July 22 was a bright day with a lot of cumulus clouds – clouds that could hide incoming aircraft from *Nisshin* and her cohort and vice versa. Unlike many seaplane tenders, the *Nisshin* was an actual warship. She was armed with six 5-inch dual purpose guns in two dual turrets, and 18 25mm guns. She was rated for 28 knots, which was why she had been on so many reinforcement runs to Guadalcanal and why American aircraft had never been able to get a clean shot on her, taking a grand total of one near miss. So she had a record of safely running the gauntlet of

American air power. At least she did under her first skipper, Captain Komazawa Katsumi. But Komazawa had been relieved last December by Captain Ito Jotaro, for whom this was his first such mission.

The day dragged on, however. Once noon came and went, tension eased a bit. They were on time for an arrival at Buin scheduled for 4:30pm. The crew started making preparations for unloading the supplies and equipment. The seaplane hangar was opened to prepare to move the tanks that were stored there. It was 1:45pm. Less than three hours to Buin …

The lookouts peered into some blue sky between the clouds, and could make out aircraft. A lot of them, and not friendly. Time seemed to stand still as every eye that could watched the specks in the sky to see what they would do. Those clouds work both ways, you know. Maybe the enemy had not seen them …

It was destroyer *Arashi* who burst that bubble. A second group of enemy planes was only 1,000 meters away distant, bearing 110 degrees True, and closing. It appeared to be "more than ten" B-17 Flying Fortresses. The guns of the *Nisshin* and her escorts opened fire. As they did so, Captain Ito ordered the *Nisshin*'s engine room to give every knot of speed it could muster. Apparently, they worked up to 34 knots, impressive for a ship rated for only 28. Ito swung the helm sharply, settling on course 120 degrees True. The B-17s' bombs all fell harmlessly into the sea off the starboard bow. Everyone knew B-17s can't hit moving ships. The crews relaxed. The enemy had shot its bolt and missed …

But the enemy had a full quiver of bolts. At 1:53, "more than forty" enemy strike aircraft spilled out of the clouds to port, 1,000 meters away. They knew exactly where and when to find the *Nisshin*. It was an ambush.

The Americans had indeed discovered the reinforcement mission. Not from the scout planes the *Nisshin* had seen during the night, as the Japanese thought, but from *Magic*. The Allies had known about the *Nisshin*'s mission since July 19. Particularly damaging was a message from 9:37pm the previous night, just before the *Nisshin* had even left Rabaul, that detailed her convoy's estimated time of arrival and planned anchorage points. Barely three months since *Magic* had provided the information to allow the ambush of Admiral Yamamoto over southeast Bougainville, *Magic* again provided the information to allow another ambush in nearly the same place. Stopping the reinforcement was a priority, but the Allies especially wanted the *Nisshin*, a nemesis that had caused so much trouble during the Guadalcanal Campaign.

So the Americans prepared to nail the nemesis. With those B-17s, plus 12 B-24 Liberators from the 13th Air Force, 18 TBF Avenger torpedo bombers from AirSols, and 16 SBD Dauntless dive bombers, also from AirSols, escorted by no fewer than 120 fighters.

Captain Ito threw *Nisshin* into a "maximum emergency turn" to port, hoping to get under the bombers and cause them to overshoot their target. He almost succeeded. The sharp turn caused the *Nisshin* to heel to starboard, which allowed one bomb to hit the port side of the Number 2 turret, ripping a 20-meter hole in the waterline below it. There was some flooding and a fire was reported near the forward magazines. The damage was serious but not critical. The seaplane carrier was still making good speed and handling well. Just to be safe, Captain Ito ordered the forward magazines flooded, so whatever fire was in their vicinity would not cook off the ammunition and blow the ship from the inside out.

But his precaution was undone by an act of carelessness. During the attack, no one had closed the hangar, which was still open to offload the tanks. And a bomb managed to find it, plunging into the open hangar and striking near the forward end of it. Its detonation caused severe damage deep inside the *Nisshin* and started a new, much larger fire. A third bomb struck the forward end of the aircraft maintenance deck, causing the fire raging in the hangar to spread.

Midships on the *Nisshin* became an inferno, with fire engulfing the innards of the ship from the aft engine room to the forward generator room, knocking out electrical power. No lights, no communications, and no power to the rudder, which caused the *Nisshin* to steam in circles ever more slowly as her speed fell to 15 knots. About 20 fighters came in from the starboard bow, brutally machine-gunning the troops packed on deck.

The Americans had finally gotten clean shots on the *Nisshin*, leaving the seaplane tender sorely hurt. But even if their skipper was new, the crew of the *Nisshin* was a veteran one. The damage control worked quickly and effectively. The jammed rudder was reset and locked on the centerline position so the ship could be steered by engine. That required the bridge to be able to send orders to the engine room, but with communications out, they had to try to use hand signals and flags raised from the bridge to signal the engine room. Yet even that failed because the smoke boiling from the hangar blocked the lines of sight. That left steering to "be done by guess." In the Shortlands southwest of Buin, packed with little islands. That was not going to end well.

And it didn't. At 1:59pm, only 20 miles from Buin, one last wave of carrier bombers bored in on the *Nisshin* in horizontal runs from 40 degrees to port. The seaplane carrier's speed had been halved, she could not steer, and many of her guns were inoperable from damage and from flooding the forward magazines. There was little Captain Ito could do but wait for the inevitable.

The wait lasted one minute. Then two bombs pierced the *Nisshin*'s port side amidships to detonate deep inside the ship. Again. The explosion was devastating, causing 30 meters of topside deck on the port side to collapse and leave a caldera-like hole and apparently venting out the starboard side. Now the *Nisshin* rapidly heeled to starboard and started settling by the bow.

It was over. Captain Ito gave the order to abandon ship. In another sign of the veteran crew of the *Nisshin*, first priority was given to getting the soldiers off the ship. Crewmen helped Imperial Japanese Army soldiers over the sides. Gunners remained at their posts trying to cover for the evacuation until they were literally washed away from their guns. A sixth bomb hit midships on the starboard side at 2:03, but it was superfluous. Two minutes later, the *Nisshin* rolled over the starboard and sank bow first. The Allied nemesis was no more.

Admiral Osugi's *Hagikaze*, *Arashi*, and *Isokaze*, already packed with 750 soldiers between them, moved in to try to rescue survivors. But the *Nisshin* had lasted just

12 minutes after the first bomb hit. That was enough time for only a handful of people to get off the ship. An ineffectual bombing visit from 17 B-17s at 4:25pm convinced the destroyers to leave for Buin where they arrived at 6:30pm. They offloaded their troops very quickly, and 90 minutes later the destroyers were back at sea. They arrived back at the site of the *Nisshin*'s sinking at 10:00pm to resume rescue work, but again they had to cut it short an hour later and speed back to Rabaul when they were attacked by more Allied aircraft in the dark. They had managed to fish only 178 survivors out of the oily water, 91 of whom were from the 630 soldiers the *Nisshin* had been carrying. Captain Ito and 1,084 officers and men went down with the *Nisshin*. It was a disaster of the first magnitude.

And it was yet another sign of how the war was slipping away from Japan. On February 28, 1942, it was the US seaplane tender *Langley* making a desperate run to Java with badly needed reinforcements, but, without air cover, she was sunk by Japanese naval aircraft. Now, not even 18 months later, the situation had completely reversed. Even though the Japanese had two airfields within range at Buin and Ballale. Even though the *Nisshin* had had fighter cover: Chief Petty Officer Shiga Masami led eight Zeros from the 201 Air Group and claimed seven AirSols aircraft destroyed and one probable; actual losses appear to have been zero, but what else could be expected with eight Zeros taking on more than ten dozen fighters.[120]

The loss of the *Nisshin* was not so much a nick or a cut as a full-fledged gash, costing the Japanese a carrier conversion. But in the immediate aftermath it was back to those nicks and cuts and what had become an eternal Japanese struggle to avoid them in the course of their rat runs. The next day, July 23, Captain Shimai, who had pulled the proverbial rabbit out of the hat with his torpedoes at the Battle of Kolombangara, was given a mission to run Guadalcanal veteran Lieutenant Colonel Yano Keiji's 2nd Battalion, 230th Infantry Regiment, 38th Division, to Kolombangara. It was something of a coincidence because US Navy Commander Arleigh Burke was given a rat run of his own to supply Colonel Liversedge at Enogai. To run 200 tons of supplies to Enogai, Burke had four destroyer-transports (*Kilty*, *Crosby*, *Talbot*, and *Waters*) to carry them; four destroyers (his own *Conway*, plus the *Patterson*, *Taylor*, and *Ellet*) to escort the four destroyer-transports carrying the 200 tons of supplies; and Admiral Merrill's force of two light cruisers (his own *Montpelier* and the *Cleveland*) and five destroyers (*Waller*, *Pringle*, *Philip*, *Maury*, and *Gridley*) to deal with any Japanese who showed up. Japanese like Captain Shimai, who had three destroyers – the *Yukikaze*, *Mikazuki*, and *Hamakaze* – and that was pretty much it.[121]

Yet running three destroyers to Kolombangara had gotten surprisingly complicated for the Japanese. To avoid a repeat of the *Nisshin* disaster, Base Air Force provided some air cover. Of course, Base Air Force had provided air cover over the *Nisshin*, too, and you see how that turned out. The Japanese also wanted to avoid a repeat of the rat runs that had been intercepted, if still mostly successful, at Kula Gulf and Kolombangara. More importantly, they wanted to avoid a repeat of the disaster at Vila-Stanmore, when, after completing their run to Vila, the Japanese destroyers *Murasame* and *Minegumo* had been ambushed by this same Admiral Merrill and this same Commander Burke and sunk with barely getting a shot off.

Captain Shimai had proven his cunning at Kolombangara; he would prove it again now. Leaving Simpson Harbor an hour before dawn on July 23, Shimai had his destroyers go southeast around the Treasury Islands west of Bougainville and avoided The Slot by using Wilson Strait to reach Ariel. In choosing this course, Shimai had guessed correctly that the Americans would be waiting for him, as Admiral Merrill was looking for a repeat of Vila-Stanmore as he came up The Slot. The three Japanese destroyers had avoided that fate. For now.

Everything worked well enough for the Japanese to reach Ariel at 11:30pm and begin disembarking their Imperial Army troops and supplies. A little less than an hour later, the floatplanes that were escorting him reported "devil boats" just to the east of him which would have put them on Kolombangara itself. Allegedly, Captain Shimai had almost finished unloading, so he cut it a bit short to head back the way he had come. Only to find TBF Avengers overhead.

Their presence revealed an Allied response that was both complete and comical. Captain Shimai's destroyers had been spotted at around 11:00pm by a Black Cat, who dropped a flare and tried to inform Admiral Merrill of the Japanese position. Neither worked out the way it was intended. The flare drew a protest from the PT boats in the area, who claimed it was illuminating them. The message never got through to Merrill, but did get through to Guadalcanal. In response, AirSols sent four Avengers and four Mitchells to attack the Japanese destroyers.

The nocturnal air strike arrived all right and managed to spot Captain Shimai's little squadron. But the friendly fire incident that resulted in the sinking of the *PT-166* and the downing of a B-25 just a few days earlier was fresh in the minds of the Americans. That incident occurred in part because the Mitchells had been told no Allied ships were in the area. What if, once again, these were Allied ships, of whose presence the aviators were not informed? What if this was Admiral Merrill's force and they had not been told? The Avengers and Mitchells held off.

Admiral Merrill's force indeed was in the Vella Gulf, having arrived at 1:00am, but they found nothing. The PT boats were busy evading bombs dropped by the Japanese floatplanes that had been escorting Captain Shimai's ships, but again, with the *PT-166* incident fresh in their minds, they blamed one of the Avengers for the splashes the PTs were busy avoiding, while the Avenger protested that he had not even dropped his munitions.

While all that was going on, Captain Burke's destroyer-transports unloaded at Enogai while his four escorting destroyers briefly bombarded Bairoko. Captain Shimai's destroyers escaped unscathed and got back to base with nary a scratch.[122]

It was during this period of July 15–24 that the Imperial Navy submarine *Ro-103* sighted enemy ships three times and was unable to get into attack position each time. On July 28, skipper Lieutenant Ichimura Rikinosuke radioed Rabaul to that effect. The

Ro-103 was never heard from again. Today, her loss remains a mystery. Speculation has been that she was sunk by a PT boat or, more likely, a mine, probably one in the mine fields laid by the busy destroyer-minelayers *Breese, Preble,* and *Gamble*.[123]

Mine-laying was seen just as one of those essential but boring activities. Like making a spear. A good spear needs not just a good point but a strong shaft. Both had been lacking in the New Georgia Campaign. General Griswold set out to fix that.[124]

The big reasons for the weakness of that shaft were the supply system that was, at best, sluggish and tangled; and medical services that were mostly nonexistent in the New Georgia area. Griswold designated Barabuni Island as supply depot for the 43rd Infantry Division and Kokorana for the 37th. Cargo ships from Guadalcanal would land supplies and equipment on these islands, from where landing craft and other small boats would transport them to Laiana or to other places that were more readily accessible.

Furthermore, construction of a road out of Laiana to the Munda trail had finally been completed on July 20, both ensuring a good flow of supplies and creating the ability to assemble supply caches close to the front line. The construction capability that made the new road possible was increased with four engineering companies, three from the 37th Division's 117th Engineer Battalion and one from the 25th Infantry Division's 65th Engineer Battalion. As New Georgia Campaign historian extraordinaire Ronnie Day explained, "Japanese respect for the engineers stood second only to that for the artillery. With some exaggeration, the Kumamoto Division historians wrote that the 'engineers that led the infantry cleared the jungle and also fought with the infantry with guns and grenades.'"[125]

Perhaps the greatest improvement came in the provision of medical care. It was mere hours after he assumed command that General Griswold asked General Harmon to send the 250-bed 17th Field Hospital from Guadalcanal to Rendova immediately. Harmon approved, and the 117th promptly set itself up on Kokorana Island. The 37th Division brought in its 112th Medical Battalion, less one company, and one company of the 25th Medical Battalion was also brought in. To make sure that casualties being evacuated from New Georgia received proper medical attention during the trip to Guadalcanal, the corps surgeon arranged with naval authorities for a naval medical officer to travel on each transport carrying patients.[126] Special provision was made for treating the war neuroses that had crippled the early efforts on New Georgia. Rest camps providing hot food, baths, clean clothes, and cots were established on the barrier islands. Colonel Hallam tried to see to it that more accurate diagnoses were made so that men suffering from combat fatigue were separated from true neurotics and sent to these camps. Perhaps most importantly, definitions and standard procedures were established. "Combat fatigue" would mean physical exhaustion; "war neurosis" would mean emotional depletion.[127]

Some reinforcements helped things, too, and General Griswold shuffled the US Army units in preparation for what he considered the final offensive to take Munda, which he had scheduled for July 25. His plan called for a complete combined arms operation. Following a naval bombardment and a heavy bombing, XIV Corps infantry, supported by artillery and US Marine tanks, would make a frontal attack on the Japanese line. The 43rd

Infantry Division on the left would take Lambeti Plantation and the airfield itself, and the 37th on the right would take Bilbilo Hill, surround the Japanese north of the airfield, and prevent them from retreating across the Kula Gulf to Kolombangara or other points north or west of New Georgia.[128]

By July 23, the bulk of the 37th Infantry Division had arrived at New Georgia and was either in action or ready to be put into action. General Griswold turned over command of all units on New Georgia except the 136th Field Artillery Battalion to the 37th's commander, Major General Robert S. Beightler. Beightler was a general from the National Guard, and turning the command over to him was a sign of confidence in his work.[129]

It meant the hard-pressed 169th Infantry Regiment was finally switched out on the front line by the 145th Infantry Regiment, though its commander Colonel Holland did not switch out because he was given back command of the 145th, his old unit. General Beightler placed the 145th on the left, with its 2nd Battalion holding a very narrow front on Reincke Ridge and its 1st Battalion was already committed to Kelley Hill; its 3rd Battalion was with Colonel Liversedge. Also with Liversedge was the 3rd Battalion of the 148th Regiment. The 148th was placed on the right, with no definite frontage, and assigned the responsibility for protecting the XIV Corps' right flank and rear, so there would be no more Colonel Tomonari-type attacks. In the center was the 161st Regiment, normally with the 25th Infantry Division but now attached to the 37th.[130] In the 43rd Division's sector, the 172nd Infantry Regiment moved right to (finally) establish contact with the 37th's left and to make room for another battalion of the 103rd Infantry.

There was a slight problem. Unbeknownst to the Americans, the Japanese had occupied a ridge on the 161st Regiment's front. When patrols established this fact, General Beightler did not want to commit the regiment to removing it before the offensive began. However, smaller units tried but failed to permanently clear it. The 161st would have to take care of it on the first day of the offensive.[131]

During all this, General Sasaki was not sitting on Kongo Hill twiddling his thumbs. He tried to make the best of what he knew to be a bad hand. He was badly outnumbered and what units he did have were mostly shadows of their former selves. He kept pushing Colonel Tomonari to quickly make a second counterattack with whatever troops he could muster on the American northern flank, but Tomonari's 13th Infantry Regiment had not recovered from the first counterattack, a repeat of which was extremely unlikely since the US Army's 148th Infantry Regiment was overlapping the Japanese line. Sasaki had wanted to bring over the freshly-landed-on-Kolombangara Major Yano and his 2nd Battalion of the 230th Infantry Regiment, but Admiral Samejima denied that request because that would violate the Southeast Area Fleet's agreement with 8th Area Army, inasmuch as it would leave Kolombangara vulnerable. Samejima eventually released one company to Sasaki. Because one company would make all the difference on New Georgia.[132]

Ultimately, Sasaki had to base his defense on a number of fortified hills: Shimizu Hill in front of the 172nd Infantry, and Horseshoe Hill in front of the 145th and 161st

Regiments northwest of Kelley Hill and west of Reincke Ridge. Major Kojima's 3rd Battalion of the 229th Infantry Regiment, along with what was left of Major Hara's 1st Battalion and one company of the 230th Regiment, held Horseshoe Hill. Major Sato's 2nd Battalion of the 229th held Shimizu Hill. And what was left of Colonel Tomonari's 13th Regiment loitered in the upper Barike trying to pull itself together. In more ways than one, it would seem.[133]

General Sasaki was in a no-win situation. Even if Colonel Tomonari could pull his troops back together, most of his strength had been lost in the earlier counterattack, while the Americans were sure to have strengthened that open flank. The chance for driving the Allies off New Georgia was gone. The best he and his troops could do was make the final Allied victory as costly and as time-consuming as possible.

General Griswold was not interested in consuming time, and the offensive actually began on time on July 25. Commander Burke sailed up with seven destroyers (*Maury*, *Gridley*, *Conway*, *Wilson*, *Taylor*, *Ellet*, and *Patterson*) taking part in a "drive-by shooting" of Lambeti Plantation. With a line of fire parallel to the opposing battle lines, it was a dangerous bombardment for US troops, but Burke had tried to avoid any friendly fire issues by scouting the target a few days earlier to choose visual checkpoints and work out some firing solutions. Good thing, too, because a morning haze reduced visibility on July 25. Nevertheless, at 6:09am, the *Maury* and *Gridley* started inflicting a little more than 30 minutes of hell in which some 4,000 5-inch shells were lobbed at the offending plantation.

Starting at 6:30, 254 aircraft – Liberators and Flying Fortresses, followed by Mitchells, and then Dauntlesses and Avengers – also began inflicting 30 minutes of hell by unloading the first of half a million pounds of fragmentation and high explosive bombs on their target area, a 1,500-by-250-yard strip beginning about 500 yards west of the 103rd Infantry's front lines. It was the largest attack ever mounted by AirSols. All the staff officers who could talk themselves into a ride went along to see what the 23rd Bombardment Squadron called the "greatest show on earth." After the bombers left – this was getting to be a theme with the Sea Eagles – the Japanese came in with 30–40 Vals escorted by 54 Zeros at about 9:40am. Well, the Zeros came in; the D3As reportedly jettisoned their bombs and fled when they saw the 29-fighter Rendova Patrol on the scene. The resulting air battle resulted in five Zeros downed for a loss of four Allied fighters, though the Japanese claimed 24.[134]

On top of all that was the artillery. Before 7:00am, the 43rd Division's supporting artillery began the first of more than 100 preparations that were fired that day. The 103rd and 152nd Field Artillery Battalions fired more than 2,150 105mm howitzer shells; the 155mm howitzers of the 136th Field Artillery Battalion threw 1,182 rounds at the Japanese.[135]

With that softening up completed or almost so, their ears probably still ringing from the explosions, at 7:00am the men of the XIV Corps began their advance.

And were stopped cold.

It was Gifu all over again. Strong combat patrols went out in the morning of July 26 to fix the location of the Japanese pillboxes as accurately as possible. So began the chiseling away of the Japanese positions. It took infantry, tanks, heavy artillery, and, for the first time in the Solomons Campaign, flamethrowers, to slowly but surely eliminate the interlocking lines of pillboxes one pillbox at a time.

The offensive devolved into three separate battles: the 43rd Division's along the Roviana beach and extending north to Shimizu Hill; the 37th Division's (less the 148th Infantry) on Bartley Ridge and Horseshoe Hill; and the 148th's on the northern flank.

Through the end of July, the 43rd Division inched its way forward, yard by yard, foot by foot, pillbox by pillbox. Too slowly for General Griswold, who, in a move that should have been made much earlier, had General Hester sacked. General Harmon replaced him with Major General John R. Hodge, commander of the Americal Division. As Harmon wrote, "Hodge was the best Div Comdr I have in area for this particular job."[136] The right tool for the right job.

The 37th Division did not move forward with anywhere near that speed. The terrain made its use of tanks and flamethrowers more problematic. While a flanking patrol managed to get to Horseshoe Hill and found it largely deserted, the 148th Regiment, knowing it was outflanking the Japanese, pushed forward almost to the strategic objective of Bibilo Hill, only to find themselves cut off by roving raiders of Colonel Tomonari's 13th Regiment, not acting in force but, again, in small groups. The 148th was compelled to destroy its heavy equipment and any supplies it could not carry and make small groups of its own to get back to American lines.[137]

Then August 1 arrived. Shimizu Hill had been captured, and with it the last piece of high ground between the 43rd Division and the Munda airfield. On the 37th Division's front, Bartley Ridge had fallen; Horseshoe Hill was about to, and the 148th Regiment was almost back to American lines.[138]

At 11:00am, the 103rd Infantry began its attack – and found practically no opposition. At 3:00pm it was almost at Lambeti Plantation. The day before, Generals Hodge and Wing, and Colonel Ross, had visited the observation posts of the 1st Battalion, 145th Infantry, from where they could see part of Munda airfield. They detected evidence of a Japanese withdrawal, which seemed to be covered by fire from the enemy still on Horseshoe Hill. Was it true? Was this another secret withdrawal from Guadalcanal?[139]

At 3:00pm, with the 43rd Division still advancing against almost no resistance, General Griswold ordered all units to send out patrols immediately to discover whether the Japanese were withdrawing. Within minutes patrols went out. They found no enemy.[140] About 90 minutes later, orders were issued to advance aggressively until solid resistance was met, in which case its location, strength, and composition were to be developed. The 103rd Infantry reached the outer taxiways of Munda airfield, while the 169th stopped just short of Bibilo Hill, both out of caution, not opposition. The 37th Division swept past Horseshoe Hill, which was now free of Japanese.[141]

On August 2, 3, 4, and 5 the advance continued all across the corps' front. The 103rd and 169th Infantry swept past the runways of the Munda airfield. Kokengolo Hill, in the center of the airfield, held up the advance temporarily, but not for long. An exception was Bibilo Hill, whose fortifications had to be reduced the usual way. It took three days of action by elements of the 169th, 172nd, 145th, and 161st Regiments, supported by Marine tanks. But it was done all the same.[142]

General Griswold telegraphed Admiral Halsey to tell him that after 12 days of fighting, "Our ground forces have wrested Munda from the Japs and present it to you as the sole owner. Our Munda operation is the finest example in all my experience of a united all-service all-American team." The South Pacific 3rd Fleet commander replied, "Consider this a custody receipt for Munda and for a gratifying number of enemy dead. Such teamwork and unrelenting offensive spirit assures the success of future drives and the implacable extermination of the enemy wherever we can bring him to grips. Keep 'em dying."[143]

So ended "the most unintelligently waged land campaign of the Pacific war[.]"[144] Munda airfield had fallen. The long national nightmare was over.

But where had the Japanese gone?

CHAPTER 8
THE HOP

While there evidently were comings and, mostly, goings on New Georgia, at Rabaul there were a lot of sittings. Among those doing a lot of sitting was Hara Tameichi's destroyer *Shigure*. He was anxious to go out.

Captain Hara got his wish soon enough. He and his one-ship destroyer division got roped into joining the *Hagikaze* and *Arashi* of Destroyer Division 4 under Captain Sugiura Kaju on a rat run to Rekata on Santa Ysabel. This trip involved carrying 100 members of the 7th Combined Special Naval Landing Force and some 100 tons of supplies. Hara and his friends arrived at Rekata at 1:00am on July 27, offloaded their passengers and cargo, and took on board one infantry battalion of about 820 men who were supposed to be sent to the Munda front. There were reportedly air attacks on the return trip, but no damage was suffered and the three destroyers reached Shortland without incident.[1]

Upon Captain Hara's return to Rabaul, he and his one-ship destroyer division got roped into joining the same two ships of Destroyer Division 4 once again, this time on a rat run to Kolombangara. Three destroyers, *Hagikaze*, *Arashi*, and *Shigure*, were loaded with 900 troops and 120 tons of supplies. Destroyer *Amagiri* would lead them through Vella Gulf and the Blackett Strait around Kolombangara to Vila from the south. Once the supplies and troops were dropped off, the quartet would hightail it back the way they had come.[2]

The Vella Gulf-Blackett Strait route was one that had been used recently, which made Captain Hara uneasy.[3] He had studied the records of the engagements of the Guadalcanal and New Guinea campaigns, and came to the conclusion that "many of them were patterned on the same formula. When a tactic succeeded it was likely to be used repeatedly and without change by the Imperial Navy, and this often proved disastrous."[4]

Despite Captain Hara's misgivings, on August 1, the *Amagiri* led the *Hagikaze*, *Arashi*, and *Shigure* out of Simpson Harbor. As darkness overtook the column, the tension increased on the bridge of the *Shigure*, especially as the ships wound their way through the narrow, twisting Blackett Strait. But the ships arrived at the rendezvous point with the Vila garrison without incident, according to Hara at any rate. The Japanese were now old hands at this, and the supplies and troops were offloaded in 20 minutes. *Hagikaze* signaled, "Let's go home!"

The *Amagiri* led the way once again as the column threaded its way through the Blackett Strait at the "truly breakneck speed," in Captain Hara's view, of 30 knots. There was good reason for the speed, as Hara was about to find out. As they passed Gizo, they tightened the column into 500-meter intervals between ships. In the darkness, Hara was able to make out "the movement of a small black object moving swiftly from the left toward *Amagiri*." He could not determine what the object was, but groaned, "Here it comes!" bracing for the explosion. But "[the]black object melted into the darkness and was gone, with no explosion, no flash, no fire. It was mystifying."

That was Captain Hara's story and he was sticking to it. The Japanese destroyers had run right into an ambush by 15 US Navy PT boats. Hara does not mention it, but the PTs reported attacking the four Japanese destroyers on the destroyers' inbound leg and being driven off by gunfire, machine guns, and searchlights. On the outbound leg, the PTs attacked again.

The view from the *Amagiri* was much different than that from the *Shigure*. "Ship ahead off port bow!" yelled the lookout.

"Look again!" shouted *Amagiri* skipper Lieutenant Commander Hanami Kohei from the bridge, "report instantly!"[5]

"Torpedo boats to the forward port!" came the answer. Hanami peered off the starboard side of the *Amagiri*'s bridge. He was able to make out a small dark silhouette in the water some 800 to 1,000 meters distant, just slightly to the right by 10 degrees – almost dead ahead. He recognized it as a US Navy torpedo boat. By Hanami's estimation, they would collide with the "devil boat" in less than 20 seconds.

"Fire! Fire!" yelled Petty Officer Mitsuaki Sawada from the gunnery position. One problem with that: they were too close to be able to hit it with their guns or torpedoes. As Lieutenant Commander Hanami later explained:

> I had come to the conclusion that it was too difficult to shoot and hit a target as small and fast as a torpedo boat, and that ramming was the best method of dealing with them. Such an opportunity had never arisen in my many previous encounters with torpedo boats, but this was a favorable situation for ramming and I decided to try it. [...] To veer away would have meant exposing our flank to torpedo attack at point blank range. My decision was to ram, and I gave the order.

"Ten degrees turn," Hanami ordered the helmsman, "full speed ahead! Ram into them!"

This is the time to point out that Hanami's immediate superior, veteran Destroyer Division 11 Commodore Captain Yamashiro, was also on the bridge. Yamashiro recalled giving the opposite order: to avoid the boat. But Hanami does not remember that, while the helmsman Coxswain Kazuto Doi, would only say, "Captain Yamashiro does not remain much in my memory." Regardless, the *Amagiri* heeled over in a starboard turn. The

Amagiri's engines roared as she worked her way up to 34 knots. The klaxon of the collision alarm wailed. There was a jarring crunch.

While Captain Hara says there was "no explosion, no flash, no fire," there was very much a fire. Flaming gasoline from the wrecked PT boat spewed all over the *Amagiri's* forward hull, deck, and bridge. "We crashed right into it," remembered Hanami. "I saw the enemy ship break in two with a tremendous roar. White gasoline flames shot out. The torpedo boat disappeared in the dark. I knew that at least one half and probably both halves sank." One of the destroyer's propellers was damaged as well, forcing Lieutenant Commander Hanami to reduce speed. The *Amagiri* signaled, "Enemy torpedo boats encountered! One rammed and sunk!"

The torpedo boat was the *PT-109*, under the command of one Lieutenant (jg) John F. Kennedy. Kennedy had kept the boat's engines idling to avoid producing a wake that had earlier attracted fire from Japanese shore batteries on Kolombangara. Low in the water and in the night "as dark as if you were in a closet with the door shut," the *109* did not see the approaching *Amagiri* until it was too late to fire the boat's torpedoes or even move.[6] The boat was cleaved in two and left to sink off Kolombangara.

The *Hagikaze* and *Arashi* opened up with machine guns to starboard, shortly thereafter joined by the *Shigure*. "Cheers of joy and laughter sounded and echoed in each of our destroyers as we continued running at top speed," said Captain Hara.[7] The *Amagiri* had to cut speed somewhat, but they drove off all the PTs with otherwise no damage and made it safely back to Rabaul.

The PT boats had done a terrible job executing the ambush. And they knew it. *PT-105* skipper Richard Keresey summarized the results:

Fifteen PT boats ventured out into Blackett Strait to attack four Japanese destroyers, the best odds PT boats ever had. We fired thirty-two torpedoes, including four from my 105. We hit nothing! The destroyers kept right on going straight down Blackett Strait and then straight back a couple of hours later.[8]

He added, "when the 109 got in the way, they ran over it." Years later, John F. Kennedy put it more succinctly, describing the night's events as "fucked up."[9]

Captain Hara would have disagreed, but not too much:

Cheers of joy and laughter sounded and echoed in each of our destroyers as we continued running at top speed. I understood the elation at our good fortune, but could not join the merrymaking. My spine was still creeping at the thought of the close shave we had had, as I recalled the loss of *Terutsuki* [normally rendered as *Teruzuki*] in December, 1942, to motor torpedo boats. This new Japanese destroyer of 3,470 tons was sunk as the result of two hits by torpedoes delivered by a couple of 50-ton torpedo boats. The same fate could have just as well befallen us this night if the enemy had spotted us and reacted a few minutes earlier.[10]

When the convoy arrived at Rabaul a few hours later, Lieutenant Commander Hanami and Captain Yamashiro went to the 3rd Destroyer Flotilla's nominal flagship *Sendai*, where they were greeted by Rear Admiral Ijuin. The baron laughed and playfully scolded them, "Why didn't your radio report say that the torpedo boat had been crushed underfoot?"[11]

Within 48 hours, the Tokyo news media were blaring with triumphant, euphoric headlines.

A Japanese destroyer had sunk a US Navy motor torpedo boat. What a major strategic coup for Imperial Japan. Arriving back at Rabaul at the same time as Captain Yamashiro and Lieutenant Commander Hanami was an "apprehensive and glum" Captain Hara. He had a very different reaction, even before he was handed a report:

> Destroyers *Mikazuki* (Destroyer Division 30) and *Ariake* (Destroyer Division 27), while on
> a transport mission to Tuluvu, New Britain, grounded near Cape Gloucester on July 27 and
> were attacked next day by B-25s which demolished them completely. Only seven crewmen
> were killed.[12]

Hara was beside himself. "How could both *Mikazuki* and *Ariake* have been so clumsy and inept as to run aground?" he asked himself.[13] Not just run aground, but run aground in the same place at the same time. That takes a certain talent, to be sure, and suggests that the decline in the skill level of the Imperial Japanese Navy was not limited to the Sea Eagles.

There wasn't much more to the story. On July 27, the *Mikazuki* led the *Ariake* on a quick reinforcement run to Tuluvu. They both ran aground on a submerged reef near Cape Gloucester. The *Ariake* was able to work herself free. She removed the troops and Captain Orita, commander of Destroyer Division 30, from the *Mikazuki* and completed the run to Tuluvu. Then the *Ariake* went back to try to pull the *Mikazuki* off the reef. But her work was interrupted by six B-25 Mitchells from the 90th Bombardment Squadron and three Mitchells from the 13th Bombardment Squadron, both from the 3rd Bombardment Group, 5th Air Force, who just plastered both destroyers. The *Ariake* was sunk, and the *Mikazuki* was left beached where she was, in sinking condition, with her bow blown off. The 3rd returned the next day with four B-25s of the 13th, three from the 90th, and seven from the 8th Bombardment Squadrons to try to finish off the *Mikazuki* with an absolutely murderous bombing attack, but just managed to wreck her some more. The *Mikazuki* did not fully sink, and had to endure the ignominy of serving as a target for bombing practice by US aircraft.[14]

Captain Hara was brooding about the loss of half of his command without his even commanding it. He does not seem to have noticed that yet another destroyer, the *Akikaze*, had been hit by the enemy. On August 2, Royal Australian Air Force PBY Catalinas found the old destroyer and secret war crime site steaming south of Rabaul and landed at least one bomb in her bridge area, causing heavy damage and 23 casualties, including skipper Sabe Tsurukichi, who was killed just one day after he had been promoted to full commander. The *Akikaze* would be out of action for the next three months.[15]

That would not have improved Captain Hara's mood, nor would that mood be improved by the plans for the next operation. On the morning of August 4, Captain Sugiura, commander of Destroyer Division 4, invited Hara and *Shigure* skipper Lieutenant Commander Yamagami Kamesaburou to a conference detailing the next rat run to Kolombangara. Except for replacing the damaged *Amagiri* with the *Kawakaze*, the operation was to be precisely the same.

Captain Hara voiced the alarm bells that were going off in his mind. "Captain Sugiura, I understood you to say that we are to repeat the mission. Does that mean we are to conduct this operation in the same way as the last one?"

"Yes, Hara. We shall go through Vella Gulf and Blackett Strait again, and unload at the Kolombangara anchorage at [11:30pm], exactly as we did last time."

"Begging your pardon, Sugiura, I do not think it wise to repeat the exact same formula again. This same procedure has already been used twice in Vella Gulf. Can't we vary the course somewhat this time? Blackett Strait by itself, with all those reefs and shoals, is unhealthy enough, without using the identical route for getting there again. How about feinting through Gizo Strait before sneaking into Blackett? Or how about just changing the timing by two hours either way?"

"Hara, I see your point but I already have my orders. To alter them in any detail such as you suggest would involve great changes for all parties concerned, especially in communications. And you know how poor the Army garrison's communication system is."[16]

There was no questioning orders in the Imperial Japanese Navy. Or in Imperial Japan, for that matter. Hara's heart sank. Captain Sugiura offered Hara's *Shigure* the role of scout for the mission, as the *Amagiri* had been the last time. But Hara declined it because the *Shigure*'s engines were in such bad shape he doubted she could make even 30 knots. So Sugiura's own *Hagikaze* would lead instead.[17]

It was with trepidation that Captain Hara had his *Shigure* follow as the tail end of a column that consisted of the lead ship *Hagikaze* followed by the *Arashi* and the *Kawakaze* as it left Simpson Harbor at 3:00am on August 6. The column headed south into intermittent squalls. As the destroyers passed Buka at 2:30pm they spotted an enemy scout plane. The *Shigure*'s radio room reported hearing an "Urgent" coded message, likely the plane's sighting report. That was ominous. Their mission was found out, Hara thought. What would Captain Sugiura do in response? Nothing, as it turned out which did not help Hara's mood.

At 7:00pm the column entered the Bougainville Strait. The *Hagikaze* led the destroyers on a column turn to 140 degrees True – southeast – and increased speed to 30 knots for the run down The Slot to Kolombangara. Orders were for the ships to maintain 500-meter intervals. But the *Shigure* huffed and puffed and could not maintain 30 knots, as Captain Hara had predicted. She kept falling further and further behind the *Kawakaze* and thus the rest of the column.

When they were northeast of Vella Lavella, navigator Lieutenant (jg) Tsukihara Yoshio reported to Captain Hara, "Sir, we are lagging 1,000 meters behind *Kawakaze*. Shall we use the overboost to gain back our lost 500 meters?" Hara was angry this was working out exactly as he had predicted it would. "No," he thundered, "this is good enough. To hell with the prescribed 500-meter distance. Don't overboost the engine!"

The *Hagikaze* led the column in rounding Boko Point and entering the Vella Gulf. Visibility to starboard was good, but the blackness of Kolombangara swallowed everything to port. Captain Hara was taking no chances. "Stand by for action! Aim all guns and torpedoes to port. Set gun range of 3,000 meters. Set torpedoes to run at two-meter depth, angle 20 degrees. Double all lookouts!" The *Shigure* sailed on this way for ten minutes. Captain Hara peered into the darkness off Kolombangara, but could see nothing. Finally, the torpedo officer Lieutenant Doi Toshio asked if it was all right to return the tubes from portside to their original starboard position.

"No!" Hara shouted. Then he caught himself. "No, Doi, for heaven's sake, no! Starboard visibility is so good that we can see the reefs of Vella Lavella. To port we see no more than 2,000 meters, and we don't know where the enemy is. Stay trained to port and be ready for action at any moment."

Like that very moment. At 9:45pm came the call from the lookout: "White waves! Black objects! … Several ships heading toward us!"

Hara immediately ordered full starboard helm, and torpedoes launched at port-side targets. But his heart sank further as he watched the *Hagikaze*, *Arashi*, and *Kawakaze* ahead of him, the last now by 1,500 meters. They were maintaining speed and course. No evasive action, no action at all to indicate they had seen the enemy, let alone the torpedoes that were certainly now on their way.

Captain Hara saw the wakes himself, the nearest 800 meters away, and again roared his order for full starboard helm. He glimpsed a fiery eruption from midships on the *Arashi* and two explosions on the *Kawakaze*. But the commodore-in-name-only had no time to worry about it now, with three torpedoes headed for his *Shigure*. "My knees almost gave in as I clutched the handrail," he remembered. "The first torpedo passed 20 meters ahead of the bow, the second was closer, and the third appeared certain to hit. It did not, however, or if it did it was just a glancing blow on the skin of the rapidly turning ship. I thought I felt a dull thud from aft but could not be sure."

The *Shigure* completed a full circle to starboard, then Hara ordered, "Port helm, half!" No more torpedoes were visible. He later remembered, "Those two minutes just passed were the most breathtaking ones of my life."

This was not going according to plan, but it was going how Captain Hara feared it would. An explosion in the vicinity of the enemy ships – ships, not boats this time – gave the crew of the *Shigure* the hope that their torpedoes had scored a hit. But it was a false hope. The American ships had made a 90-degree turn just in time to avoid Hara's spread. The explosion they had seen was one of the torpedoes exploding in the wake of one of the enemy ships.

Captain Hara asked the radio room if any messages had come in from the other destroyers. The answer was not encouraging. "*Arashi* and *Kawakaze* sent brief messages saying they were hit by torpedoes. We have heard nothing from *Hagikaze*." Hara ordered a smokescreen to hide the *Shigure* as she headed northwest away from the battle in a tactical retreat so she could reload her torpedo tubes and Hara could plot his next move. In Hara's words, his *Shigure* was at a "distinct disadvantage."[18] The Americans had pulled off the ambush, and knocked out two, maybe three of four Japanese destroyers. They had fired their torpedoes and waited for them to hit before opening gunfire. They had hidden themselves in the blackness of Kolombangara. It was something the Imperial Japanese Navy would do. Indeed, had done many, many times. Whoever was leading the Americans was good.

It was Commander Frederick Moosbrugger, a veteran destroyer skipper "whose name," opined historian C.W. Kilpatrick, "even sounded belligerent[.]"[19] For this operation, Moosbrugger commanded Task Group 31.2, which consisted of his own Destroyer Division 12, with the *Dunlap*, *Craven*, and *Maury*; and Destroyer Division 15 under Commander Rodger W. Simpson with the *Lang*, *Sterett*, and *Stack*. On August 4, Admiral Wilkinson, now in charge in place of the reassigned Admiral Turner, had ordered Moosbrugger and his task group to disrupt the Tokyo Express runs to Kolombangara through Vella Gulf. The next day, Moosbrugger and Simpson met on the *Dunlap* with PT boat officers to gather intelligence on Japanese behavior in the Vella Gulf area.[20] No doubt how the Japanese handled the failed PT ambush that led to the sinking of *PT-109* was high on the list of topics. An operational plan was worked out with the PT boats, but they ended up not taking part.[21]

No matter. Late in the afternoon of August 5, Admiral Wilkinson gave Commander Moosbrugger specific operational instructions. Both destroyer divisions of his task group were to leave Tulagi at 12:30pm on August 6, head south of the Russells and Rendova to arrive at the Gizo Strait at 10:00pm and begin sweeps of Vella Gulf. Wilkinson explained to the commodore that he believed the Japanese planned to reinforce Vila-Stanmore during the night of August 6, using destroyers and possibly a cruiser. If Moosbrugger and his ships had not found the enemy by 2:00am on August 7, he was to return at maximum speed through The Slot to Purvis Bay to avoid enemy air attack.[22]

With combat probably imminent, on the morning of August 6, Commander Moosbrugger met with Commander Simpson and most of the group's destroyer skippers. Tired of merely screening for cruisers, now that there were no cruisers available and the destroyers would be on their own, they hoped to show what they could do with a little freedom of action. This conference was intended to develop an operational plan to do just that.[23]

That plan called for Commander Moosbrugger's and Commander Simpson's destroyers to operate in two separate columns. They would pass through the Gizo Strait in division columns at 15 knots to enter Vella Gulf. When they passed Liapari Island, Simpson's destroyers were to move to Moosbrugger's destroyers' starboard quarter and sweep along the west shore of Kolombangara for barges.[24] Division 15 had traded half its torpedo tubes for 40mm guns, which were considered ideal for barge busting.

Commander Moosbrugger's destroyers were to operate seaward of Commander Simpson's. The barges were to be targeted only if no heavier targets presented themselves. If destroyers or larger ships were encountered, Moosbrugger's destroyers would close to fire torpedoes, retire to about 10,000 yards (believed to be the maximum range for Japanese torpedoes) until the torpedoes hit, then open gunfire. Simpson's ships were to wait until the torpedoes hit before opening gunfire, though they could make their own torpedo attacks if a favorable opportunity was presented.[25]

Moosbrugger's Destroyer Division 12 was given the job of engaging surface ships because it still had 44 torpedo tubes. It had operated together since 1941 and considered radar-guided night torpedo attacks its specialty.[26] Moreover, on July 27, Admiral King had given permission to disable the ineffective magnetic influence feature of the Mark 6 torpedo exploder, so now there was a chance American torpedoes might actually work.[27]

It was as if a light had finally switched on. Finally, someone in the US Navy understood that it is easier to maintain concealment, not to mention easier to hit the target, by firing torpedoes first and waiting until they are supposed to hit before opening gunfire. The Japanese had been doing this for the entire Pacific War, and the Pacific Fleet was finally catching on and incorporating it into its battle plans. At the conference, Commander Moosbrugger came right out and said one of the "assumptions" in developing the battle plan was "[t]hat in a night surface engagement under favorable conditions our primary and most devastating weapon is the torpedo."[28]

This battle plan was not Commander Moosbrugger's battle plan, actually. It was originally developed by Commander Arleigh Burke, who had rapidly become a leading US Navy theoretician on destroyer tactics. But after he developed the plan, Burke, naturally, was reassigned, leaving it to Moosbrugger to carry out.[29] It was becoming a US Navy tradition, having a commander develop a battle plan, then reassigning him just before battle. To be sure, Moosbrugger had been involved in developing the plan. Then again, Admiral Wright had been involved in developing the plan at Tassafaronga, and you see how that worked out.

Five destroyers of Commander Moosbrugger's task group left Purvis Bay at around 11:30am, a full hour ahead of schedule because the *Maury's* main feed pumps were leaking, limiting her speed to 27 knots.[30] They picked up the *Sterett*, who was quite happy to get in some surface action after her long, post-Guadalcanal layoff, and *Stack* a little before 1:00pm, and positioned themselves in a circular cruising formation with Moosbrugger's own *Dunlap* at center.[31] It was good to be the commodore's ship.

The task group moved south of the Russell Islands and southeast of the Tetapari and Rendova islands. At 5:15pm, Commander Moosbrugger received a sighting report from a PBY Catalina relayed by Guadalcanal: "Relay of plane contact. Fast fleet 4 degrees 50 minutes south, 154 degrees 40 minutes east, course 190 degrees True, speed 15." The staff made some calculations and determined that if this "fast fleet" increased speed to 24 knots, it could reach Vella Gulf at midnight.[32] Of course, while it was nice to know the position, course, and speed of the contact, it would have been nicer to know what the contact actually was. A "fast fleet"? What the hell did that mean?

Shortly after 6:00pm, the force shifted from the circular cruising formation to a column, with the *Dunlap* leading Division 12 in front and Division 15 in back, 500-yard intervals between ships.[33] At 7:30, Commander Moosbrugger ordered Battle Stations. Tension built, but so did excitement. The *Maury's* Russell Crenshaw spoke for a lot of destroyer crewmen: "At last, destroyers were going to be employed as they were designed to be: as powerful fighting ships, free to use their speed and maneuverability, deployed in a sensible formation, and provided with a clear and logical plan of action. If our force found the enemy, all hands knew what to expect."[34] The gunnery officer of the *Sterett* and, like the *Sterett*, a veteran of the Friday the 13th Battle, Commander J.D. Jeffrey, prepared for a surface action for the first time since that Friday the 13th:

> Strapping on my .45 and my life jacket, I stepped out on deck and into the blackest night I ever saw. Through the opaque void I groped upward – more by familiarity than by sight – to the gun director, the highest battle station on the ship, located directly over the bridge. The director was a metal shell, a cube of perhaps fifteen feet, that swiveled in a complete circle and housed the computers, radar, optical rangefinder, communication circuits, and controls that were the electrical-mechanical brain directing the fire of the 5-inch main battery.
>
> It took perhaps thirty minutes for our eyes to adapt to that gloom – there was no way of marking precisely the passage of time. After thirty minutes it was just as black as when we had first come out. The feeling of claustrophobia that settled on us became understandable when we realized the clouds were not much higher than the mast.[35]

At 9:59pm, the column passed Gizo Island, and passed Lipari Island to port about 15 minutes later, at which time it broke up into the offset divisional columns, Division 15 on the starboard quarter of Division 12, as prescribed in the battle plan. Course was changed to 50 degrees True – northeast – and speed cut to 15 knots. In the gun director of the *Sterett* of Division 15, Commander Jeffrey struggled to see his fellow ships as the weather worsened. "A heavy mist started to fall. I was barely able to make out the phosphorescent wakes of the first division before; now they were swallowed up by that wall of nothingness into which they had disappeared."[36]

At 10:28pm course was changed to the southeast to poke around the entrance to Blackett Strait, then a little before 10:56 both columns turned to due north to sweep the Vella Gulf.[37]

Then things started happening, sort of. Radar picked up a surface contact at 11:18pm, but the contact was determined to be false, a reflection of the column, actually; radar was not nearly as reliable in 1943 as it is today. Five minutes later, both columns changed course to 30 degrees and raised speed to 25 knots.[38] A real radar contact would come soon enough.

In the gun director of the *Sterett*, Commander Jeffrey was getting hungry. The wardroom steward had given him a cheese sandwich and an apple to take care of any hunger pangs while he was at battle stations. Jeffrey unwrapped the cheese sandwich and took a bite. "That must have been the signal," Jeffrey later theorized.[39]

The signal for the *Dunlap*, in the lead, to pick up an unidentified ship bearing 359 degrees True – almost due north – range 23,900 yards at 11:33pm.[40] Radar continued tracking the ship, and soon the range dwindled to 19,700 yards on a bearing of 351 degrees True. Commander Moosbrugger asked the other destroyers to confirm. The *Craven* replied with "I have contact." Radar continued tracking. Moosbrugger ordered course changed to 335 degrees True to reach a good firing position for torpedoes. The torpedo tubes were trained to port; the torpedo directors began making calculations.[41]

Jeffrey tossed the sandwich over the side.[42] Radar continued tracking, and the contact seemed to split up into multiple targets. The *Craven* reported, "I have three targets; looks mighty nice to me." The *Dunlap* answered, "We have four." To this point, none of the enemy ships had been sighted visually, only on radar. The *Craven*'s estimates became the general torpedo firing solution: target course of roughly 180 degrees True, speed 26 knots, track angle of 290 degrees. The time was 11:41pm. Commander Moosbrugger ordered, "Execute Eight William Two."[43]

As Admiral Ainsworth had used it earlier, "William" was the code for launching torpedoes, but the confusion present when he used it at Kula Gulf would not repeat itself here. The *Dunlap*, *Craven*, and *Maury* each launched eight torpedoes – eight actual Mark 15 torpedoes with functioning detonators.

With this launch was the coming of age of US Navy destroyers, of the US Navy. In the words of historian John Prados, "These were classic night-destroyer tactics, the kind the Japanese had so often employed against American flotillas whose own tin cans were usually restricted by conforming to a battle line of heavy ships."[44] From now on, these tactics would also be used by the US Navy, especially one destroyer commodore named Arleigh Burke.

It took only four minutes for the new, actually functioning torpedoes to make their presence felt. Though Captain Hara missed it, the lead Japanese destroyer *Hagikaze* was the first hit, starting a large fire. The good news was the fire was quickly doused; the bad news was that it was doused by the plume of water from a second torpedo hit, this one to the machinery spaces, that brought the flameless *Hagikaze* staggering to a halt. The *Arashi* was also the recipient of two torpedoes to her engine room, and she drifted to a stop. Yet another torpedo hit the *Kawakaze* beneath her bridge in one of her magazines, causing a massive explosion that wrecked the ship. The *Shigure* had been last in the Japanese column, 1,500 meters behind the *Kawakaze* due to her sick engines. Those sick engines were her salvation. Mostly.[45]

Even before his torpedoes had hit, Commander Moosbrugger had ordered, "Division One, execute upon receipt, Turn Nine" – a 90-degree turn to port to avoid the torpedoes he assumed the Japanese would launch.[46] Correctly, as Captain Hara had launched all the *Shigure*'s torpedoes. On board the *Maury* and the other destroyers, crewmen held on to anything to keep from falling as the port turn caused a heel to starboard. Eventually, the ships righted themselves, presenting a narrow stern profile to any approaching Japanese torpedoes from which they would be running away.[47] The turn ruined Hara's chance for a retaliatory hit.

While the US Navy torpedoes were hitting, Commander Simpson's destroyers were moving. On the port bow of the Japanese ships, they turned to course 230 degrees True to

cut across the Japanese bows and rake them with gunfire in a classic "crossing of the 'T.'"
"At fairly close range, we poured perhaps fifteen salvos into the hulk of that second ship,"
recalled Cal Calhoun. "Each salvo caused further damage and started new fires. When it
seemed that the target could no longer stay afloat, we checked fire to catch our breath."[48]
It may have seemed like the target, the *Kawakaze*, could no longer stay afloat, but the *Stack*
added four torpedoes just to make sure, and the *Kawakaze* rolled over and sank at 11:52pm
without having fired a shot, her flaming fuel leaving a sheet of flame on the water.[49]

In the words of Morison, "[P]anic-stricken Japanese gunners in the *Hagikaze* and the
Arashi were both flailing about, firing raggedly in all directions." At destroyers, but also at
anything they thought they saw. Commander Moosbrugger's division turned around to
join in the gunnery action. The *Sterett* and *Stack* joined in the gunfire without signal in
accordance with Commander Simpson's doctrine, and by midnight all the remaining
Japanese guns had been silenced.[50]

Except for those of the *Shigure*. Her torpedo tubes reloaded, Captain Hara went
charging back into battle. Only to be treated to one of his destroyer-mates exploding.
Hara watched in horror as "tremendous fireworks filled the sky some three miles ahead.
Torrents of flares and flaming projectiles shot up in every direction with blinding
brightness."[51] Commander Jeffrey said, "The ship virtually disintegrated before our eyes as
a gigantic column of flame rose into the air. There was only one explosion. A part of her
stern, the last visible trace of the ship, went under as a subsequent salvo exploded above
it."[52] Another survivor described it as "like a bed of hot coals thrown a thousand feet into
the air."[53] That was the *Arashi*, her magazines exploding and sending her to the depths.[54]

The American gunfire stopped, leaving Captain Hara to ponder what exactly was out
there in the darkness waiting for him. The *Shigure*'s radio room reported that hails to the
other destroyers in his force were going unanswered. Hara had also noticed the destroyer's
maneuvering was sluggish.

Additionally, Captain Hara had to consider the lives of the 250 Imperial Army troops
on his ship. With no indication there were any friendly ships left, an unknown number of
enemy ships out there, and those Imperial Army troops on his ship, Hara decided to
withdraw. "It was a hard decision but there was no alternative," he later wrote.[55] He had
Rabaul informed of the disaster and requested instructions. Their answer came quickly:
"Return to base. Ask Kolombangara to rescue survivors."[56] And with that, the *Shigure* sped
off into the night.

Leaving one floating Japanese ship behind her, the *Hagikaze*. But with no way to move,
no weapons operable, and six destroyers ganging up on her, she had only a few minutes.
Commander Simpson ordered each of his destroyers to fire two torpedoes at the hulk.
After a few hits and a series of explosions, the *Hagikaze* joined the *Kawakaze* and *Arashi*
on the floor of Vella Gulf.[57]

Commander Moosbrugger's radar showed no more enemy targets. His destroyers stopped
firing. By now they were starting to have problems. The *Maury*'s feed pump finally gave out,
one of the *Sterett*'s guns had jammed, and the concussions from the *Dunlap*'s gunfire had

knocked her radar temporarily offline.[58] Moosbrugger's Division 12 headed back down The Slot toward Tulagi, leaving behind Division 15 with orders to pick up survivors.

The three destroyers crisscrossed Vella Gulf looking for Japanese survivors. And they found quite a few of them. To skipper Commander John L. Wilfong of the *Lang*, it seemed that "the sea was literally covered with Japs" – so thick that their bodies were seen to be thrown up in the phosphorescent wake of the vessel.[59] From all sides the survivors lifted a cry that sounded like "Kow-we, Kow-we," chanted in unison with considerable volume. "It was a weird unearthly sound punctuated at times by shrieks of mortal terror." When speed was reduced and efforts were made to pick up survivors, someone in the water blew a whistle, the chanting stopped, and the men all swam away from the ship.[60] Not surprisingly, Commander Simpson's ships could not recover any survivors, and they headed back to Tulagi at 2:00am. The Japanese had lost three destroyers. Of their 700 crewmen and 820 troops, only 310 survived.[61] American casualties consisted of one cheese sandwich.

The next morning under gray skies six Allied destroyers entered Tulagi Harbor. They seemed a little wet and bedraggled, but on every masthead was two-blocked a broom – symbol of a clean sweep of Vella Gulf.[62]

Not quite, but close enough.

When last we left General Sasaki, he was nowhere to be found. The Japanese positions around the Munda airfield had been abandoned, the Imperial Army soldiers and Special Naval Landing Force troops vanished. Not in a puff of smoke, mind you, unless you are counting the voluminous quantities of explosive munitions hurled at or dropped on the Japanese defenders by Allied naval guns, aircraft, and artillery, in which case it would be a very large puff of smoke. But they had vanished nonetheless.

Admiral Nimitz's admonition to "Remember, the enemy is hurting, too" was in effect.[63] The Japanese had constructed their defensive positions with exceptional skill and cunning, but they were not supermen. For once, the Japanese had a general who was competent and could hold his own against enemies who had even just an average level of training, equipment, and leadership, but General Sasaki was still no Yamashita, never mind Rommel, Guderian, or Manstein. American chipping away at the Japanese trenches, dugouts, and pillboxes had destroyed not just defensive positions, but lives. The effects of the repeated air attacks, artillery bombardment, and infantry assaults had taken a severe toll, far more than the Allies knew.

After several days of General Griswold's offensive, the vast majority of the Japanese fortifications around Munda were literally shells of their former selves. Infantry companies that had 160–170 men at the outset had been reduced to as few as 20. The 229th Infantry Regiment, the core of the Japanese defense of Munda, was down to 1,245 effectives. To compensate for the diminution of his regiment's strength, Colonel Hirata resorted to the usual solution in the Imperial Japanese Army: he ordered the soldiers of his 229th Infantry to kill ten Americans for each Japanese killed, and to fight until death.[64]

Except too many had already fought until death. Having to be on the front line every day kept the men's nerve on edge and fatigued them greatly, but the constant bombing and bombing, as with Pistol Pete and Washing Machine Charlie on Guadalcanal, prevented men from getting anywhere close to adequate sleep and even caused nervous disorders. The provision of medical care was even worse than it had been for the Allied troops.[65]

As the Japanese defenses around Munda started buckling, General Sasaki informed Admiral Samejima that the line could not hold for much longer and requested new instructions. In response, Samejima sent 8th Fleet staff officer Commander Kisaka Yoshitane, who arrived at Kongo Hill around 1:00 on the morning of July 30. But the response he brought contained no new instructions. As recorded in Sasaki's Confidential Log, the response merely read: "Our air strength shall gradually become dominant from mid-August. The Combined Fleet shall carry out a full-scale offensive in early or mid-September with all its power. Therefore, retain Kolombangara and Munda." How many times had such messages been given before? It sounded like 8th Fleet was trying to kick the can down the road again when the road had just ended in a cliff.[66]

But maybe that was not the case. Admiral Kusaka's chief of staff, Rear Admiral Nakahara Yoshimasa, recorded a more specific version of the message to the effect that the new goal was to prevent the use of the airfield, keep the supply lines to Kolombangara secure, and prevent a breakdown in the overall plan, even if that meant enduring a temporary setback. At the very least, General Sasaki now had some specific instructions that were perhaps more reasonable than those indicated in the log. Whatever the case, Sasaki appears to have acted in line with these instructions.[67]

General Sasaki sent orders that the withdrawal would be made the night of July 31–August 1. The new defense line – again, more like a series of fortified hills – would be anchored on Kokenggolo Hill on the right. Kokenggolo Hill had been smack in the middle of the Japanese position at Munda, and though it would leave the airfield itself outside the Japanese defenses, it would leave the airfield unusable. The defense line would run east of Bilbilo Hill to protect the Munda–Bairoko Trail, and then north to what the Japanese called Hachiman Hill. In general, Colonel Hirata's 229th Regiment would hold Kokenggolo Hill on the left and Colonel Tomonari's 13th Regiment would hold Hachiman Hill on the right.[68]

Commander Kisaka appears to have brought permission from Admiral Samejima to bring Major Yano and the rest of his 2nd Battalion of the 230th Infantry Regiment over from Kolombangara. Yano's troops were indeed brought over, put under Colonel Hirata's command, and positioned in the center of the line east of Bilbilo Hill at a place called Sankaku Hill. Finally, Kisaka probably told General Sasaki that General Inamura was sending reinforcements: a battalion of the 23rd Infantry on the night of August 1, and six companies of replacements for the 13th and 229th on the night of August 6.[69]

The withdrawal to the new positions did not go smoothly, however. Withdrawing from the front line under fire is one of the most difficult tactical maneuvers, and this one was further complicated by the continued bombardment by US Army artillery, which lived up to its reputation with the Japanese as "tremendously fierce and concentrated."[70] On August 1, almost 2,000 rounds were fired; on the 2nd another 2,000 rounds; on the 3rd 7,300 rounds; and 3,600 on the 4th.[71]

By August 2, General Sasaki's line had crystallized at Kokenggolo and Bilbilo Hills and their fortifications. But how long they could hold out under the continuing pressure from US Army infantry and especially artillery? Major Kojima and four of his officers were killed when a shell made a direct hit on their dugout on Bilbilo Hill. Major Hara was killed, and what remained of his 1st Battalion was placed under Major Sato's command early on August 2. For his part, Sato was in a tunnel in Kokenggolo Hill when a direct hit collapsed the entrance, burying him and 60 others; digging them out took the entirety of the next day. Colonel Tomonari barely escaped with his life after a shell hit his headquarters. A number of staff officers were killed, but Tomonari was unharmed. Such was the caprice of war.[72]

Of more concern to General Sasaki at that moment was the caprice of his superiors. On August 3, he received orders from Admiral Samejima to secure "an area" of New Georgia and the Vila-Stanmore complex on Kolombangara. Multiple times, Sasaki asked for clarification: "What area?" Naturally, he received no answer. Sasaki's exasperation was increased by a loss of confidence in Colonel Hirata, whom he blamed for sending overly optimistic and misleading reports from the front line. A bleak message from Major Yano was the proverbial last straw.[73] In all probability, Sasaki was probably sensing that his fears of an Allied envelopment were being realized. He had to get his troops out.

At 3:00am on August 4, General Sasaki ordered a general withdrawal northward to Zieta and that farm set up by 6th Kure Special Naval Landing Force. He would set his headquarters up at the farm. Colonel Hirata was to be the rearguard until dusk, when he would withdraw to Kongo Hill and Admiral Ota's units.[74] By the end of day on August 4, both the 148th and 161st Infantry Regiments had broken through to the sea north of Kokenggolo Hill, but the Japanese troops had escaped the trap.[75] Nevertheless, while General Sasaki had carried out his orders to hold "an area" of New Georgia, with the loss of not just the airfield but of Kokenggolo Hill, he could no longer prevent its use. And, unlike Guadalcanal, the Allies were prepared to take full advantage right away.

But how could they handle the remaining Japanese troops on New Georgia? And Kolombangara?

Those wild and wacky PT boats. One never knew what they were going to do, and, likely, neither did they. It's a theme hit repeatedly within these pages. PT boats looked great in theory. Just bolt two torpedo tubes and some machine guns on a fast yacht and turn them loose on the enemy. Except all too often they turned loose on the Allies. At this point in the Pacific War, they had confirmed sinkings of just as many friendly ships (the *McCawley*) as enemy ships (the *Teruzuki*). And within these pages have been numerous friendly fire near-incidents. Whether it was threatening to torpedo the *Portland* after the Friday the 13th Action; having to be ordered to let the battleships *Washington* and *South Dakota* pass off Guadalcanal; or actually launching torpedoes at US Navy destroyers off Enogai.

But perhaps focusing on the friendly fire incidents and near-incidents is not entirely fair. The motor torpedo boat was a relatively new concept. Certainly, they were fast, maneuverable, cheap, expendable. Well, the boats were expendable. Not the crews. Lieutenant (jg) Kennedy and the survivors of *PT-109* certainly found that out. After an epic six-day struggle across places like Plum Pudding Island during which they needed the help of Melanesian scouts to survive, Kennedy and his crew were rescued by *PT-157*, which had reporters aboard, and taken back to Rendova. Kennedy himself would be treated as a hero. The fact that he had completely missed seeing a destroyer until it was cutting his boat in half was conveniently forgotten. It was hoped that John F. Kennedy would use the experience to make something of his life.

It was an example of what PT boats could do. They could not only sink ships, enemy and friendly. They could rescue downed airmen, survivors of sunken ships (enemy and friendly), and exposed coastwatchers. They could drop off scouts such as US Army Colonel Frank L. Beadle, General Harmon's chief engineer, and his party of six, whom the PTs deposited on Vella Lavella during the night of July 21–22.[76] The PTs could patrol the littoral looking for Japanese soldiers and hidden boats and barges.

One thing they could not do was lead an amphibious invasion. They had tried at Nassau Bay, and you see how that worked out. At least that's what the Japanese thought. Besides, the Japanese had much more important things to worry about than what a handful of little PT boats were doing. They knew something was going on with the Allies. Something big. In early August Japanese radio intelligence reported increased Allied radio traffic. Scout planes reported a new concentration of ships at Guadalcanal. Tokyo and Rabaul guessed a new invasion was coming. Admiral Kusaka believed the next target was Kolombangara. The island was, in fact, the next logical target.

On the front lines of this uncertainty was General Sasaki, still on New Georgia, for the moment, at least. He had complied with his orders, vague though those orders might have been, and held on to "an area" of the island. Though General Griswold's plan had called for an envelopment of the Munda base, Sasaki had correctly surmised the Allied plan of attack and was able to get almost all of his troops out of the planned trap. They had moved to hold roughly the area of Bairoko, thus protecting the supply line from and the line of retreat to Kolombangara, and Zieta, with its farm-fresh produce courtesy of the 6th Kure Special Naval Landing Force.

Even so, General Sasaki moved most of the Japanese troops off of New Georgia proper. Colonel Tomonari was ordered to take his 13th Infantry Regiment back to Kolombangara and prepare its defenses. Major Nagakari Miyoshi would hold Baanga Island with his 3rd Battalion, 23rd Infantry Regiment and two 120mm naval guns, which would shell the now-enemy-held Munda air base. Admiral Ota would defend southern Arundel Island with his Special Naval Landing Force troops. All that was left on New Georgia was Colonel

Hirata's 229th Infantry Regiment, which Sasaki positioned two kilometers east of Zieta. Also available were a little less than 1,000 troops, including antiaircraft gunners and construction personnel. Sasaki moved these troops, along with his headquarters, to Zieta, where they dug in and enjoyed that farm-fresh produce as they waited for reinforcements.[77]

And those reinforcements were coming: six companies from the 6th Kumamoto and 38th Nagoya Divisions in a mixed battalion temporarily under the command of Captain Mikami Kisaburo and thus called the Mikami Detachment. They would come in on the night of August 6–7 on four destroyers commanded by Captain Sugiura. Or they would have come in, had three of those destroyers not been sunk the night of August 6–7, taking most of the troops with them and unceremoniously dumping the rest into the Vella Gulf.[78]

With the end of General Sasaki's reinforcements came the end of General Sasaki's hopes for holding "an area" of New Georgia proper. On August 7, he ordered a general withdrawal to Kolombangara via Baanga Island. Or would have ordered a general withdrawal to Kolombangara had Rabaul not stepped in, ordering Sasaki to hold an area of New Georgia for future operations. A staff officer would come down to bring him further instructions. Sasaki just moved his headquarters to Vila and had Colonel Hirata's troops hold up at Baanga.[79] The staff officer arrived from Rabaul on August 9 and handed General Sasaki his new orders, which were … to hold an area of New Georgia for future operations. Sasaki would be notified when these "future operations" had been decided. In other words, don't call us; we'll call you.[80]

By this time, like Admiral Tanaka almost a year earlier, General Sasaki had to be exasperated with his superiors in Rabaul, even more than when they told him to hold "an area" of New Georgia. Not because they gave him contradictory orders as they had with Tanaka, but because they gave orders that at once were both vague and inflexible, demonstrating a certain detachment from the events on New Georgia. It was said that Sasaki actually felt sorry for Admiral Samejima, stuck as he was directing a land battle he didn't understand with forces not even remotely strong enough to wage it.[81]

In actuality, Admiral Samejima was relaying orders given by Imperial General Headquarters. On August 7, the army and navy operations sections agreed to withdraw from the Central Solomons and to cooperate in building up Bougainville. That would require a new agreement between the Imperial Army and the Imperial Navy, which would have to be put before the Emperor.

And the Emperor was, well, not entirely pleased with his armed forces. On June 29 he summoned Prime Minister Tojo to the Imperial Palace and, as Tojo told it, promptly gave the prime minister an imperial tongue lashing. "You keep repeating that the Imperial Army is invulnerable, yet whenever the enemy lands you lose the battle," the Emperor said. "You've never been able to repulse an enemy landing. Can't you do it *somewhere*? How is this war going to turn out?"[82]

The uncharacteristic display of imperial anger left Prime Minister Tojo shaken. Admitting the Emperor was "sorely troubled," Tojo told one of his staff, "[W]e must come up with some measure. It is extremely urgent. Without saying it's an order of the Emperor, we must insist on a definite strategic plan indicating exactly where we can stem the enemy counteroffensive and where our last defense line should be."[83]

That was the day before the Allied landings on New Georgia. And, no, the Emperor's attitude had not improved much since then. Not with the Allied invasion of Sicily that left Italy teetering and the shattering of the Wehrmacht's panzer arm at Kursk during July. On August 5, he chewed out the Army Chief of Staff Sugiyama, recently promoted to field marshal, for the defeats in New Guinea and the Solomons. "We can't continue being pushed back inch by inch. Constant setbacks will produce a great effect not only on the enemy but on the third nations. When are you going to wage the Decisive Battle?"

"Things have gone wrong for us everywhere," Sugiyama replied, "I am deeply sorry."

The Emperor was unmoved:

You may well be. If we are forced to retreat gradually like this, the uplift for our enemies, and the effect even on neutrals, will be great. Where in the world are you going to dig in? Where do you propose to fight a decisive battle? I don't think we can afford to keep being pushed back like this, bit by bit, do you?[84]

That same day, the Munda air base fell to the Allies. The Emperor was showing a disquieting talent for summoning his military aides immediately before a major disaster. It's more traditional to summon military aides after a major disaster. Like on August 8, after the Mikami Detachment wound up in the Vella Gulf, when His Majesty vented his frustration with the Imperial Navy to his chief military aide, General Hasunuma Shigeru.

"What in the world is the Navy doing?" he asked Hasunuma. "Isn't there any way we can get our men to attack the enemy? They are gradually being pushed back and losing their confidence. Couldn't they somehow deal the enemy a heavy blow somewhere?"[85] That same day, Field Marshal Sugiyama was treated to the same refrain from the throne, "Can't we take the offensive somewhere? ... Isn't there any way to strengthen the air force quickly? ... Isn't there any possibility of slapping the Americans one sharp blow?"[86]

For Imperial General Headquarters, the Emperor's anger coupled with the crumbling situation on New Georgia meant another round of meetings between the Army and the Navy. As an interim measure while those discussions went on, on August 13, Admiral Nagano issued NGS Directive No. 267, providing that the Solomons battle be waged by forces in place, which forces should withdraw to rear positions beginning in late September.[87]

In this atmosphere, four enemy PT boats did not seem all that important. Four PT boats – -104, -107, -168, and -169 – under US Navy Captain George C. Kriner left Rendova at 5:30pm on August 12. The Japanese didn't think much of it; the boats must be patrolling the Blackett Strait or the Vella Gulf. A few Louie the Lice from the 938 Air Group came out to do what lice do: make people uncomfortable or in this instance bombing and strafing for more than two hours in almost continuous attacks. The four boats became separated. One bomb exploded some 10 feet astern of PT-168, riddling the hull with holes, wounding four, and knocking all three of the boat's engines offline. Skipper Ensign William F. Griffin and his crew managed to get two engines going, but how long they would keep going was an open question. Griffin radioed for help. Lieutenant (jg) David M. Payne's *PT-106*, patrolling the area and not part of Griffin's mission, picked up the signal. Payne rounded up *PT-169* under skipper Lieutenant (jg) Philip A. Potter, Jr, who was part of the mission. Potter came alongside Griffin's boat and took off *PT-168*'s passengers so the mission could continue. *PT-106* took off -*168*'s four wounded, then escorted the limping boat through the Ferguson Passage before speeding back to Rendova to get the wounded medical treatment. Naturally, just after *PT-106* departed, -*168*'s engines went down again. *PT-103* under Lieutenant (jg) Joseph K. Roberts, in the area on a separate patrol, had to tow -*168* back to Rendova.[88]

A few hiccups, but the mission was proceeding. *PT-107* under Lieutenant (jg) William F. Barrett, Jr, reached the landing site first and started disembarking its passengers. As it did so, *PT-104* under Lieutenant (jg) Robert D. Shearer arrived, as did *PT-169*, and began dumping their passengers. But they had issues. The inflatable rubber boats they had brought along to take them to shore proved not so inflatable. Locals paddled out in canoes to take the Americans ashore. All was complete by 3:20am and the PTs headed back to Rendova. En route, at around 5:00am, they came across *PT-103* towing -*168*. *PT-107* stayed with the tow until fighter protection arrived at 6:30am. PTs -*103* and -*168* arrived back at Rendova around 9:00am.[89]

Meanwhile, the passengers the PTs had dumped – 40 officers and enlisted men – were conducting their mission in an area near the southern tip of Vella Lavella known as Barakoma. They made contact with coastwatchers Josselyn and Silvester. The previous day, August 11, Josselyn had radioed Guadalcanal that there were 40 Japanese in his area. A South Pacific Air intelligence bulletin had gone out saying, "Forty Japanese had landed on SE Coast of Vella Lavella by 12 August. They were unarmed and were taken prisoners by Allied scouts on the island." It added, "They came from Vila because of the food shortage and the terrific bombing." Of the 40 Americans whom the PT boats had just landed, 26 were from the 103rd Infantry Regiment. Their job was to take custody of the prisoners. One complication: when Captain Kriner and the Americans landed at Barakoma, they quickly found out the Japanese were not prisoners.[90]

Oh well, details. Josselyn had updated his report to the effect that there were now 140 Japanese in the area – 40 at Biloa and 100 about five miles north of Barakoma. Naturally, this update had not reached the troops who might actually have to face them. Josselyn indicated they were under surveillance but were not prisoners. Most of them appeared to be starving, ragged, armed only with "grenades, clubs and a few firearms." They were mostly survivors from the Battle of Vella Gulf. Nonetheless, they could be a problem, Captain Kriner decided, so he asked for reinforcements. At 4:45am on August 14, PTs -*103*, -*169*, -*175*, and -*180* left Rendova with 72 officers and men from the 103rd Infantry, landed them at Barakoma five hours later under the protection of four Kiwi Kittyhawks from No. 16 Squadron, then headed back.[91] Those 140 Japanese shouldn't be a problem now.

Not to the normal soldiers, at any rate. But, of the 40 Americans whom the PT boats had landed on the night of August 12–13, 26 were from the 103rd Infantry Regiment; the remaining 14 were naval pathfinders whose job was to mark beaches for an amphibious invasion. They had to remain secret, which was hard when you had about 100 soldiers around trying to capture Japanese, of whom they captured ... seven.[92] Oh, well, details.

But details were important now because the Allies were embarking on yet another amphibious invasion, even though the campaign started by their last amphibious invasion, New Georgia, wasn't even finished. Stranger yet, this invasion deviated from the *Cartwheel* plan inasmuch as they were not landing on the next major island in the Solomons chain, Kolombangara, but were instead skipping it and landing on Vella Lavella, the island on the other side of Kolombangara from New Georgia.

It was the culmination of a fast-moving series of events. Recall that on the night of July 21–22, Colonel Beadle took a party of six to Vella Lavella in a PT boat.[93] Aerial photographs had shown two locations that might be good for an airfield or two. Beadle's mission was to check out the two sites and if they weren't going to work, he was to find ones that would. Henry Josselyn and his scouts met Beadle and his team at Barakoma, then they went off to inspect the two sites. Neither proved doable. But, oddly enough, the place where they landed, Barakoma, looked workable if they put the runway almost right up against the coast. Furthermore, you could get the landing ships onto the beach.

From such humble beginnings, at least in the South Pacific, came what would become known as "island hopping." "Island hopping" isn't exactly a clear term, however. If you're going across a big ocean, you could call going from island to island "island hopping" because you're "hopping" over water. But that's not what it means. What "island hopping" means is more along the lines of "leapfrogging." You're hopping over other islands, preferably islands the enemy has strongly defended, to get to other islands that are not so strongly defended in order to cut off the aforementioned islands that are strongly defended. And leave them to "wither on the vine."

As Admiral Halsey explained it:

The nearest island north of New Georgia, Kolombangara, had a fighter strip at Vila-Stanmore and – as confirmed by a combat reconnaissance team – a garrison of 10,000 troops dug into positions as nearly impregnable as Munda's. The undue length of the Munda operation and our heavy casualties made me wary of another slugging match, but I didn't know how to avoid it.[94]

Halsey figured it out soon enough: avoid Kolombangara altogether.

Northwest of Kolombangara was Vella Lavella. These pages first got up close and personal with Vella Lavella when the survivors of the *Helena* ended up there. There were Japanese on the island, but very few. Some Imperial Army patrols and a tiny base near Horaniu for barges. The American victory at Vella Gulf had the weird consequence of actually increasing the Japanese presence on Vella Lavella as survivors of the three Japanese destroyers ended up there just as had the *Helena* survivors. But the Japanese presence on the island was still minimal.

If the Allies took Vella Lavella, Kolombangara and its 10,000 troops would be cut off. All the Allies would have to do is "hop" or leapfrog over Kolombangara to Vella Lavella. They needed the Munda airfield to provide fighter coverage for the landing because Base Air Force would mount a ferocious counterattack, especially with its base at Ballale only 60 miles away and Kahili only 30 miles beyond that.

The Seabees of the 73rd and 24th Naval Construction Battalions had the unenviable task of getting the Munda airfield into shape. Though the "Munda airfield looked like a slash of white coral in a Doré drawing of hell [...]," damage to the runway was less than expected. The Japanese appear to have made little if any effort to destroy the installations. As a result, work proceeded rapidly. On August 7, barely two days after its capture, the airfield, though rough, was reported able to handle emergency landings. Army Air Force Lieutenant Cotesworth B. Head, Jr, became the first Allied pilot to land at the airstrip on August 13 in his 44th Fighter Squadron P-40 Warhawk. The next day, the 24 F4U Corsairs of Marine Fighting 123 and 124 staged into Munda. They were quickly joined by General Mulcahy.[95] Between Munda and Segi, they had their air cover.

It was becoming a familiar theme: capturing something from the Japanese and finding they had made no effort to render that something useless to the enemy. On Guadalcanal, it was the airfield, though there were mitigating circumstances inasmuch as there were almost no defenders; as a result the Lunga airfield was captured quickly. There was no such excuse at Munda. The airfield was the obvious target of the Allies for months, yet the Japanese did little to damage it. Even worse from the Japanese standpoint, they left behind a "treasure trove" of "material of intelligence value" at Munda. Among the materials captured was a list of code designators used in communications for geographic locations in the South Pacific. Also captured was Southeast Area Fleet Operations Order No. 10, issued by Admiral Kusaka on July 18, detailing the strategy the Japanese were following in the Central Solomons.[96] It was as if the Japanese military could not conceive of anything being captured by the enemy, so they made no preparations for that possibility.

The Allies would take full advantage. Admiral Halsey issued his orders for the invasion on August 11. The landing was set for August 15, not even two days after Munda was fully operational. According to one US Army historian, "He organized his forces much as he had for the invasion of New Georgia." Not exactly. The invasion of Vella Lavella would be much smaller and simpler, not like the swarm of landings at sometimes bizarre locales on New Georgia. Like New Georgia, however, the landing force would be designated Task Force 31, though now it was under Admiral Wilkinson. Task Force 31 would land at Barakoma near the southern tip of Vella Lavella. Wilkinson planned to only occupy the southern half of the island. Naturally, Halsey chose to call this unit the "Northern Force."[97]

For his part, Admiral Wilkinson issued Operations Order No. A12-43, which defined his mission: "Commencing on Dog Day this force will seize the vicinity of BARAKOMA, VELLA LAVELLA, capture or destroy enemy forces encountered, and will construct an airfield; in order to develop VELLA LAVELLA as a base for further offensive operations." He divided the Northern Force into three echelons, consisting of an invasion group (the main body) and two other echelons.

Wilkinson then subdivided the main body into three subgroups. The Advance Transport Group consisted of seven of those fast destroyer-transports (*Stringham, Waters, Dent, Talbot, Kilty, Ward,* and *McKean*) escorted by destroyers *Nicholas, O'Bannon, Taylor, Chevalier, Cony,* and *Pringle.* Commanding this group was the veteran destroyer commodore Captain Ryan from his trusted *Nicholas,* though Admiral Wilkinson himself was in the *Cony.* The Second Transport Group, under destroyer commodore Captain Cooke, consisted of 12 landing craft escorted by destroyers *Waller, Saufley, Philip,* and *Renshaw.* The Third Transport Group, under Captain Grayson B. "Chick" Carter, consisted of three landing ships – *LST-354, -395,* and *-399,* escorted by destroyers *Conway* and *Eaton,* and submarine chasers *SC-760* and *-761.* Between all three echelons, the Allies would land 5,888 men, including the 35th Infantry Regiment of the 25th Infantry Division; the 4th Marine Defense Battalion; the 25th Cavalry Reconnaissance Troop; the 58th Naval Construction Battalion; and a naval base group. The troops were commanded by Brigadier General Robert B. McClure, assistant commander of the 25th Division, who had commanded the 35th Infantry during the Guadalcanal Campaign. Again, another commander with jungle experience who was not used for the invasion of New Georgia that turned into a quagmire from which the Allies were still extricating themselves. Moving right along, one mistake from *Toenails* that was corrected now was the ambiguity of the transfer of command from the transport force commander to the army commander. McClure would be under Wilkinson's command until he was established ashore, estimated to be September 3, when Wilkinson would turn over command to General Griswold.[98]

Putting the hard-earned and -learned lessons of Guadalcanal, the Russells, and New Georgia into use here required a delicate juggling of the invasion forces and their transports. Admiral Wilkinson planned to have the landing and offloading completed within 12 hours. The destroyer-transports of the Advance Transport Group were the fastest vessels involved in landing the troops on Vella Lavella and were scheduled to arrive at the landing zone first at 6:10am on August 15. Naturally, they were scheduled to leave Guadalcanal last, at 4:00pm on August 14. Conversely, the slowest vessels, the landing ships of the Third Transport Group, were scheduled to land last at 8:00am on August 15, and were scheduled to leave Guadalcanal first, at 3:00am on August 14. The landing craft of the Second Transport Group were in between both, leaving Guadalcanal at 8:00am on August 14 for their planned landing at 7:10am on August 15.[99] As weird as it sounds, it did, as it turned out, make sense.

The embarkation came off without a hitch and the ships left on schedule, heading south of New Georgia through Blanche Channel and Gizo Strait. To screen the vulnerable transports, picket lines of PT boats were set up the night of August 14–15. Boats based in Lever Harbor were off Vella Gulf, while boats based in Rendova patrolled off Wilson Strait and between Ganongga and Simbo. Their night was uneventful, perhaps because the attention of the Louie the Lice of the 938 Air Group was focused on two other PT escorting a transport and two landing ships to Enogai. No harm, no foul, and the PT from the pickets were back at base by dawn.[100]

In the meantime, the logic of the seemingly weird schedule of the invasion transports became apparent. The Second Transport Group passed the slower Third Transport Group, and at 3:05am the Advance Transport Group, with the fastest of the transports, passed the first two groups and took the lead. The Advance Transport Group, carrying two battalions of the 35th Regiment under Colonel Everett Brown, troops needed to actually secure the landing area, may have been the fastest of the transports, but they also had the smallest capacity. They had one hour to land their troops and get out so the Second Transport Group could get in.[101]

Sure enough, at 6:20am, the troops began landing from the Advance Transport Group. The 2nd Battalion landed at 6:24 and started heading south toward Biloa Mission. The 1st Battalion landed companies abreast six minutes later and headed north across the Barakoma River. At 6:45, the fast destroyer transports and four of the escorting destroyers headed back to Guadalcanal. Two remained: the *Cony*, with Admiral Wilkinson on board, and the *Pringle*.[102]

Then the landing craft of the Second Transport Group started to poke their way in, right on schedule. But, surely, no one expected the landing to go this easily. The landing beach was smaller than reported, and only eight of the landing craft could land at one time, instead of a dozen. When the landing ships arrived at 8:00am, on schedule, the last four landing craft were still unloading.[103]

Naturally, this was the time the Japanese chose to attack. Base Air Force was now new and improved. With not just the aircraft of Carrier Division 2 (*Ryuho*, *Junyo*, and *Hiyo*), but also the new commander of Carrier Division 2, Rear Admiral Sakamaki Munetake, who had arrived on July 20. Admiral Kusaka reorganized his command so all fighters would be at Buin under Admiral Kosaka's 26th Air Flotilla (or 6th Air Attack Force) while the land-based bombers would remain at Rabaul under Admiral Ueno's 25th Air Flotilla (or 5th Air Attack Force). The fighters from the *Ryuho* and *Junyo* were placed under the auspices of the 204 Air Group. All the Aichi D3A carrier bombers and Nakajima B5N carrier attack planes at Buin were placed under the auspices of the new, non-composite, fighterless 582 Air Group in what Kusaka designated the 2nd Mobile Air Attack Force. Evidently realizing that calling a group of aircraft "mobile" was rather superfluous, Kusaka put everything at Buin under the much-better-sounding "1st Combined Air Attack Force" under Admiral Sakamaki. It made for a confusing command structure over the roughly 220 aircraft of Base Air Force.[104]

On this day, it was the 1st Combined Air Attack Force. At 3:00am, a Japanese plane, likely from the 938 Air Group, sighted part of the invasion force off Gatukai still in the lower New Georgia islands.[105] So when that 1st Combined Air Attack Force, which had taken off from Buin at 5:00am with 47 Zeros escorting six D3As, found the Americans just before 8:00am off Vella Lavella, it was very much a shock to the Japanese system. They had done absolutely nothing to secure Vella Lavella, had not even considered the possibility the Allies would invade it. A failure of imagination. They had no garrison per se on the island; the Japanese present there were either patrols from Kolombangara, manning that tiny base at Horaniu, or survivors from sunken ships in the Vella Gulf. They were not organized for defense. Air attacks were the only way the Japanese could respond to being taken by surprise once again.

Upon arrival over Vella Lavella, the 1st Combined Air Attack Force would face an AirSols that had changed markedly in the last month, not entirely for the better. After the air attacks on July 25, Navy Fighting 11, 21, 26, 27, and 28 were all withdrawn to the US for re-equipping and retraining. Re-equipping inasmuch as their Grumman F4F Wildcats were finally being replaced, not by the Vought F4U Corsair, but by Grumman's successor to the Wildcat, the F6F Hellcat. Retraining inasmuch as the pilots would be prepared for duty on the new carriers that were coming online.[106]

Commensurate with those aircraft carriers coming online, Admiral Mitscher left AirSols to become commander of many of those carriers. His replacement was the US Army Air Force's Major General Nathan Farragut Twining. Twining, brother to the US Marines' Lieutenant Colonel Twining, was thus the first commander of AirSols and its predecessor the Cactus Air Force to come from the Army Air Force. With Twining's arrival, the top subordinate commanders, with the exception of Hansen (Photographic Command), also changed as scheduled. US Navy Captain Charles Coe took over as chief of staff, US Marine Lieutenant Colonel D.F. O'Neill took over Strike Command, US Army Air Force Brigadier General Don Strother (AAF) took over Fighter Command, and US Army Air Force Colonel William A. Matheny moved up from command of the 307th Bombardment Group to Bomber Command.[107]

Of course, with the withdrawal of all the Navy Wildcats, General Twining now faced a shortage of fighters. AirSols had 161 serviceable fighters on July 31; two weeks later that figure was down to 129.[108] Nevertheless, if the Allies lost this air battle, you can be sure that Washington would say it would be all *his* fault.

The air battle for General Twining this August 15 started with 47 Zeros and six D3As taking off from Buin at 5:00am on an armed reconnaissance mission. Warhawks of the 44th Fighter Squadron and Kittyhawks from the Kiwi No. 16 Squadron out of Segi were flying air cover when the incoming Japanese were reported at 7:41am. The 'Hawks were quickly joined by Corsairs from Marine Fighting 123 and 124 operating out of Munda. The loss of the Munda air base would cause the Japanese considerable pain. The 'Hawks pounced on the Zeros, but the D3As came in under the fighter scrum, looped around to come at their targets from the east, and made shallow dives out of the morning sun on the invasion ships. Cunning, but ineffective. Admiral Wilkinson's *Cony* was drenched by towering water columns from three near misses; *Philip* and *LST-395* also took near misses. But that was it.[109]

Lieutenant Ken Walsh of Marine Fighting 124 had already shot down a Zero before he caught up to the Vals and knocked down two of them. Then he was jumped by Zeros, who shot up his Corsair and put a 20mm shell into his starboard wing tank. He had to redline his engines to get back to Munda, where he landed safely to the cheers of the ground crews. They counted 57 holes in the F4U, and found that 20mm rounds had shot out his hydraulics and hit the main spar. He should never have made it back, and the Corsair was written off. All told, five Zeros and three Vals were shot down. Japanese pilots claimed seven enemy aircraft destroyed and eight probables – in reality, they had shot down one Warhawk, that of Army Lieutenant Robert Robb, who was killed, and damaged one more – and reported that they had "repuls[ed] fifty aircraft." They also claimed to have sunk three "large transports" and one "large landing barge."[110]

These reports only encouraged Admiral Kusaka, who kept the pressure on. Between 9:10 and 9:30am, the next attack, involving 48 Zeros led by Lieutenant Kawai Shiro of the 201 Air Group escorting 11 D3As, took off from Buin. By the time they had arrived over Barakoma around 12:30pm, the three landing ships were unloading, having moved in after the landing craft completed their work around 9:00am. This time, air cover was provided by the Corsairs from Marine Fighting 215. The radio propagandist known as Tokyo Rose had bragged that "no LST (landing ship) will be allowed to land its cargo." Aware that the landing ships had only seven machine guns apiece – for those of us who are mathematically challenged, three landing ships meant 21 machine guns – seven Zeros swept low over the beach and the landing ships to make strafing runs. Also aware that the landing ships had only seven machine guns apiece was Captain Carter, who decided to do something about it by borrowing 21 20mm cannons from Guadalcanal and deploying the heavy guns of the 4th Marine Defense Battalion's Special Weapons Section on the landing ships' main decks. The Zeros were shocked to find themselves caught in a hellish crossfire and were quickly driven away, but not before Warrant Officer Kondo Masaichi of the *Junyo* had been seriously wounded. The unexpectedly heavy antiaircraft fire ruined the Vals' attacks. Even so, the Japanese believed they had set three transports afire.[111]

Not content with the results so far, that afternoon Admiral Kusaka launched a third attack, with 45 Zeros escorting eight D3As. They were met by more Corsairs of Marine Fighting 123 and 124 and this time four Airacobras of the 12th Fighter Squadron. Once again, the attacks by the Vals were completely ineffective. Three of the Zeros were shot down, including one by the 12th's Captain Cyril Nichols; it seems the Airacobras were gaining effectiveness as interceptors, a far cry from the early days on Guadalcanal when the pilots of the 67th Fighter Squadron felt helpless in their Airacobras against the Zeros. The Japanese claimed eight victories for the loss of three fighters. But their mission had failed, not that the Japanese saw it that way. For this last attack, they claimed to have sunk one transport, two cruisers, and one destroyer. Nonetheless, the landing ships pulled up their ramps at 6:00pm and headed home. At a cost of 12 killed and 40 wounded, they had landed 4,600 troops and 2,300 tons of gear including eight 90mm antiaircraft guns, 15 days' supplies, and three units of fire for all weapons except antiaircraft guns, for which one unit was landed.[112] The day had been a success.

But the day was not yet over. To add insult to injury, the Japanese returned to Buin and entered the landing circle after a long day of combat, only to find the landing circle a little crowded. Roaring out from behind Choiseul were eight Corsairs from Marine Fighting 214, coming in line abreast, sweeping across the runway in one big strafing run, the first the Allies had ever made on the Buin/Kahili air base. One Val just about to touch down was caught in the hail of gunfire and promptly flipped over, landing on its back. Two gas trucks just off the runway refueling aircraft exploded with satisfying balls of flame. Buin was in chaos as personnel ran for cover. And just like that, the Corsairs were gone. Badly outnumbered and over an enemy air base, they knew not to stick around, so they sped away, knowing the discombobulated Zeros would not catch them. The Marine pilots claimed three Vals shot down and four destroyed on the ground.[113]

For the day, the Japanese lost nine Zeros and eight D3As. The Japanese pilots claimed the sinking of four large transports, two cruisers, and one destroyer; with four transports damaged and 29 Allied aircraft shot down. In combat, AirSols had lost Lieutenant Robb and his Warhawk and one Corsair, the pilot rescued. AirSols had a worse day at Munda itself with operational accidents, losing five fighters, with two pilots injured. Two of the fighters were Corsairs from Marine Fighting 124 who had tried to take off from opposite ends of the runway, which is not considered among the best practices for airport management. Both pilots were lucky to be alive, though one was seriously injured.[114]

And yet the day was still not over, not for Base Air Force's 5th Air Attack Force, at any rate. At 3:30pm, three G4Ms took off from Vunakanau with the job of finding the retiring invasion convoys and keeping tabs on them. They succeeded admirably, finding the Second Transport Group southeast of Gatukai and the Third Transport Group entering the Gizo Strait. Hoping for a repeat of the attack on the *Chicago*, Admiral Ueno then sent an air strike of 23 G4Ms – seven from the 752 Air Group armed with torpedoes and 16 from the 702 Air Group armed with bombs.[115]

It was the 752 Air Group who first made contact, in this case with the Second Transport Group. They went after the landing craft, but Captain Cooke skillfully handled his ships, and the destroyers *Waller*, *Saufley*, *Philip*, and *Renshaw* put up such heavy antiaircraft fire that it spoiled the aim of the Japanese pilots, and all the torpedoes missed. At least nine of the G4Ms armed with bombs found the Third Transport Group. Captain Carter's foresight with the 20mm guns on the landing ships paid off again, spoiling the Bettys' aim, resulting in no hits. For this meager result, the Japanese lost two G4Ms: one from the 752 Air Group that had a landing mishap and the second one of the tracking planes that was so badly damaged it had to ditch; the crew was rescued.[116]

But, again, that was not all. Louie the Lice had to make their appearance at 8:34pm, when they found the Third Transport Group. After an already exhausting day, Captain Carter and his sailors had to deal with the harassing floatplanes dropping flares, float lights, and the occasional bomb. The Americans had to perform evasive maneuvers, lay smokescreens, and use those 20mm guns to keep the pesky Petes at bay until midnight, when the Japanese headed back. The *Conway*'s skipper Commander Nathaniel Scudder Prime said coming out of the engagement undamaged was due to "a perfectly phenomenal supply of good luck."[117] And with that, the action of August 15, 1943, came to a merciful end.

So, now what? By the time the day's combat actions were finally completed, General McClure had the 35th Infantry Regiment dug in. The 4th Marine Defense Battalion had 16 .50cal., eight 20mm, and eight 40mm antiaircraft guns and two searchlights unlimbered and set up. They had that 2,300 tons of gear and 15 days' supplies, but much of it was scattered on the beach since the men did not like unloading transports and carrying the supplies to cache areas, so organizing them would take time. But already the Americans outnumbered the Japanese on Vella Lavella about 18 to 1. And two echelons of Allied troops were still to come.[118]

Also still to come, the full Japanese response.

When last we left Baron Ijuin Matsuji, he was congratulating Destroyer Division 11's Commodore Yamashiro and the *Amagiri*'s skipper Lieutenant Commander Hanami for winning the greatest naval victory since, at least, Trafalgar, probably the Spanish Armada, maybe even Salamis, in their destroyer sinking a torpedo boat.

Baron Ijuin had first gained some prominence in this Pacific War as the skipper of the heavy cruiser *Atago* and therefore the flag captain for Admiral Kondo, commander of the 2nd Fleet. While Admiral Kondo had been largely sidelined, Baron Ijuin was moving up in the world, to a degree. He had been given command of the 3rd Destroyer Flotilla and would officially be promoted to rear admiral, appropriate for and commensurate with a flotilla command, on November 1. Not bad for someone who finished 92nd out of his class of 95 at Etajima.[119] Then again, Matsuji was the son of Baron Ijuin Goro, Vice Chief of the Naval General Staff during the Russo-Japanese War and later Commander in Chief of the Combined Fleet.

With Admirals Akiyama and Izaki now at the bottom of the Kula Gulf, it was the pending Admiral Ijuin who was next man up. Captain Hara, who worked with Ijuin firsthand, said Ijuin was "a remarkably congenial and friendly person despite his noble rank of baron. Born with a silver spoon in his mouth, he had achieved a Navy-wide reputation as an excellent navigator."[120] The Imperial Japanese Navy did seem to reward excellent navigators, those officers like Admiral Kimura Susumu who could get you there. The question was, once they got you there, could they do anything else?

The baron's mission would be the result of some hasty deliberations in Rabaul and at Imperial General Headquarters. On Kolombangara were 10,000-plus Japanese troops dug in, ready and eager for combat. The Allies had landed on Vella Lavella. They had bypassed Kolombangara. They were not going to attack Japan's major strongpoint in the central Solomons.

What to do about it? The obvious answer, for some, was counterlanding. Lieutenant General Hyakutake Harukichi, commanding the 17th Army that was charged with defending Bougainville and the Shortlands, would provide a battalion from the 6th Division that would move by barge (now the preferred Japanese method for moving troops), Admiral Samejima would provide destroyers escort, and Admiral Sakamaki would provide air support. The operation would take place the night of August 16–17. Only General Inamura seems to have wondered exactly how one battalion was supposed to drive some 5,000 enemy troops off the island. To have any chance of success, you'd need three or four at least. And they did not have three or four battalions lying around. A counterlanding was thus off the table.

If there was to be no counterlanding, then those 10,000-plus troops on Kolombangara were cut off. Something had to be done to get them out. The first step in getting them out, Admiral Kusaka believed, was to expand the Japanese presence at that barge station at Horaniu near the northeast end of Vella Lavella. The Allied troops were at the southern end of the island and had stopped to form a perimeter, so this was workable.[121]

It would be the baron's job to land the reinforcements at Horaniu on Vella Lavella. It was a mission with which he was not totally happy. When he was briefing his skippers in his destroyer *Sazanami* on the morning of August 16, Ijuin commented, "When ordered to direct this operation, I urged the high command to discontinue the use of destroyers for transport purposes."[122] He was right, of course. But complaining to your superiors tended to not work well in the Imperial Japanese Navy. It got Admiral Tanaka an all-expense-paid trip to Burma. And it got Captain Hara, an attendee at this conference, in hot water in Rabaul. But the high command actually listened to Ijuin. Maybe it was because the baron was one of the few noblemen in the Imperial Navy. Maybe it was because of the disaster at Vella Gulf.

Ijuin continued: "Accordingly our destroyers will function purely as escorts. Escort squadrons of a year ago never had fewer than eight destroyers, but we must be content with four because of the high attrition rate of recent months." Tin cans were in short supply these days, in part because the Japanese lacked the ability to recycle their tin cans once they were sunk. (For that matter, tin was in short supply.) "But I have hand-picked these four outstanding ships, and I know that their fighting strength will be as the strength of eight."[123] Hyperbole worthy of Homer. The destroyers were the *Sazanami*, serving as Ijuin's flagship; Captain Hara's *Shigure*, *Hamakaze*, and *Isokaze*. As Hara later elaborated:

This reference to the four ships as the best at Rabaul was no mere flattery. My *Shigure* was the only one which was not of the very latest type. *Hamakaze*, hero of the July 13 battle at Kula Gulf, was one of the rare Japanese warships to be equipped at this time with radar. She and sister-ship *Isokaze* formed Destroyer Division 17, commanded by Captain Toshio Miyazaki. These and Ijuin's own flagship, *Sazanami*, formed the escort for the operation. This little squadron could boast the rare line-up of a rear admiral and two captains.[124]

The admiral asked Captain Hara to brief the skippers on the Vella Gulf disaster, of which Hara's own *Shigure* was the sole survivor. The criticism of Hara aside, *Shigure*'s survival was starting to earn the destroyer a reputation for being lucky. Hara proceeded to relate the story of the ambush in the Vella Gulf. Ijuin and the skippers listened closely, and if Ijuin had not agreed with Hara's opinions beforehand, he did afterwards. After Hara concluded his presentation, Ijuin spoke again: "I wholeheartedly endorse Hara's remarks and I commend to you his actions in that battle. Remember his cautiousness and flexibility. In the present operation our duty is to guard the convoy, not to seek duels. I disapprove of the dogged inflexibility which has proved such a detriment to our Navy."[125] Despite finishing 92nd out of 95 at Etajima, Ijuin was hardly the unthinking type, nor was he the kind to yell "Banzai!" and charge the nearest enemy at random times.

So if the destroyers were not going to run the reinforcements in to Vella Lavella, who or what was? In a word: barges.

Barges had made their appearance felt during the Guadalcanal Campaign. Early on, the Army's Major General Kawaguchi Kiyotake initially refused to move his 35th Brigade to Guadalcanal by slow transport or fast destroyer. He insisted on barges; he later relented somewhat, especially after most of his barges were shot up by American aircraft. Yet toward the end of the Guadalcanal Campaign, barges made their impact felt once again as the Japanese tried desperately to get supplies in to their languishing troops.

Though mass produced out of welded steel, the Japanese barge was often modified locally, so there was not much standardization. If there was a "typical" barge, it was the *Daihatsu* Army Type A. This was a 50-foot open creature with, when fully loaded, a top speed of 7 knots. It could carry some 70 men, 10 tons of cargo, or even one light tank. Other barges could go as much as 10 knots. It had a retractable ramp at the front. The design typically sloped down from the bow to midships then up to the stern. Looking from the beam it was difficult to tell which way it was going.[126]

This operation would have 13 barges and three motor torpedo boats carrying 390 troops (two Imperial Army companies and a platoon of Special Naval Landing Force infantry) with a close escort of one motor torpedo boat, two subchasers, two armed barges, and one armored boat, forming a Transport Unit under Lieutenant Commander Niwa Toshio. The four destroyers of Admiral Ijuin, who, like Kawaguchi, was an advocate of the use of barges instead of destroyers, would be the relatively heavy escort.[127] As such, "rat run" was not necessarily accurate, because the Transport Unit would use not destroyers but barges instead, in what the Japanese called an "ant run."

It was 5:00 the next morning, August 17, when Admiral Ijuin's four destroyers left Simpson Harbor.[128] Events quickly took a worrying turn. Not even 100 miles from Rabaul, the squadron intercepted a radio transmission from an Allied reconnaissance plane.[129] So much for surprise. They could expect an air attack any time now. Ijuin quickly requested that Buin double its scout patrols.[130]

Just as quickly, Admiral Wilkinson, who had just returned to Tulagi, responded to a scouting report sighting the barge convoy. Wilkinson quickly ordered Captain Ryan's Destroyer Division 41 (*Nicholas*, *O'Bannon*, *Taylor*, and *Chevalier*) to intercept. Ryan's destroyers had just returned to Purvis Bay after covering the landings, and had just finished refueling. Ryan left at 3:27pm and raced up The Slot at 32 knots.[131] As he did so, he received the report that Admiral Ijuin's destroyers had intercepted and thus was aware he could be facing Japanese destroyers.[132] An hour later, the *Chevalier* developed a problem with her main feed pump. But the problem had been anticipated and was quickly resolved, and the *Chevalier* soon caught up with the rest of the column.[133]

It turned into a veritable collision course. Just as Admiral Ijuin's flotilla was approaching Buin at 2:30pm, it received a message from one of the scout planes: "Three large enemy destroyers in Gizo Strait headed toward Biloa." "This information was received in our force with mixed feelings," Captain Hara later recalled. "I was relieved to know something about the enemy's movements. It was so much better than my last mission when we had to advance with no knowledge of the enemy deployment."[134]

That information showed the convoy was at risk as it moved slowly along the coast of Choiseul. Ijuin promptly increased speed to 28 knots to intercept the enemy before the enemy intercepted the convoy.[135] What was it about the Japanese and having the heavy escorts lag behind the convoy they are supposed to be guarding? The Japanese had done it at Java Sea with little in the way of ill effect. They had done it at Soenda Strait and suffered damage for it. They had done it at Cape Esperance, and it directly led to their defeat. While they may have learned from their Vella Gulf experience, they had not learned from those earlier experiences. Would it cost them now?

The sun set at 5:38pm. Clouds at about 1,500 feet obscured the full moon, limiting visibility to about three miles, which made Captain Hara very nervous because the enemy had radar, though he seems to have forgotten that the *Hamakaze* did, too.[136] By 10:00pm, Vella Lavella was in sight. Something else was in sight, too. A lookout on the *Shigure* shouted, "Enemy plane!"[137]

And here Captain Hara had been all worried about enemy destroyers. He saw a "sleek bomber" disappear into the clouds. Then he saw a second, which he identified as a Grumman TBF Avenger – not exactly a sleek bomber – drop a flare directly above the *Shigure*. The destroyers scattered, spread out, and opened fire, which the Allies had learned the hard way in the Java Sea Campaign was precisely the opposite of what you wanted to do to defend against air attack. But the Japanese had their prescribed procedure and they were sticking to it. That procedure included the destroyers zigzagging and laying smoke screen, the latter making little sense when you are dealing with aircraft that can simply fly over it.

As they did here. Vectored in by Black Cats were seven AirSols TBF Avengers from Marine Torpedo Bombing 143 armed with bombs for this moonlight attack. Four made contact with the Japanese ships. Captain Hara thought they were performing a repeat of the skip-bombing that had turned the Bismarck Sea into a Japanese nightmare. But no. Skip-bombing takes a lot of practice. The Grummans here were just dropping bombs the old fashioned way, just letting momentum and gravity do their thing, albeit not very accurately. One attack on the *Shigure* and at least two attacks on the *Sazanami*, both between 11:10 and 11:30pm, netted no hits. Hara was not impressed. "I knew [the

Sazanami would] be safe from the attack of such mediocre bomber pilots as these." The feeling was mutual, since the destroyers' antiaircraft fire was inaccurate and all seven Avengers returned safely.[138]

But the Avengers' attack had not been for naught. At 11:10pm, Captain Ryan had spotted the antiaircraft bursts from the Japanese destroyers, which continued for over an hour. "The flash of their guns and bursting shells made it very easy to locate the force," explained the *Nicholas*' skipper Lieutenant Commander A.J. Hill.[139] Captain Ryan sensed another Vella Gulf in the offing.

And when he saw the dark mass of Kolombangara swallowing anything that might be in front of it, so did Admiral Ijuin. Even though, or especially because, no enemy ships had been detected – were they invisible against the black backdrop of Kolombangara? – Ijuin immediately ordered "a 180-degree turn to the west, because of poor visibility on Kolombangara side."[140] Vella Gulf survivor Captain Hara had also sensed another Vella Gulf. "I was happy to obey that order," Hara later recalled.[141] The Japanese destroyer column reformed and headed west. After sailing for almost 30 miles, the *Sazanami* signaled: "Four enemy ships bearing 190 degrees, distant [sic] 15,000 meters."[142] Captain Hara was happy to admit, "Admiral Ijuin had kept us out of an enemy ambush."[143]

Baron Ijuin later described his thinking to Hara. "Ijuin later told me how overjoyed he was to find that the enemy was pursuing us. 'I was positive that the enemy, overconfident after his phenomenal August 6 victory, had decided to ignore the vulnerable unescorted convoy, and challenge us to a duel. I headed north to lure the enemy into battle at a safe distance from the convoy.'"[144]

The baron was exactly right. Captain Ryan wanted a replay of Vella Gulf. He had originally hoped to take out the Japanese destroyers while having two other destroyers, *Philip* and *Saufley*, whom he expected to arrive late, take care of the barges. But they ultimately had to go help the destroyer *Waller*, who was having some issues, as most ships would, with a hole in her hull, in this case caused by her sideswiping the *Philip* while maneuvering during an attack by Japanese seaplanes.[145] So his four ships would have to replay Vella Gulf and handle the barges on their own.

Captain Ryan was on his way to doing exactly that when at 12:27am, or five minutes before the *Sazanami* detected the Americans, the *O'Bannon* reported detecting enemy ships 11.5 miles away bearing 311 degrees True – northwest.[146] The Americans got a visual about four minutes later.[147] Ryan and Lieutenant Commander Hill interpreted the radar display on the *Nicholas* as showing the barges in between the US Navy tin cans and their Japanese counterparts.[148] Ryan still wanted his ambush.

Despite everything he had said about "our duty is to guard the convoy, not to seek duels," Admiral Ijuin wanted his own ambush. The *Sazanami*'s Aldis lamp flashed "Form combat column. Prepare for torpedo attack to port!"[149] At 12:32am, just after the Americans had sighted them, the Japanese destroyers turned 45 degrees to starboard to head northwest. Ijuin's combat formation had the *Sazanami* drop back with the radar-equipped *Hamakaze* following her. This placed the *Hamakaze*, northwest of and closest to the Americans. Ijuin hoped to lure the Americans to the north, away from the barges and into a full ambush by the *Shigure* and *Isokaze*, who were further northwest.

Captain Ryan's destroyers, heading northwest, were slowly closing in on the *Sazanami* and *Hamakaze* from behind. Trying to get into position to spring his trap. Then, at 12:40am, "a brilliant blue and white flare blossomed" over the Americans.[150] A Japanese Mitsubishi F1M Type 0 Observation Seaplane, which the Allies called "Pete," had found the US Navy ships and dropped a few bombs and the blue and white flare, which meant, "Enemy ships are destroyers!" to Captain Hara and the other sailors on the Japanese ships who saw it.[151] The bombs all missed, but Ryan's planned second Vella Gulf was out the window with his ships pinned and brilliantly illuminated for the Japanese by the flare.[152] Now what could Captain Ryan do?

At 12:40am, the *Nicholas* led the American destroyers on a column turn to a course due west.[153] That course change put them headed directly for the barges. Admiral Ijuin watched in horror as his own trap was thrown out the window and the precious barges were threatened.[154] That can happen when you have the escorts behind whatever they're supposed to be protecting, but the Japanese had yet to learn this. Ijuin immediately ordered a 90-degree turn to the southwest for his destroyers. Quickly calculating that his own destroyers could not reach the enemy destroyers before they attacked the barges – the distance, he believed, was 8,000 meters, Ijuin ordered: "Fire torpedoes on long-range setting!" Captain Hara thought the range was closer to 10,000 meters, and believed, "At such a range there was practically no chance of scoring hits."[155]

The American ships were on an almost parallel course and making better than 30 knots. Launching torpedoes was a desperate, not to say panic, move here. But the Type 93s shot from their tubes all the same. The *Shigure* launched her torpedoes at 12:46 at a range of 12,500 yards, followed four minutes later by those of the *Hamakaze*; a minute after that came those of *Isokaze*, and finally at 12:55 the flagship *Sazanami* unleashed hers.[156]

In the meantime, at 12:50 as Captain Ryan's destroyers were getting close to the barges, he ordered, "Emergency turn 3," an immediate 30-degree turn to starboard, which split up his column and put his destroyers in a line of bearing headed northwest.[157] At 12:53, Ryan ordered "Emergency turn 3" again.[158] This put the Americans on another line of bearing, not aimed at but passing around the barges. One minute later, Ryan said, "We'll get those barges later."[159] At 12:56 he ordered, "Emergency turn 6," a 60-degree turn to port, which reformed the column heading west and passing to the north of the barges.[160]

The sudden moves of the American destroyers made all of Admiral Ijuin's torpedoes miss. He watched the maneuvers through his binoculars and said, "What an evasion! But at least we distracted them from the convoy."[161] It made him feel better to tell himself that the Americans had seen his torpedoes, especially one that for some reason jumped out of the water, and avoided them. In reality, Ijuin had badly misjudged Ryan's intentions. The US Navy commodore had not been going after the barges. What looked like evasive maneuvers was merely trying to get around the barges to attack Ijuin's destroyers. Rather than sticking to his original interpretation of the American plan, which was correct, Ijuin had indeed panicked, though perhaps it was unavoidable, and launched his best weapon, his torpedoes, too early and at an extreme range. He did have torpedo reloads, but the torpedo tubes would have to be reloaded during combat, potentially making the normally 20–30 minute procedure take longer and definitely making it more dangerous. In the interim, he would have to use his guns.

"All guns," Ijuin thundered, "open fire!"[162] The *Sazanami* and *Hamakaze* turned south at 12:55 and crossed the American "T," with the US Navy destroyers silhouetted by the setting moon behind them. As the *Shigure* and *Isokaze* began their turns two minutes later, the Japanese opened fire at 12:57. Perhaps from the Naval Battle of Guadalcanal, Ijuin had learned the dangers of using searchlights and kept them off while his destroyers unleashed their guns on the Americans at ranges of 9,000 to 12,000 yards.[163]

Captain Hara had other ideas. His next battle order came at 12:59: "Ready four torpedoes portside!"[164] But the Americans had started shooting back, first the *Nicholas* at 12:58, one minute after the Japanese had opened fire, and her shells were falling uncomfortably close to the *Shigure* for Hara's taste.

"The next moment *Shigure* was straddled by enemy shells which fell 20 to 40 meters from the ship, kicking up pillars of water and spray," Captain Hara later wrote. "Another barrage, seconds later, bracketed our ship even more closely; and the third just barely missed us." The man who wrote the book on Japanese torpedo tactics lost his nerve momentarily. "Forgetting my own plans for a torpedo attack, I ordered smoke and a zigzag course."[165]

With less than total effectiveness. "*Shigure* weaved back and forth through the thickening smoke screen at her full 30 knots. But no matter which way we turned shells kept falling around us every six or seven seconds with breath-taking, uncanny tempo. Tension rose as we realized that any moment might bring a direct hit." That is one of the more common risks in war. "Enemy salvos were falling so close that they splashed water in my face. When the enemy range had closed to 5,000 meters I gave the word to launch and turn away. I watched the torpedoes speed on their way and, at the same time, waited for the feeling of *Shigure*'s response to her helm which was slow in coming."[166] That rudder.

Captain Hara was not the only one getting water splashed in his face by near misses. One Japanese shell landed about 50 feet from the *Chevalier*, sending up a large column of water that came down on her bridge, drenching the bridge personnel.[167] The destroyer responded by launching five Mark 15s, aimed at, apparently, Captain Hara's *Shigure* at a range of 9,000 yards.[168] Then the *Chevalier* opened up with her guns, the concussion from which launched another torpedo.[169]

Going into the teeth of the Japanese cross of his "T" and the resulting gunfire was not sitting well with Captain Ryan. It was an article of faith that you should never let the enemy cross your "T," no matter the circumstances. More than putting you at a tactical disadvantage from the enemy being able to use all his guns while you could use only, at most, your forward guns, it was also a philosophical thing. His "T" being crossed with the setting moon backlighting his ships made it worse. It was just dumb luck the Japanese had not managed to get a hit just yet. Ryan had the *Nicholas* lead the other destroyers on a course change to starboard, breaking the "T" and setting up on a course almost parallel to the Japanese but heading in the opposite direction.[170]

Which only lasted for a few minutes. The *Sazanami* and *Hamakaze* started making smoke, which disrupted efforts by US Navy lookouts to monitor their course changes. Radar, however, suggested the Japanese destroyers had changed course and were leaving. Abandoning their largely defenseless barges.

They were, "to the surprise of all of us," Captain Ryan wrote.[171] The radar of destroyer *Hamakaze* had "detected the approach of a powerful enemy force."[172] What exactly the radar showed is a mystery, but it has been suggested that the *Hamakaze*'s radar operators misread the returns from the barge convoy, which had by this time scattered.[173] Captain Miyazaki suggested to Admiral Ijuin that they retire to the northwest. Ijuin and Hara agreed, and the flotilla of four Japanese destroyers turned northwest at 1:00am and sailed off, leaving the barges to their fate.[174]

Captain Ryan's surprise turned to outrage.[175] He wanted those destroyers. "To get at them," he later wrote, "there was no other course than to damn their torpedoes and chase."[176] Damning their torpedoes and chasing them can be dangerous and costly: just ask Admiral Ainsworth.

But the commodore chased them all the same. Heading northwest on a roughly parallel course, range 15,000 yards.[177] Too far for the destroyers' 5-inch guns to shoot effectively, but Ryan tried it anyway. He was rewarded with a few near misses on the *Isokaze*, starting a few small fires that were quickly put out.[178] The Japanese destroyer had launched eight torpedoes, hoping for more of a replay of Kula Gulf and Kolombangara than Vella Gulf, but they all missed.

As far as Captain Ryan could tell, the Japanese were opening up the range. His speed was limited to 30 knots, the fastest the *Chevalier* could make with her jury-rigged feed pump. The maximum speed of Japanese destroyers, he knew, was typically 35 knots. He had no way of knowing the *Shigure* and *Isokaze* could make no more than 28 knots because of engineering, maintenance, and other issues.[179] Ryan gave up the chase at 1:21, and turned around to deal with those barges ... Where were those barges?[180]

During the fight between the destroyers, Lieutenant Commander Niwa had his convoy of barges scatter. One seasick soldier of the Mikami Battalion wrote in his diary, "This was the first time in my life I knew what fear was ... In our dizzy condition we awaited the hour wearing our life jackets, the only thing we could depend on."[181]

Almost all of the barges had made it to the north coast of Vella Lavella, many of them in a cove, and camouflaged themselves. A frustrated Captain Ryan did not locate any targets until 1:51am, and then it was only the barges' close escorts. His ships managed to sink the auxiliary subchasers *Cha-5* and *Cha-12*, as well as one armed barge, while also driving one of the motor torpedo boats aground.[182]

At this point, Captain Ryan called it quits for this battle. While disappointed that he could not find the barges, he had suffered no losses and had turned back the Japanese destroyers. Ryan had thus stopped a Tokyo Express operation. Or so he thought. He could not conceive that this time the destroyers were not carrying the troops; the barges were and the barges had made it safely to the coast of Vella Lavella. They would hide the next day and proceed to Horaniu the next night to set up the barge base.[183]

In fairness, Captain Ryan was not the only one who thought the Americans had won the engagement. So did the Emperor, who chewed out Admiral Nagano. "[Admiral,] the other day when the army dispatched a large unit, I heard that four of your destroyers guarding the troopships fled." Telling the Emperor he was incorrect was a rather unpleasant duty.[184]

Even more unpleasant was offloading troops and cargo under air attack, but the Americans were stuck with just that the morning of August 18. After the destruction of *LST-396*, Captain Cooke had two landing ships remaining. At 7:00am, they were back at Barakoma to finish offloading. Providing motivation for completing the offloading quickly were 46 Zeros and nine D3As. The strike arrived over Barakoma around 8:00am in scattered groups that did not resemble a combat formation. They were met by the Corsairs of Marine Fighting 121 and 123 and Army Air Force Airacobras from the 12th Fighter Squadron, 18th Fighter Group. Again, the Vals got no hits, but one did get a near-miss on the *LST-339* that lifted the bow and drove the landing ship further onto the beach, so it was stranded once its unloading was completed. The *LST-339*'s cunning skipper, Lieutenant John H. Fulweiler, requested the escorting destroyers speed by as close to the shore as possible. Their wakes rocked the *LST-339* enough to enable her to slide off the beach back into the water. The cost was two Corsairs shot down (one by friendly fire, the pilot recovered) and one Airacobra, with two pilots, Marine 2nd Lieutenant Lisle Harrison Foord and Army Air Force 2nd Lieutenant Jack B. Eddy, killed.[185]

Base Air Force came back with another air attack of 41 Zeros and six D3As, but inclement weather foiled their attempts at making an effective attack. Their presence on radar, however, kept the US Navy ships at general quarters, and further incursions on radar kept the ships at general quarters until 2:00am on August 19. It made for another exceedingly long day. The Americans had three aircraft shot down, two by the Japanese, with both pilots killed, and one by Marine antiaircraft batteries at Barakoma, with the pilot rescued.[186]

It was not only in Rabaul and Buin that the invasion of Vella Lavella raised alarm bells, but at Zieta as well. While the Japanese troops were scurrying ashore at Horaniu on the night of August 18–19, General Sasaki moved the 2nd Battalion of the 45th Infantry Regiment and one battery of the 6th Field Artillery Regiment from Kolombangara to Gizo Island in an effort to secure the line of retreat from Kolombangara.[187]

Meanwhile, the Japanese scheduled the evacuation of Rekata Bay for August 22. That morning, Captain Miyazaki Toshio left Rabaul in his *Hamakaze*, leading the *Shigure* and *Isokaze*, with the idea of evacuating some 750 troops of the 7th Combined Special Naval

Landing Force (some of whom had been dropped off at Rekata only a month earlier), and stuffed to the gunwales with food and supplies for men they had to leave behind. It appears that Admiral Ijuin had the destroyer *Sazanami* provide some "cover" to the transport destroyers, though her exact role, if any, remains murky.[188]

Like many operations of late, this run gave the increasingly glum Captain Hara, who had been a part of that earlier run to Rakata, a sense of foreboding:

> Our mission was a tough one under any circumstances. [...] The enemy was alerted. We had to be prepared for the worst.
>
> The approach to Rekata was dangerous because of its countless unposted reefs and shoals. Our charts, copied from British ones made in 1939, carried this note: "These islands have been only partially surveyed and, the larger portion of them being quite unknown, great caution is necessary while navigating in this vicinity."[189]

For about a year, the Japanese had been operating a seaplane base at Rekata, from where they had conducted seaplane operations, most notably nighttime harassing attacks on Guadalcanal and other targets using the infamous Louie the Louse. Yet, the Japanese had somehow not found an opportunity to update their charts on the Rekata Bay area. What had been arrogance, overconfidence, and sloppiness was now reduced to just sloppiness.

They were not even 100 miles out of Simpson Harbor when they were met by at least one and as many as three Liberators. Not Army Air Force B-24s but Navy PB4Ys, operating at 20,000 feet. The destroyers' guns opened fire, but the Liberators were above the guns' maximum altitude. They did not drop bombs, instead, as Captain Hara put it, "circling overhead, out of reach, in taunting fashion." "It was most distressing," Hara admitted.[190]

Evidently responding to calls for air cover from the destroyers, a half dozen Zeros arrived to try to drive off the Liberators. The Americans left after 20 minutes, whether due to the Zeros or other considerations is not clear. The Zeros remained over the Japanese destroyers until dusk and then returned to base.[191]

But Captain Miyazaki's troubles were far from over. As Captain Hara had explained, they had to creep along the Choiseul coast at 10 knots, threading their way through the reefs and rocks toward Rekata Bay. As they did so, they received an urgent message from the Rekata base: "Four enemy cruisers and several destroyers sighted near the mouth of Rekata Harbor."[192]

Captain Hara groaned. Stuck in the maze of reefs and shoals, they were, "like big clay pigeons for the shells and torpedoes of the enemy." His commodore's thoughts seem to have been similar, as Captain Miyazaki signaled "Put about at once and head out to sea at 24 knots, until we learn the movements of the enemy."[193]

The destroyers reversed course and headed toward the north. Maybe ten minutes after that, they intercepted a sighting report, probably from a Black Cat, describing how they had just turned around. Captain Hara was dumbfounded. "What could we do against such an opponent?"[194]

How times had changed. Some 18 months earlier, as skipper of the *Amatsukaze*, Hara Tameichi had been present at the Battle of the Java Sea. The major difference in the engagement that enabled the Japanese to win was their omnipresent floatplanes that constantly reported the movement of the Allied ships. The stage was set for the action, in fact, when a Japanese scout plane reported the Allied striking force that had been about to enter port had suddenly turned around and was heading for the Japanese. Now, the roles were reversed. Hara Tameichi didn't like that. Not one bit.

While Captain Hara was perhaps contemplating the irony, the *Hamakaze* signaled, "Rabaul orders immediate return to base without engaging. Return to Rabaul at 30 knots."[195] There would be no battle this night. Would have been no battle, anyway. There were no enemy ships in the area. What the naval infantry at Rekata had seen is anyone's guess.[196]

The Japanese were loath to just leave the troops at Rekata so on August 25 they tried again, this time with a bizarre plan only the Imperial Japanese Navy could concoct. Admiral Ijuin led a small force with the destroyers *Sazanami* and *Matsukaze* and the light cruiser *Sendai*. Their job was to serve as a decoy while Captain Miyazaki went in again with the *Hamakaze*, *Isokaze*, and *Shigure*.[197] This time, they got some friendly weather in the form of low clouds and intermittent squalls that kept the Black Cats away. Mostly. The weather did make poking through the reef and rocks "as enervating as enemy action" to Captain Hara. The destroyers arrived at Rekata at 1:00am on August 26, at which time they began embarking passengers, the speed of which was helped along by two Allied bombers that roared low over the ships and dropped their bombs, missing everybody. Having taken on board all they could, the destroyers headed back, and by 2:30am were making 30 knots.[198]

They would need every knot. At dawn the Japanese destroyers were in the open sea off of Choiseul. An hour later they were in the Bougainville Strait. So were maybe a dozen Liberators, all US Navy PB4Ys. Between the Black Cats' report and a subsequent report by a coastwatcher, General Twining decided to take a shot at the retreating Japanese.

Captain Miyazaki had his ships go to full speed, make smoke, and scatter; only the first was really an effective countermeasure against bombers. Captain Hara came so close to realizing this truth as he watched the antiaircraft fire have no visible effect on the attackers. The *Hamakaze* and *Isokaze* worked their speed up to their rated maximum of 35 knots. The *Shigure* struggled to make 30 and "was exasperatingly sluggish in responding to the helm." Hara was still unaware of the hole in her rudder.

It seemed like a recipe for disaster, but it was not. Not for the *Shigure*, anyway. After five minutes, the attack was over and the *Shigure* was untouched. The commodore's ship *Hamakaze* was not so well off. She was crawling along at reduced speed with a fire near her bow. Captain Miyazaki signaled, "One direct hit on forecastle, 36 casualties. Speed restricted to 20 knots. Am considering heading for Shortland. Miyazaki."

It made sense. Shortland was only 30 miles away. But the enemy would probably assume the Japanese destroyers would head for Shortland. What if the enemy attacked them there? The fighter protection for the Shortlands anchorage had been ineffective of late. The *Shigure* signaled, "Captain Hara strongly objects to your plan. Shortland base no longer safe. Let us return to Rabaul at 20 knots. If trouble develops, *Shigure* is prepared to tow you. Please reply." Captain Miyazaki quickly approved the counterintuitive plan. There were no more air attacks, the *Hamakaze*'s crew put the fire out, and Hara's *Shigure* led the *Hamakaze* and *Isokaze* safely into Simpson Harbor.

Captains Miyazaki and Hara headed for shore. Miyazaki was glum and embarrassed. Admiral Ijuin greeted him by holding out a piece of paper and saying, "Don't scowl, Miyazaki. Read this and cheer up." Captain Miyazaki took the piece of paper and read it. His hands began to tremble. With a weak smile, he handed it to Captain Hara. It was a message from Buin saying that the base was now under heavy air attack. Shaking Hara's hand, Miyazaki said, "Hara, you saved me and *Hamakaze* with her crew and hundreds of passengers. Had I gone to Shortland we would have been blasted to bits by now."

Maybe, maybe not. Whatever air attack Buin suffered was not exactly Pearl Harbor or Cavite. Even so, while Captains Hara and Miyazaki had not gone to Shortland, their passengers would. Two days later, the *Sendai* and *Sazanami* transported them back to Buin. The remainder of the troops at Rekata Bay were picked up by six flying boats and, reportedly, one submarine.[199]

Also being abandoned as a Japanese base was New Georgia proper. General Sasaki was pulling everyone off, but maintaining a defense line at Arundel and Baanga islands. It was from the latter that Sasaki had maintained two 120mm "Pistol Petes," or, for those of the metric persuasion, "Millimeter Mikes," of the 7th Yokosuka Special Naval Landing Force to periodically shell the Munda airfield.

The 169th Infantry Regiment of the US Army's 43rd Infantry Division was given the task of scouting Baanga. On August 11, elements of its 3rd Battalion landed on the island. They found "[e]nemy forces of undetermined strength," including the Japanese 120mm guns, "in the southern portion of the island." The next day, the 66 men of L Company were sent to occupy Baanga. According to the 43rd's report, "For some reason, they were not ordered to land where the patrol had experienced no opposition, but in a cove in the island which had not been reconnoitered."[200] What difference did it make?

The first of two tank landing barges had unloaded when the Japanese revealed that this particular cove was unique in that it was a strongpoint of their defenses. Not only were the Pistol Petes on Baanga. So were Colonel Hirata's 229th Infantry Regiment, Lieutenant Colonel Yano's 2nd Battalion of the 230th Infantry Regiment, and Major Nagakari Miyoshi's 3rd Battalion of the 23rd Infantry Regiment. L Company was caught in a murderous crossfire that drove both barges away, leaving 34 men on the beach. Efforts to reach them after dark were similarly driven back. As best as can be determined, six survived.[201]

Realizing Baanga was not going to be a pushover, General Barker, temporarily in command of the 43rd Division after General Hodge went back to the Americal Division, ordered the 3rd Battalion of the 169th Infantry to land at the tiny islet of Vela Cela on August 13 and use that as a base to advance to Baanga the following day. They established a beachhead in the mangrove swamps on the eastern side of the island, but after advancing about 600 yards they were stopped cold by yet another Gifu-style system of Japanese fortifications. Barker then committed the 2nd Battalion of the 169th Infantry, which also was stymied by the Japanese defenses. With the 169th Regiment giving a "shaky performance," Barker was forced to commit the 1st and 3rd Battalions of the 172nd Infantry Regiment. This left one battalion of the 169th Infantry and one battalion of the 172nd Infantry defending the Munda airfield.[202]

The limited troops defending Munda had the potential to become problematic, because General Sasaki had kept many troops on Baanga to take advantage of any opportunity to recapture the Munda airfield. The 120mm guns of the 7th Yokosuka Special Naval Landing Force were becoming a nuisance for operations at Munda. Finally, on August 16, the 136th Field Artillery Battalion, the saviors of Zanana Beach, started a marathon of counterbattery fire with its 155mm howitzers. "If the Japanese fired one," one historian observed, "there would be hundreds returned, along with relentless bombing." But counterbattery fire – destroying enemy artillery with your own artillery – is easier said than done, and the Pistol Petes remained a nuisance and shelled the airfield again the next morning, when an Airacobra flying up from Munda was able to see the gun flashes. At 1:20pm, AirSols sent up 13 Avengers from Marine Torpedo Bombing 233 followed by 17 Dauntlesses from Marine Scout Bombing 141. In the words of the late New Georgia historian Ronnie Day, "the amount of ordnance placed on the small target area had the effect of carpet bombing." It seems the guns of the 7th Yokosuka Special Naval Landing Force did not fire at the air base after that.[203]

It was a small but necessary Allied success in what had become, in the words of Samuel Eliot Morison, "a vicious little campaign for Baanga Island." The Japanese troops put up fierce resistance, but on August 20 they started pulling back to Arundel Island, and by August 22 all of their troops had escaped. This was becoming a theme of the campaign. Fierce fighting leading to a Japanese escape with the bulk of their troops.

Bairoko was a similar situation. General Collins expected a major fight and thought he was prepared for it. His plan was to send the 161st Infantry Regiment and the 1st Battalion of the 27th Regiment, supported by engineers and artillery, up the Bairoko Trail to a vaguely located point known as Mount Bao. There, the 161st with an artillery battalion would turn west on the Zieta Trail to another point called Mount Tirokiambo, known to the Americans as "Turkey Hill," at which time the artillery would unlimber and deploy, and the 161st would turn north to attack the west side of Bairoko Harbor in conjunction with 3rd Battalion of the 145th Regiment. The 1st Battalion of the 27th Regiment would attack the east side.[204]

In Bairoko, Admiral Ota had plans of his own, and they did not involve sitting back and waiting for the Americans to bring an end to him and his naval infantry. His barges, usually five to eight at a time, were running every night, going from Bairoko to Kolombangara and back. The *daihatsus* stayed very close to the coast in order to blend in both visually and on radar. PT boats tried to interdict this effort, but they were repeatedly stymied by artillery on Kolombangara and seaplanes from the 938 Air Group, as well as the barges' own machine guns. As Lieutenant Commander Kelly reported:

A recent conference with the Commanding Officers of the First and Fourth Marine Raider Battalions at Enogai revealed that during the period 14–19 August, 28 barges have been observed by their Observation Post to enter and leave Bairoko. On three of these nights the PT's have attacked a total of 17 barges leaving Bairoko. On each occasion the return fire from the barges and shore batteries has been so heavy that the PT's have been unable to close to effective range. Only two barges were seen to be damaged and none are believed to have sunk or been seriously disabled. Without illumination it is impossible for the PTs to see the barges which closely hug the shore. However, the PT's themselves are clearly visible against the horizon in the moonlight. Heavily armored large barges with 40mm and machine-guns escort the medium barges which carry only machine-guns and/or 20mm. In order to sink a barge, the range must be closed well within 100 yards and more than 1,000 rounds of .50-caliber and 500 rounds of 20mm are required … This requires laying to at point blank range of shore batteries and barges for approximately 10 minutes which is tantamount to sacrificing the PT boat.[205]

As far as Allied intelligence could tell, this run of barges to and from Bairoko was part of a Japanese reinforcement effort, a reinforcement effort that had to be stopped if there was to be any hope of a successful conclusion to the New Georgia campaign in the foreseeable future. So if these *daihatsus* like to make their runs at night and hide during the day, maybe attack them during the day at their bases.

That was the idea behind a bizarre scheme to send two teams of three PT boats each – two carrying demolition volunteers from the 117th Engineer Battalion, and the third to cover them – into Japanese-held coves to destroy the barges in broad daylight. At 7:25am on August 22, *PT-104* and *-169* entered Elliott (or Ringgi) Cove, just west of Vila on the southern coast of Kolombangara. *PT-105* was left to cover the entrance, where she was immediately taken under fire by Japanese shore batteries. Not taking the hint, *PT-104* and *-169* crept into the cove and started shooting at the camouflaged barges, at which point they were caught in a vicious crossfire of Japanese machine guns and small arms. *PT-105* put herself between the shore and the boats and laid a smokescreen to cover their escape.[206]

At about the same time and in about the same fashion, *PT-108* and *-125* entered Webster (or Vavohe) Cove, just west of Elliott Cove, leaving *PT-124* to cover the entrance. And in about the same fashion, *PT-108* and *-125* were caught in an even more vicious crossfire of Japanese machine guns and small arms. But this time, the Japanese hit *PT-108*. Lieutenant (jg) David M. Payne, commanding the Webster Cove expedition, was wounded immediately and fell into the charthouse, dead. Lieutenant (jg) Sidney D. Hix, normally the skipper of *PT-108* but working the helm today, took a bullet in the head, but managed to put the wheel hard over to withdraw before he, too, collapsed, dead. Badly wounded and dazed, Quartermaster 2nd Class James G. Cannon, Jr stood over

Hix's body to take the wheel and steer the boat out of danger. One Navy gunner and one Army engineer were killed as well. Only one officer and two men were not wounded. *PT-125* took *-108*'s lead in speeding out and suffered only one wounded.[207]

The next morning, the 161st Regiment entered a strangely empty Bairoko. The last run of the barges had evacuated Admiral Ota and the last of his supplies and naval infantry the previous night.[208] Like *Ke* on Guadalcanal, the Allies had mistaken Japanese withdrawal for reinforcement and allowed them to escape.

That same day, August 23, Admiral Samejima ordered General Sasaki to hold the Gizo–Kolombangara–Arundel line and to wait to be notified when the evacuation date was set. Sasaki set out to carry out the orders as best he could. On August 26, he sent two companies of the 1st Battalion of the 13th Regiment under Major Kinoshita Seishu to Arundel. Two days later Sasaki sent Yamada with two companies of the 45th Regiment to Gizo. The general also ordered Colonel Hirata's 229th Regiment to Bambari Harbor on Kolombangara.[209] The 6th Kure Special Naval Landing Force held the west coast of Kolombangara. Sasaki created a "Base Force" under the venerable Colonel Tomonari to defend Vila-Stanmore. Base Force consisted of the remainder of Tomonari's own 13th Infantry; Major Hara Hidetome's 2nd Independent Quick-Fire Battalion; Commander Takeda's 7th Yokosuka Special Naval Landing Force, minus its artillery; and the remaining mountain artillery units. As a very tiny reserve, Sasaki had the 5th and 8th Companies of the 45th Regiment, and the 3rd Company of the 13th Regiment, under his direct command.[210]

Such as at Arundel, which on August 27 felt the boots of Colonel Ross' 172nd Regiment of the 43rd Infantry Division, now under General Wing who had taken over for General Barker.[211] It took them a week to find Major Kinoshita's positions. Kinoshita saw this as indicative of "winning." General Sasaki saw this as indicative of an opportunity to counterattack and maybe push the Americans out of the northern part of Arundel or at least seize their food. Sasaki began to slowly shuttle Colonel Tomonari's 13th Regiment to the island, using the very limited supply of barges that Admiral Ota had used to escape Bairoko. First over was Major Takabayashi Uichi's 3rd Battalion.

But the Japanese reinforcement was not taking place in a vacuum. With no idea of the enemy reinforcement, General Griswold had come to the conclusion that the 43rd Infantry Division "had more than it could handle"; supposedly not a reflection of its performance but of the fact that it was tired and depleted after almost two months of combat operations. Griswold ordered in two battalions of the 27th Infantry Regiment of the 25th Infantry Division to Arundel. The detachment of the 27th was led by Colonel Douglas Sugg, who was given command of all operations on Arundel. Also landing on Arundel was B Company of the 82nd Chemical Battalion. The unit was both not as scary and more scary than its name suggested. "Chemical" was mainly a reference to its white phosphorous rounds, which were used both for making smoke and making enemy lives miserable. It was an artillery unit that featured 4.2-inch mortars, "in their South Pacific debut," according to one historian.

The mortars started causing problems for the Japanese. One battalion of the 27th moved in on September 12 and cut off Major Kinoshita's troops from their ostensible reinforcement by Major Takabayashi's troops. The US Army mortars and other artillery set up a killing ground to take out the Japanese barges. One battalion of the 169th landed to begin cutting off the Japanese all together, at least as far as they could. On September 15, the indefatigable Colonel Tomonari returned to combat by landing on Arundel with his headquarters. Tomonari's return to combat lasted exactly ten minutes. As he was sitting on a log listening to a report from a company commander, a mortar round landed at his feet and exploded. Major Takabayashi took over command of the 13th from his suddenly departed superior, only to be killed by another mortar round within 48 hours. That left everything up to Kinoshita.

General Griswold kept upping the ante, sending in five tanks from the 11th Marine Defense Battalion. On the morning of September 17, the tanks, screened by a third battalion of the 27th Infantry, drove the Japanese back. A follow-up attack on the following day was not nearly as successful, as Kinoshita knocked out two tanks.

By that time, however, General Sasaki had gotten the order from Rabaul to withdraw. He stopped the movement of the 13th Regiment on September 17 and began the withdrawal itself at 10:00pm on September 19, starting with the recently arrived 13th. The Japanese withdrew under heavy artillery fire; General Barker was firing blindly. But the Japanese did have artillery of their own: those two 120mm howitzers of the 7th Yokosuka Special Naval Landing Force started shooting again. Evidently the air strikes targeting them had not been as effective as the Americans believed. But though Barker was firing blindly, his guns drew blood all the same. The Japanese rearguard, the 12th Company, promptly lost its commander to American shells. The platoon commander had his leg blown off. The battalion commander, as he was supposed to, left in the last barge, which promptly took a mortar shell, killing him. Though painful and unpleasant, the withdrawal of Major Kinoshita's troops was completed the following night.[212] And the Allies had conquered another island, though more by default than anything else.

That left Kolombangara and Vella Lavella. The Americans had landed on Vella Lavella, but had not secured it. Kolombangara now had some 12,000 Japanese troops, dug in and well-stocked with supplies.

What happened with those troops would go a long way toward determining how the Solomons Campaign and *Cartwheel* would play out.

No one can serve two masters. Early in the Guadalcanal Campaign, for instance, Admiral Tanaka had no fewer than three instances in which his superiors gave him contradictory orders, which contributed to the disaster that campaign became. But this invocation goes much further. Any military operation must have clearly defined objectives. Moreover, those objectives must be prioritized, either in order of achievement, in order of importance, or both. Midway was perhaps the ultimate example of what happens when this dictum is not followed. Admiral Nagumo had to figure out what he was supposed to do first: knock out the air power based at Midway or knock out the American ships that were approaching. The catastrophe that resulted was not because he had chosen poorly – although he had – but because he had trouble choosing at all, resulting in a critical delay that enabled the US Navy carriers to get in the first shot, which turned out to be mostly a knockout blow.

Maybe Admiral Nagumo learned something from Midway, maybe he didn't. What is clear is that Imperial General Headquarters learned nothing from Midway. With the situation in the central Solomons deteriorating, Admiral Kusaka and General Inamura had decided to maintain a line of communication to General Sasaki's remaining troops on New Georgia. Sasaki was to hold out as long as possible, then make a slow, fighting withdrawal in order to buy time to build up the defenses on Bougainville. They began implementing this general plan.

But if you didn't like that plan, well, the Japanese had others. Like in New Guinea. At Imperial General Headquarters, the Army and Navy staffs got into a big argument as to which area should get priority in defense: New Guinea or the Solomons? Originally, way back in 1942, the Army considered New Guinea much more important while the Navy considered the Solomons more important. By the end of 1942, the positions had flipped: the Army arguing the Solomons were more important, the Navy arguing New Guinea. Now, in late 1943, the positions reversed once again. The Army argued New Guinea was more important, the Navy, the Solomons. Which was more important? Imperial General Headquarters answered in the form of a question: why not both?

Yes, once again, Imperial General Headquarters could not make a decision and instead decided to split the baby, which preserved interservice peace but obviously did the baby no good. And it would do the Japanese no good, as well, because though the impetus for the discussions that resulted in this no-decision was the central Solomons, New Guinea was heating up once again.

As strange as it may sound with the narrative of the invasions of New Georgia and Vella Lavella, *Cartwheel* was supposed to be a two-pronged advance: the Solomons and New Guinea. That is certainly divided, but the objective of both prongs was the same: Rabaul. Yet so far, it had been a lot of Solomons and very little New Guinea. But General MacArthur had a plan for that. A plan for an operation given the vaguely obscene name of "*Postern*."

The objective of *Postern* was to capture the Huon Peninsula – that sizable thumb of land that juts eastward from New Guinea toward the Vitiaz and Damphier Straits directly opposite New Britain. The Huon Peninsula had a certain geographical utility. It had the tiny port of Finschhafen. It would make a good jumping off point for an invasion of New Britain and Rabaul, the ultimate objective of *Cartwheel*. Additionally, just south of the Huon Peninsula was the Huon Gulf. On the other side of the Huon Gulf was the Papuan peninsula of New Guinea. The Huon and Papuan peninsulas formed a sort of elbow with the Huon Gulf in between. And right in the crook of that elbow was and is Lae, the principal Japanese fortress on New Guinea, known antebellum for its export of minerals, agricultural products, and Amelia Earhart. Southeast of Lae along the coast was Salamaua, another major Japanese fortress. The operational objective of *Postern* would be to neutralize and seize these two major bases.

But General MacArthur had some serious logistical problems. He had paratroopers and not enough transport aircraft from which to drop them. He had amphibious troops and not enough assault craft from which to land them. He had ground troops – plenty of ground troops – and not enough terrain suitable for their effective deployment and use. General MacArthur wanted to be Southwest Pacific commander, would work under no one else. He wanted this dilemma. He had to solve it. And, as much as these pages have been critical of Douglas MacArthur – for which there was and would continue to be ample reason – it must be acknowledged that he and his men rose to the challenge with a resourcefulness and ingenuity not often seen in this Pacific War.

The geographic key to *Postern* would be the valley of the Markham River, which runs northwest from Lae for maybe 110 miles. It was a good place for air bases, the general's staff believed. So good that you just couldn't help but build an air base there. You could just be strolling along the banks of the Markham and suddenly you'd find yourself grading a runway. You just couldn't help yourself. But the Markham was on the other side of Lae and Salamaua from the Allies in the Buna area. How to get there? That was why General MacArthur earned the big bucks. As Australian historian Peter J. Dean put it, "Operation *Postern* was a deliberate attack utilizing a coordinated effort across all domains of military power."[213] Translation: *Postern* would feature an airborne assault, an airmobile assault, an amphibious assault, and a just plain average assault, all with ample air and artillery support.

This offensive would take elements from the "island hopping" in the Aleutians and the central Solomons. Of course, island hopping would be much more difficult on New Guinea, since it was all just one island, and you couldn't just hop over it when you needed to capture targets on it. The settlements on New Guinea were kind of like islands, though, in that getting to them overland was often extremely difficult and sometimes even impossible. It was why that Japanese convoy destroyed off Lae in March could not land outside of Allied air range and had the troops march overland to Lae. There were simply no roads available through the jungle. Still, without islands, calling what General MacArthur was planning "island hopping" was just silly. The best they could do was "not-island hopping."

But not-island hopping would function much the same as island hopping. The Japanese base closest to the Allied line in New Guinea was Salamaua. Australian troops had been creeping closer and closer to Salamaua throughout the summer. There was also that business at Nassau Bay, which gave the impression of an Allied commitment to attack Salamaua. The Japanese started moving troops to a defense line south of Salamaua.

Which, in the Allies' minds, was a good thing. The idea in *Postern* was to make the Japanese believe Salamaua was the target. Hopefully, they would commit themselves to defending it. Then General MacArthur would hop over it and attack Lae instead with an amphibious operation east of Lae and a parachute operation west of Lae to seize the town in a pincer attack. More specifically, transports would land the Australian troops on the coast east of Lae near Malahang. At about the same time, the US 503rd Parachute Infantry Regiment would stage the first Allied airborne assault of the Pacific War, with its objective the village of Nadzab, some 40 miles northwest of Lae in the aforementioned Markham valley. Seizure of Nadzab would both give the Allies an air base – an old air base that could be quickly readied – for further operations in the Huon Peninsula and block Japanese reinforcements from western New Guinea.

In short, *Postern* would be a trap, a two-pronged attack to take Lae in the posterior of the Japanese defenses at Salamaua in the hopes of cutting off the Japanese defenders.

General Sir Thomas Blamey, commander of Allied ground troops in New Guinea, selected two Australian divisions for *Postern*: the 7th and 9th Divisions, both veteran units. Also selected was the aforementioned US Army 503rd Parachute Infantry Regiment, an independent unit not affiliated with a division such as the more famous 82nd and 101st Airborne divisions, as well as the US 2nd Engineer Special Brigade, which was really a unit of small boats for use by the Army. Fronting Salamaua would be the Australian 3rd Division and the US Army's 41st Infantry Division.

Of course, since *Postern* was a complicated operation, there were difficulties. Originally, the start of the offensive was set for August 1, but it was postponed ultimately to September 4. The delay did not mean that nothing was going on in the interim. Certainly not on the Japanese side. General Inamura of the 8th Area Army and General Adachi of the 18th Army planned to hold and defend both Lae and Salamaua with the approximately 10,000 troops they had available, though as many as half were sick with the usual tropical ailments. By the end of July, some 8,000 of those 10,000 troops were in the Salamaua sector.[214]

Additionally, work was continuing – slowly – on a road that would run from Wewak and Madang in western New Guinea through the Markham Valley to Lae. Once complete, supplies and reinforcements could be run into Wewak and Madang and kept at the outside of Allied air power, thus not risking another Bismarck Sea catastrophe. Of course, this road amounted to closing the barn door after the horses had run off into the Bismarck Sea and drowned, but better late than never.

The "Battle" of the Bismarck Sea in March had changed everything in New Guinea. The Japanese had not even attempted another convoy run into New Guinea since. Until June, six submarines had been running in supplies in mole runs, but that number had been reduced to three, and the Japanese were compelled to use, as they had in the Solomons, that ultimate Japanese weapon: the *daihatsu* barge. The barges would run from Tuluvu on the north coast of Cape Gloucester to Lae.

But maintaining Tuluvu itself was becoming costly. There was no road from Rabaul through the jungle to Tuluvu, so supplies had to be brought in by sea, which in a time of increasing Allied air dominance and a virtual blockade of large ship traffic through the Huon Gulf to Lae was exceedingly dangerous. It was while running supplies to Tuluvu that the destroyers *Ariake* and *Mikazuki* had run aground and been lost. After that disaster,

Captain Hara's destroyer *Shigure* had been forced to take up the slack and make a single-ship supply run to Tuluvu on September 1.[215]

Captain Hara had the *Shigure* creep along the north coast of New Britain at 18 knots. Sunset found the destroyer off Cape Hollman, about halfway between Rabaul and Tuluvu. So did a Black Cat, whose sighting report the *Shigure*'s radio operators intercepted. Hara had expected this, of course, albeit not so early. About an hour later, another sighting report was intercepted. And then another. Things were getting tense and uncomfortable. Fortunately, there was a friendly neighborhood rain squall. Hara took the destroyer into it, slowing down in the process. The enemy would not find him in the murky darkness. The contact reports stopped. Solved that problem. Everyone on the bridge relaxed. Hara allowed himself a yawn and a stretch ...

And immediately froze with his arms in the air. Others on the bridge got wide eyed, their jaws dropping. Hara had heard it. They all had heard it. Getting louder. The "high-pitched, jarring sound of dive-bombing planes." The Americans were bombing him. At night. In a rainstorm. Can they *do* that?

The answer was immaterial, they were doing just that. "With a spine-shivering roar, a plane whizzed directly over the bridge," Hara recalled. "There was a monstrous, deafening detonation followed by several explosions. Another plane thundered by the mast."

The commodore did some thundering himself. After Lieutenant Commander Yamagami ordered battle stations and a second bomb landed in the water maybe 10 meters from the ship and drenched everyone topside, Hara roared, "Hard right rudder! Immediate overboost! Flank speed!"

An overboost is like a turbocharge in a car, forcing air into the engines, albeit for a short period in the case of the overboost, in order to increase their power. Under normal conditions, increasing speed from 12 knots to 30 would take a half hour. Under combat conditions, it might take half of that. Captain Hara was trying to do it *now*. All at once. It risked wrecking the engines in even the newest of ships, let alone engines as old, overused, and poorly maintained as those of the *Shigure*. But Hara felt he had no choice. It was either the engines or the ship.

As if to emphasize the danger, the aft stack started spewing flames – burning bunker fuel – like a torch in the night. No way the enemy could miss that. And they didn't. But no more bombs fell. After a few moments, the radio room reported, "Enemy plane, in plain language, reports direct hits amidship on a destroyer, setting it afire and leaving it sinking." The report was met with incredulity, then shouts of joy, and finally laughter. Hara canceled the overboost and completed the mission without further incident.

In Rabaul the next day, Hara was met by Admiral Ijuin. When Hara told him the story, the baron "laughed until he almost choked[.]" Ijuin finally said, "I guess we can now call you the Miracle Captain, Hara."

But if it was this dangerous for Japanese ships north of New Britain, south of New Britain had to be even worse than the Bismarck Sea ambush. No way the Japanese could run ships to Lae anymore. They had to use barges.

One problem: they needed 150 barge-loads of food to keep the 10,000 troops around Lae and Salamaua supplied. They needed another 200 to bring in reinforcements and ammunition. They had … 40. And those 40 were being whittled down. Once again, barges were not the most seaworthy creatures, and the run from Tuluvu to Lae was both long and dangerous, especially in the Danphier Strait. The barges were being picked off by Allied aircraft and PT boats. General MacArthur's PT boats were far more effective in ferreting out and sinking barges than their counterparts in the Solomons. Then again, MacArthur's PT boats no longer had to worry about facing enemy warships, for the most part, and so could modify themselves specifically to handle barges.

In short, after the defeat in the Bismarck Sea, the Japanese supply system for Lae and Salamaua had been inadequate at best and was now on the brink of complete collapse. It had reduced the effectiveness of Japanese air power at Lae and Salamaua to near impotence, so much so that General MacArthur shrugged them off as little threat to his operations.

So had General Inamura, which is why he had pestered Imperial General Headquarters for additional air power. Imperial General Headquarters finally came through on July 27, when it ordered the Japanese Army Air Force's 4th Air Army, commanded by Lieutenant General Teramoto Kumaichi, to stage from the Netherlands East Indies to the Southeast Area. The 4th included the 6th and 7th Air Divisions, the 14th Air Brigade, and a few loose squadrons lying around, totaling about 250 aircraft. The headquarters arrived at Rabaul on August 6, at which time Inamura ordered it to stage into the Wewak air complex some 310 miles northwest of Finschhafen. Its mission would be escorting convoys, destroying Allied aircraft and ships, and cooperating with the 18th Army.[216] Which seemed like rather obvious priorities.

The Allies were not oblivious to the Japanese buildup of air forces at Wewak and the threat it posed for *Postern*. General MacArthur's intelligence officer General Willoughby, had pointed out that the *Toenails* operation at New Georgia showed that the Japanese air reaction to the planned landings "might be violent."[217] Such helpful foresight is why war is best left to the professionals. The 5th Air Force had to be prepared in case the Japanese reaction with its big new air force was "violent." The Dobodura air complex was deemed a little too far away to provide effective continuous fighter coverage, so a staging field was to be built in the Watut Valley west of Salamaua at a place called Tsili Tsili. A rose by any other name might smell just as sweet, but an airfield with the name Tsili Tsili was silly in the opinion of General Kenney, so he ordered it renamed Marilinan, after a village about four miles away.[218]

The biggest problem, however, was radar coverage. Japanese aircraft from Wewak or Madang could fly south of the mountains, or from New Britain across Dampier and Vitiaz Straits, and radar would not pick them up until they were almost over Lae. An Australian aviator suggested posting a picket destroyer in that radar blind spot. So the destroyer USS *Reid* was ordered to loiter in the Vitiaz Strait about 45 miles southeast of Finschhafen in the hope that her performance as radar picket destroyer would be better than that of the *Blue* and *Ralph Talbot* at Savo Island about a year earlier.[219]

However silly General Kenney thought Tsili Tsili was, by mid-August it had two complete runways and 3,000 troops. At the same time Tsili Tsili was under construction, Kenney was building an emergency airstrip at Bena Bena. Well, Kenney called it an "emergency" airstrip, but it was really a decoy to distract the Japanese from Tsili Tsili. And the Japanese took the bait. They attacked it almost daily, burning down the grass huts and bombing strips that had been cleared of grass, which looked to the Japanese like runways. The local construction workers thought it was hilarious. Despite the obvious danger, when the Japanese attacked the airfield, the local inhabitants would literally roll on the ground with laughter, cackling about how they were "making fool of the Jap man."[220]

But you can fool all the Japanese some of the time and all that. The morning of August 14, a Japanese scout plane loitered over Tsili Tsili. That evening, the 40th Fighter Squadron of the 3rd Fighter Group, flying new, improved Airacobras with oxygen and turbochargers, staged into the new base.[221] Everyone knew what came next.

The next day, to be precise, when 34 Nakajima Ki-43 fighters from the Japanese Army Air Force's 24th and 59th Air Regiments flew top cover for seven Ki-48 bombers from the 208th Air Regiment from the Dagua to arrive over Tsili Tsili a little after 9:00am. Though everyone had known what was coming, the attack came as a surprise because the Japanese had flown just under a cloud layer, evading the Lightnings patrolling just above said cloud layer, and the newly installed radar did not pick up the incoming strike. When the Japanese were finally detected, they were only a mile away.[222]

Nonetheless, there was a very active defense of Tsili Tsili. A dozen of the new and improved Airacobras from the 35th Fighter Group's 41st Fighter Squadron were escorting 24 Skytrains to the base. A dozen of the transports had already landed, and the other dozen were in the landing circle. The Airacobras saw the incoming Japanese, whom they identified as "nine medium bombers (Sallys) ... at 10,000 feet," and moved to intercept.[223]

The escorting Oscars flew their top cover a little too top and a little too far back for the Lilys, who focused on their bombing runs to the point where they took almost no evasive action. Captain Namba Shigeki, leading one of the cover elements, later lamented that "one by one the Ki-48s were shot down in flames."[224] But at least the Lilys were destroyed in the air and not on the ground like they usually were. One of the Lilys did make kind of a proto-kamikaze dive – technically a *taiatari*, literally translated as "body crashing" – on the newly built chapel. The chaplain and six or seven men inside were killed.[225]

With the bombers gone or going, the air battle developed between the Oscars and the Airacobras. No one could get a hold of the Lightnings flying over the clouds, while maybe 20 Airacobras from the 40th Fighter Squadron scrambled, no small feat when the air base was under attack, as Hickam and Clark Fields could attest. Three of the Oscars were shot down. Three P-39s of the 41st Fighter Squadron were lost, with one pilot killed; a fourth Airacobra crash landed and was written off. Most of the Skytrains were able to scatter and evade the Japanese, but not all of them. One C-47 coming in to land was shot down and its six occupants killed; a second Skytrain carrying nine vanished into the mountains and was never seen again. Other than the chapel, damage to the base was minimal.[226]

Nevertheless, the returning Japanese reported that the air base had been badly damaged, with 18 American fighters and "three or four" transports shot down. With results like that, General Teramoto decided to go for an encore late the next day, sending 33 fighters and three bombers to, in General Kenney's words, "argue the point." When they arrived, once again, a redundant-sounding train of Skytrains, 48 in this case, was coming in to Tsili Tsili. They were covered by 13 Lightnings from the newly arrived 431st Fighter Squadron of the 475th Fighter Group and 32 of a new, muscular-looking fighter plane that the Japanese had never seen before. The Americans called it the Republic P-47 Thunderbolt, these from the brand-new 348th Fighter Group. It was the fighters' second such mission of the day, but they had to abandon it to cut off the approaching Japanese, whom they estimated to be 16 bombers and 15 fighters. The interception would also see the Thunderbolt's first combat against the Japanese, combat that lasted maybe a half hour. The US Army Air Force pilots claimed nine fighters and five bombers; in actuality they had shot down three Oscars with their pilots. One Thunderbolt was reported missing, that of 2nd Lieutenant Leonard G. Leighton of the 341st Fighter Squadron, whose corpse and wrecked plane was found in the jungle several days later. A Lightning also had to be written off. Again, damage to the base was minimal.[227]

Nevertheless, the returning Japanese reported that after two days of combat, the Tsili Tsili airdrome was destroyed, with 39 Allied aircraft shot down. They had actually shot down seven. General Teramoto and his men had not fought at Guadalcanal or New Georgia, so they seem to have been unaware of the rule of thumb that you can never really destroy an air base made of dirt. Anyway, the Japanese considered the two-day series of attacks on Tsili Tsili a major success, and senior staff officers came down from Rabaul to present awards and perform a ceremonial inspection.[228]

General Kenney was not happy with the attacks on Tsili Tsili. A rather fortuitous photo reconnaissance mission over Wewak that day came back with pictures showing 225 Japanese aircraft at the complex's four air bases, with 110 aircraft, mostly bombers, at Boram, 35 fighters at Wewak city (or "Wirui" or "Wewak Central"), which had been used by the Divine Word missionaries; 60 fighters and bombers at Dagua (or "But East"), and 20 fighters at But (or "But West").[229]

That's sort of dispersed, but not completely. Though on the surface it did not seem to accomplish a lot, General Kenney's 5th Air Force had been quite busy since the Battle of the Bismarck Sea. Flying Fortresses had been making night nuisance raids on the Rabaul air complex. Like Washing Machine Charlie, but with more damage and better tuned engines. The 5th had also been hitting the Lae-Salamaua area hard, attacking it nearly every day of July. Sorties during the month totaled 400 by B-25 Mitchells, 100 by B-24 Liberators, 45 by Royal Australian Air Force A-20 Bostons, 35 by A-20 Havocs, 30 by B-17 Flying Fortresses, and seven by B-26 Marauders.[230] The constant harassment was one reason the Japanese had largely stopped using the Lae and Salamaua airdromes and had instead massed their aircraft at the Wewak complex. The Japanese had determined that Wewak was outside the range of the 5th Bomber Command. Slight problem: it wasn't.

This they learned the hard way on August 17. Their morning wakeup call came a little before 12:30am in the form of six Flying Fortresses from the 63rd Bombardment Squadron (Heavy) sweeping low over the Dagua air base, dropping fragmentation bombs on the runways and dispersal areas while machine-gunning in every direction. Thirty minutes later six Flying Fortresses from the 65th joined in the Dagua party with parachute fragmentation clusters. Another thirty minutes later it was seven Liberators from the 403rd coming in low over the But air base. When they left "the whole area was a sheet of flame." Following at 2:24am were six Liberators from the 64th, who swept the length of the runway.[231]

The only aerial opposition came from a single twin-engine fighter. Lieutenant John C. Glyer's Flying Fortress of the 63rd was caught in searchlights and attacked from behind by the fighter but was not hit. A second Fortress, piloted by Captain Robert H. Fuller of the 65th, earned "a fantastic duel with a Nip night fighter from Madang to Wewak and back again." The fighter reportedly made a dozen passes at Fuller's Flying Fortress without scoring a single hit.[232] The shooting suggested the decline in the skill level of Japanese pilots was not limited to the Naval Air Force.

While all this was going on, the 90th Bombardment Group (Heavy) came in with 25 Liberators of the 319th, 320th, 321st, and 400th Bombardment Squadrons (Heavy), whose targets were Wewak Central and Boram. One of the first to arrive at Wewak Central was a Liberator of the 320th flown by Lieutenant Lionel B. Potter. Potter found Wewak "just too quiet and peaceful – not a light or sign of life anywhere." Naturally, that jinxed it. Four searchlights snapped on, quickly joined by five more, and the antiaircraft fire became "awfully damn accurate." Even so, Potter and his fellow Liberators completed their bombing mission at Wewak Central and headed back.[233]

A similar if more deadly story played out at Boram. The Japanese were caught with their pants down – literally in most cases – but they recovered quickly enough to respond with antiaircraft fire that was "extremely heavy and accurate" and searchlights that were "annoying." And some things that were worse than annoying. The crews attacking Boram watched in horror as the Liberator piloted by 2nd Lieutenant Joseph M. Casale of the 321st Squadron burst into flames and started a fiery glide downward. As it did so, it may have clipped a second Liberator, flown by Lieutenant Charles F. Freas of the 400th. In any event, Freas' bomber staggered southward for 20 minutes before disappearing into a swamp.[234] While there were some grouchy Oscars flying around that night, the Army Air Force crews, again, reported twin-engine aircraft taking swipes at the bombers.

The twin-engine fighter would have been a Kawasaki Ki-45 *Toryu* ("Dragonslayer") Type 2 Two-Seat Fighter. Rather than say that mouthful, the Allies simply gave it the reporting name "Nick." The Ki-45s, from the 13th Air Regiment under Captain Ashai Rokuro, were operating out of Boram as night fighters. Despite their earlier inaccuracy, they are believed to have shot down at least 2nd Lieutenant Casale's Liberator and possibly

Lieutenant Freas' as well; the 13th's reports would claim one shot down and one probable. A third Liberator, from the 64th, got lost after its radio malfunctioned; it ran out of fuel and had to ditch off the southern coast of New Guinea. Two .50cal. waist machine guns detached during the ditching and flew through the passenger compartment, killing two and fatally injuring a third, while a fourth flew out of a hole torn in the aircraft by the crash and was never seen again. The six survivors were rescued.[235]

But that was just the beginning. General Kenney had been waiting for this day for a long, long time. His bombers had always had the range to hit Wewak, but his fighters had not. Wewak was too well defended with its own fighters and antiaircraft artillery to attack without fighter escort. Kenney was not going to risk his few precious bombers and their crews in an unescorted attack on such a fortress, so he did not attack. He attacked pretty much everywhere else: Gasmata, Madang, Lae, Salamaua, even the Netherlands East Indies. But not any of the four airfields at the Wewak air complex. The Japanese assumed the lack of bombing attacks on Wewak meant it was outside the range of Allied bombers.

But you know what they say happens when you assume. General Kenney was a believer that half of war was 90 percent mental, or something like that, and wanted the Japanese to believe Wewak was out of range. That was where the new forward air base at Tsili Tsili came in. Fighters based or topped off there did have the range to escort the bombers all the way to Wewak. First chance Kenney got, he was going for a full-scale attack on the Wewak air base complex. And, with Tsili Tsili having been operational for only a few days, he did.

Beginning at 6:00am, 24 B-25 Mitchells of the 71st and 405th Bombardment Squadrons (Medium), 38th Bombardment Group (Medium), took off from Durand Field near Port Moresby. At the same time, 37 B-25 gunships from the 8th, 13th, and 90th Bombardment Squadrons (Medium), 3rd Bombardment Group (Medium), modified the Pappy Gunn way, took off as well. Scheduled to join them were 99 Lightnings from six squadrons of the 35th, 49th, and 475th Fighter Groups. The base at Tsili Tsili, however silly its actual name, was paying off.[236]

Or not. The rendezvous went badly awry, causing most of the squadrons to abort. One that did not abort was the 405th under Captain William Ruark. A dozen Mitchell gunships, they continued up the Markham Valley. Then most of them discovered that their auxiliary fuel tanks – potential bombs even when empty – would not release. One pilot, Captain Garrett E. Middlebrook, ordered upper turret gunner Staff Sergeant Robert S. Emminger to hook his parachute harness to the exposed ribs of the fuselage above the tank, and then "jump up and down on the son-of-a-bitch." It worked. Unfortunately, the other pilots had not been so resourceful. With strict radio silence, Middlebrook could not tell them his solution, and they, too, had to abort.[237]

All but Middlebrook. And one gunship Middlebrook saw "flying straight as an arrow" toward Wewak. He joined up on the wing of the Mitchell, flown by Captain William N. Gay. Joining up on the other wing was the Mitchell of Lieutenant Berdines Lackness. As far as they could tell, they were all that remained of the massive strike force: three medium bomber "Gunnships." Heading toward Japan's biggest base in New Guinea. Without fighter protection.

After wondering to himself "where duty ended and insanity began," Captain Middlebrook chose what the others had already decided: they were going to attack.[238]

The worst that could happen was: they would all be killed. They could live with that.

As the sun rose over Wewak Central, the enthusiasm of the Japanese senior staff officers who had arrived from Rabaul to give awards after the supposed victory at Tsili Tsili was rather dampened when they saw the two Ki-21 Type 97 heavy bombers that had brought them here had been reduced to tangles of blackened metal by the previous night's activities. They met with the intelligence officer, then headed for the area headquarters, located in a former church of Bishop Lörks's vicariate, overlooking Wewak.

The intelligence officer, Captain Yamanaka Akira, was the chain-smoking senior officer at Wewak Central that morning, though his stinky cigarette smoke was harder to detect among the charred, smoldering wrecks along the runways.[239] The still very large numbers of surviving aircraft were being prepared to launch a major air attack, even as they sat in nice rows, wingtip to wingtip, along the runway, all the better for an inspection by senior staff. Yamanaka remained troubled. These were the same people who insisted that Wewak was outside the range of Allied bombers. Moreover, of those two most important commodities in any military operation, information and communications, Yamanaka was dealing with a shortage of both, especially the latter. The phone lines were down. That was bad. Wewak did have radar – that was still not operational four months after it was brought in. Consequently, they were dependent on sighting reports that required those phone lines and radios. Captain Yamanaka did have a little information, including a rather curious report from a distant lookout post. Two P-38 Lightnings had been reported at high altitude heading toward Wewak. That was odd. Only two Lightnings? At high altitude? Why would they do that …? Yamanaka knew. He ordered the phone lines repaired as soon as possible, if not sooner. The troops, tied up getting ready for the inspection, struggled to carry out his order. In the meantime, another lookout post, this one at Hansa Bay, reported in by radio: a formation of enemy aircraft was approaching Wewak from the southeast. With rising horror, Yamanaka made some calculations: those aircraft would arrive at Wewak in 20 minutes.

Twenty minutes. Twelve hundred seconds. And all the planes at his base and the other Wewak-area bases were lined up, wingtip to wingtip, armed and fueled, waiting for inspection and then action. And his phone lines were down. Well, not all of them. A few of them had been repaired. Captain Yamanaka got a warning off to But air base, 30 miles away. But that was all. In desperation, Captain Yamanaka and the men of his intelligence unit started running down the runway of Wewak Central, shouting and waving. Trying to get the attention of the pilots and the ground crews. To warn them. Some of the fighters had their engines turning over.

It was too late. Appearing behind him just over the treetops were three twin-engine aircraft. B-25 Mitchells. Roaring in low. Spitting fire. A lot of fire. Yamanaka hit the dirt.

Those three Mitchells were the first of seven Gunnships from the 90th Bombardment Squadron (Medium). In the lead was Captain Philip H. Hawkins, described by one newspaper correspondent as "a typical Texan from the Panhandle with a drawl as soft as the wool tops on his flying boots[.]"[240] Captain Hawkins led his strafers in low, as in, as low as 20 feet. At 280 knots. Each Gunnship, just as Pappy Gunn had designed them, with eight .50cal. machine guns. For the mathematically challenged, three Gunnships over the runway meant 24 .50cal. machine guns. All firing at once, a total of more than 100 rounds per second, creating an opaque dust cloud that swept over the runway and everything on either side of it.

That dust cloud was a wave of destruction. Many of the .50cal. rounds thumped into the ground or trees or bushes. Others thunked into metal – of the aircraft parked side by side, wingtip to wingtip, for that inspection; of vehicles, of fuel tanks that exploded. Still others made far more strickening sounds.

In three waves, Captain Hawkins' seven Gunnships fired 6,000 rounds of .50cal. ammunition. But that was not all. Oh, not even close. As the Gunnships were gunning, they were also bombing, releasing what were called "parafrag bombs," short for parachute fragmentation bomb. The parafrag bomb, an invention of General Kenney himself back in the 1920s, was a small 23lb bomb scored to break into 1-inch fragments on detonation. It was equipped with a small parachute that slowed the bomb's descent, allowing it to be dropped in a low-level attack while giving the attacking aircraft time to get clear before the bomb exploded. Because the parafrag bomb was so small, a lot of them could be dropped at once, filling an area a half a mile long with shrapnel.[241]

Captain Hawkins' Gunnships dropped 177 of these parafrag cluster bombs. Clinging to the dubious safety of the ground, Captain Yamanaka could only glimpse as the carnage unfolded around him. Explosions of gas tanks, both on the aircraft and in fueling vehicles; flying metal; flying bodies and pieces of bodies; blood, guts, and gasoline spewing everywhere.[242]

The entire attack was over in a matter of minutes, a short period of time that did not seem to fit the destruction and death Captain Yamanaka beheld when he finally pushed himself up off the ground. All those beautiful planes that only minutes before had been arranged so neatly – too neatly, Yamanaka knew, had known – were at best perforated; others were recognizable burning hulks; still others were piles of twisted metal. Fires were burning everywhere. Maybe 70 men had been killed the night before. Yamanaka could see this would be much worse.

If misery loves company, Wewak Central had a lot of love this day. Three miles away at Boram, Major Donald P. Hall, commanding officer of the 3rd Bombardment Group, was leading six Gunnships from the 8th Bombardment Squadron, followed by eight of the

13th Bombardment Squadron. Roaring in low over the treetops, when they cleared the trees – there were a lot of trees around the airfields, it would seem – the sight that greeted Hall and his aviators left them stunned. There were 60 to 70 aircraft parked in straight rows, wingtip to wingtip, on either side of the runway. Some had their engines turning over, many were surrounded by ground personnel. All Hall and his pilots had to do was line them up and shoot them up. It was too easy. One bomber was moving down the runway. Hall and his group of three opened fire, catching the bomber as it lifted off, sending it crashing back to the runway, blocking it. In the words of General Kenney, Hall's Gunships swept over Boram "like a giant scythe." The 8th attacked in two waves of three, followed by the 13th, which by itself fired approximately 12,500 rounds of .50-caliber ammunition and dropped 95 clusters of parafrags on Boram.[243]

Some 20 miles away at Dagua, Captain Gay was leading what he and his men feared were the only three Mitchells to make the attack. Roaring in from the east at 280 knots, also at treetop level, Gay and his aviators were also stunned by what they saw. "God, it was unbelievable," Captain Middlebrook wrote. He counted "at least forty to fifty" twin-engine bombers lined up along the southern length of the strip, and several Oscars on the opposite side. He also noticed three Oscars taking off at the far end of the runway. It seems that Captain Yamanaka's warning to But air base had been relayed to Dagua, as well, just in time to get those three Nakajima Ki-43s air borne.

For the time being, it would not matter. Captain Middlebrook lined up the machine-gun-filled nose of his Gunship with the row of bombers on the ground and pressed the firing button:

> The first twin-engine Sally bomber which my tracers poured into exploded, and the concussion caused an identical plane alongside it to jump several feet into the air before settling back to earth, where it too began to burn. I saw the tail section upon a third bomber disintegrate while the wing of yet another was shredded. Two Japanese soldiers were running toward the jungle along the south edge of the runway. They ran alongside another bomber just as my firepower reached it. The violent explosion formed a fireball which engulfed the two Japs, causing them to instantaneously disappear from the face of the earth.[244]

But that warning from Captain Yamanaka would have more consequences than just those three Oscars. But air base, the original recipient of Yamanaka's message, had not been attacked because the Gunships assigned to it from the 71st Bombardment Squadron had aborted. But was able to scramble more fighters. As Captain Gay, Captain Middlebrook, and Lieutenant Lackness finished their attack run, ten to 15 Oscars Ki-43s jumped them. Middlebrook would later describe it as an appropriate moment "to flee for our lives and to place our faith in those Wright Cyclone engines."[245]

They did, and the Ki-43s followed. Captain Gay led his flight over the water and had the other Mitchells form on him in a tight formation to maximize their defensive firepower, shooting down one Oscar in the process. Diving as close as they dared to the wavetops, Gay's Mitchells led the Oscars on a less-than-merry chase of some 300 miles for about an hour, the Oscars gradually dropping out one by one until the last ones turned away near Salamaua. Exhausted, soaked with perspiration, Gay and his men reached Dobodura safely.[246]

At the Port Moresby air complex and its Advanced Echelon headquarters, the mood was jubilation as reports of the wildly successful attack on Wewak came in. Returning air crews stepped off their planes to find reporters waiting for them. "It was a cinch," Captain Hawkins told Alan Dawes of the Sydney *Telegraph*. "Except for the Bismarck Sea battle, which was a job of a different order, this was the most successful mission I have ever been on." At Advanced Echelon headquarters, Whitehead told reporters he was "delighted with the success of the mission and with the performance of the air personnel."[247]

"Photographs reveal the total destruction of 120 enemy planes and severe damage to at least another 50," claimed General MacArthur in a statement from Brisbane. "Heavy casualties were inflicted on his air and ground crews, who were completely surprised and unable to escape the machine gun and bombing attacks as our planes strafed and re-strafed the fields in numberless passes. It is estimated that 1500 enemy air personnel were killed."[248]

Well … not exactly. It has been claimed that 63 percent of all statistics are made up, including this one.[249] General MacArthur's quote was among those 63 percent. He had no idea how many aircraft were destroyed or how many Japanese were killed. The 90th Squadron rather conservatively claimed about 15 aircraft destroyed or damaged at Wewak. The 8th Squadron claimed at least 15 of 40 to 60 aircraft had been destroyed and 25 to 30 left burning at Boram, while the 13th Squadron that had followed the 8th at Boram reported that of 70 to 80 aircraft on the runway, "all [were] believed destroyed or severely damaged." The two Lightnings assigned to photograph the targets for battle damage assessments – the two Lightnings that had been reported to Captain Yamanaka before the attack – had run out of film after they had photographed just one airfield. The keeper of the 8th Photo Reconnaissance Squadron war diary later noted: "Although no accurate estimate of the damage can be assessed, it is assumed that 70 to 80 planes were destroyed on the ground."[250] 80. 120. It was all the same to MacArthur.

Nevertheless, if General MacArthur wanted revenge for the destruction of his Far East Air Force on the ground at Clark Field, if the US Army Air Force wanted revenge for the destruction of their Warhawks on the ground at Pearl Harbor's Hickam Field, they had it. The results of the attacks had been devastating. Colonel Tanikawa Kazuo, a staff officer in the 8th Area Army, later acknowledged that "the scale and suddenness of the 17 August raid took the Japanese defenses completely by surprise." The Japanese would call it "The Black Day of August 17."[251]

Just like Hickam Field, the Japanese had been caught with their aircraft stupidly parked next to each other, wingtip to wingtip. Just like Clark Field, the Japanese had lost the ability to even contest Allied air superiority. The raids of August 17 were followed by a second, less successful series of raids on August 18, in which the Mitchell of Major Ralph

Cheli, commanding the 405th Bombardment Squadron (Medium), was set afire during an attack on Dagua. Cheli continued leading the attack, then his plane crash-landed, after which he was captured by the Japanese and later murdered. Nevertheless, Cheli had completed his mission. Afterwards, Japan's 13th Air Regiment had only two serviceable aircraft remaining, while the 68th had only two Ki-61s, and the 78th none at all. The strength of the 4th Air Army was reduced to an operational strength of just over 30 planes. Thereafter it averaged only 100 planes. "It meant a virtual end to air operations in New Guinea for the time being" and "the prospect of the New Guinea operation [was] much gloomier."[252]

With Wewak thus neutralized, General MacArthur could go forward with *Postern*. Rear Admiral Arthur S. Carpender, General MacArthur's naval commander, decided with Wewak more or less off the table it was feasible to send what few warships he had further up the New Guinea coast. On August 20, Carpender in Brisbane sent orders to Captain Jesse H. Carter at Milne Bay:

Inasmuch as there is good reason to believe that the enemy is moving both supplies and troops from Finschhafen to Salamaua, you will select four destroyers and make a sweep of Huon Gulf – during darkness 22–23 August – and follow this with a bombardment of Finschhafen. Targets of opportunity are to be destroyed.[253]

This operation itself would be small, but it would have a few firsts. It would be the first time Allied warships had ventured so far up the New Guinea coast. More significantly, it would be the first time Allied warships had bombarded Japanese positions in New Guinea. After all the pressure on General MacArthur's land and air units, one of Admiral Carpender's staff commented, "It will be worthwhile to prove the Navy is willing to pitch in, even if we get nothing but coconuts."[254]

Though on this operation the US Navy didn't find even coconuts. Captain Carter selected the *Perkins* as his flagship and led the destroyers *Smith*, *Conyngham*, and *Mahan* to Buna for a quick briefing and a discussion of air cover. On the evening of August 22, Carter's ships swept Huon Gulf and found nothing. The real fun began at 1:21 the next morning, August 23, when Carter's ships lobbed 540 5-inch shells at Finschhafen in 10 minutes before returning safely to Milne Bay. The bombardment did not accomplish much, but the message it sent to the Japanese was clear: there were no more safe havens on New Guinea.[255]

But to keep those safe havens unsafe, the pressure had to be maintained which, in turn, put more pressure on the Allied 5th Air Force to maintain that pressure. During the remainder of August, Liberators carried out 102 additional sorties, and Mitchells added 21 against land targets in the Wewak area. From the first Wewak raid until the end of the month, B-25 gunners claimed 22 enemy aircraft shot down for a loss of two Mitchells in combat and three from other causes; Liberator gunners claimed 35 enemy aircraft against three B-24s destroyed in combat and one in an accident; American fighters entered claims for 69 enemy planes shot down. Six Lightnings were lost in combat and three Lightnings and four Thunderbolts from other causes. Official Allied figures showed over 200 Japanese aircraft destroyed on the ground at the Wewak air complex. The actual total may be half that figure.[256]

By the end of August, General Kenney's intelligence staff estimated the Japanese had 118 operational aircraft in New Guinea, primarily at Wewak. It was the result of considerable reorganization by the Japanese after the crippling strikes on Wewak. The 13th Air Regiment had to switch from using the Ki-45 to Ki-43s left behind by the 1st Air Regiment. The 24th Air Regiment remained in situ, but lost Warrant Officer Saito Chiyoji, credited at that time with 21 victories and noted as a "P-38 killer," when he was shot down and killed on August 20. The 68th and 78th Air Regiments had been withdrawn to Manila to re-equip with newer Kawasaki Ki-61 Army Type 3 fighters. The 78th returned to Wewak in late August, the 68th in early September.[257] Nevertheless, for Kenney and his staff, the numbers were discouraging.

More discouraging was the number of enemy aircraft on New Britain – the Rabaul complex, Gasmata, and Cape Gloucester – which was believed to be more than 280 aircraft, plus 54 at Kavieng and 113 in the Shortlands complex – Kahili and Ballale. Kenney was also responsible for air operations in the Netherlands East Indies, where, it was estimated, the Japanese had 345 aircraft. In other words, the Japanese still had 910 planes facing the 5th Air Force.[258]

It forced General Kenney to make some tough choices. To keep the pressure on for *Postern*, he had to continue pounding all the coastal strongholds, particularly Wewak, to keep them down. That meant, as Kenney informed MacArthur, he "didn't have enough strength to handle the Jap air forces at both Rabaul and Wewak." He would have to stop attacking Rabaul until *Postern* was well under way. General MacArthur tacitly approved.[259]

So did the Australian 3rd Division and elements of the US Army's 41st Infantry Division, who were creeping forward toward Salamaua. On August 24, the Australian 5th Division, under the command of Major General E.J. Milford, relieved the 3rd. They continued the push toward the Francisco River, the last natural barrier before Salamaua.

The 3rd and later the 5th Divisions were facing thousands of troops of the Imperial Japanese Army's 51st Division under Lieutenant General Nakano Hidemitsu outside Salamaua. Some 25 miles away at Lae, the Japanese were keeping some 6,000 troops, including parts of the 80th, 41st, and 21st Infantry Regiments; artillery from the 21st Independent Mixed Brigade and the 14th Field Regiment; the 5th Sasebo Special Naval Landing Force; and a hodgepodge of engineers and logistics troops.[260] However, about two thirds of those troops were positioned to stop an advance on Lae from Salamaua. Just as the Allies had intended.[261]

This was why General MacArthur was using maneuver in the form of Rear Admiral Daniel Barbey's VII Amphibious Force. Barbey had the destroyers *Conyngham* and *Flusser*; fast destroyer-transports *Brooks*, *Gilmer*, *Sands*, and *Humphreys*; 13 landing ships; 34 landing craft; and transports carrying the Australian 9th Division under Major General

George Wootten. They were escorted by destroyers *Mugford* and *Drayton* commanded by Lieutenant Commander H.G. Corey, and covered by Captain Carter's destroyers *Perkins*, *Smith*, *Mahan*, and *Lamson*.[262] They left Milne Bay on September 1 and crept up the coast, putting in at Buna and Morobe. They started their final run to the Lae beaches on the evening of September 3.[263]

At this late hour, General Kenney began to have visions of Bismarck Sea in reverse, which could be caused by, he feared, Japanese air attacks out of Rabaul, which he had not attacked in the month-and-a-half he had been focusing on Wewak. He wanted to hit Rabaul one last time, but his own heavy bombers were targeting Lae – again. Somehow, he finagled nine Royal Australian Air Force Catalinas from No. 11 and 20 Squadrons out of Cairns to stage through Milne Bay to attack Rabaul the night of September 3–4. Their orders were to attack and linger over the airfields to "disturb the sleep and nerves of the enemy," like Washing Machine Charlie had. They did attack Vunakanau, Lakunai, and Rapopo, but found the antiaircraft defenses were too hot and quickly departed without loss but also without doing much damage.[264] One out of two wasn't bad.

At 6:18am on September 4, 18 minutes after dawn, Captain Carter's destroyers conducted a 10-minute bombardment of the invasion beaches. Then 16 landing craft from the fast destroyer transports started for the beaches carrying the first echelon of the 9th Division, which hit the beach at 6:31am some 18 miles east of Lae and found no opposition. Two minutes later more 9th Division troops also landed 18 miles east of Lae, east of the Bulu River. They found a small group of Japanese who ran away. They may have been some of those Special Naval Landing Force troops who never surrender.[265] After another 15 minutes the landing craft and then the landing ships moved in. All assault troops had landed by 8:30, and by 10:30 1,500 tons of supplies had been landed. All of it was outside the range of the guns of the Japanese 14th Field Regiment. General Nakano was completely unprepared for the landing and needed to redeploy his troops to counter it. To buy time, he had to beg for air support.

And he got it, at least to the extent the Japanese could provide it. Around 7am, before most of the Allied fighters were on station, three Japanese Army Air Force twin-engine bombers, possibly with six fighters as escort, made a cameo that damaged a few of the landing craft, killing three and wounding nine.[266]

There would be a relaxing interval of seven hours before the next Japanese air attack because fog had Base Air Force socked in, but as soon as it was clear, Admiral Kusaka and Base Air Force came through, as much as they could, anyway. A dozen G4Ms from the 702 Air Group and eight D3As from the 582 came in escorted by 61 Zeros from three air groups – eight from the 201, 14 from the 253, and 39 from the 204.[267] By this time, the invasion transports were getting ready to leave and 5th Fighter Command had arrived to provide air cover in the form of 40 Lightnings, 20 Thunderbolts, and even a few P-40s (from the 35th, 39th, and 341st Fighter Squadrons, with the 9th and 432nd joining them) who were vectored in by the radar picket destroyer *Reid*, then operating off Finschhafen.[268] Nevertheless, the Sea Eagles fought past the defending fighters – only to miss the main convoy and landing beach, where 1,500 tons of supplies were stacked in vulnerable mounds, and instead, off Cape Ward Hunt, attacked landing ships and craft who had already discharged their passengers and cargo. Landing craft *LCI-339* suffered a direct hit from a Val forward of her conning tower and had to be beached in sinking condition. A Betty put a torpedo into the port side aft of landing ship *LST-471*, *LST-473* suffered two hits and two near misses from bombs, but effective damage control kept both afloat. Forty-nine were killed and 56 wounded. The destroyer *Conyngham* was damaged by near misses. Some three hours later around 5:00pm, an undetermined number of Ki-43 fighters showed up and shot up an ammunition dump, killing two and wounding 12.[269]

Once again, the Japanese effort had been too little, too late, and too costly. Base Air Force admitted the loss of three G4Ms (matching the claims by American fighters) and four Zeros, while five D3As, seven G4Ms, and three Zeros sustained damage. The surviving crews claimed to have shot down 23 Lightnings, with four more considered "uncertain." The actual number lost was two, with three others damaged. The Japanese aviators also claimed to have badly damaged two destroyers and two transports and sunk four transports and a cruiser. As there was no cruiser present during this invasion, it could not have been sunk. Nevertheless, the Japanese sank it.[270]

Meanwhile, Generals Kenney and MacArthur discussed the seizure of Nadzab, scheduled for the following day. It involved a parachute assault by the 503rd Parachute Infantry Regiment. It would be not just the first parachute assault of the Pacific War but the first parachute assault by all 1,700 paratroopers of the 503rd.[271] That was significant – and a potential problem.

In the course of discussing the details of covering and supporting the Nadzab operation, General Kenney casually mentioned that he would be in one of the bombers to see how things went off. General MacArthur said he didn't think Kenney should go. Kenney replied that he had obeyed MacArthur's orders to keep out of combat and that, with Wewak's air force out of the picture and a fog stopping Base Air Force in Rabaul from interfering, he didn't expect any trouble. Furthermore:

> in any case this was to be my big day. If everything went all right, I would still be his Allied Air Force Commander. If the show went sour, I would be what a lot of his staff already thought I was. Furthermore, they were my kids and I was going to see them do their stuff.[272]

General MacArthur patiently listened to his air force commander make his case. Finally, MacArthur said, "You're right, George, we'll both go. They're my kids, too." General Kenney was aghast.

> "No, that doesn't make sense," I objected. "Why, after living all these years and getting to be the head general of the show, is it necessary for you to risk having some five-dollar-a-month Jap aviator shoot a hole through you?"

General MacArthur looked at Kenney in all seriousness and said, "I'm not worried about getting shot. Honestly, the only thing that disturbs me is the possibility that when we hit the rough air over the mountains my stomach might get upset. I'd hate to get sick and disgrace myself in front of the kids."[273]

General Kenney arranged to have three B-17s fly just above and to one side of the troop carriers as they approached Nadzab for the parachute jump. Kenney put General MacArthur in one and himself in a second, keeping the third B-17 for mutual protection in case Japanese fighters showed up. MacArthur suggested that they go in the same plane but Kenney countered that he "didn't like to tempt fate by putting too many eggs in one basket." The Southwest Pacific commander laughed but agreed.[274]

General MacArthur tells a somewhat different story:

It was a delicate operation involving the first major parachute jump in the Pacific war. The unit to make the jump was the United States 503rd Parachute Regiment. I inspected them and found, as was only natural, a sense of nervousness among the ranks. I decided that it would be advisable for me to fly in with them.

I did not want them to go through their first baptism of fire without such comfort as my presence might bring to them.[275]

The morning of September 5, 84 Skytrains of the 54th Troop Carrier Wing loaded the US 503rd Parachute Infantry Regiment and the 2nd Battalion of the 4th Australian Field Regiment and started taking off at 8:25am; all were in the air in 15 minutes. They gathered their escort of some 100 fighters. After crossing the Owen Stanleys, six squadrons of Liberator Gunships gave a drubbing to the old Nadzab airfield and, at 10:22am, the first paratrooper made his jump. General MacArthur was watching from the B-17 Flying Fortress *The Talisman* and quickly determined these paratroopers making their first combat jump "did not need me."

One plane after another poured out its stream of dropping men over the target field. Everything went like clockwork. The flame-throwers ate away the tall, irregular blotches of tropical Kunai grass; holes in the field were patched up, and the follow-up transports began to discharge their loads of infantry troops.[276]

General Kenney was similarly impressed:

The seizure of Nadzab by the paratroopers on September 5th went off so well that it is still hard for me to believe that anything could have been so perfect. At the last minute the Australian gunners who were to man the battery of 25 pounders decided to jump with their guns. None of them had ever worn a parachute before but they were so anxious to go that we showed them how to pull the ripcord and let them jump. Even this part of the show went off without a hitch and the guns were ready for action within an hour after they landed.

When we got back to Port Moresby, General MacArthur swore that it was the most perfect example of discipline training he had ever seen.[277]

The staid tones of the statements by MacArthur and Kenney perhaps belie the emotion and excitement of the situation at Nadzab. Kenney wrote General Arnold saying MacArthur was watching from a nearby B-17 and "jumping up and down like a kid."[278] Be that as it may, less than two hours after the jump, the entire aerial armada of Skytrains was safely back at base.[279] There was no resistance because there were no Japanese, and within 24 hours the old air base was declared secure. And the Skytrains began ferrying in the Australian 7th Division.

The campaign began to move quickly from this point. The Japanese at Lae and Salamaua were now hemmed in on three sides. Cooler heads in Imperial General Headquarters prevailed on General Nakano to hold out as long as possible, but to withdraw if he could not hold Salamaua. That directive became moot on September 8 when General Adachi ordered Nakano to abandon Salamaua and pull back to Lae, which he began on September 11. Two days later, Salamaua fell to the Allies.[280]

But Adachi soon saw that not even Lae was defensible now and the entire 51st Division was in serious danger of being cut off completely. He ordered Lae abandoned, with the troops ordered to go overland to the north coast of the Huon Peninsula. Adachi hoped to at least hold Finschhafen; to that end, he ordered the 20th Division at Madang to move to Finschhafen.[281] The Australian 7th Division driving in from the Markham valley and the Australian 9th Division driving in from the east met only delaying forces. They began something of a race between each other as to who would reach Lae first. The last Japanese units evacuated Lae on September 15, to join a hellish retreat through the jungle. The next day, Lae was liberated.

General MacArthur saw that the conclusion of the Lae-Salamaua Campaign had been quick. Much quicker than he had anticipated, with far fewer casualties. That was the result of moving all the chess pieces into position beforehand. Now he saw another opportunity and another threat.

General MacArthur's *Elkton* plan called for the capture of Finschhafen as a step toward gaining control of the Vitiaz and Dampier Straits separating New Britain from New Guinea. The plan had set the tentative date for the move against Finschhafen at six weeks after Lae was secured. The rapid fall of Lae and Salamaua encouraged moving up that timetable. Another factor was the Imperial Army's 20th Division heading for Finschhafen, about which Allied intelligence was aware. Ultimately, on September 17, MacArthur approved a plan for landing near Finschhafen on September 22.[282]

From six weeks to less than a week? If Admiral Halsey could invade Vella Lavella on the fly, why couldn't the same be achieved with Finschhafen? Rear Admiral Daniel Barbey, commander of the 7th Amphibious Force, had just enough time to slap together eight tank landing ships, 16 infantry landing craft, four destroyer-transports (*Brooks*, *Gilmer*, *Sands*, and *Humphreys*), and ten destroyers (*Conyngham*, *Henley*, *Perkins*, *Smith*, *Reid*,

Mahan, Lamson, Flusser, Mugford, Drayton). More elements of the Australian 9th Division were selected for this operation.[283]

After a short bombardment by the destroyers *Lamson, Mugford, Flusser,* and *Drayton,* the landing itself took place as scheduled on September 22 at 4:45am on a beach some six miles north of Finschhafen. In less than five hours, the feeble opposition had been easily overcome, 5,300 troops and tons of supplies had been landed, and the invasion fleet was on its way back. The destroyer *Reid* reprised her role as radar picket destroyer.[284]

This was a good thing, because everyone knew an aerial counterattack was coming. Despite the Japanese Army Air Force still having possession of the Wewak air base complex, the air attacks on this day came from Base Air Force. Admiral Kusaka had to risk the G4M land attack planes he had been carefully husbanding. That husbanding allowed him to send all of eight G4Ms from the 751 Air Group on a torpedo attack on the withdrawing invasion fleet, escorted by 38 Zeros (23 from the 253 Air Group, 12 from the 201, and three from the 204). It was a pointless attack on the now-empty ships that came at a disastrous time for the Japanese: a shift change in the fleet's fighter cover. Instead of the three squadrons that would have been defending the fleet, the Japanese had to face five. Of the eight G4Ms, only one – that flown by Flight Chief Petty Officer Kuramasu Jitsuyoshi – returned to Vunakanau. Seven Zeros were shot down, including the 201 Air Group's leading fighter ace, Chief Petty Officer Okumura Takeo. All for three Lightnings shot down, two of the pilots killed; and no torpedo hits.[285]

The Australian troops quickly consolidated their beachhead and began the drive toward Finschhafen. Other elements of the 9th Division – those that had been landed east of Lae during *Postern* – were moving up from Lae. It was another pincer operation. Less than 48 hours after landing, one of Finschhafen's airfields was captured.

But unlike Lae and Salamaua, Finschhafen and the Huon Peninsula would not be quick. Finschhafen itself fell to the 9th Division on October 2, but only after heavy resistance by the Japanese that was overcome only by hand-to-hand fighting and close air support. Even then, the Japanese had been defeated, not destroyed, and the remnants of the Finschhafen garrison would join up inland with the Imperial Army's 20th Division. Two more months of fighting on the Huon Peninsula lay ahead.[286]

Still, Lae, Salamaua, and Finschhafen. In less than one month.

The *Cartwheel* was finally turning.

———

The *daihatsu*. The barge.

No matter how many local modifications the Japanese made, the *daihatsu* was still slow and barely seaworthy. Yet, somehow, the *daihatsu*s had resisted the efforts of US Navy destroyers to clear them from the sea. So this thankless job was given to the PT boats.

Except the PT boats had their own issues in dealing with the *daihatsu*s. All four of the PT boat squadrons in the Solomons had been making night patrols of the waters around the New Georgia islands since late July. They had sunk several of the Japanese barges, but had not made a dent in the number of barges available. Admiral Halsey was less than impressed, saying:

> The use of PT boats as barge destroyers leaves much to be desired. … However, steps have been taken locally to improve their effectiveness, when so employed, by equipping them with a 37mm. or 40mm. single AA gun. Work is now underway on the conversion of three 77-foot MTB's into motor gunboats by removal of torpedo tubes and depth charges to provide space and weight compensation for an additional 40mm. single AA gun and armor.[287]

That meant, yes, an arms race between Japanese *daihatsus* and PT boats. As the *daihatsus* added armor and machine guns, the PT boats had to add heavier guns, which meant taking off the torpedo tubes, useless as they were against the barges. At least in Admiral Halsey's South Pacific command area. In General MacArthur's command area, the PT boats had always been used exclusively against barges, with decent results due to their 40mm cannons.

By September 15, the Japanese had a plan in place for the evacuation of Kolombangara that they would eventually call *Se*. It was the brainchild of Admiral Samejima, who since his arrival had managed to insert himself into pretty much everything in Rabaul. *Se* was based on a memorandum of understanding between Admiral Kusaka and General Inamura issued August 30. The memorandum had three main points: 1. The operation would start in late September and end no later than late October; 2. the evacuation would be carried out using only small boats running through either Vella Lavella or Choiseul; and 3. the Imperial Army would contribute something called the 2nd Shipping Engineer Group, with at least 30 barges.[288] If a "Shipping Engineer Group" sounds like a bizarre euphemism only the Japanese could concoct, remember the Americans had something called "attack cargo ships."

Working with the commander of the 2nd Shipping Engineer Group, Major General Yoshimura Masayoshi, as well as Admiral Ijuin, Admiral Samejima scheduled *Se* for two stages between September 28 and October 20, attempting to take advantage of the new moon. Admiral Kusaka managed to snag a dozen more destroyers from Combined Fleet for Ijuin to escort the convoys. Kusaka also sent the submarine *Ro-109* to the Kolombangara area because … well, he had his reasons. The admiral also arranged for Base Air Force to provide some air cover, with the emphasis on "some," mostly by the seaplanes of the 938 Air Group.[289]

Kusaka no longer had Kosaka to provide that air cover, because Kosaka and his staff went back home on September 1, with Admiral Sakamaki taking over. But Kusaka still had Kisaka, whom he sent to Vila on September 15 to explain the plan to General Sasaki and Admiral Ota and iron out any wrinkles with them. General Yoshimura's barges, dubbed "The 17th Army Sea Battle Unit," would make two runs, September 28 and

October 2, to take Sasaki's and Ota's troops from Kolombangara to Choiseul. Kisaka explained that the staging bases on Choiseul would be Sumbi Point and Sambi Point.[290] Sasaki did convince Kisaka of the logistical and security need for three staging areas on Kolombangara from which the troops would leave: Bambari Harbor, Tuki Point, and Wilson (or Hambare) Harbor on the west coast.[291]

Se would be a difficult job, much more difficult than *Ke*, the evacuation of Guadalcanal. A total of 12,435 men were to be moved, using 18 torpedo boats, 38 large landing craft, and 70–80 *daihatsus*.[292] There would be no deception here, no trying to convince the Allies that the Japanese were reinforcing the island for another offensive. So General Yoshimura had to find a way to hide 18 torpedo boats, 38 large landing craft, and 70–80 *daihatsus* from prying eyes, whether reconnaissance planes or scouting coastwatchers.

And at first General Yoshimura did not hide the boats very well. On September 20, the *daihatsus* drove out of Buin in droves, heading to Sumbi Point. Admiral Ijuin was tasked with covering the movement with his 3rd Destroyer Flotilla. The baron chose as his flagship the destroyer *Akigumo*, which was among the newest of the available destroyers, albeit not the very newest, but definitely the most controversial. Even today there is heated debate as to whether the *Akigumo* was the first member of the *Yugumo* class of destroyers – which would make it the *Akigumo* class of destroyers – or, more accurately, the last member of the nearly-identical-but-not-quite-as-good *Kagero* class of destroyers.[293]

Anyway, in typical Imperial Japanese Navy fashion, Admiral Ijuin divided his force into an "attack group" consisting of his flagship *Akigumo* and definite *Yugumo*-class destroyers *Isokaze* and *Kazegumo*; an "escort group" of the *Yunagi* and the finally returned *Amagiri*; and a "transport group" that included the *Fumizuki* and *Minazuki*; a "feint group" of the *Shigure*, *Matsukaze*, and the *Yugumo*-class destroyer *Yugumo*; and – finally – a fairly nebulous group that here will be called the "cameo group" with the *Samidare* and *Satsuki*, whose job apparently was to show up fashionably late for one or more cameos.[294] Why did Ijuin divide his force this way? Because he could.

The problem for Admiral Ijuin as well as General Yoshimura was that Royal Australian Navy Volunteer Reservist and veteran Choiseul coastwatcher Sub Lieutenant Alexander Nicol Anton "Nick" Waddell reported the presence of barges, and AirSols sent eight Corsairs from Marine Fighting 215 to clean them up, destroying five of the eight barges they found. Yoshimura called it an "inauspicious start to the operation," but he persisted. Yoshimura made his way from Buin to Sumbe Head, arriving on September 25 to a welcome from the 7th Yokosuka Special Naval Landing Force. It's not like he had anything better to do, and it could easily have been a lot worse.

Very easily, because the Japanese on Choiseul were paying their typical level of attention to operational security. Sub Lieutenant Waddell ended up with a copy of General Yoshimura's preliminary plan but bureaucratic bungling prevented the information from getting to AirSols in time to make use of it.[295]

Reagardless, Allied intelligence was aware the Japanese were doing ... something. Either reinforcing Kolombangara or evacuating Kolombangara which narrowed the possibilities, to be sure. Admiral Halsey tried to throw a wrench into whatever it was the Japanese were doing by splitting up Admiral Merrill's cruiser force into two cruiser mini-forces, or "task groups." Merrill kept the light cruisers *Montpelier* and *Denver* with destroyers *Waller, Renshaw, Eaton,* and *Cony,* while Captain Frank E. Beatty, skipper of the light cruiser *Columbia,* took the other group with the *Columbia* and *Cleveland* and destroyers *Charles Ausburne, Dyson, Claxton,* and *Spence.* Halsey kept sending these task groups up The Slot to ambush the Japanese and the Japanese kept not falling into the ambush. The repeated trips were wearing out the US Navy crews. As one of the *Montpelier's* men wrote in his diary, "We have been very busy for the past 5 days and nights looking for Jap warships in their own backyard but we could not find any. [...] Every day we would leave Tulagi at 4pm for our trip up the Slot and we would not return until the next day at noon."[296]

He quickly got a break. On the night of September 25–26, both *Columbia* and *Cleveland* reported sighting torpedo wakes, which narrowly missed the *Columbia.* Someone also reported possible contact with a surfaced submarine, which could have been *Ro-109* but was more likely *Ro-105.* Halsey yanked the cruisers out after that, keeping one task group at Tulagi just in case. He would have to use only destroyers to break up the Japanese effort, which intelligence had determined would run from September 29 to October 2.[297]

The actual Japanese evacuation effort began on September 27, however, which was close enough for government work. US government work, anyway. General Yoshimura sent out his barges to make the six-hour run from Choiseul to Kolombangara. Admiral Wilkinson thoughtfully sent Captain Martin J. Gillan with the destroyers *Charles Ausburne, Claxton, Dyson, Spence,* and *Foote* up to make that six-hour run in a small, slow, barely-seaworthy barge a little less boring. Gillan's ships stumbled across a group of 17 barges commanded by Lieutenant Commander Tanegashima. When we last saw Tanegashima, he was skipper of the destroyer *Murasame* as the destroyer sank into the dark waters of Kula Gulf, a victim of Admiral Merrill's ambush off Vila-Stanmore. That he had gone from commanding a destroyer to commanding a group of barges shows what Combined Fleet thought of *him.* Be that as it may, Gillan's five destroyers managed to sink only four of the barges. The rest of Tanegashima's and Yoshimura's barges made it to Kolombangara. Not a good start for the US Navy tin cans.[298]

It would not improve much. The next day the barges were nowhere to be found, the Japanese having skillfully camouflaged them and tucked them in hideaways along the Kolombangara coast. Japanese security was tight and no information concerning the barges came out of the island. Over the island was something else, however. At 1:05pm, a PB4Y Liberator from Navy Bombing 102 on a reconnaissance mission found Admiral Ijuin's ships heading south at a position northeast of Green Island – about as generic a name as you could get in an area full of green islands. The crew counted eight destroyers before being chased off by Zeros, who finally made a substantive, if not totally effective, appearance.

The crew undercounted by only three. The baron had his *Akigumo* with the *Shigure*, *Samidare*, *Isokaze*, *Yugumo*, *Amagiri*, and *Kazegumo*. Captain Kanaoka, killer of the *Strong*, was commanding the transport group, this night consisting of the *Fumizuki*, *Matzukaze*, *Minazuki*, and *Satsuki*. Admiral Ijuin and his men knew that these days, when you saw one Allied plane, more always followed. This time it was in fact another variant of the Consolidated heavy bomber: SB-24s – five, to be precise, from the 394th Squadron of the 5th Bombardment Group (Heavy) based on Guadalcanal – which were given the unofficial name "Snoopers." They were equipped with radar for making nighttime bombing attacks, not with just search radar but with more precise fire-control radar linked to the bomb release so the munitions would be dropped at the perfect time to get a hit. Or not, since on this night an hour-long attack that began at 7:20pm got no hits.[299]

In the interim, the Japanese barges had made their way from Kolombangara to Choiseul. For reasons known only to Admiral Wilkinson, there were no Allied destroyers present to interfere; they evidently had something better to do that night. So the barges made their way to Choiseul, where they would discharge their passengers, who would then board the destroyers. Except for one group carrying 735 men from Bambari Harbor who missed the signal identifying the *Amagiri* and instead made for Vella Lavella. By the time they realized their mistake, the *Amagiri* had left. She obviously didn't want to run into – or over – more PT boats. These troops had to return to Bambari Harbor to enjoy the sights, sounds, heat, and humidity of Kolombangara for another night. The rest of the troops – 1,950 men – were taken aboard Captain Kanaoka's destroyers for the ride to Rabaul. AirSols scrubbed a scheduled attack on Kahili at 5:47am on September 29 and launched 27 Liberators without fighter escort in a last-ditch attempt to stop Ijuin's ships, only to be stopped themselves by bad weather and a successful intercept by Zeros, which were driven off with no loss to either side. While this was going on, one other Liberator, a US Navy PB4Y, found the Japanese destroyers rounding the northern tip of Buka. This particular battle was over. The Allies had lost.[300]

The losing would continue. At 9:15 that same morning of September 29, AirSols showed up at Sambi Pont with 17 Dauntlesses and 12 Avengers, with an escort of 56 fighters, on what was essentially a social call since the Japanese recorded no damage. At 8:00pm on that busy September 29, Lieutenant Commander Tanegashima led 11 barges carrying 1,000 troops on the run from Kolombangara to Choiseul. This time the US Navy was ready, or at least the US Navy thought so. Captain Frank R. Walker's Destroyer Squadron 4, consisting of the *Patterson*, *Foote*, *Ralph Talbot*, and *McCalla*, after avoiding a few air attacks, was on hand and on the prowl for barges, of which they found one about halfway in between Kolombangara and Choiseul at 10:20pm. Walker ordered the *McCalla* to deal with this barge, only for the destroyer to find yet more barges. With surface visibility in The Slot down to less than two miles – on this night, there were frequent squalls and, remember, there was no moon – Tanegashima ordered the barges to scatter. Lieutenant Colonel Yano, whose unit was part of this transport, ordered his own barge to full speed, shells splashing all around, running the engine so hard it turned red with the heat. No barges were damaged.[301]

Captain Walker's destroyers could not say the same. When the *McCalla* was returning to the destroyer formation off Sambi Point, her gyro malfunctioned, causing her to lose steering control. She ran into the *Patterson*, smashing the latter's bow, killing three and injuring ten. The *McCalla*'s bow fell off as she tried to back away, while the *Patterson*'s bow fell off as Walker's destroyers crept back to Purvis Bay at a blazing ten knots. The *McCalla* needed three months of repair, the *Patterson* six.[302] This was adding injury to insult. State of the art US Navy destroyers were being bested by barges, defeated by *daihatsu*s. Worse than defeat, it was embarrassing.

The next night, September 30, US Destroyer Division 42 under Commander Alvin D. Chandler with the destroyers *Radford*, *Saufley*, and *Grayson* was on hand trying to make up for the previous embarrassments. It started out well. Chandler detected the Japanese shortly after 9:00pm approximately 13 miles northwest of Tuki Point. Visibility was poor again, but Chandler decided to actually do something about it, having his own *Radford* fire off some starshells. And, wonder of wonders, they actually worked, illuminating part of the area and revealing a reported 12 barges in a formation of two columns. There were actually four. Chandler opened fire and scored a direct hit on one barge that carried troops of the 3rd Battalion of the Japanese 23rd Regiment. Ninety men who had caused the Americans troubles on Baanga Island, including Major Nagakari and his command staff, were no more. The other three *daihatsu*s made it to Sambi Point, but only one was undamaged, offloading 73 men. A second disembarked 91, but lost six men killed. The third one disembarked 65, then promptly sank as a result of battle damage. Not the best performance by the Americans, but far better than the previous night's, simply because Chandler, who believed he had destroyed six barges, was more proactive and refused to just accept the negatives of the hand he had been dealt.[303]

By this time, Admiral Samejima had ordered *Se* to go to Phase Two, which looked a lot like Phase One, only more of it. The remaining 48 barges would depart Choiseul on the night of October 1 as originally scheduled, but these would be reinforced by three torpedo boats and two armed vessels. Maybe barges, maybe boats. Admiral Ijuin would send down destroyers as a decoy to American forces. On the night of October 2, he would bring down his main force, with three destroyers taking the troops from Tuki Point and the barges going to Choiseul.

But the more the Japanese acted, the more evidence they revealed of their plans and intentions. Allied intelligence was slowly putting together those plans and intentions, enabling some attempted countermoves. That same day, Commander Chandler's destroyers got a new friend in the veteran *La Vallette*. Chandler had his tin cans race up The Slot for a scheduled rendezvous with Captain Gillan, who now had his own destroyer

Charles Ausburne, with the *Claxton*, *Dyson*, *Spence*, and *Selfridge*. Except Admiral Wilkinson had ordered Gillan's destroyers to switch places on this mission with the destroyers of Captain Cooke – *Waller*, *Renshaw*, *Eaton*, and *Cony* – who were then escorting Admiral Merrill's cruisers *Montpelier* and *Denver*, who in turn were holding back waiting for some determination of what Japanese naval units were coming down for the night. Not everyone received the order to switch, however, including Commander Chandler's own *Radford*, so Chandler was about to receive support from a unit different than the one he was expecting. It might seem minor, but in warfare and especially in night warfare the smallest mistakes can get magnified. The stage was set for a friendly fire incident that, for once, did not involve PT boats, or, as the *Radford*'s venerable skipper Commander Romoser put it, "The apparent failure of some units to receive this despatch created an embarrassing conflict which might well have endangered the entire operations [sic] as planned for the night."[304]

Though Romoser didn't know even the half of it. Admiral Ijuin's decoy force of four destroyers – probably the *Shigure*, *Samidare*, *Matsukaze*, and *Yugumo* – was coming down, as the baron had planned.[305] But for a decoy to serve as a decoy, the enemy must be aware of the decoy. And none of the enemy was aware of the decoy force. That is, until 9:20pm when a Black Cat from Patrol Squadron 54 reported three approaching Japanese destroyers off northwest Choiseul. That was rather late in this particular game. And without the desired effect, though a beneficial one for the Japanese nonetheless. Ever since the *Columbia* and *Cleveland* reported close calls with approaching Japanese submarine torpedoes, Admiral Merrill had been under standing orders forbidding him from committing his cruisers unless enemy heavy units were present. Destroyers did not qualify as "heavy units," so at 10:04pm, when he was off Visuvisu Point, Merrill had the *Montpelier*, *Denver*, and Captain Gillan's destroyers head back while Captain Cooke sped up to try to make the rendezvous with Commander Chandler's destroyers that Captain Gillan was originally to have kept. It was all so confusing.

And it would quickly get even more so. Commander Chandler's destroyers had been loitering off Kolombangara since about 7:30pm watching for barges and waiting for the aforementioned rendezvous. A little more than two hours later, they detected Admiral Merrill's ships on radar. Then at 10:00pm, Chandler got a message from Captain Cooke to join up with him, which had to come as a surprise to Chandler since he was supposed to join with Captain Gillan and no one had told him otherwise until now. The American units were already in disarray, and combat had not yet even begun.

Naturally, it was now, when he was speeding off to join Captain Cooke, that the *Radford*'s radar detected Japanese barges. Commander Romoser was not happy about that. The *La Vallette*, immediately behind the *Radford*, had been given the role of "illuminator" this evening, and she did so admirably, firing a spread of starshells that revealed a large group of barges. Commodore Chandler started firing on them with his 5-inch main batteries.

Watching from Sambi Point was General Yoshimura. With the new moon, the night was darker than usual, so Yoshimura was treated to the spectacle of gun flashes, starshells, explosions, and tracers, knowing his barges were somewhere in the middle of all of it. Yoshimura recalled that he was so absorbed by it he "could neither sit nor stand, only pray to the gods," presumably while lying down.[306]

But at about 11:00pm Captain Cooke ordered Commodore Chandler to cease firing and join him, because the Black Cat just reported those destroyers she had found were now stopped off of Vella Lavella. And Chandler dutifully complied; but as he did so, the *Radford* detected something about 5,000 yards just east of south. Chandler's ships "were unable to develop [the contact] due to orders to join up." Instead, the American destroyers had to pick their way through what they reported were wrecked and burning Japanese barges. "Numerous contacts" appeared on the SG search radar, but the fire-control radar could not lock on to any of them, reportedly because the range was so short.

It was around 11:30pm when Commander Chandler's ships finally hooked up with Captain Cooke's ships, and together they began a dash to the northwest to deal with those Japanese destroyers. Except the Black Cat had reported the destroyers retiring northward. The Americans would never catch them. Worse, the Americans had attracted the attention of the 938 Air Group, whose seaplanes were providing some cover to the nighttime activities of the *Se* operation. At 11:39, as many as four floatplanes began bombing runs on the American destroyers. The *Saufley* suffered "considerable damage to personnel and material" from three near-misses that killed two and wounded 11. Cooke called it a night and headed back.

As useless and even counterproductive as the usual Japanese predilections for decoys usually proved to be, this time the gambit had actually worked. The presence of the Japanese destroyers had distracted the Americans from the barges long enough for the barges to escape. Commander Romoser thought they might have sunk three barges; Japanese records admit only two, but in this case, it was two in a short period of time. Commander Chandler's tactics were working, slowly but effectively. The distraction, however, saved a lot of Japanese lives. But there's just no pleasing some people. As a postwar Japanese summary of this action put it, "[S]ince the small craft unit came between our surface forces and the enemy's we lost the opportunity for an engagement."[307] But that can happen when the escorts let their charges get ahead of them, between them and the enemy. After Java Sea, Soenda Strait, and Cape Esperance, that had become almost a Japanese trademark.

That wasn't the way Admiral Ijuin did things. Mission focused, he just wanted to get in, complete the mission, and get out. He did not have images of "decisive battle" dancing in his head. But it had not been Ijuin who had developed the operational plan here; it was Admiral Samejima. And Samejima wanted a clear victory, not just a mission completed.

The baron would get another bite at the proverbial apple, however. Pursuant to the operational plan for this last withdrawal from Kolombangara, at 5:00am the next day,

October 2, Ijuin left Simpson Harbor with a force of at least eight destroyers.[308] A little more than an hour later, the guns of the 7th Yokosuka Special Naval Landing Force at Vila fired their last rounds; evidently, the Allied air strikes had not destroyed them after all. General Sasaki and Admiral Ota readied the remaining units. At Vila were elements of the aforementioned 7th Yokosuka under Commander Takeda Koshiin and the 2nd Independent Quick Fire Battalion under Major Hara Hidetome; they would make their way to Bambari Harbor. At Wilson Harbor were elements of the 6th Kure Special Naval Landing Force under Commander Okumura Saburo and the 1st Battalion of the 13th Infantry Regiment under Major Kinoshita. Worrying about everything that could go wrong in getting his men off Kolombangara, Sasaki had already ordered the runways and installations at Vila destroyed; not that it mattered, since the Allies thought Vila was a bad site for an air base.[309]

General Sasaki was right to be worried. He did not want any of his men trapped on Kolombangara. He did not want the destroyers due to take them away to be sunk, or for the road from Vila to Bambari Harbor that his engineers had painstakingly cut to be blocked. Those fears became more real when at 11:00am, General Barker's guns began shelling said road; to impress the visiting General Harmon, it was said. Not impressing Harmon was the effort of AirSols to clean up the Bambari Harbor evacuation area with 12 Avengers, 25 Dauntlesses, and six Mitchells. Attacking low to avoid a thunderstorm, in an hour-long attack the Americans only managed to damage some barges. But it had to have alarmed Sasaki that AirSols now knew his evacuation point at Bambari Harbor. It simply could not be helped; the new road was bound to attract attention.[310]

For their part, the Americans were not so much playing mix-and-match with destroyers, as they had done both earlier and recently in the war and as the Japanese were doing now, as they were playing mix-and-match with destroyer divisions. Admiral Wilkinson had swapped out Commander Chandler's division of destroyers for another division of destroyers under Commander Harold O. Larson, with the grizzled veteran *Ralph Talbot*, not-quite-as-grizzled veteran *Taylor*, and brand-spanking-new *Terry*. The switch might be explained by the damage to the *Saufley* and efforts to repair it. What is not explained is why the *Renshaw* was ordered to Nouméa at this time. It was probably just one of those things. But it left Captain Cooke with only the *Waller*, *Eaton*, and *Cony* to work with Larson's group.[311]

The stage was set for another clash of the tin cans. With some tins caught in the middle. The *daihatsu*s began driving at dusk. Lieutenant Commander Tanegashima was waiting with 2,100 men for the four destroyers, probably the *Fumizuki*, *Minazuki*, *Amagiri*, and *Yunagi*. Three destroyers were for transport; the fourth, either the *Amagiri* or (more likely) the *Yunagi*, was there for close cover. Tanegashima was able to load 1,450 troops by around 10:35pm, when the destroyers had to cut the loading short. The Americans were coming.

The warning had come in from the 938 Air Group. Commander Larson's destroyers had passed Visuvisu Point at around 6:00pm and went to battle stations. They knew that they were entering a combat zone with more than just water craft. Sure enough, at around 8:20pm, six Louie the Lice began harassing the Americans, dropping the usual litany of red, green, and white flares to mark the destroyers' position and floatlights to indicate their course. The Americans were veterans, however – except for the *Terry* – and shrugged it off.[312] Let Louie the Louse come; as long as he didn't drop any bombs he wasn't a real threat. Larson's crew were going after anything barge or bigger.

It started with just barge. At 9:09pm, the *Ralph Talbot*, leading Commander Larson's destroyers, found a barge 4,330 yards away. The American column made a firing pass, each ship firing in succession. The barge was reported sunk at 9:35. Lather, rinse, repeat, which they did at 9:35. As respected historian Vincent P. O'Hara put it, "The waters appeared to be full of enemy small craft, giving onlookers the impression of a shooting gallery. The gallery shot back, however[...]"[313] The *Ralph Talbot* was hit twice, disabling the Number 6 20mm mount, requiring it to be immediately replaced with a spare so it could continue in action.[314]

Lather, rinse, repeat, which they did at 10:00, minus the disabled gun. Twelve minutes later, Commander Larson's ships passed Captain Cooke's ships. Cooke was trying to coordinate an attack with Larson's destroyers, but because the voice radio channel was "overloaded," his maneuvering orders did not get through to his own other two destroyers, *Cony* and *Eaton*. While he sorted it out, Larson went on alone. After another three minutes, the *Ralph Talbot's* radar detected "five surface ships, proceeding at 25–28 knots, maneuvering radically." These were the transport destroyers, heading northwest for the relative safety of Shortland. Larson could not cut them off, but he maneuvered into attack position and at 11:25pm unleashed half salvos of torpedoes from a range of 7,500 yards. As soon as he fired, the Japanese veered hard to starboard about 90 degrees, heading away from him and his torpedoes, the perfect maneuver to make them miss.[315]

Commander Larson tried again at 11:43pm. All missed, again. This time, the problem was not the torpedoes. Nonetheless, that was it for them, so Larson opened fire with his guns at a range of about 8,000 yards. The ineffectiveness of the second torpedo attack convinced the Americans that their targets were "probable torpedo or gunboats of 600 to 1,000 tons," so they were mildly surprised with the return "heavy calibre fire." They exchanged shells for about two minutes before the Japanese turned away. Larson's destroyers managed three hits, apparently on the *Minazuki*, all duds. This time, the problem was not the torpedoes.[316]

All this time, Captain Cooke was trying to get back into the game. He got his chance at 12:08am when Commander Larson reported he had picked up on radar a large target and that he was out of torpedoes. Larson's ships got out of the way as Cooke's destroyers roared through at 32 knots to pick up the chase where Larson had left off. The *Waller*, *Cony*, and *Eaton* were catching up to the Japanese destroyers – much too slowly. Cooke kept up the chase for 20 minutes "until it was apparent that the enemy could not be closed for effective gun or torpedo fire." It was just as well. The Japanese had loosed 14 torpedoes at their pursuers, which they believed to be three cruisers and three destroyers. If Cooke had continued, he might have had a repeat of Tassafaronga, Kula Gulf, and Kolombangara.[317]

Watching all this was Admiral Ijuin with four destroyers – probably the *Akigumo*, *Isokaze*, and *Kazegumo*, and, maybe, the *Satsuki* – at the mouth of Vella Gulf. One might think an extra four destroyers could have helped out in the combat between the Japanese transport destroyers and the Americans, maybe even given the Americans another bloody nose. "Since our ships were in a confused tangle," says one Japanese history, "[Ijuin's ships] refrained from participating in the action."[318] Well, that was his story and he was sticking to it.

Of course, in the midst of all this were the Japanese barges. Lieutenant Commander Tanegashima now had an extra 600 men he needed to get to Choiseul. And he had to do it with six US Navy destroyers hunting the barges. Commander Larson's division claimed to have sunk six barges – one each at 12:36am, 1:16, 1:27, 1:40, 1:58, and 2:10am. Captain Cooke claimed "six barges definitely sunk and twelve damaged out of a total of approximately thirty encountered. In addition it is believed very few of the remaining twelve escaped without some damage."[319] In other words, six barges sunk and 12 damaged. According to the Japanese, he was almost half right:

Tanegashima Transport Group boarded 2,117 soldiers on seventeen barges and later transferred 1,450 soldiers to the destroyers, which joined the group from the attacking squadron. On the way to Sumbi, the transport group was attacked for two hours starting from [12:30] by the enemy destroyers and torpedo boats. As a result, five barges sank but the rest arrived safely at Sumbi.[320]

For their part, General Sasaki and Admiral Ota arrived at Sambi Point at 4:00am, where they hid out for the rest of the day to avoid air attacks. The next night, they finally met General Yoshimura. Like the rest of the Japanese troops on Choiseul, they started making their way to Buin using barges, hiding in the daylight, creeping along the coast at night, with little way to stop them. And they got back to the Shortlands safely.

For a military with a reputation for never retreating, the Japanese were getting good at this whole retreating thing. Or this "turning around and advancing" thing, because this rickety retreat saved the vast majority of the estimated 12,000 Japanese combatants from New Georgia and Kolombangara. One Japanese history says that the *daihatsus* carried a total of 5,400 men to safety, while the destroyers carried 4,000, for a total of 9,400. Even that number may be low, because it seems no muster was taken on Choiseul. All these combatants saved in the face of already significant and growing Allied air and naval superiority. For whatever reason, the US Navy and AirSols could not cut off New Georgia and Kolombangara.[321]

They could have cut off New Georgia and Kolombangara, the Americans fussed, if not for those meddling barges. According to the *Waller*'s skipper, Lieutenant Commander W.T. Dutton:

Barges are difficult targets to hit and to keep under fire. Once fire is opened they appear to disappear in splashes both visually and in the radar screen. [...] Frequently after it had appeared that all targets had been destroyed firing would be checked but further illumination a minute late[r] would reveal the continued presence of barges. Whether these were the same or additional barges was very often a matter of doubt.[322]

Russell Crenshaw had a similar opinion:

Encountering Daihatsu, bristling with machine guns, in the middle of a black night was another matter. Hitting a small target of little freeboard with five-inch, particularly under full radar control, was not easy. DesDiv 15's 40mm guns, using tracer control, offered a better solution and would most probably outrange anything carried on the enemy barges. The 40mm ammunition, however, was designed for AA use over friendly forces and was fused to self-destruct at 4000 yards, so it could not be used at ranges greater than two miles.[323]

That was hardly the end of the excuses by US Navy commanders for their relatively ineffective showing against Japanese barges. Captain Cooke added another two:

Speed. The speed used while operating against barges was 20 knots. This is acknowledged to be high. It gives a high rate of change when barges are encountered on opposite courses and cuts down the time barges are within range. Barges are difficult to see at best due to their low silhouette. However, due to the possible presence of submarines and of aircraft, it is believed that a speed much less than 20 knots would hazard own ships unnecessarily.

Searchlights. The only illumination used was star shells. Had searchlights been used the damage inflicted would have been greater no doubt. The same arguments used against low speed apply to the use of searchlights.[324]

The *Waller's* Lieutenant Commander Dutton had similar complaints, and added one more:

The relative large size of splash pips [on radar] make it impossible to remain in effective radar control, while the short range and high or at least moderately high speed advisable in waters probably containing enemy torpedo craft create a high rate of change of bearing which lowers the effective time of illumination of each starshell.[325]

It seems that after almost two years of war, the Japanese had finally found the Achilles heel of the US Navy: barges. Forget the glamorous, cutting-edge aircraft carriers and tactics of *Kido Butai*. Forget the giant superbattleship *Yamato* and her sister *Musashi*. Forget the incredible specs of the Mitsubishi A6M "Zero" fighter. Forget the Type 93 "Long Lance" torpedo. All they needed was a barge. The *daihatsu*, to be exact. Because, it seems, even state-of-the-art US Navy warships could not see, could not shoot, could not hit, could not sink this barely-seaworthy metal or wood boat with a top speed of 10 knots. All the Japanese had to do at Midway was advance with an armada of barges and the Americans would have been helpless. The entire campaign, the entire war would have been different if the Japanese had just committed a few more *daihatsu*s.

If this sounds preposterous, that's because it is. One can argue that a US Navy destroyer equipped with radar and sonar and armed with a 5-inch main battery, 40mm guns, and .50cal. machine guns is not the perfect tool to destroy a small, slow-moving-if-very-maneuverable barge. Fair enough. That the aforementioned destroyer would fare so poorly against the aforementioned barge, so much so that the Japanese were shocked by how small their losses were in the *Se* operation, is indeed preposterous.

And, yet, here we are. Maybe General Kawaguchi was right.

"Ijuin did not distinguish himself in his first fight, but he obtained acceptable results."[326]

That was how historian Vincent P. O'Hara described Admiral Ijuin's performance off Horaniu. Put another way, Ijuin accomplished his mission, but little else. His proximate mission had been to get 400 troops (two Army companies and a Special Naval Landing Force platoon) to Horaniu. And he did. In an Imperial Navy where the tendency among the officers was to try to turn every mission, no matter how mundane, into the Great Decisive Battle to Defeat the US Navy and Win the Pacific War, the baron's focus on his assigned mission and avoidance of vainglory were a rarity. That mission focus was needed once again. Because his next mission would be to evacuate those same 400 troops, give or take 200 or so.

After the escape from Kolombangara, there were still Japanese in the central Solomons, some 600 troops in desperate shape, stranded on Vella Lavella. Of whom 400 were the troops Admiral Ijuin had landed with "acceptable results." The rest were a hodgepodge of Army, Special Naval Landing Force, or survivors of sunken Japanese ships in Vella Gulf, with nothing in the way of organization. The closest thing they had had to a base was the station they had set up at Horaniu, and that had fallen to the Americans on September 14 after heavy artillery fire had chased away the ramshackle understrength battalion of green Japanese troops commanded by a junior grade lieutenant. Now the Japanese were strewn from Tambala Bay in the north to Marquana Bay in the south.[327]

"There was never any real ground combat on Vella Lavella," says one history. Maybe not in a Battle of Kursk sense, but there would be combat. In contrast to General MacArthur's Southwest Pacific, Admiral Halsey decided to give a non-American unit a leading combat role. That unit was the New Zealand 3rd Division under Major General Harold E. Barrowclough. The New Zealand 14th Brigade Group, who would take point in clearing the island, landed on September 18, the same day Barrowclough took over command on Vella Lavella from General McClure.

Also changing command on Vella Lavella at around that time were the Japanese, if appointing someone to a completely new command counts as changing command. On September 21, the Imperial Army's Captain Tsuruya Yoshio arrived on Vella Lavella. Certainly not the level of brass the Allies were using. Tsuruya set about concentrating all the scattered Japanese troops at Marquana Bay. These Japanese had had almost no supplies – no food, ammunition, or medical gear – so Tsuruya, smart officer that he was, made supplies his first priority.

The Japanese had a plan for that. On September 27, the fishing boat *Hinode Maru*, carrying 10 tons of supplies and a radio set, put in at Tambala Bay. This solved that problem, or would have, except, after a brief firefight that killed two, the boat was promptly captured by the enemy – a patrol of those newly landed Kiwis. Might call it a metaphor for the Japanese in the Guadalcanal-Solomons Campaign. Decent plan or at least decent concept, inept execution. For the Japanese presence on Vella Lavella, such as it was, the capture was an abject catastrophe. The 938 Air Group was compelled on the night of September 28 to begin dropping food, ammunition, medical supplies, and batteries for what was rather grandiosely called the "Tsuruya Unit."[328]

Nevertheless, the ragged, hodgepodge Tsuruya Unit quickly showed itself capable of "real combat." The task of locating and eliminating the Japanese on Vella Lavella had been given to the 14th Brigade under, appropriately enough, Brigadier General Leslie Potter. In an area famous for land crabs, Potter decided to try a pincer movement to trap the Japanese. The 35th Battalion under Lieutenant Colonel C.F. Seward, with a battery of artillery and the 14th's headquarters, would come up from the south, while the 37th Battalion under Colonel A.H.L Sugden would land at Doveli Cove, east of Tambala Bay, and come down from the north. The Japanese would be trapped between them.

But "trapped" can be a matter of perspective. Were the Japanese trapped with the Kiwis, or were the Kiwis trapped with the Japanese? As Lieutenant Colonel Seward's troops headed toward Marquana Bay on September 26, two platoons they had sent forward were cut off and surrounded, having to fight just to stay alive until they were rescued on October 2, with a dozen killed and ten wounded. Three companies Seward sent forward to clear the jungle south of the bay ran into what Seward called a "hornet's nest" of machine guns. Two days of attacks only earned the Kiwis 18 dead and ten wounded. This was certainly "real ground combat" to them. General Potter scrambled to move Colonel Sugden's 37th Battalion into a position to take the Japanese from the opposite side from the beleaguered 35th.

Of course, the Japanese were beleaguered themselves. The "Tsuruya Unit was now cornered all the way with its back against Marquana Bay," says the official Japanese history. "Supplies were not reaching them. There was little food and ammunition. The troops were hanging by a thread." Melodrama in a military history, rare as it is, is always welcome. The melodrama certainly had an effect on Admiral Samejima, who on October 3 told Captain

Tsuruya that his troops would be evacuated on the night of October 5–6. He probably should have first told his superior, Admiral Kusaka, who promptly put a stop to it. But Samejima persisted and Kusaka ordered the evacuation for the night of October 6–7.[329]

Baron Ijuin's lineup for this evacuation would look very similar to his lineup for putting them on Vella Lavella in the first place, except he had more of it. He had two "support groups" lined up. One, under Ijuin's direct command, had his flagship destroyer *Akigumo* and destroyers *Isokaze*, *Kazegumo*, and *Yugumo*.[330] A second support group under Captain Hara, finally getting his chance to command more than one ship at a time, would consist of the destroyers *Shigure* and *Samidare*. Both were to act in support of the transport groups, of which there were two. A destroyer transport group under Captain Kanaoka Kunizo with the destroyers *Fumizuki*, *Matsukaze*, and *Yunagi*; and a "sub-chaser transport group" under Captain Nakayama Shigoroku that consisted of only four actual subchasers but included about 20 barges.[331] Hara admitted, "His force was disproportionately strong for the minor evacuation effort on which he was embarked."[332] It was a sign of the importance that was attached to this operation.

The baron planned to conduct the operation here in a very similar manner to how he conducted the engagement off Horaniu:

> Being a navigation expert he was inclined toward elaborate maneuvers, and the memory of having successfully outmaneuvered the enemy in the same area seven weeks earlier could not but influence him further. Tired as he was, new concepts could not be expected.
>
> The four ships of his first group were capable of making 35 knots. Accordingly, in our conference on tactics, Ijuin had told us that he would maneuver to lure the enemy into position where my two destroyers could make a disconcerting thrust so that the third group of destroyers could reach the transport convoy without opposition. Our nine destroyers were thus deployed in separate groups to confuse the enemy as to our actual strength.[333]

It was an Imperial Japanese Navy tradition. Most military organizations seek to divide their enemies' forces. The Japanese much preferred to divide their own. Again, as far as combat is concerned, it had not worked at Coral Sea, or Midway, or Eastern Solomons, or Santa Cruz, or Guadalcanal. But the Japanese figured it had to work eventually.

So in the early morning of October 6, Admiral Ijuin's force left Simpson Harbor on what looked like a humanitarian mission to rescue Japan's own troops, but was more like a propaganda mission to convince the world, not to say itself, that its withdrawal from the central Solomons was "voluntary" after "pinning down" or even "annihilating" the enemy.[334]

If the enemy was indeed pinned down or annihilated, they had a funny way of showing it. As they passed the eastern coast of Bougainville, Admiral Ijuin's communications people intercepted a coded enemy message. It had to be a sighting report, either from one of the ever-annoying coastwatchers or, more likely, from a scout plane. That the enemy knew of their movements so soon was "disconcerting" to Captain Hara.[335] In response, Admiral Ijuin increased the intervals between his ships from 500 to

1,000 meters.[336] In terms of antiaircraft defense, it was stupid, but that was Japanese doctrine and they were sticking to it.

That increased distance would come in handy, though not for the reasons Admiral Ijuin was considering. At around 5:00pm, "several planes did approach from the direction of Choiseul[.]" At the same time, a heavy rainstorm approached as well and overtook Ijuin's ships.[337] That increased distance would be useful for avoiding collisions or running aground. The storm gave the baron's ships cover for about a half hour. When the storm cleared, there were no enemy aircraft to be seen.[338] For that matter, it was just about sunset. Not that sunset had been protection from air attacks lately. Admiral Ijuin informed Captain Hara that the First Support Group would rush ahead toward Vella Lavella. Hara's Second Support Group was to "slow to nine knots and stand by east of Shortland to meet the barges," which were expected to depart soon.[339] It made sense; for once, the Japanese escorts were in position to screen their charges, not vice versa. Ijuin and his ships took off down Bougainville Strait at 26 knots. "Darkness added considerably to the hazard of these waters but his ships made it without incident. It was a fine demonstration of his talent as a navigator."[340]

Captain Hara, with the *Shigure* and *Sazanami*, held back as ordered, creeping through Bougainville Strait, meeting the "transport convoy" heading down the Center Route at a "leisurely" 9 knots.[341] Everything going leisurely, except for Admiral Ijuin. He was almost at Horaniu when he spotted "four" destroyers, "in the direction of the assembly point at approximately [9:00pm … But] a battle did not develop because the enemy was lost from sight due to a squall that restricted the field of vision."[342] Then the baron was handed a note: "A scout plane from Rabaul has spotted four enemy cruisers and three destroyers cruising westward north of Vella Lavella." That was bad. If the scout report was right, the enemy was here, and much more powerful than Ijuin had expected. The baron nodded and ordered his group to be ready to reverse course.[343] It was at around this time that Captain Kanaoka and his transport destroyers aborted their mission and headed back, though the Sub-chaser Transport Group continued onward.[344]

When Captain Hara got the report, he was shocked both at the size of the enemy force and that it was at Horaniu so soon. With the odds now stacked against them, maybe this whole dividing our forces thing was not such a good idea. Hara was anything but shocked when at 10:10pm he received the order from the admiral for Hara's two destroyers to join him "as quickly as possible." The commodore immediately ordered his destroyers to race up at 30 knots.[345] At 10:29, Admiral Ijuin tried to speed up the rendezvous by heading west. That wasn't quite good enough. Six minutes later, Hara radioed, "Cannot find you because of poor visibility. Request that *Yugumo* hoist a blue stern light."[346] The baron had his ships turn hard to port as the *Yugumo* hoisted the blue lamp.[347] It was hoped that the Americans didn't see it. Because as the Japanese destroyers settled on their new westerly course, the *Kazegumo* reported dark shapes approaching from the east.[348]

Admiral Ijuin's column swung to a southwesterly course at 10:40, hoping to get the *Shigure* to see the *Yugumo*'s blue light special without showing it to the Americans. Sure enough, Captain Hara had sighted the blue light at 10:38, and now the *Shigure* and *Samidare* were five miles behind the *Yugumo*.[349] Ijuin finally caught sight of the Americans coming from the east at 10:39.[350] What were they? The scout plane had reported four cruisers and three destroyers. That's what these looked like. Range was, what? 10,000 meters? That looked about right. The baron set up for a repeat of the engagement off Horaniu. Not that that encounter was a spectacular success, but it was a success. He would be happy with that against these odds. Ijuin led his ships west southwest at high speed for a torpedo-firing run against the four cruisers and three destroyers.[351]

The baron was half right, sort of. His opposition at this time consisted of three US Navy destroyers: a newcomer to the Pacific War in the *Selfridge*, carrying Captain Frank R. Walker, commander of Destroyer Squadron 4; and Pacific War veterans *Chevalier* and *O'Bannon*. Admiral Wilkinson had indeed gotten the scout plane's earlier report. But he was stuck. Almost all of his destroyers were committed to convoy duty. Except for Captain Walker's three, though Wilkinson could and did squeeze three destroyers – veterans *Ralph Talbot*, *Taylor*, and *La Vallette* – of Destroyer Squadron 8 under Captain Harold O. Larson out of escorting the convoys.

Times, they were a-changin'. This was setting up to be the third straight naval engagement of destroyers versus destroyers. As R.H. Roupe, Yeoman 2nd Class from the *Chevalier*, later explained:

> Destroyers began to play an increasingly important part in the Solomons campaign. They were fast and maneuverable and heavily armed, and the inevitable ship losses which Slot duty entailed were not the serious blows to fleet strength which the loss of battleships and cruisers would have been. It was a grueling experience but destroyers were tough and could take it.
>
> We established ourselves in Purvis Bay, a snug, angular little harbor toward the southeastern end of Florida Island, the Tulagi base. In groups of three and four and five we made almost nightly runs up the Slot toward Bougainville, never knowing what we might encounter, and meeting usually anything from planes to Japanese task forces.[352]

By this time, Captain Walker's men were getting a little tired of high-speed runs up and down The Slot. They had started October 5 by leaving Tulagi at 10:00am with orders to patrol between Vella Lavella and Tiposako, Choiseul from 9:00pm to 3:30am the morning of October 6.[353] But they found nothing except Tiposako and headed back down The Slot.

This was getting old. As Yeoman Roupe recalled, "We made a couple of runs up the Slot and encountered nothing beyond the usual snooper planes. Enemy activity along the little water passage seemed to have quieted[.]"[354]

Not quieted enough. At 9:45 the next morning, while returning down The Slot from their previous trip up The Slot, Captain Walker's ships were ordered to turn around and go up The Slot again, this time at 20 knots. Destroyers are fuel hogs, however, as their high rate of speed means they get poor gas mileage and they are the smallest ships, so their fuel bunkers are tiny. That means they are always looking for their next fuel break. By this time, Walker estimated that his fuel bunkers were down to 65 percent. He turned around, as ordered, but headed up at 17 knots to save fuel.[355]

At about 11:30, Admiral Wilkinson elaborated on his earlier orders. They read as follows: "Proceed to a point 10 miles southwest of Tipi Sako Point, Choiseul; arrive by 2100; operate in vicinity to intercept barge traffic."[356] Wilkinson and Walker were apparently among the very exclusive group of people in the world who knew where Tipi Sako or Tiposako Point was. This Pacific War was no longer being fought in places you never heard of, but in places you can't find on any map.

But Captain Walker wouldn't need to find Tipi Sako or Tiposako, because at about 7:00pm Admiral Wilkinson changed his orders again. This time, Walker's destroyers were to rendezvous with Captain Larson's destroyers "in position 10 miles west of Sauka Point, Vella Lavella." Another place that did not and does not show up on too many maps or searches. The combined group, operating under Walker's command, was to "Intercept and destroy enemy evacuation force consisting of unknown number of destroyers, 3 PTs and 6 SCs expected off northwest Vella Lavella at [10:30pm] with embarkation about one hour later." Destroyers *Selfridge*, *O'Bannon*, and *Chevalier* "were further directed to intercept enemy if rendezvous were [sic] delayed."[357]

That "unknown number of destroyers" had to be sticking out in Captain Walker's mind as he plodded northwest toward Vella Lavella. Admiral Wilkinson later clarified that the unknown number could be as many as nine, and that they had passed through the Bougainville Strait at 8:00pm.[358] So, the admiral had just ordered Walker's three destroyers, if their rendezvous with Captain Larson's three destroyers was delayed, to proceed and engage nine Japanese destroyers. Three on nine, or in the lowest common denominator, one on three. What could go wrong?

By 7:00pm, Captain Walker's little force was ten miles south of Kekasa, Choiseul, on a course of 350 degrees True – roughly north northwest – and a speed now up to 21 knots.[359] Couldn't worry about fuel too much when he was about to enter combat. He saw friendly aircraft returning from an attack on the Kahili air base, dropping flares over Kekasa as a waypoint on the trip home. Presumably wanting to stay out of their flares, Walker changed course away from Kekasa to 250 degrees – southwest.[360] On the *Chevalier*, tension increased as the crew suspected something very serious was going on. "Before the night had worn very far along we began to realize with increasing uneasiness that there was something different going on from what we had been led to look for," Yeoman Roupe recalled. There was too much activity, for one thing. "The darkness seemed filled all around us with a secret, stirring life which was menacing and mysterious."[361]

Life that was about to reveal itself. At 7:40, radar picked up an unidentified aircraft seven miles to the southwest. Captain Walker led his ships on a starboard turn to

290 degrees True – west northwest, trying to avoid the plane. It soon became evident that wasn't working, so he changed course again to 340 degrees True – north northwest – at 8:11pm, just as one of those Type 0 Observation Seaplanes appeared.[362] It was annoying. "Enemy planes were shadowing us, remembered Yeoman Roupe. "They stayed discreetly out of range of our guns and dropped flares – regularly and persistently. Strange yellowish lights descended and bobbed up and down far out on the water, winking on and off like signal lights with the rise and fall of intervening swells."[363]

Japanese floatplanes operating at night had been a menace ever since the Java Sea Campaign, when Admiral Doorman's efforts at getting his Combined Striking Force around blocking Japanese cruisers to hit a Japanese invasion convoy were foiled by floatplanes doing exactly what this floatplane was doing now – reporting his every move, keeping his force illuminated with parachute flares, and marking his course with floatlights. They continued during the Guadalcanal Campaign with Louie the Louse, among many others. And at Horaniu they had revealed the American destroyers to the Japanese. Here they were again.

Their presence was not just a tactical benefit to the Japanese, but had a psychological benefit as well by unnerving the Allied sailors as they had during the Java Sea Campaign. As Yeoman Roupe explained, "They gave us the impression of being surrounded by unseen and intangible forces gathering quietly on the dark perimeter of our vision to close in suddenly without warning. Slowly, with mounting tension, we understood that the night might hold more than the expected routine patrol. Something was up!"[364] Lieutenant Commander McDonald of the *O'Bannon* agreed, commenting, "It was quite evident that something was taking place this particular night [...] we had come to the conclusion that unless there was something going on, the Japs would not go to the trouble of tracking us the way they were doing."[365]

Like many a commander before him, including Admiral Doorman, Captain Walker led his destroyers, now the *Selfridge* leading the *Chevalier* and then the *O'Bannon*, on more course changes – to the southwest, to the northwest, back to the southwest, then to the southeast – trying to shake that floatplane. That never works. And it did not work here. That last turn took Walker's ships into a squall. He changed course again to the northwest and increased speed, first to 23 and then to 25 knots. The Pete found him again. Walker tried juking him again, to the southwest, to the west southwest.[366] And so on, and so forth, but nothing worked. As Samuel Eliot Morison so memorably put it, "everywhere that Walker went, 'Pete' was sure to go."[367]

They had lost the advantage of surprise. That was ominous. "Something's in the wind," Captain Walker told his men over the voice radio. "When we round this corner, close the gap and be ready for anything. I want to get the fish off without guns if possible. Every man alert standing by."[368] Walker had indeed learned from the Japanese how to ambush with torpedoes. The only problem was that thanks to that Pete, ambush was no longer possible.

The commodore led his destroyers on a port turn to course 210 degrees True – south southwest.[369] "We swung sharply to the left," Yeoman Roupe recalled. "The Captain quietly told the bridge talkers to pass the word for all hands to stand alert. We did so. Someone on my circuit immediately queried, 'What's up?' I said I didn't know.

"There was a sudden stir of excitement, and the bridge communicator buzzed into life.

"'We've made radar contact with four ships, Captain,' came the Exec's voice."[370]

According to Captain Walker, it was at 10:31pm when, as he wrote it, "SURFACE RADAR CONTACTS OBTAINED ALMOST SIMULTANEOUSLY BY ALL THREE SHIPS."[371]

They had detected two groups. One was at a bearing of 277 degrees True – just north of due west – at a range of 19,500 yards. A second group was at a bearing of 281 degrees True – just north of the bearing of the first – also at a range of 19,500 yards. The American radar operators and gunnery officers started tracking the targets. Both groups appeared to be changing course from easterly through north toward the west. Looked like four ships in column in each group, with the second group off the starboard quarter of the first group.[372]

Captain Walker sent a wireless telegraph reporting "Eight enemy destroyers sighted" to Admiral Wilkinson – four times – but he never got an acknowledgment.[373] Walker then tried to call Captain Larson's destroyers. Using the code name for Larson, "Gay," he called out, "Hello? Gay's group? Come in. Any one in Gay's group. Come in please."[374] There was no response. Larson's group was racing up at 30 knots, but he was still 20 miles away and outside the range of the Talk Between Ships voice radio. For now, Walker's little force was on its own.

Yeoman Roupe tried thinking comforting thoughts: "We were outnumbered this time – four against three. On a previous occasion we had been even up, and had routed the enemy without difficulty. Maybe this slight tipping of the scales in their favor wouldn't make much difference. Maybe they would turn tail and run."[375]

Not exactly. At 10:45, the enemy came into sight. As best as the Americans could tell, the three US Navy destroyers were facing "one column of five [destroyers] with middle ship somewhat larger (possibly cruiser) and a second column of four [destroyers]."[376]

At this news, Yeoman Roupe was not entirely hopeful:

Five more ships showed up on the radar screen – four destroyers, and what appeared to be a light cruiser. Nine ships – eight destroyers and a cruiser – against three destroyers. The odds now were more than overwhelming. They were astronomical. If we had any sense, we were the ones to turn tail and run.

Nine ships! Holy Christopher! The sweat broke out on my forehead.[377]

Three on nine, or one on three. Would not, could not wait for Captain Larson to arrive to make it six on nine, or two on three. Captain Walker, at the head of his little destroyer column and in the *Selfridge* leading the *Chevalier* and then the *O'Bannon* third, led his ships to course 240 degrees True – southwest – and a speed of 30 knots.[378] And charged in.

Once again, Yeoman Roupe was not entirely pleased: "We were going in, no doubt about that, though it looked like a suicide mission. These Navy skippers were fire-eaters. They wouldn't back down in the face of the whole Jap fleet, regardless of odds."[379]

Not exactly. There has been considerable criticism of Captain Walker for charging his three destroyers against nine Japanese destroyers, knowing the advantage of surprise had been lost, without waiting for Captain Larson's three destroyers to arrive. Such criticism ignores two facts. First, the Japanese had made it a common practice of having their destroyers charge in no matter the odds, and they had repeatedly been successful, Tassafaronga being the biggest case in point. Second, these simply were his orders. Admiral Wilkinson had informed Walker of the possibility of facing nine Japanese destroyers, and sent him in with only three destroyers anyway. Not just sent him in, but sent him in "to intercept enemy if rendezvous [with Larson's ships] were [sic] delayed." In other words, Walker was ordered not to wait, but to immediately attack. Nevertheless, orders or no orders, Captain Walker was going in three on nine. What could go wrong?

Things had already gone wrong for Admiral Ijuin, and they were largely his own fault. The baron had badly underestimated the distance to the American ships as 10,000 meters. And, not to belabor the point, he had a nine to three advantage in ships, but he was apparently overly influenced by the scout plane's report of "four enemy cruisers and three destroyers." The admiral thought he was facing cruisers.

As Captain Walker was charging in, Admiral Ijuin was getting some good news. Captain Nakayama, leading the Sub-chaser Transport Group, radioed he was 20 miles southwest of Horaniu, on track to arrive there shortly. It meant the barges would pass behind the enemy destroyers. Hopefully, Ijuin could keep them occupied so they didn't notice the barges sneaking behind them.[380]

At the same time, the baron was realizing he had made a mistake. Apparently based on their recent experience in the Solomons with US Navy cruisers like the *Honolulu*, *Helena*, and *St Louis*, the Japanese had come to believe "A cruiser packs ten times the firepower of a destroyer[.]" Captain Hara speculated, "Ijuin must have been thinking of this and recalling how accurate radar-controlled guns can be. Ijuin knew that in rain and darkness, without effective radar, his warships would be no match for so powerful an enemy force."[381]

At 10:45, Admiral Ijuin noticed that "the enemy column appeared to have maintained its course, but it was still farther away than it should have been."[382] The baron led his column on a turn to course 162 degrees True – roughly south southeast. Three minutes later, he ordered a simultaneous starboard turn of 45 degrees for all ships to course 207 degrees True – roughly south southwest.[383] This meant he would be breaking the column. Thus, his destroyers changed formation from a column to a line in a right echelon, the line of bearing approximate to their previous course of 162 degrees True, with the *Akigumo* in front and the other destroyers behind and to the right of her, heading south southwest. Three minutes later, the baron ordered another simultaneous turn, this time to port and a course of 115 degrees True – southeast. His ships were not back in column, but in a left echelon in a line of bearing of 162 degrees True, with the *Akigumo* in front and the other destroyers behind and to the left of her, heading southeast.[384]

No one knows what exactly Admiral Ijuin was trying to accomplish with this series of maneuvers, and, likely, neither did he. According to Captain Hara, "Ijuin has never offered any reason, excuse, or alibi for this action other than to acknowledge his mistake." Hara speculates as to the baron's reasoning. "It is my belief that he made this move to lure the enemy southward and thus ensure [sic] that the Japanese convoy remain free from attack."[385]

The effects of these maneuvers, however, are known. As Captain Hara explains:

> A simultaneous turn is an extremely difficult maneuver. It requires precision timing and is even more difficult of execution by destroyers speeding in tight column formation. In order to execute this movement it is absolutely essential that the flagship be fully aware of the exact situation and attitude of every ship in the column. As a result, all flagship communication lines were tied up in talking with each of the other three ships, and contact was lost with *Shigure* and *Samidare* of the second group.[386]

Communications and information, those two most important commodities of any military operation.

The second effect was tactical. Admiral Ijuin's best, most logical bet to fight this battle was to cross in a column in front of Admiral Walker's destroyer column – in other words, leading his column southeast across the bows of the American column heading southwest – thus crossing the American "T" in naval parlance. This would allow the Japanese to use all their guns while the Americans could only use at most their forward guns.

But what the baron actually did was more like dotting the American "I." The Japanese were indeed crossing the front of Captain Walker's column, but not in a column of their own. They were crossing in a left echelon. And they were in a left echelon such that the *Yugumo*, at 3,000 meters away the closest ship to the Americans, was crossing the American "T," but also fouling the range of the three destroyers now stacked behind her – three more dots above the dot provided by the *Yugumo*. The *Kazegumo*, *Isokaze*, and, furthest from the Americans, *Akigumo*, could neither fire their guns nor launch their torpedoes out of a fear of hitting the *Yugumo*.[387] To make matters even worse, the Japanese were in this strait jacket of a formation backlit by the moon.

Naturally, from the Japanese standpoint, when they are in their worst tactical position, this was the time, 10:55, that Captain Walker radioed his ships "Partial salvo," quickly followed by, "Execute William."[388] The new-and-improved American torpedoes, now with Torpex, swished out of their tubes, three from the *Selfridge*, five from the *Chevalier*, and six from the *O'Bannon*.[389]

At that point, for reasons known only to her skipper Commander Osako Higashi, the destroyer *Yugumo* peeled out of the Japanese line toward the American column and at 10:56 launched eight Type 93 torpedoes.[390] One minute later, as the *Yugumo* was scurrying back to the dubious protection of the Japanese line, Captain Walker ordered his ships to open fire: "Execute Dog."[391]

The *Yugumo*, closest to the US Navy destroyers, took her first hit, from a 5-inch shell, at 10:58 and quickly took a few more in succession.[392] But she gamely returned fire as she headed back to the south, where Admiral Ijuin had ordered a 90-degree starboard turn to reform his column. The *Kazegumo*'s field of gunfire had been cleared when the *Yugumo* charged alone at the Americans, so she got off a few shots as she headed south with the *Isokaze* and *Akigumo*, who could not open fire, making smoke to cover their movement.[393] Captain Hara's two destroyers had not attracted any attention yet, but Captain Walker wanted starshells fired to try to change that, and ordered the *Chevalier*, "Be prepared to illuminate."[394]

The *Chevalier*'s Yeoman Roupe recalled the opening of gunfire:

Both sides began firing at once. The quiet darkness of the sea was suddenly transformed into a flaming hell of fire and thunder. The Japs were so close you could hear their guns roaring between the salvos from our own, and the flashes of their gunfire were great red splotches spreading in a long line directly off the port beam. We were firing at murderously close range.

A tremendous explosion flamed among those hulking black shapes paralleling our course and spitting death as they passed. One of them was immediately enveloped in an inferno of smoke and fire. It swerved and fell behind, burning fiercely.[395]

The *Yugumo* had taken at least five hits from the 5-inch guns of Captain Walker's destroyers, who mistook the destroyer for the light cruiser *Yubari*. Her rudder was quickly disabled; by 11:00pm fires had blossomed on her superstructure, she began losing speed and was soon unable to keep up with Admiral Ijuin's column.[396]

And then Yeoman Roupe's world went black:

Things went suddenly black. I reeled off into a great empty void, where I seemed to float like a disembodied spirit. I could see nothing. I wondered vaguely where I was, and how I had got there. Everything was strangely quiet.

My brain struggled desperately to adjust itself. Dimly I remembered that I was supposed to be wearing phones, and that we had been in the midst of battle.

I groped shakily in the darkness. Very faintly I thought I heard the tinkle of falling glass. My hands reached my head and I felt for the phones. They were still there. But one earpiece was missing, and that side of my face was warm with sticky wetness. Slowly my head cleared, and I could see a little. I was half-sitting on the deck, yards away from the annunciator. I got up painfully and stumbled back to it, wading through a pile of debris with which the deck was littered. My head began to pound. I put a hand to my forehead, and encountered a lump the size of a hen's egg on my right temple.

I reached the annunciator and leaned against it for support, fighting panic and nausea. The quiet was unearthly. I couldn't hear a sound.

Full consciousness gradually returned. I looked around, to find that the pilothouse was a mass of wreckage. The radio had been blasted off the bulkhead and lay on the deck in twisted ruins. The binnacle was smashed. The navigator's desk hung grotesquely by a single remaining shred of steel. A 20mm gun mount had crashed through the forward bulkhead. Pieces of glass and other unrecognizable debris covered the deck.

Chief Weber appeared suddenly beside me and asked if I was all right.

"I guess so," I said. "What happened?"

"Torpedo," he said briefly. "Go and take a look up forward."[397]

[…]

I went out on the wing and looked over the side. The whole forward structure of the ship was gone, clear back to the bridge. Dark whirlpools of water gurgled along the crumpled steel plates below. The bridge itself hung precariously over the water.[398]

It was indeed a torpedo, one of the eight Type 93s from the *Yugumo*. Yeoman Roupe was hardly the only one to lose consciousness. So did skipper Lieutenant Commander George R. Wilson, many of the bridge crew, and others.

As Wilson reported it:

There were two distinct concussions, the first being the explosion of the torpedo and the second, almost simultaneously being Gun 2 magazine. All personnel on the bridge were stunned. I was thrown to the deck and I presume somehow between the compass binnacle and the wheel, since that is where I found myself when I came to. My first thought was to warn the *O'Bannon* that I was out of control swinging right. […] In the meantime, still a bit dazed, I inquired as to extent of the damage. I was informed that the entire bow forward of the bridge had been blown off. All communications were out.[399]

Not all communications; at 11:02, one minute after she was hit, the *Chevalier* was able to radio, "I am hit."[400]

The *Yugumo*'s Type 93 had lanced into the handling room for the Number 2 5-inch mount, detonating the 5-inch ammunition therein. The explosion blew off the bow as far as the bridge. The *Chevalier* kept moving forward, which in her shape was extremely dangerous. "The wreckage of the bow and the hole in IC room and forward fireroom had caused the ship to start submerging like a submarine."[401]

Still, a single torpedo hit is usually enough to sink a destroyer. A torpedo hit in a handling room – a magazine – would normally destroy a destroyer almost instantly. Instead, the damage was very similar to what happened to the *Minneapolis* and *New Orleans* at Tassafaronga. It could have been worse. Much worse.

And, just as Lieutenant Commander Wilson ordered his executive officer Lieutenant Commander Hansen to survey the damage, a jarring metallic crunch signaled that it was worse. It was not a torpedo hit, as Wilson had initially thought. The destroyer *O'Bannon*, moving at full speed at, "unfortunately," the prescribed 500-yard interval from the *Chevalier* and evidently unable to see what was ahead of her due to dense smoke produced by the flashless powder, had plowed through the *Chevalier*'s starboard propeller shaft into her starboard side after engine room.[402]

The *O'Bannon*'s skipper Lieutenant Commander McDonald was preparing to train his torpedo tubes to starboard to target Captain Hara's destroyers when he saw the *Chevalier* get hit by the *Yugumo*'s Long Lance. He quickly ordered hard right rudder, but the *Chevalier* was heading to starboard as well, with her bow breaking off. With the *Chevalier*'s after section "more or less diving and closing my bow very rapidly[,]" McDonald realized there was no way to avoid it. He sounded the collision alarm and ordered emergency full astern to at least limit the speed and thus limit the damage. The *O'Bannon*'s bow penetrated the *Chevalier* by maybe 10–12 feet.[403] McDonald immediately radioed, "I have just collided with [*Chevalier*]."[404]

On the beleaguered *Chevalier*, all power was lost and the ship came to a stop. However, "the bow, if such it could be called, came up some." Lieutenant Commander Wilson went so far as to say, "I believe she would have gone on under in spite of everything if *O'Bannon* had not stopped our headway."[405] The *O'Bannon* was like that, though. Recall that in the wee hours of July 5, the destroyer *Strong* took a torpedo in Kula Gulf off Rice Anchorage, from a source about which the US Navy was still uncertain. It was the *Chevalier* who came to the stricken destroyer's aid, if you could call it that, when she plowed into the port side of the *Strong*'s bow. In abandoning the *Strong*, many of her crewmen were able to just walk from the main deck of the *Strong* to the main deck of the *Chevalier*. The *Chevalier* had hit the *Strong*, however, in the course of trying to avoid colliding with the *O'Bannon*. The *O'Bannon* was also coming to the *Strong*'s aid, but came on too fast too close to the *Chevalier*. The *Chevalier*'s executive officer ordered emergency full speed to get out of the *O'Bannon*'s way. She was not entirely successful. The *O'Bannon* grazed the *Chevalier*'s stern, knocking out the latter's starboard depth charge rack and smoke screen generator. It was by going full speed to avoid the *O'Bannon* or at least minimize the damage that the *Chevalier* had collided with the *Strong*.

So, this was the second time the *O'Bannon* had collided with another ship. Not just collided with another ship, but collided with the same other ship, the *Chevalier*. That has to be a record of some sort. Nevertheless, in both collisions, there were some positive effects. Some, but not all, obviously. While the *O'Bannon* and the *Chevalier* were locked together, motionless, and helpless, as if to taunt them, that annoying Pete floatplane dropped a floatlight that "beautifully illuminated" them. That was just insulting.[406] But the insult was quickly returned. At 11:03, one of the *Chevalier*'s Mark 15 torpedoes, much slower than the Japanese Type 93 that had hit her, buried itself in the *Yugumo*'s starboard side.[407] According to Captain Walker, the *Yugumo* "exploded with tremendous violence," to the point where the lookouts thought she had "disintegrated."[408] Not exactly, but the descriptions suggest that like the *Chevalier*, she was hit in the magazine. The *Yugumo* sank two minutes later.[409]

That left the destroyer USS *Selfridge* and Captain Walker against now five Japanese destroyers. One on five. Except Admiral Ijuin, demoralized after watching the *Yugumo* explode and sink, continued leading his three destroyers south behind the smokescreen, continuing to believe he was facing enemy cruisers, not destroyers; and then turned westward to retire.

Captain Walker had the *Selfridge*, all by herself, turn to course 300 degrees True – west northwest – to deal with the second Japanese group.[410]

But while the exchange was going on between the *Chevalier* and the *Yugumo* Captain Hara had noticed the *Selfridge* coming for him with a favorable angle for radar-controlled guns and an unfavorable angle for Hara's torpedoes. At 10:56, his *Shigure* led the *Samidare* on a hard right turn to a course almost due west. Hara was actually nervous:

> How could we best oppose the "powerful" enemy force, still believed to consist of four cruisers and three destroyers? If the enemy took the initiative he could wallop us. How could we seize the initiative? In the excitement I had the feeling of not being able to breathe deeply enough, and suddenly realized that I was panting.[411]

Hyperventilating aside, two minutes later, after the *Selfridge* had turned to starboard, the *Shigure* led the *Samidare* on another hard right turn to north northwest. As Hara explained it:

> We were 8,500 meters from our intended targets. The idea of running parallel and ahead of the enemy column was one of the formulas worked out in my torpedo manual. My running ahead discouraged the enemy from attacking with torpedoes, and permitted me to choose my own time and angle for launching at him.[412]

And he should know. Hara wrote the book. As he will tell you. Over and over and over again.

"Prepare guns and torpedoes for fight to starboard!" the Japanese commodore ordered. Captain Walker was bringing the *Selfridge*'s guns to fire full broadsides to his port side. Concerned about this radar-directed fire, Captain Hara ordered yet another hard right to throw off the American firing solutions. The *Samidare*'s skipper, Lieutenant Commander Sugihara Yoshiro, asked by radio if they were going to fight on this new course. "With all the restraint I could muster" to what he considered Sugihara's "stupid" question, Hara thundered, "Tell him we will turn left again before opening on the enemy!"[413]

After about 500 meters, Captain Hara ordered a left turn and the release of the Type 93s, angle 50 degrees to starboard, range of 7,500 meters. At 11:01, the *Shigure* and

Samidare launched 16 Type 93s. As the last Type 93 left the tubes, shell splashes rose on both sides of the *Shigure*. Captain Walker's *Selfridge*, all by herself, had opened fire with her 5-inch guns. "The first enemy salvo had straddled us," Hara recalled, "The enemy's aim – undoubtedly radar-controlled – was spectacular, but neither of my ships was hit."[414] Not that spectacular, it would seem. Nevertheless, Hara felt compelled to return fire as his men struggled to reload the torpedo tubes.

As this exchange of gunfire was going on, at 11:07 or so the lookouts on the *Selfridge* saw a torpedo porpoise off the port side. The destroyer came left to avoid it, only to be told about 30 seconds later that another torpedo was approaching from starboard.[415]

One minute later, the Long Lance burrowed into the *Selfridge's* starboard side just forward of the Number 2 5-inch mount. Like the *Chevalier*, the bow was entirely blown off forward of the bridge. The destroyer lost all power except for an emergency generator aft and stumbled to a stop. Except for the Talk Between Ships voice radio circuit, the *Selfridge* lost all communications and radar.[416]

Captain Walker used the only functioning method of communication left, the Talk Between Ships voice radio, to call for help from Captain Larson or his other destroyers. He got no response, so he resorted to getting rid of the code wheels for deciphering messages, and damaging electronic countermeasures.[417]

Captain Hara started poking around for both the results of his torpedo attack and the reported cruisers. When he spotted dark specks on the horizon, he concluded these must be the cruisers fleeing. Finding nothing else, he turned the *Shigure* and *Samidare* for Rabaul.

Still out there was Admiral Ijuin and his three remaining destroyers *Akigumo*, *Isokaze*, and *Kazegumo*. While heading toward the west, according to Captain Hara, at 11:13pm the *Akigumo's* lookouts mistook the *Chevalier* and *O'Bannon* for four enemy cruisers. Historian Samuel Eliot Morison suggests that Hara is relating a garbled second-hand account of that Pete floatplane reporting four cruisers approaching from the south, and the baron wanted no part of any more cruisers.[418] Either way, Ijuin turned the column to the northwest. Six minutes later, the three destroyers launched 24 Type 93s at the *Chevalier* and *O'Bannon* at a range of 16,000 yards.[419] They all missed. One sinking, barely navigable ship and one ship running slowly because of a damaged bow. It was not the high point in Japanese torpedo practice. The baron took his three remaining destroyers and headed back. The "four cruisers" approaching from the south were, naturally, Captain Larson's destroyers.

The *Ralph Talbot*, *Taylor*, and *La Vallette* had seen flashes of gunfire in the distance ahead of them, but by the time they passed the sinking *Yugumo* – only her bow remained above water – and arrived on the scene, the Japanese had left 15 minutes earlier; the battle was over.[420] Captain Larson's ships investigated the area around Marquana Bay until 12:20am. Then they moved in to help Captain Walker's crippled ships.[421]

The *Chevalier* was not so much disabled as she was dead. The *O'Bannon* had tried to come alongside, earning an ineffective bombing attack from the Pete in the process, but her damaged bow made that impossible. Given that she had already hit the *Chevalier* twice, it was probably a good idea for her to keep her distance anyway. She finally gave up, moved a thousand yards off the port beam, and started signaling by Aldis lamp.

"They want to know if you think we can stay afloat much longer, Captain," one of the signalmen said.

The men of the *Chevalier* had tried everything. Jettisoning all topside weight, including depth charges (set on safe), torpedoes (fired at the hulk of the *Yugumo*), and ammunition. They had tried to move at 5 knots; it only brought more water in. It was no use.

"Tell them 'negative,'" Lieutenant Commander Wilson replied. "Tell them our engineering spaces are flooding, and we are settling slowly."

Another exchange by Aldis lamp. The signalman returned. "They say, 'We are standing by,'" he interpreted.[422]

With resignation, Lieutenant Commander Wilson gave the order to abandon ship. The crew assembled on the fantail and calmly went over the side. Some went to rafts and floater nets, others just swam for the destroyer *O'Bannon*. The ever-helpful floatplanes of the 938 Air Group even dropped a floatlight to illuminate the area with the *Chevalier*'s survivors.

Or did they? According to the *Chevalier*'s engineering officer Lieutenant George Gowen:

> When we finally abandoned ship, I went over the port side aft and swam to a life raft I had cut loose earlier. Other crew members were already aboard, and they began shouting to me as I approached. "Put it out," they hollered. Finally, I understood. I had gone into the water with my 4-cell flashlight in my hip pocket. The water shorted it out and it was shining back up into the sky. I emptied the batteries into the sea and my shipmates finally let me aboard. The history of the battle states that there was a flare from a Japanese plane that had been dropped in the water. I still think it was my flashlight.[423]

With Lieutenant Gowen perhaps taking the phrase "Light up your ass" a little too literally, everyone headed for the *O'Bannon*. Once Lieutenant Commander Wilson came on board, he reported that he guessed the *Chevalier* would remain afloat for about another 90 minutes or so. The veteran Lieutenant Commander McDonald assured Wilson that he would see the *Chevalier* sunk before he had the *O'Bannon* leave the area. McDonald then asked the skipper of the *La Vallette*, Commander Robert Taylor, "to relieve [the *Chevalier*'s] suffering" if she had not sunk by the time they had to leave.[424]

Yeoman Roupe made it to the *O'Bannon*. He turned back to take one last look:

> The *Chevalier* lay low in the water, a dim, black shape against the faintly luminous sky. The missing forward structure gave her a curiously truncated appearance. She looked like the ghost of a ship, dark and lifeless and without motion save for a sluggish roll as the

ground swells caught her and set her to wallowing idly. I thought of the day I had first seen her, a proud, trim little greyhound of the fleet tied up at a dock in Norfolk on a chilly evening in late October. Almost a year had passed, and during that time I had known no other home.

I took a last, long look and turned away. I knew that I would never see the *Chevalier* again ...[425]

Never seeing was a theme on this night, because the Americans never saw the barges. When Larson arrived on the scene, he poked around in the dark of Marquana Bay until 12:20am, but found no barges. They were there, however. They landed at 1:50am. The seaplanes of the 938 Air Group kept the Allied artillery silent while all 589 men of the Tsuruya Unit boarded the barges, which left at 3:10am, reaching Buin safely. That Japanese secret weapon, the *daihatsu*, had foiled the Americans again. No mere warship could resist the power of the barge.[426]

Certainly not the *Chevalier*, not any more; maybe not even the *Selfridge*. With the bow gone, skipper Lieutenant Commander George E. Peckham took to sailing the destroyer backwards while damage control parties tried to shore up enough of the bulkheads to enable her to move forward in the more traditional manner. At 12:51am, the *Taylor* came up to take off Captain Walker and most of the crew. Walker promptly radioed AirSols requesting fighter protection at dawn. At around 3:15am, Peckham, with a skeleton crew, tried moving the *Selfridge* forward slowly. The bulkheads held and she started slowly down The Slot with the rest of the tin cans.[427]

Except for two that were left behind. The *Chevalier*, which was abandoned and unable to move, and the *La Vallette*, which had the painful job of finishing her off. The *La Vallette* moved off by about a mile and fired one torpedo – one perfectly aimed torpedo that, 45 seconds after launch, lanced into the *Chevalier*'s after magazines. According to Commander Taylor, "the *Chevalier* blew up with the biggest explosion I have ever seen. Flames and great balls of fire rose to at least 500 feet." It left smoke so thick it "furnished excellent cloud cover from Jap planes."[428]

They would need it. As the sun rose above the horizon, with the Americans still west of Vella Lavella, Captain Walker could see that AirSols had come through: two flights of Lightnings from the 339th Fighter Squadron were overhead. Another flight of Lightnings plus a flight of Corsairs from Marine Fighting 214 were available if needed, but for now they had a different agenda: searching for the crew of a downed B-25 Mitchell. Joining them at around 7:20 were a dozen Zeros from the 204 Air Group, who also had a different agenda. A short but spirited shootout some 25 miles northwest of Vella Lavella left one Zero pilot killed and two Lightnings damaged. The Japanese did not bother the retiring American ships for the rest of the day, and the destroyers reached Purvis Bay on October 8.[429]

And with that, the night combat engagement the Americans would call the Battle of Vella Lavella came to an end. "[H]istorians who have written about it since have levied criticism at all concerned," said historian Ronnie Day.[430] Ijuin for his handling of the battle, Walker for not waiting for Larson's destroyers. There's just no pleasing some people.

Certainly not Admiral Ijuin's superiors in Rabaul. "[D]espite his many blunders, Ijuin's escort mission worked out pretty much as planned. And so it was his victory."[431] Nevertheless, on returning to Rabaul, Captain Hara found the baron "shaken and ashamed:"

> [Ijuin] was not openly rebuked, but the high command showed its appraisal of the action by presenting a ceremonial sword to me and daggers to Lieutenant Commander Kinuo Yamagami of *Shigure* and Yoshiro Sugihara of *Samidare*. No rewards or citations were given to anyone in Ijuin's group for the action, Japan's first naval victory in the theater in almost three months.[432]

But is it a victory if neither side considers it a victory? Despite the success of the evacuation, it seems that Admiral Ijuin and Rabaul did not consider it a Japanese victory. Neither did the Americans. "[A]s in the case of Kula Gulf and Kolombangara," wrote Morison, "the firm conviction of victory on the American side really nullified the actual victory of the Japanese."[433] What Morison really meant was that, whatever the Japanese victory, it was not nearly enough to make a difference in a New Georgia Campaign that was a major defeat because with Vella Lavella, the New Georgia campaign was essentially complete. The Japanese were now out of the central Solomons – New Georgia, Kolombangara, and Vella Lavella. The Shortlands complex – Buin, Ballale, etc. – was about to change from forward bases to the front line.

After a fashion. The quick strike that the Allies had hoped for turned into the proverbial and literal quagmire. A quagmire that badly delayed the advance and, despite overwhelming Allied superiority, allowed most of the Japanese to escape. The success of the evacuation stunned the Japanese. Lieutenant Commander Imai Akijiro, chief of staff of the 8th Combined Special Naval Landing Force, expressed just how improbable the Japanese success had been:

> The enemy was guarding the Kolombangara area very cautiously. Forty sea miles from Kolombangara to Choiseul, they had surrounded the area with torpedo bombers, destroyers, and cruisers. We had to go through the siege, close to being unarmed, with twice as many passengers as we should have, on slow motor barges. It was like sending the troops to sea just so they could get sunk. At worst, we all could have died. Even if we were successful, we thought we would probably lose half the troops. It was a miracle that 90% of the troops were actually transported.[434]

Historian John Prados had this chilling bit of wisdom: "Had Japanese offensives been conducted as meticulously as their evacuations, the Allied Powers in the South Pacific might truly have been driven onto the ropes."[435] In that sense, New Georgia and indeed the entire South Pacific was a near-run thing.

As Admiral Halsey summed up the New Georgia Campaign: "Our original plan allotted 15,000 men to wipe out the 9,000 Japs on New Georgia; by the time the island was secured, we had sent in more than 50,000. When I look back [...], the smoke of charred reputations still makes me cough."[436]

The admiral's smoking habit notwithstanding, there was a reason for that. A very good reason. A man whose reputation was not charred: Imperial Japanese Army General Sasaki Minoru. Perhaps the biggest honor any military commander can be given is the respect of his enemy. Sasaki had more than earned the respect of his Allied adversaries. Historian John Miller, Jr would explain:

> No account of the operation should be brought to a close without praising the skill, tenacity, and valor of the heavily outnumbered Japanese who stood off nearly four Allied divisions in the course of the action, and then successfully evacuated 9,400 men to fight again. The obstinate General Sasaki [...] deserved his country's gratitude for his gallant and able conduct of the defense.[437]

His country expressed its gratitude by attaching General Sasaki to General Inamura's 8th Area Army in Rabaul for the rest of the war.

CHAPTER 9
DOMINOES

Although Admiral Ijuin and his superiors did not consider what Captain Hara called "Japan's first naval victory in the theater in almost three months" much of a naval victory, they celebrated the outcome at Vella Lavella all the same.[1]

The day after the engagement, there was a sword presentation ceremony and dinner at the officers' club. Almost all of the brass at Rabaul were there, including Admiral Kusaka and Admiral Samejima. Captain Hara's description starts with a big warning flag: "Great quantities of *sake* were served[.]" The party really got going when it was joined by "the usual geisha girls assigned by the Navy Ministry to the major forward bases as morale boosters." A depressed Captain Hara – he told himself his depression was because this party should have involved his entire crew, not the top brass – just wanted to get drunk and forget it all, so he drank all the *sake* he could.

Admiral Kusaka proclaimed a toast to Captain Hara's destroyer *Shigure*. "The life expectancy of Rabaul-based destroyers has averaged something under two months. Yet one old ship has now fought steadily for almost three months without a scratch or the loss of a single member of her crew," the Southeast Area Fleet commander announced. "Let's drink a toast to Captain Hara, Commander Yamagami, and all the men of the great *Shigure*!" The party got even louder. Too loud.

One of the staff officers, undoubtedly with the liquid courage of *sake*, decided to speak his mind: "Admiral Kusaka, I have long desired, but never dared, to ask certain questions. May I ask them now?" The once-boisterous party came to a screeching halt. Everyone stared in shock. No one talks to an admiral like this. But Kusaka, a laid-back sort who was generally loved by his men, merely nodded. The staff officer went on.

You have just noted the brief life expectancy of a destroyer. Must we put up with such a situation? Why do all our big ships just sit at Truk? Are we going to celebrate next October 26 as the anniversary of the last battle in history in which our carriers took part? During the past year our destroyers have not only been conducting their unglamorous transport missions, but they have also been bearing the full brunt of all actions in these waters. Forgive my rudeness. This is no criticism of you, but we all know that your 11th Air Fleet has been shore-based since the start of the war. In this critical theater, why do destroyers have to shoulder the entire burden without the support of our carriers, battleships and cruisers?

The tension increased. Admiral Kusaka was silent. The whole room was silent. Though Hara does not mention it, at least a few in the room, including him, had to be thinking about the fate of Admiral Tanaka, who had also spoken what everyone was thinking. Admiral Samejima tried to smooth things over. "I understand that Commander in Chief Koga is preparing for a decisive naval action in which all our big ships will be deployed." As if everyone in the room had not heard that one before. Multiple times. The staffer was having none of it. He began shouting drunkenly.

"When? When are these ships going to do something? They have been out of action for a full year, and that year has been like a century for our destroyers. In this time the enemy has caught up and surpassed us!" Another officer, a friend of the drunken staffer, stepped in, pleading exhaustion. Again, the staffer was having none of it.

"And what is Imperial Headquarters doing in Tokyo? Announcements blare every day that we are bleeding the enemy white in the Solomons. It is we who are being bled white, not the enemy."

Now two of his friends stepped in and dragged him from the room as he tearfully sobbed, "*Yugumo* is sunk. Poor *Yugumo* is sunk with so many of my friends."

After yet another uncomfortable moment, Captain Hara staggered over to Admiral Samejima with the ceremonial sword.

"I wish to return this sword, Admiral, because I do not deserve it. Even if I did deserve it, what use is a sword on board ship?" The uncomfortable silence returned with a vengeance. Captain Miyazaki recovered quickly from his shock and came over to Hara, as the staff officer's friends had, saying, "You are tired, Hara. Let us go home and get some rest."

And like the staff officer, Captain Hara was having none of it. "No, thank you, Miyazaki," Hara waved, "I want to exchange this sword for *sake* for my wonderful crew. They are the ones who should be rewarded. Not me. Admiral Samejima, buy drinks for my men." Now Hara's own commander Admiral Ijuin stepped in. "All right, Hara. I'll buy drinks for your men, but now we are all tired and it is time to turn in." The commodore does not seem to remember much after that, or maybe even before that. Hara woke up the next morning with "a terrible hangover."

To top it off, Commander Yamagami told him that Admiral Ijuin and Captain Miyazaki had had to drag a "bellowing" Hara from the party. Hara's fears of an official sanction for his behavior proved unfounded, likely because Kusaka, Samejima, and Ijuin agreed with him. Meanwhile, when the story of Hara's performance reached the enlisted men, his popularity with them increased.[2]

Maybe that popularity would help the men of the *Shigure* perform better. Maybe it wouldn't. Maybe it would, but it wouldn't matter. Admiral Kusaka, though not an aviator, was very popular with the aviators of Base Air Force. Yet Kusaka's popularity among his air crews had not been able to stop or even slow down the erosion in the performance and skill of Base Air Force.

Then again, that erosion could only partly be blamed on Admiral Kusaka. He was not in charge of pilot training back in the Home Islands, which might charitably be called inept. He was not in charge of approving Japanese aircraft designs, which placed performance above all other considerations, including and especially the safety of the aviators. He was in charge of air operations in the Southeast Area, and that was all. Admiral Kusaka was certainly among those most uncomfortable at this disastrous sword presentation ceremony. He would have been even more so had he known it represented yet another switch in places between Imperial Japan and the Allies. In August 1942, a conference among Allied commanders to iron out details of the imminent invasion of Guadalcanal had been held on board the carrier *Saratoga*, then near Koro in the Fiji Islands. The conference quickly degenerated into a shouting match between the carrier commander, Admiral Fletcher, and the amphibious force commander, Admiral Turner, which presaged the disastrous Battle of Savo Island that crippled the early Guadalcanal Campaign. But by the end of that campaign, it was Japanese conferences that were becoming shouting matches, even involving physical altercations. The sword presentation ceremony showed that this state of affairs had not improved.

Guadalcanal. That was really where all this had started. Midway had changed everything in terms of the mindsets of both the Japanese and the Allies, as well as stripping the Japanese of the overwhelming power of *Kido Butai*. But Guadalcanal was ultimately a Japanese miscalculation whose consequences were becoming more and more catastrophic. The initial Japanese attacks of the Pacific War, the so-called "Centrifugal Offensive," had been carefully researched, planned, and conducted. Generally, the Japanese would seize an air base, which would give them the air range and momentum to seize the next air base. It was like dominoes. Consider the eastern prong of the Japanese advance in the Java Sea Campaign. When Jolo fell to the Japanese in December 1941, it would cause Menado to fall in January 1942, which would cause Balikpapan to fall that same month, which would cause Kendari to fall in early February, which would cause Bali to fall that same month, which would help cause Java to fall in March. The Japanese had set up their dominoes perfectly.

In the South Pacific, however, things were different. Japanese troops had captured Rabaul in February 1942. The fall of Rabaul would cause Bougainville and the Shortlands to fall a month later, which would cause Guadalcanal to fall in July and August 1942. That was the Japanese plan. Except the move to Guadalcanal was not carefully researched, planned, and conducted. It was done on the fly. And Guadalcanal did not fall. The Bougainville-Shortlands domino did not cause Guadalcanal to fall. The Japanese had not set their dominoes properly. They missed a domino: Munda. The

Japanese recognized their error. They set up the Munda domino, but it was too late. Not only was the Guadalcanal domino not going to fall because of the new Munda domino, it was wobbling in the other direction, and would instead cause the Munda domino to fall. And when the Munda domino fell, the Bougainville-Shortlands domino, now the next domino in line, started looking more and more wobbly, especially with Allied forces now on Vella Lavella, having just completed construction of a new airfield at Barakoma.

In fact, not just dominoes, but walls seemed to be threatening to fall in on the Japanese. On September 8, Italy had formally surrendered to the Allies. That meant the Italian Navy was no longer a factor in the Mediterranean, which in turn meant the British Royal Navy could reinforce the Eastern Fleet in the Indian Ocean and threaten the southwestern flank of the Greater East Asia Co-prosperity Sphere in Burma (another place that was far from prosperous, though unlike the Solomons it was actually in Asia).

With the southwest threatened in Burma and the southeast threatened in the Solomons and New Guinea, Japan needed a new defense strategy. Already, even before the collapse of the Italian Fascist government, the chiefs of the Imperial Japanese Army and Navy General Staffs had reported to the Emperor on August 24 their plans for the conduct of future operations. The main points were as follows:

- In the southeast area, which is the area east of eastern New Guinea through the Solomons, holding operations would be carried out, by holding the current front and defeating any enemy attacks.
- By next spring, defenses in the Banda Sea, western New Guinea, the Carolines and the Marianas would be strengthened, and Army and Navy forces readied, and a counteroffensive launched when the opportunity presented itself.[3]

This policy was formally approved on September 24 and was memorialized in an Imperial Conference held on September 30, 1943, in which new "Guidelines for the Future Conduct of War" and a new "Estimate of the World Situation" were also adopted. Informally, the new strategic concept outlined in these guidelines has been called the "Absolute National Defense Zone" or the "Absolute Defense Sphere." This policy designated the Kuriles, Bonins, Marianas, western Carolines and western New Guinea, and the area west of this line, as the zone in the Pacific Ocean that absolutely had to be held to ensure Japan's survival.[4]

In line with this new strategic policy, that same September 30, Imperial General Headquarters issued Navy Section Directive No. 280. It restated the new strategic policy:

The absolute defense sphere will be narrowed to the line running from the Bunda [sic] Sea to the Caroline Islands. While engaging in delaying action in the Southeast Area, strong points for a counter offensive will be formed in the area from the North of Australia to the central Pacific ocean.[5]

Its operational policy stated:

> The Imperial Army and Navy will, in close co-operation, fight off the advancing enemy in key sectors of the Southeast area and make every effort toward extended warfare, meanwhile rapidly building springboards for the launching of counter-operations in strategic locations from the North-of-Australia area (northwest New Guinea and the areas around the Banda and Flores Seas) to the Central Pacific area (the Caroline, Marshall, Mariana and Gilbert Island groups; Wake, Marcus, Nauru and Ocean Islands) and preparing strength for a counteroffensive calculated to deal a decisive blow to the advancing enemy. Everything possible will be done to rout the enemy before his attack is set and break his will to fight.[6]

Despite not being within this Absolute National Defense Zone and having been changed from a "crucial front" to a "holding front," the Southeast Area would still play a critical part. According to the directive, "Our forces will endeavor to defeat the advancing enemy in key locations in the Southeast Area from east of eastern New Guinea to the Solomon Islands and hold out there as long as possible."[7]

To "particularly emphasize" the point:

> The defense of key locations focusing on Rabaul in the Bismarck Archipelago and Bougainville Island areas will be strengthened and efforts made to hold them as long as possible. Everything possible will be done to supply and hold key areas on the west shore of Dampier Strait and in northern New Guinea.[8]

To just plain "emphasize" the point, "Until Japan's real line of defense is completed, the enemy advance from the Southeast for a major counterattack will be held in that area."[9]

But Imperial General Headquarters went a bit further:

1. A defensive stand was to be adopted with Rabaul as the ultimate point of resistance. To this end, strategic areas in the Admiralties and New Ireland were to be strengthened.
2. Efforts would be made to hold the area around the Dampier Strait for as long as possible.
3. Since Bougainville was not only the strongest of Rabaul's outposts but also the strategic key point for checking enemy advances in the Central Pacific, every effort was to be made to drive off the advancing enemy and hold the island. The southern part of Bougainville surrounding Shortland Bay was to be the principal point in the island's defense, with only partial forces assigned to the defense of the northern section.[10]

In practice it meant General Inamura's 8th Area Army had to deal with two lines of wobbly dominoes. In New Guinea, the fall of Buna/Gona/Sanananda had led to the fall of Lae/Salamaua, which had led to the latest falling domino: Finschhafen. The small port was not completely secured as of yet, and the Japanese 18th Army was still on the Huon Peninsula in the vicinity of Finschhafen trying to recapture it, but having little success in so doing. With Finschhafen in Allied hands, the only barrier to Douglas MacArthur's troops landing on New Britain proper was the Vitiaz and Dampier Straits. But at Finschhafen, this particular line of dominoes could split: it could go into New Britain and thus Rabaul, or it could move west along the north coast of New Guinea, or both.

So where would MacArthur go next? Madang? Wewak? Rook Island? This was a rhetorical question because obviously the next domino would be on New Britain, but where? Cape Gloucester? Arawe? Gasmata? The Allies had to land somewhere; they could not sail the distance to Rabaul in one shot. That was Japan's best hope. Wherever the Allies landed, they would not have an easy time marching overland to position troops to attack Rabaul proper, because New Britain had few roads through its mountainous jungle. But this worked both ways: because New Britain had few roads through its mountainous jungle, the Japanese had to supply and reinforce their bases using ships. Allied air power had turned these reinforcement efforts into potential disasters – or even literal disasters, like the Lae convoy – the consequence of which was that while the Japanese had a defensive presence in most of the likely targets for an amphibious landing in New Britain, with the exception of the area around Rabaul they were not strong enough anywhere to repel such an invasion, nor could they be easily reinforced.

In the northern Solomons, the Japanese faced a completely different set of problems. This was another set of dominoes, converging at Rabaul with that set from New Guinea – or were they more like spokes in a cartwheel? Bougainville and the Shortlands were defended by General Hyakutake's 17th Army. When last we saw Hyakutake, he was busy messing up the Guadalcanal Campaign for the Japanese and, no, he had not gotten much better since then.

These days, General Hyakutake's assignment was to mess up the Solomons Campaign for the Japanese. His 17th Army had some 20,000 troops, mostly of the 6th Kumamoto Division, whose most famous accomplishment was the Rape of Nanking, and, no, the 6th had not gotten much better since then, either. Some 15,000 of these troops were positioned in southern Bougainville.[11] Also available to General Hyakutake were a considerable number of naval infantry. Some elements of the 8th Fleet headquarters remained after Admiral Samejima pulled it back to Rabaul. There were also 6,800 naval infantry of the 1st Base Force, mostly at Buin; and some 5,000 men of the 4th South Seas Garrison Unit who were positioned on the outer islands of the Shortlands. Most of these naval troops were static and could not be moved, but they could still fight in defense.[12]

Also firmly in defense now was Admiral Kusaka and his 11th Air Fleet's (1st) Base Air Force. By the beginning of November, Base Air Force was authorized to have 312 fighters, 96 carrier bombers, 24 carrier attack planes, 144 medium land attack planes, and 24 reconnaissance planes, for a total of 600 aircraft.[13] What Base Air Force actually had available was not anywhere remotely close to that figure, but it remained exceedingly dangerous, especially defending what for all intents and purposes was its home turf, as the Cactus Air Force had been on Guadalcanal.

The Japanese were better positioned than they had ever been to keep these Solomons dominoes from falling, but they were going against an enemy with momentum who had them outnumbered and outgunned, or so they thought.

Recall the Joint Chiefs Directive of March 28, 1943, which set the goals for 1943 for General MacArthur and Admiral Halsey. First, they were to set up airfields on Woodlark and Kiriwina, two sizable island groups north of Milne Bay. Second was to seize the Huon Peninsula – Lae, Salamaua, Finschhafen, and Madang – of New Guinea and occupy western New Britain. Third was to seize and occupy the Solomon Islands as far as southern Bougainville. While they had not yet completed the plan, General MacArthur and Admiral Halsey were on track to accomplish all of those goals. Except a new complication had developed, one of which the Japanese were not aware. Admiral Nimitz had begun siphoning off resources from the South Pacific such as warships, transport ships, supplies, and air units to prepare for his offensive in the Central Pacific. While General MacArthur had his own resources to pursue operations in New Guinea and New Britain, Halsey would find himself more and more strapped for combat power as he tried to complete the Joint Chiefs' plan and move on southern Bougainville.

Which was precisely where General Hyakutake and even Imperial Japanese Headquarters expected the Allies to land. Thus, the Allies were going to land right in the teeth of strong Japanese defenses at Buin and the Shortlands.

Right?

EPILOGUE:
THE *AKIKAZE* RESUNK

Japanese attempts to cover up the war crimes of the Imperial Army and Navy were similar in some ways to the efforts of officials of the Third Reich in the dying days of World War II. But Japan began this process far too late to be able to do much with the mass graves because by the time it started most of those graves were no longer in Japanese-controlled territory. In fact, the biggest effort started only after the Pacific War ended:

> From when a ceasefire was announced on August 15, 1945, until August 28, 1945 – when the first American troops arrived in Japan – the Japanese military and civil authorities invested a large amount of work in destroying compromising archival materials, especially those related to the war years between 1942 and 1945. Field units were ordered to burn materials that would have provided evidence of violence and torture against POWs, among other things. It is estimated that 70 percent of the existing sources were destroyed in these two weeks, [citation omitted] leaving behind a gap in history that can never be filled again and providing former war criminals with a chance to lead ordinary lives. Regardless of this intense purge of Japan's official documentation of the war, the U.S. military was still able to collect more than 350,000 documents related to the war and the crimes committed during it.[1]

Unlike the Third Reich, the Japanese still had possession of most of these records because the Allies were not yet in physical possession of Japanese central military facilities. Down the memory hole they went. Compromising orders, suspicious supply requests, revealing reports, dropping prisoner counts, transportation records, anything and everything Japanese authorities could identify in those two weeks. Gone. Burned. As it is, eyewitness testimony is the least reliable form of evidence, and the vast majority of the eyewitnesses were dead, buried in mass graves hidden deep in the jungle.

The gambit was mostly successful. Maybe the worst of the war criminals, Tsuji Masanobu, escaped justice altogether, at least as far as anyone can tell. The renowned "god of operations" who was instrumental in the Japanese conquest of Malaya and Singapore, Tsuji also organized the *Sook Ching* in Singapore and had a major hand in the Bataan Death March, which he opposed, but only because he wanted all the American and Filipino prisoners killed. He also crippled the final Japanese effort to capture Guadalcanal by conniving to have one of the commanders of that offensive, General Kawaguchi Kiyotake, removed the day before the attack, largely because Kawaguchi was not enough of a war criminal for Tsuji. His star falling after the defeat on Guadalcanal, Tsuji was sent to China and eventually Burma, where he spent the rest of the war. In perhaps the most contemptible display of craven cowardice by any major figure in either the Pacific or European Theaters, at the end of the war, Tsuji disguised himself as a Buddhist monk and escaped Burma and Thailand to hide out in China and Indochina, where he advised the Viet Minh against the French. He returned to Japan in 1949, after the war crimes trials had been completed and amnesty granted, and was elected to the Diet twice, his fight with Kawaguchi resuming. Tsuji went to Vientiane in 1961, probably to advise the Viet Cong or maybe the Pathet Lao, and was never seen again.

However, it seems probable that no amount of burning, shredding, or feeding to the dog incriminating documentation was necessary to mostly preserve the fog of mystery that continues to surround the massacre of the defenseless missionaries and lay staff on the *Akikaze*. Even now, almost eight decades later, about all that is known for sure is that the crew of the *Akikaze* murdered a bunch of civilians in the afternoon of March 18, 1943. "A bunch of civilians" is the proper term, because even precise number of people killed is not known for certain. The best guesses are about 60.

Exactly why the Japanese murdered these religious "neutral civilians" has never been conclusively determined, nor has the identity of the officer who issued the order "to dispose of all neutral civilians on board." The Imperial Japanese Navy and, especially, the Imperial Japanese Army were no strangers to war crimes, largely because of a *bushido* culture that treated enemies who surrendered rather than died in combat or through *seppuku* as less than honorable, less than human. However, relatively few war crimes were ordered by higher commands. Fewer still were treated during the war with the secrecy that was attached to the handling of the missionaries and other civilians who were murdered on board the *Akikaze*, as opposed to after the war, when the aforementioned destruction of incriminating documents took place.

The idea the Japanese had that the increasing submarine and air attacks on supply and troop convoys were the result of these Roman Catholic and Lutheran clergy passing information concerning these convoys to the Allies was obviously preposterous. Yet while Japanese fear of clergy may have been irrational in this case, another Japanese fear was not: that downed Allied air crews would be assisted by the missionaries.

The only hint the Japanese gave as to why the "disposal" of the civilians was ordered was a rather vague explanation that several downed Allied airmen were not only hiding in the area, but had contacted the mission with the help of what the Japanese described as "local people who harbored anti-Japanese sentiment."[2] At least one specific incident would seem to fit this description. In late February, Melanesian locals had passed a note to Father Manion from a downed air crew. The crew was from the Consolidated B-24 Liberator flown by Lieutenant McMurria of the 321st Bombardment Squadron, forced down at sea off Wewak on January 20.

In a driving rainstorm that morning, Lieutenant McMurria and his nine crewmates had left Port Moresby's 5-Mile Airfield (or Ward Drome) on a scouting mission over the shipping lanes between the Wewak/Madang area in New Guinea and the Bismarcks. Based on previous reports, they had expected to find a small Japanese presence in Wewak, with one identified antiaircraft position. They were stunned to find a harbor full of ships and, worse, an airfield full of aircraft, a contingent on loan from the carrier *Junyo*. This was the day after the first convoy of the 20th Division had arrived in Wewak. Lieutenant McMurria and his crew also found a lot more than one antiaircraft gun, both on land and in the harbor. His intelligence information proven wrong in the most dangerous fashion, McMurria was livid. "We were alone, looking down at all those goddamn Japanese while supposedly flying a routine reconnaissance mission," he would write much later.[3] McMurria had a right to be angry about their predicament, but, objectively speaking, it was not entirely fair. While the presence of the *Junyo*'s Zeros was several days old, the transports in the harbor had arrived in the last 24 hours. The entire purpose of his reconnaissance mission was to update that intelligence.

Updating that intelligence, however, had just put Lieutenant McMurria and his crew in mortal danger. He ordered the bomb load jettisoned to lighten the heavy bomber and then poured on the speed to try to escape. But the antiaircraft guns on the ships in the harbor and on shore poured on the gunfire. They managed to nick the Liberator's Number 3 engine, depriving it of the power necessary to get over the Owen Stanley Mountains back to friendly territory, and ultimately disabling it. As the B-25 staggered, the *Junyo*'s Zeros scrambled. With their chances of escape now reduced to almost zero, at 9:20am, McMurria radioed they were being attacked by fighters. The *Junyo*'s Zeros started shooting up the crippled bomber, especially with devastating 20mm explosive rounds. McMurria was forced to ditch offshore.[4]

The B-24 Liberator was notorious for reacting poorly to ditching. When the Liberator struck the water, it broke in two. The front section sank immediately while the rear floated for a few minutes. Two crewmen went down with the bomber.

Exactly one four-man life raft deployed before the Liberator sank. Lieutenant McMurria and his seven surviving crewmates had to cling to that raft for two and a half days until they were able to stagger ashore on Wokeo Island.[5] Friendly Melanesian locals found the wounded, exhausted aviators and cared for them for almost two months until they had mostly recovered.

Yet Lieutenant McMurria and his men knew they could not stay on Wokeo. Their very presence put the Melanesians in danger and stretched their very limited food supply. It was around this time that Lieutenant McMurria found out about the presence of the Divine

Word missionaries on Kairiru. After much pleading, the natives agreed to contact St John's mission. It was a desperate gamble, but one McMurria had to take. And it was one that failed. His message had been carried to Father Manion, who, as stated earlier, advised McMurria to turn himself in to the Japanese.[6]

With one desperate gamble having failed, Lieutenant McMurria and his men turned to another, even more desperate gamble: they would sail to the coast of New Guinea and then walk to Port Moresby – over those 13,000-foot Owen Stanley Mountains, through some of the deadliest territory in the world, featuring aggressive insects, nasty diseases, ravenous crocodiles, annoying plants, and, last but not least, Japanese troops. With assistance from the locals on Wokeo, the Americans left on March 7 or so.[7] It was maybe a week later when Japanese troops showed up on Wokeo Island looking for the Americans. They found nothing tying the islanders to the airmen. A healthy bribe of two chickens convinced the Japanese to leave without further ado.[8]

The visit of the Japanese to Wokeo occurred at about the same time as the order to remove the clergy from Kairiru and Manus. At least one historian, Bruce Gamble, and one investigator, Father Ralph M. Wiltgen of the Society for the Divine Word, have drawn a connection between Lieutenant McMurria's message to Kairiru, carried by "local people who harbored anti-Japanese sentiment," and the order to remove the missionaries.[9] The incident may have been the trigger – the proverbial straw that broke the camel's back – but was not the cause. Rear Admiral Kamata Michiaki and his 2nd Special Base Force had been campaigning for an order to remove the missionaries almost since the unit's arrival in Wewak, and the Divine Word missionaries in particular had already been accused of spying for the Allies, though exactly when those charges began is unclear. Moreover, it was not just the Divine Word personnel who were removed, but Lutheran missionaries from the Liebenzell Mission on Manus, where there was a Japanese air base.

The biggest questions remain the identity of the parties responsible for the order to move the missionaries and the order to "dispose" of them. Part of the reason for this lack of clarity is simply the high level of activity and, indeed, intrigue during this period in the Japanese-held South Pacific. Submarine attacks on convoys were a growing problem. Air attacks on convoys were a growing problem, culminating in the catastrophe not quite in the Bismarck Sea. There was also the ominous growth of Allied air power in the Buna area, which directly threatened Rabaul. There was the pending change in command of the 8th Fleet, with Admiral Mikawa preparing to turn things over to Admiral Samejima.

But Admiral Samejima was not the only new party coming to Rabaul. So was the Japanese Gestapo in the form of the 6th Field Kempeitai, due to arrive in Rabaul in late March. They would take charge of any prisoners of war or civilian internees. Until then, Kairiru and Manus were under the jurisdiction of the Navy and thus the Tokkeitai, the military police of the Imperial Japanese Navy. Though formed only in July 1942, in part to protect the Imperial Navy and its personnel from the excesses of the Kempeitai, the Tokkeitai was "fully as vile" as the Kempeitai, and more than capable of its own intrigues.[10]

In short, there were a lot of moving pieces in the Japanese-held South Pacific at this time. It was a toxic brew in which Bishop Lörks and his fellow missionaries were trapped, into which Lieutenant McMurria and his crew had now blundered.

After the war, Australian investigators trying to determine the fate of the missionaries were faced with sieving this toxic brew to figure out who was responsible for the order and who gave the order. In any military, they are not necessarily the same thing. Complicating the investigation was the fact that so many of the participants, including the central figures, Sabe Tsurukichi and Kami Shigetoku, had been killed during the war.

Post-war investigators, as well as historians, found these deaths to be rather convenient for the main suspects in this war crime: Vice Admiral Mikawa and his chief of staff Rear Admiral Onishi Shinzo. Onishi denied responsibility, claiming that they had not issued the order to the *Akikaze* because the *Akikaze* was not part of the 8th Fleet, but of the 11th Air Fleet. It was a curious response whose potential significance does not seem to have been recognized. When he realized the investigators were not buying that explanation, Onishi changed his story and claimed Lieutenant Kami had issued the order without any authorization. Onishi said the first and last time he heard of the massacre was at the end of March 1943, when Lieutenant Kami orally reported to him and Mikawa that a "small number of German missionaries" had been executed on the *Akikaze*.[11]

For his part, Admiral Mikawa stated that he had never seen or heard of the *Akikaze* and the destroyer was never part of his command. He claimed that he had not only not ordered the executions of the civilians aboard the *Akikaze*, but had never ordered the civilians to be moved in the first place. Mikawa corroborated Onishi's claim that the first he heard of the executions was on March 26, when Lieutenant Kami told him and Onishi a "small number of German missionaries" had been executed "on a destroyer." Mikawa claimed to have been shocked and outraged by the information, but was unable to investigate it because of the pending change in command of the 8th Fleet.[12]

Post-war investigators and historians such as Tanaka Yuki have been understandably suspicious of Admirals Mikawa and Onishi. Tanaka basically called Mikawa and Onishi liars who changed their stories when they were found out, because they knew everyone who could corroborate or refute their stories was conveniently dead.[13] But there is likely less here than meets the eye. The *Akikaze* was technically part of the 11th Air Fleet – that is, Base Air Force – which was commanded by Mikawa's superior Vice Admiral Kusaka. *Akikaze*'s supply run to Wewak, which immediately preceded the stop at Kairiru, was a mission for Base Air Force.[14] The destroyer had a history of working assignments from Base Air Force; recall that on the first day of the Pacific War the *Akikaze* was positioned between Formosa and Luzon as a rescue ship for any aviators downed during the Japanese attack on the Clark Field complex.

And the *Akikaze* had continued performing missions for Base Air Force. It was the *Akikaze* who escorted the aircraft transports *Mogamigawa* and *Kinryu Maru*s in early July

1942 to reinforce the seaplane base at Tulagi and, critically, drop off troops to begin construction of a certain air base at Guadalcanal's Lunga Point. While the *Akikaze* spent most of her time escorting convoys or individual ships, those were often Base Air Force missions. For instance, in late July 1942 she had escorted the aforementioned *Mogamigawa Maru* from Rabaul to Lae and back. In the first week of August she escorted the aircraft transport again, to Kavieng and back. After two transport runs to the emergency air base at Buka and back, the *Akikaze* escorted the seaplane carrier *Akitsushima* on two missions making the rounds of Rabaul, Buka, and Shortland, sandwiching the missions around a run to Rekata Bay. On October 20, Lieutenant Commander Sabe took command of the destroyer and immediately escorted the *Akitsushima* again, this time on a circuit of Rabaul, Shortland, and Rekata Bay. In early October she escorted the *Taiyo* on an aircraft transport run to Rabaul, and so on.[15]

From the standpoint of the 8th Fleet, however, while the *Akikaze* may have been under the fleet's authority at times, she was a nonentity. With all those battles and troop convoy runs in the Solomon Islands, the times *Akikaze*'s name is seen are few and far between because she was escorting convoys for Base Air Force. Not all of her missions were for Base Air Force, because Base Air Force simply did not have enough work to keep a destroyer continuously occupied, so she also performed some escort missions for 8th Fleet. The denial could be explained as simply a matter of command technicalities and flawed memory.[16]

Admiral Mikawa would speculate as to why Lieutenant Kami would have sent out the order. In a word, coastwatchers. Japanese frustration with the coastwatchers was palpable. It seemed every time they moved ships or aircraft in the Solomons or New Guinea, the Allies quickly found out about it and would adopt countermeasures. Local commanders had complained to Mikawa about the coastwatchers and asked that he do something about them. Which he did, but, aside from the area of Buka and northwestern Bougainville, his efforts were ineffective, and he did not have the manpower to increase those efforts. The 8th Fleet staff was not happy with this state of affairs. Mikawa believed that Lieutenant Kami issued the order without getting his or Onishi's approval as an overreaction to those complaints by 2nd Special Base Force. Mikawa also indicated that another staff officer in charge of civilian affairs, Commander Ando Norisaka, might have collaborated with Kami to issue the order.[17]

Oddly, not mentioned in playing a role here, although it had to have done so, was the debacle that took place in, or rather just outside, the Bismarck Sea. The loss of so many ships and men at one time was a serious emotional blow. The disaster could be seen as evidence of Allied spies in New Guinea and the Bismarcks. The Japanese were themselves outraged at what they believed was Allied ruthlessness and even hypocrisy in machine-gunning lifeboats, rafts, anything that could float, and concentrations of survivors in the water. The civilian internees were the only target immediately available for a strike at the enemy who had hurt Japan so much.

It has been argued that Admiral Mikawa's speculation was entirely without merit due to the Japanese procedure for issuing orders by radio and wireless telegraph. Tanaka Yuki:

> In relation to ship movements and other secret matters, any order form was required to have the signature of the staff officer, if he originated the order, as well as the signatures of both the chief of staff and commander in chief. The order form containing these three signatures was then delivered via the staff officer in charge of signals to the staff cipher officer. The order was then encoded and sent to each ship's captain, the commander of the naval base force, and the naval garrison unit. [End note omitted.] Therefore, if Mikawa's claim is correct and the order issued by Kami and Ando to move the civilians from Kairiru and Manus and execute them on the *Akikaze* was given to the staff officer in charge of signals, then Kami could not have passed it on to the staff cipher officer because he did not have the signatures of the chief of staff and the commander in chief. If, for some reason, the staff officer in charge of signals had handed over the order to the staff cipher officer, knowing that the form was missing the two signatures, then in turn the cipher officer could not – or should not – have been able to encode the order.[18]

The thinking here appears to be that because no order could go out over the wireless without the signatures of both Admirals Mikawa and Onishi, they both had to know about and approve the order when it was sent. But this thinking can be turned on its head: because no order could go out over the wireless without the signatures of both Admirals Mikawa and Onishi, the order did not go out over the wireless.

The *Akikaze* did not receive the order to dispose of the missionaries by wireless, but by a courier with a sealed envelope containing the orders. In modern times, this is a rather unusual way of transmitting orders, usually reserved for times when radio, telephone, or wireless communications are out or unreliable, which was not the case here; or when extreme secrecy is necessary. Why would extreme secrecy be necessary here? The Japanese had never been shy about war crimes. At one point in the early days of the China Incident, there had been press coverage of a "contest" between two officers over how many Chinese prisoners of war they could decapitate with their *katana*s. War crimes were especially common in the Imperial Japanese Army, but also took place with disturbing regularity in the Imperial Navy. The massacre of the survivors of the US Navy destroyer *Edsall* by elements of the Special Naval Landing Force near Makassar City on Celebes and the murder of three US Navy aviators shot down at Midway – *Yorktown* TBD Devastator pilot Ensign Wesley Osmus on the destroyer *Arashi*, and *Enterprise* Dauntless pilot Ensign Frank O'Flaherty and his gunner, Aviation Machinist's Mate 2nd Class Bruno P. Gaido, on the destroyer *Makigumo* – are cases in point.

Then again, there appears to be no indication that the aforementioned war crimes of the *Arashi* and *Makigumo* were ordered from higher commands. The US Navy aviators were murdered on the initiative of the destroyers' skippers. The *Akikaze*

Massacre was, by a preponderance of the evidence, not on the skipper's initiative, but was instead ordered by higher command, which is by itself curious.[19] And these orders from higher command were hand-delivered by courier, not sent by the usual radio or wireless telegraph. Since the end of the Pearl Harbor attack, the Japanese had not been especially careful with communications security. The Imperial Navy believed its communications codes were unbreakable and even if they were not, the Japanese language was, they believed, indecipherable to barbaric white people. They thought nothing of sending even the most sensitive of information by radio or wireless telegraph. But not this. Why?[20]

The answer might be found in the often-overlooked order to Chief Petty Officer Ichinose on Manus to assemble the civilians from the Liebenzell Mission for transport to Rabaul. Ichinose later said the order was jointly signed by the Chief of Staff of the 8th Fleet and the 81st Naval Garrison Unit. The latter was likely Ichinose's parent unit, and was under the jurisdiction of the 8th Base Force, which itself answered to 8th Fleet. But the signature of the Chief of Staff of the 8th Fleet – that is, Admiral Onishi – is curious. Staff officers often issue orders in the name of their commander – that's what the staff is for – but in such cases the order is still usually attributed to the commander, not the staff officer. Not here, which suggests it was in Onishi's own name, not Admiral Mikawa's. Why?

Because, more than likely, Admiral Mikawa did not issue the order. Admiral Onishi did. Or, more accurately, someone on Onishi's behalf issued the order. Plus, as Mikawa later explained, "In the Japanese Navy, occasionally when certain officers gave an order to a subordinate, in order to give it weight, they would say that the order came from a superior officer even if they originated it themselves ..."[21]

It should be remembered that what is known about the order to execute the missionaries and lay people comes almost entirely by hearsay. The orders themselves, termed "confidential," were delivered in a sealed and secured envelope for the skipper's eyes only by the liaison on that boat in Kavieng. As far as anyone can tell, the orders themselves were never seen except by Lieutenant Commander Sabe. However, after the orders arrived, Sabe was regularly seen with Captain Amaya, Sabe's immediate superior as commander of Destroyer Division 34 (and largely superfluous on this trip) and "a very close friend," so it is reasonable to presume that Amaya saw the orders as well. Beyond that, however, in all likelihood nobody saw the order.

The most complete explanation available comes from Lieutenant Commander Kuroki. An extremely depressed Sabe had told Kuroki:

> On orders from the 8th Fleet Headquarters we stopped over at Lorengau Island and took several missionaries aboard my ship, the *Akikaze*. On the return trip to Rabaul, an order for the disposal (*Shobun*) of the missionaries was received from 8th Fleet Headquarters, and although I felt that the order was mysterious, we had to dispose of the missionaries before reaching port in accordance with this order.[22]

There was more to this conversation, however, than what was said. As reported by the Divine Word's Father Ralph M. Wiltgen, who investigated the *Akikaze* Massacre postwar:

> [Kuroki] sensed that the so-called order which Sabe said he had received from the 8th Fleet Headquarters was not a bona fide order. A bona fide order would need the consent of both the commander in chief and the chief of staff of the 8th Fleet Headquarters. Knowing well the characters of both these men, and considering the matter from the standpoint of common sense, Kuroki felt that the order in question may have been issued in the form of an order but without the approval of the commander in chief and the chief of staff. Kuroki's suspicions went even further. He was convinced that Sabe had received not an order, but a request. "Some personnel of 8th Fleet Headquarters issued it as a request of the staff officer," Kuroki said, "and Sabe, feeling that I might press into it, simply said that it was an 8th Fleet order."[23]

That last speculation on Kuroki's part about receiving a "request" and not an order is likely incorrect. The version of the order as Sabe related to Kuroki is consistent with what witnesses aboard the *Akikaze* reported. Sublieutenant Kai said Sabe told him "that an order came from the 8th Fleet to execute the missionary passengers, the Third Party Nationals."[24] According to Lieutenant Takahashi, Sabe said words to the effect of, "This order has just arrived and compels us to dispose of all internees on board."[25] Dr Sugiura later explained, "I seem to recall that the ship captain said after dinner that he had received a very difficult order."[26] Machinist Petty Officer Ishigami Shinichi said that after the *Akikaze* arrived in Rabaul but before the crew was allowed to disembark, Sabe said words to the effect of, "the killing of these foreigners was done in accordance with orders received from higher up, that it was a very regrettable incident, and that we should not discuss this matter with our friends or comrades or with anyone after reaching port."[27]

In response to Kuroki's questions, Sabe repeated his description of the order as "mysterious"; he did not know if 8th Fleet had the authority to issue such an order.[28] Kuroki wondered if 8th Fleet had actually issued such an order at all.[29] Not just for the reasons described – that is, a conflation of "request" and "order" – but something perhaps darker. He wondered if it was sent out without their authorization.

The odd arrangement of the order conjures up the possibility that the weird secrecy surrounding it was not to avoid scrutiny by the Allies, either during or after the war, but to avoid scrutiny by Admiral Mikawa. Mikawa denied even ordering the civilians to be moved, let alone ordering them to be "dispose[d] of." The probability is that Mikawa was being truthful, if the order as related by Chief Ichinose is any indication. The movements of the *Akikaze* were ordered by Base Air Force. The orders concerning the civilians, first to transport them, then to "dispose of" them, are separate from the movement orders to the *Akikaze*. They may not have required both Mikawa's and Onishi's signatures for coding.

But if they did, it explains why the order was sent by courier to the *Akikaze* – because they could not get Mikawa to sign off on such an order.

This would be consistent with what is known about Mikawa Gunichi. If Mikawa was guilty of ordering the *Akikaze* Massacre, it would not only be the only war crime of which he was guilty, but the only war crime he was even accused of committing. Mikawa was a veteran admiral, with a reputation for being aggressive but also being thoughtful and careful – his victory at Savo Island being one example of both. Mikawa was soft-spoken, known for being concerned about the welfare of those under his command, and respected by his Allied adversaries. In an Imperial Japanese military with far more than its share of rapists, sadists, and thugs, Mikawa was one of the good guys. Ordering the *Akikaze* Massacre would be highly out-of-character for him. That is not to say Admiral Mikawa was not responsible for the massacre. People under his command committed the massacre. As their commanding officer, he bears responsibility. But that is a separate issue from whether he ordered it. More than likely, he did not.

Admiral Onishi is another matter. Chief Petty Officer Ichinose's statements implicate Onishi in ordering at least the movement of the civilians. But there may have been other parties at play here. The relatively shallow stream of conversation between Sabe and Kuroki contained one more piece of gold: "Sabe further confided to Kuroki that when he went to report to the 8th Fleet Headquarters, 'he sensed that the act had been taken in accordance with the opinion of Commander Ando.'"[30]

The reference here is to one Commander Ando Kenei, 8th Fleet Headquarters gunnery staff officer since July 1942. One of his duties as gunnery officer was handling prisoners of war. Ando had authority to send them wherever he wanted, but he usually just turned them over to the 8th Base Force Headquarters. Ando controlled supply operations by ships from Rabaul to the combat areas, so he had some authority over the *Akikaze*.[31] Kuroki later described Ando as "a highly nervous person. He was a very thoughtful person, but he often did things on his own initiative. The operations at that time being violent and dangerous, he became very nervous. Whenever I met him, he generally upbraided me and issued illogical orders."[32]

Admiral Mikawa had this to say about Ando:

> In regard to the possibility that Staff Officer Ando, who handled civil administration in my headquarters, might have arbitrarily and without my permission caused this incident, I doubt very much that the said staff officer carried out such an incident arbitrarily, since he was well aware that my policy was to protect carefully the human element in this area, especially the German missionaries, from the standpoint of civil administration. However, this officer had a quick mind and could be called a rash person and, according to the nature of the affair, it seemed that he often did things without first speaking to the Chief of Staff, so I always warned him about such a characteristic. I suppose the other staff officers who

worked side by side with this officer every day must know even more about his daily working habits and his nature.[33]

This Commander Ando seems to have been rather famous in the Southeast Area Fleet. In support of Admiral Mikawa, Admiral Kusaka testified:

> [...] I wish to repeat that it is impossible to believe that Mikawa issued the order. It is my opinion that, because it was such a busy time, one of his subordinates who held extremist views and who was directly concerned with the handling of prisoners of war and foreign nationals took matters into his own hands without orders from Mikawa and did this infamous deed. Such incidents are extremely regrettable from the standpoint of military discipline. They constitute very rare examples, but it cannot be said that they did not occur. [...]
>
> [...I]f a certain staff officer of the 8th Fleet wanted to send such a message to the captain of the *Akikaze*, I think he could have done it. If that had been the case, I think the captain of the *Akikaze* probably obtained the impression that the order was issued after approval was given by Mikawa and Onishi. However, such action on the part of a staff officer is a serious violation of the Japanese Naval Regulations.[34]

Tanaka Yuki's statements notwithstanding, the *Akikaze* was part of Base Air Force. She certainly received occasional missions from 8th Fleet, but mostly when it did not conflict with her duties for Base Air Force. Her March 1943 mission in making the rounds from Rabaul to Kavieng, Wewak, Manus, back to Kavieng, and then back to Rabaul was a mission delivering supplies to 11th Air Fleet bases in these locales. The naval security for these bases – 2nd Special Base Force in Wewak; 8th Base Force in Rabaul, Kavieng, and Manus – was under the command of 8th Fleet, which was itself under the commander of Base Air Force. This was why 2nd Special Base Force complained to 8th Fleet about the civilians on Kairiru: that was the chain of command. It's not clear if 8th Fleet passed on 2nd Special Base Force's concerns to Base Air Force, but in terms of the civilians' fate it probably would not have mattered. Based on his reputation, Vice Admiral Kusaka was little more likely to order a war crime than Vice Admiral Mikawa was.

But the *Akikaze*'s mission would take her to Wewak, close to where the civilians were being held on Kairiru. It would not have taken much to divert the *Akikaze* to Kairiru, as it would not interfere with her duties for Base Air Force; moreover, Manus was, to a degree, on the way back to Kavieng. This was a chance to deal with the civilians by piggybacking it on the *Akikaze*'s existing mission for Base Air Force.

The complaints from Admiral Kamata and the 2nd Special Base Force had reached Admirals Mikawa and Onishi. Mikawa was not doing anything about it, which, he admitted, irked his staff. Onishi was likely one of those irked, as was Lieutenant Kami.

Moreover, the Tokkeitai was also probably involved, anxious to tie up this proverbial loose end before the 6th Field Kempeitai arrived in Rabaul to take charge of security. The two agencies were not exactly friends. For that matter, neither were the two services; the Imperial Navy and Army hated each other almost as much as they hated the Allies. If these missionaries were in Vunapope when the 6th Field Kempeitai arrived, they could reveal that the Tokkeitai had not secured them for almost three months of the Japanese occupation. The Tokkeitai may not have wanted to deal with such uncomfortable questions.[35]

The Tokkeitai preferred to deal with other matters. Like extortion. Take, for instance, the Japanese-occupied island of Borneo. Starting in October 1943, the Tokkeitai began what it described as an "investigation into an "active 'anti-Japanese' organization." The organization was reported to consist of rich Chinese merchants, indigenous rulers ... everyone with substantial sums of money.[36] That was, of course, just a coincidence.

So began a reign of terror against the people of Borneo. Two different campaigns to eradicate this "active 'anti-Japanese' organization" resulted in the executions of some 1,500 people, including the Sultan of Pontianak and his two sons, whom the Japanese publicly beheaded. After each execution, the Tokkeitai appropriated the victim's cash and businesses.[37] The Imperial Navy officer in charge who gave the go-ahead to the Tokkeitai for these crush-for-cash campaigns? Admiral Kamata. Postwar, Kamata was tried by a Dutch military tribunal for these and other crimes, convicted, and executed.

With that last piece of personnel information in line, Divine Word Father Wiltgen, who has done more than anyone to uncover the *Akikaze* Massacre, developed a hypothesis as to what happened:

> At dawn on March 17th (if not earlier), the airmen were captured on the coast near the mouth of the Sepik River. News of this was immediately sent by telegraph to the 2nd Special Base Force Headquarters at Wewak where the exchange of letters between the Vokeo airmen and the Kairiru missionaries was already known. Rear Admiral Kamata and his staff at Wewak, already suspicious of the missionaries, would naturally surmise that the missionaries had counseled and organized the escape. Unable to punish the missionaries of Kairiru directly because they had already sailed off to Rabaul, Kamata wired the news of the captured American airmen to Staff Officer Ando at Rabaul and implied that this might be sufficient proof of complicity to warrant death for the missionaries. The amount of time which elapsed for the Murik-Wewak-Rabaul communications was hardly half an hour.
>
> In order to keep the execution request as secret as possible, it was not sent telegraphically from Rabaul to the *Akikaze* or even to Kavieng, but instead as sealed orders by seaplane to Kavieng where the *Akikaze* had been instructed to await an important communication from the 8th Fleet Headquarters. The *Akikaze* lay drifting off Kavieng with its engines turned off from 8:30 that morning, March 17th until 10:13, taking on no passengers and performing

no other duty, but only awaiting the sealed orders from Rabaul. When the seaplane finally arrived, a liaison boat from shore got the sealed orders from the seaplane and transferred them to the captain of the *Akikaze*. Capt. Sabe read Ando's request, the *Akikaze* left Kavieng, and then preparations for the executions got under way.[38]

While impossible to prove, this scenario seems eminently reasonable, if perhaps understated. Admiral Kamata browbeat Commander Ando into issuing the order. Knowing his superiors would never tolerate such an order, Ando was forced to send it by courier. The orders included admonitions against sending a notice by radio or wireless that the orders were carried out, instead to report in person to 8th Fleet headquarters. The injunctions on mentioning the murders were, again, to keep the news from Mikawa. For a while, at least. Mikawa would eventually find out. Kami told him and Onishi together, in part to give Onishi some cover for knowing about it, but Kami told them too late for Mikawa to do anything about it, including launch a serious investigation. Mikawa was not happy about this, as reported by Father Wiltgen:

Senior Staff Officer Kami was a man of intelligence and very fine character, Mikawa said. If the execution order had been issued by the 8th Fleet and had gone through the proper channels then, Mikawa said, "Staff Officer Kami should have, by all means, reported the *Akikaze* captain's and another officer's story to me either that night or early the next morning." But Kami did not report this until after March 25th. This fact, Mikawa stated, and also the fact "that the *Akikaze*'s captain had not come to me or to the chief of staff either before or after the incident indicates, I believe, that there was some wrong involved in the incident."[39]

This does bring up the probability that Kami was involved as well, which makes sense as the final report was made to him.

Like so many other war crimes, the *Akikaze* Massacre went unpunished. Lieutenant Commander Sabe and Sublieutenant Terada were later killed during the Pacific War. Admirals Mikawa and Onishi were tried and acquitted on directed verdicts. It was not quite as simple as the evidence, however. There were serious jurisdictional issues – no Australians were victims of this massacre. Germans and Americans were, but the Germans were in no position to prosecute the matter. On July 18, 1947, all the evidence was turned over to the US government, who appears to have taken no further action.[40] The vast majority of the victims of the *Akikaze* Massacre were German citizens. Before the end of the European War, the German Reich was at best indifferent to the plight of these missionaries and seems to have been completely uninterested in what happened to them. After the end of the European War, there was no German government to prosecute the case on behalf of the missionaries. That was the primary jurisdictional issue with the *Akikaze* Massacre case: who had the jurisdiction to pursue it? That seems like semantics, however. Legal cover to justify doing nothing. The US government was the last hope for prosecuting the case because a few of the missionaries were American citizens. But the US was uninterested in it as well. Maybe US investigators were just overwhelmed with the sheer volume of Japanese war crimes against American citizens.

The sad result was that Bishop Lörks, the missionaries, the lay staff, and the other civilians thus had no one to speak for them when they were no longer able to speak for themselves. As a consequence, the *Akikaze* Massacre has been largely forgotten.

NOTES

Prologue

1 Mary Taylor Huber, *The Bishop's Progress: A Historical Ethnography of Catholic Missionary Experience on the Sepik Frontier* (Washington, DC, and London: Smithsonian Institution Press, 1988), 104. Subsequently, one of Josef Lörks' admiring clergy called himself, "A servant of this servant of the servants of God."

2 Huber, *Bishop's Progress*, 100–1.

3 Huber, *Bishop's Progress*, 100–1.

4 Mark Felton, *Slaughter at Sea: The Story of Japan's Naval War Crimes* (Barnsley, UK: Pen & Sword, 2007), 1580.

5 The Roman Catholic Vicariate of Central New Guinea is now the Diocese of Wewak. David M. Cheney, "Diocese of Wewak," *The Hierarchy of the Catholic Church: Current and historical information about its bishops and dioceses* (https://www.catholic-hierarchy.org).

6 When some of the tribes such as the Herero and the Nama rebelled against the predations of German rule in 1904, the German army drove them out into the desert and sealed off their routes back. Trapped in the desert, thousands of Herero and Nama – the vast majority of both tribes – died of thirst. The few survivors who made it out or avoided it were confined to concentration camps, used as slave labor, and just plain executed. Today, the Kaiserreich's treatment of the Herero and the Nama is considered genocide. If any of these actions by a German Reich sounds vaguely familiar, it should: some historians call it a template for the *Endlösung der Judenfrage* and *Generalplan Ost* by Nazi Germany that followed some three decades later.

7 In short, because central New Guinea was a vicariate and not yet a diocese, the head of the vicariate was a Vicar Apostolic, who is a titular bishop.

8 Huber, *Bishop's Progress*, 102.

9 Huber, *Bishop's Progress*, 101.

10 Except where otherwise noted, the account of the events on the *Akikaze* comes from Ralph M. Wiltgen, "The Death of Bishop Loerks and his companions, Part I: The Execution," *Verbum SVD* 6:4 (1964), 363–97; and Ralph M. Wiltgen: "The Death of Bishop Loerks and his companions, Part II: The Trial," *Verbum SVD* 7:1 (1965), 14–44. Many thanks to archivist Andrew Rea and the Chicago Province of the Society of the Divine Word for providing a copy of Father Wiltgen's work, which is otherwise extremely difficult to find.

11 *Kiyosumi Maru* (which mistakenly lists the destroyer *Akizuki* as an escort) and *Yugumo* TROMs; Douglas MacArthur, *Reports of General MacArthur Volume II – Part I: Japanese Operations In The Southwest Pacific Area* (Washington, DC: Government Printing Office, 1966, 1994 reprint), 188–89; Peter J. Dean, *MacArthur's Coalition: US and Australian Operations in the Southwest Pacific Area, 1942–1945* (Lawrence: University of Kansas Press, 2018). Huber, *Bishop's Progress*, 131; Gordon L. Rottman, *Japanese Army in World War II: The South Pacific and New Guinea, 1942–43* (Oxford and New York: Osprey, 2005), Kindle edition, 1656; Wiltgen, "Part I: The Execution," 363; Wiltgen: "Part II: The Trial," 22. While most historians identify the naval infantry unit as the "2nd Special Naval Base Force" or "2nd Special Base Force," Leland Ness, in his respected work *Rikugun: Guide to Japanese Ground Forces 1937–1945, Volume I: Tactical Organization of Imperial Japanese Army & Navy Ground Forces* (Solihull, UK: Helion, 2014), Kindle edition, 6412, Table 8.3, does not, instead identifying two units called the "2nd Base Force," one formed prewar on Formosa and deactivated in March 1942, and a second one formed in November 1942 for Wewak. It is the latter that is called the "2nd Special Naval Base Force" in most histories. The difference is not entirely academic, as a "Base Force" and a "Special Base Force" had slightly different functions. It is

not clear how or even if those differences are applicable here. It should be pointed out that the 8th Special Base Force (Ness, *Rikugun, I*, 6381) was formed in Rabaul in February 1942, but Ness lists it in multiple charts (*Rikugun, I*, 6386, 6412) as the 8th Base Force. The Japanese naval forces in the Pacific were reorganized on April 10, 1942, and it may be that the 2nd and 8th Special Base Forces were redesignated at that time.

12   There were so many Catholic priests imprisoned at Dachau Concentration Camp near Munich that the Nazis gave them their own barracks.

13   Who exactly this "third country" was the Japanese never specified. Presumably, it was the Vatican.

14   Yuki Tanaka, *Hidden Horrors: Japanese War Crimes in World War II*, 2nd ed. (Lanham, Boulder, New York, London: Rowman & Littlefield, 2018), Kindle edition, 4641–49.

15   Wiltgen, "Part I: The Execution," 364.

16   Huber, *Bishop's Progress*, 131, 228–29.

17   Wiltgen, "Part I: The Execution," 364–66.

18   Wiltgen, "Part I: The Execution," 368.

19   Wiltgen, "Part I: The Execution," 368–69.

20   Wiltgen, "Part I: The Execution," 367.

21   The Vicariate Apostolic of Eastern New Guinea is now the Archdiocese of Madang. Cheney, "Archdiocese of Madang," *Hierarchy of the Catholic Church* (https://www.catholic-hierarchy.org); "Papua New Guinea," *Hagiography Circle: An Online Resource on Contemporary Hagiography* (http://newsaints.faithweb.com/index .htm); "History," *Society of the Divine Word: Chicago Province* (https://www.divineword.org/history/).

22   "Papua New Guinea," *Hagiography Circle* (http://newsaints.faithweb.com/index.htm).

23   Wiltgen, "Part I: The Execution," 371.

24   But, the location of the Catholic mission is pronounced "boot."

25   Wiltgen, "Part I: The Execution," 370. Father Wiltgen mistakenly lists McMurria's rank as captain.

26   Wiltgen, "Part I: The Execution," 370–71. While it is often reported that Lieutenant McMurria requested the missionaries' help in the escape of him and his remaining crew, apart from the ambiguous request for "other supplies" mentioned by Father Wiltgen, there is no indication here that McMurria requested such assistance.

27   Wiltgen, "Part I: The Execution," 370–71.

28   Wiltgen, "Part I: The Execution," 371. The general contents of the note come from Bruce Gamble, *Target: Rabaul: The Allied Siege of Japan's Most Infamous Stronghold, March 1943–August 1945* (Minneapolis, MN: Zenith Press, 2014), 48.

29   Wiltgen, "Part I: The Execution," 371.

30   Wiltgen, "Part I: The Execution," 377–78; Tanaka, *Hidden Horrors*, 4711. The Imperial Japanese Navy had a rank of "sublieutenant" which was the equivalent of the US Navy's "lieutenant junior grade."

31   Wiltgen, "Part I: The Execution," 377–78. Wiltgen renders the surname of the commander of Destroyer Division 34 as "Amagaya." Elsewhere, including *The Imperial Japanese Navy Page* (www.combinedfleet.com), it is rendered as "Amaya" (see e.g. *Soya* TROM).

32   Wiltgen, "Part I: The Execution," 379–80. Theo Aerts (ed.), *The Martyrs of Papua New Guinea: 333 Missionary Lives Lost During World War II* (Port Moresby: University of Papua New Guinea Press and Bookshop, 2009), 124, 127; G.W.L. Townsend, *District Officer: From untamed New Guinea to Lake Success, 1921–46* (Sydney: Pacific Publications, 1968), 225n; Gamble, *Target: Rabaul*, 48. Just how many civilians were picked up from Kairiru and Manus remains unclear.

33   Wiltgen, "Part I: The Execution," 377, 380–81. Lawrence Molom, one of the schoolchildren who was watching these events, later said, "The top Japanese officer waiting for [Bishop Lörks] on the shore then ordered a big and burly soldier to go and hurry him up." The identification here of "[t]he top Japanese officer" as Lieutenant Commander Yagura is a deduction based on the fact that he was, in fact, the top Japanese officer on site and that his orders from Admiral Kamata included "officially transferr[ing the missionaries] from the charge of the 2nd Special Base Force to the charge of the captain of the *Akikaze*."

34   Tanaka, *Hidden Horrors*, 4652; Wiltgen, "Part I: The Execution," 377, 381–82.

35   Tanaka, *Hidden Horrors*, 4652; Wiltgen, "Part I: The Execution," 377, 381–82.

36   Wiltgen, "Part I: The Execution," 381–82.

37   Wiltgen, "Part I: The Execution," 382–84.

38   Wiltgen, "Part I: The Execution," 382.

39   Wiltgen, "Part I: The Execution," 368–69. The Liebenzell Mission is now known as the Evangelical Church of Manus. It is under the jurisdiction of the American branch of the Liebenzell Mission. Aerts, *Martyrs of Papua New Guinea*, 124.

40   Wiltgen, "Part I: The Execution," 383–84.

41 Wiltgen, "Part I: The Execution," 383–84.

42 Aerts, *Martyrs*, 124, 127; Townsend, *District Officer*, 225n; Gamble, *Target: Rabaul*, 48.

43 Wiltgen, "Part I: The Execution," 384; Townsend, *District Officer*, 225n. "Chamorra" is normally a term for a female native of Guam.

44 Wiltgen, "Part I: The Execution," 382.

45 Aerts, *Martyrs*, 127.

46 Aerts, *Martyrs*, 127–28; Wiltgen, "Part I: The Execution," 385.

47 Wiltgen, "Part I: The Execution," 386, 391.

48 Wiltgen, "Part I: The Execution," 386, 391.

49 Wiltgen, "Part I: The Execution," 387, 391; Wiltgen, "Part II: The Trial," 40; Aerts, *Martyrs*, 128.

50 At the war crimes tribunal after the war, Sublieutenant Kai testified, "I have never interrogated [the missionaries from Kairiru]." Wiltgen, "Part II: The Trial," 29.

51 Wiltgen, "Part I: The Execution," 391. Father Wiltgen says Bishop Lörks "was probably the victim meant by (Lieutenant) Takahashi's statement: 'The missionary was called out first.' On an earlier occasion Takahashi had referred to Bishop Loerks as 'the missionary.'"

52 It is not clear where the questioning took place. Claims that it took place on the bridge (see, e.g., Tanaka, *Hidden Horrors*, 4705) seem to be incorrect given Lieutenant Takahashi's testimony that he watched the proceedings from the bridge. More likely the questioning took place in the corridor beneath the bridge.

53 Wiltgen, "Part I: The Execution," 388.

54 Wiltgen, "Part I: The Execution," 388.

55 Chief Petty Officer Oimoto Yoshiji, the gun captain of the third gun, testified: "I saw Lt. (jg) Terada aim his (Model 38) rifle at the missionary (Lörks). There were no obstructions or persons between the two. I heard the sound of the rifle and saw the victim move and his blood flow. I saw someone cut the rope by which the victim had been hanging and watched the body fall into the sea." Wiltgen, "Part I: The Execution," 389.

Chapter 1

1 USS *Trigger Report of Fourth War Patrol* ("*Trigger* Report"), 1.

2 *Trigger* Report, 1.

3 *Trigger* Report, 2.

4 *Trigger* Report, 2–3.

5 *Trigger* Report, 3.

6 *Trigger* Report, 3–4. During World War II, at least two US submarines, the *Tang* and the *Tullibee*, were sunk by their own torpedoes making circular runs, while it is now believed that her own torpedo making a circular run contributed to the sinking of a third US submarine, the *Grunion*. (See generally Peter F. Stevens, *Fatal Dive: Solving the World War II Mystery of the USS* Grunion (Washington, DC: Regnery, 2012).) At least one US Navy ship, the destroyer *Porter*, was sunk by a circular torpedo run. The Imperial Japanese Navy, the Royal Navy, and the *Kriegsmarine* do not appear to have had similar issues with their torpedoes making circular runs, suggesting another major design flaw in US torpedoes.

7 *Trigger* Report, 4.

8 *Trigger* Report, 4.

9 The account of the *Trigger*'s March 15 attacks comes from *Trigger* Report, 5–6.

10 Put simply, a "gyro angle" is the difference between the direction in which the launching torpedo tube is pointing and the direction in which the torpedo is supposed to travel. When the torpedo is launched, the gyro will turn the torpedo 45 degrees. The gyro is necessary because submarines and surface ships with fixed torpedo tubes cannot always face in precisely the direction in which they want the torpedo to travel.

11 *Trigger* Report, 6–7.

12 *Trigger* Report, 7–8; *Choan Maru No. 2 Go* TROM.

13 Mark E. Stille, *The Imperial Japanese Navy in the Pacific War* (Oxford: Osprey, 2014), Kindle edition, 4201–8; *Sawakaze* TROM.

14 Literally. Yamamoto was an avid and skilled poker player.

15 *Akikaze* and *Tachikaze* TROMs.

16 *Hakaze* TROM.

17 *Akikaze* TROM.

18 The *Akikaze*'s wartime exploits, if you could call them that, come from the *Akikaze* TROM.

19 *Yakaze* TROM; Stille, *Imperial Japanese Navy*, 4208.

20 *Akikaze*, *Mogamigawa Maru*, and *Kinryu Maru* TROMs.

21 United States Strategic Bombing Survey, *The War Against Japanese Transportation, 1941–45* (Washington, DC: Transportation Division, United States Strategic Bombing Survey, 1947), 2; David C. Evans and Mark Peattie, *Kaigun: Strategy, Tactics, and Technology in the Imperial Japanese Navy 1887–1941* (Annapolis: Naval Institute Press, 1997), 392.

22 USSBS, *The War Against Japanese Transportation, 1941–45*, 48.

23 Wiltgen, "Part II: The Trial," 29–30.

24 Although, to be sure, Japanese submarines had no issues attacking defenseless hospital ships. Ask the *Centaur* for details.

25 Rather confusingly for some people, "Shortland" is both the name for an island group and that island group's dominant island.

26 Thomas Alexander Hughes, *Admiral Bill Halsey: A Naval Life* (Cambridge, MA: Harvard University Press, 2016), Kindle edition, 3431.

27 Hughes, *Admiral Bill Halsey*, 3431–47.

28 John B. Lundstrom, *The First Team and the Guadalcanal Campaign: Naval Fighter Combat from August to November 1942* (Annapolis, MD: Naval Institute Press, 1984), Kindle edition, 12150.

29 Williamson Murray and Allan R. Millett, *A War to be Won: Fighting the Second World War* (Cambridge, MA; London: Belknap Press of Harvard University Press, 2000), 591.

30 Richard B. Frank, *Guadalcanal: The Definitive Account of the Landmark Battle* (New York: Penguin, 1992), 319; Lundstrom, *First Team*, 8370.

31 Morison, *History of United States Naval Operations in World War II, Vol V: The Struggle for Guadalcanal August 1942–February 1943* (Edison, NJ: Castle, 1949), 244; Stephen Howarth, *The Fighting Ships of the Rising Sun: The Drama of the Imperial Japanese Navy 1895–1945* (New York: Atheneum, 1983), 313.

32 Calhoun, *Tin Can Sailor*, 1686.

33 It was the Imperial Japanese Navy's version of the ancient maxim of "divide and conquer," though while most militaries sought to divide their enemies' forces, the Japanese much preferred to divide their own.

34 Jonathan Parshall, "Akizuki class," *Imperial Japanese Navy Page* (www.combinedfleet.com).

35 Allyn Nevitt, "*Akizuki* class notes," *Imperial Japanese Navy Page* (www.combinedfleet.com).

36 Tanaka, "Struggle for Guadalcanal," 206–7.

37 Tameichi Hara, Fred Saito, and Roger Pineau, *Japanese Destroyer Captain: Pearl Harbor, Guadalcanal, Midway – The Great Naval Battles as Seen Through Japanese Eyes* (Annapolis: Naval Institute Press, 1967), Kindle edition, 154; Dennis Letourneau and Roger Letourneau, *Operation KE: The Cactus Air Force and the Japanese Withdrawal From Guadalcanal* (Annapolis: Naval Institute Press, 2012), Kindle edition, 8–9.

38 Steven Bullard (trans.), *Japanese Army Operations in the South Pacific Area: New Britain and Papua Campaigns, 1942–43* (Canberra: Australian War Memorial, 2007), vi.

39 *Junyo* TROM.

40 *Tenryu* and *Gokoku Maru* TROMs; Matome Ugaki, Donald M. Goldstein, and Katherine V. Dillon (ed.), *Fading Victory: The Diary of Admiral Matome Ugaki* (Pittsburgh: University of Pittsburgh Press, 1991), 308.

41 Ballalai; Balalai; Ballelei; Ballalae; Balalae; Ballali. According to the *Pacific Wrecks* website, "The island has at least five different spellings, all pronounced 'Bal-a-lai.'" "Broken Wings of Ballale: The Tragic Salvage History of the Last Undisturbed World War II Airfield," *Pacific Wrecks* (www.pacificwrecks.com).

42 There is apparently considerable debate as to whether the footpath through the Owen Stanley Mountains via the village of Kokoda is properly called "Kokoda Trail" or "Kokoda Track." Karl James, "The Kokoda 'Track' or 'Trail'?," *Australian War Memorial* (www.awm.gov.au).

43 Vunakanau was also called "Rabaul West," "West Airfield," "Rabaul Upper Airfield" or "Rabaul No. 2" by the Japanese. "Vunakanau Airfield (Rabaul West, West Airfield, Rabaul Upper, Rabaul No. 2) ENB PNG," *Pacific Wrecks* (www.pacificwrecks.com).

44 Lakunai was also called "Lakunai Airfield," "Lakunai Drome," "Lakunai Airdrome," "East Airfield," "*Rabinjikku* (Rabaul Lower)" or "Rabaul No. 1." "Lakunai Airfield (Rabaul East, East Airfield, Rabaul No. 1) East New Britain Province PNG," *Pacific Wrecks* (www.pacificwrecks.com).

45 Volcanic ash is different from what we normally think of as "ash," meaning the burnt aftermath of a fire. Volcanic ash is actually pulverized rock. It is very fine and is thus difficult to filter out. It is also jagged-edged. As a result, volcanic ash can be very damaging, especially to the engines and control surfaces of aircraft.

46 Ugaki, Goldstein, and Dillon, *Fading Victory*, 277.

47 The Wau airfield consisted of a single rough 3,100-foot runway with a 10 percent slope heading directly for a mountain, requiring aircraft to approach from the northeast and land uphill, with no mulligans on the landing, and to take off downhill. Craven and Cate, *Army Air Forces*, 136.

48   *Yoshinogawa Maru* TROM. Her TROM has the escort as the *PB-39* but the *PB-39*'s TROM does not mention it, though the TROMs of smaller combatants and noncombatants were often incomplete. Time is from *Nautilus* Report, 7.

49   Multiple sources report that it was a Japanese seaplane that found and attacked the submarine. However, Cressman (*Official Chronology*) is very specific that the aircraft came from the 582 Air Group. The re-designated 2nd Air Group, the 582 was a mixed group of both Zero fighters and Aichi Type 99 (Val) carrier bombers. If the aircraft came from the 582, it was most likely a Type 99 carrier bomber and not a seaplane.

50   Charles R. Hinman, "The Loss of USS *Argonaut* (SS-166)," *On Eternal Patrol* (http://www.oneternalpatrol.com /uss-argonaut-166-loss.html).

51   *PB-1* TROM; Cressman, *Official Chronology*.

52   *Toa Maru* TROM.

53   *W-17* TROM.

54   *Kimposan Maru* TROM.

55   *Soya* TROM. The particulars of this attack are rather shaky in their documentation. The *Soya* mistakenly dated the attack as January 28. Additionally, the TROM erroneously lists the skipper of the *Greenling* as Lieutenant Commander James D. Grant. Grant took over at the beginning of the *Greenling*'s next war patrol in February 1943. Lieutenant Commander Henry C. Bruton commanded the *Greenling* during this war patrol and signed her report upon its completion. For his part, Bruton in his patrol report says he fired only one torpedo, which ran under the target and did not explode. See *Greenling*, Patrol Report, 13.

56   *Senzan Maru* TROM; Eric Hammel, *Air War Pacific Chronology: America's Air War Against Japan in East Asia and the Pacific 1941–1945* (Pacifica, CA: Pacifica Military History, 1998), Kindle edition, 4267.

57   *Kitakami, Oi, Sanuki Maru* and *Sagara Maru* TROMs. The sister ships *Kitakami* and *Oi* are best known for their temporary conversion to what the Japanese called "torpedo cruisers" and what Imperial Japanese Navy historian Jonathan Parshall called "torpedo boats on steroids (for want of a better designation)."

58   *Junyo* TROM; Gamble, *Target: Rabaul*, 4; "Wewak Airfield (Wirui, Wewak Central)," *Pacific Wrecks* (www.pacificwrecks.com).

59   Gamble, *Target: Rabaul*, 6; "B-24D-20-CO Liberator Serial Number 41-24101," *Pacific Wrecks* (www.pacificwrecks.com).

60   *Junyo* TROM.

61   *Gokoku Maru* TROM.

62   *Yasukuni, Hakozaki,* and *Aratama Maru* TROMs; *Hatsuyuki* TROM.

63   *Aratama, Shinkyo,* and *Juzan Maru* TROMs.

64   missing text

65   *Wahoo* Report, 3; *Harusame* TROM; Blair, *Silent Victory*, 383; Theodore Roscoe, *United States Submarine Operations in World War II* (Annapolis: Naval Institute Press, 1949) 205–6; David Jones and Peter Nunan, *U.S. Subs Down Under: Brisbane 1942–1945* (Annapolis: Naval Institute Press, 2005), 96–97.

66   *Kenkon Maru* TROM.

67   The *Nautilus* had become such a nuisance to *Kido Butai* that the destroyer *Arashi* was detached to attack the submarine, thereby holding the *Nautilus* down and preventing the submarine from pursuing as *Kido Butai* moved on. When this was completed, the *Arashi* sped on to catch up with *Kido Butai*. US Navy carrier dive bombers spotted the *Arashi* and the very large wake caused by her high speed. The Americans followed the *Arashi* to *Kido Butai*.

68   *Akizuki* TROM.

69   *Akitsushima* and *Hakaze* TROMs.

70   *Nichiun Maru* TROM.

71   *Keiyo Maru* TROM.

72   *Keiyo Maru* TROM.

73   Howard, "The Oil Slick In Blackett Strait."

74   *Ch-18* TROM.

75   *Ch-18* TROM.

76   *Ch-18* TROM.

77   *Suruga Maru* TROM.

78   Cressman, *Official Chronology*, "*Koshin Maru* Class Auxiliary Transport," *Imperial Japanese Navy Page* (www.combinedfleet.com).

79   *Oshio* TROM.

80   *Kitakami, Oi, Sanuki Maru* and *Sagara Maru* TROMs.

81   *Yasukuni, Ukishima* and *Kiyokawa Maru* TROMs; *Isonami, Akigumo,* and *Nagatsuki* TROMs. The *Ukishima Maru* TROM does add this comment: "Note one source shows UKISHIMA MARU arriving [in] Palau as early as 5 February and it is possible the ship was detached and steamed ahead."

82   *Aratama, Shinkyo,* and *Juzan Maru* TROMs.

83   The Type 0 Reconnaissance Seaplane must not be confused with the Type 0 Observation Seaplane.

84   *Gokoku Maru* TROM.

85   *Kirikawa Maru* TROM. According to *Imperial Japanese Navy Page,* the *Kirikawa Maru* was sunk "probably with all hands." Which would be curious by itself. It would mean either the *Kirikawa Maru* was scuttled by friendly ships with men still on board, or all the men aboard the *Kirikawa Maru* were killed by the air attack but the ship was left afloat.

86   *W-22* TROM. *W-22* seems to have been slightly east or southeast of the position of the air attack, suggesting she was left behind. *Ch-26* is not mentioned in connection with this submarine attack.

87   *W-22* TROM.

88   *W-22* TROM.

89   McAulay, *The Battle of the Bismarck Sea 3 March 1943* (Maryborough, Qld.: Banner Books, 2008), Kindle edition, 942.

90   Lawrence J. Hickey, *Ken's Men Against the Empire: The Illustrated History of the 43rd Bombardment Group During World War II, Volume I: Prewar to October 1943 The B-17 Era* (Boulder, CO: International Historical Research Associates, 2016), 133.

91   Hickey, *Ken's Men,* 133; McAulay, *Bismarck Sea,* 1087. The Japanese Army Air Force and Naval Air Force were organized in such fashions that were not directly analogous to Western air forces, or, in fact, to each other, and trying to present their activities, particularly those of the Army Air Force, in a readable fashion for the English-speaking reader can be a challenge. At the start of the Pacific War, the Japanese Naval Air Force's *kokutai* often operated using the name of their home base. Thus, the home base of the Takao Air Group was at Takao, on Formosa, and the home base of the Tainan Air Group was at Tainan, also on Formosa. However, starting on October 1, 1942 and finishing on November 1, 1942, the Japanese Naval Air Force's *kokutai* designations were changed completely into a numeric code. There is a long-standing disagreement as to how that redesignation of the Japanese Naval Air Force units should be translated. It is instinct among Westerners, to use the example here of the 751 (the former Kanoya) Air Group, to reference it as the "751st Air Group." However, to consider these designations as ordinals appears to be inaccurate inasmuch as each digit in the new designation referred to a particular characteristic of the unit. To use the "751" example again, the "7" meant a land attack plane unit, the "5" meant its home base was in the Sasebo Naval District, and the "1" meant the unit was formerly a named unit. Since the Kanoya had been a mixed air group, the fighter component was spun off on November 1, 1942 as part of the 253 Air Group, the "2" denoting "single-engine carrier fighter" unit, the "5" again the Sasebo district, and the "3" again formerly a named unit (Mark Peattie, *Sunburst: The Rise of Japanese Naval Air Power, 1909–1941* (Annapolis: Naval Institute Press, 2013), 256). In short, the new numeric designation was not an ordinal but a code.

92   It was said that the pilots themselves removed the radios because they were so unreliable and went so far as to saw the Zero's wooden antenna off to gain an extra knot of speed (Davis, *Lightning Strike,* 3830). The fact that the antenna was wooden might help explain why their radios were so unreliable.

93   Samuel Eliot Morison, *History of United States Naval Operations in World War II, Vol VI: Breaking the Bismarcks Barrier 22 July 1942–1 May 1944* (Edison, NJ: Castle, 1950), 55–6; McAulay, *Bismarck Sea,* 1054.

94   McAulay, *Bismarck Sea,* 1444; *Kyokusei Maru* TROM.

95   John Prados, *Islands of Destiny: The Solomons Campaign and the Eclipse of the Rising Sun* (New York: NAL Caliber, 2012), Kindle edition, 255.

96   Gamble, *Fortress Rabaul,* 316.

97   *Kiriha Maru* TROM; Allyn Nevitt, "Who Sank the Triton?," *The Imperial Japanese Navy Page,* (www.combinedfleet.com).

98   Ronnie Day, *New Georgia: The Second Battle for the Solomons* (Bloomington, IN: Indiana University Press, 2016), Kindle edition, 947.

99   Vincent P. O'Hara, *The US Navy Against the Axis: Surface Combat 1941–1945* (Annapolis: Naval Institute Press, 2007), Kindle edition, 3723.

100 Hara, Saito, and Pineau, *Destroyer Captain,* 164.

101 Nevitt, "Who Sank the Triton?"

102 *Momoyama Maru* TROM; Hickey, *Ken's Men, I,* 153. Vernon J. Miller ("An Analysis of US Submarine Losses During World War II, Part V," *Warship* 46 (April 1988), 48–59, 58) suggests that the distant depth charging the

Trigger heard on March 15 was actually the air attack that fatally damaged the *Momoyama Maru*. This is highly unlikely, as that air attack took place on March 13, two days before the depth charging reported by the *Trigger*.

103 *Nagaura* TROM.
104 Wiltgen, "Part I: The Execution," 373.
105 *Ch-24* TROM.
106 *Momoha Maru* TROM.
107 *Nagaura* TROM.
108 *Ch-24* and *Tasmania Maru* TROMs.
109 *Ch-22* TROM.
110 *Ch-24* TROM; Roscoe, *Submarine Operations*, X.
111 *Tonei Maru* TROM.
112 Wiltgen, "Part I: The Execution," 367.
113 Wiltgen, "Part I: The Execution," 369.
114 Wiltgen, "Part I: The Execution," 366.
115 Wiltgen, "Part I: The Execution," 366.
116 *Aoba* TROM; Wiltgen, "Part I: The Execution," 373.
117 Wiltgen, "Part I: The Execution," 373.
118 Wiltgen, "Part I: The Execution," 373. Back in August 1942 at the start of the Guadalcanal Campaign, Admiral Mikawa had derided the 18th Cruiser Division, which had the old light cruisers *Tenryu* and *Tatsuta* and, sometimes, the *Yubari*, as "rabble." Loxton and Coulthard-Clark, *Shame*, 125. Mikawa was compelled to use the *Tenryu* and *Yubari* during his counterattack that resulted in the Battle of Savo Island, the biggest defeat for the US Navy in its history, in which the *Tenryu* in particular played a significant part.
119 Wiltgen, "Part I: The Execution," 373.
120 Wiltgen, "Part I: The Execution," 373; *Akikaze* TROM.
121 Wiltgen, "Part I: The Execution," 373, 375. Father Wiltgen mistakenly says the *Akikaze* arrived at Kairiru "on the morning of March 16th, Ash Wednesday." This is a typo. In 1943, Ash Wednesday was on March 10, as Father Wiltgen says on page 375.
122 Wiltgen, "Part I: The Execution," 375.
123 Wiltgen, "Part I: The Execution," 375. It should be pointed out that Father Wiltgen, a member of the Society of the Divine Word, is very even-handed in his account of the *Akikaze* Massacre. For instance, he takes no issue with the Japanese moving the missionaries from Kairiru because the Japanese wanted to build a base there. His issue is the Japanese murdering those missionaries for no apparent reason.
124 Wiltgen, "Part I: The Execution," 373, 375, 377.
125 Wiltgen, "Part I: The Execution," 377. She arrived at Simpson Harbor at 5:28am on March 3 and was back in Rabaul at 4:28pm on March 4 where she arrived on March 11 at about 9:30pm.
126 Nevitt, "Who Sank the Triton?"
127 Wiltgen, "Part I: The Execution," 377.
128 Wiltgen, "Part I: The Execution," 382.
129 Kai testified on the stand, "I do not know very much about the Christian religion." Wiltgen, "Part II: The Trial," 29.
130 Wiltgen, "Part I: The Execution," 376.
131 Tanaka, *Hidden Horrors*, 4670–77.
132 Wiltgen, "Part I: The Execution," 383.
133 Wiltgen, "Part I: The Execution," 384.
134 Wiltgen, "Part I: The Execution," 384–85.
135 Wiltgen, "Part I: The Execution," 385. Prologue notes that *Akikaze* left at 3:35pm (after starting engines.)
136 Wiltgen, "Part I: The Execution," 386.
137 Wiltgen, "Part I: The Execution," 386–87.
138 Wiltgen, "Part I: The Execution," 387.
139 *Hakaze* and *Tachikaze* TROMs; Wiltgen, "Part I: The Execution," 386–87, 392.
140 Wiltgen, "Part I: The Execution," 387.
141 Tanaka, *Hidden Horrors*, 5231, 5498.
142 Wiltgen, "Part I: The Execution," 387.
143 Wiltgen, "Part I: The Execution," 387.
144 Wiltgen, "Part I: The Execution," 388, 390; Tanaka, *Hidden Horrors*, 4698–707.
145 Wiltgen, "Part I: The Execution," 388.
146 Wiltgen, "Part I: The Execution," 388, 390.

147 Wiltgen, "Part I: The Execution," 389.

148 Wiltgen, "Part I: The Execution," 388; Tanaka, *Hidden Horrors*, 4707.

149 Wiltgen, "Part I: The Execution," 389–90.

150 Wiltgen, "Part I: The Execution," 389.

151 Wiltgen, "Part I: The Execution," 389.

152 Wiltgen, "Part I: The Execution," 389.

153 Wiltgen, "Part I: The Execution," 390.

154 Wiltgen, "Part I: The Execution," 390.

155 Wiltgen, "Part I: The Execution," 390.

156 Wiltgen, "Part I: The Execution," 390.

157 Aerts, *Martyrs*, 133; Wiltgen, "Part I: The Execution," 389–90.

158 Wiltgen, "Part I: The Execution," 391; Tanaka, *Hidden Horrors*, 4719.

159 Felton, *Slaughter at Sea*, 1580.

160 Wiltgen, "Part I: The Execution," 391.

161 Wiltgen, "Part I: The Execution," 391.

162 Wiltgen, "Part I: The Execution," 392. In fairness to what sounds at first glance to be a preposterous excuse, some investigators into the mystery of the merchant ship *Mary Celeste*, found abandoned and adrift but in seaworthy condition in the Atlantic off the Azores in December 1872, suggested that a rogue sea wave had swept the crew off the ship.

163 Wiltgen, "Part I: The Execution," 392.

164 Wiltgen, "Part I: The Execution," 392.

165 Wiltgen, "Part I: The Execution," 392. Kai mistakenly calls it the "8th Special Base Force."

Chapter 2

1 Gitta Sereny, *Albert Speer: His Battle with the Truth* (New York: Knopf, 1995), 267–68.

2 Samuel Eliot Morison, *The Two-Ocean War: A Short History of the United States Navy in the Second World War* (Boston; Toronto; London: Little, Brown, and Company, 1963), 35.

3 Eisenhower Diaries, March 10.

4 "Foreign Relations of the United States, The Conferences at Washington, 1941–1942, and Casablanca, 1943 Document 114," Office of the Historian, United States Department of State, https://history.state.gov/historicaldocuments/frus1941-43/d114.

5 "Foreign Relations of the United States, The Conferences at Washington, 1941–1942, and Casablanca, 1943 Document 114;" Frank, *Guadalcanal*, 7–8; Vice Admiral George Carroll Dyer, USN (Ret.), *The Amphibians Came to Conquer: The Story of Admiral Richmond Kelly Turner* (Washington, DC: U.S. Government Printing Office, 1971), 234, 239–40.

6 Frank, *Guadalcanal*, 6.

7 Brig Gen Samuel B. Griffith, USMC (ret.), *The Battle for Guadalcanal* (Toronto; New York; London; Sydney: Bantam, 1980), 5.

8 William Manchester, *American Caesar: Douglas MacArthur 1880–1964* (New York: Back Bay Books, 1978), Kindle edition, 5591.

9 Griffith, *Battle for Guadalcanal*, 9–10.

10 Dyer, *Amphibians*, 243.

11 Maurice Matloff and Edwin M. Snell, *United States Army in World War II: The War Department, Volume III:* "Strategic Planning for Coalition Warfare 1941–1942" (Washington: Office of the Chief of Military History, Department of the Army, 1953), 157.

12 Murray and Millett, *A War to be Won*, 2606.

13 Thomas B. Buell, *Master of Seapower: A Biography of Fleet Admiral Ernest J. King* (Annapolis: Naval Institute Press, 1980), Kindle edition, 4466.

14 Walter R. Borneman, *The Admirals: Nimitz, Halsey, Leahy, and King – The Five-Star Admirals Who Won the War at Sea* (New York; Boston; London: Little, Brown, and Company, 2012), 284.

15 John Toland, *The Rising Sun: The Decline and Fall of the Japanese Empire 1936–1945* (New York: Random House, 1970), Kindle edition, 7676; Frank, *Guadalcanal*, 33; James D. Hornfischer, *Neptune's Inferno: The US Navy at Guadalcanal* (New York: Bantam, 2011), Kindle edition, 497; Borneman, *Admirals*, 284.

16 Manchester, *American Caesar*, 5591; Buell, *Master of Seapower*, 3949.

17 Borneman, *Admirals*, 280.

18 Admiral Nimitz's first suggestion to head the South Pacific Command was Vice Admiral William S. Pye, whose main claim to fame was, in a meeting on December 6, 1941, loudly declaring, "The Japanese will not go to war with the United States. We are too big, too powerful, and too strong." Gordon Prange, *At Dawn We Slept: The Untold Story of Pearl Harbor* (New York: Penguin, 1981), 470.

19 Dyer, *Amphibians*, 252–53.

20 William Tuohy, *America's Fighting Admirals: Winning the War at Sea in World War II* (St. Paul, MN: Zenith Press, 2007), Kindle edition, 1156–64.

21 Prados, *Islands of Destiny*, 36.

22 In the designation "JN-25," "JN" means "Japanese Navy" and "25" references this being the 25th such code identified.

23 Lundstrom, *Black Shoe*, 313.

24 Frank, *Guadalcanal*, 34.

25 Frank, *Guadalcanal*, 35.

26 Prados, *Combined Fleet Decoded*, 235–36.

27 Dean, *MacArthur's Coalition*, 2439, 1844–64.

28 Quote is from Dean, *MacArthur's Coalition*, 2095; Alan Rems, *South Pacific Cauldron: World War II's Great Forgotten Battlegrounds* (Annapolis: Naval Institute Press, 2014), Kindle edition, 550–54.

29 Hammel, *Air War Pacific Chronology*, 2151.

30 Hammel, *Air War Pacific Chronology*, 2151–71.

31 Twining, *No Bended Knee*, 88.

32 Johnson, *Pacific Campaign*, 200.

33 Johnson, *Pacific Campaign*, 201.

34 Johnson, *Pacific Campaign*, 204.

35 William J. Owens, *Green Hell: The Battle for Guadalcanal* (Central Point, OR: Hellgate Press, 1999), 15.

36 Jack London, *The Cruise of the Snark*, 208–09.

37 Rakata Bay should not be confused with and has no relation to the Rakata peak of Krakatoa.

38 John Wukovits, *Admiral "Bull" Halsey: The Life and Wars of the Navy's Most Controversial Commander* (New York: St. Martin's Press, 2010), 33.

39 Wukovits, *Halsey*, 33.

40 Wukovits, *Halsey*, 33.

41 Lundstrom, *First Team*, 8345; Frank, *Guadalcanal*, 318–19.

42 Fleet Admiral William F. Halsey, USN, *Admiral Halsey's Story* (Pickle Partners Publishing, 2013), Kindle edition, 2362.

43 Hornfischer, *Neptune's Inferno*, 3930.

44 Hornfischer, *Neptune's Inferno*, 3930.

45 Halsey, *Story*, 2498.

46 Hornfischer, *Neptune's Inferno*, 3964.

47 Toland, *Rising Sun*, 8834.

48 Eric Hammel, *Carrier Strike: The Battle of the Santa Cruz Islands October 1942* (Pacifica, CA: Pacifica Military History, 1999), Kindle edition, 1899.

49 Halsey, *Story*, 2502–20.

50 Halsey, *Story*, 2578.

51 Lundstrom, *First Team*, 9234.

52 Frank, *Guadalcanal*, 371.

53 Halsey, *Story*, 2577.

54 Lundstrom, *First Team*, 9250.

55 Lundstrom, *First Team*, 9519–40.

56 Lundstrom, *First Team*, 9552. There are two commonly held myths regarding this order. The first is that it read "Attack, Repeat, Attack," which comes from Admiral Halsey himself (*Story*, 2593) paraphrasing the order. The second is the timing of the order, which, again thanks in part to Admiral Halsey (Story, 2593), is commonly believed to have been the early morning hours of October 26. In fact, official ComSoPac records (CTF 61 242350) show the order as going out early afternoon on October 25.

57 *Shokaku* TROM.

58 Lundstrom, *First Team*, 10945.

59 Halsey, *Story*, 2610–29.

60 Commander Edward P., USN. Stafford, *The Big "E"* (New York: Ballantine, 1962),198–99.

61 Stafford, *The Big "E,"* 198–99.

62 Hughes, *Admiral Bill Halsey*, 3447.

63 Prados, *Islands of Destiny*, 390.

64 Prados, *Islands of Destiny*, 391.

65 Halsey, *Story*, 2650.

66 Hammel, *Starvation*, 6636.

67 Morison, *Struggle*, 235–36.

68 Lundstrom, *First Team*, 12622.

69 Historian Eric Hammel called Admiral Scott "an authentic tiger." Eric Hammel, *Guadalcanal: Decision at Sea: The Naval Battle of Guadalcanal November 13–15, 1942* (Pacifica, CA: Pacifica Military History, 1988) Kindle edition, 1846.

70 Frank, *Guadalcanal*, 433.

71 Frank, *Guadalcanal*, 433 n. 2.

72 Murphy, *Fighting Admiral*, 186.

73 Hammel, *Guadalcanal*, 1863.

74 Hornfischer, *Neptune's Inferno*, 254; J.E. Bennett, "Callaghan Was Calm and Collected at Guadalcanal," *Shipmate 59* (April 1996), 18.

75 Hornfischer, *Neptune's Inferno*, 254.

76 Lieutenant C.G. Morris and Hugh B. Cave, *The Fightin'est Ship: The Story of the Cruiser* Helena (Holicong, PA: Wildside Press, 1944), 44.

77 Morison, *Struggle*, 244; Calhoun, *Tin Can Sailor*, 1686.

78 Appendix I TBS Logs of *Helena* and *Portland*. The message is sometimes reported as "Cease firing, own ships." See, e.g., C.W. Kilpatrick, *The Night Naval Battles in the Solomons* (Pompano Beach, FL: Exposition-Banner, 1987), 91. It may seem like a curious wording, as if Admiral Callaghan wanted to specify he was ordering "our" ships to cease fire, but not "their" ships. He seems to have been trying to say that "our" ships were being hit by friendly fire.

79 Grace, *Night Action*, 147–48; Hornfischer, *Neptune's Inferno*, 333.

80 McCandless, "San Francisco."

81 Calhoun, *Tin Can Sailor*, 2018.

82 Hammel, *Guadalcanal*, 5818.

83 Hornfischer, *Neptune's Inferno*, 7076; Hammel, *Guadalcanal*, 5809.

84 Halsey, *Story*, 2891.

85 In the opinion of the ONI Narrative (75, n. 83), "The 5½ minutes of 16-inch shell fire required to destroy the battleship *Kirishima* contrasts significantly with the extraordinary aerial and torpedo pounding absorbed by her sister ship, the [*Hiei*], 2 days before."

86 Frank, *Guadalcanal*, 503.

87 Frank, *Guadalcanal*, 501–2.

88 Frank, *Guadalcanal*, 504.

89 Crenshaw, *Tassafaronga*, 61.

90 Morison, *Struggle*, 314.

91 Crenshaw, *Tassafaronga*, 76.

92 See, e.g., Frank, *Guadalcanal*, 517; Morison, *Struggle*, 314.

93 Crenshaw, *Tassafaronga*, 75–76.

94 Frank, *Guadalcanal*, 531; Lt. Col. John B. George, *Shots Fired in Anger* (Buford, GA: Canton Street, 2012), Kindle edition, 321–24. Gifu Prefecture, whose capital is Gifu, is located on Honshu in roughly the center of the Home Islands. One of the few landlocked prefectures, Gifu's central position has earned it the historical if unofficial title of The Crossroads of Japan.

95 George, *Shots Fired*, 315–17.

96 George, *Shots Fired*, 321.

97 Dean, *MacArthur's Coalition*, 2118.

98 Dean, *MacArthur's Coalition*, 2118; Paul M. Edwards, *Between the Lines of World War II: Twenty-One Remarkable People and Events* (Jefferson, NC: McFarland, 2010), Kindle edition, 2113.

99 Edwards, *Between the Lines*, 2101–13.

100 Rems, *South Pacific Cauldron*, 613–37.

101 Dean, *MacArthur's Coalition*, 2118.

102 Rems, *South Pacific Cauldron*, 637.

103 Drea, "World War II: Buna Mission," *HistoryNet* (www.historynet.com); Edwards, *Between the Lines*, 2124.

104 Rems, *South Pacific Cauldron*, 646–48.

105 Rems, *South Pacific Cauldron*, 637.

106 Rems, *South Pacific Cauldron*, 637.

107 Eichelberger, *Our Jungle Road*, 36–37.

108 Rems, *South Pacific Cauldron*, 637.

109 Eichelberger, *Our Jungle Road*, 61.

110 Eichelberger, *Our Jungle Road*, 43, 54–55. Eichelberger (44–46) tells the story of his senior aide, Captain Daniel K. Edwards. On December 5, a bullet from a Japanese sniper believed to be the same sniper who had wounded General Waldron "whizzed past [Eichelberger's] stomach and struck Edwards in the side." Eichelberger made sure Edwards was taken out of the combat area and then the general returned to the front. Later, as he was headed back to his headquarters, Eichelberger stopped at the forward wounded station, where the doctor told him Edwards' wound was so severe he would likely die because he could not be moved and they did not have the equipment on hand to treat him. Deciding "if he were going to die, he might as well die on the hood of my jeep," Eichelberger lashed Edwards to the hood of his Jeep and rushed him back to the nearest field hospital, whose surgeons saved Edwards' life. The afternoon of December 7 (51–52), that same field hospital was bombed by the Japanese and badly damaged. Eichelberger found that Edwards had survived the bombing by rolling himself under his cot. The general again transported Edwards on the hood of his Jeep for treatment before the captain was flown out.

111 Eichelberger, *Our Jungle Road*, 64–65.

112 Eichelberger, *Our Jungle Road*, 65.

113 Eichelberger, *Our Jungle Road*, 64.

114 Manchester, *American Caesar*, 327.

115 Rems, *South Pacific Cauldron*, 680; Manchester, *American Caesar*, 327.

116 Manchester, *American Caesar*, 326.

117 Rems, *South Pacific Cauldron*, 719–23.

118 Morton, *United States Army in World War II: The War in the Pacific: Strategy and Command: The First Two Years* (Washington: Center of Military History, United States Army, 1962), 370.

119 Morton, *First Two Years*, 370.

120 Morton, *First Two Years*, 370.

121 Morton, *First Two Years*, 370–71.

122 Morton, *First Two Years*, 370–71.

123 Morton, *First Two Years*, 370–71.

124 Morton, *First Two Years*, 370–71.

125 Morton, *First Two Years*, 372.

126 *Naganami, Kawakaze, Suzukaze, Makinami, Isonami, Inazumi, Kuroshio, Kagero, Oyashio*, and *Arashio* TROMs; Frank, *Guadalcanal*, 547.

127 Louis B. Dorny, *US Navy PBY Catalina Units of the Pacific War* (Oxford: Osprey, 2013), Kindle edition, 1482–1508. The radio altimeter became so critical that if it failed during a night mission the aircraft immediately returned to base.

128 Morison, *Struggle*, 331.

129 Frank, *Guadalcanal*, 545–46.

130 Frank, *Guadalcanal*, 546.

131 Letourneau and Letourneau, *KE*, 130.

132 Letourneau and Letourneau, *KE*, 129–30.

133 Morison, *Struggle*, 353.

134 Action Report – USS *La Vallette* (for January 30, 1943), 4.

135 Frank, *Guadalcanal*, 581.

136 John Wukovits, "Battle of Rennell Island: Setback in the Solomons," *World War II* magazine (March 2000), 3.

137 *I-1* TROM.

138 Prados, *Islands of Destiny*, 225–26.

139 Prados, *Islands of Destiny*, 230.

140 Miller, *Guadalcanal*, 348.

141 Miller, *Guadalcanal*, 348.

142 Hammel, *Air War*, 4618–38.

143 William Wolf, *13th Fighter Command in World War II: Air Combat Over Guadalcanal and the Solomons* (Atglen, PA: Schiffer, 2004), 100–01.

144 Morison, *Bismarcks Barrier*, 89.

145 Wolf, *13th Fighter Command*; Eric Hammel, *Coral and Blood* (Pacifica, CA: Pacifica Military History, 2009), Kindle edition, 1749.

146 *Maikaze* and *Isokaze* TROMs.

147 Kenney, *Reports*, 175–76; Gamble, *Fortress Rabaul*, 278.

148 Capt. Matthew K. Rodman, *War of Their Own: Bombers over the Southwest Pacific* (Maxwell AFB, AL: Air University Press, 2005), 57.

149 Watson, *The Fifth Air Force in the Huon Peninsula Campaign January to October 1943 (AAFRH-13)* (Washington: AAF Historical Offices, Headquarters, Army Air Forces, 1946), 84.

150 Watson, *Fifth Air Force*, 84.

151 Rodman, *War of Their Own*, 28.

152 Rodman, *War of Their Own*, 29.

153 Rodman, *War of Their Own*, 29.

154 Rodman, *War of Their Own*, 30.

155 Kenney, *Reports*, 143.

156 Hickey, *Ken's Men*, 102; McAulay, *Bismarck Sea*, 461; Gamble, *Fortress Rabaul*, 279.

157 Gamble, *Fortress Rabaul*, 279.

158 Martha Byrd (*Kenneth N. Walker: Airpower's Untempered Crusader* (Maxwell Air Force Base, AL: Air University Press, 1997), 113; "Whitehead, Ennis Clement (1895–1964)," *Pacific War Online Encyclopedia* (http://pwencycl.kgbudge.com); Hickey, *Ken's Men*, 102, 104; Gamble, *Fortress Rabaul*, 280–81. Gamble says Major Lindbergh was flying the plane; Hickey says the plane was normally Captain Daniels' but on this day it was being piloted by Bleasdale. Both Hickey and Gamble list Bleasdale as a major, but casualty records list him as a lieutenant colonel.

159 Gamble, *Fortress Rabaul*, 279–80; Hickey, *Ken's Men*, 105–07.

160 *Keifuku* and *Kagu Maru* TROMs.

161 Gamble, *Fortress Rabaul*, 282.

162 Gamble, *Fortress Rabaul*, 282.

163 Hickey, *Ken's Men*, 107.

164 Hickey, *Ken's Men*, 109–10; Douglas Gillison, *Australia in the War of 1939–1945: Series Three (Air) Volume I – Royal Australian Air Force, 1939–1942* (Canberra: Australian War Memorial, 1962), 674.

165 Cressman, *Official Chronology*, Craven and Cate, *Army Air Forces*, 136; *Maikaze* and *Isokaze* TROMs.

166 Cressman, *Official Chronology*.

167 Dean, *MacArthur's Coalition*, 4305.

168 Gillison, *Royal Australian Air Force*, 679–80.

169 Craven and Cate, *Army Air Forces*, 136.

170 McAulay, *Bismarck Sea*, 406; Craven and Cate, *Army Air Forces*, 137.

171 Gann, *Fifth Air Force*, 19–20.

172 Prados, *Islands of Destiny*, 251.

173 Kenney, *Reports*, 198.

174 Kenney, *Reports*, 197–98.

175 Kenney, *Pappy Gunn*, 41.

176 Kenney, *Pappy Gunn*, 43.

177 Kenney, *Pappy Gunn*, 45.

178 Rodman, *War of Their Own*, 59.

179 Rodman, *War of Their Own*, 59.

180 Gamble, *Fortress Rabaul*, 300–01.

181 McAulay, *Bismarck Sea*, 1680, 1781.

182 Martin Caidin, *Fork-Tailed Devil: The P-38* (Dering Harbor, NY: iBooks, 2001), Kindle edition, 3727.

183 Hickey, *Ken's Men*, 139–40.

184 Ikuhiko Hata, Yashuo Izawa, and Christopher Shores, *Japanese Naval Air Force Fighter Units and Their Aces* (London: Grub Street, 2011), Kindle edition, 1244; Hickey, *Ken's Men*, 139–40; Eric Gene Salecker, *Fortress Against The Sun: The B-17 Flying Fortress In The Pacific* (Conshocken, PA: Combined Publishing, 2001), Kindle edition, 5640–45; Gamble, *Fortress Rabaul*, 309.

185 Gillison, *Royal Australian Air Force*, 693.

186 Rodman, *War of Their Own*, 67.

187 Rodman, *War of Their Own*, 68.

188 Rodman, *War of Their Own*, 69.

189 Gamble, *Fortress Rabaul*, 310.

190 Murphy, *Skip Bombing*, 116–17.

191 Murphy, *Skip Bombing*, 116–17.

192 McAulay, *Bismarck Sea*, 2912–39.

193 Hickey, *Ken's Men*, 143.

194 David Dexter, *The New Guinea Offensives. Australia in the War of 1939–1945. Series 1 – Army. Volume 6* (Canberra: Australian War Memorial, 1961), 10–11.

195 Kenney, *Reports*, 205–06.

196 Miller, *CARTWHEEL*, 9–10.

197 Miller, *CARTWHEEL*, 10.

198 Miller, *CARTWHEEL*, 10.

199 Dyer, *Amphibians*, 493.

200 Dyer, *Amphibians*, 494; Crenshaw, *Destroyer*, 2144.

201 Dyer, *Amphibians*, 493–94.

202 Miller, *CARTWHEEL*, 12.

203 Halsey, *Story*, 3322–36.

Chapter 3

1 Day, *New Georgia*, 1195, 1571; Hara, Saito, and Pineau (*Destroyer Captain*, 162–3) quote Rear Admiral Takama Tamotsu, commander of the 4th Destroyer Flotilla, as saying, "One thing is certain: the Army did not provide proper air cover for the Bismarck Sea convoy."

2 Toland, *Rising Sun*, 9719–37.

3 Prados, *Islands of Destiny*, 256.

4 Prados, *Islands of Destiny*, 256–57.

5 Gamble, *Fortress Rabaul*, 320.

6 Day, *New Georgia*, 1193.

7 Prados, *Islands of Destiny*, 257.

8 Prados, *Islands of Destiny*, 255–56.

9 Prados, *Islands of Destiny*, 255–56.

10 Day, *New Georgia*, 1209; Prados, *Islands of Destiny*, 261; Hata, Izawa, and Shores, *Japanese Naval Air Force*, 1294; Japanese Monograph No. 122: "Outlines of Southeast Area Naval Air Operations Part III (November 1942–June 1943)" (General Headquarters US Far East Command, Military History Section, 1950) (hereinafter "Monograph 122"), 37.

11 Day, *New Georgia*, 1209; Prados, *Islands of Destiny*, 261; Hata, Izawa, and Shores, *Japanese Naval Air Force*, 1294.

12 "Rapopo Airfield (Rabaul South, South Airfield, Rabaul No. 3)," *Pacific Wrecks* (www.pacificwrecks.com).

13 Hickey, *Ken's Men*, 156.

14 Hickey, *Ken's Men*, 156.

15 Hickey, *Ken's Men*, 156.

16 Hickey, *Ken's Men*, 156; Eric M. Bergerud, *Fire In The Sky: The Air War In The South Pacific* (Boulder, CO: Westview Press, 2000), Kindle edition, 3484–88.

17 Murphy, *Skip Bombing*, 130.

18 Gamble, *Target: Rabaul*, 30.

19 Murphy, *Skip Bombing*, 130.

20 Gamble, *Target: Rabaul*, 30–31.

21 "How to Make a Volcano Explode (or not)," *Research Associates: The Best in WW2 Aviation History* (https://airwarworldwar2.wordpress.com).

22 Prados, *Islands of Destiny*, 261; Hata, Izawa, and Shores, *Japanese Naval Air Force*, 1294.

23 Prados, *Islands of Destiny*, 261; Monograph 99, 13. *Rikko* was the Japanese abbreviation for *rikujo kogeki-ki* (land-based attack aircraft); Osamu Tagaya and Mark Styling, *Mitsubishi Type 1 Rikko 'Betty' Units of World War 2* (Oxford: Osprey, 2001), Kindle edition, 22.

24 Day, *New Georgia*, 1213.

25 Masatake Okumiya, Jiro Horikoshi, and Martin Caidin, *Zero!* (Pickle Partners Publishing, 2014), Kindle edition, 3687.

26   The numbers and composition are an amalgamation of Gamble (*Fortress Rabaul*, 321) and Hata, Izawa, and Shores (*Japanese Naval Air Force*, 1294), who are the only sources who give information as to the specific numbers and units involved, and even they do not agree.

27   Hammel, *Air War*, 5146; Wolf, *13th Fighter Command*, 131; ComAirSoPacFor and VMF-221 war diaries.

28   Gamble, *Fortress Rabaul*, 321; Hata, Izawa, and Shores, *Japanese Naval Air Force*, 1294, 7789.

29   Monograph 99, 12; Monograph 122, 37; "Ballale Airfield," *Pacific Wrecks* (www.pacificwrecks.com); Major E.C. Milliken, "Report on War Crimes on Ballale Island," *Roll of Honour: Britain at War* (http://www.roll-of -honour.org.uk). Ballale is also spelled "Ballale," "Ballalai," and other variants.

30   Prados, *Islands of Destiny*, 258.

31   Okumiya, Horikoshi, and Caidin, *Zero!*, 3722.

32   Except where otherwise noted, the account of Admiral Yamamoto's last night on the *Musashi* comes from Hiroyuki Agawa, *The Reluctant Admiral: Yamamoto and the Imperial Navy* (Tokyo; New York: Kodansha, 1979), 339–40. Davis (*Lightning Strike*, 3390) says Yamamoto's shogi partner that night was Commander Watanabe. Day (*New Georgia*, 1193) says Yamamoto's presence was necessary to solve the command conflict between Admirals Kusaka and Ozawa.

33   Davis, *Lightning Strike*, 3390.

34   Prados, *Islands of Destiny*, 258; Davis, *Lightning Strike*, 3390; Gamble, *Fortress Rabaul*, 322.

35   According to Prados (*Islands of Destiny*, 258), "Any doubts that Yamamoto intended to lead in person, not simply visit the front, were dispelled when the admiral and Ugaki turned up replete with their stewards and the fancy dishware, tablecloths, and silverware used to serve meals aboard flagship *Musashi*." Who knew that men going into heavy combat could be so inspired by china and dinnerware?

36   Agawa, *Reluctant Admiral*, 342–43.

37   Prados, *Islands of Destiny*, 259; Davis, *Lightning Strike*, 3390.

38   Prados, *Islands of Destiny*, 259.

39   Gamble, *Fortress Rabaul*, 322.

40   Agawa, *Reluctant Admiral*, 343.

41   *Aoba* TROM.

42   *O'Bannon* War Diary; ComDesRon 21 War Diary, *Ro-34* TROM.

43   Ernest A. Herr, "The Maine Potato Episode," *Destroyer History Foundation* (www.destroyerhistory.org).

44   Ernest A. Herr, "The Maine Potato Episode," *Destroyer History Foundation* (www.destroyerhistory.org).

45   John Wukovits, *Tin Can Titans: The Heroic Men and Ships of World War II's Most Decorated Navy Destroyer Squadron* (Boston: Da Capo Press, 2017), Kindle edition, 2481–91.

46   Davis, *Lightning Strike*, 3428.

47   Prados, *Islands of Destiny*, 262.

48   Okumiya, Horikoshi, and Caidin, *Zero!*, 3722.

49   Davis, *Lightning Strike*, 3428–46.

50   Okumiya, Horikoshi, and Caidin, *Zero!*, 3740.

51   Okumiya, Horikoshi, and Caidin, *Zero!*, 3740.

52   Okumiya, Horikoshi, and Caidin, *Zero!*, 3740–58.

53   Davis, *Lightning Strike*, 3446; Michael John Claringbould, *Operation I-Go: Yamamoto's Last Offensive New Guinea and the Solomons, April 1943* (Kent Town, Australia: Avenmore, 2020), 37; Monograph 99, 13. Davis has the scouts reporting 31 ships, Claringbould has them each reporting 33, and Monograph 99 gives the breakdown of ships reported that add up to 26.

54   Davis, *Lightning Strike*, 3446.

55   Claringbould, *I-Go*, 36–37; Day, *New Georgia*, 1218; Monograph 122, 39.

56   Day, *New Georgia*, 1213; Hata, Izawa, and Shores, *Japanese Naval Air Force*, 1294–1309; Claringbould, *I-Go*, 33, 36; Monograph 122, 40.

57   Day, *New Georgia*, 1213; Hata, Izawa, and Shores, *Japanese Naval Air Force*, 1294–1309; Claringbould, *I-Go*, 33–34, 36–38, 50.

58   Except where specified otherwise, the story of the *Aaron Ward* comes from USS *Aaron Ward* "Report of enemy action resulting in loss of *Aaron Ward*" ("*Aaron Ward* Loss Report"), generally.

59   Morison, *Bismarcks Barrier*, 121.

60   Day, *New Georgia*, 1234.

61   Day, *New Georgia*, 1213.

62   Prados, *Islands of Destiny*, 262.

63   Prados, *Islands of Destiny*, 262; Wolf, *13th Fighter Command*, 132; Claringbould, *I-Go*, 35.

64 Prados, *Islands of Destiny*, 262.

65 Tuohy, *Fighting Admirals*, 1912.

66 Day, *New Georgia*, 1234.

67 Prados, *Islands of Destiny*, 263. Henderson Field had used a three-stage system of readiness: "Green," "Yellow," and "Red." "Green" meant remain calm, all is well. If a Japanese air attack was detected or suspected within an hour or so, "Yellow" alert would be declared, by which the four enlisted Marines who formed the "Pagoda Watch" raised a red flag, naturally, and cranked a siren. If everyone needed to take cover immediately, like for an imminent air attack or a bombardment, "Red" alert would be declared, in which the Pagoda Watch would raise a black flag, naturally, and sound the siren. On a select few occasions, Henderson Field would implement a fourth stage of readiness, "Very Red," which would presumably require raising a very black flag.

68 Day, *New Georgia*, 1234; Robert Sinclair Parkin, *Blood on the Sea: American Destroyers Lost in World War II* (Cambridge, MA: Da Capo Press, 1995), 137.

69 Prados, *Islands of Destiny*, 263; Morison, *Bismarcks Barrier*, 120.

70 Morison, *Bismarcks Barrier*, 120 n. 5; Barrett Tillman, *US Marine Corps Fighter Squadrons of World War II*, (Oxford, Osprey, 2014), Kindle edition, 41; Hammel, *Air War*, 5205; Wolf, *13th Fighter Command*, 132–3; Claringbould, *I-Go*, 61; ComAirSoPacFor; VMF-213, -214, and -221 war diaries. Marine Fighting 213's War Diary entry starts with "This day will go down in the annals of the Squadron as the most exciting day of all as it was the day of its initial contact with the enemy."

71 Claringbould, *I-Go*, 61; Astor, *Semper Fi*, 2828.

72 Hata, Izawa, and Shores, *Japanese Naval Air Force*, 1294–1309; Claringbould, *I-Go*, 47.

73 Astor, *Semper Fi*, 2810; Hammel, *Aces*, 2097.

74 Hammel, *Aces*, 2097.

75 Gamble, *Fortress Rabaul*, 323; VMF-221 War Diary; Day, *New Georgia*, 1256; Hammel, *Aces against Japan*, 2118–32.

76 Amphibious Force, South Pacific Force War Diary, April 7; Morison, *Bismarcks Barrier*, 121–22; Claringbould, *I-Go*, 47; USS *Taylor* War Diary.

77 Morison, *Bismarcks Barrier*, 121–22.

78 Morison, *Bismarcks Barrier*, 122.

79 Morison, *Bismarcks Barrier*, 122.

80 W. F. Craven and J.L Cate (editors), *Army Air Forces in World War II, Vol. IV:* "The Pacific: Guadalcanal to Saipan August 1942 to July 1944" (Washington, DC: Office of Air Force History, 1983), 213; Hata, Izawa, and Shores, *Japanese Naval Air Force*, 1309; Claringbould, *I-Go*, 60.

81 Hammel, *Aces*, 2097.

82 Hammel, *Aces*, 2097–118.

83 Day, *New Georgia*, 1256; Hata, Izawa, and Shores, *Japanese Naval Air Force*, 1309, 7789–90; Gamble, *Fortress Rabaul*, 325. Monograph 99 (13) says 21 Japanese aircraft "went down in suicide attacks or failed to return."

84 Bates, *Battle of Savo Island*, 219–20.

85 H.P. Willmott, *The Battle of Leyte Gulf: The Last Fleet Action* (Bloomington, IN: Indiana University Press, 2005), 784–85.

86 Willmott, *Leyte Gulf*, 795–98.

87 *Ro-34* TROM.

88 Prados, *Islands of Destiny*, 265.

89 Monograph 122, 41; Claringbould, *I-Go*, 75–83; Hammel, *Air War*, 5244; Hata, Izawa, and Shores, *Japanese Naval Air Force*, 1328.

90 Claringbould, *I-Go*, 76.

91 Claringbould, *I-Go*, 76.

92 Gamble, *Fortress Rabaul*, 324; Gillison, *Royal Australian Air Force*, 700.

93 Kenney, *Reports*, 225.

94 Kenney, *Reports*, 225.

95 Hickey, *Ken's Men*, 170–71.

96 Hickey, *Ken's Men*, 170–71; Prados, *Islands of Destiny*, 265.

97 Monograph 122, 42.

98 Monograph 99, 14.

99 Tagaya, *Rikko*, 1273; Hata, Izawa, and Shores, *Japanese Naval Air Force*, 1328; Claringbould, *I-Go*, 90.

100 Ugaki, Goldstein, and Dillon, *Fading Victory*, 327; Tagaya, *Rikko*, 1273; Hata, Izawa, and Shores, *Japanese Naval Air Force*, 1328; Claringbould, *I-Go*, 90, 146.

101 Kenney, *Reports*, 227.
102 Kenney, *Reports*, 227; Claringbould, *I-Go*, 92–93.
103 Kenney, *Reports*, 227; Hickey, *Ken's Men*, 171; Claringbould, *I-Go*, 93–94.
104 Kenney, *Reports*, 228; Ugaki, Goldstein, and Dillon, *Fading Victory*, 329; Hata, Izawa, and Shores, *Japanese Naval Air Force*, 1328; Claringbould, *I-Go*, 97–98; Monograph 122, 42.
105 Gamble, *Fortress Rabaul*, 326; Craven and Cate, *Army Air Forces*, 160; Hickey, *Ken's Men*, 171. Craven and Cate (based on and written by Watson, *Fifth Air Force*, 123) say the fuel dump hit by the Japanese was at Kila. Hickey shows photos suggesting it was at Wards, which was flatter than Kila. There is also no other reference to Kila as a target of this Japanese attack.
106 Kenney, *Reports*, 228–29.
107 Kenney, *Reports*, 229.
108 Ugaki, Goldstein, and Dillon, *Fading Victory*, 329.
109 Ugaki, Goldstein, and Dillon, *Fading Victory*, 327–28.
110 Gamble, *Fortress Rabaul*, 327.
111 Davis, *Lightning Strike*, 3522.
112 Toland, *Rising Sun*, 9755; Davis, *Lightning Strike*, 3522–60.
113 Agawa, *Reluctant Admiral*, 369.
114 Davis, *Lightning Strike*, 5017.
115 Davis, *Lightning Strike*, 3516–44, 5006; Prados, *Islands of Destiny*, 269.

Chapter 4

1 Ugaki, Goldstein, and Dillon, *Fading Victory*, 329; Tagaya, *Rikko*, 1273–88; Hata, Izawa, and Shores, *Japanese Naval Air Force*, 1344–48; Claringbould, *I-Go*, 109.
2 Ugaki, Goldstein, and Dillon, *Fading Victory*, 329; Hata, Izawa, and Shores, *Japanese Naval Air Force*, 1344; Claringbould, *I-Go*, 119; Monograph 122, 44 (with differing fighter contribution figures).
3 Claringbould, *I-Go*, 110.
4 Or Kana Kope. Or Kana Kopa.
5 Claringbould, *I-Go*, 110.
6 Claringbould, *I-Go*, 110–12.
7 Claringbould, *I-Go*, 110–12.
8 Claringbould, *I-Go*, 119–20, 122–23.
9 Claringbould, *I-Go*, 119–20, 122–23.
10 Claringbould, *I-Go*, 117–18.
11 Claringbould, *I-Go*, 117–18.
12 Claringbould, *I-Go*, 118; "Richard I. Bong, P-38 Pilot 49th Fighter Group, 9th Fighter Squadron and 5th Fighter Command: Highest Scoring American Ace of World War II," *Pacific Wrecks* (www.pacificwrecks.com).
13 Claringbould, *I-Go*, 119–20.
14 Claringbould, *I-Go*, 121; Morison, *Bismarcks Barrier*, 126.
15 "MV Gorgon (MS Gorgon)," *Pacific Wrecks* (www.pacificwrecks.com); "MS Van Heemskerk," *Pacific Wrecks* (www.pacificwrecks.com); Claringbould, *I-Go*, 121–22; Morison, *Bismarcks Barrier*, 126–27. Claringbould says the *Gorgon* was struck by two 250kg bombs, which could only have come from the land attack planes.
16 Ugaki, Goldstein, and Dillon, *Fading Victory*, 329; Claringbould, *I-Go*, 115–18; Prados, *Islands of Destiny*, 266–67.
17 Davis, *Lightning Strike*, 3502.
18 Ugaki, Goldstein, and Dillon, *Fading Victory*, 330.
19 Monograph 122, 45.
20 Ugaki, Goldstein, and Dillon, *Fading Victory*, 329; Monograph 122, 45.
21 Okumiya, Horikoshi, and Caidin, *Zero!*, 3711.
22 Gamble, *Fortress Rabaul*, 331.
23 Davis, *Lightning Strike*, 3718–38.
24 Agawa, *Reluctant Admiral*, 346; Ugaki, Goldstein, and Dillon, *Fading Victory*, 351.
25 Davis, *Lightning Strike*, 3738.
26 Dick Lehr, *Dead Reckoning: The Story of How Johnny Mitchell and His Fighter Pilots Took on Admiral Yamamoto and Avenged Pearl Harbor* (New York: HarperCollins, 2020), Kindle edition, 275.
27 Amalgamation of Lehr, *Dead Reckoning*, 275, and Agawa, *Reluctant Admiral*, 347.
28 Lehr, *Dead Reckoning*, 274–75.
29 Ugaki, Goldstein, and Dillon, *Fading Victory*, 352.

30 Ugaki, Goldstein, and Dillon, *Fading Victory*, 352–53.

31 Davis, *Lightning Strike*, 3795–814; Hampton, *Operation Vengeance*, 3641; Ugaki, Goldstein, and Dillon, *Fading Victory*, 353.

32 Gargill R. Hall, *Lightning Over Bougainville: The Yamamoto Mission Reconsidered* (Washington and London: Smithsonian Institution Press, 1991), 145–48; Dan Hampton, *Operation Vengeance: The Astonishing Aerial Ambush That Changed World War II* (New York: HarperCollins, 2020), Kindle edition, 3634–41. Konishi's given name is sometimes rendered as "Seizo."

33 Davis, *Lightning Strike*, 3815; Lehr, *Dead Reckoning*, 275.

34 Gamble, *Fortress Rabaul*, 337; Carroll V. Glines, *Attack on Yamamoto* (Atglen, PA: Schieffer Military History, 1993), 105–06; Lehr, *Dead Reckoning*, 289. The idea that the 20mm cannon at the back of each of the G4Ms was useless because Admiral Yamamoto and his entourage had piled their luggage in the 20mm cannon position is dismissed here as absurd.

35 Hall, *Lightning*, 110; Davis, *Lightning Strike*, 4027.

36 Hall, *Lightning*, 110.

37 Ugaki, Goldstein, and Dillon, *Fading Victory*, 353, with an allowance that the landing base was Buin and not Ballale. Ugaki insists their destination was Ballale and Commander Watanabe's message indicated such, but both Ugaki's pilot Hayashi (Hall, *Lightning*, 146–48) and escorting Zero pilot Yanagiya (Hall, *Lightning*, 110–11) are insistent that the destination was in fact Buin. Except for his insistence that they were landing on Ballale, everything else in Ugaki's account is taken as true.

38 Glines, *Attack*, 96.

39 Agawa, *Reluctant Admiral*, 350.

40 Except where noted otherwise, the description of the decryption of Admiral Yamamoto's itinerary and the reaction thereto comes from Prados, *Islands of Destiny*, 269.

41 Davis, *Get Yamamoto*, 11.

42 Davis, *Lightning Strike*, 3620; Prados, *Islands of Destiny*, 269; Davis, *Get Yamamoto*, 11.

43 Davis, *Lightning Strike*, 3620; Davis, *Get Yamamoto*, 43. For clarification, the word "Setsua" in the original message was a coded reference to the date, April 18, and "Chuko" was a coded reference to *Rikko*, the Japanese shorthand for "land attack plane" such as the Mitsubushi G4M Type 1 Land Attack Plane.

44 Glimes, *Attack*, 4–6; Prados, *Islands of Destiny*, 269–70; Davis, *Get Yamamoto*, 11–12.

45 Glimes, *Attack*, 6–7; Kyodo News, "Use of Outdated Code Led to Ambush That Killed Yamamoto, U.S. Files Show," *Japan Time*, 9/29/2008.

46 Except where otherwise noted, details of Commander Layton's conversation with Admiral Nimitz come from Davis, *Get Yamamoto*, 5–9, and E.B. Potter, *Nimitz* (Annapolis: Naval Institute Press, 1976), Kindle edition, 233.

47 Davis, *Get Yamamoto*, 7–8.

48 Carl von Clausewitz (1780–1831), Prussian general and military theorist. Sort of a German Sun Tzu. Authored famous study of military theory, *Vom Kriege* ("On War").

49 Gordon William Prange, *At Dawn We Slept: The Untold Story of Pearl Harbor* (New York: Penguin, 1981), 11.

50 The full scenario is detailed in Davis, *Get Yamamoto*, 14–20. Prados, *Islands of Destiny*, 270.

51 Davis, *Lightning Strike*, 3658.

52 Davis, *Lightning Strike*, 3699–718.

53 Hall, *Lightning*, 126.

54 Glines, *Attack*, 28.

55 Don Hollway, "Death by P-38," *Aviation History Magazine*, 3/4/2012.

56 Glines, *Attack*, 29–30.

57 Hall, *Lightning*, 131. Major Condon said of Admiral Halsey's message, "It was secret, mentioned no name, but they knew who it was." Well, except for Major Mitchell.

58 Hollway, "Death by P-38"; Davis, *Lightning Strike*, 3757.

59 Hollway, "Death by P-38."

60 Davis, *Lightning Strike*, 3775.

61 Davis, *Lightning Strike*, 3775.

62 Glines, *Attack*, 30–31.

63 Glines, *Attack*, 33.

64 Wolf, *13th Fighter Command*, 139.

65 Davis, *Lightning Strike*, 3889.

66 Wolf, *13th Fighter Command*, 139.

67 Hall, *Lightning*, 70–72.

68 Hollway, "Death by P-38," says the briefing was given the night before and has the quote, "Yamamoto's supposed to be coming to Bougainville tomorrow morning." The quote is altered here because Mitchell did not brief the pilots or confirm that the target was Admiral Yamamoto until the Sunday morning briefing.

69 Glines, *Attack*, 38.

70 Davis, *Lightning Strike*, 3949.

71 Glines, *Attack*, 57–58.

72 Glines, *Attack*, 58.

73 Davis, *Lightning Strike*, 3948.

74 Glines, *Attack*, 38–39.

75 Davis, *Lightning Strike*, 3909.

76 Davis, *Lightning Strike*, 3901, 4007–27.

77 Davis, *Lightning Strike*, 4007.

78 The course and time information comes from Davis, *Lightning Strike*, 4027–66.

79 Glines, *Attack*, 60.

80 Glines, *Attack*, 61.

81 Hall, *Lightning*, 73.

82 Glines, *Attack*, 60.

83 Glines, *Attack*, 61.

84 Davis, *Lightning Strike*, 3870.

85 Glines, *Attack*, 61–62; Hollway, "Death by P-38." In a comment to Hollway, retired Air Force pilot Joseph Roberts commented:

> Fine article. I just have one small correction. Doug Canning is the last of the surviving Operation *Vengeance* pilots living at this time (Jan 2014). He has always maintained that he broke radio silence to say "Bogeys at 10 o'clock," not 11 o'clock, and not 9 o'clock, as others have reported.
>
> A fellow named Jablonski (it's late now, and I don't have his book in front of me) wrote a book about the Air War in WWII back decades ago. He is one of the few who've gotten this right. Doug laughs about this today, but is still insistent that he said "9 o'clock."

The issue is likely a discrepancy of which pilots adjusted their positional clocks for Daylight Saving Time. The narrative here is going with Roberts' comment.

86 Hall, *Lightning*, 75.

87 Davis, *Lightning Strike*, 4129.

88 Davis, *Lightning Strike*, 4148; Toland, *Rising Sun*, 9774.

89 Davis, *Lightning Strike*, 4166.

90 Davis, *Lightning Strike*, 4166.

91 Glines, *Attack*, 68.

92 Hall, *Lightning*, 88, 111–13.

93 Agawa, *Reluctant Admiral*, 351.

94 Ugaki, Goldstein, and Dillon, *Fading Victory*, 354.

95 Glines, *Attack*, 68.

96 Ugaki, Goldstein, and Dillon, *Fading Victory*, 354.

97 Ugaki, Goldstein, and Dillon, *Fading Victory*, 354–55; Hall, *Lightning*, 152–53.

98 Ugaki, Goldstein, and Dillon, *Fading Victory*, 354–55.

99 Glines, *Attack*, 71.

100 Glines, *Attack*, 71.

101 Glines, *Attack*, 71–72.

102 Glines, *Attack*, 72.

103 Glines, *Attack*, 69.

104 Davis, *Lightning Strike*, 4254.

105 Davis, *Lightning Strike*, 4322.

106 Davis, *Lightning Strike*, 4322.

107 Hall, *Lightning*, 114–15.

108 Hall, *Lightning*, 113–14.

109 Gamble, *Fortress Rabaul*, 342.

110 Hall, *Lightning*, 115.

111 Hampton, *Operation Vengeance*, 4334–47.

112 Glines, *Attack*, 98; Hampton, *Operation Vengeance*, 4334–47.

113 Glines, *Attack*, 98; Davis, *Lightning Strike*, 4447.

114 Davis, *Lightning Strike*, 4358.

115 Hall, *Lightning*, 89.

116 Except where specified otherwise, the story of Lieutenant (jg) Metke's PBY Catalina comes from Wolf, *13th Fighter Command*, 147–48.

117 Davis, *Lightning Strike*, 4296–303. Yanagiya Kenji apparently found out in a 1988 interview with Cargill Hall (*Lightning*, 114) that he had shot down Lieutenant Hine. Yanagiya had not known he had shot down an enemy plane on this mission and seemed uncomfortable with that knowledge. That's not uncommon for fighter pilots when their targets are personalized. The entire experience of the mission and its aftermath was evidently painful for Yanagiya, who was the only one of Admiral Yamamoto's escorts to survive the war. Yanagiya should be commended and remembered for sharing his experience with his former enemies to give a more accurate historical perspective.

118 Except where otherwise noted, the account of the return of the Lightning pilots was based on Davis, *Lightning Strike*, 4389–444.

119 Wolf, *13th Fighter Command*, 149.

120 Wolf, *13th Fighter Command*, 149.

121 Davis, *Lightning Strike*, 4358.

122 Wolf, *13th Fighter Command*, 149.

123 Davis, *Get Yamamoto*, 187; Davis, *Lightning Strike*, 4464–81.

124 Davis, *Lightning Strike*, 4481.

125 Prados, *Islands of Destiny*, 274.

126 Agawa, *Reluctant Admiral*, 355. Admiral Ugaki actual said the drugs might "cure his 'R.'" "R" was a euphemism for *rimbyo*, the Japanese word for gonorrhea.

127 Agawa, *Reluctant Admiral*, 355–56; *W-15* TROM.

128 Except where noted otherwise, the account of the Imperial Japanese Army party comes from Agawa, *Reluctant Admiral*, 357–62.

129 Agawa, *Reluctant Admiral*, 358–59. What struck Lieutenant Hamasuna and his men most was the thick wad of clean white toilet paper Admiral Yamamoto was carrying in one of his breast pockets. There was an "extreme shortage" of toilet paper in the Imperial Army. One member of the search party was said to have commented, "You get to use good paper when you get to be C. in C.!" Rank has its privileges.

130 Davis, *Lightning Strike*, 4702.

131 Agawa, *Reluctant Admiral*.

132 *W-15* TROM.

133 Glines, *Attack*, 106.

134 Agawa, *Reluctant Admiral*, 365.

135 Agawa, *Reluctant Admiral*, 365.

136 Agawa, *Reluctant Admiral*, 365.

137 Many historians simply do not buy the "official" reports on Admiral Yamamoto and his party. Historian Bruce Gamble (*Fortress Rabaul*, 342–43) makes the point that the surrounding fireball would have resulted in burnt, disfigured remains. Similarly, Donald Davis (*Lightning* Strike, 4740) points out that .50-caliber bullets and/or flying shrapnel did not make neat holes and would have caused ghastly disfigurement. Gamble concludes, "Ultimately, so many details regarding Yamamoto's condition were whitewashed that it is difficult to accept any of them at face value."

138 Okumiya, Horikoshi, and Caidin, *Zero!*, 3898–919.

139 Davis, *Lightning Strike*, 4767.

140 Prados, *Islands of Destiny*, 281.

141 Toland, *Rising Sun*, 9824.

Chapter 5

1 The geographic and environmental description of New Georgia and its island group comes from Shaw and Kane, *Isolation of Rabaul*, 41–42.

2 Allyn D. Nevitt, "The Destruction of DesDiv 15," *The Imperial Japanese Navy Page* (www.combinedfleet.com).

3 *Oyashio* TROM. (Time adjusted from Japan Standard Time to local.)

4 Day, *New Georgia*, 1026–47. Curiously, there seems to be no agreement as to exactly how Destroyer Division 15 got to Vila. Readers should be aware of the disagreement as to what route Destroyer Division 15 took to Vila and make their own judgments.

5   *Oyashio* TROM; Day, *New Georgia*, 1042–48.

6   Nevitt, "The Destruction of DesDiv 15."

7   Nevitt, "The Destruction of DesDiv 15"; *Kuroshio* TROM; Morison, *Bismarcks Barrier*, 115.

8   Morison, *Bismarcks Barrier*, 114; Day, *New Georgia*, 1026; "Mining of Blackett Strait During Night of 6–7 May, Action Report of." The track chart of the mine laying shows the mines did not completely cover the Ferguson Passage. According to Lieutenant Commander Romoser, the entire minefield was laid without a single premature explosion or a single "floater."

9   Lord, *Lonely Vigil: Coastwatchers of the Solomons* (New York: Open Road, 1977), Kindle edition, 219.

10 *Oyashio* TROM; Day, *New Georgia*, 1047.

11 Day, *New Georgia*, 1048–54; ComAirSoPacFor, VMF112, VMF213 war diaries.

12 J.M.S. Ross, *Official History of New Zealand in the Second World War 1939–45: Royal New Zealand Air Force* (Wellington: War History Branch, Department of Internal Affairs, 1955), 182; Barrett Tillman, *SBD Dauntless Units*, 1033–50.

13 ComAirSoPacFor, VMF112 and 213 war diaries.

14 *Oyashio*, *Kagero*, and *Kuroshio* TROMs. For some reason, there has been a belief that the Japanese destroyer *Michishio* was also involved in this action. In this version, the *Michishio* was a fourth destroyer involved in this reinforcement effort and was damaged by air attack as she retreated toward Shortland. Such actions would have been extremely difficult for the *Michishio* because she was at that moment in a drydock in Yokosuka Navy Yard, having come there all the way from the South Pacific where her engines had been damaged by air attacks on Admiral Tanaka's convoy on November 13, 1942. See Nevitt, "The Destruction of DesDiv 15" and *Michishio* TROM.

15 Morison, *Bismarcks Barrier*, 111–12; Hammel, *Air War*, 4990–5010; Ross, *New Zealand*, 177; *Kazagumo* TROM.

16 Cressman, *Official Chronology*.

17 "Minelaying Missions to Buin, Tonolei, and Shortland Harbor Areas, Bougainville Island, Report of" (Serial 002474 20 Nov 1943), 7; Hammel, *Air War*, 5693–733; Morison, *Bismarcks Barrier*, 112.

18 Glines, *Attack*, 123.

19 The full text of Lodge's submission can be found at Glines, *Attack*, 115–17.

20 Davis, *Lightning Strike*, 4579–97.

21 Glines, *Attack*, 118–19.

22 Halsey, *Story*, 3347.

23 Gline, *Attack*, 119.

24 Davis, *Lightning Strike*, 4579.

25 Davis, *Lightning Strike*, 4579.

26 Davis, *Lightning Strike*, 4579–97.

27 Davis, *Lightning Strike*, 4952.

28 Davis, *Lightning Strike*, 5070.

29 Clay Blair, Jr, *Silent Victory: The US Submarine War Against Japan* (Annapolis: Naval Institute Press, 1975), 372.

30 "The Loss of USS *Argonaut* (SS-166)," *On Eternal Patrol* (http://www.oneternalpatrol.com/uss-argonaut-166-loss.html).

31 Blair, *Silent Victory*, 372. The loss of the *Argonaut* sparked controversy and questions as to why this boat incapable of combat had been vectored to intercept the heavily escorted, empty convoy as it headed back toward Rabaul.

32 Rear Admiral Richard H., USN (Ret.) O'Kane, *Wahoo: The Patrols of America's Most Famous WWII Submarine* (Novato, CA: Presidio, 1987), Kindle edition, 116.

33 Kent G. Budge, "Fife, James, Jr. (1897–1975)," *The Pacific War Online Encyclopedia* (http://pwencycl.kgbudge.com).

34 Blair, *Silent Victory*, 375.

35 *Kiriha Maru* TROM; "Triton (SS-201)," *United States Submarine Losses In World War II* (Washington, DC: Naval History Division, Office of the Chief of Naval Operations, 1963).

36 *Kiriha Maru* TROM; "Triton (SS-201)," *United States Submarine Losses In World War II*.

37 *Kiriha Maru* TROM; "Triton (SS-201)," *United States Submarine Losses In World War II*.

38 Blair, *Silent Victory*, 376.

39 *Keiyo Maru* TROM.

40 "Grampus (SS-207)," *United States Submarine Losses World War II* (Washington, DC: Naval History Division, Office of the Chief of Naval Operations 1963 (Revised 2017))(https://www.history.navy.mil/content/history/nhhc/research/library/online-reading-room/title-list-alphabetically/u/united-states-submarine-losses/grampus-ss-207.html), 37–38; Ed Howard, "USS *Grampus* (SS-207)," *U.S. Submarines Lost In WWII*.

41 There is a line of thinking that asserts there is no evidence the *Grampus* received the orders to go patrol Vella Gulf with the *Grayback* (see, e.g., Howard, "USS *Grampus* (SS-207)") and/or no evidence the *Grampus* was in Vella Gulf on the night of March 5–6, 1943 (see, e.g., Day, *New Georgia*, 4916, n. 10). With all due respect to these fine historians, neither assertion is true. The report by *Grayback*'s skipper Lieutenant Commander Stephan that his boat saw and heard what appeared to be another submarine in the area of Vella Gulf assigned to *Grampus* is indeed evidence. It is not conclusive evidence, but in legal terms it is evidence of probative value.

42 Task Force 63 (titled incorrectly as Task Force "Thirty-three") War Diary.

43 Day, *New Georgia*, 4916 n. 10. Day cites the "938th Air Group," but this is assumed to be a typo. The 938 Air Group was not activated until April. The 958 Air Group was in the area and had executed attacks on what was believed to be the *Grampus*.

44 *Concise History, Volume 4*, 88.

45 "Triton (SS-201)," *United States Submarine Losses World War II*, 40–41.

46 Blair, *Silent Victory*, 375.

47 Ed Howard, "USS *Triton* (SS-201)," *SubSoWesPac: U.S. Submarines Lost In WWII* (www.subsowespac.org).

48 Nevitt, "Who Sank the Triton?"

49 Nevitt, "Who Sank the Triton?"

50 *Momoyama Maru* TROM. Vernon J. Miller ("An Analysis of US Submarine Losses During World War II, Part V," *Warship* 46 (April 1988), 48–59, 58) suggests that the distant depth charging the *Trigger* heard on March 15 was actually the air attack that fatally damaged the *Momoyama Maru*. This is highly unlikely, as the air attack took place on March 13, two days before the depth charging reported by the *Trigger*.

51 Nevitt, "Who Sank the Triton?" *Imperial Japanese Navy Page*; Cressman, *Official Chronology*.

52 *Nagaura* TROM.

53 *Ch-24* TROM.

54 *Momoha Maru* TROM.

55 *Nagaura* TROM.

56 See Jeffrey R. Cox, "Under Water No One Can Hear You Scream," for full details as to the scenario and evidentiary research involved.

57 Wolf, *13th Fighter Squadron*, 165.

58 Wolf, *13th Fighter Squadron*, 164.

59 Wolf, *13th Fighter Squadron*, 165.

60 Tagaya, *Rikko*, 1302–10.

61 Wolf, *13th Fighter Command*, 163.

62 Day, *New Georgia*, 1068, 4939 n. 23.

63 Day, *New Georgia*, 1326–36.

64 Day, *New Georgia*, 1336; Wolf, *13th Fighter Command*, 166; Tagaya, *Rikko*, 1310.

65 *Nashville* War Diary.

66 Day, *New Georgia*, 1063–71; Morison, *Bismarcks Barrier*, 115–16; Cressman, *Official Chronology*.

67 Day, *New Georgia*, 1347; Hata, Izawa, and Shores, *Japanese Naval Air Force*, 1363–70, 7790; Monograph 122, 53, 55 (with discrepancy regarding the number of fighter planes and units). American units are from Wolf, *13th Fighter Command*, 166; and Hammel, *Air War*, 5613.

68 Day, *New Georgia*, 1347; Hata, Izawa, and Shores, *Japanese Naval Air Force*, 1363–70, 7790; Monograph 122, 53, 55; Wolf, *13th Fighter Command*, 166; and Hammel, *Air War*, 5613.

69 Day, *New Georgia*, 1348–57; Monograph 122, 52.

70 William N. Hess, *49th Fighter Group: Aces of the Pacific* (Oxford: Osprey, 2013), Kindle edition, 874.

71 Tagaya, *Rikko*, 1316–30; Wolf, *5th Fighter Command*, 278; Hammel, *Air War*, 5633. Tagaya says the escort was 33 Zeros, while Wolf says 32. The difference may be that one Zero had to turn back due to mechanical difficulties.

72 Tagaya, *Rikko*, 1316–30; Wolf, *5th Fighter Command*, 278; Hammel, *Air War*, 5633; Hata, Izawa, and Shores, *Japanese Naval Air Force*, 1405.

73 Hata, Izawa, and Shores, *Japanese Naval Air Force*, 1405; Wolf, *5th Fighter Command*, 281.

74 Except where otherwise noted, the account of the attack on the *Niagara* comes from Captain Robert J., Jr., USNR (Ret.) Bulkley, *At Close Quarters: PT Boats in the United States Navy* (Washington: Naval History Division, 1962), 110–11.

75 Day, *New Georgia*, 1339.

76 Gray Book, May 23rd, 1943. Curiously, with respect to the scuttling of the *Niagara*, Admiral Nimitz commented, "In several instances during the war ships have been abandoned and/or sunk while there was still a reasonable chance for salvage." One wonders to what "several" ships Nimitz was referring.

77 Wolf, *13th Fighter Command*, 166; Monograph 122, 55. Oddly, the ComAirSoPacFor War Diary has this attack taking place the following night.

78 Hammel, *Air War*, 5693.

79 Wolf, *13th Fighter Command*, 166.

80 Day, *New Georgia*, 1363.

81 Tagaya, *Rikko*, 1330.

82 Day, *New Georgia*, 1363.

83 Day, *New Georgia*, 1367.

84 Day, *New Georgia*, 1367.

85 Hata, Izawa, and Shores, *Japanese Naval Air Force*, 1405; Wolf, *5th Fighter Command*, 170.

86 Hata, Izawa, and Shores, *Japanese Naval Air Force*, 1405–24; Day, *New Georgia*, 1363–84; Wolf, *13th Fighter Command*, 171.

87 Wolf, *13th Fighter Command*, 170–71; Ross, *New Zealand*, 184; VMF-112-124 war diaries.

88 Lieutenant Moore's crew was massacred as it bailed from a burning B-17 by three clippedwing Zeros from the 204 and/or 253 Air Groups. With the 204 Air Group involved in the June 7 fighter sweep, there is a significant chance that the pilot that tried to machine-gun 2nd Lieutenant Logan in midair was one of the pilots that machine-gunned Moore's crew.

89 Tillman, *US Marine Corps*, 883; Robert Sherrod, *History of Marine Corps Aviation in World War II* (Washington, DC: Combat Forces Press, 1952), 140.

90 The story of Lieutenant Matson comes from Wolf, *13th Fighter Command*, 171.

91 Tillman, *US Marine Corps*, 883.

92 Hata, Izawa, and Shores, *Japanese Naval Air Force*, 1405–24; Davis, *Lightning Strike*, 5290; Day, *New Georgia*, 1363–84 and n. 27; Henry Sakaida, *Imperial Japanese Navy Aces 1937–45* (Oxford: Osprey, 1998), Kindle edition, 943.

93 Prados, *Islands of Destiny*, 244.

94 Day, *New Georgia*, 1384.

95 Amphibious Force, South Pacific Force War Diary; Dyer, *Amphibians*, 510–12; Wolf, *13th Fighter Command*, 171; Day, *New Georgia*, 1431; Monograph 122, 59. Dyer has seven Bettys attacking at dusk, with an unspecified number arriving after that were supposed to be aided by flares, but the flares were "luckily faulty." Monograph 122 says, "18 land medium bombers turned back due to poor weather."

96 Hata, Izawa, and Shores, *Japanese Naval Air Force*, 1424.

97 Ross, *New Zealand*, 185–86; Wolf, *13th Fighter Command*, 171.

98 Bruce R. Porter and Eric Hammel, *Ace! A Marine Night-Fighter Pilot in World War II* (Pacifica, CA: Pacifica Press, 1985), 126.

99 Porter and Hammel, *Ace!*, 127.

100 Porter and Hammel, *Ace!*, 129.

101 Porter and Hammel, *Ace!*, 132.

102 Hata, Izawa, and Shores, *Japanese Naval Air Force*, 1424; Wolf, *13th Fighter Command*, 171; Day, *New Georgia*, 1384 and n. 28.

103 Hata, Izawa, and Shores, *Japanese Naval Air Force*, 1424; Wolf, *13th Fighter Command*, 171; Day, *New Georgia*, 1384.

104 Day, *New Georgia*, 1384; Wolf, *13th Fighter Command*, 172.

105 Day, *New Georgia*, 1384; Hata, Izawa, and Shores, *Japanese Naval Air Force*, 1424.

106 Day, *New Georgia*, 1384–1405; Wolf, *13th Fighter Command*, 172; Amphibious Force, South Pacific Force War Diary; Hata, Izawa, and Shores, *Japanese Naval Air Force*, 1424.

107 Day, *New Georgia*, 1392; Wolf, *13th Fighter Command*, 171–72, 176; "June 16, 1943: Today in World War II Pacific History," *Pacific Wrecks* (www.pacificwrecks.com); Ross, *New Zealand*, 186.

108 John Stanaway, *P-38 Lightning Aces of the Pacific and CBI* (Oxford: Osprey, 1997), Kindle edition, 304.

109 Day, *New Georgia*, 1406–17.

110 Day, *New Georgia*, 1405; Wolf, *13th Fighter Command*, 176.

111 Wolf, *13th Fighter Command*, 172, 174.

112 Stanaway, *Lightning Aces*, 294–304; Wolf, *13th Fighter Command*, 172–74.

113 Stanaway, *Lightning Aces*, 294–304; Hammel, *Air War*, 5952; Wolf, *13th Fighter Command*, 174, 176.

114 "Spark III (LST-340)," *DANFS*. Note that the *LST-340* was later renamed the USS *Spark*, hence the entry in *DANFS*.

115 "Spark III (LST-340)," *DANFS*.

116 "Celeno," *DANFS*.

117 Hata, Izawa, and Shores, *Japanese Naval Air Force*, 1424; Davis, *Lightning Strike*, 5290; Day, *New Georgia*, 1417; Sherrod, *Marine Corps Aviation*, 140.

118 "Spark III (LST-340)" and "Celeno," *DANFS*.

119 Day, *New Georgia*, 1417.

120 Day, *New Georgia*, 1417.

121 Day, *New Georgia*, 1417.

122 Day, *New Georgia*, 1444.

123 Wolf, *13th Fighter Command*, 176.

124 Day, *New Georgia*, 1444.

125 *Kamikawa Maru* TROM; USS *Scamp* (SS-277) Report of Second War Patrol, Period from April 19, 1943 to June 4, 1943, 8–10.

126 This *Myoko Maru* is of no relation to the *Myoko Maru* that General MacArthur's bombers had forced aground outside Lae the previous January. The Japanese had numerous cases of multiple *Marus* sharing the same name. It can be confusing.

127 *Myoko Maru*, TROM.

128 *Ro-102* TROM.

129 George Odgers, *Australia in the War of 1939–1945: Series Three (Air) Volume II – Air War Against Japan, 1943–1945* (Canberra: Australian War Memorial, 1968), 147.

130 Gill, *Royal Australian Navy*, 257–58.

131 Richard Carleton, "A Grave Mistake," *60 minutes* (May 18, 2003), Nine Network (https://web.archive.org/web/20060828010512/http://sixtyminutes.ninemsn.com.au/sixtyminutes/stories/2003_05_18/story_838.asp).

132 Gill, *Royal Australian Navy*, 257.

133 Odgers, *Air War*, 147; Gill, *Royal Australian Navy*, 259.

134 Odgers, *Air War*, 148.

135 Odgers, *Air War*, 148.

136 Odgers, *Air War*, 148; Stevens, *Critical Vulnerability*, 239–40.

137 Stevens, *Critical Vulnerability*, 222.

138 *I-174* TROM; Odgers, *Air War*, 149–51; Gill, *Royal Australian Navy*, 260–61; Stevens, *Critical Vulnerability*, 242.

139 *I-174* TROM; Odgers, *Air War*, 149–51; Gill, *Royal Australian Navy*, 261.

140 *I-174* TROM.

141 *I-174* TROM.

142 This scenario is an amalgamation of Odgers, *Air War*, 151; and *I-174* TROM. Odgers has the Beaufort detecting the submarine on radar and following the wake, but both disappeared within one minute. The TROM has the same, except for the disappearance. Instead, the Beaufort bombs the *I-174* and misses, compelling the submarine to crash dive. After staying under for 35 minutes, the *I-174* surfaced, only to be bombed and compelled to crash dive again. After staying under for another 25 minutes, the submarine surfaced again and continued on.

143 Gill, *Royal Australian Navy*, 261; Stevens, *Critical Vulnerability*, 233–34; Odgers, *Air War*, 151.

144 *I-174* TROM.

145 Action Report USS *LST-469*, 1.

146 Action Report USS *LST-469*, 1–2; *I-174* TROM.

147 Stevens, *Critical Vulnerability*, 233–34.

148 Odgers, *Air War*, 151; Stevens, *Critical Vulnerability*, 235.

149 The story of the attack on the *I-178* comes from Odgers, *Air War*, 151–52; Stevens, *Critical Vulnerability*, 235; Gill, *Royal Australian Navy*, 261; *Concise History, Volume 3*, 71, 77; and *I-178* TROM.

150 Stevens, *Critical Vulnerability*, 235.

151 So talented was Lieutenant Nambu Nobukiyo that after the war he would rise to Rear Admiral in the Japan Maritime Self Defense Force.

152 *I-174* TROM; Stevens, *Critical Vulnerability*, 235.

153 *I-174*, *I-177*, and *I-178* TROMs.

154 Cressman, *Official Chronology*; *I-178* TROM; Gill, *Royal Australian Navy*, 260.

155 *O'Bannon* War Diary; *Ro-103* TROM; "Aludra I" and "Deimos I" *DANFS*.

156 *Ro-103* TROM.

Chapter 6

1   The son of Publius Cornelius Scipio Africanus Major adopted a son himself, who became known as Publius Cornelius Scipio Aemilianus Africanus Minor Numantinus.
2   Or Sasaki Noburu. Or Sasaki Akira.
3   Stille, *Solomons*, 655.
4   Stille, *Solomons*, 655; Rottman, *Japanese Army*, 1425.
5   Day, *New Georgia*, 1590.
6   Day, *New Georgia*, 1590–625.
7   Day, *New Georgia*, 1625–43.
8   Day, *New Georgia*, 1643–63.
9   Lord, *Lonely Vigil*, 186.
10 Lord, *Lonely Vigil*, 186; Rottman, *Japanese Army*, 1425.
11 Lord, *Lonely Vigil*, 186; Day, *New Georgia*, 1773; Monograph 99, 26.
12 Lord, *Lonely Vigil*, 175.
13 Shaw and Kane, *Isolation of Rabaul*, 41, 44–45; Lord, *Lonely Vigil*, 178.
14 Day, *New Georgia*, 1492; Morton, *Strategy and Command*, 401.
15 Morton, *Strategy and Command*, 401–02.
16 Day, *New Georgia*, 1511 and n. 7.
17 Day, *New Georgia*, 1511.
18 Dyer, *Amphibians*, 563–66.
19 Dyer, *Amphibians*, 537; Morison, *Bismarcks Barrier*, 144
20 Dyer, *Amphibians*, 537–39.
21 Day, *New Georgia*, 1511; Dyer, *Amphibians*, 537–39.
22 *Honolulu* War Diary.
23 USS *Montpelier* "Action Report, Bombardment of Poporang Island, night of June 29–30, 1943."
24 *Saratoga* War Diary.
25 Day, *New Georgia*, 1557.
26 Miller, *Cartwheel*, 71.
27 Lord, *Lonely Vigil*, 178–79.
28 Lord, *Lonely Vigil*, 182–83.
29 Lord, *Lonely Vigil*, 182–83.
30 Lord, *Lonely Vigil*, 183.
31 Dyer, *Amphibians*, 510–11; Day, *New Georgia*, 1773.
32 USS *Pringle* War Diary.
33 Morison, *Bismarcks Barrier*, 136.
34 Bulkley, *Close Quarters*, 188; Day, *New Georgia*, 1791–811; Philip Bradley, *Hell's Battlefield: The Australians in New Guinea in World War II* (London: Allen and Unwin, 2012), Kindle Edition, 4209; Dexter, *New Guinea*, 94–96.
35 Morison, *Bismarcks Barrier*, 136–37.
36 Day, *New Georgia*, 1811.
37 Dyer, *Amphibians*, 541.
38 Onaiavisi Passage is also known as Onaiavisi Entrance, Honiavasa Passage, Honiavasa Entrance, or somesuch. Dume is also known as Sasavele.
39 Dyer, *Amphibians*, 541.
40 Dyer, *Amphibians*, 545.
41 Morison, *Bismarcks Barrier*, 149.
42 Lord, *Lonely Vigil*, 185.
43 Dyer, *Amphibians*, 574.
44 Except where otherwise noted, the account of the Wickham operation comes from Day, *New Georgia*, 1981–2006; Eric Hammel, *Munda Trail: The New Georgia Campaign June–August 1943* (Pacifica, CA: Pacifica Military History, 1989), Kindle edition, 1270–363.
45 The narrative of the attempted landings at Viru Harbor come from Dyer, *Amphibians*, 567–70; and Day, *New Georgia*, 2006–54.
46 Day, *New Georgia*, 2054; Dyer, *Amphibians*, 571–72.
47 Prados, *Islands of Destiny*, 286.
48 Japanese Monograph No. 99 – "Southeast Area Naval Operations, Part II: Feb.–Oct. 1943," 26.
49 Day, *New Georgia*, 1791, 1811; *Ro-101* TROM; Prados, *Islands of Destiny*, 284.

50 Day, *New Georgia*, 1850; Dyer, *Amphibians*, 538.

51 Dyer, *Amphibians*, 547–48.

52 Dyer, *Amphibians*, 550; Wolf, *13th Fighter Command*, 181.

53 Hata, Izawa, and Shores, *Japanese Naval Air Force*, 1445.

54 Hata, Izawa, and Shores, *Japanese Naval Air Force*, 1442; Day, *New Georgia*, 1830–50.

55 Day, *New Georgia*, 1850.

56 Hammel, *Munda Trail*, 1163–85.

57 Monograph 99, 27. The site of General Sasaki's headquarters is disputed. Most accounts have his headquarters located atop a hill immediately north of the Munda runway in the middle of the base complex. The hill is called "Kokengolo," "Kokenggolo," or somesuch. (See e.g. Hammel, *Munda Trail*, 1594.) Citing *Senshi Sosho*, historian Ronnie Day placed both General Sasaki's and Admiral Ota's headquarters next to each other at a place Day calls "Kongo Hill which Day locates maybe 1,500 yards north of the Munda base." The Japanese called it "Kongōyama" – "Golden Mountain." The Americans eventually took to calling it "Twin Hills" because it has two peaks. This narrative here goes with Day's account.

58 Day, *New Georgia*, 1850.

59 Tagaya, *Rikko*, 1360.

60 Day, *New Georgia*, 1871.

61 VMF-221 Action Report of June 30, 1943, 2; Day, *New Georgia*, 1871.

62 Dyer, *Amphibians*, 560.

63 Wolf, *13th Fighter Command*, 182.

64 Tagaya, *Rikko*, 1360.

65 Hata, Izawa, and Shores, *Japanese Naval Air Force*, 1442.

66 Wolf, *13th Fighter Command*, 182.

67 Day, *New Georgia*, 1871–94.

68 Day, *New Georgia*, 1871–94; Wolf, *13th Fighter Command*, 182.

69 Day, *New Georgia*, 1871–94; Tillman, *US Marine Corps*, 903; Monograph 99, 29.

70 Dyer, *Amphibians*, 559.

71 Dyer, *Amphibians*, 560. Admiral Turner absolved Rodgers of any blame for the loss of the *McCawley*, and rightfully so; Rodgers was awarded the Silver Star for his efforts.

72 Dyer, *Amphibians*, 561.

73 Miller, *Cartwheel*, 49–50.

74 Miller, *Cartwheel*, 55.

75 Miller, *Cartwheel*, 56–57.

76 Tagaya, *Rikko*, 1360. "Squadron" is used here in place of the Japanese term *chutai*, which usually in the Naval Air Force meant six to nine aircraft, much smaller than a "squadron" in the US Army Air Force, Navy, or Marines. In the case of a *Rikko* unit a standard *chutai* was composed of nine aircraft, plus three in reserve. Hence the dozen aircraft of the 1st Chutai.

77 Day, *New Georgia*, 1894.

78 Monograph 140, 10; Hata, Izawa, and Shores, *Japanese Naval Air Force*, 1459; Hammel, *Air War*, 6130.

79 Hammel, *Munda Trail*, 1605.

80 Sherrod, *Marine Corps*, 148–49; Day, *New Georgia*, 1905; Hata, Izawa, and Shores, *Japanese Naval Air Force*, 1458; "July 2, 1943: Today in World War II Pacific History," *Pacific Wrecks* (www.pacificwrecks.com).

81 Day, *New Georgia*, 1905; Wolf, *13th Fighter Command*, 184; Sherrod, *Marine Corps*, 148–49.

82 Sherrod, *Marine Corps*, 148–49; Day, *New Georgia*, 1905–25; Wolf, *13th Fighter Command*, 184; Hata, Izawa, and Shores, *Japanese Army Air Force*, 1459–66.

83 Sherrod, *Marine Corps*, 148–49; Day, *New Georgia*, 1905; Hata, Izawa, and Shores, *Japanese Naval Air Force*, 1458; Wolf, *13th Fighter Command*, 184; Monograph 99 (29); Monograph 140, 5, 6, 10; "July 2, 1943: Today in World War II Pacific History," *Pacific Wrecks* (www.pacificwrecks.com). The specifics of the Japanese Naval Air Force participation in the two attacks of July 2 are unclear.

84 Hata, Izawa, and Shores, *Japanese Naval Air Force*, 1458.

85 VMF-213 War Diary; "Kashi Maru (Kasi Maru)," *Pacific Wrecks* (www.pacificwrecks.com).

86 Allyn D. Nevitt, "Introduction: The Niizuki," *Imperial Japanese Navy Page* (www.combinedfleet.com); *Yubari*, *Nagatsuki*, *Minazuki*, *Satsuki*, *Mikazuki*, and *Mochizuki* TROMs.

87 *Hatsuyuki* TROM.

88 *Nagatsuki*, *Minazuki*, and *Mikazuki* TROMs.

89 *Amagiri* and *Hatsuyuki* TROMs.

90 Day, *New Georgia*, 1941; *Nagatsuki* TROM; Prados, *Islands of Destiny*, 286.

91 *Niizuki, Yubari, Satsuki, Yunagi, Mochizuki,* and *Minazuki* TROMs.

92 *Yunagi* TROM.

93 Day, *New Georgia*, 1941.

94 Day, *New Georgia*, 1941–62.

95 Cressman, *Official Chronology*.

96 Hammel, *Munda Trail*, 1499–526; Miller, *Cartwheel*, 92–94; Morison, *Bismarcks Barrier*, 155.

97 Miller, *Cartwheel*, 92–94; Morison, *Bismarcks Barrier*, 155.

98 Miller, *Cartwheel*, 93–94.

99 Dyer, *Amphibians*, 579.

100 Hata, Izawa, and Shores, *Japanese Naval Air Force*, 1457; Day, *New Georgia*, 1919 and n. 30; Wolf, *13th Fighter Command*, 185.

101 Day, *New Georgia*, 1962.

102 Day, *New Georgia*, 1919; Hata, Izawa, and Shores, *Japanese Naval Air Force*, 1457; Commander South Pacific War Diary; Wolf, *13th Fighter Command*, 185. Day identifies the Japanese Army fighters as Ki-43s. Hata, Izawa, and Shores identify them as Ki-61s. The narrative here goes with both.

103 "Action Report, Night Bombardment of Vila-Stanmore and Bairoko Harbor, Kula Gulf, 4–5 July 1943" ("Ainsworth Rice Report"), 4; Day, *New Georgia*, 2073–93.

104 Alfred Samuels, *The USS* Ralph Talbot *and her Gallant Men* (Charlottesville, VA: Publishers Syndication International, 1991), Kindle edition, 2320.

105 "Action Report of Bombardment of Kula Gulf Area and Circumstances of Sinking of U.S.S. *Strong*, July 5, 1943" ("*Strong* Report"), 1.

106 Dyer, *Amphibians*, 580; *Talbot* War Diary.

107 *Strong* Report, 1; USS *Chevalier* "Action Report – Shore Bombardment Kula Gulf Area, July 4–5, 1943" ("*Chevalier* Rice Report"), 2; Day, *New Georgia*, 2093.

108 Ainsworth Rice Report, 3; "Action Report of Bombardment of Kula Gulf Area and Circumstances of Sinking of U.S.S. *Strong*, 5 July 1943, Amplifying Report" ("*Strong* 2nd Report"), 1; *Chevalier* Rice Report, 2.

109 Ainsworth Rice Report, 3–4; *Strong* Report, 1.

110 Dyer, *Amphibians*, 581; Samuels, *Ralph Talbot*, 2320; "Actions by Surface Ships – Reports of." Enclosure (B) "Narrative of Landing at Rice Anchorage, Kula Gulf, on July 5, 1943" ("*Ralph Talbot* Rice Report").

111 *Ralph Talbot* Rice Report, 1; Samuels, *Ralph Talbot*, 2320–43.

112 USS *Nicholas* "Action Report – Vila Plantation – Bairoko Harbor Bombardment, July 5, 1943" ("*Nicholas* Rice Report"), 2.

113 *Nicholas* Rice Report, 2.

114 John J. Domagalski, *Sunk in Kula Gulf: The Final Voyage of the USS* Helena *and the Incredible Story of Her Survivors* (Washington, DC: Potomac, 2012), Kindle edition, 890.

115 *Strong* Report, 2.

116 Alton B. Grimes, "Stories of USS *Strong*," *Destroyer History Foundation* (www.destroyerhistory.org).

117 Domagalski, *Sunk in Kula Gulf*, 890.

118 *Chevalier* Rice Report, 7; Domagalski, *Sunk in Kula Gulf*, 893.

119 Domagalski, *Sunk in Kula Gulf*, 900.

120 Domagalski, *Sunk in Kula Gulf*, 911; Tony DiGiulian, "Naval Propellants – A Brief Overview," *NavWeaps: Naval Weapons, Naval Technology and Naval Reunions* (www.navweaps.com).

121 Domagalski, *Sunk in Kula Gulf*, 900–17.

122 Domagalski, *Sunk in Kula Gulf*, 911; *Chevalier* Rice Report, 7.

123 Ainsworth Rice Report, 4.

124 Harding, *Castaway's War*, 10; Rear Admiral Joseph H. Wellings (ret.), "The Night *Strong* Was Sunk: 4–5 July 1943 in Kula Gulf," *Shipmate* 40 (July/Aug 1977), 3.

125 *Strong* Report, 2.

126 Wellings, "The Night *Strong* Was Sunk," 3.

127 *Strong* Report, 2–3; Wellings, "The Night *Strong* Was Sunk," 3.

128 Wellings, "The Night *Strong* Was Sunk," 3.

129 Wellings, "The Night *Strong* Was Sunk," 4.

130 Wellings, "The Night *Strong* Was Sunk," 4.

131 *Chevalier* Rice Report, 4–5.

132 Wellings, "The Night *Strong* Was Sunk," 4.

133   *Chevalier* Rice Report, 4–5, 7.

134   Wellings, "The Night *Strong* Was Sunk"; Morison, *Bismarcks Barrier*, 158; Task Unit 36.1.4 "Action Report – Shore Bombardment of enemy positions on Kolombangara Island and New Georgia Island (Kula Gulf) on the night of July 4–5, 1943" ("McInerney Rice Report"), 2; *Chevalier* Rice Report, 5–6.

135   Morison, *Bismarcks Barrier*, 158; *Chevalier* Rice Report, 5–7; Wellings, "The Night *Strong* Was Sunk," 4; *Strong* 2nd Report, 2; Harding, *Castaway's War*, 95–96.

136   *Chevalier* Rice Report, 5–6; Wellings, "The Night *Strong* Was Sunk," 4–5.

137   Wellings, "The Night *Strong* Was Sunk," 5; USS *Strong* "Action Report of Bombardment of Kula Gulf Area and Circumstances of Sinking of USS *Strong*, 5 July 1943, Amplifying Report," 2–3.

138   *Chevalier* Rice Report, 6.

139   Dyer, *Amphibians*, 581.

140   Dyer, *Amphibians*, 582; *Chevalier* Rice Report, 8.

141   USS *Gwin* "Action Report – Landing at Rice Anchorage, 5 July, 1943" ("*Gwin* Rice Report"), 2; *Ralph Talbot* Rice Report, 2; Alton B. Grimes, "USS Strong (DD 467) World War II Operations," *Destroyer History Foundation* (www.destroyerhistory.org).

142   Miller, *Cartwheel*, 95–96; Dyer, *Amphibians*, 581.

143   Day, *New Georgia*, 2124; Miller, *Cartwheel*, 95–96.

144   Ainsworth Rice Report, 2; McInerney Rice Report, 3.

145   Pompey's actual name was Gnaeus Pompeius. "Magnus" ("The Great") was his cognomen. To this day, there is no agreement as to how Pompey got the nickname "The Great."

146   Monograph 99, 32.

147   Monograph 99, 31.

148   Allyn D. Nevitt, "Introduction: The *Niizuki*."

149   Stille, *Imperial Japanese Navy*, 5841–43.

150   The Type 21 Radar is also known as the No. 21 Radar, No. 21(2) Radar, Type 2 Model 1 Mark 2 Radar, or somesuch.

151   Nevitt, "Introduction: The *Niizuki*"; Harding, *Castaway's War*, 86.

152   Day, *New Georgia*, 2102.

153   What is presented here is an amalgamation of Harding, *Castaway's War*, 86–87; O'Hara, *US Navy*, 3792. Most histories do not indicate the order in which Captain Kanaoka arranged his destroyer column, and there is disagreement among those that do.

154   Day, *New Georgia*, 2111.

155   Harding, *Castaway's War*, 86–87.

156   Nevitt, "Introduction: The *Niizuki*"; Harding, *Castaway's War*, 87.

157   Harding, *Castaway's War*, 87–88.

158   Harding, *Castaway's War*, 87–88; Nevitt, "Introduction: The *Niizuki*"; Day, *New Georgia*, 2102.

159   *Yubari* TROM; Morison, *Bismarcks Barrier*, 112 and n. 26.

160   Day, *New Georgia*, 2124 and n. 52; Wolf, *13th Fighter Command*, 185–86; Hata, Izawa, and Shores, *Japanese Naval Air Force*, 1466–73. Monograph 140 says the Japanese sent seven bombers and 36 fighters.

161   Nevitt, "Introduction: The *Niizuki*."

162   Domagalski, *Sunk in Kula Gulf*, 1063; Kilpatrick, *Naval Night Battles*, 185.

163   Day, *New Georgia*, 2752.

164   Morison, *Bismarcks Barrier*, 163.

165   Kilpatrick, *Naval Night Battles*, 185; O'Hara, *US Navy*, 3820.

166   Kilpatrick, *Naval Night Battles*, 185; Hammel, *Kula Gulf*, 177.

167   Kilpatrick, *Naval Night Battles*, 185; Hammel, *Kula Gulf*, 177.

168   Day, *New Georgia*, 2773.

169   Kilpatrick, *Naval Night Battles*, 186.

170   O'Hara, *US Navy*, 3849.

171   Morison, *Bismarcks Barrier*, 166.

172   Morison, *Bismarcks Barrier*, 166.

173   Hammel, *Kula Gulf*, 217.

174   Admiral Akiyama ordering the launch of torpedoes is a deduction based on Anthony Tully ("Located/Surveyed Shipwrecks of the Imperial Japanese Navy," *The Imperial Japanese Navy Page* (www.combinedfleet.com)), who reports that the torpedo tubes on the wreck of the *Niizuki* were intact and trained in as if in the middle of a reload. That the tubes had been trained back in to load the second batch of torpedoes suggests that Admiral Akiyama had time to order the torpedoes launched before the bridge was hit.

175 Prados, *Combined Fleet Decoded*, 491; Tully, "Located/Surveyed Shipwrecks of the Imperial Japanese Navy."

176 Kilpatrick, *Naval Night Battles*, 187.

177 Ainsworth Kula Gulf Report, 7.

178 Domagalski, *Sunk in Kula Gulf*, 1009.

179 Domagalski, *Sunk in Kula Gulf*, 992–1001.

180 Domagalski, *Sunk in Kula Gulf*, 992–1049.

181 Kilpatrick, *Naval Night Battles*, 183.

182 Russell Sydnor, Jr. Crenshaw, *South Pacific Destroyer: The Battle for the Solomons from Savo Island to Vella Gulf* (Annapolis: Naval Institute Press, 1998), Kindle edition, 2515.

183 Crenshaw, *South Pacific Destroyer*, 2515.

184 Crenshaw, *South Pacific Destroyer*, 2514.

185 USS *Radford* "Night Surface Engagement off Kula Gulf during night of July 5–6, 1943; Action Report of" ("*Radford* Kula Gulf Report"), 1; Domagalski, *Sunk in Kula Gulf*, 1032; Morison, *Bismarcks Barrier*, 161.

186 *Radford* Kula Gulf Report, 1.

187 *Radford* Kula Gulf Report, 1.

188 Crenshaw, *South Pacific Destroyer*, 2514.

189 *Radford* Kula Gulf Report, 1.

190 *Radford* Kula Gulf Report, 2; Crenshaw, *South Pacific Destroyer*, 2514.

191 Crenshaw, *South Pacific Destroyer*, 2531.

192 *Radford* Kula Gulf Report, 2; Commander Task Force 18 "Action Report – Night Engagement off Kula Gulf during night of 5–6 July 1943" ("Ainsworth Kula Gulf Report"), 1–2.

193 Commander Task Group 36.1.4 "Surface Engagement with Enemy (Japanese) Forces off Kula Gulf, New Georgia Group, Solomon Islands on the Night of July 5–6, 1943; report of" ("McInerney Kula Gulf Report"), 1; Crenshaw, *South Pacific Destroyer*, 2535.

194 Crenshaw, *South Pacific Destroyer*, 2535.

195 Ainsworth Kula Gulf Report, 2–4.

196 Ainsworth Kula Gulf Report, 4.

197 Kilpatrick, *Naval Night Battles*, 185; *Radford* Kula Gulf Report, 10.

198 Ainsworth Kula Gulf Report, 6.

199 Kilpatrick, *Naval Night Battles*, 185.

200 Crenshaw, *South Pacific Destroyer*, 2595.

201 Kilpatrick, *Naval Night Battles*, 185; Ainsworth Kula Gulf Report, 6.

202 Ainsworth Kula Gulf Report, 6.

203 Ainsworth Kula Gulf Report, 6; Domagalski, *Sunk in Kula Gulf*, 1133.

204 *Radford* Kula Gulf Report, 2.

205 USS *O'Bannon* "Engagement with Enemy Surface Forces off Kolombangara, Kula Gulf, early morning, 6 July 1943" ("*O'Bannon* Kula Gulf Report"), 2.

206 Kilpatrick, *Naval Night Battles*, 186.

207 Ainsworth Kula Gulf Report, 7.

208 Kilpatrick, *Naval Night Battles*, 186; Ainsworth Kula Gulf Report, 6. Admiral Ainsworth does not give the times when he ordered battle formation or the course change, only saying that the latter came one minute after the former. Crenshaw (*South Pacific Destroyer*, 2567) says Admiral Ainsworth ordered battle formation at 1:44am and the course change one minute later.

209 *O'Bannon* Kula Gulf Report, 2.

210 Crenshaw, *South Pacific Destroyer*, 2567.

211 *Radford* Kula Gulf Report, 10.

212 *Radford* Kula Gulf Report, 10; Domagalski, *Sunk In Kula Gulf*, 1133; "USS *St Louis* Action Report, First Battle of Kula Gulf 5–6 July 1943" ("*St Louis* Kula Gulf Report"), 14.

213 *Radford* Kula Gulf Report, 10; Crenshaw, *South Pacific Destroyer*, 2584.

214 *St Louis* Kula Gulf Report, 2.

215 Ainsworth Kula Gulf Report, 6–7.

216 Ainsworth Kula Gulf Report, 7.

217 McInerney Kula Gulf Report, 2.

218 Kilpatrick, *Naval Night Battles*, 186.

219 *Radford* Kula Gulf Report, 10; *St Louis* Kula Gulf Report, 2; Ainsworth Kula Gulf Report, 6.

220 Crenshaw, *South Pacific Destroyer*, 2584.

221 Ainsworth Kula Gulf Report, 7.

222 *O'Bannon* Kula Gulf Report, 6.

223 *O'Bannon* Kula Gulf Report, 6.

224 *O'Bannon* Kula Gulf Report, 6. Captain McInerney's actual quote was, "Gunfire or William?" "William" was the code word for launching torpedoes.

225 Kilpatrick, *Naval Night Battles*, 186.

226 *O'Bannon* Kula Gulf Report, 6.

227 Ainsworth Kula Gulf Report, 7; Crenshaw, *South Pacific Destroyer*, 2585–606.

228 *St Louis* Kula Gulf Report, 2.

229 *O'Bannon* Kula Gulf Report, 6.

230 Ainsworth Kula Gulf Report, 7.

231 Kilpatrick, *Naval Night Battles*, 187.

232 Kilpatrick, *Naval Night Battles*, 187.

233 Ainsworth Kula Gulf Report, 7.

234 Kilpatrick, *Naval Night Battles*, 187; Crenshaw, *South Pacific Destroyer*, 2615.

235 Crenshaw, *South Pacific Destroyer*, 2615.

236 Lieutenant C.G. (USNR) Morris and Hugh B. Cave, *The Fightin'est Ship: The Story of the Cruiser Helena*, (Holicong, PA: Wildside Press, 1944), 84.

237 Morris and Cave, *Fightin'est Ship*, 84–85.

238 Ainsworth Kula Gulf Report, 7.

239 O'Hara, *US Navy*, 3857.

240 *St Louis* Kula Gulf Report, 2–3.

241 *St Louis* Kula Gulf Report, 3.

242 *O'Bannon* Kula Gulf Report, 6.

243 *St Louis* Kula Gulf Report, 3.

244 Wukovits, *Tin Can Titans*, 2721.

245 Hammel, *Kula Gulf*, 211; Kilpatrick, *Naval Night Battles*, 187.

246 Morison, *Bismarcks Barrier*, 166–67.

247 *O'Bannon* Kula Gulf Report, 7; *St Louis* Kula Gulf Report, 14.

248 Kilpatrick, *Naval Night Battles*, 188.

249 Kilpatrick, *Naval Night Battles*, 188–89.

250 Kilpatrick, *Naval Night Battles*, 188; *Radford* Kula Gulf Report, 3.

251 McInerney Kula Gulf Report, 3; *O'Bannon* Kula Gulf Report, 3.

252 *Radford* Kula Gulf Report, 12; *St Louis* Kula Gulf Report, 15.

253 *St Louis* Kula Gulf Report, 15; *Radford* Kula Gulf Report, 12.

254 Kilpatrick, *Naval Night Battles*, 190.

255 *Radford* Kula Gulf Report, 3.

256 McInerney Kula Gulf Report, 3.

257 *Radford* Kula Gulf Report, 12.

258 Ainsworth Kula Gulf Report, 8; *Radford* Kula Gulf Report, 12.

259 *O'Bannon* Kula Gulf Report, 3.

260 *Radford* Kula Gulf Report, 3.

261 *O'Bannon* Kula Gulf Report, 8.

262 *O'Bannon* Kula Gulf Report, 8. During this time there was no standardization to voice radio logs from the Talk Between Ships circuit. Some logs used exact quotes as much as possible, some paraphrased. Some used local time, others used a different time. Some would use the code words verbatim, others translated the code words and put the translations in the log. For the ease of understanding, this narrative has endeavored to translate coded TBS transmissions, but any word substitutions for code words are indicated by [brackets].

263 *Radford* Kula Gulf Report, 3.

264 *O'Bannon* Kula Gulf Report, 8.

265 Morison, *Bismarcks Barrier*, 168.

266 McInerney Kula Gulf Report, 4.

267 Ainsworth Kula Gulf Report, 9; Crenshaw, *South Pacific Destroyer*, 2720.

268 *O'Bannon* Kula Gulf Report, 9.

269 Crenshaw, *South Pacific Destroyer*, 2720.

270 Morison, *Bismarcks Barrier*, 168–69.

271 Ainsworth Kula Gulf Report, 11.
272 *O'Bannon* Kula Gulf Report, 10.
273 *O'Bannon* Kula Gulf Report, 10.
274 *O'Bannon* Kula Gulf Report, 10.
275 *O'Bannon* Kula Gulf Report, 10; *Radford* Kula Gulf Report, 14–15.
276 *Radford* Kula Gulf Report, 15.
277 *O'Bannon* Kula Gulf Report, 10; *St Louis* Kula Gulf Report, 18.
278 *Radford* Kula Gulf Report, 15.
279 *Radford* Kula Gulf Report, 16. Time is from *O'Bannon* Kula Gulf Report, 10, because the *Radford*'s times seem to be about three minutes fast.
280 *Radford* Kula Gulf Report, 16.
281 *St Louis* Kula Gulf Report, 18.
282 *O'Bannon* Kula Gulf Report, 11.
283 *O'Bannon* Kula Gulf Report, 11.
284 *Radford* Kula Gulf Report, 16.
285 *Radford* Kula Gulf Report, 16.
286 Wukovits, *Tin Can Titans*, 2721.
287 Wukovits, *Tin Can Titans*, 2731.
288 Morris and Cave, *Fightin'est Ship*, 44.
289 Casten, USS *Helena*, 87.
290 Morris and Cave, *Fightin'est Ship*, 85.
291 "U. S. S. Helena (CL50) Loss In Action Kula Gulf, Solomon Islands 6 July, 1943. War Damage Report No. 43" ("*Helena* Loss Report"), 4–5; Domagalski, *Sunk in Kula Gulf*, 1342.
292 USS *Helena* "Events I Observed During and After the Action of 6 July, 1943" ("Cook Kula Gulf Report"), 1.
293 Cook Kula Gulf Report, 1.
294 *Helena* Loss Report, 7.
295 *Helena* Loss Report, 5, 7–9 and Plate I.
296 Cook Kula Gulf Report, 1.
297 *Helena* Loss Report, 5, 7–9 and Plate I.
298 Cook Kula Gulf Report, 1.
299 Domagalski, *Sunk in Kula Gulf*, 1390; *Helena* Loss Report, 10.
300 Domagalski, *Sunk in Kula Gulf*, 1372.
301 Morris and Cave, *Fightin'est Ship*, 85.
302 Casten, USS *Helena*, 87.
303 *Helena* Loss Report, 18 and Plate II.
304 *Helena* Loss Report, 4.
305 Morris and Cave, *Fightin'est Ship*, 87.
306 *Helena* Loss Report, 1; Domagalski, *Sunk in Kula Gulf*, 1342.
307 Domagalski, *Sunk in Kula Gulf*, 1356–72.
308 *Helena* Loss Report, 2. Captain Cecil mentions the aft turrets firing two or three rounds per gun, but says nothing about the remaining forward turrets.
309 O'Hara, *US Navy*, 3881.
310 Lord, *Lonely Vigil*, 193; *Helena* Loss Report, 4.
311 Morris and Cave, *Fightin'est Ship*, 89.
312 *O'Bannon* Kula Gulf Report, 11.
313 Wukovits, *Tin Can Titans*, 2741.
314 McInerney Kula Gulf Report, 4.
315 USS *Nicholas* "Action Report" ("*Nicholas* Kula Gulf Report"), 4.
316 *Radford* Kula Gulf Report, 4.
317 Morison, *Bismarcks Barrier*, 172; O'Hara, *US Navy*, 3912.
318 Morison, *Bismarcks Barrier*, 167–168; O'Hara, *US Navy*, 3912.
319 O'Hara, *US Navy*, 3923.
320 Morison, *Bismarcks Barrier*, 167–68; *Amagiri* TROM.
321 Morison, *Bismarcks Barrier*, 168; *Hatsuyuki* TROM.
322 Morison, *Bismarcks Barrier*, 168; O'Hara, *US Navy*, 3985; *Nagatsuki* TROM.
323 Crenshaw, *South Pacific Destroyer*, 2833.

324 Crenshaw, *South Pacific Destroyer*, 2833.
325 *Amagiri* TROM.
326 *Nicholas* Kula Gulf Report, 10; Morison, *Bismarcks Barrier*, 137.
327 Morison, *Bismarcks Barrier*, 174; *Mochizuki* TROM.
328 Morison, *Bismarcks Barrier*, 174.
329 Day, *New Georgia*, 2834–44.
330 Day, *New Georgia*, 2844.
331 Day, *New Georgia*, 2844; Morison, *Bismarcks Barrier*, 191.
332 Day, *New Georgia*, 2844; Morison, *Bismarcks Barrier*, 174–75.
333 Day, *New Georgia*, 2844.
334 Morison, *Bismarcks Barrier*, 171; Day, *New Georgia*, 2810; Tully, "Located/Surveyed Shipwrecks of the Imperial Japanese Navy."
335 Morison, *Bismarcks Barrier*, 174–75; Hammel, *Air War*, 6183–94; Wolf, *13th Fighter Command*, 187; Day, *New Georgia*, 2844–56; Tully, "Located/Surveyed Shipwrecks of the Imperial Japanese Navy."
336 *Nagatsuki* TROM.
337 Day, *New Georgia*, 2824.
338 Day, *New Georgia*, 2848.
339 Miller, *Cartwheel*, 99.
340 Miller, *Cartwheel*, 99–100.
341 Samuel B. Griffith, "Action at Enogai," *Marine Corps Gazette* 28, 3 (Mar 1944), 15.
342 Griffith, "Action at Enogai," 15.
343 Griffith, "Action at Enogai," 15.
344 Miller, *Cartwheel*, 101.
345 Morison, *Bismarcks Barrier*, 176.
346 Miller, *Cartwheel*, 101.
347 Day, *New Georgia*, 2498–532; Griffith, "Action at Enogai," 16; Miller, *Cartwheel*, 101.
348 Day, *New Georgia*, 2553–71; Miller, *Cartwheel*, 103; Griffith, "Action at Enogai," 18–19.
349 Day, *New Georgia*, 2571; Tagaya, *Rikko*, 1385; Hata, Izawa, and Shores, *Japanese Naval Air Force*, 1472–79; "William E. Sage," *Missing Marines* (www.missingmarines.com). Hata, et al., have the 55 Zeros escorting eight *Rikko*. The Japanese fighter pilots claimed 15 victories and four probables, despite facing only five fighters. Monograph 140 shows no Japanese air attack on this day.
350 Wolf, *13th Fighter Command*, 188; Hammel, *Air War*, 6234; Day, *New Georgia*, 2571; Harding, *Castaway's War*, 119–20; Hata, Izawa, and Shores, *Japanese Naval Air Force*, 1476.
351 Craven and Cate, *Guadalcanal*, 232.
352 Day, *New Georgia*, 2139–54.
353 Hammel, *Munda Trail*, 1704.
354 Hammel, *Munda Trail*, 1740–58; Miller, *Cartwheel*, 108.
355 Miller, *Cartwheel*, 108–09, 112–13.
356 Miller, *Cartwheel*, 108–09, 112–13.
357 Day, *New Georgia*, 2139.
358 Craven and Cate, *Guadalcanal*, 231.
359 Miller, *Cartwheel*, 110–11; Day, *New Georgia*, 2154.
360 Day, *New Georgia*, 2173.
361 Day, *New Georgia*, 2173.
362 Day, *New Georgia*, 2173.
363 Hammel, *Munda Trail*, 1865.
364 Hammel, *Munda Trail*, 1882–1901.
365 Day, *New Georgia*, 2848; *Satsuki* and *Yugure* TROMs. Curiously, neither the *Chokai's* nor the *Sendai's* TROMs mention this operation.
366 Miller, *Cartwheel*, 104–05; Day, *New Georgia*, 2154.
367 Hammel, *Munda Trail*, 2011.
368 Miller, *Cartwheel*, 114–15.
369 Miller, *Cartwheel*, 114–15.
370 Morison, *Bismarcks Barrier*, 177.
371 Dyer, *Amphibians*, 590–91.
372 Hammel, *Munda Trail*, 2011–30.

373 Miller, *Cartwheel*, 115.
374 Commander, Cruiser Division 12 War Diary.
375 Morison, *Bismarcks Barrier*, 177–79.
376 Morison, *Bismarcks Barrier*, 177–79.
377 Dyer, *Amphibians*, 582–83.
378 USS *Honolulu* War Diary.
379 USS *Taylor* "Action Report, Morning of July 12, 1943," 2–3.
380 *Ro-101* TROM.
381 USS *Taylor* "Action Report, Morning of July 12, 1943," 3.
382 Day, *New Georgia*, 2869.
383 Day, *New Georgia*, 2869–91; Wolf, *13th Fighter Command*, 188–89; Hata, Izawa, and Shores, *Japanese Naval Air Force*, 1476.
384 Miller, *Cartwheel*, 115–16.
385 Miller, *Cartwheel*, 116.
386 Hata, Izawa, and Shores, *Japanese Naval Air Force*, 1476.
387 Hata, Izawa, and Shores, *Japanese Naval Air Force*, 1476.
388 Day, *New Georgia*, 2336.
389 *Ro-101* TROM.
390 *Ro-101* TROM.
391 Izaki is sometimes rendered as "Isaki."
392 *Jintsu* TROM.
393 Kilpatrick, *Naval Night Battles*, 200; Day, *New Georgia*, 2917.
394 Kilpatrick, *Naval Night Battles*, 201.
395 Morison, *Bismarcks Barrier*, 180.
396 O'Hara, *US Navy*, 3962.
397 S.D. Waters, *The Royal New Zealand Navy* (Wellington: Historical Publications Branch, 1956), 317.
398 McInerney Kula Gulf Report, 8.
399 Waters, *Royal New Zealand Navy*, 317.
400 Commander Task Force 18 Action Report, "Night Engagement off Kolombangara during night of 12–13 July 1943" ("Ainsworth Kolombangara Report"), 3.
401 Crenshaw, *South Pacific Destroyer*, 3014.
402 Crenshaw, *South Pacific Destroyer*, 3014.
403 Kilpatrick, *Naval Night Battles*, 201; Crenshaw, *South Pacific Destroyer*, 3014.
404 O'Hara, *US Navy*, 3956.
405 Commander Task Group 36.1.4, "Surface Engagement with Enemy (Japanese) Forces off Kula Gulf, New Georgia Group, Solomon Islands on the Night of July 12–13, 1943 (second engagement); report of" ("McInerney Kolombangara Report"), 2.
406 Kilpatrick, *Naval Night Battles*, 201.
407 Kilpatrick, *Naval Night Battles*, 201.
408 Waters, *Royal New Zealand Navy*, 318. The *Jintsu* TROM has Captain Shimai's given name as Zenjiro.
409 O'Hara, *US Navy*, 3994, n. 32.
410 O'Hara, *US Navy*, 3994, n. 32.
411 Kilpatrick, *Naval Night Battles*, 201; Crenshaw, *South Pacific Destroyer*, 3050.
412 McInerney Kolombangara Report, 11.
413 Kilpatrick, *Naval Night Battles*, 201; O'Hara, *US Navy*, 3994.
414 O'Hara, *US Navy*, 3994.
415 Ainsworth Kolombangara Report, 3; McInerney Kolombangara Report, 2.
416 USS *Radford* Action Report of Night Engagement off Kolombangara during the night of 12–13 July 1943 ("*Radford* Kolombangara Report"), 1.
417 *Radford* Kolombangara Report, 1; McInerney Kolombangara Report, 2, 11.
418 Kilpatrick, *Naval Night Battles*, 202; McInerney Kolombangara Report, 11.
419 O'Hara, *US Navy*, 3994; Crenshaw, *South Pacific Destroyer*, 3070.
420 McInerney Kolombangara Report, 2, 11.
421 McInerney Kolombangara Report, 12.
422 Crenshaw, *South Pacific Destroyer*, 3092; McInerney Kolombangara Report, 12.
423 Kilpatrick, *Naval Night Battles*, 202.

424 Crenshaw, *South Pacific Destroyer*, 3113.

425 O'Hara, *US Navy*, 3994.

426 Crenshaw, *South Pacific Destroyer*, 3113.

427 Crenshaw, *South Pacific Destroyer*, 3113.

428 O'Hara, *US Navy*, 3994.

429 O'Hara, *US Navy*, 3994.

430 Waters, *Royal New Zealand Navy*, 318; Kilpatrick, *Naval Night Battles*, 202.

431 Kilpatrick, *Naval Night Battles*, 203.

432 Waters, *Royal New Zealand Navy*, 318; Kilpatrick, *Naval Night Battles*, 203.

433 Morison, *Bismarcks Barrier*, 184.

434 Waters, *Royal New Zealand Navy*, 318.

435 Morison, *Bismarcks Barrier*, 184.

436 Morison, *Bismarcks Barrier*, 184.

437 O'Hara, *US Navy*, 4016–31.

438 Kilpatrick, *Naval Night Battles*, 187.

439 Crenshaw, *South Pacific Destroyer*, 3179.

440 Crenshaw, *South Pacific Destroyer*, 3179; McInerney Kolombangara Report, 3.

441 Crenshaw, *South Pacific Destroyer*, 3156.

442 Crenshaw, *South Pacific Destroyer*, 3179; O'Hara, *US Navy*, 4031; Waters, *Royal New Zealand Navy*, 319.

443 Kilpatrick, *Naval Night Battles*, 187.

444 Kilpatrick, *Naval Night Battles*, 187.

445 *Jintsu* TROM.

446 Waters, *Royal New Zealand Navy*, 321–22.

447 Waters, *Royal New Zealand Navy*, 322.

448 Kilpatrick, *Naval Night Battles*, 203–04.

449 Kilpatrick, *Naval Night Battles*, 203.

450 Morison, *Bismarcks Barrier*, 186; Crenshaw, *South Pacific Destroyer*, 3222; McInerney Kolombangara Report, 12.

451 O'Hara, *US Navy*, 4031.

452 Crenshaw, *South Pacific Destroyer*, 3222.

453 Crenshaw, *South Pacific Destroyer*, 3222.

454 O'Hara, *US Navy*, 4052; Waters, *Royal New Zealand Navy*, 319.

455 Waters, *Royal New Zealand Navy*, 319.

456 *Jintsu* TROM.

457 Crenshaw, *South Pacific Destroyer*, 3222.

458 Crenshaw, *South Pacific Destroyer*, 3222.

459 Crenshaw, *South Pacific Destroyer*, 3244.

460 Crenshaw, *South Pacific Destroyer*, 3244.

461 Crenshaw, *South Pacific Destroyer*, 3266.

462 Crenshaw, *South Pacific Destroyer*, 3266.

463 Kilpatrick, *Naval Night Battles*, 204.

464 Crenshaw, *South Pacific Destroyer*, 3266.

465 O'Hara, *US Navy*, 4052.

466 Ainsworth Kolombangara Report, 5.

467 *Honolulu* Kolombangara Report, Enclosure (A) Commanding Officer's Statement, 2.

468 *St Louis* Kolombangara Report, Enclosure (B) TBS Log, 3.

469 Crenshaw, *South Pacific Destroyer*, 3287.

470 Ainsworth Kolombangara Report, 5.

471 *Honolulu* Kolombangara Report, 3.

472 USS *Woodworth* Action Report ("*Woodworth* Kolombangara Report"), 2.

473 *St Louis* Action Report, Second Battle of Kula Gulf, 12–13 July 1943 ("*St Louis* Kolombangara Report"), 26.

474 *St Louis* Kolombangara Report, 1, 14.

475 *Honolulu* Kolombangara Report, 4.

476 *Honolulu* Kolombangara Report, 5.

477 USS *Gwin* (433) Night Action off Kula Gulf on 12–13 July, Loss of USS *Gwin* ("*Gwin* Kolombangara Report"), 3; *Woodworth* Kolombangara Report, 3.

478 *Woodworth* Kolombangara Report, 3; *Buchanan* Kolombangara Report, 4.

479 The *Woodworth*'s Gordinier did note (*Woodworth* Kolombangara Report, 3) in his report, "The lack of a [SG] radar was keenly felt," while the *Buchanan*'s Myhre (*Buchanan* Kolombangara Report, 5) was slightly more circumspect, "Although it was probably a coincidence, it is to be noted that *Buchanan* and *Woodworth*, the two ships suffering battle damage from collision, were the only two non-SG ships present." Otherwise, the After Action Reports' descriptions of the lead-up to the collision cannot be easily reconciled with the other, to put it mildly.

480 Morison, *Bismarcks Barrier*, 187.

481 *Honolulu* Kolombangara Report, Enclosure (A) Commanding Officer's Statement, 2–3.

482 Crenshaw, *South Pacific Destroyer*, 3309.

483 Kilpatrick, *Naval Night Battles*, 205; *St Louis* Kula Gulf Report, Enclosure (B), TBS Log, 3.

484 Crenshaw, *South Pacific Destroyer*, 3332.

485 Kilpatrick, *Naval Night Battles*, 205; *St Louis* Kula Gulf Report, Enclosure (B), TBS Log, 3.

486 *St Louis* Kula Gulf Report, Enclosure (B), TBS Log, 3.

487 *St Louis* Kula Gulf Report, Enclosure (B), TBS Log, 3.

488 *Gwin* Kolombangara Report, 3.

489 *Gwin* Kolombangara Report, 3.

490 Morison, *Bismarcks Barrier*, 190.

491 Morison, *Bismarcks Barrier*, 190.

492 The night naval surface battle of July 5–6, 1943 took place northwest of Kolombangara at the entrance to Kula Gulf and is therefore known as the Battle of Kula Gulf. The night naval surface battle of July 12–13, 1943 also took place northwest of Kolombangara at the entrance to Kula Gulf and is therefore known as the Battle of Kolombangara.

493 Day, *New Georgia*, 2982.

Chapter 7

1 Day, *New Georgia*, 2844; Morison, *Bismarcks Barrier*, 191.

2 Except where noted otherwise, the story of Lieutenant Commander Chew and the other *Helena* survivors comes from Lord, *Lonely Vigil*, 194–212.

3 Lord, *Lonely Vigil*, 194–95.

4 DesRon 21 Rescue of Survivors of *U.S.S. Helena* from the Island of Vella La Vella (New Georgia Group); report of (hereinafter "McInerney *Helena* Rescue Report"), 1.

5 McInerney *Helena* Rescue Report, 1.

6 Lord, *Lonely Vigil*, 208–09; Wukovits, *Tin Can Titans*, 2743; Morison, *Bismarcks Barrier*, 193.

7 DesRon 12 Rescue of approximately 164 *Helena* survivors from Vella Lavella, Solomon Islands, 16–17 July, 1943 (hereinafter "Ryan *Helena* Rescue Report"), 1.

8 McInerney *Helena* Rescue Report, 1–2.

9 McInerney *Helena* Rescue Report, 2.

10 Morison, *Bismarcks Barrier*, 193; Wukovits, *Tin Can Titans*, 2743–62.

11 Ryan *Helena* Rescue Report, 4.

12 Ryan *Helena* Rescue Report, 2, which says a stop at Lambu Lambu was always part of the plan, which Ryan had developed with Sweeney. Not telling Sweeney about the stop at Lambu Lambu would have been an egregious error and a sign of incompetence. The narrative here goes with Ryan.

13 Ryan *Helena* Rescue Report, 5.

14 McInerney *Helena* Rescue Report, 1.

15 Day, *New Georgia*, 3202.

16 Halsey, *Story*, 3420.

17 Hughes, *Admiral Bill Halsey*, 4953–954; Miller, *Cartwheel*, 121.

18 Miller, *Cartwheel*, 120–21.

19 Miller, *Cartwheel*, 121.

20 Halsey, *Story*, 3420.

21 Miller, *Cartwheel*, 123.

22 Dyer, *Amphibians*, 586.

23 Potter, *Bull Halsey*, 225; Dyer, *Amphibians*, 586; Day, *New Georgia*, 2316.

24 Dyer, *Amphibians*, 586–87.

25 Hughes, *Admiral Bill Halsey*, 4975.

26 Dyer, *Amphibians*, 587.

27 Miller, *Cartwheel*, 135.

28 Day, *New Georgia*, 2345.

29 Miller, *Cartwheel*, 135; Day, *New Georgia*, 2345.

30 Day, *New Georgia*, 2345.

31 Hammel, *Munda Trail*, 2602.

32 Day, *New Georgia*, 2345–55, 2609.

33 Day, *New Georgia*, 2355. Day says, "The only account available (the 6th Division history, based largely on the recollections of Major Kinoshita and his orderly, Corporal Kaga Dennosuke) presents a confused picture of what occurred between 14 and 17 July. What emerges with some clarity, however, is that Tomonari's troops had a rough time."

34 Col. (Ret.) Joseph E. Zimmer (*The History of the 43rd Infantry Division, 1941–1945* (Bennington, VT: Merriam Press, 2015), Kindle edition, 43) gives the time as 5:00pm. Some of the sources do not agree on the times but I am largely following Day, *New Georgia*, 127; and Brian Altobello, *Into The Shadows Furious: The Brutal Battle For New Georgia* (Novato, CA: Presidio Press, 2000), 290–301.

35 Whether Major Hara's troops committed this attack is still a matter of debate and some conjecture that runs the full spectrum. Hammel (*Munda Trail*, 4738) flat-out says the attacking unit was Major Hara's. Day's description of the attack (*New Georgia*, 2393–99) says it was conducted by "parties of Japanese" and concedes that what happened "is not at all clear," though his placement of the incident implies they were Colonel Tomonari's men. He does not mention Hara's men until their return to what he calls "the Kure 6th Farm" near Zieta, well to the north, on July 19. Miller (*Cartwheel*, 137 n. 9) splits the difference: Japanese records do not indicate just what the main body of the 13th actually did during the period 17–19 July. The various raids could not have been the work of the entire unit. The main body apparently never got into action at all. The 170 hungry survivors of Major Hara's Viru garrison may have caused some of the trouble to the Americans, for on 18 or 19 July they reached Munda after marching overland from Viru and infiltrating the American lines from the rear.

36 Hammel, *Munda Trail*, 2612; Zimmer, *History of the 43rd*, 42.

37 Hammel, *Munda Trail*, 2621.

38 Zimmer, *History of the 43rd*, 42; Day, *New Georgia*, 2365; Major Charles D. (Ret.) Melson, "Up the Slot: Marines in the Central Solomons," *World War II Commemorative Series* (Washington, DC: History and Museums Division, Headquarters, U.S. Marine Corps, 1993), 20.

39 Hammel, *Munda Trail*, 2621.

40 Hammel, *Munda Trail*, 2621.

41 Day, *New Georgia*, 2370.

42 Day, *New Georgia*, 2370.

43 Altobello, *Shadows Furious*, 277.

44 Day, *New Georgia*, 2376.

45 Miller, *Cartwheel*, 136.

46 Hammel, *Munda Trail*, 2639.

47 Hammel, *Munda Trail*, 2649. General Hester was not at the 43rd's forward command post on Zanana Beach, but where he was seems to be disputed in different sources.

48 Day, *New Georgia*, 1711.

49 Miller, *Cartwheel*, 136.

50 Brig. Gen. (Retired) Harold R. Barker, *History of the 43rd Division Artillery: World War II 1941–1945* (Providence, RI: John F. Greene, Co., Inc., 1961), 53–54.

51 Barker, *Artillery*, 55.

52 Barker, *Artillery*, 55.

53 Major John N. Rentz, "Marines in the Central Solomons," (Washington, DC: Historical Branch, Headquarters, U.S. Marine Corps, 1952), 83.

54 Day, *New Georgia*, 2378.

55 Hammel, *Munda Trail*, 2657.

56 Day, *New Georgia*, 2378–86, 5282–92; Melson, "Up the Slot," 17.

57 Rentz, "Marines in the Central Solomons," 84.

58 Rentz, "Marines in the Central Solomons," 84.

59 Day, *New Georgia*, 2386; Miller, *Cartwheel*, 136 and n. 8.

60 Hammel, *Munda Trail*, 2562.

61 Miller, *Cartwheel*, 136.

62 Hammel, *Munda Trail*, 2714–21.

63 Miller, *Cartwheel*, 136; Hammel, *Munda Trail*, 2711–31.

64 Zimmer, *43rd*, 43.

65 Miller, *Cartwheel*, 136.

66 Barker, *Artillery*, 55.

67 Rentz, "Marines in the Central Solomons," 84.

68 Rentz, "Marines in the Central Solomons," 84.

69 Rentz, "Marines in the Central Solomons," 84.

70 Rentz, "Marines in the Central Solomons," 84. They were eventually awarded the Navy Cross.

71 Day, *New Georgia*, 2393–406.

72 Miller, *Cartwheel*, 136.

73 Hara, Saito, and Pineau, *Destroyer Captain*, 148.

74 Hara, Saito, and Pineau, *Destroyer Captain*, 158.

75 *Shigure* TROM; Hara, Saito, and Pineau, *Destroyer Captain*, 159.

76 Hara, Saito, and Pineau, *Destroyer Captain*, 159.

77 Hara, Saito, and Pineau, *Destroyer Captain*, 159.

78 Hara, Saito, and Pineau, *Destroyer Captain*, 160.

79 Hara, Saito, and Pineau, *Destroyer Captain*, 160.

80 Hara, Saito, and Pineau, *Destroyer Captain*, 168–69.

81 *Nagara* TROM; Pressman, *Official Chronology*; USS *Silversides* "Report of 5th War Patrol," 6.

82 Except where noted otherwise, the details of the attacks on the *Chincoteague* come from "War Damage Report No. 47 U.S.S. Chincoteague (AVP24) Bomb Damage, Saboe Bay, Santa Cruz Islands 17 July, 1943" (hereinafter "*Chincoteague* Damage Report"), 2–7.

83 *Thornton* War Diary.

84 *Thornton* War Diary.

85 *Thornton* War Diary.

86 *Thornton* War Diary.

87 *Thornton* War Diary.

88 *Thornton* War Diary.

89 Wolf, *13th Fighter Command*, 191; VMSB-132, VMF-122, -213, and -221 war diaries; Barrett Tillman, *Corsair: The F4U in World War II and Korea* (Annapolis: Naval Institute Press, 1979), Kindle edition, 58; Robert J. Cressman, *The Official Chronology of the U.S. Navy in World War II* (Washington, DC: Contemporary History Branch, Naval Historical Center, 1999); Hammel, *Air War*, 6311–19; Sam S. Britt Jr, *The Long Rangers: A Diary of The 307th Bombardment Group (H)* (Spartanburg, SC: Reprint Company Publishers, 1990), 51–52; Ross, *Official History*, 192–93.

90 Hata, Izawa, and Shores, *Japanese Naval Air Force*, 1492–99, 7791; *Hatsuyuki* and *Yunagi* TROMs; Wolf, *13th Fighter Command*, 191; Hammel, *Air War*, 6311–19; Morison, *Bismarcks Barrier*, 206; "July 17, 1943," *Pacific Wrecks* (www.pacificwrecks.com). For some reason, Cressman (*Official Chronology*) lists the *Hatsukaze* as being damaged in this strike, but the *Hatsukaze's* TROM has her docked at Kure in the Home Islands for repairs at this time.

91 Hammel, *Air War*, 6335–42; Wolf, *13th Fighter Command*, 191–92; Britt, *Long Rangers*, 52; "July 17, 1943," *Pacific Wrecks* (www.pacificwrecks.com); Hata, Izawa, and Shores, *Japanese Naval Air Force*, 1499; MAG 12 Record of events, Fighter Command, Guadalcanal, February 1, 1943 to July 25, 1943 (hereinafter "MAG 12 War Diary"), 17; "TBF-1 Avenger Bureau Number 05923," *Pacific Wrecks* (www.pacificwrecks.com).

92 *RO-106* TROM; Richard Seaman, "LST 342 (Tank Landing Ship 342)," *The Flying Kiwi* (http://www.richard-seaman.com/index.html).

93 Hara, Saito, and Pineau, *Destroyer Captain*, 169.

94 Day, *New Georgia*, 3045; *Yugure* TROM.

95 *Yugure* TROM.

96 *Yugure* TROM and "Editorial Notes [to *Yugure* TROM]" by Anthony Tully, Managing Editor, CombinedFleet.com.

97 *Kumano* TROM; *Yugure* TROM and "Editorial Notes [to *Yugure* TROM]"; Prados, *Islands of Destiny*, 297.

98 *Kiyonami* TROM; *Yugure* TROM; and "Editorial Notes [to *Yugure* TROM]."

99 United States Army Air Forces, *The Crusaders: A History of the 42nd Bombardment Group (M)* (1946), 38.

100 United States Army Air Forces, *The Crusaders*, 38.

101 *Kiyonami* TROM; United States Army Air Forces, *The Crusaders*, 38.

102 *Minazuki* TROM.

103 *Yugure* TROM.

104 *Yugure* TROM; Hara, Saito, and Pineau, *Destroyer Captain*, 169.

105 Hara, Saito, and Pineau, *Destroyer Captain*, 169.

106 Day, *New Georgia*, 3097.

107 Bulkley, *Close Quarters*, 119–20.

108 Rentz, "Marines in the Central Solomons," 111.

109 Destroyer Squadron 22 "Action Report, Night 17–18 July 1943"; Office of Naval Intelligence, *Combat Narratives: Solomon Islands X, Operations in the New Georgia Area 21 June – 5 August 1943*, 48–49; Bulkley, *Close Quarters*, 119.

110 Rentz, "Marines in the Central Solomons," 111.

111 Miller, *Cartwheel*, 130.

112 Miller, *Cartwheel*, 129–30; Rentz, "Marines in the Central Solomons," 111.

113 Rentz, "Marines in the Central Solomons," 111.

114 Rentz, "Marines in the Central Solomons," 117.

115 Rentz, "Marines in the Central Solomons," 117.

116 Day, *New Georgia*, 2696; Tillman, *SBD Dauntless*, 1011–17.

117 Day, *New Georgia*, 2696; Tillman, *SBD Dauntless*, 1011–17.

118 Day, *New Georgia*, 2696–705 n. 23; Hata, Izawa, and Shores, *Japanese Naval Air Force*, 1499; Wolf, *13th Fighter Command*, 192; Cressman, *Official Chronology*; Day.

119 The account of the ambush of the *Nisshin* comes from the *Nisshin* TROM and A.P. Tully, "Neglected Disaster: Nisshin," *Imperial Japanese Navy Page* (www.combinedfleet.com).

120 Hata, Izawa, and Shores, *Japanese Naval Air Force*, 1499.

121 Day, *New Georgia*, 3123; *ONI, Solomon Islands X*, 49–50.

122 Day, *New Georgia*, 3137; *ONI, Solomon Islands X*, 50–51.

123 *Ro-103* TROM.

124 Miller, *Cartwheel*, 139.

125 Miller, *Cartwheel*, 139–40; Day, *New Georgia*, 3171.

126 Miller, *Cartwheel*, 140; Day, *New Georgia*, 3171–78.

127 Miller, *Cartwheel*, 140; Hammel, *Munda Trail*, 2831.

128 Day, *New Georgia*, 3150.

129 General Beightler would turn out to be the only National Guard general to lead his division from start to finish in the war. Day, *New Georgia*, 3150.

130 Miller, *Cartwheel*, 137–39; Day, *New Georgia*, 3150–57.

131 Miller, *Cartwheel*, 139; Day, *New Georgia*, 3157–64.

132 Day, *New Georgia*, 3178–85.

133 Miller, *Cartwheel*, 146; Day, *New Georgia*, 3185–92.

134 Miller, *Cartwheel*, 146–47; Day, *New Georgia*, 3198; Hammel, *Air War*, 6450; Hata, Izawa, and Shores, *Japanese Naval Air Force*, 1501.

135 Miller, *Cartwheel*, 146–47.

136 Miller, *Cartwheel*, 148–49.

137 Miller, *Cartwheel*, 154–57.

138 Miller, *Cartwheel*, 154–57.

139 Miller, *Cartwheel*, 158.

140 Miller, *Cartwheel*, 158–59.

141 Miller, *Cartwheel*, 159.

142 Miller, *Cartwheel*, 163–64.

143 Halsey, *Story*, 3478–86.

144 Morison, *Bismarcks Barrier*, 177.

Chapter 8

1   Monograph 99, 44; *Hagikaze, Arashi,* and *Shigure* TROMs.

2   Hara, Saito, and Pineau, *Destroyer Captain*, 170.

3   Hara, Saito, and Pineau, *Destroyer Captain*, 169. Hara seems to have garbled two different incidents with the later run of the *Ariake* that ended in her loss.

4   Hara, Saito, and Pineau, *Destroyer Captain*, 164.

5   The account from aboard the *Amagiri* comes from William Doyle, *PT-109: An American Epic of War, Survival, and the Destiny of John F. Kennedy* (New York: William Morrow, 2015), 5–7, 100–20.

6   Doyle, *PT-109*, 81.

7   Hara, Saito, and Pineau, *Destroyer Captain*, 171.

8   Doyle, *PT-109*, 104.

9   Doyle, *PT-109*, 104.

10   Hara, Saito, and Pineau, *Destroyer Captain*, 171–73.

11   Doyle, *PT-109*, 7–8.

12   Hara, Saito, and Pineau, *Destroyer Captain*, 173.

13   Hara, Saito, and Pineau, *Destroyer Captain*, 173.

14   Hammel, *Air War Pacific Chronology*, 6493–513; *Mikazuki* TROM; "History of the 3rd Bombardment Group (L), AAF, from Activation, 1 July 1919 to 31 March 1944," 61–62.

15   *Akikaze* TROM.

16   Except where noted otherwise, the Japanese account of the Vella Gulf battle comes from Hara, Saito, and Pineau, *Destroyer Captain*, 173–80.

17   Hara, Saito, and Pineau, *Destroyer Captain*, 175.

18   Hara, Saito, and Pineau, *Destroyer Captain*, 179.

19   Raymond C. Calhoun, *Tin Can Sailor: Life Aboard the USS Sterett, 1939–1945* (Annapolis: Naval Institute Press, 1993), Kindle edition, 2571–90; Kilpatrick, *Night Naval Battles*, 211.

20   DesDiv12 Action Report for Night of August 6–7, 1943 – Battle of Vella Gulf (hereinafter "Moosbrugger Vella Gulf Report"), 6.

21   Moosbrugger Vella Gulf Report, 6.

22   Moosbrugger Vella Gulf Report, 2–3.

23   Moosbrugger Vella Gulf Report, 7; Morison, *Bismarcks Barrier*, 213.

24   Moosbrugger Vella Gulf Report, 4, 8.

25   Moosbrugger Vella Gulf Report, 4, 8–9.

26   Calhoun, *Tin Can Sailor*, 2590.

27   Crenshaw, *South Pacific Destroyer*, 3814.

28   Moosbrugger Vella Gulf Report, 8.

29   Ken Jones, *Destroyer Squadron 23: Combat Exploits of Arleigh Burke's Gallant Force* (Uncommon Valor Press, 2016), Kindle edition, 135.

30   Moosbrugger Vella Gulf Report, 9; Crenshaw, *South Pacific Destroyer*, 3882.

31   Moosbrugger Vella Gulf Report, 3; "Action Report of USS *Dunlap* (384), Battle of Vella Gulf 6–7 August 1943" ("*Dunlap* Vella Gulf Report"), 2; Calhoun, *Tin Can Sailor*, 2552.

32   Kilpatrick, *Naval Night Battles*, 212.

33   *Dunlap* Vella Gulf Report, 2.

34   Crenshaw, *South Pacific Destroyer*, 3882.

35   Calhoun, *Tin Can Sailor*, 2632.

36   Moosbrugger Vella Gulf Report, 10; Calhoun, *Tin Can Sailor*, 2673.

37   Moosbrugger Vella Gulf Report, 10; *Dunlap* Vella Gulf Report, 3.

38   Moosbrugger Vella Gulf Report, 10; *Dunlap* Vella Gulf Report, 3.

39   Calhoun, *Tin Can Sailor*, 2673.

40   *Dunlap* Vella Gulf Report, 4.

41   *Dunlap* Vella Gulf Report, 4.

42   Calhoun, *Tin Can Sailor*, 2673.

43   Moosbrugger Vella Gulf Report, 10; *Dunlap* Vella Gulf Report, 4. Because all the reports of the target course and speeds were slightly different, the *Dunlap*, for example, actually used a solution of 176 degrees True, speed 27 knots, track angle 290 degrees.

44   Prados, *Islands of Destiny*, 303.

45   Kilpatrick, *Night Naval Battles*, 214.

46   Moosbrugger Vella Gulf Report, 11; Crenshaw, *South Pacific Destroyer*, 3924.

47   Crenshaw, *South Pacific Destroyer*, 3424–95.

48   Calhoun, *Tin Can Sailor*, 2695.

49   Morison, *Bismarcks Barrier*, 219; O'Hara, *US Navy*, 4170.

50   Morison, *Bismarcks Barrier*, 219; DesDiv15 Action Report for Night of 6–7 August, 1943 (hereinafter "Simpson Vella Gulf Report"), 4.

51   Hara, Saito, and Pineau, *Destroyer Captain*, 180.

52   Calhoun, *Tin Can Sailor*, 2695.

53   Roscoe, *Destroyer Operations*, 235.

54   O'Hara, *US Navy*, 4170.

55   Hara, Saito, and Pineau, *Destroyer Captain*, 180.

56   Hara, Saito, and Pineau, *Destroyer Captain*, 180.

57   O'Hara, *US Navy*, 4170.

58   Calhoun, *Tin Can Sailors*, 2715.

59   ONI Narrative, 6.

60   ONI Narrative, 6.

61   Hara, Saito, and Pineau, *Destroyer Captain*, 180.

62   Calhoun, *Tin Can Sailors*, 2736.

63   Potter, *Nimitz*, 196.

64   Miller, *Cartwheel*, 159.

65   Miller, *Cartwheel*, 159.

66   Day, *New Georgia*, 3341–48.

67   Day, *New Georgia*, 3341–48. The narrative goes with Day as recent scholarship over Miller (*Cartwheel*, 159) gives a different version of these events.

68   Day, *New Georgia*, 3348–54.

69   Day, *New Georgia*, 3348–54.

70   Day, *New Georgia*, 1711.

71   Day, *New Georgia*, 3376.

72   Day, *New Georgia*, 3376–82.

73   Day, *New Georgia*, 3389.

74   Day, *New Georgia*, 3382–89.

75   Day, *New Georgia*, 3396–404.

76   Miller, *Cartwheel*, 174.

77   Day, *New Georgia*, 3392, 3407; Miller, *Cartwheel*, 171–72. The narrative concerning the movement of General Sasaki's headquarters goes with Day over Miller, who says the headquarters was first moved to Baanga, then on August 8 moved to Kolombangara.

78   Miller, *Cartwheel*, 172; Day, *New Georgia*, 3459.

79   Day, *New Georgia*, 3540.

80   Day, *New Georgia*, 3540.

81   Day, *New Georgia*, 3540.

82   Toland, *Rising Sun*, 9892.

83   Toland, *Rising Sun*, 9900.

84   Toland, *Rising Sun*, 10333–43; David Bergamini, *Japan's Imperial Conspiracy* (London: William Morrow, 1971), 990.

85   Toland, *Rising Sun*, 10343.

86   Bergamini, *Imperial Conspiracy*, 990.

87   Prados, *Islands of Destiny*, 306–07.

88   Miller, *Cartwheel*, 174; Bulkley, *Close Quarters*, 134–35; Monograph 140, 16.

89   Bulkley, *Close Quarters*, 134–35.

90   Reg Newell, *The Battle for Vella Lavella: The Allied Recapture of Solomons Island Territory, August 15–September 9, 1943* (Jefferson, NC: McFarland, 2016), Kindle edition, 53.

91   Newell, *Vella Lavella*, 54; Bulkley, *Close Quarters*, 135.

92   Miller, *Cartwheel*, 174–75.

93   Miller, *Cartwheel*, 174.

94   Halsey, *Story*, 3603.

95   John A. DeChant, *Devilbirds: The Story of United States Marine Corps Aviation in World War II* (New York and London: Harper, 1947), 109; Craven and Cate, *Guadalcanal*, 235–36; Prados, *Decoded*, 500; Miller, *Cartwheel*, 165; Wolf, *13th Fighter Command*, 199.

96   Prados, *Decoded*, 494, 500.

97   Miller, *Cartwheel*, 175.

98   Newell, *New Georgia*, 55; Morison, *Bismarcks Barrier*, 228–29; Day, *New Georgia*, 3617.

99   Miller, *Cartwheel*, 176–77; Newell, *Vella Lavella*, 55. With the "Third Transport Group" and the "Second Transport Group," why there had to be an "Advance Transport Group" instead of a "First Transport Group" will remain a mystery.

100 Morison, *Bismarcks Barrier*, 230; Day, *New Georgia*, 3628; Newell, *Vella Lavella*, 56.

101 Day, *New Georgia*, 3628–38; Miller, *Cartwheel*, 178–79.

102 Day, *New Georgia*, 3638; Miller, *Cartwheel*, 179; Morison, *Bismarcks Barrier*, 230; Newell, *Vella Lavella*, 58.

103 Day, *New Georgia*, 3638.

104 Day, *New Georgia*, 3565–74.

105 Miller, *Cartwheel*, 179.

106 Hammel, *Air War*, 6453.

107 Day, *New Georgia*, 3574–85.

108 Day, *New Georgia*, 3585.

109 Monograph 140, 26; Hata, Izawa, and Shores, *Japanese Naval Air Force*, 1509; Miller, *Cartwheel*, 179; Day, *New Georgia*, 3638–50; Newell, *Vella Lavella*, 62–63; Morison, *Bismarcks Barrier*, 230.

110 Monograph 140, 26; Monograph 99, 47; Hata, Izawa, and Shores, *Japanese Naval Air Force*, 1509; Day, *New Georgia*, 3638–50; Morison, *Bismarcks Barrier*, 230; Tillman, *US Marine Corps*, 42; Newell, *Vella Lavella*, 63; Wolf, *13th Fighter Command*, 200.

111 Hata, Izawa, and Shores, *Japanese Naval Air Force*, 1509; Day, *New Georgia*, 3650; Hammel, *Air War*, 6712–22; Morison, *Bismarcks Barrier*, 231. Monograph 140 has the number of Zeros as 48; Hata, et al., have it as 45.

112 Monograph 140, 26; Hata, Izawa, and Shores, *Japanese Naval Air Force*, 1509; Newell, *Vella Lavella*, 64; Miller, *Cartwheel*, 180. Monograph 140 has the number of Zeros as 45; Hata, et al., have it as 24.

113 Morison, *Bismarcks Barrier*, 231–32; Day, *New Georgia*, 3663.

114 Day, *New Georgia*, 3663–72; Miller, *Cartwheel*, 180.

115 Day, *New Georgia*, 3672–81; Tagaya, *Rikko*, 1391. The identification of all 16 G4Ms armed with bombs as coming from the 702 Air Group is a supposition. Usually, but not always, all aircraft of the same unit were armed with the same loadout to maintain unit integrity.

116 Day, *New Georgia*, 3672–81; Tagaya, *Rikko*, 1391.

117 Morison, *Bismarcks Barrier*, 232.

118 Miller, *Cartwheel*, 180.

119 "Ijuin Matsuji (1893–1944)," Budge, *The Pacific War Online Encyclopedia* (http://pwencycl.kgbudge.com/).

120 Hara, Saito, and Pineau, *Destroyer Captain*, 191.

121 Prados, *Islands of Destiny*, 307.

122 Hara, Saito, and Pineau, *Destroyer Captain*, 183.

123 Hara, Saito, and Pineau, *Destroyer Captain*, 183.

124 Hara, Saito, and Pineau, *Destroyer Captain*, 184.

125 Hara, Saito, and Pineau, *Destroyer Captain*, 184.

126 Kilpatrick, *Naval Night Battles*, 219–20.

127 Monograph 99, 49; Miller, *Cartwheel*, 182; Newell, *Vella Lavella*, 7; Day, *New Georgia*, 3688–94; Morison, *Bismarcks Barrier*, 234; Prados, *Islands of Destiny*, 306.

128 Hara, Saito, and Pineau, *Destroyer Captain*, 184.

129 Hara, Saito, and Pineau, *Destroyer Captain*, 184.

130 Hara, Saito, and Pineau, *Destroyer Captain*, 184.

131 USS *Nicholas* Action Report – Engagement with Enemy Surface Units off Vella Lavella Island, British Solomon Islands, August 17–18, 1943 ("*Nicholas* Horaniu Report"), 1; O'Hara, *US Navy*, 4222; Morison, *Bismarcks Barrier*, 188.

132 O'Hara, *US Navy*, 4222.

133 Kilpatrick, *Naval Night Battles*, 221; Night Action North of Vella Lavella By Desdiv 41 (Task Unit 31.2) August 17–18, 1943 ("Ryan Horaniu Report"), 3.

134 Hara, Saito, and Pineau, *Destroyer Captain*, 184.

135 Hara, Saito, and Pineau, *Destroyer Captain*, 184.

136 Hara, Saito, and Pineau, *Destroyer Captain*, 184.

137 Hara, Saito, and Pineau, *Destroyer Captain*, 184.

138 Hara, Saito, and Pineau, *Destroyer Captain*, 185; Day, *New Georgia*, 3701.

139 *Nicholas* Horaniu Report, 1.

140 Hara, Saito, and Pineau, *Destroyer Captain*, 186.

141 Hara, Saito, and Pineau, *Destroyer Captain*, 186.
142 Hara, Saito, and Pineau, *Destroyer Captain*, 186.
143 Hara, Saito, and Pineau, *Destroyer Captain*, 186.
144 Hara, Saito, and Pineau, *Destroyer Captain*, 186.
145 Ryan Horaniu Report, 1, Enclosure B TBS Log, 1.
146 *Nicholas* Horaniu Report, 2.
147 *Nicholas* Horaniu Report, 2.
148 *Nicholas* Horaniu Report, 2.
149 Hara, Saito, and Pineau, *Destroyer Captain*, 186.
150 Hara, Saito, and Pineau, *Destroyer Captain*, 185.
151 Hara, Saito, and Pineau, *Destroyer Captain*, 185. The Type 0 Observation Seaplane should not be confused with the Type 0 Reconnaissance Seaplane.
152 *Nicholas* Horaniu Report, 2.
153 Ryan Horaniu Report, Enclosure A Composite Track Chart; USS *Chevalier* Action Report – Enemy surface forces night of 17–18 August, 1943 ("*Chevalier* Horaniu Report"), 2, which has the time as 12:43. The TBS log does not show this course change, but Captain Ryan stated in his report (Ryan Horaniu Report, 1) it was standard procedure to execute column turns in a follow-the-leader manner without signaling.
154 Hara, Saito, and Pineau, *Destroyer Captain*, 185.
155 Hara, Saito, and Pineau, *Destroyer Captain*, 185.
156 O'Hara, *US Navy*, 4235. Hara (Hara, Saito, and Pineau, *Destroyer Captain*, 186) is not specific as to whose torpedoes were launched when.
157 *Nicholas* Horaniu Report, 2; Ryan Horaniu Report, Enclosure (B) TBS Log, 3.
158 Ryan Horaniu Report, Enclosure (B) TBS Log, 3.
159 Kilpatrick (*Naval Night Battles*, 222) and O'Hara (*US Navy*, 4235) both have Captain Ryan broadcasting to his ships his comment, "We'll get those barges later." However, it should be noted that the comment does not show up in the TBS logs submitted by Ryan or the destroyer *O'Bannon*.
160 Ryan Horaniu Report, Enclosure (B) TBS Log, 3. The TBS Log reads, "Emergency turn 6" but it probably meant "Emergency 6 turn" because Ryan's track chart (Enclosure (A)) shows a turn to port at this time.
161 Hara, Saito, and Pineau, *Destroyer Captain*, 187.
162 Hara, Saito, and Pineau, *Destroyer Captain*, 187.
163 O'Hara, *US Navy*, 4235–54.
164 Hara, Saito, and Pineau, *Destroyer Captain*, 188.
165 Hara, Saito, and Pineau, *Destroyer Captain*, 188.
166 Hara, Saito, and Pineau, *Destroyer Captain*, 188.
167 *Chevalier* Horaniu Report, 3.
168 *Chevalier* Horaniu Report, 3; Morison, *Bismarcks Barrier*, 236.
169 *Chevalier* Horaniu Report, 3.
170 Ryan Horaniu Report, Enclosure A Composite Track Chart.
171 Ryan Horaniu Report, 1.
172 Hara, Saito, and Pineau, *Destroyer Captain*, 189.
173 Hara, Saito, and Pineau, *Destroyer Captain*, 190; O'Hara, *US Navy*, 4274.
174 Hara, Saito, and Pineau, *Destroyer Captain*, 189.
175 Morison, *Bismarcks Barrier*, 236.
176 Ryan Horaniu Report, 1.
177 O'Hara, *US Navy*, 4274.
178 Hara, Saito, and Pineau, *Destroyer Captain*, 189.
179 Hara, Saito, and Pineau, *Destroyer Captain*, 189.
180 Hara, Saito, and Pineau, *Destroyer Captain*, 189.
181 Day, *New Georgia*, 3715.
182 O'Hara, *US Navy*, 4277–83. The subchasers *Cha-5* and *Cha-12* must not be confused with the subchasers *Ch-5* and *Ch-12*, respectively, which were completely different craft.
183 Prados, *Islands of Destiny*, 308.
184 Prados, *Islands of Destiny*, 308; Bix, *Hirohito*, 466.
185 Monograph 140, 27; Day, *New Georgia*, 3723–32. Day says the numbers were 48 Zeros and ten D3As.
186 Day, *New Georgia*, 3723–32; Morison, *Bismarcks Barrier*, 237.
187 Miller, *Cartwheel*, 182.

188 Hara, Saito, and Pineau, *Destroyer Captain*, 193; Day, *New Georgia*, 3732. Hara says the "[d]amaged *Isokaze* was replaced by *Minazuki*," but the *Isokaze*'s TROM indicates she was on this mission while the *Minazuki*'s TROM says she was in drydock at Kure for repairs and refitting after her damage in the July 20 air attack. Both Hara and Day insist the mission consisted of only three destroyers. However, the *Sazanami*'s TROM insists she participated in this mission as "cover," which in the Imperial Japanese Navy parlance could mean anything from accompanying the three destroyers to staying in port.

189 Hara, Saito, and Pineau, *Destroyer Captain*, 193.

190 Hara, Saito, and Pineau, *Destroyer Captain*, 194.

191 Hara, Saito, and Pineau, *Destroyer Captain*, 194.

192 Hara, Saito, and Pineau, *Destroyer Captain*, 194.

193 Hara, Saito, and Pineau, *Destroyer Captain*, 194.

194 Hara, Saito, and Pineau, *Destroyer Captain*, 194.

195 Hara, Saito, and Pineau, *Destroyer Captain*, 195.

196 Day, *New Georgia*, 3732.

197 Day, *New Georgia*, 3732–41; Hara, Saito, and Pineau, *Destroyer Captain*, 195; *Sazanami* and *Matsukaze* TROMs. *Matsukaze*'s presence with the *Sendai* and *Sazanami* is a deduction by process of elimination.

198 Except where noted otherwise, the Japanese account of the August 25–26 mission to Rekata comes from Hara, Saito, and Pineau, *Destroyer Captain*, 195–97.

199 Day, *New Georgia*, 3741; *Sendai* and *Sazanami* TROMs.

200 Zimmer, *History of the 43rd*, 47; Day, *New Georgia*, 3896.

201 Day, *New Georgia*, 3896–902; Miller, *Cartwheel*, 171–72.

202 Day, *New Georgia*, 3902–09; Miller, *Cartwheel*, 172; Zimmer, *History of the 43rd*, 47–48.

203 Miller, *Cartwheel*, 172, 184; Day, *New Georgia*, 3909–15.

204 Day, *New Georgia*, 3930–36.

205 Bulkley, *Close Quarters*, 131.

206 Bulkley, *Close Quarters*, 135–36; Day, *New Georgia*, 3944–51.

207 Bulkley, *Close Quarters*, 135–36; Day, *New Georgia*, 3951.

208 Day, *New Georgia*, 3951.

209 Bambari Harbor is also known as Jack Harbor for reasons the narrative has been unable to check.

210 Day, *New Georgia*, 3959–65.

211 General Barker's command of the 43rd Infantry Division was always intended to be temporary. General Wing's promotion to division command over Barker was specifically addressed as not reflective of any fault on Barker's part but simply the result of Wing's outstanding performance. Barker went back to commanding the 43rd's artillery.

212 Day, *New Georgia*, 4024–30.

213 Dean, *MacArthur's Coalition*, 5797–804.

214 Morison, *Bismarcks Barrier*, 254.

215 The story of the *Shigure*'s mission to Tuluvu comes from Hara, Saito, and Pineau, *Destroyer Captain*, 198–200.

216 Miller, *Cartwheel*, 195; Morison, *Bismarcks Barrier*, 258–59.

217 Miller, *Cartwheel*, 193.

218 Miller, *Cartwheel*, 196; Kenney, *Reports*, 253, 271.

219 Miller, *Cartwheel*, 193.

220 Kenney, *Reports*, 262–63.

221 Gamble, *Target: Rabaul*, 95.

222 Gamble, *Target: Rabaul*, 95; Hata, Izawa, and Shores, *Japanese Army Air Force Fighter Units*, 1025.

223 Gamble, *Target: Rabaul*, 96.

224 Gamble, *Target: Rabaul*, 96.

225 Gamble, *Target: Rabaul*, 96.

226 Hata, Izawa, and Shores, *Japanese Army Air Force Fighter Units*, 1025; Hickey, *Ken's Men*, 255–56; "Dagua Airfield (But East)," *Pacific Wrecks* (www.pacificwrecks.com); Craven and Cate, *Guadalcanal*, 177; Morison, *Bismarcks Barrier*, 259; Hammel, *Air War*, 6708–16; Kenney, *Reports*, 276. The account of this attack has been pieced together.

227 Gamble, *Target: Rabaul*, 97; Hickey, *Ken's Men*, 256; Hammel, *Air War*, 6730; Kenney, *Reports*, 276. Curiously, Hammel has the Army Air Force claiming to have shot down two Kates, six Zeros, and seven Oscars.

228 Gamble, *Target: Rabaul*, 98.

229 Gamble, *Target: Rabaul*, 96; Kenney, *Reports*, 276.

230 Miller, *Cartwheel*, 196.

231 Hickey, *Ken's Men, Volume I*, 256–57.

232 Gamble, *Target: Rabaul*, 99.

233 Gamble, *Target: Rabaul*, 99.

234 Gamble, *Target: Rabaul*, 99.

235 Gamble, *Target: Rabaul*, 99; Hata, Izawa, and Shores, *Japanese Army Air Force Fighter Units*, 1025; Hickey, *Ken's Men*, 256–58; Hammel, *Air War*, 6738–46; Kenney, *Reports*, 276–77; Craven and Cate, *Guadalcanal*, 178–79.

236 Gamble, *Target: Rabaul*, 100.

237 Gamble, *Target: Rabaul*, 100–01.

238 Gamble, *Target: Rabaul*, 100–01.

239 Except where noted otherwise, the account of Captain Yamanaka at Wewak Central comes from Gamble, *Target: Rabaul*, 101–03.

240 Gamble, *Target: Rabaul*, 103.

241 Gamble, *Target: Rabaul*, 102; Baker, *It Wasn't So Jolly*, 310; Kent G. Budge, "Parafrag Bombs," *The Pacific War Online Encyclopedia* (http://pwencycl.kgbudge.com/).

242 Gamble, *Target: Rabaul*, 103.

243 Kenney, *Reports*, 179.

244 Gamble, *Target: Rabaul*, 103–04.

245 Gamble, *Target: Rabaul*, 104.

246 Gamble, *Target: Rabaul*, 104.

247 Gamble, *Target: Rabaul*, 104–05.

248 Gamble, *Target: Rabaul*, 105.

249 *Dilbert*.

250 Craven and Cate, *Guadalcanal*, 179; Gamble, *Target: Rabaul*, 105.

251 Gamble, *Target: Rabaul*, 105; Kenney, *Reports*, 278.

252 Hata, Izawa, and Shores, *Japanese Army Air Force Fighter Units*, 1025; Miller, *Cartwheel*, 199; Hiroyuki Shindo, "Japanese Air Operations over New Guinea during the Second World War," *Journal of the Australian War Memorial*, No. 34 (June 2001), 16.

253 Morison, *Bismarcks Barrier*, 259.

254 Morison, *Bismarcks Barrier*, 260.

255 Morison, *Bismarcks Barrier*, 260.

256 Craven and Cate, *Guadalcanal*, 180; Hiroyuki Shindo, "Japanese Air Operations."

257 Gamble, *Target: Rabaul*, 115; Hata, Izawa, and Shores, *Japanese Army Air Force Fighter Units*, 1025.

258 Gamble, *Target: Rabaul*, 115.

259 Gamble, *Target: Rabaul*, 116.

260 Dean, *MacArthur's Coalition*, 6222.

261 Dean, *MacArthur's Coalition*, 6222.

262 Morison, *Bismarcks Barrier*, 261–62.

263 Miller, *Cartwheel*, 203.

264 Gamble, *Target: Rabaul*, 127.

265 Miller, *Cartwheel*, 203–04.

266 Craven and Cate, *Guadalcanal*, 183; Gamble, *Target: Rabaul*, 127–28.

267 Monograph 140, 30; Tagaya, *Rikko*, 1402; Gamble, *Target: Rabaul*, 127–28; Hata, Izawa, and Shores, *Japanese Naval Air Force*, 1528; Craven and Cate, *Guadalcanal*, 183–84; Miller, *Cartwheel*, 204–05. The identification of the 582 Air Group as the D3As unit is an assumption based on it being the only D3A unit in Base Air Force.

268 Miller, *Cartwheel* 204–5; Wolff, *5th Fighter Command*, 345–5.

269 Morison, *Bismarcks Barrier*, 263–64.

270 Gamble, *Target: Rabaul*, 128.

271 George C. Kenney, *General Kenney Reports: A Personal History of the Pacific War* (Washington, DC: U.S. Government Printing Office, 1997), 288–89; MacArthur, *Reminiscences*, 179.

272 Kenney, *Air War in the Pacific*, 288–89.

273 Kenney, *Air War in the Pacific*, 289.

274 Kenney, *Air War in the Pacific*, 289.

275 MacArthur, *Reminiscences*, 179.

276 MacArthur, *Reminiscences*, 179, 218.

277 Kenney, *Reports*, 292.

278 Kenney, *Reports*, 292–93.

279 Craven and Cate, *Guadalcanal*, 184–85; Miller, *Cartwheel*, 208–09.

280 Miller, *Cartwheel*, 211; Craven and Cate, *Guadalcanal*, 186.

281 Miller, *Cartwheel*, 211; Craven and Cate, *Guadalcanal*, 186.

282 Miller, *Cartwheel*, 217.

283 Miller, *Cartwheel*, 217–18; Task Force 76 War Diary.

284 Miller, *Cartwheel*, 218; Craven and Cate, *Guadalcanal*, 187–88.

285 Monograph 140, 34; Tagaya, *Rikko*, 1405–11; Hata, Izawa, and Shores, *Japanese Army Air Force Fighter Units*, 1535; Craven and Cate, *Guadalcanal*, 187–88; Hammel, *Air War*, 7332.

286 Craven and Cate, *Guadalcanal*, 188.

287 Bulkley, *Close Quarters*, 131.

288 Day, *New Georgia*, 4077–84.

289 Day, *New Georgia*, 4091–97; Monograph 99, 51–52.

290 Or Sumbe Head. Or Sambe Head. Or somesuch.

291 Day, *New Georgia*, 4091–97.

292 Miller, *Cartwheel*, 185.

293 For a more detailed explanation of the ambiguity of the *Akigumo*, see Nevitt, "*Kagero* Class Notes" and Nevitt, "*Yugumo* Class Notes," both at *The Imperial Japanese Navy Page* (www.combinedfleet.com).

294 O'Hara, *US Navy*, 4297. O'Hara says a third member of the "transport group" was the destroyer *Yayoi*. The *Yayoi* was sunk almost exactly a year earlier off Goodenough Island. But a review of the Japanese destroyers' tabular records of movement does not reveal the identity of the third destroyer, if there was one.

295 Day, *New Georgia*, 4104.

296 Day, *New Georgia*, 4112–20 and n. 5; USS *Denver* and Task Group 39.2 War Diaries; Morison, *Bismarcks Barrier*, 241; Fahey, *Pacific War Diary*, 52.

297 Day, *New Georgia*, 4112–20 and n. 5; USS *Denver* and Task Group 39.2 War Diaries; Morison, *Bismarcks Barrier*, 241; *Ro-105* TROM.

298 Morison, *Bismarcks Barrier*, 241; Day, *New Georgia*, 4091, 4126–33.

299 Day, *New Georgia*, 4133–40.

300 Day, *New Georgia*, 4140–48; O'Hara, *US Navy*, 4305.

301 Day, *New Georgia*, 4155–62; O'Hara, *US Navy*, 4305.

302 Day, *New Georgia*, 4140–48; O'Hara, *US Navy*, 4305–12.

303 "USS *Radford* Operations Against Japanese Barges in Kolombangara-Choiseul Area on Nights of Sept. 30–Oct. 1 and Oct. 1–2, Action Report of" ("*Radford* Barge Report"), 2; Day, *New Georgia*, 4162–69; O'Hara, *US Navy*, 4312–20.

304 *Radford* Barge Report, 4.

305 Trying to identify the three Japanese destroyers Admiral Ijuin sent down as the decoy force on October 1, 1943 has been an exercise in frustration. None of the Japanese destroyer TROMs show for this date anything that could be considered within the realm of going anywhere near Kolombangara or Choiseul. The number and identification of the destroyers here is an educated guess based on 1. The aforementioned *Southeast Naval Operations, Part II*; 2. The composition of Ijuin's "feint group" of destroyers (*Shigure*, *Matsukaze*, and *Yugumo*); and 3. The formal assignment earlier on October 1 of the *Samidare* to Captain Hara's Destroyer Division 27.

306 Day, *New Georgia*, 4182.

307 Monograph 99, 53.

308 Finding information on the Japanese destroyers in the combat on the night of October 2–3 has been another exercise in frustration. This construction is just the narrative's best estimate based on the sources available, but absent additional information, other constructions could work just as well. Readers should be aware of the uncertainties over who was involved and are invited to make their own judgments.

309 Day, *New Georgia*, 4188.

310 Day, *New Georgia*, 4188–95.

311 Day, *New Georgia*, 4188; *Renshaw* War Diary.

312 USS *Ralph Talbot* Actions By Surface Ships – Report of. Enclosure (B) Narrative of Surface Actions of October 2nd and 3rd, 1943 ("*Ralph Talbot* October 2–3 Report"), 1; USS *Waller* Action Report, Operations against Japanese barges and small craft operating between Kolombangara and Choiseul Solomon Islands 1–3 October, 1943 ("*Waller* Barge Report"), 5; O'Hara, *US Navy*, 4327–38.

313 O'Hara, *US Navy*, 4338.

314 *Ralph Talbot* October 2–3 Report, 1.

315 *Ralph Talbot* October 2–3 Report, 1; Destroyer Squadron 22 Action Report, Operations Against Japanese Barges and Small Craft Nights of 1–2 and 2–3 October 1942 ("Cooke Barge Report"), 3.

316 *Ralph Talbot* October 2–3 Report, 1.

317 Cooke Barge Report, 4; O'Hara, *US Navy*, 4344; Monograph 99, 53.

318 Monograph 99, 53.

319 Cooke Barge Report, 4.

320 O'Hara, *US Navy*, 4352.

321 Monograph 99, 53–54; Day, *New Georgia*, 4209.

322 *Waller* Barge Report, 6–7; O'Hara, *US Navy*, 4352–59.

323 Crenshaw, *South Pacific Destroyer*, 3800.

324 Cooke Barge Report, 4.

325 *Waller* Barge Report, 6–7.

326 O'Hara, *US Navy*, 4287.

327 Day, *New Georgia*, 3772–91, 4216.

328 Day, *New Georgia*, 4223–36.

329 Day, *New Georgia*, 4242.

330 *Kazegumo* is sometimes rendered as *Kazagumo*.

331 Hara, Saito, and Pineau, *Destroyer Captain*, 203. Hara has Captain Kanaoka's given name as "Kunizo"; other sources render his given name as "Yuzo."

332 Hara, Saito, and Pineau, *Destroyer Captain*, 204.

333 Hara, Saito, and Pineau, *Destroyer Captain*, 203.

334 Morison, *Bismarcks Barrier*, 243.

335 Hara, Saito, and Pineau, *Destroyer Captain*, 203. Morison (*Bismarcks Barrier*, 244) says it was at least one scout plane from AirSols.

336 Hara, Saito, and Pineau, *Destroyer Captain*, 204.

337 Hara, Saito, and Pineau, *Destroyer Captain*, 204.

338 Hara, Saito, and Pineau, *Destroyer Captain*, 204.

339 Hara, Saito, and Pineau, *Destroyer Captain*, 204. Sunset was at 5:31pm.

340 Hara, Saito, and Pineau, *Destroyer Captain*, 204.

341 Hara, Saito, and Pineau, *Destroyer Captain*, 204.

342 Hara, Saito, and Pineau, *Destroyer Captain*, 204. Monograph 99, 56.

343 Hara, Saito, and Pineau, *Destroyer Captain*, 204. Despite the known issues with the accuracy of eyewitness testimony and information received secondhand, the narrative here goes with Hara over Morison (*Bismarcks Barrier*, 245), who has the report as one cruiser and four destroyers.

344 The actions of the Destroyer Transport Group are left deliberately ambiguous because there is no agreement when Captain Kanaoka turned his transport destroyers around or under whose authority.

345 Hara, Saito, and Pineau, *Destroyer Captain*, 205.

346 Hara, Saito, and Pineau, *Destroyer Captain*, 204.

347 Hara, Saito, and Pineau, *Destroyer Captain*, 204.

348 O'Hara, *US Navy*, 4406.

349 Hara, Saito, and Pineau, *Destroyer Captain*, 205; O'Hara, *US Navy*, 4406.

350 O'Hara, *US Navy*, 4406.

351 Hara, Saito, and Pineau, *Destroyer Captain*, 207.

352 R.H. Roupe, "Hell and High Water: The story of a gallant warship and her crew – the destroyer *Chevalier*, which fought a good fight until sunk by superior forces in the night action of Vella Lavella," *Destroyer History Foundation* (www.destroyerhistory.org).

353 Advance Preliminary Report of Battle Action – *Selfridge*, *O'Bannon* and *Chevalier* with Enemy Forces off Sauka, Vella Lavella Night 6–7 October 1943 ("Walker Vella Lavella Preliminary Report"), 1.

354 Roupe, "Hell and High Water."

355 Walker Vella Lavella Preliminary Report, 1.

356 Kilpatrick, *Naval Night Battles*, 228.

357 Walker Vella Lavella Preliminary Report, 2.

358 Walker Vella Lavella Preliminary Report, 2.

359 Walker Vella Lavella Preliminary Report, 3.

360 Walker Vella Lavella Preliminary Report, 3.

361 Roupe, "Hell and High Water."

362 Walker Vella Lavella Preliminary Report, 3. The Type 0 Observation Seaplane should not be confused with the Type 0 Reconnaissance Seaplane.

363 Roupe, "Hell and High Water."

364 Roupe, "Hell and High Water."

365 USS *O'Bannon* Action Report – engagement with enemy surface units north of Vella La Vella [sic] during late ovening [sic], 2–3.

366 Walker Vella Lavella Preliminary Report, 3.

367 Morison, *Bismarcks Barrier*, 245.

368 Roupe, "Hell and High Water"; USS *Selfridge* – Night Engagement with Japanese Destroyers Northwest of Vella Lavella Island on October 6, 1943 – Report of ("*Selfridge* Vella Lavella Report"), Enclosure (C), TBS Log, 1.

369 Walker Preliminary Report, 4.

370 Roupe, "Hell and High Water."

371 Walker Vella Lavella Preliminary Report, 4.

372 Walker Vella Lavella Preliminary Report, 4.

373 Morison, *Bismarcks Barrier*, 246; Walker Vella Lavella Preliminary Report, 4. Captain Walker added, "There was much interference on the circuit from an army station (3000 kcs)."

374 *O'Bannon* Vella Lavella Report, Enclosure (D), TBS Log, 15.

375 Roupe, "Hell and High Water."

376 Walker Vella Lavella Preliminary Report, 5.

377 Roupe, "Hell and High Water."

378 Walker Vella Lavella Preliminary Report, 5.

379 Roupe, "Hell and High Water."

380 Hara, Saito, and Pineau, *Destroyer Captain*, 206.

381 Hara, Saito, and Pineau, *Destroyer Captain*, 204–05.

382 Hara, Saito, and Pineau, *Destroyer Captain*, 204–05.

383 Hara, Saito, and Pineau, *Destroyer Captain*, 204–05; Morison, *Bismarcks Barrier*, 247–49.

384 Hara, Saito, and Pineau, *Destroyer Captain*, 204–05; Morison, *Bismarcks Barrier*, 247–49.

385 Hara, Saito, and Pineau, *Destroyer Captain*, 207.

386 Hara, Saito, and Pineau, *Destroyer Captain*, 207.

387 Hara, Saito, and Pineau, *Destroyer Captain*, 207.

388 Walker Vella Lavella Preliminary Report, 5; *O'Bannon* Vella Lavella Report, Enclosure (D), TBS Log, 3.

389 Walker Vella Lavella Preliminary Report, 5; Kilpatrick, *Naval Night Battles*, 230.

390 Hara, Saito, and Pineau, *Destroyer Captain*, 208.

391 *O'Bannon* Vella Lavella Report, Enclosure (D), TBS Log, 3.

392 Time comes from O'Hara, *US Navy*, 4420.

393 Hara, Saito, and Pineau, *Destroyer Captain*, 238. O'Hara (*US Navy*, 4420 and n. 21), citing Japanese National Institute for Defense Studies, *Naval Operations in Southeast Area, Part 2*, 83, says both the *Kazegumo* and the *Akigumo* were able to open fire, in addition to the *Yugumo*, during this time. O'Hara admits that this is an unusual claim, since most studies say that only the *Yugumo* and *Kazegumo* were able to get off a few shots. However, Hara is very specific that "*Isokaze* and *Akigumo* could not even fire their guns."

394 *Chevalier* Vella Lavella Report, 3.

395 Roupe, "Hell and High Water."

396 O'Hara, *US Navy*, 4420; Walker Vella Lavella Preliminary Report, 6.

397 Roupe, "Hell and High Water."

398 Roupe, "Hell and High Water."

399 *Chevalier* Vella Lavella Report, 3.

400 Walker Vella Lavella Preliminary Report, 6.

401 *Chevalier* Vella Lavella Report, 3.

402 *O'Bannon* Vella Lavella Report, 4; *Chevalier* Vella Lavella Report, 3.

403 *O'Bannon* Vella Lavella Report, 4.

404 *O'Bannon* Vella Lavella Report, Enclosure (D) TBS log, 6.

405 *Chevalier* Vella Lavella Report, 3.

406 *O'Bannon* Vella Lavella Report, 4.

407 Allyn D. Nevitt, "The Battle of Vella Lavella," *The Imperial Japanese Navy Page* (www.combinedlfeet.com); Hara, Saito, and Pineau, *Destroyer Captain*, 208.

408 Walker Preliminary Report, 6.

409 Imperial Japanese Navy records usually are given in terms of Japan Standard Time, no matter where the action took place. Local time was two hours ahead, and converted to 12-hour format would be 11:05pm. However, Hara does say that when the *Yugumo* was hit by the torpedo at 11:03, she "exploded almost immediately, staggered drunkenly for several minutes, and sank." Nevitt ("The Battle of Vella Lavella") gives the time as 2310 (11:10pm), which, if Hara's "staggered drunkenly for several minutes" is accurate, may be closer to the actual time of *Yugumo*'s sinking.

410 Walker Preliminary Report, 6.

411 Hara, Saito, and Pineau, *Destroyer Captain*, 210.

412 Hara, Saito, and Pineau, *Destroyer Captain*, 210.

413 *Samidare* TROM; Hara, Saito, and Pineau, *Destroyer Captain*, 210.

414 Hara, Saito, and Pineau, *Destroyer Captain*, 210.

415 Walker Vella Lavella Preliminary Report, 7; Times are from Final Report of Battle Action – *Selfridge*, *O'Bannon* and *Chevalier* with Enemy Forces off Sauka, Vella Lavella Night 6–7 October, 1943 ("Walker Vella Lavella Final Report"), 1. Walker's Vella Lavella Preliminary Report somehow got 10 minutes ahead, and he had to correct it in the Vella Lavella Final Report.

416 Walker Vella Lavella Preliminary Report, 7.

417 Walker Vella Lavella Preliminary Report, 7.

418 Hara, Saito, and Pineau, *Destroyer Captain*, 210; Morison, *Bismarcks Barrier*, 250.

419 Hara, Saito, and Pineau, *Destroyer Captain*, 211.

420 Samuels, *Ralph Talbot*, 3011; Morison, *Bismarcks Barrier*, 250.

421 Morison, *Bismarcks Barrier*, 250.

422 Roupe, "Hell and High Water."

423 George Gowen, [untitled], *Destroyer History Foundation* (www.destroyerhistory.org).

424 *Chevalier* Vella Lavella Report, 6; *O'Bannon* Vella Lavella Report, 8.

425 Roupe, "Hell and High Water."

426 Day, *New Georgia*, 4309. Morison (*Bismarcks Barrier*, 251) says the barges entered Marquana Bay at 1:10am and left at 3:05.

427 Morison, *Bismarcks Barrier*, 250–51; Day, *New Georgia*, 4303.

428 Morison, *Bismarcks Barrier*, 251; USS *La Vallette* "Night Action West of Vella Lavella, October 6–7, 1943" (hereinafter "*La Vallette* Report"), 2.

429 Day, *New Georgia*, 4309–18; Morison, *Bismarcks Barrier*, 251–52; Hammel, *Air War*, 7521–28.

430 Day, *New Georgia*, 4326.

431 Hara, *Japanese Destroyer Captain*, 212.

432 Hara, *Japanese Destroyer Captain*, 212.

433 Morison, *Bismarcks Barrier*, 252.

434 Day, *New Georgia*, 4073–77.

435 Prados, *Islands of Destiny*, 310.

436 Halsey, *Story*, 3432.

437 Miller, *Cartwheel*, 188.

Chapter 9

1 The account of the sword presentation ceremony comes from Hara, Saito, and Pineau, *Destroyer Captain*, 213–14.

2 Hara, Saito, and Pineau, *Destroyer Captain*, 213–14.

3 Dean, *Australia 1943*, 81–82.

4 Dean, *Australia 1943*, 82; Monograph 140, 37.

5 Monograph 140, 37.

6 Monograph 100, 2; Dean, *Australia 1944–45*, 52.

7 Monograph 100, 2–3, 4.

8 Monograph 100, 3.

9 Monograph 100, 3–4.

10 Monograph 100, 4–5.

11 Miller, *Cartwheel*, 238; Monograph 100, 7.

12 Monograph 100, 7.

13 Monograph 100, 10.

Epilogue

1   Frank Jacob, *Japanese War Crimes during World War II: Atrocity and the Psychology of Collective Violence* (Santa Barbara, CA, and Denver, CO: ABC-CLIO, 2018), 4.

2   Gamble, *Target: Rabaul*, 48.

3   Gamble, *Target: Rabaul*, 4.

4   Gamble, *Target: Rabaul*, 5.

5   Or Vokeo Island. Or Roissy Island.

6   Gamble, *Target: Rabaul*, 46.

7   Gamble, *Target: Rabaul*, 46–47.

8   Gamble, *Target: Rabaul*, 47.

9   Gamble, *Target: Rabaul*, 48.

10   Kent G. Budge, "Tokkeitai," *The Pacific War Online Encyclopedia* (http://www.pwencycl.kgbudge.com/).

11   Tanaka, *Hidden Horrors*, 4735–61. Tanaka says that Admiral Onishi said the *Akikaze* was part of the "11th Fleet." The Imperial Japanese Navy had no "11th Fleet," but it did have an "11th Air Fleet," so that correction has been made in the narrative.

12   Tanaka, *Hidden Horrors*, 4732–42.

13   Tanaka, *Hidden Horrors*, 4761.

14   Nevitt, "Who Sank the Triton?"

15   *Akikaze* TROM.

16   It should be noted that in his discussion of the Guadalcanal Campaign, Admiral Tanaka was occasionally mistaken as to the identities of ships under his command.

17   Tanaka, *Hidden Horrors*, 4742–52.

18   Tanaka, *Hidden Horrors*, 4752–61.

19   Huber (*Bishop's Progress*, 229) relays a statement from the Society for the Divine Word's Father John Tschauder suggesting that there were no orders to dispose of the civilians and that Lieutenant Commander Sabe acted on his own. There appears to be no corroborating evidence for this statement, however, and considerable evidence against it.

20   Or at least not this order to the *Akikaze*. The order could have been sent to Kavieng by radio or wireless, but that would seem to defeat the purpose of not sending it by same to the *Akikaze*, so it's fairly safe to assume the order was sent by courier to Kavieng as well.

21   Wiltgen, "Part I: The Execution," 393.

22   Wiltgen, "Part I: The Execution," 393.

23   Wiltgen, "Part I: The Execution," 393.

24   Wiltgen, "Part I: The Execution," 387.

25   Wiltgen, "Part I: The Execution," 387.

26   Wiltgen, "Part I: The Execution," 387.

27   Wiltgen, "Part I: The Execution," 391.

28   Wiltgen, "Part I: The Execution," 393.

29   Wiltgen, "Part I: The Execution," 393.

30   Wiltgen, "Part I: The Execution," 393.

31   Wiltgen, "Part I: The Execution," 393.

32   Wiltgen, "Part II: The Trial," 31.

33   Wiltgen, "Part I: The Execution," 393.

34   Wiltgen, "Part II: The Trial," 22.

35   Felton (*Slaughter at Sea*, 1564) suspected the accusations of "spying" were completely fabricated by the Tokkeitai, "giving them a reason to kill them within Japanese military law."

36   Felton, *Slaughter at Sea*, 1500–06.

37   Felton, *Slaughter at Sea*, 1513–18.

38   Wiltgen, "Part II: The Trial," 42.

39   Wiltgen, "Part II: The Trial," 34.

40   D.C.S. Sissons, *The Australian War Crimes Trials and Investigations (1942–51)* (Canberra: D.C.S. Sissons, 2006), 54.

BIBLIOGRAPHY

Aerts, Theo (ed.), *The Martyrs of Papua New Guinea: 333 Missionary Lives Lost During World War II*. Port Moresby: University of Papua New Guinea Press and Bookshop, 2009.

Agawa, Hiroyuki, *The Reluctant Admiral: Yamamoto and the Imperial Navy*. Tokyo; New York: Kodansha, 1979.

Altobello, Brian, *Into the Shadows Furious: The Brutal Battle for New Georgia*. Novato, CA: Presidio Press, 2000.

Blair, Clay, Jr, *Silent Victory: The US Submarine War Against Japan*. Annapolis: Naval Institute Press, 1975.

Bulkley, Captain Robert J., Jr, USNR (Ret.), *At Close Quarters: PT Boats in the United States Navy*. Washington: Naval History Division, 1962.

Calhoun, C. Raymond, *Tin Can Sailor: Life Aboard the USS Sterett, 1939–1945*. Annapolis: Naval Institute Press, 1993. Kindle edition.

Claringbould, Michael John, *Operation I-Go: Yamamoto's Last Offensive New Guinea and the Solomons, April 1943*. Kent Town, Australia: Avenmore, 2020.

Craven, W.F.; and Cate, J.L. (eds.), *Army Air Forces in World War II, Vol. IV*: "The Pacific: Guadalcanal to Saipan August 1942 to July 1944." Washington, DC: Office of Air Force History, 1983.

Crenshaw, Russell Sydnor, Jr, *South Pacific Destroyer: The Battle for the Solomons from Savo Island to Vella Gulf*, Annapolis: Naval Institute Press, 1998. Kindle edition.

Cressman, Robert J., *The Official Chronology of the U.S. Navy in World War II*. Washington, DC: Contemporary History Branch, Naval Historical Center, 1999.

Crocker, Mel, *Black Cats and Dumbos: WW II's Fighting PBYs*. Huntington Beach, CA: Crocker Media Expressions (2nd ed.), 2002.

Davis, Donald A., *Lightning Strike: The Secret Mission to Kill Admiral Yamamoto and Avenge Pearl Harbor*. New York: St. Martin's, 2005. Kindle edition.

Day, Ronnie, *New Georgia: The Second Battle for the Solomons*. Bloomington, IN: Indiana University Press, 2016. Kindle edition.

Domagalski, John J., *Sunk in Kula Gulf: The Final Voyage of the USS* Helena *and the Incredible Story of Her Survivors*. Washington, DC: Potomac, 2012. Kindle edition.

Dull, Paul S., *A Battle History of the Imperial Japanese Navy (1941–1945)*. Annapolis: Naval Institute Press, 1978.

Dyer, Vice Admiral George Carroll, USN (Ret.), *The Amphibians Came to Conquer: The Story of Admiral Richmond Kelly Turner*. Washington, DC: U.S. Government Printing Office, 1971.

Evans, David C. (ed.), *The Japanese Navy in World War II in the Words of Former Japanese Naval Officers* (2nd ed.) Annapolis: Naval Institute Press, 1986. Kindle edition.

Fuller, Richard, *Shokan: Hirohito's Samurai*. London: Arms and Armour Press, 1992.

Gamble, Bruce, *Fortress Rabaul: The Battle for the Southwest Pacific, January 1942–April 1943*. London: Zenith Press, 2013. Kindle edition.

Gamble, Bruce, *Target: Rabaul: The Allied Siege of Japan's Most Infamous Stronghold, March 1943 – August 1945*. London: Zenith Press, 2013. Kindle edition.

Glines, Carroll V., *Attack on Yamamoto*. Atglen, PA: Schieffer Military History, 1993.

Goldstein, Donald M.; and Dillon, Katherine V. (ed.), *The Pacific War Papers: Japanese Documents of World War II*. Dulles, VA: Potomac, 2004.

Hall, R. Cargill, *Lightning Over Bougainville: The Yamamoto Mission Reconsidered*. Washington and London: Smithsonian Institution Press, 1991.

Halsey, Fleet Admiral William F., USN, *Admiral Halsey's Story*. Auckland: Pickle Partners Publishing, 2013. Kindle edition.

Hammel, Eric, *Air War Pacific Chronology: America's Air War Against Japan in East Asia and the Pacific 1941–1945*. Pacifica, CA: Pacifica Military History, 1998. Kindle edition.

Hammel, Eric, *Munda Trail: The New Georgia Campaign June–August 1943*. Pacifica, CA: Pacifica Military History, 1989.

Hammel, Eric, *The Naval Battle of Kula Gulf July 5–6, 1943*. Pacifica, CA: Pacifica Military History, 2016. Kindle edition.

Hara, Tameichi; Saito, Fred; and Pineau, Roger, *Japanese Destroyer Captain: Pearl Harbor, Guadalcanal, Midway – The Great Naval Battles as Seen Through Japanese Eyes*. Annapolis: Naval Institute Press, 1967. Kindle edition.

Hata, Ikuhiko; Izawa, Yasuho; and Shores, Christopher, *Japanese Naval Air Force Fighter Units and Their Aces*. London: Grub Street, 2011. Kindle edition.

Jones, David; and Nunan, Peter, *U.S. Subs Down Under: Brisbane 1942–1945*. Annapolis: Naval Institute Press, 2005.

Kenney, George C., *General Kenney Reports: A Personal History of the Pacific War*. Washington, DC: U.S. Government Printing Office, 1997.

Kilpatrick, C.W., *The Night Naval Battles in the Solomons*. Pompano Beach, FL: Exposition-Banner, 1987.

Lacroix, Eric; and Wells, Linton, II., *Japanese Cruisers of the Pacific War*. Annapolis: Naval Institute Press, 1997.

Lord, Walter, *Lonely Vigil: Coastwatchers of the Solomons*. New York: Open Road, 1977. Kindle edition.

McMurria, Capt. James Austin (USA), *Fight for Survival!: An American Bomber Pilot's 1,000 Days as a P.O.W. of the Japanese*. Spartanburg, SC: Honoribus Press, 2005.

Morison, Samuel Eliot, *History of United States Naval Operations in World War II, Vol VI: Breaking the Bismarcks Barrier 22 July 1942–1 May 1944*. Edison, NJ: Castle, 1950.

Morris, Lieutenant C.G. (USNR), and Cave, Hugh B., *The Fightin'est Ship: The Story of the Cruiser Helena*. Holicong, PA: Wildside Press, 1944.

Newell, Reg, *The Battle for Vella Lavella: The Allied Recapture of Solomons Island Territory, August 15-September 9, 1943*. Jefferson, NC: McFarland, 2016. Kindle edition.

O'Hara, Vincent P., *The US Navy Against the Axis: Surface Combat 1941–1945*. Annapolis: Naval Institute Press, 2007. Kindle edition.

Odgers, George, *Australia in the War of 1939–1945: Series Three (Air) Volume II – Air War Against Japan, 1943–1945*. Canberra: Australian War Memorial, 1968.

Okumiya, Masatake; Horikoshi, Jiro; and Caidin, Martin, *Zero!* Auckland: Pickle Partners Publishing, 2014. Kindle edition.

Prados, John, *Islands of Destiny: The Solomons Campaign and the Eclipse of the Rising Sun*. New York: NAL Caliber, 2012. Kindle edition.

Rems, Alan, *South Pacific Cauldron: World War II's Great Forgotten Battlegrounds*. Annapolis: Naval Institute Press, 2014. Kindle edition.

Rentz, Major John N., "Marines in the Central Solomons". Washington, DC: Historical Branch, Headquarters, U.S. Marine Corps, 1952.

Roscoe, Theodore, *United States Destroyer Operations in World War II*. Annapolis: Naval Institute Press, 1953.

Roscoe, Theodore, *United States Submarine Operations in World War II*. Annapolis: Naval Institute Press, 1949.

Ross, J.M.S., *Official History of New Zealand in the Second World War 1939–45: Royal New Zealand Air Force*. Wellington: War History Branch, Department of Internal Affairs, 1955.

Sakai, Saburo; Caidin, Martin; and Saito, Fred, *Samurai*. New York: J. Boylston & Company, 2001. Kindle edition.

Samuels, Alfred, *The USS Ralph Talbot and her Gallant Men*. Charlottesville, VA: Publishers Syndication International, 1991. Kindle edition.

Sherrod, Robert, *History of Marine Corps Aviation in World War II*. Washington, DC: Combat Forces Press, 1952.

Stille, Mark E., *The Imperial Japanese Navy in the Pacific War*. Oxford: Osprey, 2014. Kindle edition.

Stille, Mark E., *The United States Navy in World War II: From Pearl Harbor to Okinawa*. Oxford: Osprey, 2021. Kindle edition.

Tanaka, Yuki, *Hidden Horrors: Japanese War Crimes in World War II*. Lanham, MD: Rowman & Littlefield Publishers, 2018. Kindle edition.

Toland, John, *The Rising Sun: The Decline and Fall of the Japanese Empire 1936–1945*. New York: Random House, 1970. Kindle edition.

Ugaki, Matome; Goldstein, Donald M.; and Dillon, Katherine V. (ed.), *Fading Victory: The Diary of Admiral Matome Ugaki*. Pittsburgh: University of Pittsburgh Press, 1991.

INDEX